Research Anthology on Applying Social Networking Strategies to Classrooms and Libraries

Information Resources Management Association
USA

Volume II

Published in the United States of America by
IGI Global
Information Science Reference (an imprint of IGI Global)
701 E. Chocolate Avenue
Hershey PA, USA 17033
Tel: 717-533-8845
Fax: 717-533-8661
E-mail: cust@igi-global.com
Web site: http://www.igi-global.com

Library of Congress Cataloging-in-Publication Data

Names: Information Resources Management Association, editor.
Title: Research anthology on applying social networking strategies to
  classrooms and libraries / Information Resources Management Association,
  editor.
Description: Hershey PA : Information Science Reference, 2022. | Includes
  bibliographical references. | Summary: "This reference book presents
  contributed chapters that describe the applications, tools, and
  opportunities provided by the intersection of education and social
  media, considering the ways in which social media encourages learner
  engagement and community participation"-- Provided by publisher.
Identifiers: LCCN 2022030171 (print) | LCCN 2022030172 (ebook) | ISBN
  9781668471234 (hardcover) | ISBN 9781668471241 (ebook)
Subjects: LCSH: Social media in education. | Libraries and social media. |
  Online social networks--Educational applications | Online social
  networks--Library applications.
Classification: LCC LB1044.87 .R46 2022 (print) | LCC LB1044.87 (ebook) |
  DDC 371.33/44678--dc23/eng/20220920
LC record available at https://lccn.loc.gov/2022030171
LC ebook record available at https://lccn.loc.gov/2022030172

British Cataloguing in Publication Data
A Cataloguing in Publication record for this book is available from the British Library.

For electronic access to this publication, please contact: eresources@igi-global.com.

List of Contributors

Table of Contents

Section 2
Development and Design Methodologies

Volume II

Section 3
Tools and Technologies

Section 5
Organizational and Social Implications

Section 6
Managerial Impact

Section 7
Critical Issues and Challenges

Preface

The introduction of social media has given many communities the opportunity to connect and communicate with each other at a higher level than ever before. Many organizations, from businesses to governments, have taken advantage of this important tool to conduct research and enhance efficiency. Libraries and educational institutions have also made use of social media to enhance educational marketing, engage with learning communities, adapt educational tools, and more.

Staying informed of the most up-to-date research trends and findings is of the utmost importance. That is why IGI Global is pleased to offer this four-volume reference collection of reprinted IGI Global book chapters and journal articles that have been handpicked by senior editorial staff. This collection will shed light on critical issues related to the trends, techniques, and uses of various applications by providing both broad and detailed perspectives on cutting-edge theories and developments. This collection is designed to act as a single reference source on conceptual, methodological, technical, and managerial issues, as well as to provide insight into emerging trends and future opportunities within the field.

The *Research Anthology on Applying Social Networking Strategies to Classrooms and Libraries* is organized into seven distinct sections that provide comprehensive coverage of important topics. The sections are:

1. Fundamental Concepts and Theories;
2. Development and Design Methodologies;
3. Tools and Technologies;
4. Utilization and Applications;
5. Organizational and Social Implications;
6. Managerial Impact; and
7. Critical Issues and Challenges.

The following paragraphs provide a summary of what to expect from this invaluable reference tool.

Section 1, "Fundamental Concepts and Theories," serves as a foundation for this extensive reference tool by addressing crucial theories essential to implementing social networking into classrooms and libraries. The first chapter, "Social Media and the Future of the Instructional Model," by Prof. Soha Abdeljaber of Rising Leaders Academy, USA and Prof. Kathryn Nieves Licwinko of New Jersey City University, USA, provides the latest information on social media and its application in the instructional model. The chapter contains information on how social media enhances learning, especially at times where remote learning is necessary, such as COVID-19. The last chapter, "Facebook in the International Classroom," by Prof. Inna P. Piven of Unitec Institute of Technology, New Zealand, explores international students' learning experiences with Facebook-based activities within the eight-week study term known as the intensive mode of course delivery. By implementing participant observation and two asynchronous Facebook focus groups, the study investigates the potential values of Facebook for learning from international students' perspective.

Section 2, "Development and Design Methodologies," presents in-depth coverage of the design and development of social networking implementation. The first chapter, "Bridging Activities: Social Media for Connecting Language Learners' in-School and Out-of-School Literacy Practices," by Prof. Ellen Yeh of Columbia College Chicago, USA and Prof. Svetlana Mitric of University of Illinois at Chicago, USA, applies pedagogically-focused project design by using Instagram as a platform to investigate how the use of social media such as Instagram in a multimodal digital storytelling model could bridge the skills English language learners (ELLs) learn in the classroom to out-of-school literacy practices. The last chapter, "Social Media, Cyberculture, Blockchains, and Education: A New Strategy for Brazilian Higher Education," by Prof. Matheus Batalha Moreira Nery of Uninassau, Brazil; Prof. Magno Oliveira Macambira of Universidade Estadual de Feira de Santana, Brazil; Prof. Marlton Fontes Mota of Universidade Tiradentes, Brazil; and Prof. Izabella Cristine Oliveira Rezende of Uninassau, Brazil, contributes to the debate of the uses of social media, cyberculture, and blockchain technology for the development of educational strategies. It reviews the existing scientific literature on social networking, social media, cyberculture, and blockchains related to Brazil.

Section 3, "Tools and Technologies," explores the various tools and technologies used in classrooms and libraries for social networking. The first chapter, "Using Social Media in Creating and Implementing Educational Practices," by Profs. Inna P. Piven and Robyn Gandell of Unitec Institute of Technology, New Zealand, examines the use of social media as a couse management tool, the use of social media to enhance student-centered learning and the need for institutional support for using social media in educational contexts. The last chapter, "Is Twitter an Unexploited Potential in Indian Academic Libraries? Case Study Based on Select Academic Library Tweets," by Prof. Swapan Kumar Patra of Tshwane University of Technology, South Africa, maps the Indian libraries' Twitter activities, taking academic libraries as case study.

Section 4, "Utilization and Applications," describes the opportunities and challenges of social networking implementation. The first chapter, "Navigating the Shortcomings of Virtual Learning Environments via Social Media," by Profs. Puvaneswary Murugaiah and Siew Hwa Yen of School of Distance Education, Universiti Sains Malaysia, Penang, Malaysia, uncovers the shortcomings of the use of virtual learning environments (VLEs) for language learning in several Malaysian institutions of higher learning. It also highlights the use of social media in addressing the barriers. The last chapter, "Nexus Between Social Network, Social Media Use, and Loneliness: A Case Study of University Students, Bangladesh," by Prof. Md. Aminul Islam of University of Liberal Arts Bangladesh, Bangladesh and Prof. Bezon Kumar of Rabindra University, Bangladesh, explores how real-life social network and social media use are related to loneliness among university students in Bangladesh.

Section 5, "Organizational and Social Implications," includes chapters discussing the impact of social networking on education and library organizations and beyond. The first chapter, "Identifiable Problems in Social Media: Concerning Legal Awareness Within Academic Libraries," by Prof. Amy D. Dye-Reeves of Murray State University, USA, serves as a primer for academic librarians on helping patrons with disabilities receive, protect, and understand disseminated content on a multitude of popular social media networking platforms. The content of the chapter provides introductory material on the Americans with Disabilities Act (ADA) and the Family Educational Rights and Privacy Act. The last chapter, "Using Twitter to Form Professional Learning Communities: An Analysis of Georgia K-12 School Personnel Discussing Educational Technology on Twitter," by Profs. Charles B. Hodges, Lucas John Jensen, and Mete Akcaoglu of Georgia Southern University, USA, diescusses teacher professional development taking place on Twitter in Georgia, USA.

Section 6, "Managerial Impact," covers the internal and external impacts of social networking within education and library administration. The first chapter, "Social Media in Tertiary Education: Considerations and Potential Issues," by Prof. Ann M. Simpson of Unitec Institute of Technology, New Zealand, addresses some of the considerations and potential issues that impact our use of social media in the higher education classroom. It examines social media as an educational tool in higher education, possible pedagogies for social media use, potential educational contexts, and privacy concerns raised by social media use in educational environments. The last chapter, "Social Media Integration in Educational Administration as Information and Smart Systems: Digital Literacy for Economic, Social, and Political Engagement in Namibia," by Profs. Sadrag Panduleni Shihomeka and Helena N. Amadhila of University of Namibia, Namibia, explains that there are various groups on Facebook where youthful education administrators can use to post educational information and discuss pertinent issues concerning their institutions.

Section 7, "Critical Issues and Challenges," presents coverage of academic and research perspectives on challenges to social networking in education and libraries. The first chapter, "Making Social Media More Social: A Literature Review of Academic Libraries' Engagement and Connections Through Social Media Platforms," by Prof. Elia Trucks of University of Denver, USA, explores how academic libraries have used social media for broadcasting information, responsive communication, and engagement. The last chapter, "Social Media Usage for Informal Learning in Malaysia: Academic Researcher Perspective," by Prof. Mohmed Y. Mohmed Al-Sabaawi of Department of Management Information Systems, College of Administration and Economics, University of Mosul, Iraq; Prof. Halina Mohamed Dahlan of Information Systems Department, Azman Hashim International Business School, Universiti Teknologi Malaysia, Malaysia; and Prof. Hafiz Muhammad Faisal Shehzad of Department of Computer Science and IT, University of Sargodha, Pakistan, explores the use of social media for informal learning, barriers, benefits, and effect of individual factors.

Although the primary organization of the contents in this multi-volume work is based on its seven sections, offering a progression of coverage of the important concepts, methodologies, technologies, applications, social issues, and emerging trends, the reader can also identify specific contents by utilizing the extensive indexing system listed at the end of each volume. As a comprehensive collection of research on the latest findings related to social networking in education and library practices, the *Research Anthology on Applying Social Networking Strategies to Classrooms and Libraries* provides pre-service teachers, teacher educators, faculty and administrators of both K-12 and higher education, librarians, archivists, government officials, researchers, and academicians with a complete understanding of the applications and impacts of social networking. Given the vast number of issues concerning usage, failure, success, strategies, and applications of social networking applied to classrooms and libraries, the *Research Anthology on Applying Social Networking Strategies to Classrooms and Libraries* encompasses the most pertinent research on the applications, impacts, uses, and strategies of social networking.

Chapter 27
Impact of Balancing Techniques for Imbalanced Class Distribution on Twitter Data for Emotion Analysis:
A Case Study

Shivani Vasantbhai Vora
CGPIT, Uka Tarsadia University, Bardoli, India

Rupa G. Mehta
Sardar Vallabhbhai National Institute of Technology, Surat, India

Shreyas Kishorkumar Patel
Sardar Vallabhbhai National Institute of Technology, Surat, India

ABSTRACT

Continuously growing technology enhances creativity and simplifies humans' lives and offers the possibility to anticipate and satisfy their unmet needs. Understanding emotions is a crucial part of human behavior. Machines must deeply understand emotions to be able to predict human needs. Most tweets have sentiments of the user. It inherits the imbalanced class distribution. Most machine learning (ML) algorithms are likely to get biased towards the majority classes. The imbalanced distribution of classes gained extensive attention as it has produced many research challenges. It demands efficient approaches to handle the imbalanced data set. Strategies used for balancing the distribution of classes in the case study are handling redundant data, resampling training data, and data augmentation. Six methods related to these techniques have been examined in a case study. Upon conducting experiments on the Twitter dataset, it is seen that merging minority classes and shuffle sentence methods outperform other techniques.

DOI: 10.4018/978-1-6684-7123-4.ch027

INTRODUCTION AND MOTIVATION

Information technology is used in every field of human life and make human's life improved and more accessible. This tool became valued elements of life because it opened many doors to individuals. It firmly entrenched in human lives and facilitated their lives. Continuously growing technology strengthens individual creativity, makes our daily life more accessible, and gives us the facility to predict and cater to our needs. A deep understanding of human behavior is needed in machines and computers to understand our needs. The key part of human behavior is about perceiving and communicating emotions. It also motivates to take actions, influence the quality of decision making, and enhance the ability to empathize and communicate. Machines and computers must deeply understand emotions to anticipate human needs (Chatterjee A et al. (2019)). Emotion recognition and detection are closely related to sentiment analysis. Identification of sentiment intends to detect neutral, negative, or positive feelings from the content (Liu, B. (2012)).

In contrast, Emotion Analysis aims to identify and recognize feelings through text phrases, like joy, happiness, anger, disgust, fear, sadness, surprise, and many more (Picard R. W. (2000)). Recently, an identification of emotion has become a popular application of NLP. It has potential applications in Artificial intelligence (Damani S et al. 2018), Psychology (Druckman J. N. et al. 2008), Human-computer interaction (S. Brave et al.2009), Political science (Valentino N. A. et al. 2011) help in preventing suicide, or measuring the communal well-being (Van der Zanden R. et al. 2014), and Marketing (Bagozzi R. P. et al. 1999) etc.

WhatsApp, Facebook, and Twitter are prominent messaging platforms used by many online users to interact with each other. Statics given by (Statista, 2021) – "by the 3rdquarter of 2020, there are around 187 million daily active users of Twitter worldwide." In varied fields like researchers in marketing, analytics for political parties or social scientists look into twitter data in order to study human behavior in physical world. Tweets are rich sources of textual data containing the emotions of users. These data inherit the imbalanced emotion class distribution. In imbalanced dataset, data samples of one class are higher or lower than that of other group of classes. Figure 1 illustrates an imbalanced data. On encountering a imbalance class distribution problem in the training data, the results of classification task is influenced by majority class (Zhao C. et al. 2020).

Most machine learning classification algorithms are unable to manage imbalanced distribution of classes and are likely to get influenced by majority classes (Kothiya, Y. (2020, July 17)).

In the research literature, various approaches are proposed to cater to the imbalance class distribution issues in the data classification. These approaches are broadly categorized as algorithmic centered approaches and pre-processing methods or data level approaches.

Re-sampling techniques (Kotsiantis S. et al. 2006), reducing redundant data (Y.K. (2019, May 15)), and augmentation of text data are data-level approaches that are included as a solution to handle imbalance distribution of classes. The techniques are utilized to obtain an approximately equal count of samples in the classes. Assumptions created to favor the minority class and change the costs to get the balance classes, is the algorithmic-centered approach. (Kotsiantis S. et al. 2006).

In the machine learning (ML) community, the imbalanced class distribution gained extensive attention as it has produced many research challenges. It demands the experimental comparisons of approaches to take care of the imbalanced data set. A case study focuses on various data-level methods to deal with the imbalance distribution of emotion classes in Twitter data.

Figure 1. Imbalance distribution of class (Zhao C. et al. 2020)

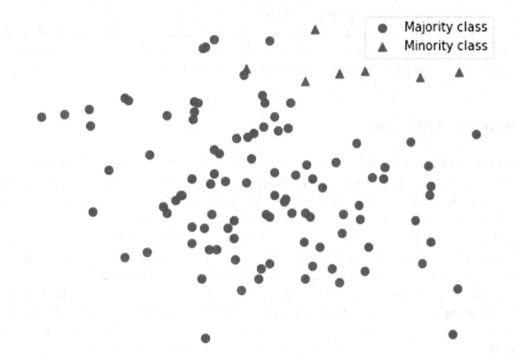

Contribution and Plan of the Report

- A case study focuses on tackling the imbalance multiclass emotion classification of tweets using various techniques such as resampling, reducing redundant data, augmentation of text data. It focuses on effectively processing imbalanced data while including the proposed model that inferred emotions from tweets. The study intends to bridge the gap between imbalanced learning and emotion analysis.
- This study's primary goal is to compare various approaches for balancing classes and enhance the proposed deep learning (DL) based model's efficiency and accuracy.

The rest of this chapter is organized as follows: Section 2 describes a literature review. The Proposed methodology is explained in section 3. Section 4 discusses the experiment setup. The analysis of experimental results is discussed in section5. Section 6 is the conclusion and future work that remarks the findings of this study in the end of the chapter.

LITERATURE REVIEW

In the research literature, Kotsiantis S. et al. 2006 discuss various approaches at the data and the algorithm level for managing class imbalanced data. Many different resampling approaches are proposed at the data level like random over-sampling, Synthetic Minority Over-Sampling (SMOT), and random under-sampling, etc.,. Various classification algorithms and techniques are updated to manage the imbalanced class distribution. Ensemble learning, leveraging the class weights parameter during the training of models, etc., is examples under the latter category.

The study focuses on different data-level methods to deal with imbalanced multiclass emotion analysis for Twitter data. Strategies such as resampling, handling redundant data, data augmentation methods for NLP task are used in the case study for balancing classes and enhance the efficiency and accuracy of the proposed deep learning model.

Twitter Emotion Analysis

Although emotion Recognition based on speech and images has been worked on a lot at this point, text-based emotion detection is in its early stage in natural language processing, including how recently it has drawn ample of attention. The emotion-detection algorithms are at large, put down to two categories, namely, Machine learning (ML) based methods and dictionary based methods.

When the vocabularies such as linguistic rules, ontologies, lexicons, or bags of words are used it is considered as Lexicon based approaches, whereas when the algorithms based on linguistic features, it falls into the category of Machine learning (ML) approaches (Canales L.et al. 2014).

The limitations of lexicon-based methods (Strapparava c. Et al. 2008, ma c. Et al. 2005, Balahur a. Et al. 2011, Sykora m. D. Et al. 2013, Bandhakavi a. Et al. 2017, pp. 102-108, Bandhakavi a. Et al. 2017, pp. 133-142, Chaumartin f. R. 2007, al Masum et al. 2007, Ortony a. Et al. 1988, Neviarouskaya a. Et al. 2010, Deerwester s. Et al. 1990, gill a. J. Et al. 2008, Wang x. Et al. 2013) concerning scalability and domain customization can be overcome by machine learning approaches (Mohri m. Et al. 2012, Hasan m. Et al. 2014, ACM, Sigkdd, Hasan m. Et al. 2014, Wang w. Et al. 2012, Roberts k. Et al. 2012, Suttles j. Et al. 2013, Balabantaray r. C. Et al. 2012, Seol y. S. Et al. 2008, li w. Et al. 2014, lee s. Y. M. Et al. 2010). It can also learn emotional signals that are not explicitly expressed.

The Conventional machine learning techniques required heavy feature engineering as well as a substantial expertise in the domain to create a model to transform raw input into a feature vector which enables a classifier to identify patterns in the input.

Deep learning-based (DL) methods are basically the method of representation learning. It has multiple levels of representation that are obtained by composing non-linear components which transforms a raw input at one level into a abstract higher level (LeCun Y. et al. 2015). The key advantage of deep learning methods is that the layers of features are learned from data using learning procedure. The DL methods perform feature engineering so there is no requirement to design hand-crafted features (LeCun Y. et al. 2015).

Deep learning-based architectures and algorithms have shown considerable success in speech and image domains. They also show favorable results in many NLU tasks such as question answering, topic classification, language translation, and sentiment analysis (LeCun Y. et al. 2015).

Lately, many approaches using deep learning (DL) models for emotion recognition from the text format have been proposed.

In (Zahiri S. M. et al. 2017), the author classifies emotion in a transcript of TV show. Transcripts are well-scripted, but the text data from social media such as tweets and textual dialogue are crowded by internet slang. spell errors etc. Some recent researches are on understanding the various emotions of tweets (Abdul-Mageed M. 2017, Köper M. 2017). In (Felbo B. 2017), authors learn representation based on emojis and uses it for identification of emotions. An author used pretrained LSTM model that is trained with lots of tweets and the emoticons appears in tweets. The work done by Mundra S.2017 is the sole study that addresses the difficulty of emotion identification in textual conversation of English language.

The study says that the deep learning methods give promising results for emotion detection in text. Also, deep learning-based algorithms require very less feature engineering, and so they can conveniently take advantage of available computation and data, as it increases in the amount. It motivated us to move to deep learning approaches for recognized emotion from the text.

Deep Learning Based Emotion Analysis for Imbalanced Class Distribution

Imbalance class distribution is a common problem in classification tasks. Model's performance will degrade due to imbalanced distribution of class. A balanced class distribution is not possible for real-world application domains.

To balance the minority class samples, researchers utilize data over-sampling methods to generate synthetic data from original training data. Method such as synthetic minority oversampling technique (SMOT) performs well for random numerical data (Chawla N. V. et al. 2002) and AdaSyn (He H. et al. 2008). A deep learning model CycleGAN that is the type of generative adversarial networks (GAN) performs well for images (Almahairi, A. et al. 2018). Synthetic text and images generally suffers from semantic or contextual information loss, whereas this is not the case with numeric data. The resulting text frequently turns out to have poor text structure and grammar, thus losing its meaning. Recently, research on tackling imbalanced dataset involves semantic text generation using deep language models. In (Shaikh S. et al. 2021), the authors proposed an LSTM-based model for sentence-level text generation to cater to imbalance distribution of classes in NLP domain applications. Three highly imbalanced datasets from two different domains were used evaluate the performance of LSTM and GPT-2 models for document-level sentence generation. Experimental results show overall improved classification accuracy for the proposed model (Shaikh S. et al. 2021).

In (Cong Q. et al. 2018), authors proposed a model for identification of depression in highly imbalanced social media data. They proposed a deep learning based model (X-A-BiLSTM) that consists of two modules: one is XGBoost module that increases the samples in minority classes and other one is an attention based BiLSTM model that enhances performance of classification task. An author utilizes real-world depression dataset. The dataset used is the Reddit Self-reported Depression Diagnosis (RSDD) dataset. Results illustrate that the approach remarkably performs well with the previous (SOTA) state-of-the-art models on the same dataset.

A research study in (Jamal N. et al. 2019) proposed a hybrid method of a deep learning-based model for emotions recognition on a highly imbalanced tweets data. The proposed model works in four stages:

1. Pre-processing steps are help in getting useful features from raw tweets and filtering out the noisy data.
2. The importance of each feature is computed using entropy weighting method.
3. Further, each class is balanced using a class balancer.
4. Principal Component Analysis (PCA) is applied to get normalized forms from the high correlated features.

At last the TensorFlow with Keras module is recommended to predict good-quality features for identification of emotions. A data set of 1,600,000 tweets that is collected from the 'Kaggle' was analyzed with the suggested methodology. Upon comparing it with the various states of art techniques on various training ratios, it is seen that the recommended methodology outperforms all of them.

Several researchers in different learning settings have studied imbalanced learning for emotion detection. However, we found very few papers that directly address imbalanced emotion classification for Twitter data (Shaikh S. et al. 2021, Jamal N. et al. 2019).

A study focuses on deep learning-based emotion detection for highly imbalanced Twitter data. The next sections describe the methodology used to balance the imbalanced class distribution of text data.

Handle Redundant Data

Twitter dataset comprises of duplicate tweets and a lots of similar tweets. Discarding identical tweets will help to bring down the size of the majority class. Tweet dataset contains multiple tweets with similar semantic meaning. Removing the redundant tweets will help in balancing the classes. One of the beneficial approaches is that the validation set can remove redundant tweets (Kotsiantis S. et al. 2006). There is a range of techniques to represent tweets like word2vec embedding, TF-IDF embedding, BOW representations, etc. The similarity of tweets is measured using different similarity metrics such as Jaccard similarity, cosine similarity, etc. Siamese LSTM models to find out similar tweets have been proposed in the research domain (Cohen E. (2018, September 16)).

Merge minority classes is the approach to merge multiple minority classes that have numerous overlapping features (Multi-Class Emotion Classification for Short Texts, 2018). This trick may help out to enhance the f1-score of the classification task.

Resample Training Dataset

Oversampling the tweets of minority classes or under sampling tweets of majority classes is the straightforward method for balancing the imbalanced tweet data set. Another resampling method is to make new synthetic tweets from minority classes with SMOTE (Synthetic Minority Over-sampling Technique) (Chawla N. V. et al. 2002) algorithm.

Undersampling is an approach to balance the majority classes by eliminating tweets randomly. It may cause information loss from tweets and lead to inadequate model training (Y.K. (2019d, May 15)).

Oversampling is the process to replicate minority class tweets randomly. Random under-sampling suffers with information loss issue and random over-sampling may cause the problem of over fitting. To be precise, if the instances in the dataset are randomly replicated, then the learned model would fit too closely with the training data, resulting into unseen cases to be less generalized (Hoens T. R. et al. 2013).

To conquer this issue, (Chawla N. V. et al. 2002) came up with a SMOTE approach that creates synthetic data instead of taking same samples that already exist in the dataset. In this algorithm, the synthetic instances are introduced to each sample from the minority class, along the line segments connecting any or all of the nearest neighbours of the k minority class (Chawla N. V. et al. 2002). In the feature space, the Euclidean Distance between its data points help evaluates the nearest neighbours, this is essential for the technique. SMOTE works in the feature space such that it selects close examples and draws a line between them, then at a point along this line it draws a new sample.

Data Augmentation

Recently, research on tackling imbalanced dataset involves data augmentation methods of texts. Data augmentation of text can be done by tokenizing documents into a sentence, shuffling and joining them again to generate new sentences. Semantic text generation is also done by replacing adjectives, verbs, etc., with its synonym. A word's synonym is found using any pre-trained word embeddings or lexical dictionaries such as Wordnet, SentiWordNet, etc. ((I. (2019b, March 1)), (T. (2018a, November 16))).

(Zhang X. et al. 2015), Introduced the use of synonyms in their research work. While experimenting, it is found that text augmentation can be done by replacing words or phrases with their synonyms. In a very time effective way a huge amount of data can be generated if there is leverage existing thesaurus. The geometric distribution helps the authors to replace the selected word with its synonym (Zhang X. et al. 2015). Another interesting way was utilization of K-NN algorithm with cosine similarity to find a analogous word for replacement was suggested by (Wang W. Y. et al. 2015).In place of using static word embedding to replace the target word, (Fadaee M. et al. 2017) used the contextualized word embedding. In their work of data augmentation for machine translation with lower resources, they perform text augmentation to validate the model. The experiment proves that by leveraging text augmentation, the machine translation model gets enhanced.

(Kobayashi S. 2018), proposes to employ a bi-directional language model in the research work of data augmentation using contextual word embedding. Upon having selected the target word, the model predicts all probable substitutions by providing the surrounding words. Author applied the language model (LM) approach with sequential model RNN and convolution model CNN on six datasets, and the results turned out to be positive. (Kafle K. et al. 2017) presented an alternate approach for data augmentation. Here, the whole sentence is generated instead of just replacing a single few words.

Machine language translation is another interesting method of data augmentation for text. The technique helps to increase samples of minority classes. The technique used machine translation model to translate English language text to any language text and again converting back to English text. In this way, the essential details of the input texts are preserved, but word order or sometimes new words with similar meanings are introduced as new records, thus increasing the number of insufficient classes ((T. (2020a, September 7)), (Es, S. (2021b, April 9))). It may help out to enhance the f1-score of the classification task.

A case study focuses on tackling the imbalance multiclass emotion classification of tweets using various techniques such as resampling, reduced redundant data, augmentation of text data. It also focuses on effectively processing imbalanced data while including the proposed model that inferred emotions from tweets. The study intends to bridge the gap between imbalanced learning and emotion analysis.

This study's primary goal is to compare different techniques for balancing classes and enhance the proposed deep learning model's efficiency and accuracy.

PROPOSED APPROACH

Emotion recognition from the tweets is an area in Natural Language Processing (NLP), which is the study of interpreting the emotion expressed in text. A study of emotion detection using a deep learning-based approach is shown in Figure 2.

Proposed approach work in two phases. The first phase balances the dataset's class distribution using different data level strategies such as handling redundant data, resampling techniques, and data augmentation approach.

In second phase, pre-processing of a balanced dataset has been done with different methods and tools. Pre-processing techniques replace contraction words with proper words, remove punctuation, numbers, URLs, replace line space and extra white space, replace emoticons with related appropriate words, and demojized the emojis in tweets using emot library available in python.

The proposed model utilized the pre-trained embedding of GloVe (Global Vectors) as weights of the Embedding layer. The Glove Twitter pre-trained model with 200 dimensions is used to embedding the pre-processed Twitter data.

Glove embedding data fed to recurrent neural network (RNN), a deep learning (DL) based model for the text classification task. For twitter classification, the proposed model utilizes the biLSTM model with different layers.

Figure 2. Proposed framework for emotion detection

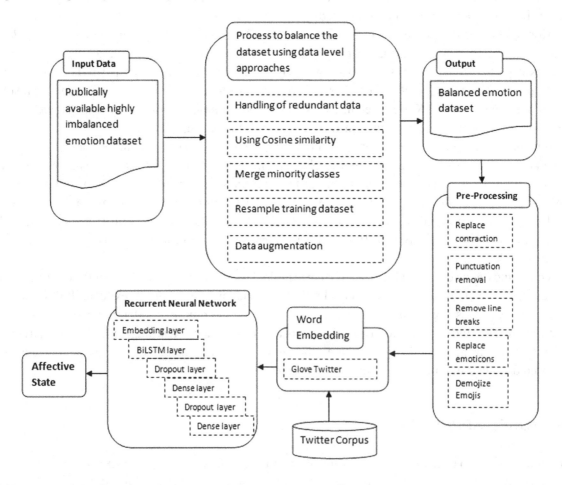

A sequential model RNN is the type of ANN that specialize in the processing the sequential data. RNNs designed to deal with sequential data by sharing their internal weights. The Long Short-Term Memory networks (LSTMs), an extension of the RNN was introduced In 1997. In LSTM, the vanishing and exploding of the gradient issues are avoided by the unique connection of the recurrent cells (Sepp Hochreiter et al. 1997). Generally the LSTMs maintain information from the past because the sequence is processed in only one direction. The bidirectional LSTM (BiLSTM) combine output from two LSTM layers that processed in opposite directions. One processed forward through time, and another processed backwards through time to retrieve information from both states simultaneously (Schuster M. et al. 1997).

EXPERIMENTAL SETUP

Dataset

Experiments performed on a publically available emotion dataset from Kaggle (Emotion, 2020). The emotion dataset has 40,000 tweets with its 13 emotion labels. The dataset is highly imbalanced with a different number of tweets in each emotion category. Detail of imbalanced dataset provided in Table 1.

For the emotion dataset, 80% used for training, 20% for testing and another 20% used for validation. The training dataset has 25,600 tweets, 6400 tweets are in the validation set, and 8000 tweets are in the test set. The cleaning operations are performed on train, validation and test tweets datasets. Details of the dataset are available in Table 2.

Table 1. Class details of emotion dataset

Emotion Classes	# Tweets	Emotion Classes	# Tweets	Emotion Classes	# Tweets
neutral	8504	love	3837	empty	806
worry	8441	surprise	2178	enthusiasm	758
happiness	5206	fun	1774	boredom	178
sadness	5154	relief	1525		
anger	110	hate	1323		

Table 2. Emotion dataset

Dataset	Classes	Train	Validation	Test
Emotion dataset from Kaggle	13 (neutral, worry, happiness, sadness, anger, love, surprise, fun, relief, hate, empty, enthusiasm, and boredom)	25600	6400	8000

Pre-Processing Techniques

Pre-processing techniques replace contraction words with proper words, remove punctuation, numbers, URLs, replace line space and extra white space, replace emoticons with related appropriate words, and demojized the emojis in tweets using emot library available in python. Figure 3 describes the pre-processing techniques.

Removal of Punctuations, Digits, Twitter Handles ('@'), Special Characters

Basically, the twitter users are denoted by their twitter handles that start with a '@' sign. These handles do not give any significant meaning to the text and so they are to be removed. Tweets also contain punctuations, numeric information and special characters. These are also unnecessary as they do not convey many emotions with their meaning. It can quickly be done using Regular Expression available in python libraries. It uses simple methods to find characters and patterns in a string.

Example: "@abc 102 Not out Excellent!!" will become "Not out Excellent

Remove Unicode Strings and Noise

To get a clean dataset is not always possible. The Unicode strings like "\u002c" and "\x06" and some non-English characters were left behind by the crawling method that was used to create the dataset. These strings have to be removed or replaced by some regular expressions.

Replacing Contractions

Yet another approach in pre-processing is to replace the contractions, which is replacing words like "won't" and "don't" by "will not" and "do not", respectively.

Lowercasing

A common pre-processing method is to convert all the words into lowercase. This will merge a lot of words thereby reducing the dimensionality of the problem.

Lemmatization

Lemmatization typically refers to doing things correctly using a vocabulary and morphological examination of words, generally aimed solely at eliminating infection endings and restoring the basic term referenced as a lemma. Lemmatization is done by using different modules and available open-source libraries.

Spell Check

Examining the word's spelling is one of the primary necessities for any form of text processing. There are various paths available in Python to check the spelling of terms and correct their respective words.

Removing Stop Words

The function words that have high frequency that it their presence across all the sentences is high are called stop words. This reduces their importance in getting analyzed because they don't hold much necessary information in regards to the sentiment analysis. This collection of words is never pre-defined; it may change by adding or removing some words, based on the application.

Figure 3. Flow of data pre-processing

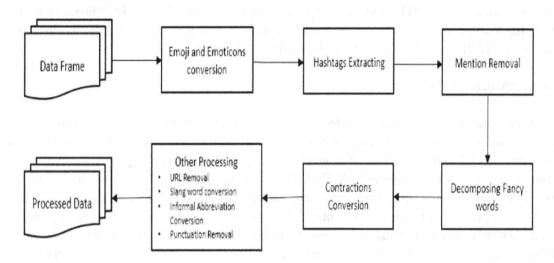

Replacing Elongated Words

Sometimes there are words which have characters that have been wrongly (thought purposely) repeated more than once, e.g. "greeeeat", these are called as elongated words. The need is to replace these words with their source words in order to merge them. If this wasn't done then these different words would never be considered in evaluation due to their low frequency of occurrence.

Replacing Emoticons and Demojized Emojis

An emoji is defined as a unique combination of keyboard characters like letters, numbers and punctuation marks to express a human facial expression. They are like small images that can be fitted into text also express an emotion or idea. The name "emoji" is derived from the Japanese characters 'e' for picture + 'mo' for writing + 'ji' for character, making its literal meaning to be 'picture-character' (Subramanian D. (2020b, January 7)).

Emojis and emoticons play a fundamental role in human computer-mediated communications. They use a proxy of emotional communication to process tweets by considering emoticons information. Emot library available in Python libraries used to replace emoticons with appropriate words. With the help of Demojize function of Python, emojis replaced with suitable words.

Pre-Trained Word Embedding – GloVe

Experiments have been done with Glove that is pre-trained with billions of tweets (Pennington J. et al. 2014) word embedding as an embedding layer of the model.

The proposed model used the pre-trained embeddings of GloVe (Global Vectors) as weights of the Embedding layer. The model used a Glove Twitter pre-trained model with 200 dimensions. The accuracy and complexity of the model increase as the size of training data and vocabulary size increases. The model used GloVe embeddings trained with Twitter data.

Glove Twitter pre-trained model trained with 2B tweets and has 27B tokens and 1.2M vocab. It is available in uncased, 25d, 50d, 100d, & 200d vectors with a size of 1.42 GB. The GloVe Twitter Embedding has a dataset of 27 Billion tokens which contains slangs commonly used while writing a tweet. Hence GloVe Twitter is favorable when dealing with Twitter data.

Classification Model

The experimental study is to create a model whose task is to understand emotions as a multiclass classification problem where for the given input through tweets, the model will provide probabilities of varied emotion classes like – neutral, fear, anger, sadness, and joy and more.

Figure 4 describes the proposed EMOTWEET_TL deep learning model architecture. The neural network's proposed architecture comprising the embedding unit and a (biLSTM) bidirectional LSTM unit (64 dim). The LSTM unit learns semantic and sentiment feature representation. Initially, using the pre-trained word embedding, each tweet is given to the bidirectional LSTM. Text-based transfer learning techniques such as Glove embedding used as embedding layer and leverage them to perform effectively on downstream tasks. To predict the final emotion class label, the features proceed through a dense layer with the Relu non-linear function and then through the output layer with the softmax non-linear function. A dropout layer (Srivastava N. et al. 2014) was added between the bidirectional LSTM layer and to the first dense layer with Relu activation function and another dropout layer was added between the dense layer and the prediction layer (p=0.2) to improve the generalization of the network.

The Adam optimizer is used to train the model. For multiclass classification, the categorical cross-entropy loss function is utilized. F1-score, recall and precision were used as performance measures of the model.

Strategies used for Balancing Imbalanced Data

The experimental study focuses on different data-level methods to deal with imbalance multi-class emotion analysis. The strategies used in experiments are discussed below.

Handling of Redundant Data

For handling redundant tweets, the experiments have performed with two techniques. In the first technique, similar tweets are identified from the majority class. Such tweets are either deleted or added to the validation set to reduce the majority class size. The second technique merges similar minority classes.

Figure 4. EMOTWEET_TL: Proposed model for inferring emotions from tweets

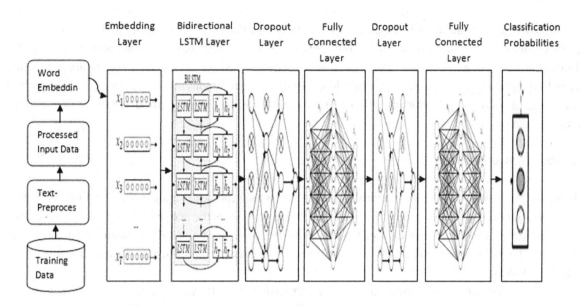

Using Cosine Similarity

tweets with similar semantic meaning or duplicate tweets are finding out using a cosine similarity measure. The tweets are used in validation sets also. Removing such duplicate and similar semantic meaning tweets will aid to reduce the size of the majority classes. In an experimental study, the tweets' similarity is identified using a cosine similarity metric with a threshold of 40% similarity.

Merge Minority Classes

It is the approach to merge multiple minority classes that have numerous overlapping features. The 13 emotions have been converted into 5 emotions such as neutral, happy, sad, hate, and anger. (It will add in handling the redundant data-merge similar classes-The native dataset is consists of 40,000 tweets that are divided into 13 emotion classes. These five classes are also the same as in (Bouazizi M. et al. 2017).

Resample Training Dataset

The experimental study used the SMOTE method to generate synthesized new tweets for minority classes. For creation of a new synthetic minority class instance, begin with randomly selecting a minority class instance namely 'p' and figure out its k-nearest class neighbors. Now randomly choose any one of these k-nearest minority neighbors namely 'q' and connect the two together, making a line segment in the feature space. The convex combination of these instances 'p' and 'q' generate the synthetic instance. Experiments have been performed with k=5. All minority classes have been balanced with the same number of tweets of majority class (here neutral class has maximum tweets - 8504 tweets). SMOTE algorithm is used to generate synthesized new data.

Data Augmentation

Simple data augmentation methods are used to increase similar tweets for minority classes. In the first approach, tokenizing tweets into words, shuffling and joining them again to create new tweets. NLTK library is used to tokenize tweets. The second approach replaces words of tweets with synonyms found using Pydictionary. It is a Dictionary Module for Python to get synonyms, translations, meanings, and Antonyms of words (PyDictionary, 2020). The synonym replacement method is helpful to generate semantic texts.

Performance Metrics

The use of an evaluation metrics is a vital to rate the classification performance of a learning algorithm. The broadly used metrics for evaluating classification algorithm is the accuracy and error. In the imbalances datasets, it seen that there exists a bias towards the majority class while, measuring performance. Therefore, these famous metrics' values do not show the classifier's ability to predict examples from minority classes.

Theoretically, various evaluation metrics like Precision, Recall, and F-measure etc. have been put forward to measure the classifier performance while dealing with imbalanced data problems.

To measure the correctly classified positive class samples, a Precision metric is used and defined as:

$$Precision = \frac{TP}{TP + FP}.$$

where TP and FP stands for the count of true-positive and false-positive respectively.

Now the Recall is used to measure the proportion of correctly identified the real positive samples and is calculated using:

$$Recall = \frac{TP}{TP + FN}.$$

where FN stands for the counts of false-negative.

In general, there is a trade-off between precision and recall. This relationship can give an inherent view of the performance of the classifier using the F-measure metrics. F-measure is basically a harmonic mean of precision and recall (Chicco D. et al. 2020). It is calculated using:

$$F - measure = 2 * \frac{Presicion * Recall}{Precision + Recall}.$$

In the experimental study, a highly imbalanced dataset is used so precision, recall and F-measures are used as evaluation metrics for evaluating model performance.

EXPERIMENT RESULTS AND ANALYSIS

Experiments performed on a highly imbalanced emotion dataset. It is balanced using above mentioned techniques and applied to the proposed model EMOTWEET_TL and infer emotion from it. Results are shown in Table 3.

In the study, an emotion dataset with 13 emotion classes is used. Data distributions of classes are highly imbalanced and described in Table1. To balance data distributions of minority classes, different techniques such as resampling, handling redundant data in majority classes, and data augmentation methods are used. After applying the methods mentioned above, the prepared balanced dataset is fed to the proposed EMOTWEET_TL model that infers tweets' emotion.

The experimental study conducted with the baseline method gives an f1-score 0.17. In the Baseline method, the imbalanced dataset is fed to the proposed model and evaluates its performance. The results of the dataset, balanced with the SMOTE method, give poor performance. F1-score is only 0.028. The performance of the model is decreasing with much difference in F1-score.

One observation of SMOTE algorithm's poor performance is that it does not take neighboring samples from other classes while generating synthetic samples. This can lead to an increase in the overlapping of classes and may introduce additional noise. The literature study indicates that the performance of the SMOTE is degrading with text data because the vectors created from the text data has high dimensions, and SMOTE is not very effective for high dimensional data (Chawla N. V. et al. 2002).

The technique's performance that used cosine similarity to filter out similar tweets from majority classes is almost equal to a baseline method. The F1-score of the method is 0.18. The technique finds similar tweets with a cosine similarity threshold of 40%. Due to the small amount of similar tweets identified with a given threshold, the majority class tweets not reduced much in size. So the impact of the method on this dataset is not much as compared to other techniques. A prior experiment was conducted with 65% threshold but identified a very less number of similar tweets.

Data augmentation methods such as shuffle words, shuffle sentences and replacing synonyms in tweets give better results than the baseline method. Their F1-score are 0.36, 0.48 and 0.38 respectively. Almost it is +0.20 points higher than the baseline method. The new tweets generated using these methods are similar to their class tweets, and it is one of the reasons for better performance. The Shuffle sentence method gives better performance than the shuffle words method. In the shuffle words method, a tweet is tokenized and shuffles these tokens and again joining them may change the context of some tweets and may cause the model's effectiveness. Whereas in the shuffle sentences method, tweets are tokenized by sentences and shuffle sentences to create a new tweet, so the context of sentences did not change, and performance may improve. These prominent methods are performed well as a merging minority classes method. The F1-score of this method is 0.48. Similar minority classes are merged, and as a result, it reduces the number of classes in the dataset. The merging method performs well over other methods of experimental study. Better performance of the methods due to below reasons:

CONCLUSION AND FUTURE WORK

Emotion detection from the Twitter dataset is confronted with the class imbalance problem. Most machine learning and deep learning classification algorithms are not equipped to manage imbalanced distribution of classes and are likely to get influenced by majority classes.

Table 3. Performance of the proposed model for different techniques to balancing class distribution of the dataset

Method		Train			Validation			Test		
		Precision	Recall	F1-score	Precision	Recall	F1-score	Precision	Recall	F1-score
Baseline		0.65	0.2	0.30	0.44	0.10	0.18	0.44	0.10	0.17
Handling Redundant Data	Using cosine similarity	0.71	0.22	0.34	0.39	0.12	0.18	0.39	0.12	0.18
	Merging Minority classes	0.78	0.62	0.69	0.53	0.45	**0.49**	0.53	0.44	**0.48**
Resample Training Dataset	SMOTE	0.69	0.014	0.028	0.67	0.012	0.023	0.70	0.014	0.028
Data Augmentation	Shuffle Words	0.80	0.28	0.42	0.73	0.24	**0.37**	0.72	0.24	**0.36**
	Shuffle sentences	0.84	0.30	0.52	0.78	0.35	**0.48**	0.77	0.35	**0.48**
	Synonym	0.86	0.30	0.44	0.78	0.26	**0.39**	0.77	0.25	**0.38**

• It reduces the number of classes of the dataset.

• It balances the distribution of data in all merged classes.

A way to address this challenge is to use different strategies for balancing imbalance class distribution in a case study are handling redundant dataset, resampling training dataset and data augmentation. Five methods related to the techniques mentioned above examined in a case study. In a case study, experiments are conducted on Twitter dataset collecting from Kaggle to infer emotions from the tweets. A Twitter dataset is in the English language. The obtained results show that merging minority classes with similar classes and shuffle sentence methods for data augmentation give better performance than other techniques.

In future work, we intend to extend our study to incorporate more advanced techniques for data augmentation, such as generating new semantic tweets using biLSTM models and using machine language translation techniques.

Reduce the majority classes' size by filtering out semantically similar tweets using the Siamese LSTM model instead of a cosine similarity measure to get the more accurate and efficient performance of the model. An experimental study will perform with more datasets on the same domain and with different domain datasets.

REFERENCES

Abdul-Mageed, M., & Ungar, L. (2017, July). Emonet: Fine-grained emotion detection with gated recurrent neural networks. In *Proceedings of the 55th annual meeting of the association for computational linguistics (volume 1: Long papers)* (pp. 718-728). 10.18653/v1/P17-1067

Al Masum, S. M., Prendinger, H., & Ishizuka, M. (2007, November). Emotion sensitive news agent: An approach towards user centric emotion sensing from the news. In *IEEE/WIC/ACM International Conference on Web Intelligence (WI'07)* (pp. 614-620). IEEE. 10.1109/WI.2007.124

Almahairi, A., Rajeshwar, S., Sordoni, A., Bachman, P., & Courville, A. (2018, July). Augmented cyclegan: Learning many-to-many mappings from unpaired data. In *International Conference on Machine Learning* (pp. 195-204). PMLR.

Bagozzi, R. P., Gopinath, M., & Nyer, P. U. (1999). The role of emotions in marketing. *Journal of the Academy of Marketing Science*, *27*(2), 184–206. doi:10.1177/0092070399272005

Balabantaray, R. C., Mohammad, M., & Sharma, N. (2012). Multi-class twitter emotion classification: A new approach. *International Journal of Applied Information Systems*, *4*(1), 48–53. doi:10.5120/ijais12-450651

Balahur, A., Hermida, J. M., & Montoyo, A. (2011, June). Detecting implicit expressions of sentiment in text based on commonsense knowledge. In *Proceedings of the 2nd Workshop on Computational Approaches to Subjectivity and Sentiment Analysis (WASSA 2011)* (pp. 53-60). Academic Press.

Bandhakavi, A., Wiratunga, N., Massie, S., & Padmanabhan, D. (2017). Lexicon generation for emotion detection from text. *IEEE Intelligent Systems*, *32*(1), 102–108. doi:10.1109/MIS.2017.22

Bandhakavi, A., Wiratunga, N., Padmanabhan, D., & Massie, S. (2017). Lexicon based feature extraction for emotion text classification. *Pattern Recognition Letters*, *93*, 133–142. doi:10.1016/j.patrec.2016.12.009

Bouazizi, M., & Ohtsuki, T. (2017). A pattern-based approach for multi-class sentiment analysis in Twitter. *IEEE Access: Practical Innovations, Open Solutions*, *5*, 20617–20639. doi:10.1109/ACCESS.2017.2740982

Brave, S., & Nass, C. (2009). Emotion in human–computer interaction. In *Human-computer interaction fundamentals* (Vol. 20094635). CRC Press. doi:10.1201/b10368-6

Canales, L., & Martínez-Barco, P. (2014, October). Emotion detection from text: A survey. In *Proceedings of the workshop on natural language processing in the 5th information systems research working days (JISIC)* (pp. 37-43). 10.3115/v1/W14-6905

Chatterjee, A., Gupta, U., Chinnakotla, M. K., Srikanth, R., Galley, M., & Agrawal, P. (2019). Understanding emotions in text using deep learning and big data. *Computers in Human Behavior*, *93*, 309–317. doi:10.1016/j.chb.2018.12.029

Chaumartin, F. R. (2007). UPAR7: A knowledge-based system for headline sentiment tagging. In *SemEval (ACL Workshop)* (pp. pp-422). 10.3115/1621474.1621568

Chawla, N. V., Bowyer, K. W., Hall, L. O., & Kegelmeyer, W. P. (2002). SMOTE: Synthetic minority over-sampling technique. *Journal of Artificial Intelligence Research*, *16*, 321–357. doi:10.1613/jair.953

Chicco, D., & Jurman, G. (2020). The advantages of the Matthews correlation coefficient (MCC) over F1 score and accuracy in binary classification evaluation. *BMC Genomics*, *21*(1), 1–13. doi:10.118612864-019-6413-7 PMID:31898477

Cohen, E. (2018, September 16). *How to predict Quora Question Pairs using Siamese Manhattan LSTM.* Medium. https://blog.mlreview.com/implementing-malstm-on-kaggles-quora-question-pairs-competition-8b31b0b16a07

Cong, Q., Feng, Z., Li, F., Xiang, Y., Rao, G., & Tao, C. (2018, December). XA-BiLSTM: A deep learning approach for depression detection in imbalanced data. In *2018 IEEE International Conference on Bioinformatics and Biomedicine (BIBM)* (pp. 1624-1627). IEEE.

Damani, S., Raviprakash, N., Gupta, U., Chatterjee, A., Joshi, M., Gupta, K., & Mathur, A. (2018). *Ruuh: A deep learning based conversational social agent.* arXiv preprint arXiv:1810.12097.

Deerwester, S., Dumais, S. T., Furnas, G. W., Landauer, T. K., & Harshman, R. (1990). Indexing by latent semantic analysis. *Journal of the American Society for Information Science, 41*(6), 391–407. doi:10.1002/(SICI)1097-4571(199009)41:6<391::AID-ASI1>3.0.CO;2-9

Druckman, J. N., & McDermott, R. (2008). Emotion and the framing of risky choice. *Political Behavior, 30*(3), 297–321. doi:10.100711109-008-9056-y

Emotion. (2020, January 7). *Kaggle.* https://www.kaggle.com/icw123/emotion

Es, S. (2021b, April 9). *Data Augmentation in NLP: Best Practices From a Kaggle Master.* Neptune. Ai. https://neptune.ai/blog/data-augmentation-nlp

Fadaee, M., Bisazza, A., & Monz, C. (2017). Data augmentation for low-resource neural machine translation. arXiv preprint arXiv:1705.00440. doi:10.18653/v1/P17-2090

Felbo, B., Mislove, A., Søgaard, A., Rahwan, I., & Lehmann, S. (2017). Using millions of emoji occurrences to learn any-domain representations for detecting sentiment, emotion and sarcasm. arXiv preprint arXiv:1708.00524. doi:10.18653/v1/D17-1169

Gill, A. J., French, R. M., Gergle, D., & Oberlander, J. (2008). Identifying emotional characteristics from short blog texts. In *30th Annual Conference of the Cognitive Science Society* (pp. 2237-2242). Washington, DC: Cognitive Science Society.

Hasan, M., Agu, E., & Rundensteiner, E. (2014). Using hashtags as labels for supervised learning of emotions in twitter messages. ACM SIGKDD workshop on health informatics.

Hasan, M., Rundensteiner, E., & Agu, E. (2014). *Emotex: Detecting emotions in twitter messages.* Academic Press.

He, H., Bai, Y., Garcia, E. A., & Li, S. (2008, June). ADASYN: Adaptive synthetic sampling approach for imbalanced learning. In *2008 IEEE international joint conference on neural networks (IEEE world congress on computational intelligence)* (pp. 1322-1328). IEEE.

Hochreiter, S., & Schmidhuber, J. (1997). Long short-term memory. *Neural Computation, 9*(8), 1735–1780. doi:10.1162/neco.1997.9.8.1735 PMID:9377276

Hoens, T. R., & Chawla, N. V. (2013). Imbalanced datasets: from sampling to classifiers. *Imbalanced learning: Foundations, algorithms, and applications,* 43-59.

I. (2019b, March 1). *NLP (data augmentation)*. Kaggle. https://www.kaggle.com/init927/nlp-data-augmentation#Introduction-to-Data-Augmentation-in-NLP

Jamal, N., Xianqiao, C., & Aldabbas, H. (2019). Deep learning-based sentimental analysis for large-scale imbalanced twitter data. *Future Internet, 11*(9), 190. doi:10.3390/fi11090190

Kafle, K., Yousefhussien, M., & Kanan, C. (2017, September). Data augmentation for visual question answering. In *Proceedings of the 10th International Conference on Natural Language Generation* (pp. 198-202). 10.18653/v1/W17-3529

Kobayashi, S. (2018). Contextual augmentation: Data augmentation by words with paradigmatic relations. arXiv preprint arXiv:1805.06201. doi:10.18653/v1/N18-2072

Köper, M., Kim, E., & Klinger, R. (2017, September). IMS at EmoInt-2017: Emotion intensity prediction with affective norms, automatically extended resources and deep learning. In *Proceedings of the 8th Workshop on Computational Approaches to Subjectivity, Sentiment and Social Media Analysis* (pp. 50-57). 10.18653/v1/W17-5206

Kothiya, Y. (2020, July 17). *How I handled imbalanced text data - Towards Data Science*. Medium. https://towardsdatascience.com/how-i-handled-imbalanced-text-data-ba9b757ab1d8

Kotsiantis, S., Kanellopoulos, D., & Pintelas, P. (2006). Handling imbalanced datasets: A review. *GESTS International Transactions on Computer Science and Engineering, 30*(1), 25–36.

LeCun, Y., Bengio, Y., & Hinton, G. (2015). Deep learning. *Nature, 521*(7553), 436-444.

Lee, S. Y. M., Chen, Y., & Huang, C. R. (2010, June). A text-driven rule-based system for emotion cause detection. In *Proceedings of the NAACL HLT 2010 Workshop on Computational Approaches to Analysis and Generation of Emotion in Text* (pp. 45-53). Academic Press.

Li, W., & Xu, H. (2014). Text-based emotion classification using emotion cause extraction. *Expert Systems with Applications, 41*(4), 1742–1749. doi:10.1016/j.eswa.2013.08.073

Liu, B. (2012). Sentiment analysis and opinion mining. *Synthesis Lectures on Human Language Technologies, 5*(1), 1-167.

Ma, C., Prendinger, H., & Ishizuka, M. (2005, October). Emotion estimation and reasoning based on affective textual interaction. In *International conference on affective computing and intelligent interaction* (pp. 622-628). Springer. 10.1007/11573548_80

Mohri, M., Rostamizadeh, A., & Talwalkar, A. (2012). *Foundations of machine learning*. Academic Press.

Multi-Class Emotion Classification for Short Texts. (2018, March 17). *Github*. https://tlkh.github.io/text-emotion-classification/

Mundra, S., Sen, A., Sinha, M., Mannarswamy, S., Dandapat, S., & Roy, S. (2017, May). Fine-grained emotion detection in contact center chat utterances. In *Pacific-Asia Conference on Knowledge Discovery and Data Mining* (pp. 337-349). Springer. 10.1007/978-3-319-57529-2_27

Neviarouskaya, A., Prendinger, H., & Ishizuka, M. (2010, August). Recognition of affect, judgment, and appreciation in text. In *Proceedings of the 23rd International Conference on Computational Linguistics (Coling 2010)* (pp. 806-814). Academic Press.

Ortony, A., Clore, G. L., & Collins, A. (1988). *The cognitive structure of emotions*. Cambridge University Press.

Pennington, J., Socher, R., & Manning, C. D. (2014, October). Glove: Global vectors for word representation. In *Proceedings of the 2014 conference on empirical methods in natural language processing (EMNLP)* (pp. 1532-1543). 10.3115/v1/D14-1162

Picard, R. W. (2000). *Affective computing*. MIT Press. doi:10.7551/mitpress/1140.001.0001

PyDictionary. (2020, July 9). *PyPI.* https://pypi.org/project/PyDictionary/

Roberts, K., Roach, M. A., Johnson, J., Guthrie, J., & Harabagiu, S. M. (2012, May). EmpaTweet: Annotating and Detecting Emotions on Twitter. In Lrec (Vol. 12, pp. 3806-3813). Academic Press.

Schuster, M., & Paliwal, K. K. (1997). Bidirectional recurrent neural networks. *IEEE Transactions on Signal Processing, 45*(11), 2673–2681. doi:10.1109/78.650093

Seol, Y. S., Kim, D. J., & Kim, H. W. (2008, July). Emotion recognition from text using knowledge-based ANN. In *ITC-CSCC: International Technical Conference on Circuits Systems, Computers and Communications* (pp. 1569-1572). Academic Press.

Shaikh, S., Daudpota, S. M., Imran, A. S., & Kastrati, Z. (2021). Towards Improved Classification Accuracy on Highly Imbalanced Text Dataset Using Deep Neural Language Models. *Applied Sciences (Basel, Switzerland), 11*(2), 869. doi:10.3390/app11020869

Srivastava, N., Hinton, G., Krizhevsky, A., Sutskever, I., & Salakhutdinov, R. (2014). Dropout: A simple way to prevent neural networks from overfitting. *Journal of Machine Learning Research, 15*(1), 1929–1958.

Strapparava, C., & Mihalcea, R. (2008, March). Learning to identify emotions in text. In *Proceedings of the 2008 ACM symposium on Applied computing* (pp. 1556-1560). 10.1145/1363686.1364052

Subramanian, D. (2020b, January 7). *Emotion analysis in text mining | Towards AI.* Medium. https://pub.towardsai.net/emoticon-and-emoji-in-text-mining-7392c49f596a

Suttles, J., & Ide, N. (2013, March). Distant supervision for emotion classification with discrete binary values. In *International Conference on Intelligent Text Processing and Computational Linguistics* (pp. 121-136). Springer. 10.1007/978-3-642-37256-8_11

Sykora, M. D., Jackson, T., O'Brien, A., & Elayan, S. (2013). Emotive ontology: Extracting fine-grained emotions from terse, informal messages. *IADIS Int. J. Comput. Sci. Inf. Syst, 2013*, 19–26.

T. (2018a, November 16). *Using Word Embeddings for Data Augmentation.* Kaggle. https://www.kaggle.com/theoviel/using-word-embeddings-for-data-augmentation

T. (2020a, September 7). *Using Google Translate for NLP Augmentation.* Kaggle. https://www.kaggle.com/tuckerarrants/using-google-translate-for-nlp-augmentation

Valentino, N. A., Brader, T., Groenendyk, E. W., Gregorowicz, K., & Hutchings, V. L. (2011). Election night's alright for fighting: The role of emotions in political participation. *The Journal of Politics, 73*(1), 156–170. doi:10.1017/S0022381610000939

Van der Zanden, R., Curie, K., Van Londen, M., Kramer, J., Steen, G., & Cuijpers, P. (2014). Keshia Curie, Monique Van Londen, Jeannet Kramer, Gerard Steen, and Pim Cuijpers. Web-based depression treatment: Associations of clients' word use with adherence and outcome. *Journal of Affective Disorders, 160*, 10–13. doi:10.1016/j.jad.2014.01.005 PMID:24709016

Wang, W., Chen, L., Thirunarayan, K., & Sheth, A. P. (2012, September). Harnessing twitter" big data" for automatic emotion identification. In *2012 International Conference on Privacy, Security, Risk and Trust and 2012 International Conference on Social Computing* (pp. 587-592). IEEE.

Wang, W. Y., & Yang, D. (2015, September). That's so annoying!!!: A lexical and frame-semantic embedding based data augmentation approach to automatic categorization of annoying behaviors using# petpeeve tweets. In *Proceedings of the 2015 Conference on Empirical Methods in Natural Language Processing* (pp. 2557-2563). 10.18653/v1/D15-1306

Wang, X., & Zheng, Q. (2013, March). Text emotion classification research based on improved latent semantic analysis algorithm. In *Proceedings of the 2nd International Conference on Computer Science and Electronics Engineering* (pp. 210-213). Atlantis Press. 10.2991/iccsee.2013.55

Zahiri, S. M., & Choi, J. D. (2017). *Emotion detection on tv show transcripts with sequence-based convolutional neural networks.* arXiv preprint arXiv:1708.04299.

Zhang, X., Zhao, J., & LeCun, Y. (2015). *Character-level convolutional networks for text classification.* arXiv preprint arXiv:1509.01626.

Zhao, C., Xin, Y., Li, X., Yang, Y., & Chen, Y. (2020). A heterogeneous ensemble learning framework for spam detection in social networks with imbalanced data. *Applied Sciences (Basel, Switzerland), 10*(3), 936. doi:10.3390/app10030936

This research was previously published in Data Preprocessing, Active Learning, and Cost Perceptive Approaches for Resolving Data Imbalance; pages 211-231, copyright year 2021 by Engineering Science Reference (an imprint of IGI Global).

Chapter 28
Social Media, Cyberculture, Blockchains, and Education:
A New Strategy for Brazilian Higher Education

Matheus Batalha Moreira Nery
Uninassau, Brazil

Magno Oliveira Macambira
Universidade Estadual de Feira de Santana, Brazil

Marlton Fontes Mota
ⓘ https://orcid.org/0000-0003-3585-9862
Universidade Tiradentes, Brazil

Izabella Cristine Oliveira Rezende
Uninassau, Brazil

ABSTRACT

A new world is emerging to higher education worldwide. In Brazil, higher education took a significant turn in the last years with the substantial reductions of government investments in social justice policies. To compensate for the downturn of enrollment of new students in on-campus programs, universities started to invest heavily in distance education online programs and social media strategies. This new trend brought to the core of their strategy the necessity to develop new information and communication technologies to make the students' experience more enjoyable, to facilitate the learning process, and to increase enrollments. This process will enable professors and educators to create inspiring links with their students and within the cyberculture environment. The main objective of this chapter is to contribute to the debate of the uses of social media, cyberculture, and blockchain technology for the development of educational strategies. Therefore, it will review the existing scientific literature on social networking, social media, cyberculture, and blockchains related to Brazil.

DOI: 10.4018/978-1-6684-7123-4.ch028

INTRODUCTION

Brazilian Higher Education has evolved significantly in the past decade. However, it still encounters numerous challenges, especially regarding increasing enrollments and also developing strategies for quality in education. The goal set up for the last administration, President Dilma Rousseff's terms (2011-2016), was to achieve 33% higher education enrollment in the 18-24-year-old age group by 2024 (IBGE, 2016). Nevertheless, the new government has already indicated in their rhetoric that it is in their plans to diminish the public funding for private universities, which nowadays concentrates the majority of enrollments in Brazilian HEI (MEC, 2017).

This scenario started to change in 2015 when the Brazilian government created new rules for the students to have access to government student loans. This new set of rules pumped a crisis in private HEI and forced them to reorganize their strategy to attain a market that is still suffering from the Brazilian economic constraints (MEC, 2017). Facing such adversities, the strategy of Brazilian private institutions shifted from mostly been focus on undergraduate programs funded mostly by government student loans to develop strategies to try scaling up the enrollments in new online distance learning programs, which are not supported by public funds. This new strategy is in compass with new Brazilian government officials' vision to the future of Brazilian higher education, and strategy to scale up enrollments in online graduate programs has already started to be implemented by some institutions in Brazil (Nery, 2018a).

Beyond the new ideas and initiatives by the government, Brazilian HEI is still facing a lot of challenges to develop themselves as institutions that can provide a good service to Brazil's society. Competing in the education global scenario is a distant dream for most institutions of the country. Most of them are still facing problems with the Brazilian government's decision to defund students' loan programs and, at the same time, due to this crisis, are trying to attract students to enroll in their programs using aggressive commercial strategies. The necessary technology to perform in outstanding quality online undergraduate and graduate programs to students still needs to be implemented in most institutions. However, around the world, new technology is assisting universities to achieve a new level o development and increasing the quality of education (Nery, 2018b). Among them, it is the development of strategies in social media and blockchains technology for education, which has already indicated that can change the sector's ways of interacting with knowledge.

The Internet has become a powerful environment for today's enterprises to market their products and services. Universities and colleges are no exception in this trend, as they are continually looking forward to maintaining or expanding their students' enrollments. In Brazil, a new strategy has arisen in this scenario. Led by the necessity of lower the marketing cost of their operation and at the same time creating an online narrative that can help them attract more students, universities, and colleges started to create hashtags to stimulated their stakeholders to actively share information and knowledge about the institution to other users. These hashtags have created a massive block of information about academic programs, research initiatives, and enrollment opportunities.

The research on social media has already advanced in this scenario worldwide. There is a complex body of research work being formed by researches that are using hashtags to analyze important areas, such as political context (Bruns & Burgess, 2011). Others focused on social justice problems such as the uses of racialized hashtags, knew as "blacktags", which implies the uses of social media to do a harmful, racist, humor online (Sharma, 2013). Social media is also a linguistic marketplace and hashtags are used to bolster the visibility of the online content published by its users. Page (2012) has argued that self-branding practices can reinforce the hierarchies that are part o the offline social contexts, as also are being used by large corporations to create a synthetic personalization that can enable new narratives and broadcast talks about products or services.

However a powerful tool to congregate information and discussions about different subjects, recent research also found that most hashtags are used only for a very short amount of time. That makes a challenge for companies that are interested in using this tool. As preferences by the general public keep changing from time to time, the discussions in social media move fast to different directions (Kywe et al, 2012). Predicting hashtags popularities are also a huge challenge that presents itself as of economic importance for companies that are eager to direct information to their public. The main issue for these companies is to identify the features that can be used to describe the new hashtags, so the target public can easily identify them (Ma, Sun & Cong, 2013). Nevertheless, hashtags are the tool that enables its users to build a complex set of meanings in social media, in a massive block of information (Zappavigna, 2015).

Therefore, this chapter aims at analyzing the scientific literature on the social media phenomenon in three distinct ways. First, the authors present a review of the basic concepts of social networking, emphasizing the research development on social behavior made during recent years by organizational psychology. This section contributes to the notion that recent developments in social media are based on behavioral analyzes developed by psychology. Secondly, the authors present an analysis of cyberculture as a theoretical concept important to understanding the uses of hashtags, and other social media tools, in the educational online context. This section is expected to contribute to the understanding that online social environments are underpinned by an online culture over which higher education institutions have no control, much less hegemony. Therefore, they need to constantly work on understanding the narratives developed in these environments. Third, and finally, the authors discuss the challenges and necessities in Brazil related to the implementation of new online tools and strategies, and Blockchain technology. Blockchains are a tool that will modify the forms of interaction between the academic community and higher education institutions. Thus, it is hoped that this last section will contribute to the understanding that the modifications proposed by the blockchain tools are important to rethink the entire context in which higher education institutions are inserted today.

The goal is to better understand whether the uses of social media in Brazil will ultimately lead to the creation of educational narratives among professors, students, and the community that can go beyond the commercial strategy, reaching academic strategies. In the final remarks, the author presents a suggestion to universities' leadership regarding how to improve those strategies to create a more sustainable model of students, professors, and stakeholder interactions. Evidently, this study has limitations. The most important of these is that, in addition to the theoretical conception and discussion of some concepts related to blockchains and social media, this study focuses on regional issues and presents some elements in a case study perspective on Brazil. This study is expected to intensify the discussions on the technological transformations necessary for the development of higher education in Brazil so that the country can be updated on the best educational practices developed around the world.

The Basis of Social Networking: Social Behavior Research Development

Psychology was already interested in the study of behavior in social networks, long before the development of online websites and social media apps used by the massive population. In this field of science, several meanings are attributed to a social network. Naively, without formal analysis, the social networks can be understood as an interwoven set of wires, ropes, and wires, in systems reminiscent of a network, such as the media, sewage, gas and rail transport. In the social sciences, however, there are a wide variety of definitions for this concept. Although they all have different levels of complexity, they all converge to the sense of connection, bonding, and interaction (Santos, 2004). Generally, these concepts use metaphors or examples to facilitate the understanding of the behavior associated with it. Table 1 presents the most relevant definitions in social sciences to the social network concept.

Table 1. Social network concepts found in the literature

Definitions	Author
"A group of individuals who, in a grouped or individual way, relate to others for a specific purpose, characterized by the existence of information flows. Networks can have many or few actors and one or more classes of peer relations. A network consists, therefore, of three basic elements: nodes or actors, links or relations and flows."	Velásquez & Norman (2005)
"A network is a set of relationships. More formally, a network contains a set of objects (in mathematical terms, nodes) and mapping or description of the relationships between objects or nodes. The simplest form of a network contains two objects, 1 and 2, and a relation that unites them. We 1 and 2, for example, can be people, and the relationship that unites them may be 'they are standing in the same room."	Kadushin (2004, pp. 3)
"Social networks are a recent set of methods for the systematic study of social structures."	Degenne & Forse (1999).
"Set of nodes or actors (people or organizations) linked by social relations or ties of specific types. A bond or relationship between the two actors has both force and content. Content includes information, advice or friendship, shared interests or belongings, and typically some level of trust."	Granovetter (1998, pp. 219)
"The perspective of social networks encompasses theories, models, and applications that are expressed in terms of relational concepts or processes."	Wasserman & Faust (1994, pp. 4)
"A network is composed of a set of relationships or bonds between actors (individuals or organizations). A bond between actors has content (the type of relationship) and form (strength or intensity) of the relationship. The content of the relationship may include information and flow of resources, advice or friendship [...] in fact, any kind of social relations can be defined as a bond."	Powell & Smith-Doerr, (1994, pp. 378)

Note: The authors prepared this table based on the literature review for this chapter.

Although these concepts are elucidative and demonstrate the importance of studying behavior in different social contexts, its definitions cannot be parsimonious in conceptualizing social networks entirely as a field of study. Barnes (1972) argues that this lack of consensus is already justified since it is a field of knowledge related to both Psychology and social sciences that have been worked on both the conceptual and the methodological dimensions in the last three decades.

These attempts to outline social network behavior are more pragmatic when this phenomenon is defined in a structuralist perspective, which seeks to understand the dynamics of social relations based on a set of micro-theories from disciplines of the social and STEM sciences. One way to exemplify this argument comes from the work of Watts & Strogatz (1998). They elaborated the concept of "small worlds", which refers to the phenomenon that occurs when individuals, generally referred to as actors in a network, are highly grouped (shaping different and well-defined clusters), but at the same time connect to actors from outside their groups through a small number of intermediaries. Differently, from random networks, the distance between individuals diminishes, more and more, with the entry of new participants. In modern times, the use of hashtags facilitates the flow of information between members of a group in a social network. In higher education, where new media are increasingly used to attract new students, the direction these narratives are taking is of vital importance.

In structural terms, there are cohesive subsets of actors who have relatively strong, direct, intense and frequent links (Wasserman & Faust, 1994), which allows them to have their norms, values, orientations, and subcultures (Scott, 2000). Also, cohesion accommodates the basis for solidarity, identity and collective behavior in greater intensity among actors within the group than with those outside it. However, in a natural context, these groups are not in isolation, but connected, albeit loosely. In this situation, the role of intermediation assumed by certain actors in a network is emphasized. The ties established by them allow communication between different groups.

Kogut & Walker (2001) argue that this type of social configuration is less susceptible to fragmentation. It ensures greater stability of the structure and allows organizations and institutions to manage social relations behavior. The concept of small worlds joins many others in this perspective that highlights the dynamics of social relations, allowing more precise analysis at different levels: (a) The group as a whole; (b) subgroups; (c) and the role of the individual in social networking dynamics. This possibility has already been widely explored by organizations and institutions worldwide (Santos, 2004). Figure 1 presents the evolution of social network theoretical research:

Figure 1. Evolution of social network theory
Note: The authors prepared this figure based on the literature review for this chapter.

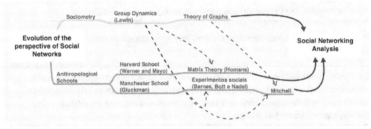

Note: The authors based on the literature review for this chapter prepared this figure.

Three currents influenced the development of the social network theoretical framework. The first one is due to sociometric analysts in 1930, influenced by psychological Gestalt Theory, as it is shown in Figure 1 blue line. Its core was to analyze the characteristics of the social configurations of patients. For Jacob Moreno, these configurations, graphically represented by sociograms, are the result of interpersonal choices, represented by attraction or repulsion, or, for example, friendship or enemies, and other types of relationship that people engage with (Silva, 2013). The sociograms were images formed by actors of a certain group, who presented themselves as points connected by lines indicating a relation between them and other actors in the same social network. These lines represented positive and negative affective relations between them, denouncing the social configuration of the subject under analysis in terms of likes or dislikes. It is a friend of or is an enemy of, among other ways of systematizing the relations under analysis. Among Moreno's contributions, one that stands out is the notion of social configuration and the attempt to represent it in a systematized way. This notion is of fundamental importance for social media analysis, as people are connected and also develop relationships online through the uses of hashtags.

The second major contribution to the development of methods of social network analysis came from the Harvard University in the 1930s, through studies that were made under the leadership of the anthropologist Radcliffe-Brown, Lloyd Warner, and Elton Mayo, as it is described in Figure 1 yellow line.

These authors were interested in the development of social networking in small American communities and industrial plants. Among the studies conducted, there is the research on the Hawthorne industrial plant, which contributed greatly to the evolution of social network analysis and also to what became the School of Human Relations within management studies. The studies of Mayo and his collaborators were aimed at remedying a frustration of the managers of the Western Electric Company, who found no direct cause between the changes produced in some working conditions and the efficiency of the workers. The main contribution of this study to the analysis of social networks was the form used to present its results. The authors organized the data with the use of the sociograms to represent the existing relationships in the target group of the research (Scott, 2000).

The sociograms constructed by the researchers presented a great similarity, not only with the organizational charts used by the management but mainly with the diagrams of electrical circuits produced by the factory and scattered on the walls in the workplaces. These diagrams had the function of describing particularities of the behavior of the groups, such as involvement in games, mutual aid, friendship, etc. The study of the Hawthorne plant encouraged other researchers to use sociograms instead of the conventional diagrams used by anthropologists, thus contributing to the development of social network analysis. Despite these contributions, this initial study did not present a well-defined method for the construction of sociograms. They were presented much more on an artistic style than reliable data analysis. There was no mathematical basis for its construction. The subgroups identified were elaborated from the speech of the workers themselves who were recognized in clicks, using the nomenclatures of the employees themselves, such as "The front gang" or "The back gang". Scott (2000) points out that the conclusions of this work are only attempting to explain how these structures influenced the behavior of the individuals involved in these groups.

Another set of important contributions came from the studies of two small communities, Yankee City and Old City (Scott, 2000). The researchers noted that, in addition to the various subgroups that made up the societies, some of them, called clicks, would be cohesive enough to form norms of conduct that were tacitly established and accepted. Thereafter, there was a significant effort to understand the internal structure of these clicks developed during the research. In the 1940s, based on a re-reading of the reports of Old City and based on Moreno's sociometry, George Homans constructed a theoretical framework for understanding group behavior. This structure was decomposed into two systems: the internal, composed by the feelings that emerged in the interaction between the actors of the group (which is now called informal network); and the external system, which is related to the issues of adaptation to the environment in which the group is located (Scott, 2000).

That innovation ultimately led to the third branch of contribution to the field originated from a group of researchers known as the Manchester School for their links to the Department of Social Anthropology in this institution. Influenced by Radcliffe-Brown's ideas, Max Gluckman was concerned with developing a structural approach that appropriated two dimensions that he considered central to the study of societies: (a) Conflict; (b) and power (Scott, 2000). These two dimensions are integral elements of any community structure and therefore would be present in the dynamics of social transformations. As an example, John Barnes and Elizabeth Bott, two researchers from Manchester School, researched kinship relations also using sociometric studies. These studies led to the use of algebraic and matrix methods for the analysis of roles. It is the proposition of defining structuring as the articulation or arrangement of elements to form the whole (Scott, 2000). From then on, the concept of personal order as a pattern of connections that an individual has with a group of people and the connections that these people have with each other would define the analysis of social networks (Mitchell, 1969). These concepts became the basis to understand social behavior in a more complex environment such as social media platforms.

Cyberculture, Education, and Communication and Information Technology

Understanding social networking is an important milestone in a comprehensive analysis of the transformations that are currently underway in social media, cyberculture, and education. The communication challenges posed by digital technologies in the new millennium have given rise to several debates about the best use of its contents and information. The massive changes in information content available online through social media has awakened new forms of social behavior (Gorini, 2017).

The fast incorporation of communication and information technologies into the daily life of society has evidenced new ways of living, thinking and building relationships that begin to emerge in a process of interaction and participation, conceiving the creation of multiple connections in dynamic networks of communities virtual communities. These relations, especially the ability to constantly sharing ideas online has reached an unprecedented level of cultural evolutionary transformation. They have become part of a hybrid cultural model, where information is processed in constant feedback of narratives and signs. For that purpose, Lemos (2004) pointed out that the cyberculture concept is the work of increasing exchange and social interaction, in various formats, due to the "futurism of modern technoculture" that transforms itself into "present postmodern cyberculture". Therefore, cyberculture is the movement of plural connections and the sharing of private life. It is also the result of popularization in access to new communication and information technologies, such as social media websites and apps.

The role played by the users of social media allows the diffusion of experiences as an actor-issuer of languages and signals, while at the same time acting as a receiver of other people's information, realigned in a necessary interrelation. Cyberspace presents cyberculture as a place of encounters, and also disagreements, reconfigurations, and ruptures. It is in cyberspace that the process of communication gains the freedom to conceptualize the autonomy of the social media users, but at the same time, it promotes the plurality of narratives and meanings that is valuable to educational institutions as learning spaces. The transformative impacts of the Internet emphasize the development of new ways of exploring digital content. This transformation became a new imperative for colleges and universities. This new perspective and the advancement of the so-called virtual society are contributing to the development of tools and devices capable of re-creating structures for sharing and learning (Linhares & Chagas, 2017).

A practical example is the so-called hashtags, which are conceptualized by Grespan & Ratt (2017) as keywords, which are intended to mark the theme of the content that people are sharing in social networks. This tool enables the subject coded in a hashtag to be accessed and retransmitted unlimitedly. There is a dynamic interaction in the use of the hashtag, involving those who are interested in a specific subject. With cyberculture, the constant changes in the traditional systematic educational environment and the evolvement of new online spaces have caused significant variations in the teaching-learning process in an attempt to establish new limits for the frontiers of pedagogical practices. The flow of information in social media leads to the adoption of new ways of reading and writing, and in particular, generates the need to be connected. Hence, collaboratively, hashtags can index content and become a facilitator in the convergence between formal, non-formal and informal knowledge (Zappavigna, 2015). This idea is similar to defended by Scott (2000) about the internal features of social networking, where the users' feelings can emerge in interactions through social media. Now, these features are catalog by hashtags.

Hashtags are presented as the shortest route for the engagement of social networks to encounter with education. Shared knowledge, extracted from digital content, suggests a new realignment in the practices and the uses of knowledge. The hashtags fit the idea of mobility of information, concentrating elementary aspects on the multi-culturally of the world. It is possible to build pedagogical activities and practices from the application of specific hashtags, which promote the search for elements that represent the multiple facts and realities experienced by the students. Likewise, it is possible to understand the shortening of time and space, in the interpretation of information collected by its users, when in approaches that align similar themes (Mota, Porto & Porto, 2018). Over time, they have been behaving like tools that categorize collaborative content for the process of autonomy and creativity of the social media user. And, it makes possible the classification of systematized information, creating the possibility of correlating other information made available, informally, in the cyberspace environment.

Working also as a self-promotion tool, hashtags are an articulated element at social media. Besides being a way of marking a discourse, they are not end in itself, since it generates multiples social behavior that reflects a certain culture that takes form in cyberculture. The applicability of the use of hashtags in the promotion of systematic knowledge, based on the users' experiences, besides promoting the reflection and the search for new knowledge about a certain theme, impels the preservation of its memory. In social media, hashtags are the way to re-dimension information, facilitating its visibility, besides allowing the indexation of specific contents. It allowed the necessary spatial amplitude to the plural essence of cyberculture, which changed the way experimentation of spaces. From the use of instant messaging applications and the insertion of social media into the cultural process of virtualized society, the technologies of writing and reading have undergone significant transformations. And in this context, the communication practices that are carried out in cyberspace promote the construction of a verbal and symbolic language, as a reflection of the cultural behavior about the sharing of users' personal feelings and experiences (Levy, 2015).

These new communicative processes in cyberspace have made learning mobility easier, changing the ways students and professors interact with knowledge, which with cyberculture and new digital technologies, has become socialized, shared and interactive. It is up to the HEI to consider the need to conceive education in a perspective directed to a new pedagogy of communication (Linhares & Chagas, 2017). The best use of digital technology, its applications, tools, and devices, can be the differential in developing an orderly compilation of social media thinking. Through the use of hashtags, it is possible to share information instantly, organize the posts of images and narratives, and create spaces of production of new knowledge, from educational and communicational experiences.

Therefore, the cultural process in cyberspace enables the creation of learning ecosystems, from the stimulus to criticality and reflection. The use of hashtags provides a greater articulation for the production of knowledge, acting as a model of content codification that facilitates the joint discovery of learning. Compatible with the demand for personal and professional interests, hashtags have become an indispensable element for publications on social networks, especially to make relevant the profile of the user and to socialize experiences. And in this scenario, they will be able to broaden and reconfigured the practices of writing and reading online, which is already becoming extremely relevant to educational practices and methodologies. A new communicative aspect can be mediated by the use of hashtags in HEI, resizing the role of the reader-writer, who will work more intensely on their autonomy in the production of knowledge.

Creating New Social Networking Technology: Blockchains' Brazilian Challenges

Currently, information and communication technologies need to meet the expectations of their increasingly ambitious users. For this reason, it is of the utmost importance to reduce the time and cost of software development, otherwise, they become obsolete and useless by the time that they realize to the general public. This is an important reality in social media, as its framework keeps evolving and, also, the community formed by its users keeps pushing for innovations. Also, creating complex technological systems involves people from different disciplines, each communicating in their way. This can lead to communication problems among stakeholders, directly affecting the results (Aiguier et al., 2012). Hence, in education, for example, the introduction of new technologies requires that those involved be consistently integrated into strategies that can assist them to evolve its practices.

One of the strategies to minimize these problems is the application of different levels of modeling and transformation models, as prescribed by Model-Oriented Approaches (Zohrevand et al., 2011). This approach provides promising ways to automate the software process and are therefore more flexible to deal with the challenges that users face in their educational realities. The Model-Oriented Approaches allows developers to focus on software generation without the involvement of platform-specific concepts. This can lead to reduced development costs, improved software consistency, maintenance, and quality (Zohrevand et al., 2011; Lazarte et al., 2010). This strategy can be an efficient way of handling and solving problems of interoperability, heterogeneity, and alignment between business and technology solutions, especially for HEI.

This strategy is based on the idea of generating code through models created through modeling languages such as UML. This factor allows the developer to focus on software generation without the involvement of platform-specific concepts (ZOHREVAND et al., 2011). MacDonald et al. (2005) define Model-Oriented Approaches as a way of separating business logic from its implementation. This allows the programmer to focus on solving the problem, rather than worrying about the details of the technology (Zohrevand et al., 2011). Model-Oriented Approaches uses software construction models to simulate, estimate, understand, communicate, and produce code (Lazarte et al., 2010).

In this context, it is important to understand that Model-Oriented Approaches entails reducing development costs, improving software consistency, maintenance, and quality. Due to these factors, Lazarte et al. (2010) place it as an efficient way of handling and solving problems of interoperability, heterogeneity, and alignment between the business and technological solutions. This is of important value when one considers the necessity of Brazilian HEI to develop a new approach in terms of communication and information technology. Brazil is still far behind other countries in terms of the development of software for education. Blockchains are already being used and are largely developed in other countries, however, in Brazil, it is mostly used to simplify the academic process, such as validation of academic credits and degree certificates. Experimental research has demonstrated that this process can be implemented in other areas of academic management bringing value to these organizations that are willing to development blockchains technology (Palma et al, 2019).

Brazilian development banks have already shown the potentiality of this tool to deal with problems that surround large corporations with a substantial portfolio of clients. For the public banks, it increases the funding transparency, and, most importantly, allows for a simplification of day-to-day operations, reducing costs (Arantes Junior et al, 2018). However, in reality, the authors argue that is not easier to implement blockchains solutions and mostly this process requires social and technological transitions.

That's the mail challenge also to implement blockchains in higher education institutions, especially in those where its culture presents resistance to change.

The implementation of new technology brings with it a new risk that needs to be compensated with the possibility for a company or a sector to acquire a competitive advantage. For universities, it is crucial to be able to collect information through knowledge management. In the contemporary world of academia, sharing perspectives and knowledge in social media is an ultimate challenge for these institutions. Blockchain technology is becoming a force in that direction, as it enables institutions to freely share knowledge and information without losing its rightful ownership of intellectual capital. Pradipto et al (2019) have found that most universities and colleges around the world must have a concern and awareness about the possibilities that may outcome of these new strategies of sharing knowledge as information and communication technology advances.

Such cultural, technological and social problems need to be solved for blockchains evolve as a vibrant technology in Brazil. For this reason, the university projects must cover all phases of the software development process addressing both social networking issues, as linked by social behavior psychology analysis, and social media and cyberculture elements, such as the hashtags uses. This is because the time and cost of development need to be reduced, as new software always has the risk to encounter an aversive environment and it is released to the general public. Also, universities and colleges need to understand blockchains as a challenge to achieve success in a new environment where the rationality involved requires from academic players an increasing abstraction level to design possibilities for new information and communication technology.

Final Considerations

The digital culture, so-called Cyberculture, is the effect of a communicational process, carried out through cyberspace. It is constantly evolving with the creation of a community that enables the production of a continuous, virtual and interconnected world. Blockchains and information and communication technology will have a key role in the development of cyberculture. In it, the exchange of information is promoted in a constant flow of meanings that surpass the time and space barrier. In this perspective, the information is processed in a continuous, fluid and convergent way, altering the structures of the resulting knowledge. By fostering the insertion of a variety of sources of knowledge, digital culture provokes maximum interactivity for greater effectiveness in the communication process, making possible the incorporation of systematic educational knowledge in this new learning environment.

Looking at how cyberculture is changing and how these changes across different social networking platforms change behavior in higher education institutions is of paramount importance. To this end, it is important to envision solutions beyond the minimization of paperwork and cost reductions that many blockchain-supported processes provide. One must act where much of the narrative about social behavior is developing. For example, these processes can facilitate communication between social network users and higher education institutions. In Brazil, as well as in other countries, communication is essential. However, many of the academic problems recurrently experienced by the academic community largely stem from communication failures between students, teachers, and administrative staff. A key recommendation to minimize these problems would be to use blockchains applications to facilitate communication and network integration of the many different actors that make up the academic community.

Also, the inexhaustible range of cyberspace leads to multiple forms of collaborative learning. Cyberculture bridges between formal knowledge and cognitive experiences, which inhabit the subjectivities of individuals and groups, as social networking theory has already demonstrated. In this context, language-mediated by the versatility of the communicative universe in digital culture favors the insertion of hashtags as an adequate resource to promote the inclusion and the engagement of tools and devices to pedagogical practices. The functionality of the hashtag provides the imperative to make the memory of conscious connectivity constant. After all, just as digital culture fosters the multiplicity of sources of knowledge production, it compares in the dispersion of this same knowledge, to dynamically update the virtual contents shared in cyberspace.

As faster as cyberculture is evolving, the dynamic of blockchains technology is also altering the way HEI around the world interact and share with knowledge. This new front is surrounded by yet but social and cultural obstacles. Universities and colleges will have to address them to overcome the berries that make collected and share information reality of a large population of scholars and HEI administrators. Information and communication technology is crucial for the development of HEI on a global level. Therefore, it is time for Brazilian HEI to start to work in this direction.

REFERENCES

Aiguier, M., Golden, B., & Krob, D. (2012). Modeling of complex systems II: A minimalist and unified semantics for heterogeneous integrated systems. *Applied Mathematics and Computation, 218*(16), 8039–8055. doi:10.1016/j.amc.2012.01.048

Arantes, G. M., Jr., D'Almeida., J. N., Jr., Onodera, M. T., Moreno, S. M. de B. M., & Almeida, V. da R. S. (2018). Improving the Process of Lending, Monitoring and Evaluating through Blockchain Technologies An Application of Blockchain in the Brazilian Development Bank (BNDES). *2018 IEEE Confs on Internet of Things, Green Computing and Communications, Cyber, Physical and Social Computing, Smart Data, Blockchain, Computer and Information Technology, Congress on Cybermatics.*

Barnes, J. A. (1972). *Social Networks Module in Anthropology.* Reading, MA: Addison Wesley.

Brazilian Institute of Geography and Statistics (IBGE). (2016). *Indicadores PIB.* Retrieved in August 31, 2016, from https://www.ibge.gov.br/home/

Bruns, A., & Burgess, J. E. (2011). The use of Twitter hashtags in the formation of ad hoc publics. In *Proceedings of the 6th European Consortium for Political Research (ECPR) General Conference 2011.* University of Iceland.

Degenne, A., & Forse, M. (1999). *Introducing Social Networks.* London: Sage Publications. doi:10.4135/9781849209373

Gorini, P. (2017) Hashtag em Disputa: Um Estudo Sobre Identidade e Memória Nas Redes Sociais [Hashtag in Dispute: A Study on Identity and Memory in Social Networks]. *XI Encontro nacional de história da mídia. São Paulo.* Available in: http://www.ufrgs.br/alcar/encontros-nacionais-1/encontros-nacionais/11o-encontro-2017/gt-2013-historia-da-midia-digital/hashtag-em-disputa-um-estudo-sobre-identidade-e-memoria-nas-redes-sociais/view

Granovetter, M. (1983). The Strength of Weak Ties: A Network Theory Revisited. *Sociological Theory, 1*, 201–233. doi:10.2307/202051

Grespan, C. L., & Ratt, C. G. T. (2017). Hashtags e sociabilidade: potencialidades e possibilidades da Ciberdemocracia [Hashtags and sociability: potentialities and possibilities of cyberdemocracy]. *Artefactum. Revista de estudos em Linguagens e Tecnologia, 14*(1).

Kadushin, C. (2004). Too Much Investment in Social Capital? *Social Networks, 26*(1), 75–90. doi:10.1016/j.socnet.2004.01.009

Kogut, B., & Walker, G. (2001). The small world of Germany and the durability of national networks. *American Sociological Review, 66*(3), 317–335. doi:10.2307/3088882

Kywe, S. M., Hoang, T. A., Lim, E. P., & Zhu, F. (2012). On Recommending Hashtags in Twitter Networks. In K. Aberer, A. Flache, W. Jager, L. Liu, J. Tang, & C. Guéret (Eds.), Lecture Notes in Computer Science: Vol. 7710. *Social Informatics. SocInfo 2012.* Berlin: Springer.

Lazarte, I. M., Tello-Leal, E., Roa, J., Chiotti, O., & Villarreal, P. D. (2010) Model-driven development methodology for B2B collaborations. *Proceedings - IEEE International Enterprise Distributed Object Computing Workshop, EDOC,* 69–78.

Lemos, A. (2004). Ficção científica cyberpunk: o imaginário da cibercultura [Science fiction cyberpunk: the imaginary of cyberculture]. *Revista Conexão, 3*(6).

Levy, P. (2015). A inteligência coletiva: por uma antropologia do ciberespaço [Collective intelligence: by an anthropology of cyberspace]. São Paulo: Edições Loyola.

Linhares, R., & Chagas, A. M. (2017). Aprendizagens no ciberespaço: por uma pedagogia da comunicação em uma educação mestiça [Learning in cyberspace: through a pedagogy of communication in a mestizo education]. In Educação no ciberespaço: novas configurações, convergências e conexões. EDUNIT.

Ma, Z., Sun, A., & Cong, G. (2013). On predicting the popularity of newly emerging hashtags in Twitter. *Journal of the American Society for Information Science and Technology, 64*(7), 1399–1410. doi:10.1002/asi.22844

Ministério da Educação (MEC). (2017). *MEC Transparência* [MEC Transparency]. Available on: http://portal.mec.gov.br/secretaria-de-regulacao-e-supervisao-da-educacao-superior-seres/transparencia/30000-uncategorised

Mitchell, J. C. (1969). The concept and use of social networks. In *Social Networks in urban Situations.* Manchester, UK: Manchester University Press.

Mota, M. F., Porto, C. de M., & Porto, I. de M. (2018). "Antes mundo era pequeno, porque terra era grande": a antevisão da interatividade digital dos mundos na poesia atemporal de Gilberto Gil, e o seu encontro com a educação [Before, the world was small, because the land was great: the preview of the digital interactivity of the worlds in the timeless poetry of Gilberto Gil, and his encounter with education]. In Educiber: Diálogos ubíquos para além da tela e da rede. Aracaju: EDUNIT.

Nery, M. B. M. (2018a). Brazil's Social Justice Policies for Higher Education: What can we learn from Asia? *Asian Journal of Distance Education, 13*(1), 88 – 108. Webpage: http://www.asianjde.org/2018v13.1.Nery.pdf

Nery, M. B. M. (2018b). Science Without Borders' Contributions to Internationalization of Brazilian Higher Education. *Journal of Studies in International Education. Journal of Studies in International Education, 22*(5), 371–392. doi:10.1177/1028315317748526

Page, R. (2012). The linguistics of self-branding and micro-celebrity in Twitter: The role of hashtags. *Discourse & Communication, 6*(2), 181-201.

Palma, L. M., Vigil, M. A. G., Pereira, F. L., & Martina, J. E. (2019). Blockchain and smart contracts for higher education registry in Brazil. *International Journal of Network Management, 29*(Special Issue), E2061. doi:10.1002/nem.2061

Powell, W. W., & Smith-Doerr, L. (1994). *Networks and Economic Life. The Handbook of Economic Sociology*. Russell Sage Foundation and Princeton University Press.

Pradipto, Y. D., Barlian, E., Suprapto, A. T., Buana, Y., Bawono, A., Garnaditya, D., & Pangaribuan, C. H. (in press). *The role of blockchain technology as a mediator between knowledge management and sustainable competitive advantage*. Academic Press.

Santos, M. V. (2004). *Redes sociais informais e compartilhamento de significados sobre mudança organizacional: estudo numa empresa petroquímica* [Informal social networks and sharing of meanings about organizational change: study in a petrochemical company] (Masters degree dissertation). UFBA.

Scott, J. (2000). *Social Network Analysis a Handbook*. Sage Publications.

Sharma, S. (2013). Black Twitter? Racial Hashtags, Networks and Contagion. *New Formation, 78,* 46-64.

Silva, E. D. C. (2013). *Consentimento Organizacional: um construto bi ou unidimensional?* [Organizational Consent: a bi-dimensional or one-dimensional construct?] (Doctoral thesis). Universidade Federal da Bahia.

Velásquez, A., & Norman, A. G. (2005). Manual introductorio al análisis de redes sociales: medidas de centralidad [Introductory manual to the analysis of social networks: measures of centrality]. Mexico: Universidad Autónoma Del Estado de México: Universidade Autónoma Chaping Press.

Wasserman, S., & Faust, K. (1994). *Social network analysis: methods and applications*. Cambridge, UK: Cambridge University Press. doi:10.1017/CBO9780511815478

Watts, D. J., & Strogatz, S. H. (1998). Collective Dynamics of "Small-World" Networks. *Nature, 393.* PMID:9623998

Zappavigna, M. (2015). Searchable talk: The linguistic functions of hashtags, Social Semiotics. *Journal Social Semiotics, 25*(3), 274–291. doi:10.1080/10350330.2014.996948

Zohrevand, Z., Bibalan, Y. M., & Ramsin, R. (2011). Towards a framework for the application of Model-Driven Development in Situational Method Engineering. *Proceedings - Asia-Pacific Software Engineering Conference, APSEC,* 122–129. 10.1109/APSEC.2011.55

Section 3
Tools and Technologies

Chapter 29
Using Social Media in Creating and Implementing Educational Practices

Robyn Gandell
Unitec Institute of Technology, New Zealand

Inna Piven
Unitec Institute of Technology, New Zealand

ABSTRACT

Social media use has become ubiquitous in the everyday lives of many people around the world. Combined with smartphones, these interactive websites provide a vast array of new activities and immediate access to a world of information for both teachers and students. Research into the use of social media in educational practice is growing. In this chapter, the authors examine the use of social media from the perspective of lecturers and learning designers in a tertiary education institute in New Zealand. Data from a qualitative, interview-based research investigation highlights three key themes: 1) the use of social media as a course management tool; 2) the use of social media to enhance student centered learning; and 3) the need for institutional support for using social media in educational contexts.

INTRODUCTION

Over the last twenty years social media websites, particularly commercial social media sites, have increased in number and functionality (Tess, 2013; Chaffey, 2017). This has happened as, and perhaps because of, developments in smartphone technology where millions of people now have everyday access to handheld computers and an increasing array of applications (Smith, 2010). Using smartphones, it is now possible to easily record, edit and post photos, videos and other media to social media sites where they can be viewed, potentially by millions of people but more likely by friends and relatives. With such large numbers of people worldwide interacting through social media sites everyday (Chaffey, 2017), social interactions are changing and this has the potential for significant change in classroom

DOI: 10.4018/978-1-6684-7123-4.ch029

social interactions as well. The early reaction of many lecturers and teachers to mobile phones was to ban use of these devices in the classroom. As smartphones evolved, educators and institutions realized that these devices allowed unprecedented access to information and to the world from the classroom. In addition, with the growth of online Learning Management Systems (LMS) and blended learning in education, some educators realized that social media could also offer a way to enhance the learning and teaching in the classroom.

Although there is a growing body of literature on social media, the research into the benefits and challenges for tertiary learning is still emerging (Salmon, 2015; Tess, 2013). This research provides a snapshot of lecturers' and learning designers' use of social media platforms in a tertiary education context. The study investigates the experiences of these educators, their use of social media in learning and teaching, and their understanding of how social media fits within a pedagogical framework and best teaching practices. In seeking to understand what is happening in these courses from a lecturer's and learning designer's perspective we posed the following research question:

How is social media effectively integrated in learning design and development within the tertiary educational context?

BACKGROUND

Social media is a new social and cultural reality characterized by unlimited opportunities for connection, communication, information seeking and knowledge sharing. As Piven and Breazeale (2016) state; "the most noticeable changes in all aspects of our collective, private and public lives are connected to the emergence of social media" (p. 283). In a multitude of ways, social media plays an important role in day-to-day practices and experiences within the education sector. For example, the recent global survey of higher education social media usage by Hootsuite (2017) reported that over 90% of education providers across the globe are now engaged with social media. While marketing and communication departments remain the most common users, there is a high adaption of social media by academic staff as well. The report also confirms that a changing student profile is the key driver behind social media adaptation by educators. As Benson (2016) states, "this new generation of students has provoked the proliferation of technology resources that could be used by academic staff to facilitate students' learning experience" (as cited in Kofinas, Al-Shawakbeh, & Lim, 2016, p. 268).

Indeed, in the past ten years, institutions, teachers and learning designers have become increasingly aware of the possibilities offered by social media for learning and teaching. If used appropriately, some researchers report, social media can lead students to more effective self-directed learning (McLoughlin & Lee, 2010; Salmon et al, 2015), better communication and collaborative skills (Rambe, 2012), and development of educational communities (Bosch, 2009). Griesemer believes that social media can help to improve students' learning experiences by preparing them "to enter a workforce that is not geographically constrained... and have highly developed online collaboration skills" (Griesemer, 2012, p. 9).

In response to ongoing technological development and challenges associated with a "mobile society" (Samovar & Porter, 2003, p. 1), educators have begun to take social media seriously and attempted to implement new teaching approaches or redesign existing ones. However, academic research into the meaning of these new approaches, and their possible implications for learning processes, course design and delivery, is still emerging. Moreover, some studies reveal mixed findings on the place of social media in education. Nonetheless, Hootsuite's global survey shows that the number one goal for tertiary education for 2018 is to develop a clear social media strategy. At this point, given social media's role in society, there is a need for academic research into the concrete teaching practices of, and experiences with, the use of social media to understand its implications for tertiary education. This study intends to contribute to that understanding.

METHODOLOGY

The study follows a grounded theory methodology, in which knowledge and ideas are understood to develop from social interaction and personal experiences (Corbin & Strauss, 2015). The world, and the knowledge in the world, is seen as ever changing so that understanding the world requires analyzing the way people interact and construct knowledge (Corbin & Strauss, 2015). To understand the use of social media in tertiary education the authors, therefore, needed to explore tertiary educators experiences in using social media in their personal learning and teaching, actions and interactions.

In this research, qualitative interviews are employed to explore lecturers' and learning designers' experiences in creating and implementing educational practices using social media. This method allows for investigation into the current use of social media in learning and teaching from the perspective of those using these social media tools in the tertiary context. The outcomes of these interviews are analyzed thematically to uncover key themes. The authors also use these interviews to examine best practices in the practical use of social media in blended learning in tertiary education contexts.

Grounded theory rejects notions of a universal truth and researchers certainly recognize that this research does not provide universality in the results. However, the authors hope this research provides some insight into the state of learning and teaching using social media that can be further explored. In addition, the authors acknowledge that research approaches of individual researchers (ranging from participant interviews to researcher transcription and analysis) are influenced by the researchers' own perspectives. To minimize this influence, the authors, use a variety of methods including using the independent analysis by two researchers, rechecking the analysis with interviewees and self-reflection on the analysis.

The five participants selected for interview were chosen from educationalists in a single tertiary institute in New Zealand. This institute provides programs from pre-degree to master's thesis study including vocational programs, certificate, diploma and degree qualifications in a variety of disciplines. The participants were lecturers and course developers who had been engaged in tertiary teaching for at least five years, although some had been teaching for much longer and at different tertiary institutions. All had used a variety of social media platforms in their teaching and course development; one participant for more than two years and the other four participants for over five years. Participants taught not only in different programs such as business, bridging education, sport and education, but also in courses from pre-degree to master's levels, and usually across several of these levels. One participant had taught in pre-degree, degree and masters programs. Three of the participants were female and two were male with their ages ranging from 35-55 years of age. The researchers acknowledge that using five participants is not a representative sample. However, the varied background of the participants enabled researchers to gather a wide variety of responses from these educationalists and thus a better understanding of the uses of social media in a tertiary context. Ethics approval was sought from the participants' tertiary institution and participants were invited to take part in the research. Prior to interviews, informed consent was gained from all participants.

From each individual participant interview transcription, the researchers extracted and gathered together evolving units of meaning. These units of meaning were then collated into emerging themes and compared across all of the participant interviews. These themes were clustered into categories across participant interviews from which three key themes emerged: 1) social media as a classroom management tool; 2) social media as an enabler of student-centered teaching practice; and 3) institutional support and management issues related to social media use in teaching.

DATA ANALYSIS AND KEY THEMES

Theme 1: Social Media as a Course Management Tool

The first key theme to emerge from this study identifies that although social media gained acceptance and a "spotlight" role in education as "a shift towards new… subject formation" and "collaborative modes of enquiry" (Hemmi, Bayne, & Landt, 2009, p. 29), first and foremost it is perceived by many educators as a course management tool. In this regard, a wide array of different aspects of course management have been identified and grouped around the theme defined as "social media as a course management tool".

Social media as a course management tool refers to the extent to which social media has been effectively integrated into course design and delivery. There are several relevant categories that emerged during the data analysis:

- Aligning social media with course learning outcomes
- Reinforcing student engagement & monitoring study progress
- Setting course rules and expectations
- Managing course information & student access to course materials
- Facilitating group collaboration

Aligning Social Media Use With Course Learning Outcomes

In the discussion of the application of social media to course design, participants point to learning outcomes as one of the deciding factors and defining components for course organization, delivery and activities:

We made sure that every week we would be saying to students – we have got these questions [on Facebook] and they are aligning to these learning outcomes.

I have 5 learning outcomes and 13 weeks to teach. When I look at the course calendar I try to identify the best way to use social media.

A part of the learning outcomes is communication and how you work within a team and engagement, this includes a FB group.

However, the focus on the alignment between course learning outcomes and social media is more an exception than a common practice. Participants note that the changes they implemented to course design were not necessarily driven by learning outcomes or specific pedagogical approaches:

We didn't have any real infrastructure...I do think that pedagogy still needs to occur and part of that is to make sure it is in alignment with learning outcomes, assessments and graduate profile.

We set up [Facebook group] very quickly. We don't have any measurements. A lot of the time with new staff we are just kind of muddling along with what works for now.

The examples above indicate that participants tend to emphasize the practical rationality of using social media in course delivery, rather than a required pedagogy for new learning environments. In this respect, McLoughlin & Lee (2010) note that "teachers who adapt social software tools should not do so merely to appear conversant with the tools, but to ensure integration of the tools with sound pedagogical strategies" (p. 38). Whether or not this integration can be achieved easily, a discussion is critical as there is an obvious need to make the learning processes not just manageable, but meaningful for students.

Reinforcing Student Engagement and Monitoring Study Progress

The responses provided by participants show that the decision to incorporate social media into course delivery is often motivated by "quite an honest reflection on students", specifically on their engagement with the course:

We were not happy with the engagement of students... And we tried to reframe the lecture to be more a conversation. Students can engage with the content before attending a lecture. So it was a bit of a change for the institution at this point.

According to the participants, social media provides distinct opportunities to design engaging and interactive courses. For example, one of the research participants learned that social media helped him and his colleague improve students' attendance. By posting course revision questions on Facebook, they were able to achieve a better attendance rate:

Every week we set a series of questions for students to reflect on, that are going to be answered during the next lecture. What we have noticed that for a number of students the attendance at a lecture was a little higher. We didn't publish the answers on Facebook. You have to come along next week to find out.

One participant who intensively uses Tumblr in her courses believes that social media makes it easier to keep track of student progress and provide timely feedback. The features of the social media platform enabled participants to see, for example, not only if assignments are completed but also the student's effort behind that assignment.

It also shows evidence of work, quantity, regularity, a variety [of students' posts] by using archive feature. [Students] cannot find excuses for not doing work. If students are not doing work, it is obvious. [You can] keep an eye on progress and you can support immediately.

The data also shows that some participants use specific social media features such as Facebook polls to check students' understanding of the course content:

We used a polling feature. We asked questions and provide a number of options and then see where students are sitting with that. An idea was... what is their prior knowledge coming to the session.

In a very general sense, social media can perform functions that are typically assigned to learning management systems. As Wang, Woo, Quek, Yang and Liu (2012) conclude, "the Facebook group can be used as LMS as it has certain pedagogical, social and technological affordances" (p. 428). However, determining the extent to which social media can be used as a supplement or even a substitute to a LMS is a difficult task and this is evident throughout the interview data. While participants recognize the limitations of the institutional LMS in terms of informal learning and communication, they feel that it is too early to give social media a central role in learning and teaching. As this research shows a LMS, such as Moodle, and social media can exist in parallel:

There was no connection between the two. It was a case of ...we are not going to use Moodle forums, our conversation will happen on FB instead...It [Facebook] is a really powerful connecting tool, which we can leverage to create a socially constructive type of learning.

This finding concurs with a study by Garmendía and Cobos (2013) who assume that "LMS have a limited functionality to support educational activities from a socio-constructive perspective" (p. 68). Similarly, the study by Dabbagh and Kitsantas (2011) reported that institutionally approved LMS do not allow informal learning to occur. According to Dabbagh and Kitsantas, in contrast with LMS, social media "can facilitate the creation of personal learning environments" that "support a learner-centered pedagogy and foster self-regulated learning" (p. 3).

Setting Course Rules and Expectations

Another important aspect that emerges is participants strong belief of a need for rules and expectations for course-related communications on social media. Aside from the occasional discussions with students about ethical challenges associated with interactivity on social media, participants recognize the importance of creating a "code of conduct" or "social rules". One participant went the extra mile, creating Tumblr exemplars to encourage students to adopt ethical social media practices.

We always did at the start of every new semester what we called an expectation session. It would really be about making students think about themselves in this learning environment, what are their expectations of the teaching staff and what are their expectations regarding the other learners... What we said is that nothing's gonna change when we go to online space. You want this collaborative supportive learning environment in the classroom. Do you want that online as well? This was our kind of structure-setting method. So our first tutorial or a laboratory session guided students through how to use Moodle, what is a Facebook site, what kind of things to expect in different places.

You have a variety of students with different capabilities and skills in terms of communication... Facebook allows raising opinions. It's important not to take it [comments/opinions] personally...Once you draw the line and say "This is what we do", then it makes a lot easier. Students start recognizing the value.

While participants point out differences in teaching, with the use of LMS and social media, in certain aspects these platforms are remarkably similar. There is a fundamental commonality that has everything to do with the institutional control over learning processes. Even on social media where acceptance for "supporting informal learning" (Garmendía & Cobos, 2013, p. 68) and "personal learning environments" (Dabbagh & Kitsantas, 2011) is growing, these participants seem to follow a highly formalized procedure of knowledge production and distribution.

Managing Course Information and Students Access to the Course Materials

A number of participants state that social media allows them to organize and manage course information more effectively. In this regard, participants generally emphasize 'simplicity', 'seamlessness', 'all-in-one' and 'easy-to-use' as the persistent qualities of social media that apply equally well to course information management, activities design and content distribution:

Lots of different resources can be stored e.g. links, photos, quotations, video links and chat.

It [course content] is all there and they [students] share with each other. So if someone is not there, then it doesn't matter.

It [social media] is also a sharing platform for the assessments – they can share documents, images and presentations.

An interesting point was made in regard to the possibility of quickly and easily modifying the course content when needed. It seems to be an important quality of social media as well, particularly when it comes to group work and class discussions:

Students can reblog and change a caption to a comment.

Whatever they have [sketches, notes on a piece of paper] – it goes to social media to a Facebook group. I asked them to record their presentations [at home], then to upload presentations on FB. I also asked students to provide constructive feedback on their classmates' work.

Most important to highlight in this context is that participants feel that, in contrast to Moodle, social media offers a more convenient way to make course information and any course-related activities and updates available to students in a timely fashion. The study shows that participants often use Facebook "as a forum to post information about the class and what was happening".

We know forums are pretty dead now, it's very difficult to get students use them. [Students) were not using Moodle forums, they weren't engaging with anything. All of the institutional emails went to their institutional student accounts that they never checked... Instead they were [on Facebook] on their phones...

Moodle isn't so user-friendly. You can have people hanging out there and having a conversation...

Having said that, the comparison of Moodle and social media, specifically Facebook, did not lead to an assumption that social media could replace the LMS. This is in contrast to Wang et al., (2012) who, as mentioned above, claimed that participants viewed social media as an adjunct to LMS.

I don't see how the course can be completely taught on social media yet. It's still a part of, not a whole.

If there is an assignment or slides – they go on Moodle.

There is an agreement between all participants that social media may best be used as a collaborative platform for group projects, course information updates, timely feedback, and after-class revision activities. For example, it was quite common among participants to use social media for debriefing topics covered in class by asking students clarifying questions. One participant mentioned that she uses Facebook for tutorials: "*I asked students questions and they responded*". There is not enough evidence to suggest that social media had also been incorporated in the assessment practices, excluding formative. However, a number of participants have begun to develop summative assessments with social media components to enrich students' learning experiences within real world contexts.

Facilitating Group Collaboration

What has become evident during the data analysis is that participants agree that social media helps them facilitate group collaboration. More precisely, the participants believe that social media allows for better group work and collaborative learning. This takes can take different forms: from those that are strictly focused on group assignment completion to those that encourage follow up discussions and peer feedback.

All assessments are mainly group assessments…The final assessment is running the event, so it's a lot of intense group work. They [students] have a lot of documents and FB gives them the chance to post quick questions.

The data also reveals that participants believe that collaborative learning on social media resulted in students' "better judgments and personal reflection" and overall, students' active contributions to the group work:

I usually get students into groups based on their specializations (marketing, sales, finance). I ask them to work on different business ideas or on a particular project. Once they finish it, they are expected to present [their projects] to other groups…I believe that it's critical to have more conversations on the subject matter… it can help them [students] to move forward.

Participants also pointed out that social media is an effective instrument in encouraging self-regulated group work:

If [students] not contributing, this was obvious to group who could work out what to do instead of a lecturer having to intervene.

Realizing the advantages of social media, some participants are able to extend student group projects far beyond the Facebook closed groups, focusing on productive collaboration between students and relevant industry partners through various tasks and interactions on social media:

[My] papers are completely practical. The whole aim has been to create an event from scratch working as a team. We typically team up with an organization that runs an event...We create an event schedule – event postings under their name.

Another participant strongly believes that assessments that incorporate social media, either for group projects or students' self-directed learning, support a smoother transition from the classroom to industry for students:

I want to produce employable students...we are going to be proactive, on top of the game. My assignments are based on real companies. Many of them have FB page. What you do? You like the page, see what the company is doing, their latest tweets or the latest updates on their FB page. As a lecturer you can say "hey, your assignment is based on that company, go and check their page". And they start getting feeds from it...Being connected to the industry online, they learn the language they speak.

At this stage, it is important to note that participants often refer to students' careers and employability as the primary drivers behind activities designed for social media:

We want to teach students how to build their personal brands on social media. People have their own brands now and they don't stay with one company forever.

A social media presence can be important. A lot of companies now do look at social media...So there is a responsibility students need to realize – what they put on Facebook may be available to people. It makes them more employable.

This result is supported by McLoughlin and Lee's study (2010) that highlighted an educational need to move towards "a social and participatory pedagogy" that supports students "personal life goals" in the changing job markets where "individuals are expected to have multiple career paths..." (p. 31).

In concluding these findings on social media as a course management tool, it is important to note that, despite the positive experiences presented above, the adaptation of social media as a course design and delivery tool is not straightforward. One research participant raises some doubts as to what extent a teacher should be involved in online learning spaces such as Facebook closed groups:

I'm not a part of students' conversation...I'm not in the groups. I have been in a previous class. I was worried that they are aware I was watching. So it can stop some of the process. This time around I have decided not to be a part of the groups...I do check how the group is going. Who is sitting on social media but not coming to class. Are they active?

This example indicates something particularly interesting about the current stage of social media use in education. On the one hand, understanding the advantages of social media, the participants intensively used it for group projects and students' independent study, or even for supporting students' "transition from classroom to the industry". On the other hand, in many cases the course groups on social media were created, owned and controlled by research participants. This means that course materials, the way they were presented and distributed to students, course discussions, content and activities had been decided and developed by teachers. From the institutional point of view this is not surprising, as social media is still a new and challenging learning space for education. Moreover, teachers and learning designers are greatly limited by specific institutional policies and arrangements within which social media can be adapted and applied to the course design. The result is somewhat consistent with the findings of Hemmi, Bayne, and Landt (2009) on social technologies in higher education: "we found a tendency for both teachers and learners to 'rein in' these potential radical and challenging effects of the new media formations, to control and constrain them within more orthodox understanding of …formal learning" (p. 29).

Even though the research participants welcome social media as "a new learning space" that "gives students some room" to have control over the course, managing and regulating students' learning were still strong priorities for participants.

Theme 2: Student-Centered Teaching Practices

The second key theme to emerge from this study is the use of social media to enhance student-centered teaching practices. Student-centered teaching refers to teaching practices that are responsive to students' individual and group learning needs. Educators using these practices take on the role of assistant to the student's learning, encourage students to become active, independent participants in the learning process, and use knowledge as a tool rather than a goal of learning (Baeten, Kyndt, Struyven & Dochy, 2010).

Research on social media in education often mentions collaboration, community building, creation of new content and forming personal identities as uses of social media in education (Tess, 2013). However, there is little mention of the use of social media as a tool for student-centered learning and teaching. At least some features of student-centered learning are mentioned by all participants in this research and one lecturer in particular specifically explores a student-centered learning pedagogy in her use of social media.

Using Social Media to Understand Students' Background and Knowledge

In order to be able to support and respond to individual students' learning needs, participants in this research use social media to learn about and better understand their students' background, skills and knowledge. All the participants report that social media platforms appear to make information on student skills and knowledge more accessible.

You know a lot about your students through Facebook. What skills they could bring in. Are they weak at English or they are weak at the subject? And based on that you help them. It makes it so easy for learning to occur.

[Social media is] familiar so it automatically makes them feel comfortable. [Social media] shows other student capabilities. Start with what the student knows and respect that. Using a variety of media to capture students and their world tapped into more skills.

[Social media allows] to know your learner, what commitments they have. I had a student… Through connecting with him on FB I realized he was a young parent with young kids and he actually needed a bit more support. What they see is support – the teacher can help me out if I need it.

An idea was… what is their prior knowledge coming to the session.

Using Social Media to Support Students and Encourage Independence

The participants' interest extends beyond just knowing their students. This knowledge of students' strengths and requirements allows the lecturers to support, scaffold and guide the students' learning more effectively. These lecturers also wanted to build on the students' prior understanding and to encourage students to use their own knowledge and worldviews in their learning. These actions both increase students' confidence and independence and their understanding of knowledge as a tool, important aspects of student-centered learning (Baeten et al, 2010).

It is student-centered; it is co-constructivist. Students build their own efficacy and knowledge. [The learning is] student directed and the lecturer scaffolds.

I would ask them to start with "What is the best way for you to communicate?"

We are facilitators we don't know everything.

Students can bring more of their world. Students as the center of their knowledge. Build own efficacy and knowledge, start with what student knows and respect that.

If someone wasn't contributing [on the social media site] this was obvious to group who could work out what to do instead of lecturer having to intervene.

[Students] ease with it and so it makes students more confident increases learning especially less academic students.

Lecturers as Assistants to Learners and Learning

Using social media enables lecturers to access students' work as it progresses, often in real time. This means lecturers are able to provide not only more immediate feedback and support, but also make interventions that are focused on individual need. Rather than supplying more general teacher-led directions, lecturers can assist with individual students' learning needs and highlight students' questions and concerns. This support encourages more active independent learning, further enhancing student-centered learning.

The last 5-10 minutes we quickly scrolled through that FB page and noticed some questions that came up more than few times - do we want to explore more? This kind of use is really powerful. Instant feedback you probably wouldn't get out elsewhere.

[You can] keep an eye on progress and you can support immediately. I displayed files on board as shared and this spurred students to complete and share documents. Instant feedback.

[Social media allows] being reactive to their [students] needs.

They can challenge me .. it can help them to move forward.

Culturally Inclusive

Key student-centered learning for one of the participants in this research means ensuring a safe cultural space where students can express their own knowledge, cultural identity and background. In a bicultural tertiary context, this place for cultural identity is essential (Ministry of Education, n.d). Creating a bicultural environment may allow those who feel outside the norm to find a place for self-expression, countering the predominantly western cultural framework of social media platforms. The lecturer below references the NZ Early Childhood Curriculum document, Te Whariki, as her students are Early Childhood pathway students. In this curriculum particular emphasis is placed on bicultural and inclusive practice (Ministry of Education, 1996).

I wanted a way students could be themselves and bring whanau, traditional knowing etc., and bring this to their work...I wanted the course to privilege their knowledge...Students in center of their knowledge, experts in own cultures.

Much research into the use of social media in learning and teaching centers around social collaboration. This data suggests that, as well as collaboration, using social media platforms facilitates lecturers to incorporate student-centered teaching practice into their courses. For participants in this research, social media allows better access to understanding their students' skills and learning needs. This knowledge of the students helps the lecturers to respond and scaffold student learning in a more individual and focused way and in a more timely manner, thus encouraging students to become more independent learners. In addition, allowing students a place in the class to bring their own knowledge and identity, particularly cultural identity, further increases students' confidence and encourages independent learning and use of their prior knowledge as a resource. By using social media in their courses, lecturers are assisting rather than directing student learning, encouraging independent learning and applying rather than accumulating knowledge. All these aspects give a strong sense of student-centered practice in the research participants' social media-based teaching practice and suggests an interesting avenue for further research.

Theme 3: Institutional Support

Social media platforms provide tools that can support good teaching practice by improving student-teacher interactions (Tess, 2013). As with any new tool, lecturers need guidance with best practice, ongoing discussions with colleagues and access to communities of practice. These are aspects of the social resources provided by the community, society and institutions that support and enable implementation of any new technologies (Warschauer, 2003). Without these social resources, particularly institutional support, implementation of new technology is impeded (Warschauer, 2003).

In addition, the use of commercial platforms adds some ethical and safety risks for students, staff and the institution. Commercial social media sites are developed and promoted for commercial gain, and access to these sites typically requires users to agree that their individual data will be collected and sold. It is usually not possible to opt out of these conditions (Fuchs, 2014). Social media sites are also designed to allow open access and the significance of this to students' safety needs to be considered both by lecturers and institutions.

A significant theme identified by the participants in this research centers around the lack of institutional support. Both social resources and institutional management of ethical and safety risks are highlighted by the participants as a concern in their implementation of social media in their courses.

Support for Teaching Practice

While participants use social media platforms as part of good teaching practice, they feel that the institute and senior staff provide little support and sometimes actively discourage their use of social media. Although blended and online learning are embedded in the institute's learning and teaching, participants' report that their use of social media does not seem to be accepted as an aspect of this type of learning. Lack of support from senior staff and academic advisors leads many participants to keep their use of social media to themselves and a few supportive colleagues. In comparison with other online tools, participants' use of social media appears to be less acceptable as a valid learning and teaching tool. In particular, participants mention lack of advice from experienced lecturers and little access to best practice teaching resources.

The decision was made between my colleague and myself. We were mavericks. The department had quite an old school type senior staff. So our attitude was let's just do it and see how it works. And then talk to senior staff about what we have done because they would get a lot of barriers we were already working through from the staff.

I wasn't sure if I should be doing that. Some people from [our academic advisory team] thought it was a bad idea, so I kept it low. But I thought the students are there, the concepts are there. I'm very confident about it

No training [in using social media]

A lot of the time with new staff we just kind of muddling along with what works for now. Eventually we make it official, and put a structure around. But it's definitely better to have more advice.

We didn't have any real infrastructure [for using social media].

Safety Issues

As Tess (2013) notes, the choice to use social media often comes from the educators rather than the institution and this certainly seems to be the case for the educators in this research. However, social media platforms, and particularly commercial social media platforms, are not without risks. Most staff institute some measures to increase students' safety: closed groups; instructions about the safety features of platforms; and how to communicate online. Although probably rare events, both trolling and stalking can and do occur on social media platforms and, as some authors have noted, use of social media can have deleterious effects (Lin et al, 2016; Tess 2013). Not all staff seem to recognize these safety issues.

For me privacy settings are much better on Instagram. I have stopped posting pictures of my son on Facebook. I now use Instagram as a very private account and only accepted close family.

You have access to personal accounts of students and see things about them. Whilst I'm not interested that's what I can see. I don't think that's appropriate for them or for me.

The biggest question was always around the privacy of the students and how we can maintain a closed network.

And a lot of people didn't understand social media, how it works, can we really engage on social media, so their questions were the same as most people who are very resistant. What does it mean to the students, how can they be safe in this space?

[Tumblr] feels safer, no nasty comments and can't get trolled or be stalked. I've had mine public and never had any problems.

Ethical Issues

Not unexpectedly, most participants use commercial social media platforms themselves and appear to choose these platforms in their teaching. As the top ten most popular social media platforms (Chaffey, 2017) are commercial businesses, the likelihood, as for participants in this research, is that lecturers and designers choose to use commercial social media platforms. The priority of these platforms is to collect and sell data to other businesses. This raises issues around student awareness of this collection and sale of their data and the ethics, for educators and tertiary institutions, colluding in this practice. Although some concerns are expressed for online safety, most participants do not seem to consider exposing students to data collection by third parties as an issue for their students, themselves or their institution.

Having data collected is part and parcel of using social media – it's a free platform.

Who stores the data…so we tried to stay away from that and really used it as a tool for engagement and another space for students' learning, not assessing.

Not all students are comfortable engaging with social media platforms (Salmon, Ross, Pechenkina, & Chase, 2015). Furthermore, some consideration must be taken into the power relationship between lecturers and their students. Although none of these lecturers insist that students sign up to social media platforms, the power relationship between lecturer and student can coerce students into joining social media platforms that their lecturer seems to endorse. Students may assume that the lecturer requires the use of a particular social media platform or that not using that platform could affect their grade for the course.

We had one or two students throughout the course of 3 years who said, "we don't like FB, we don't want to use it". With those students what we did – we sat down and explain why we're using social media, what the purpose was and they actually said they felt they see value in what we try to do. And it was only one student ever who didn't sign up for an account. What we did for these students, we emailed them with information we give everyone else.

One student told me that he is not so keen on using the Internet, he is kind of old school. And I asked him that what he wanted to do future wise. And I said 'To be honest, you need to get on with that because today if you want to be successful you need to have the understanding at least of how we use these things.

[You] shouldn't make anyone who refuses. You can't make them and neither should you.

I don't think anyone's told us any guidelines around it [social media] and that's shocking.

Policies for using social media platforms in learning and teaching, a code of conduct, and ethics for staff and students are essential for the safety of students, staff and tertiary institution. However, policies which might cover the use of social media in these tertiary institutions are myriad and often contradictory (Willems, Adachi, & Grevtseva, 2016). Although lecturers in this study are generally not concerned with these issues, this may be because at present the use of social media in their teaching is limited. Social media platforms "serve interests and priorities other than (and in many cases opposed to) those of learning" (Friesen and Lowe, 2011, p. 11). With this in mind, tertiary institutions have a duty of care to staff and students to plan for the safe and ethical use of social media in tertiary education.

SOLUTIONS AND RECOMMENDATIONS

As discussed earlier, social media is changing the way learning is designed and delivered to students. The integration of social media in course content areas, resources, activities and assessment practices is expected to continue. This study acknowledges that social media is not the only avenue for tertiary education, but rather a supporting tool for some aspects of course management and student-centered teaching practices. Based on key themes presented in this study, the following solutions and recommendations can be put forward:

1. There is a need to create and test what Dalsgaard (2006) calls "social software" that can "move e-learning beyond learning management systems and engage students in an active use of the web as a resource for their self-governed, problem-based and collaborative activities". According to study participants, existing learning management systems do not perform well in the context of collaborative learning and cannot be considered as a stand-alone platform for delivering education.
2. The findings of this study suggest that in order to effectively use social media in teaching, educators need to recognize students' pre-existing experiences, knowledge and skills. This approach suggests that teachers should incorporate this information into the course curriculum and teaching and involve students in course design. This could allow designing and delivering courses in ways that encourage "participation, community connections, social interaction and global networking" (McLoughlin, & Lee, 2010, p. 38).

3. The findings also reveal that a broad-scale discussion about ethical and legal issues around social media is needed "in order to guide faculty members and administrators through the decision related to social media use" (Cain & Fink, 2010, p. 7). The integration of social media in learning and teaching also requires a systematic approach to professional and constructive dialog with students.

FUTURE RESEARCH DIRECTIONS

As with many new educational tools, social media is being implemented into learning and teaching, while research into these practices lags behind. In addition, the emerging research into social media in education often focuses on issues of collaborative learning, communities of practice and creation of content, possibly reflecting the perceived personal uses of social media. The research in this chapter highlights some different uses of social media in tertiary education showing that, in practice, learning designers and lecturers find social media platforms beneficial as learning management tools and in increasing student-centered learning practices. Further research is needed to explore these aspects of social media in education.

These research findings also suggest that social media may be useful in supporting other teaching practices outside the previously mentioned social and content generation aspects. This research shows how educators are already engaged in using social media in interesting and different ways in their teaching, so that researching these practices is not only essential but urgent. Action-based research into current practices would provide a means to engage with this current use of social media in education.

Future research into teaching practice of course relies on the support of educational institutions. As is seen in this chapter, educational institutions can be ambivalent towards the use of social media in education. For further research to occur, educational institutes need to accept that their lecturers will continue to use social media in their teaching and should therefore support the investigations needed to increase the understanding of the best practice use of social media in education.

CONCLUSION

The use of social media in tertiary institutes has grown as social media use has expanded into everyday life. These platforms were not created for education purposes but were developed to be easily accessible and simple to use. Driven by commercial gains, social media companies will continue to develop intuitive, easy to use and engaging platforms drawing in both students and educators as users. In contrast, online education learning management systems were designed, initially at least, as a repository for resources and for the use of educators not students. Although LMS have become more interactive, students are now more familiar using social media sites to connect and post content and appear more engaged with social media platforms.

It is not only the ease of use that drives educators to social media sites. Lecturers recognize significant benefits to using social media in both greater efficiency of learning management and increased student involvement in their learning. These advantages are tempered by educators' concerns with the support that educational institutions provide with resources, best practice and minimization of risk, issues that need to be addressed if the full advantages of using social media in learning and teaching can be realized.

In conclusion the authors hope this research will inspire further development of new teaching practices into the use of social media in tertiary education and further research that will inform these practices.

REFERENCES

Bosch, T. E. (2009). Using online social networking for teaching and learning: Facebook use at the University of Cape Town. *Communication, 35*(2), 185–200.

Cain, J., & Fink, J. L. III. (2010). Legal and ethical issues regarding social media and Pharmacy education. *American Journal of Pharmaceutical Education, 74*(10), 1–8. doi:10.5688/aj7410184 PMID:21436925

Chaffey, D. (2017). *Global social media research summary 2017*. Retrieved from http://www.smartinsights.com/social-media-marketing/social-media-strategy/new-global-social-media-research/

Corbin, J., & Strauss, A. (2015). *Basics of qualitative research: Techniques and procedures for developing grounded theory* (4th ed.). Thousand Oaks, CA: SAGE.

Dabbagh, N., & Kitsantas, A. (2011). Personal Learning Environments, social media, and self-regulated learning: A natural formula for connecting formal and informal learning. *Internet and Higher Education., 15*(1), 3–8. doi:10.1016/j.iheduc.2011.06.002

Dalsgaard, C. (2006). Social software: E-learning beyond learning management systems. *European Journal of Open, Distance and E-Learning, 2006*(2). Retrieved from http://www.eurodl.org/index.php?p=archives&year=2006&hal&article=228

Friesen, N., & Lowe, S. (2012). The questionable promise of social media for education: Connective learning and the commercial imperative. *Journal of Computer Assisted Learning, 28*(3), 183–194. doi:10.1111/j.1365-2729.2011.00426.x

Fuchs, C. (2014). *Social media: A critical introduction*. London: Sage. doi:10.4135/9781446270066.n2

Garmendía, A., & Cobos, R. (2013). Towards the extension of a LMS with social media services. In *Proceedings of the 10th International Conference on Cooperative Design, Visualization, and Engineering*. Berlin: Springer. 10.1007/978-3-642-40840-3_11

Griesemer, A. (2012). Using social media to enhance students' learning experiences. *Quality Approaches in Higher Education, 3*(1), 8–11.

Hemmi, A., Bayne, S., & Landt, R. (2009). The appropriation and repurposing of social technologies in higher education. *Journal of Computer Assisted Learning, 25*(1), 19–30. doi:10.1111/j.1365-2729.2008.00306.x

Hootsuite. (2017). *Social campus report: A global survey of higher education social media usage*. Retrieved from https://hootsuite.com/resources/social-campus-report#

Kofinas, A. K., Al-Shawakbeh, A., & Lim, A. S. (2016). Key success factors of using social media as a learning tool. In V. Benson, R. Tuninga, & G. Saridakis (Eds.), *Analyzing the strategic role of social networking in firms growth and productivity*. IGI Global; doi:10.4018/978-1-5225-0559-4

Lin, L. Y., Sidani, J. E., Shensa, A., Radovic, A., Miller, E., Colditz, J. B., ... Primack, B. A. (2016). Association between social media use and depression among U.S. young adults. *Depression and Anxiety*, *33*(4), 323–331. doi:10.1002/da.22466 PMID:26783723

McLoughlin, C., & Lee, M. J. W. (2010). Personalised and self-regulated learning in the Web 2.0 era: International exemplars of innovative pedagogy using social software. *Australasian Journal of Educational Technology*, *26*(1), 28–43. doi:10.14742/ajet.1100

Ministry of Education. (1996). *Te Whariki*. Wellington: Learning Media Limited. Retrieved from https://www.education.govt.nz/assets/Documents/Early-Childhood/te-whariki.pdf

Ministry of Education. (n.d.). *Frameworks for bicultural education – He anga mō te mātauranga ahurea rua*. Retrieved from https://www.education.govt.nz/early-childhood/teaching-and-learning/assessment-for-learning/kei-tua-o-te-pae-2/bicultural-assessment-he-aromatawai-ahurea-rua/frameworks-for-bicultural-education-he-anga-mo-te-matauranga-ahurea-rua/

Piven, I., & Breazeale, M. (2016). Desperately seeking customer engagement: The five-sources model of brand value on social media. In V. Benson, R. Tuninga, & G. Saridakis (Eds.), *Analyzing strategic role of social networking in firms growth and productivity*. IGI Global; doi:10.4018/978-1-5225-0559-4

Roblyer, M. D., McDaniel, M., Webb, M., Herman, J., & Witty, J. V. (2010). Findings on Facebook in higher education: A comparison of college faculty and student uses and perceptions of social networking sites. *Internet and Higher Education*, *13*(3), 134–140. doi:10.1016/j.iheduc.2010.03.002

Salmon, G., Ross, B., Pechenkina, E., & Chase, A. (2015). The space for social media in structured online learning. *Research in Learning Technology*, *23*(1), 28507. doi:10.3402/rlt.v23.28507

Samovar, L. A., & Porter, R. E. (2003). *Intercultural communication: A reader* (10th ed.). Belmont: Thomson Learning.

Tess, P. (2013). The role of social media in higher education classes (real and virtual): A literature review. *Computers in Human Behavior*, *29*(5), A60–A68. doi:10.1016/j.chb.2012.12.032

Wang, Q., Woo, H. L., Quek, C. L., Yang, Y., & Liu, M. (2012). Using the Facebook group as a learning management system: An exploratory study. *British Journal of Educational Technology*, *43*(3), 428–438. doi:10.1111/j.1467-8535.2011.01195.x

Willems, J., Adachi, C., & Grevtseva, Y. (2016, January). Working with social media in tertiary education: A contested space between academics and policies. In ASCILITE Adelaide 2016: Show Me the Learning (pp. 648-653). Australasian Society for Computers in Learning in Tertiary Education.

ADDITIONAL READING

Benson, V. (2014). *Cutting-edge technologies and social media use in higher education*. IGI Global. doi:10.4018/978-1-4666-5174-6

Bicen, H., & Uzunboylu, H. (2013). The use of social networking sites in education: A case study of Facebook. *Journal of Universal Computer Science*, *19*(5), 658–671.

Carpenter, J. P. (2014). Twitter's capacity to support collaborative learning. *International Journal of Social Media and Interactive Learning Environments*, *2*(2), 103–118. doi:10.1504/IJSMILE.2014.063384

Ha, J., & Shin, D. H. (2014). Facebook in a standard college class: An alternative conduit for promoting teacher-student interaction. *American Communication Journal*, *16*(1), 36–52.

Manca, S., & Ranieri, M. (2016). Yes for sharing, no for teaching!: Social media in academic practices. *The Internet and Higher Education*, *29*, 63–74. doi:10.1016/j.iheduc.2015.12.004

Pitrick, R. M., & Holzinger, A. (2002). Student-centered teaching meets new media: Concept and case study. *Journal of Educational Technology & Society*, *5*(4), 160–172.

Rodrigue, J. E. (2011). Social media use in higher education: Key areas to consider for educators. *MERLOT. Journal of Online Learning and Teaching / MERLOT*, *7*(4), 539–550.

Voorn, R. J. J., & Kommers, P. A. M. (2013). Social media and higher education: Introversion and collaborative learning from the student's perspective. *International Journal of Social Media and Interactive Learning Environments*, *1*(1), 59–73. doi:10.1504/IJSMILE.2013.051650

KEY TERMS AND DEFINITIONS

Collaborative Learning: Groups of students work together to complete a task which is designed to enhance teamwork, knowledge sharing and building, and learning from each other.

Course Management: Course management is the process of creating, implementing, and coordinating the learning and teaching activities in order to achieve the course specification and defined learning outcomes.

Institutional Support: As part of the social resources required to assist implementation of new (educational) practices, this support consists of the resources an organization provides including financial, policies, and guidelines.

Learning and Teaching: Educational practices that students and teachers engage in to promote acquisition and application of knowledge.

Learning Design: The teaching-learning process of enhancing students' learning experiences by creating relevant course content areas, resources, activities, and assessments.

Learning Management System: A digital "all-in-one" course management application that organizes course activities and resources, and delivers administrative functions for the course.

Student-Centered Teaching: An educational practice whereby students, as the focus of the learning and teaching, are supported by teachers to become independent learners.

Tertiary Education: Learning in an educational institute that occurs post-secondary school. This may be academic or vocational learning.

Tumblr: A microblogging service that incorporates elements of social media as users can follow each other, "like" each others' content, and/ or "reblog" content posted by other users. The platform allows users to post a variety of content including images, text, videos, links, and audio.

This research was previously published in Global Perspectives on Social Media in Tertiary Learning and Teaching; pages 91-117, copyright year 2018 by Information Science Reference (an imprint of IGI Global).

Chapter 30
Applying Twitter as an Educational Tool for Concept Learning and Engaging Students

Armand A. Buzzelli
Robert Morris University, USA

E. Gregory Holdan
Robert Morris University, USA

Daniel R. Rota
Robert Morris University, USA

ABSTRACT

The challenge of engaging students beyond a typical class meeting session is a longstanding issue in educational research. This chapter outlines Twitter as a potential tool for enhancing student engagement while also enhancing concept learning. Twitter's efficient microblogging format allows instructors to share information quickly in real-time, while the hashtag feature enables a user to develop a list or repository of targeted tweets. These functions among others make the popular platform an educational tool that instructors should consider implementing carefully while modeling a good electronic footprint for their students.

INTRODUCTION

The challenge of engaging students in a traditional college classroom setting is a longstanding issue. Researchers have reported that only a small number of students engage in class discussions in a typical college classroom (Fassinger, 1995; Nunn, 1996; Weimer, 2013). Since the inception of popular social media platforms such as Facebook, Twitter, Pinterest, and Instagram communication continue to explode in popularity and global use. This chapter focuses on using the microblogging network Twitter to promote communication, enhance concept learning and engaging students beyond the constraints of an on-ground class session.

DOI: 10.4018/978-1-6684-7123-4.ch030

According to statistics from a survey conducted by the Pew Research Center (2018) almost half (45%) of all young adults (18-to 24-year olds) use Twitter. Despite sharing features with other social media networks, Twitter has distinct characteristics that make it unique. Twitter shares characteristics with other social media networks, yet it is distinctive in a variety of ways. The most notable difference is that it serves as a micro-blogging tool that supplies participants with a "retweet" function (Kieslinger, Ebner, & Wiesenhofer, 2011). A re-tweet is provides attestation of content created by other users while also serving as a form of admiration (or sarcastic disdain) for another user's comment. Retweeting helps distribute information to a broad audience while helping Twitter users expand their influence (Boyd, Golder, & Lotan, 2010).

While a popular tool, research also supports the contentions of educators who are wary of infusing Twitter into their teaching. A study reported that Twitter caused students to get distracted off task from their coursework (Dhir, Buragga, & Boreqqah, 2013). The Crimes Against Children Research Center at the University of New Hampshire estimated that in one year approximately 2,322 sex crime arrests were made in which the perpetrator initiated a relationship using social media (Wolak, Finkelhor, Mitchell, & Ybarra, 2010). While students logged into social media accounts may be at risk, there are a number of cases where educators have found legal trouble because of their social media use (Eckes, 2013; Downey, 2011; Oppenheim, 2013).

While there are inherent risks in using Twitter, the platform continues to grow in popularity with young adults and teens, making it attractive as a potential educational tool. It is therefore imperative for educators to understand how to safely model online behavior and customize their social media use to meet the needs of their classes. Twitter has made a positive impact on informal learning, class dynamics, motivation, and academic development (Dhir, Buragga, & Boreqqah, 2013). Further, McKerlich, Riis, Anderson, and Eastman (2011) reported that Twitter enhanced both the student learning environment and a learning outcome in a college setting. Much like in-class communication, students need to be properly motivated and gain a feeling that Twitter content is relevant in order for it to be effective (Rinaldo, Tapp & Laverie, 2011).

Twitter's website explains that hashtags were organically created by Twitter users employing the # symbol to mark keywords or topics in a tweet. Truman and Miles (2011) reported that Twitter hashtags could be used like interactive flash cards for both live in-class and out of class review. Twitter is an effective forum for flashcards because as students tweet flashcards in live time, their ideas may serve as prompts that inspire other classmates. Similarly, students are able to post each individual flashcard in real time, as opposed to the instructor compiling a list from student emails and discussion board posts. They are also easily accessible in one repository on Twitter by searching for the hashtag.

The purpose of this chapter is to provide some tools and best practices for using Twitter as a tool for engaging students in the process of concept learning. While the anonymity of Twitter can lead to confrontation and even volatile discourse, the efficient and free flowing nature of the instrument has the potential to add value in education when used properly.

ENGAGING STUDENTS

Bill is a first year undergraduate, commuter student who lives in a quiet one-bedroom apartment in the city. Bill commutes to his job as a data entry specialist on the subway and quietly scrolls along on his smartphone. He has a full day ahead of him, taking lists of information and inputting them into a corporate database for eight hours and before catching the subway back across the city to go to his night class. Bill is a first-generation college student and he needs his weekly income to supplement the cost associated with attending an elite private university he attends in the evenings. Bill is self-sufficient at work and completes his daily tasks with limited interaction with his supervisor or other colleagues. Around midday, Bill uses his lunch break to indulge in his favorite past time: surfing his Twitter feed on the iPhone tucked under his desk.

Once Bill completes his workday, he makes his nightly one-hour trek to his college class crosstown and settles in for an introductory macroeconomics course; part of his requirement for graduation. As the instructor uses the duration of the three-hour class period to lecture about principles of supply and demand, Bill hides his phone under his desk and gets lost in a Twitter debate about NFL free agency. He tweets about being bored in class and his friends share retweet his post in approval. Bill notices that the same three outgoing students engage in the conversation with the instructor while the remainder of his class appear to be completely mentally checked out. On his last subway ride home to his apartment, Bill comes to a disturbing conclusion: he has not audibly spoken a word all day.

Student experiences like Bill's are surprisingly normal in a traditional face-to-face classroom format. Studies from Fassinger (1995), Nunn (1996), and Weimer (2013) all reported that despite the perception that face-to-face classroom provides speaking opportunities, only a few students generally participate in class discussions and interaction between students and instructors may be limited. Participants in a study from the Duke University social relationships illustrated this point by citing class as the place where they feel the highest level of loneliness (Asher & Weeks, 2012). Consequently, educators must search for ways to engage students who are not interacting during a typical class session.

There are varied barometers of student engagement, including the quality of student work, the duration of times students spend on educationally purposeful activities, student interest in course material, interactions between students that are educationally purposeful, and interactions between the student and instructor (Krause & Coates, 2008; Hu & Kuh, 2001; Kuh, 2009; Junco, Heiberger, & Loken, 2011; Welch & Bonnan-White, 2012). These are just some of the measures of student engagement and serve as principles of a larger doctrine. Gamson (1987), developed a framework for student engagement built on seven tenets of best practices for faculty:

1. Encourage contact between students and faculty.
2. Develop reciprocity and cooperation among students.
3. Uses active learning techniques.
4. Give prompt feedback.
5. Emphasize time on task
6. Communicate high expectations.
7. Respect diverse talents and ways of learning.

Fredricks et al. (2011) broke down the elements of engagement into psychometric categories of behavioral, emotional, and cognitive aspects of student engagement. Behavioral aspects include attention the student gives, attendance, time-on-task, preparation for class, participation in class, concentration on material, participation in school-based activities, effort put forth, persistence towards completing assignments, adherence to classroom rules, and risk behaviors such as skipping school. Emotional aspects of student engagement cover how the student feels about school. Within the emotional category are the students' general feeling about school (e.g. happy, anxious, sad, or other emotions), expressing interest and enjoyment about school related items or activities, reporting fun and excitement, feeling safe, having supportive or positive relationships with teachers, having supportive or positive relationships with peers, having family support for learning, and expressing feelings of belonging. Cognitive aspects of student engagement include self-regulation and cognitive strategy use. Self-regulation refers to a "set of metacognitive, motivational, and behavioral techniques the learner can use to manage the learning process," while cognitive strategy use refers to "questions about the use of deep or shallow strategies to learn, remember, and understand material". Cognitive aspects of student engagement essentially refer to how invested the student is in his or her own learning. This also includes the student taking ownership of his or her own learning. Table 1 provides an overview of common elements of engagement found in the literature.

RESEARCH ON ENGAGEMENT

Chickering and Gamson (1987) advised that the responsibility for improving education fell on both the students and the teachers, but that all constituents must think of themselves as educators. Esteve Del Valle, Gruzd, Haythornthwaite, Paulin and Gilbert (2017) found that barriers for instructors incorporating social media included a lack of familiarity or technical support from their institution. This may provide an opportunity for students who are more familiar with a social media platform to provide guidance and instruction to both peers and their faculty. Research has reported that faculty need to be active participants in Twitter discourse to better engage students (Buzzelli, Bissell & Holdan, 2015; Evans, 2017; Buzzelli, Holdan, Lias, Rota & Evans, 2019). It is essential for instructors to engage with the platform on a regular basis in order to both assess its impact, but also to maintain a relevant conversation.

Several studies have tried to determine if Twitter can create more engagement in students when incorporated in the classroom. Welch and Bonnan-White (2012) found that students who reported enjoying using Twitter would perceive themselves as more engaged in class than those who did not enjoy Twitter. In a study conducted by Junco, Heiberger, and Loken (2011), students who used Twitter had a significantly greater increase in engagement than the control group, as well as higher semester grade point averages. Jacquemin, Smelser, and Bernot (2014) reported that students, as compared to faculty, who used social media more frequently in their personal lives, were more amenable to including social media in their academic lives.

Evans (2017) found that there is value in using Twitter as it both does no harm, and increases certain elements of student engagement such as curiosity and interest about the subject or material, and engagement with peers and the instructor while out of class. He also found that student-participants did not like using Twitter, mostly because it was mandatory and used in more than one class in a student's schedule. Despite the negative feedback, student-participants reported gains in perceived engagement within specific elements of engagement. These reported gains were more prevalent in out-of-class engagement than in-class engagement, though both student-participants and instructor-participants shared positive experiences in that regard with the instructors talking in class about tweets that the students had made. This study illustrated that Twitter does have the potential to increase student engagement, though measured planning must be considered to avoid potential challenges.

Table 1. Common elements of engagement in literature by category

Category	Element
Behavioral or Physical	• Adherence to classroom rules • Asking questions, raising hand in class • Attendance • Attention • Concentration • Effort (general effort put forth) • Participation in class • Participation in school activities • Persistence • Preparation for class • Risk behaviors such as skipping school
Cognitive	• Curiosity about the subject or material • Interest in the subject or material • Kinds of strategies used to learn, remember, and understand the material • Motivation to focus on and complete assignments; motivation to achieve • Self-regulation strategies used to achieve goals • Student takes ownership of his or her learning
Emotional	• Expressing feeling of belonging • Expressing interest and enjoyment in class • Feeling happy or anxious about class • Feeling safe • How does the student feel about class • Reporting fun and enjoyment about class • Student confidence, self-efficacy
Environmental and Supportive	• Academic challenge of the curriculum • Diversity of the classroom • Relevant and interesting choices of literacy activities • Relevant and interesting texts • Supportive campus climate • Supportive instructor, teacher involvement • Supportive family/home environment
Social	• Effort student puts forth in interaction with instructor • Effort student puts forth in interaction with peers • Level of interactions with peers outside the classroom (related to course materials) • Student discusses the current class in casual conversation with friends and family • Student involvement in educationally purposeful activities with other students

(Evans, 2017)

Additional studies have likewise demonstrated the importance of being strategic with the delivery of tweets. Wadhwa, Latimer, Chatterjee, McCarty, and Fitzgerald (2017) determined that tweets included images, hashtags, and those published in the morning hours had the highest user engagement rate for a Twitter feed. Semiz and Berger (2017) found that the student engagement rate was higher for tweets sent in the evening compared to other times of the day, while tweets sent on Saturday and Sunday created better engagement than tweets during the week. Additionally, Semiz and Berger (2017) found that calling out individuals by their Twitter handle created positive engagement with communications.

TWITTER IN EDUCATION

A growing body of literature exists about Twitter's use in education. The micro-blogging aspect of Twitter is what differentiates it from other social networks (Kieslinger, Ebner, & Wiesenhofer, 2011). Twitter has some other unique features that make it an excellent educational tool. From a social standpoint, Twitter is distinguished by the ability to "retweet" tweets from other users. A re-tweet affirms or efficiently enables the sharing of tweets from other members of the Twitter network. Research from Boyd, Golder, and, Lotan (2010) reported that re-tweeting allowed information to reach broader audiences and helped connect users in a broader network.

College student participants in a study by Ricoy and Feliz (2016) reported that as they became more proficient with Twitter their learning experience improved and that the character restrictions of the tool helped them synthesize complex ideas and helped them with information selection. Higher education students that used Twitter as a means of formative peer-assessment showed improved involvement, motivation, and satisfaction of their subject area (Fernandez-Ferrer & Cano, 2016). While participants in the same study had not improved learning, the findings indicate that the tool can still benefit students in a variety of ways.

A study by Fox and Bird (2017) focused on the application of Twitter in a K-12 educational setting. They found that teachers should be careful and strategic in their use of social media as schools and teacher unions develop guidelines. They also found that more teachers believe Twitter offers a social media space more conducive to professional and personal uses than does Facebook. It is suggested that in order for basic education teachers to capitalize on the educational potential of social media tools like Twitter, they must be educated and reassured by administrators and professional organizations that their appropriate use of these technologies is encouraged.

MEMORY AND CONCEPT LEARNING

While engaging students through social media is one reason to incorporate Twitter into teaching, the free-flowing and efficient communication of the platform makes it suitable to support reviewing and teaching concepts. Studies in educational psychology dating back to the 19th century in have examined the effects of spacing the study of concepts versus massed practice sessions. Ebbinghaus (1885) studied memory and practice effect by testing subjects on their recall of nonsense syllables and spacing out practice in varying durations. His study offered a concept called serial position effect, which included recency and primacy. Recency effect describes the increased recall of the most recent information because it is still in the short-term memory. Primacy effect creates better memory of the first items in a list due to increased rehearsal and commitment to long-term memory. Any comparison of spaced and massed practice is somewhat subjective and based on the exercise, Underwood (1961) determined that spaced practice occurred when trial intervals are greater than 15 seconds; massed practice, when intervals are two to eight seconds.

Dempster (1989) found that "spacing effects can best be understood in terms of the 'accessibility' hypothesis, and that spaced repetitions have considerable potential for improving classroom learning" (p. 309). Likewise, Koriat (1993) proposed the accessibility hypothesis, offering that participants base their judgments on retrieved information rather than basing them on the familiarity of the cues. The theory was influenced by research on cued recall from Tulving and Pearlstone (1966) where subjects who were non-cued had reportedly had information reach their memory stage but not their retrieval stage in contrast to those who received spaced cues. Future studies by Glenberg (1979), Raaijmakers (2003), and Pavlik and Anderson (2005) supported their findings. Correspondingly, Bahrick (1979) established that when spacing was moved closer together the recall of subjects worsened. All of this research supports the assertion that an instructor should develop strategic opportunities for spaced practice for important concepts in their courses.

The mobility and ability to pre-schedule content delivery through Twitter makes it a suitable tool to space information to learners and aid in concept learning. Bruner, Goodnow, and Austin (1967) defined concept attainment as "the search for and listing of attributes that can be used to distinguish exemplars from non-exemplars of various categories" (p.233). Seels and Glasgow (1990) described a process to help instructors identify important concepts for teaching by "defining what is to be learned, planning an intervention that will allow the learning to occur, and refining the instruction until the objectives are met" (p. 3).

In addition to providing examples of concepts during instruction, conflicting research exists on providing non-examples to assist in concept learning. Learning outcomes have varied across research when teaching with non-examples (Smoke, 1933; Morrisett & Hovland, 1959, Tennyson, Wooley & Merrill, 1972). A study that will be discussed in more detail in the next section by Buzzelli, Holdan, Rota, and McCarthy (2016) reported that reviewing examples and non-examples of concepts through Twitter was no less effective for students as a reviewing traditional study guide.

USING TWITTER TO TEACH CONCEPTS

Buzzelli, Holdan, Rota, and McCarthy (2016) attempted to determine if the efficient 280-character per tweet communication style of Twitter could be used as a pedagogical tool for reviewing class material. They used tweets about concept criterial attributes, as well as examples and non-examples, of major concepts to assist student learning of concepts through a distributed practice regimen. Their research questions were as follows:

Research Question One: Does utilizing Twitter as a distributed practice tool serve as a more effective review tool than a traditional end-of-unit study guide for concept learning?
Research Question Two: Does Twitter encourage student engagement in the overall class discussion?

OVERVIEW OF METHODOLOGY

Subjects were randomly placed into two groups. One treatment group received tweets with characteristics, examples, and non-examples of 15 primary concepts from their course material, while another group received the same information in a review worksheet. Immediately following the treatment, each group was tested for concept learning and the scores from each group were compared. The concept test itself was developed by the host professor and consisted of 15 multiple choice questions that covered the concepts reviewed in the study.

Once the experiment started, tweets with concept characteristics and an example and a non-example were created for each concept. Pre-scheduled tweets went out three times per day per concept. In a typical day, tweets for two class concepts were tweeted, and those tweets would be staggered by an hour in the morning, afternoon, and night. The same tweets for each concept were then tweeted out again later in the experiment to create a spacing effect. For ease of access, each of the tweets was followed by a hashtag that was developed for the class.

Following the first exam in the study, the conditions of the study were reversed and the Twitter review group from the initial study became the new control group and the control group became the Twitter group for the following unit. The same methodology was used to provide the treatment group Tweets spaced out over a four-week unit for review, while the control group received a traditional worksheet review prior to the exam.

Throughout the two units, all instruction was provided in the same format from the same professor with the exception of Twitter use for the one randomly selected group of students. The dependent variable in this experiment was the post-test scores for students. The independent variable was the review method, which was distributed practice through Twitter for the treatment group and a traditional end of unit worksheet for the control group.

At the completion of the experiment, students were also surveyed about their experiences using Twitter. Results were reported in aggregate, and open-ended responses were coded and reported based on common findings.

RESULTS

An independent-samples t-test was conducted to compare performance on the Twitter review and traditional worksheet review conditions. There was no significant difference in the scores for Twitter (M=12.30, SD=1.34) and traditional review (M=12.00, SD=1.41) conditions; $t(18) = .487$, $p = 0.632$. These results suggest that using Twitter for review in an introductory college history course may be as effective as a traditional end-of-unit review worksheet.

While there is a lack of substantial quantitative data that shows the effect of applying Twitter as a review tool, the results are not surprising considering a study by Smith and Tirumala (2012) found that students who used Twitter did not have improved scores in questions that tested memory of class content. Other researchers (Dunlap & Lowenthal, 2009; Paul & Ianitti, 2012; Trueman and Miles, 2011; et. al.) have demonstrated that Twitter can be used as both an instructional tool and a way to provide supplementary communication with students. This study supported literature that illustrates a variety of ways that Twitter can be incorporated into the instructional environment.

CONCLUSION

As a vehicle to engage students, Twitter has a great deal to offer educators, from behavioral, cognitive, emotional, social, and supportive perspectives. Twitter can be used to support the various pedagogies that require student active engagement, including, but not limited to concept learning; it can be used in mastery learning, cooperative learning, and peer tutoring. The platform is a terrific device to provide advance organizers; or to energize and add new layers to class discussions (Luo, Shah, & Crompton, 2019; Ferris, & Cheng, 2018).

The ability to use Twitter as a news feed on a continuum from real-time national and local news to instructor (course provided) information is invaluable and have the potential to connect educators who are geographically isolated (Carpenter, Tani, Morrison, & Keane, 2018). Twitter provides a convenient platform to receive timely information from professional organizations such as AECT (Association for Educational Technology) or NCTM (National Teachers of Mathematics) or shared interests such as professional sports teams, musicians, or even travel destinations. Those passive examples of students and colleagues sharing information about their non-academic interests have the potential to enhance learning communities and grow the bond between students and instructors (Draper, Buzzelli, & Holdan, 2016). As one of several popular social media, Twitter can be certainly be used as a one-way communication device to get information out to students, but more powerful is the ability to engage students in meaningful communications, such as sharing information, and discussions. Students do not have to sit in class "alone" and listen to other students voice opinions and share information...the venue allows all students to be a part of learning environment, not just the most vocal.

One aspect of Twitter, not unlike a teacher giving a student praise of some sort for a response, is the emotional aspect of having a tweet shared/retweeted and in a non-threatening environment when a student is ready to share or respond, and not have to worry about being the first with a raised hand to be called upon. While Twitter cannot be looked at as a "silver bullet" to engage students, research outlined in this chapter supports the claim that Twitter is a valid instructional tool that when used properly and creatively by an instructor. The uses of Twitter to engage students is limited only by the imagination of a teacher. There are literally hundreds of uses of Twitter and this chapter covers a few. The journey through Twitter for an instructor and his or her classroom can be an enjoyable and rewarding one. It is just a matter selecting an engagement strategy that best suits your classroom.

REFERENCES

Asher, S. R., & Weeks, M. S. (2012). *Social relationships, academic engagement, and well-being in college: Findings from the Duke social relationships project.* Academic Press.

Bahrick, H. P. (1979). Maintenance of knowledge: Questions about memory we forgot to ask. *Journal of Experimental Psychology. General, 108*(3), 296–308. doi:10.1037/0096-3445.108.3.296

Boyd, D., Golder, S., & Lotan, G. (2010, January). Tweet, tweet, retweet: Conversational aspects of retweeting on Twitter. In *System Sciences (HICSS), 2010 43rd Hawaii International Conference on* (pp. 1-10). IEEE.

Bruner, J., Goodnow, J. J., & Austin, G. A. (1967). *A study of thinking.* New York: Science Editions.

Buzzelli, A., Bissell, J., & Holdan, G. (2015). Analyzing Twitter's impact on student engagement in college instruction. *International Journal of Information and Communication Technology Education*, *12*(2), 3–14.

Buzzelli, A., Holdan, E. G., Rota, D., & McCarthy, J. (2016). Utilizing Twitter for Concept Learning. *International Journal of Information and Communication Technology Education*, *12*(1), 64–76. doi:10.4018/IJICTE.2016010106

Buzzelli, A. A., Holdan, G., Lias, A. R., Rota, D. R., & Evans, T. Z. (2019). Rethinking Twitter: Unique Characteristics of Twitter Render It an Instructional Asset. In Advanced Online Education and Training Technologies (pp. 163-184). IGI Global.

Carpenter, J., Tani, T., Morrison, S., & Keane, J. (2018, March). Exploring the education Twitter hashtag landscape. In *Society for Information Technology & Teacher Education International Conference* (pp. 2230-2235). Association for the Advancement of Computing in Education (AACE).

Chickering, A., & Gamson, Z. (1987). Seven principles for good practice in undergraduate education. *AAHE Bulletin*, *40*, 3–7.

Dempster, F. (1989). Spacing effects and their implications for theory and practice. *Educational Psychology Review*, *1*(4), 309–330. doi:10.1007/BF01320097

Dhir, A., Buragga, K., & Boreqqah, A. A. (2013). Tweeters on campus: Twitter a learning tool in classroom. *Journal of Universal Computer Science*, *19*(5), 672–691.

Downey, M. (2011, October 11). Court rules against ashley payne in facebook case. but more to come. *Atlanta Journal Constitution*. Retrieved from http://blogs.ajc.com/get-schooled-blog/2011/10/10/court-rules-against-ashley-payne-in-facebook-case/

Draper, J., Buzzelli, A. A., & Holdan, E. G. (2016). Patterns of Twitter Usage in One Cohort-Based Doctoral Program. *International Journal of Doctoral Studies*, *11*, 163–183. doi:10.28945/3453

Dunlap, J. C., & Lowenthal, P. R. (2009). Tweeting the night away: Using Twitter to enhance social presence. *Journal of Information Systems Education*, *20*(2), 129–135.

Ebbinghaus, H. (1885). Memory. New York: Teacher's College, Columbia University.

Eckes, S. (2013, September). Strippers, beer, and bachelorette parties: regulating teachers' out-of-school conduct. *Principal Leadership*. Retrieved from https://www.nassp.org/Content/158/PL_sept13_casesinpt.pdfhttps://www.nassp.org/Content/158/PL_sept13_casesinpt.pdf

Esteve Del Valle, M., Gruzd, A., Haythornthwaite, C., Paulin, D., & Gilbert, S. (2017). *Social media in educational practice: Faculty present and future use of social media in teaching*. Academic Press.

Evans, T. (2017). *Twitter in the Higher Education Classroom: Exploring Perceptions of Engagement* (Doctoral dissertation). Robert Morris University.

Fassinger, P. A. (1995). Understanding classroom interaction: Students' and professors' contributions to students' silence. *The Journal of Higher Education*, 82–96.

Fernandez-Ferrer, M., & Cano, E. (2016). The influence of the internet for pedagogical innovation: using twitter to promote online collaborative learning. *International Journal of Educational Technology in Higher Education,* 13-22.

Ferris, M., & Cheng, S. (2018). Using Twitter to Energize the Introductory Statistics Class. *Technology Innovations in Statistics Education, 11*(1).

Fox, A., & Bird, T. (2017). The challenge to professionals of using social media: Teachers in England negotiating personal-professional identities. *Education and Information Technologies*, *22*(2), 647–675. doi:10.100710639-015-9442-0

Fredericks, J. A., McColskey, W., Meli, J., Mordica, J., Montrose, B., & Mooney, K. (2011). Measuring student engagement in upper elementary through high school: a description of 21 instruments. *Issues and Answers Report, 98*, 26-114. Retrieved from http://ies.ed.gov/ncee/edlabs

Glenberg, A. M. (1979). Component-levels theory of the effects of spacing of repetitions on recall and recognition. *Memory & Cognition, 7*(2), 95–112. doi:10.3758/BF03197590 PMID:459836

Hu, S., & Kuh, G. D. (2001) *Being (Dis) Engaged in Educationally Purposeful Activities: The Influences of Student and Institutional Characteristics.* Paper presented at the American Educational Research Association Annual Conference, Seattle, WA.

Jacquemin, S., Smelser, L., & Bernot, M. (2014). Twitter in the higher education classroom: A student and faculty assessment of use and perception. *Journal of College Science Teaching*, *43*(6), 22–27.

Junco, R., Heiberger, G., & Loken, E. (2011). The effect of Twitter on college student engagement and grades. *Journal of Computer Assisted Learning*, *27*(2), 119–132. doi:10.1111/j.1365-2729.2010.00387.x

Kieslinger, B., Ebner, M., & Wiesenhofer, H. (2011). Microblogging practices of scientists in e-learning: A qualitative approach. *International Journal of Emerging Technologies in Learning, 6*(4), 31–39.

Koriat, A. (1993). How do we know that we know? The accessibility model of the feeling of knowing. *Psychological Review*, *100*(4), 609–639. doi:10.1037/0033-295X.100.4.609 PMID:8255951

Krause, K., & Coates, H. (2008). Students' engagement in first-year university. *Assessment & Evaluation in Higher Education, 33*(5), 493–505. doi:10.1080/02602930701698892

Kuh, G. (2009). What student affairs professionals need to know about student engagement? *Journal of College Student Development, 50*(6), 683–706. doi:10.1353/csd.0.0099

Luo, T., Shah, S. J., & Crompton, H. (2019). Using Twitter to Support Reflective Learning in an Asynchronous Online Course. *Australasian Journal of Educational Technology, 35*(3).

McKerlich, R., Riis, M., Anderson, T., & Eastman, B. (2011). Student perceptions of teaching presence, social presence and cognitive presence in a virtual world. *Journal of Online Learning and Teaching / MERLOT, 7*(3), 324.

Morrisett, L. Jr, & Hovland, C. I. (1959). A comparison of three varieties of training in human problem solving. *Journal of Experimental Psychology, 58*(1), 52–55. doi:10.1037/h0044703 PMID:13664884

Nunn, C. E. (1996). Discussion in the college classroom: Triangulating observational and survey results. *The Journal of Higher Education, 67*(3), 243–266. doi:10.2307/2943844

Oppenheim, R. (2013, May 9). *High school teacher files an appeal in case of social media related resignation*. Retrieved from http://www.californiabusinesslitigation.com/2013/05/high_school_teacher_files_an_a.html

Paul, J. E., & Iannitti, N. (2012). On beyond clickers: Twitter as a classroom response system. *The Journal of Health Administration Education, 29*(4), 319–328.

Pavlik, P. Jr, & Anderson, J. (2005). Practice and forgetting effects on vocabulary memory: An activation-based model of the spacing effect. *Cognitive Science, 29*(4), 559–586. doi:10.120715516709cog0000_14 PMID:21702785

Pew Research Center. (2018). *Social Media Use in 2018 A majority of Americans use Facebook and YouTube, but young adults are especially heavy users of Snapchat and Instagram*. Retrieved from http://www.pewinternet.org/2018/03/01/social-media-use-in-2018/

Raaijmakers, J. G. (2003). Spacing and repetition effects in human memory: Application of the SAM model. *Cognitive Science, 27*(3), 431–452. doi:10.120715516709cog2703_5

Ricoy, M. C., & Feliz, T. (2016). Twitter as a learning community in higher education. *Journal of Educational Technology & Society, 19*(1), 237.

Rinaldo, S. B., Tapp, S., & Laverie, D. A. (2011). Learning by tweeting: Using Twitter as a pedagogical tool. *Journal of Marketing Education, 33*(2), 193–203. doi:10.1177/0273475311410852

Seels, B., & Glasgow, Z. (1990). *Exercises in instructional design*. Merrill Publishing Company.

Semiz, G., & Berger, P. D. (2017). Determining the Factors that Drive Twitter Engagement-Rates. *Archives of Business Research, 5*(2). doi:10.14738/abr.52.2700

Smoke, K. L. (1933). Negative instances in concept learning. *Journal of Experimental Psychology, 16*(4), 583–588. doi:10.1037/h0073724

Tennyson, R. D., Woolley, F. R., & Merrill, M. D. (1972). Exemplar and nonexampler variables which produce correct concept classification behavior and specified classification errors. *Journal of Educational Psychology, 63*(2), 144–152. doi:10.1037/h0032368

Trueman, M. S., & Miles, D. G. (2011). Twitter in the classroom: Twenty-first century flashcards. *Nurse Educator, 36*(5), 183–186.

Tulving, E., & Pearlstone, Z. (1966). Availability versus accessibility of information in memory for words. *Journal of Verbal Learning and Verbal Behavior, 5*(4), 381–391. doi:10.1016/S0022-5371(66)80048-8

Underwood, B. J. (1961). Ten years of massed practice on distributed practice. *Psychological Review, 68*(4), 229–247. doi:10.1037/h0047516

Wadhwa, V., Latimer, E., Chatterjee, K., McCarty, J., & Fitzgerald, R. T. (2017). Maximizing the tweet engagement rate in academia: Analysis of the AJNR Twitter feed. *AJNR. American Journal of Neuroradiology, 38*(10), 1866–1868. doi:10.3174/ajnr.A5283 PMID:28663265

Weimer, M. (2013). *Learner-centered teaching: Five key changes to practice*. John Wiley & Sons.

Weimer, M. (2013). *Learner-centered teaching: Five key changes to practice*. John Wiley & Sons.

Welch, B. K., & Bonnan-White, J. (2012). Twittering to increase student engagement in the university classroom. *Knowledge Management & E-Learning: An International Journal, 4*, 325–345.

Wolak, J., Finkelhor, D., Mitchell, K. J., & Ybarra, M. L. (2010). Online "predators" and their victims. *Psychology of Violence, 1*(S), 13–35. doi:10.1037/2152-0828.1.S.13

This research was previously published in the Handbook of Research on Diverse Teaching Strategies for the Technology-Rich Classroom; pages 125-137, copyright year 2020 by Information Science Reference (an imprint of IGI Global).

Chapter 31

Facebook Page as a Digital Pedagogical Tool in the Business Studies Class

Helgaardt Hannes Meintjes
https://orcid.org/0000-0003-4639-8803
Carolina Akademiese Skool, South Africa

Micheal M van Wyk
https://orcid.org/0000-0001-5536-1362
University of South Africa, South Africa

ABSTRACT

Web 2.0 technologies and electronic teaching aids can be used to greatly advance the transmission of knowledge in the school setting. However, the investigation at hand attempted to go a step further by showing the potential benefits of incorporating the Grade 12 Business Studies curriculum into a Facebook page as a digital pedagogical tool to enhance learners' subject knowledge competence and academic performance. An exploratory mixed method research design was adopted. The data was collected using a specifically created Facebook page and an online open-ended questionnaire. Findings revealed the success of the intervention as a supportive teaching strategy and it is suggested that Business Studies teachers should be empowered through receiving training on the use of social media tools in their occupation. Further research is needed across other grade levels or at the same grade level but at other schools to gain an enhanced understanding of learners' responses to Facebook as a supportive teaching tool.

INTRODUCTION

For the past decade, we have seen tremendous numbers of new web developments across the globe. As a matter of fact, Alexander (2006:33) believes that social media software has surfaced as an important component of the Web 2.0 movement, leading to the rise of blogs, wiki's, trackback, video blogs, podcasting and numerous other social networking tools such as Facebook and MySpace. Because of the

DOI: 10.4018/978-1-6684-7123-4.ch031

development of social networking applications, there has been a growing interest in how social media can be applied as an effective teaching strategy worldwide. In recent years, social network communities have undergone rapid and sophisticated development for use in education (Van Wyk 2013:525). The social media landscape is a burgeoning environment within local-, distance-, and open education contexts (Van Wyk 2012:2).

Social media applications and ICTs for educational purposes bring both opportunities and challenges to the classroom. These Web 2.0 technologies and electronic teaching aids could be used to great effect to advance education in schools. Most schools are adapting Web 2.0 technologies in particular to advance their school image on the school's webpage. Mostly, teachers use and communicate via short message services (SMS), mobile phones, chat rooms, iPods, iPads, social networks and e-mail. Moreover, the new mobile generation has grown up with technology and is competent in a technological world (Elam, Stratton & Gibson 2007:23). Emanating from the increased usage of ICT and Web 2.0 technologies in teacher education programmes, teachers in particular have been exposed to various electronic teaching aids (electronic whiteboards, etc.) and Web 2.0 technologies (Facebook, blogs, podcasts and social bookmarking). Some schools and teachers have taken advantage of this exposure by using electronic teaching aids and social media in their daily lesson planning. Teachers are indeed called upon to make a paradigm shift in their teaching style to accommodate a new group of learners called the digital natives. These learners, who use ICT and social media as a means to communicate or to share personal information, should be catered for on a daily basis. Teachers are thus urged to make use of these electronic teaching media and Web 2.0 technologies as, in the view of Prensky (2001:1): "Our students have changed radically. Today's students are no longer the people our educational system was designed to teach". The challenge for teachers concerns how to use social media to enhance learners' learning experiences (VanDoorn & Eklund 2013:1). Saikaew, Krutkam, Pattaramanon, Leelathakul, Chaipah & Chaosakul (2011:2) stated that students spend a lot of time socialising with their friends through Facebook, which means that they devote less time to self-study. Because of the emergence of new technologies, educators must find meaningful ways to incorporate these technologies into the classroom. The big problem that educators experience is to decide which technology to incorporate so that the learning objective can still be achieved. It is evident that modern-day learners are visually stimulated and consequently e-books are being introduced at schools, rendering textbooks something of the past. In order to retain the interest of Business Studies learners, it has become essential to incorporate modern technology and for purposes of this study, it was decided to make use of a Facebook page to achieve this goal. The researchers selected this topic out of a sincere desire to get learners to become more active in the learning experience, and to bring them a form of learning that they find enjoyable through employing efficient and effective learning strategies. By establishing a Facebook page, the educator (i.e. the researchers) created an active learning environment that current learners are able to relate to. The researchers regard it important that learners should have the opportunity to collaborate in discussions outside the classroom to come up with possible subject-related solutions that are monitored by the educator who plays an advisory role. The Facebook page was used to communicate homework, assignments, class discussions and content that supports the subject, such as newspaper articles and video clips from YouTube.

The aim of the study is to explore how learners experience the use of a Facebook page as a supportive teaching and e-learning strategy in the Business Studies class. The primary research question is: *How can Facebook as social media tool be used to support Business Studies learners in enhancing learners' subject knowledge competence?* What are learners' perceptions of the use of a Facebook page as a supportive teaching strategy? How do learners experience the use of a Facebook page to assist and support them with specific learning content in Business studies?

The next section of this chapter proposes the literature review within which the use of Facebook page as a supportive tool in teaching Business Studies to enhance grade 12 learners' knowledge, skills and values could be contextualised.

LITERATURE REVIEW

It is essential to place this study in the context of certain theoretical frameworks to justify the selection of subjects, the variables being studied and the design (McMillan & Schumacher 2010:74). It is also important to apply suitable theories to show a logical link between the research question and the methodology. New opportunities and dilemmas have emerged since the world has become a global village and the use of the internet in teaching and learning. In response to this shift, innovative theories of learning have been created and according to Del Valle García Carreño (2014:108), teachers are obliged to continue seeking new strategies for their teaching and learning. She also maintains that most learning theories to date have relied on the notion of classroom attendance as well as teaching and evaluation strategies, but the 21st century has given rise to opportunities to explore alternative skills and styles such as e-learning, e-portfolio and e-blogs, amongst others. Del Valle García Carreño (2014) further points out that modern day connectivity creates a space for a learning model that recognises the tectonic shift in society and that the field of education has been slow to recognise new learning tools. These observations prompted the researchers to undertake the present study, looking at the introduction of a Business Studies Facebook page as an additional supportive teaching strategy to connect and integrate a specific group of learners that share the same interests.

According to Johnson and Johnson (2005), Social Interdependence Theory is a classic example of the interaction of theory, research and practice. The underlying principle of this theory, that is, that the way goals are structured determines how individuals interact, which in turn creates specific outcomes. More than seven decades ago Social Interdependence Theory has been modified, extended, and refined on the basis of the increasing knowledge about, and application of the theory (Johnson & Johnson 2005). The Social Interdependence Theory will be applied during the research to determine how the participants interact on the Facebook page that was created by the teacher, who is known as the researchers for the purpose of this study. The researchers were dependent on the respondents to take part actively in the activities posted on the Facebook page to complete the research and the respondents were dependend on the researchers to post subject-related activities and to respond and interact to the online comments and answers that the participants posted.

The researchers in this study was concerned with how the education system responds to the net (internet) generation. Communities of practice (CoPs) constitute groups of people who share a concern or a passion for something they do and who learn how to do it better as they interact on a regular basis (Lave & Wenger 1998). It is important to incorporate the three components in the CoPs to understand better, how the education system responds to the *net generation*. An online community of Business Studies learners were created through the creation of the Facebook page to get a better understanding of how teachers and learners can interact on a social media platform to support teaching and learning.

Indeed Bandura (2001) emphasises that the social-cognitive learning theory is a theoretical perspective in which learning by observing others is the focus of study. Furthermore Bandura distinguishes between three modes of agency namely, direct personal agency, proxy agency that relies on others to act on one's best to secure desired outcomes, and collective agency exercised through socially coordinated and inter-dependent effort. While computer-integrated lessons are widely recognised as an essential contributor to the productive use of computers in teaching and learning, very little research has focused on identifying the effectiveness of how social media can be incorporated as an alternative supportive teaching strategy. This research examines how social media, such as a Facebook page can be incorporated based on Social Cognitive Theory. The social interaction between a teacher and learners on a subject-related Facebook page can contribute to the subject knowledge through social learning.

WEB-TECHNOLOGY FOR CLASSROOM INSTRUCTION

Bute (2013:79) is of the view that diverse tools for learning, knowledge and information sharing are already in use. After the development of Web 2.0, the use of these tools has improved in leaps and bounds. This has changed the overall teaching and learning process. Furthermore, Hunter-Brown (2012:19) argues that technology has allowed learners to access much more information than in the past and at a much faster rate. Moreover, Bryan (2006:34) concurred that Web 2.0 technologies have encouraged the evolution of e-learning, where participants are more interactive. The introduction of e-learning has enhanced the inte-gration of formal and informal learning. In view of the latter, learners of today have access to the universe via the internet. Information is literally in the palm of their hand. Therefore, learners no longer have to go to a personal computer or a computer lab to log onto the internet and seek information and ideas that pique their interests. Regardless of a learner's location, smartphones and other handheld devices have been developed to allow access to the internet through various applications such as Facebook. Holladay (2010), however, cautions that it may appear as if the world is at the learner's fingertips, but that there is also concern about the risk. As Fletcher (2011:14) perceptively states: "there is no way we are going to meet our goals in education without a significant improvement in our application of technology".

In view of the above, Lam (2009:334) makes it clear that the use of Web 2.0 tools as educational motivators creates a classroom of autonomy, connectedness and active participation. Lam (2009) further claims that using Web 2.0 tools increases student motivation, but he believes that further research is needed and that such research would benefit the educational environment. According to Hunter-Brown (2012:24), teachers incorporate blogs, wikis or social networks in their classrooms to motivate their learners. Hunter-Brown (2012:22) goes further by claiming that the many forms in which Web 2.0 tools appear (e.g. podcasts) have been applied with great success in a number of schools. Podcasts are simply audio files that can be downloaded and played on computers, MP3 players, iPods, tablet computers and smartphones. The same author agrees that Facebook can be used as a link to podcasts and that this can be effortlessly integrated into the classroom environment and offer students motivational and interac-tive lessons (Hunter-Brown 2012:23). In other words, educators can utilise Web 2.0 tools in numerous ways. A study by Kitsis (2010:52) revealed that her introduction of blogging into the curriculum had motivated students who had formerly almost never turned in traditional homework. They were motivated to such an extent that they became regular contributors to her blog. Emanating from the findings of the study, Kitsis (2010) still employs face-to-face components in the lessons but the addition of blogging has increased the students' participation and motivation levels. It is my view as a researcher that with Grade 12 Business Studies learners there are certain needs levels or hierarchies that need to be met in order to motivate these learners to learn and participate in the subject. This study suggests that these various needs can be met by social networking applications such as Facebook.

USING SOCIAL MEDIA IN TEACHING AND LEARNING

With the progression of technology, innovative methods of communication have appeared and are being used in the academic field. Moreover, Bute (2013:75) accentuates that social media constitutes newly emerged communication networks that are not only used for sharing information but also for education, transfer of knowledge and for building a universal community of academics. According to Goble (2012) and Kithcart (2011), the term social media first became known in 1994, when the first web-based social networking site (i.e. Geocities) was founded. These researchers furthermore stated that Facebook, the most popular social media application, was launched in 2004 and that Twitter followed in 2006. Furthermore, they claim that Facebook became the most successful social media application because of its particular features that set it apart from other social media platforms. Cowan (2008:55) rightly points out that *"educators attempting to integrate technology into their teaching face a variety of challenges in today's classrooms"*. The first obstacle that must be addressed is to determine what type of technology to use and how to incorporate it successfully.

Hunter-Brown (2012:45) correctly pointed out that many educators agree that incorporating technology into their curriculum has academic value and she further states that some educators also believe technology can generate a level of interaction as an instructional management tool. Along the same lines Loving and Ochoa (2011) conducted a study in which Facebook was utilised as a classroom management solution by librarians and educators. In essence the study showed that the educators were able to utilise Facebook by creating a class page that learners could submit work on, be made aware of deadlines and objectives, as well as communicate with the educators and fellow learners. The researchers found that while there are many factors that offer numerous instructional prospects, there are also several privacy concerns. With this in mind, educators who choose to utilise this medium must ensure that privacy protocols are in place. There are plenty of privacy options available through Facebook and the use of these will ensure that the focus remains academic. This feature of Facebook is what prompted Loving and Ochoa (2011), amongst many others, to select the particular application for incorporation into the curriculum. These authors (2011) found that communicating with students through messages gave the instructor confidence and that the ease of creating a closed environment for the students to discuss assignments privately was extremely beneficial.

Facebook in Teaching and Learning

When it comes to using Facebook in education, opinions differ, particularly with regard to the time involved in preparing and conducting educational activities on the social media platform. Furthermore, Van Wyk (2012:2) stated that blogs as a form of learning enrich students' learning experiences and bring about deeper learning. In addition, Cain (2008:6) and Gallop (2008:74) are also strongly of the opinion that web technologies can only enhance learning, with the former stating: *"social networking sites such as Facebook provide individuals with a way of maintaining and strengthening social ties, which can be beneficial in both social and academic settings"*. Gallop (2008:74) emphasised that the use of technology or social media is not essential for effective learning but rather how skilfully technology or social media is applied during the learning experience; he goes on to say that, the degree to which learning principles are incorporated into the students' environment determines the effectiveness of the learning tools. In a similar vein Van Wyk (2014a:371) argues that by selecting various social media tools such as blogs or wikis, educators can create differentiated learning paths that can be combined to create active learning environments to accommodate the student of today. In fact, several studies have demonstrated that these personalised and customised learning environments may be better suited to address the diverse needs of today's generation (Van Wyk 2014a:371).

In addition, Baran (2010) discussed the huge role that Facebook plays in the lives of millions of students, a fact that leaves many wondering whether it is a good or bad thing. Munoz and Towner (2009:4) reported that *"in addition to the incredible usage rate among students there are a number of unique features that make it amenable to educational pursuits"*. These researchers furthermore explain that Facebook "indirectly" creates a learning environment by connecting students to each other. In the same vein Skerrett (2010:81-81) states that *"the Facebook event represented an opportunity to hold conversations about gender, male privilege, and more generally hegemonic power structures that circulate throughout social networking sites"*. Furthermore, Fogg-Phillips *et al.* (n.d.:2) also reassert that Facebook has the power to enhance learning inside the classroom and beyond, but advise that the interaction between learners in the educational setting must be open, transparent and secure.

Instead of finding themselves opposed to the use of Facebook, teachers can apply Facebook constructively as a teaching tool for supporting students' continuous learning experience. When the curriculum permits for self-directed online learning, learners can learn more than what is taught during class because they are able to create meaning for themselves beyond the classroom and beyond the teacher's objectives (Fogg-Phillips *et al.* n.d.:13). Furthermore, these researchers claim that to incorporate digital learning opportunities into the curriculum meets the needs of the *net generation* and their digital learning styles, hence enhancing their learning. Thus, teachers need to give serious thought to how best to meet their learners' needs through Web 2.0 and other networking tools (English & Duncan-Howell 2008:596). The present learner profiles, referred to as the net generation or as digital natives, have challenged the 21st century's teaching and learning environment (Van Wyk 2013:525; Van Wyk 2014a:370). Again, teachers need to be cognisant of how young people connect and interact on the web so that a more appropriate and more inclusive digital experience can be created for them in and outside the classroom. However, teachers also need to be aware that not all learners (especially those in rural areas) have the means to readily access the internet since, as pointed out by Fogg-Phillips *et al.* (n.d.:14), the use of a mobile-only to connect to the internet is 25 per cent and under in developing countries.

Since millions of students around the world use Facebook regularly and with ease, this entertainment-oriented social media platform lends itself for use as a supportive learning tool (Saikaew *et al.* 2011:1). Although there are various tools available for e-learning, Facebook seems to be one of the most useful because students generally respond to discussions speedily and are comfortable enough in their "space" to share their information and opinions (Saikaew *et al.* 2011:1). Baran's (2010:148) study, which examined Facebook being utilised as a formal instruction environment, noted, *"not all students are ready to embrace the use of social networking tools such as Facebook in formal teaching, learning and assessment"*. This particular study (Baran, 2010) revealed that certain students are indeed more interested in socialising than in the educational component of the experience. This can be a problem when teachers want to integrate social media applications such as Facebook into their curriculum since it could distract students from their subject content as opposed to enhancing their learning. Thus, the planning of

Facebook use should be done in such a way as to include the best aspects of the traditional classroom along with the advantages of real-time and mobile learning.

STUDENT PERCEPTIONS OF HOW SOCIAL MEDIA CAN SUPPORT THEIR LEARNING

In a study carried out by Van Wyk (2012:3), the majority of students indicated that they used Mxit, Facebook, Twitter and SMS as their preferred social media tools for communication. What emerged from students' postings in this study is that social media encouraged collaboration with peers and facilitated a platform where they gave their peers support or advice (Van Wyk 2012:4). Students argue that social media is characterised as Web 2.0-based e-learning that emphasises dynamic participation, collaboration and sharing knowledge and ideas with one another (Van Wyk 2013:529; Van Wyk 2014a:370). Ophus and Abbitt (2009) reported comparable data, indicating that students were mostly supportive of using a social networking system in their education. Likewise, McCarthy (2012) reported supportive attitudes from students for the use of Facebook as an academic tool, highlighting responses indicating Facebook is a platform familiar to students and that it allows access to academic information on a system that they constantly engage with. Furthermore, students' feedback reflected that they found social media a useful learning tool for promoting and supporting the e-learning experience (Van Wyk 2013:529). However, Van Wyk's (2013) findings also revealed, as did Baran's (2010), that many of the students used social media tools to interact socially rather than using them to discuss or complete subject-related matter (Van Wyk 2014a:375).

On a more positive note, some students confirmed that the establishment of the social media group enabled them to foster trust between the members and that social media applications provided them with a functional platform on which to communicate with each other and reflect on the academic work. Despite these possibilities, there are still numbers of students who avoided communication and kept things superficial (Van Wyk 2012:4-6). Gallop (2008:75-77) also reported overall positive results with students claiming that they believed technology helped them to learn.

RESEARCH DESIGN AND METHODOLOGY

The interpretive paradigm describes reality as people's personal experiences of their immediate world. The researchers' stance towards reality is inter-subjective and empathic. The social constructivist paradigm sees reality as socially constructed and sees systems of meaning as originating on a social rather than an individual level (Van Wyk & Toale, 2015). This research adopts an exploratory mixed method design to describe how a Facebook page can be used as a supportive teaching strategy in the Business Studies class at Carolina Akademiese Skool in South Africa. The motivation for using this is first to explore Grade 12 learners' views and experiences on the Facebook page regarding specific topics the researchers taught for the duration of the study on the Facebook page to enhance their knowledge, skills and attitudes in Business Studies. Secondly, an online questionnaire was designed to determine Grade 12 learners' experiences regarding supporting their learning through a Facebook page. Finally, this pragmatic approach was used through qualitative and quantitative research including an extensive literature review to achieve triangulation for the study. Marshall's (1996:522) study emphasised that the selection of a study sample is a very important step in any research project since it is rarely practical, efficient, or ethical to study entire populations. Marshall (1996:523) further asserted that sample sizes for qualitative investigations tend to be small and that this adequately answers the research question, which is why the researchers have chosen to use convenience sampling by focusing on the current fifteen Grade 12 Business Studies learners from Carolina Akademiese Skool. The main sampling strategy was purposeful sampling that consists of convenience sampling. As indicated earlier, the researchers created a Facebook page to incorporate into the Grade 12 Business Studies class as a supportive teaching strategy. The Business Studies Facebook page was incorporated over a period of ten weeks according to CAPS (Curriculum Assessment Policy Statement). Observations of how the learners used the Facebook page provided the researchers with a clear picture of the types of activities the learners became engaged in. All data was collected as screenshots and the Facebook page is still available on the internet. The researchers compiled the online closed-ended questionnaire and posted the Surveymonkey link on the Facebook page for learners to complete after they already had six weeks of access to the page. The format of an online questionnaire facilitated ease of storage, retrieval, and qualitative analysis. This enabled the researchers to easily export the data and statistics and provided ready access without the need for transcription. Thus, the researchers could refer back to the participants' responses effortlessly in the case of needing to verify the data after the analysis had already been completed. Various activities were loaded onto the Facebook page that were related to the subject content with the intent to gather information deemed pertinent to the study. The researchers also prepared additional follow-up questions in case it turned out that inconsistent data was yielded. Informal interviews were also conducted during class time. The informal interviews took the form of an open discussion, and various questions were asked based on the Business Studies class and the teacher teaching Business Studies through a Facebook page as a supportive teaching strategy.

The researchers were cognisant of the obligation to respect the rights, needs, desires and values of the participants. Permission to embark on the research was requested from the Mpumalanga Department of Education, Carolina Akademiese Skool and from the participants. In ensuring ethical soundness of the research, the researchers adhered to certain principles cited by Guba and Lincoln (1994:300), namely informed consent, an explanation to participants of the voluntary nature of their participation, assurances of safety in participation as well as privacy, confidentiality, anonymity and trust. Ethical clearance (Ref no 2017/07/12/90233522/12/MC) for the study was also requested from the University of South Africa (UNISA).

RESULTS

Learner perceptions of the use of a Facebook page as a supportive teaching strategy

To provide a further analysis of the use of Facebook as a supportive teaching strategy, learners were presented with 15 questionnaire items for scoring. These items aimed to collect learner opinions about the following: (1) the teacher's sharing of subject-related information; (2) the rate of information-sharing via Facebook; (3) the application's potential as communication platform between teacher and learners; (4) the opportunity to communicate with the teacher outside the classroom; (5) the potential it offers for sharing and exchanging files, links, information, polls and videos; (6) the opportunity it presents for group members to learn from each other; (7) boosting learner confidence through the opportunity to ask questions on the page as opposed to during class time; (8) assisting learners to think more deeply about the subject content; (9) helping learners to make connections between ideas and preparing them for class participation; (10) supporting learners to organise their learning; (11) making the learning process more visible; (12) improving learner interest in Business Studies; (13) promoting understanding of the subject content; (14) potential to boost students' marks; and (15) whether learners thought the Facebook page might distract them from their learning at school.

Table 1. Mean standard deviation, percentages of learner perceptions of the use of a Facebook page as supportive teaching strategy

Statements	Mean	SD	Strongly Disagree	Disagree	Neutral	Agree	Strongly Agree
1. Educator sharing subject-related information	4.41	0.731	0%	0%	20%	**50%**	30%
The majority of respondents (50%) agreed to strongly agreed (30%) that the educator shared subject-related information on the Facebook page (mean = 4.41; SD = 0.731) with the Grade 12 Business Studies class, and 20% indicated a neutral response.							
2. Facebook conveys information quickly	4.68	0.781	0%	0%	10%	**60%**	30%
The majority of respondents (60%) agreed to strongly agreed (30%) that information is rapidly conveyed (mean = 4.68; SD = 0.781) through the Business Studies Facebook page.							
3. Communicating information from the educator to the learner	4.48	0.721	0%	0%	40%	**60%**	0%
Sixty per cent (60%) of the respondents held that the educator communicated information to the learners (mean = 4.48; SD = 0.721) and the minority of 40% had a neutral response.							
4. It creates the opportunity to communicate easily with the educator outside the classroom	4.88	0.789	0%	0%	0%	**70%**	30%
An overwhelming majority of the respondents (70%) agreed and strongly agreed (30%) that the Facebook page creates (mean = 4.88; SD = 0.789) an opportunity to easily communicate with the educator outside the classroom.							
5. Members of the page can exchange and share files, links, information, polls and videos with one another	4.68	0.781	0%	0%	10%	**60%**	30%
The majority of the respondents agreed (60%) to strongly agreed (30%) that members of the Facebook page can exchange and share information (mean = 4.68; SD = 0.781) such as files, links, information, polls and videos with one another and merely (10%) were undecided.							
6. Members of the page learn from each other	4.03	0.811	0%	0%	33.33%	**33.33%**	33.33%
Of the respondents, 33.3% strongly agreed, 33.3% agreed and 33.3% indicated a neutral response (mean = 4.03; SD = 0.811) on the statement that members of the Facebook page learn from each other.							
7. You have more confidence to ask questions on the Facebook page than during class time	4.48	0.731	0%	20%	10%	**50%**	20%
The respondents had a mixed response in that 50% agreed and 20% strongly agreed that they have more confidence (mean = 4.48; SD = 0.731) to ask questions on the Facebook page than during contact time. The minority (20%) disagreed and a mere 10% were indecisive.							
8. 9. It helped me think more deeply about the subject content of Business Studies	4.78	0.788	0%	0%	30%	**70%**	0%
The majority of the respondents agreed (70%) that the Facebook page let them think more deeply (mean = 4.78; SD = 0.788) about the Business Studies subject content and 30% had a neutral response.							
10. It helped me to make connections between ideas and prepare myself better for classroom participation	4.55	0.751	0%	0%	50%	**50%**	0%

continues on following page

Table 1. Continued

Statements	Mean	SD	Strongly Disagree	Disagree	Neutral	Agree	Strongly Agree
Of the respondents, 50% were neutral and 50% agreed that the Facebook page (mean = 4.55; SD = 0.751) helped them to make better connections in the subject and better prepared them for classroom participation.							
11. It supported me and organised my learning in the subject	4.62	0.780	0%	0%	20%	**70%**	10%
The majority of the respondents agreed (70%) to strongly agreed (10%) that the Facebook page supported them and organised their learning (mean = 4.62; SD = 0.780) in the subject, with 20% being neutral.							
12. Most obviously, the Facebook page supports me by making the learning process more visible	4.68	0.761	0%	0%	30%	**50%**	20%
The majority of the respondents agreed (50%) to strongly agreed (20%) that the Facebook page supported them (mean = 4.68; SD = 0.761) by making the learning process more visible, and 30% were indecisive.							
13. My interest in Business Studies improved because of the use of the Facebook page	4.28	0.721	0%	0%	30%	**40%**	30%
The majority of the respondents agreed (40%) to strongly agreed (30%) that use of the Facebook page improved their interest (mean = 4.28; SD = 0.721) in the subject, with the minority (30%) being indecisive.							
14. Facebook as a supportive teaching strategy promotes my understanding of the subject content	3.88	0.981	10%	0%	20%	**60%**	10%
The majority of the respondents agreed (70%) that the Facebook page promoted their understanding of the subject content (mean 3.88; SD = 0.981). .							
15. Do you think that you and your peers will achieve better results if the Facebook page is integrated into lessons?	4.18	0.701	0%	0%	30%	**40%**	30%
The majority of the respondents agreed (40%) to strongly agreed (30%) that they would achieve better results (mean 4.18; SD = 0.701) if the Facebook page is incorporated into lessons, with 30% indicating a neutral response.							
16. The Facebook page distracted me from my educational work	3.48	0.981	20%	60%	20%	**0%**	0%
The majority of the respondents disagreed (60%) to strongly disagreed (20%) that the Facebook page caused a distraction (mean = 3.48; SD = 0.981) with regard to their educational work, and 20% were indecisive.							

Scale: SD-Strongly disagree; D-Disagree; N-Neutral; A-Agree; SA-Strongly agree

Based on the information presented in table 1, overall Grade 12 learners agreed to strongly agreed that the Facebook page for Business Studies did indeed assist and support them in their learning. All of the learners responded to these 15 items in the questionnaire, with the exception of item six where there was a 90% response rate. For item (1), 50% of the learners agreed that the teacher shared subject-related information, 30% strongly agreed and 20% gave a neutral response. This indicates that subject-related information can be shared on a Facebook page for curriculum purposes. With regards to conveying information quickly through the Facebook page, the majority (60%) of the learners agreed, 30% strongly agreed and only 10% were neutral. This points to the conclusion that Facebook is an effective teaching tool for communicating quickly and effectively because most of the learners have access to Facebook in the palm of their hands. For item (3) relating to communication from teacher to learner, 60% agreed and 40% gave a neutral response. With regards to the next item, 70% of the learners indicated that they agreed that the Facebook page creates an opportunity to communicate easily with the educator outside the classroom and 30% indicated strong agreement. This suggests that learners do indeed experience the use of Facebook as a supportive teaching tool and they relate to it in a very positive manner. For item (5) the majority (60%) of the learners agreed that members of the page can exchange and share files, links, information, polls and videos with one another, 30% reported strong agreement and only 10% gave a neutral response. Although the results indicate that the majority of the learners agreed that a variety of information can be shared, it must be noted that none of the learners shared any files, links, polls or videos on the Facebook page during the research period. With regards to whether learners felt they could learn from each other on the Facebook page, the learners who strongly agreed, agreed and were neutral showed equal scores of 33.3%.

Item (7) revealed that 50% of the learners agreed that they have more confidence to ask questions on the Facebook page than during class, and equal percentages of 20% strongly agreed and disagreed, with 10% feeling neutral. With regards to whether they thought the Facebook page helped the learners to think more deeply about the subject content, an overwhelming 70% indicated that they agreed and 30% had a neutral response. It is therefore important to highlight that the educator was successful in taking the subject content outside the classroom in order for learners to learn actively outside the classroom by incorporating the Facebook page into lesson activities. Responses to item (9) demonstrated that half of the students (50%) agreed and the other half (50%) had a neutral response towards whether the Facebook page helped them to make connections between ideas and better prepared them for classroom participation. Even though only 50% indicated that they were better prepared for classroom participation this still represents a significant number of learners who reported drawing benefit from an interactive Facebook page. Furthermore, 70% of the learners agreed that the Facebook page supported them and organised their learning in the subject, 20% indicated a neutral response and 10% strongly agreed; thus presenting more concrete evidence that the majority of the 21st century learners report benefits from the use of technologies such as a Facebook page as supportive teaching strategy.

With regards to whether they felt the Facebook page supports the learners by making the learning process more visible, 50% agreed, 30% indicated a neutral response and 20% reported strong agreement. Again the majority of learners find it favourable to learn from a screen instead of only from a textbook. Concerning whether the Facebook page improved their interest in Business Studies, 40% agreed, 30% strongly agreed and the other 30% indicated a neutral response. The researcher noticed a great improvement in the quality of classroom discussions after the Facebook page had been incorporated into the Business Studies class; learners who were normally reserved during contact time started to participate. With regards to whether their understanding of the subject content improved, 60% agreed, 20% had a neutral opinion and 10% strongly agreed, although it must also be noted that 10% reported strong disagreement.

For item (14) relating to improved learner performance, 40% agreed and 30% strongly agreed, with 30% reporting a neutral response. Finally, concerning the question of whether they felt the Facebook page was a distracting factor, 60% disagreed and 20% reported strong disagreement and 20% were neutral. Bearing all the learner feedback in mind, the researcher believes that social media applications such as Facebook definitely have a place in 21st century curricula and that indeed it may be crucial to include these technologies in order to keep abreast of the rapidly changing world we live in and its teaching and learning environments.

Learners' perceptions of a Facebook page to assist and support them with specific learning content in Business Studies

Components of the third term Grade 12 Business Studies curriculum according to the CAPS Business Studies document (DoE 2011:41), were incorporated via the Facebook page as educational tool; the results of which are described below.

Table 2. Investment securities

CAPS Topic:	Investment securities
Content in lesson plans:	Different types of investment
Facebook activities by Grade 12 learners:	The Sharenet (2016) link was shared and a share certificate was published (refer to screenshot 4.3, 4.4 and 4.5). Comparison between different investment opportunities was shared through a Fin24 (2016) link (screenshot 4.6). Link to South African retail bonds website (screenshot 4.7 and 4.8).
Assessment:	Article about Johannesburg Stock Exchange (JSE) was shared. Each learner identified one of the Top 15 listed companies and the type of certificate presented. Learners compared the three different investment opportunities and commented on what they thought was the best investment opportunity and why. Learners used www.rsaretailbonds.gov.za to answer the questions from the Facebook page. One of the CAPS Business Studies recommendations for resources is the internet and the purpose was to bring practice into the classroom and to make the textbook come alive.

Figure 1.

The following topics were incorporated into the Facebook page lesson plans prescribed by the CAPS Business Studies document (DoE 2011:41), namely, Investment securities (Different types of investment), Investment insurance (Compulsory and non-compulsory insurance), and Overinsurance and underinsurance (Learner Presentations: Verbal and non-verbal presentation).

Table 3. Grade 12 Business Studies learners' presentations

CAPS Topic:	Presentations
Content in lesson plans:	Verbal and non-verbal presentation
Facebook activities by Grade 12 learners:	All the activities on the Facebook page were used by the teacher in the form of a presentation via a data projector during class time to explain verbal and non-verbal presentation.
Assessment:	The learners identified photographs and written material as forms of non-verbal communication and the explanations by the teacher and videos as forms of verbal communication. According to the CAPS Business Studies document, learners must accurately and concisely identify and distinguish between verbal and non-verbal presentation of a variety of business-related information. The Facebook page created the ideal opportunity to recapitulate presentation of business information in verbal and non-verbal formats as required by the CAPS Business Studies guideline.

Table 4. Grade 12 Business Studies learners' perception about using a Facebook page to assist and support learning content

Statements	Mean	SD	SD	D	N	A	SA
1. It helped me to distinguish between assurance and insurance	4.78	0.761	0%	0%	0%	70%	30%
The majority of respondents (70%) agreed to strongly agreed (30%) that the Facebook page assisted and helped them (mean = 4.78; SD = 0.761) to distinguish between assurance and insurance in the Grade 12 class.							
2. I understand what compulsory and non-compulsory insurance are	4.54	0.693	0%	0%	10%	40%	50%
The majority of respondents (40%) agreed to strongly agreed (50%) that the Facebook page helped them (mean = 4.54; SD = 0.693) to understand what compulsory and non-compulsory insurance are.							
3. It assisted me to understand the difference between compound and simple interest	4.68	0.781	0%	0%	30%	60%	10%
The majority of respondents (60%) agreed to strongly agreed (10%) that the Facebook page helped them (mean = 4.68; SD = 0.781) to understand the difference between compound and simple interest. The minority (30%) were indecisive.							
4. It supported me to understand and calculate overinsurance and underinsurance	4.68	0.781	0%	0%	30%	60%	10%
The majority of respondents (60%) agreed to strongly agreed (10%) that the Facebook page helped them (mean = 4.68; SD = 0.781) to understand and calculate over- and underinsurance. The minority (30%) were indecisive.							
5. It helped me to understand why life insurance and retirement annuities are important	3.78	0.661	0%	0%	40%	30%	30%
The majority of respondents (30%) agreed to strongly agreed (30%) that the Facebook page helped them (mean = 3.78; SD = 0.661) to understand why life insurance and retirement annuities are important. The minority (40%) were indecisive.							
6. It supported me to understand the extent to which a particular form of ownership can contribute to the success or failure of a business	4.08	0.631	0%	0%	40%	50%	10%
The majority of respondents (50%) agreed to strongly agreed (10%) that the Facebook page helped them (mean = 4.08; SD = 0.631) to understand the extent to which a particular form of ownership can contribute to the success or failure of a business. The minority (40%) were indecisive.							
7. It assisted me to be able to understand and distinguish between verbal and non-verbal presentation	4.08	0.721	0%	0%	20%	50%	30%
The majority of respondents (60%) agreed to strongly agreed (10%) that the Facebook page helped them (mean = 4.08; SD = 0.721) to understand and distinguish between verbal and non-verbal presentation. The minority (20%) were indecisive.							
8. It empowered me to understand the criteria for a logical and effective presentation	4.18	0.761	0%	0%	30%	50%	20%
The majority of respondents (50%) agreed to strongly agreed (20%) that the Facebook page helped them (mean = 4.18; SD = 0.761) to understand the criteria for a logical and effective presentation. The minority (30%) were indecisive.							
9. It supported me to know how to handle and respond to feedback in a non-aggressive and professional manner	3.88	0.561	0%	0%	40%	40%	20%
The majority of respondents (40%) agreed to strongly agreed (20%) that the Facebook page supported them (mean = 3.88; SD = 0.561) to know how to handle and respond to feedback in a non-aggressive and professional manner. The minority (40%) were indecisive.							
10. I am pleasantly surprised at how the Business Studies Facebook page assisted and supported my understanding and learning in the subject	4.83	0.861	0%	0%	11.11%	88.89%	0%
The majority of respondents (88.89%) agreed that the Facebook page surprised them (mean = 4.83; SD = 0.861) in terms of how it assisted and supported their understanding and learning in the subject. A marginal percentage (11.11%) were indecisive.							

Scale: SD-Strongly disagree; D-Disagree; N-Neutral; A-Agree; SA-Strongly agree

Based on the information presented in table 4, it is evident that the Grade 12 learners agreed to strongly agreed that the Business Studies Facebook page assisted and supported them in their learning.

Open-Ended Question

As seen below, the researcher has deemed it relevant to include some of the overwhelmingly positive learner comments, which illustrate their belief that the Business Studies Facebook page is an appropriate teaching tool:

- **Respondent One:** *"It gives us a better outlook and perspective towards Business Studies, and additional information and resources regarding our work in the classroom"*.
- **Respondent Two:** *"Yes because it helps me understand more about the subject"*.
- **Respondent Three:** *"I'm more interested in technology, ever since I've started using the Facebook page "Cas BStudies" my level of understanding within the subject has highly increased. The page has been extremely useful, mentally it has groomed me"*.

DISCUSSION OF FINDINGS

It was found in this study that respondents showed overwhelming positivity towards the social networking tool and further indicated that the Facebook page should indeed be utilised as a supportive teaching strategy. Gallop (2008:74) agrees that *"social networking sites such as Facebook provide individuals with a way of maintaining and strengthening social ties, which can be beneficial in both social and academic settings"*. The literature review yielded several studies, which have been conducted regarding the educational benefits of social media tools in the classroom (Gallop 2008; Van Wyk 2014b). Furthermore, it emerged from the respondent comments that subject knowledge was indeed enhanced and this was supported by literature. Some of the comments included in the Facebook entries were as follows: *"It gives us a better outlook and perspective towards Business Studies, and additional information and resources regarding our work in the classroom"*, *"Yes, because it helps me understand more about the subject"*, and *"My level of understanding within the subject has highly increased. The page has been extremely useful, mentally it has groomed me"*. The findings of Gallop (2008:75-77) and Van Wyk (2014b) concur with these positive sentiments expressed by learners, thus confirming that the incorporation of social media into the learning space supports and enhances the e-learning experience. Moreover, Bute (2013:79) expressed a view pointing at the diversity of tools available in the public sphere for learning, knowledge and information; tools that are improving at a rapid pace. Similarly, Hunter-Brown (2012:19) argued that technology has allowed learners to access much more information than in the past and at a much faster rate, thus improving subject knowledge. The researchers succeeded in incorporating a Business Studies Facebook page for learners to improve their subject knowledge by completing interactive activities on the page as a supportive teaching strategy. Learners argue that social media is characterised as Web 2.0-based e-learning that emphasise dynamic participation, collaboration and sharing knowledge and ideas with one another (Van Wyk 2013:529; Van Wyk 2014a:370). The researchers share Lam's (2009:334) view that the use of Web 2.0 tools as educational motivators creates a classroom of autonomy, connectedness and active participation, and is also in strong agreement with Lim (2010:73) who remarked on the multifunctionality of a Facebook page in presenting subject content. In order for

Facebook to be beneficial as a supportive teaching strategy, all learners must have equal access to the necessary technology. Although the present study found that many learners had limited access to the internet through not being able to afford data bundles or not being near Wi-Fi hotspots, the researchers purchased data bundles for all participants and made a personal Wi-Fi router available to them during contact time; an arrangement which is not feasible in the long run. Consequently, some learners only had limited time to access the Facebook page and were not able to continue their participation outside the classroom environment; thus constituting a serious obstacle.

CONCLUSION AND RECOMMENDATIONS

This chapter has argued that teachers can use a Facebook page as a supportive teaching and e-learning strategy in the Business Studies class effectively. Therefore, the study has shown that the Facebook as social media tool could be used to support Business Studies learners in enhancing learners' subject knowledge competence. Furthermore, Business Studies learners get opportunities to participate actively in the learning process even after formal teaching time, such as through posting comments and engaging in online discussions, interact with fellow classmates, grows the learner's individuality and self-assertion and fosters the learner's enthusiasm for learning by encouraging learners to get involved in interesting activities. These educational gains from this study suggests that educators should constantly be alert and on the lookout for opportunities to meet the needs of their learners through Web 2.0 technologies and other networking tools. It is important to be cognisant of the fact that not all learners have ready access to the internet, especially those from rural areas. The Department of Education must address the poor (or indeed no) access to the internet in schools in order for teachers to incorporate ICT successfully. It is recommended that larger sample sizes of teachers, schools and learners must be investigated since this will be extremely advantageous to the education system. It is recommended that workshops be offered on how to incorporate Facebook pages as a supportive teaching strategy within the Economics and Business Management field by inviting other educators in the circuit and region to understand the importance of ICT in education. The researchers suggest that the use of a Facebook page as a supportive teaching strategy should be introduced to various subject clusters. It can also be expanded to the district and to provincial level to empower all teachers and learners older than 13 years. The researchers recommend that teachers form support teams and motivate local businesses to invest in the teaching of Business Studies at school so that learners can be provided with the necessary equipment for incorporating ICTs. Although the purpose of this study was to explore the use of a Facebook page as a supportive teaching strategy in the Grade 12 Business Studies class, the information that was gleaned can only be used to grant a small overview of its effectiveness and cannot be generalised to a wider population. Not all learners who indicated that they would participate in the focus group discussion eventually completed the survey. The most apparent need in terms of further research concerns the fact that more research needs to be conducted across all grades of the high school curriculum and using greater sample sizes.

REFERENCES

Alexander, B. (2006). *Web 2.0. A new wave of innovation for teaching and learning?* Available at: http://net.educause.edu/ir/library/pdf/ERM0621.pdf

Bandura, A. (2001). *Social Cognitive Theory: An Agentic Perspective*. Available at: http://www.annualreviews.org/doi/pdf/10.1146/annurev.psych.52.1.1

Baran, B., & Cagiltay, K. (2010). The Dynamics of Online Communities in the Activity Theory Framework. *Journal of Educational Technology & Society, 13*(4), 155–166.

Bryan, A. (2006). Web 2.0: A new wave of innovation for teaching and learning. *EDUCAUSER Review, 41*(2), 32–44.

Bute, S. J. R. (2013). Integrating Social Media and Traditional Media within the Academic Environment. In Social Media in Higher Education – Teaching in Web 2.0. Information Science Reference (IGI Global).

Cain, J. (2008). Online social networking issues within academia and pharmacy education. *American Journal of Pharmaceutical Education, 72*(1), 44–54. doi:10.5688/aj720110 PMID:18322572

Del Valle Garcia Carreňo, I. (2014). Theory of Connectivity as an Emergent Solution to Innovative Learning Strategies. *American Journal of Educational Research, 2*(2), 107–116. doi:10.12691/education-2-2-7

DoE (Department of Education). (2011). *National Curriculum Statement. Curriculum and Assessment Policy Statement: Further Education and Training Phase Grades 10 – 12 (Business Studies)*. Pretoria: Government Printers.

Elam, C., Stratton, T., & Gibson, D. D. (2007). Welcoming a new generation to college: The millennial students. *Journal of College Admission, 195*(2), 20–25.

Fisher, M., & Baird, D. (2006). Making eLearning Work: Utilizing Mobile Technology for Active Exploration, Collaboration, Assessment, and Reflection in Higher Education. *Journal of Educational Technology Systems, 35*(1), 3–30. doi:10.2190/4T10-RX04-113N-8858

Fletcher, G. (2011). Digital learning-and school reform-now! *The Journal, 38*(3), 14–16.

Fogg-Phillips, L., Baird, D., & Fogg, B.J. (n.d.). *Facebook for educators*. Retrieved from http://circlesofinnovation.valenciacollege.edu/files/2014/05/Facebook-for-Educators.pdf

Gallop, R. (2008). *Do blogs help students to learn?* Retrieved from http://insight.glos.ac.uk/tli/resources/lathe/documents/issue%202/case%20studies/gallop.pdf

Guba, E. G., & Lincoln, Y. S. (1994). Competing paradigms in qualitative research. In N. K. Denzin & Y. S. Lincoln (Eds.), *The handbook of qualitative research*. Thousand Oaks, CA: Sage.

Holladay, J. (2010). Cyberbullying the stakes have never been higher for students-or schools. *Teaching Tolerance, 38*, 42–45.

Hunter-Brown, S. R. (2012). *Facebook as an instructional tool in the secondary classroom: A case study* (PhD thesis). Liberty University, Lynchburg, VA.

Johnson, D. W., & Johnson, R. T. (2005). *New developments in social interdepence theory*. Available at: http://www.ncbi.nlm.nih.gov/pubmed/17191373

Kitsis, S. (2010). The virtual circle. *Educational Leadership, 68*(1), 50–54.

Lam, P. (2009). Quasi-Experimental research into the effects of an international collaboration project on Hong Kong secondary school students' learning motivation. *International Journal of Learning, 16*(7), 325–337. doi:10.18848/1447-9494/CGP/v16i07/46437

Lim, T. (2010). The use of Facebook for online discussions among distance learners. *Turkish Online Journal of Distance Education, 11*(4), 72–81.

McCarthy, J. (2012). International design collaboration and mentoring for tertiary students through Facebook. *Australasian Journal of Educational Technology, 28*(5), 755–775. doi:10.14742/ajet.1383

McMillan, J. H., & Schumacher, S. (2006). *Research in education: Evidence-based inquiry* (6th ed.). Boston: Pearson.

McMillan, J. H., & Schumacher, S. (2010). *Research in education: Evidence-based inquiry* (7th ed.). Boston: Pearson.

Ophus, J. D., & Abbitt, J. T. (2009). Exploring the potential perceptions of social networking systems in university courses. *MERLOT Journal of Online Learning and Teaching, 5*(4), 639–648.

Prensky, M. (2001). Digital natives. Digital immigrants. *On the Horizon, 9*(5). Available at: http://www.marcprensky.com/writing/Prensky%20-%20Digital%20Natives,%20Digital%20Immigrants%20-%20Part1.pdf

Saikaew, K. R., Krutkam, W., Pattaramanon, R., Leelathakul, N., Chaipah, K., & Chaosakul, A. (2011). *Using Facebook as a supplementary tool for teaching and learning*. Available at: http://gear.kku.ac.th/~krunapon/research/pub/usingFB4Learning.pdf

Van Wyk, M. M. (2014a). Blogs as an e-learning strategy in supporting economics education students during teaching practice. *Journal of Communication, 5*(2), 135–143. doi:10.1080/0976691X.2014.11884833

Van Wyk, M. M. (2012). Using blogs as a means of enhancing reflective Teaching Practice in open distance learning ecologies. *African Education Review, 10*, 47–62. Available at: http://www.unisa.ac.za/contents/conferences/odl2012/docs/submissions/ODL-010-2012EDITFinal_vanWykM.pdf

Van Wyk, M. M. (2013). Exploring students' perceptions of blogs during teaching practice placements. *Mediterranean Journal of Social Sciences, 4*(14), 525-533. Available at: http://www.mcser.org/journal/index.php/mjss/article/view/1634/1639

Van Wyk, M. M. (2014b). Using social media in an open distance learning teaching practice course. *Mediterranean Journal of Social Sciences, 5*(1), 370–377. Available at: http://www.mcser.org/journal/index.php/mjss/article/view/2224

Van Wyk, M. M., & Toale, M. (2015). Research design. In O. Chinedu & M. Van Wyk (Eds.), *Educational research: An African approach*. Cape Town: Oxford University Press.

VanDoorn, G., & Eklund, A. A. (2013). *Face to Facebook: Social media and the learning and teaching potential of symmetrical, synchronous communication*. Available at: http://files.eric.ed.gov/fulltext/EJ1005279.pdf

KEY TERMS AND DEFINITIONS

Web 2.0 Technologies: Are online-networked technologies like social media. Facebook, Twitter, WhatsApp, blogs are some of the most popular social media tools that students are using either for socialization or for learning. These Web 2.0 technologies or social network tools are characterized by greater user interactivity, sharing, collaboration, more pervasive network connectivity, and enhanced communication channels.

This research was previously published in the Handbook of Research on Digital Learning; pages 57-74, copyright year 2020 by Information Science Reference (an imprint of IGI Global).

Chapter 32

Instagram as a Learning Space to Introduce Virtual Technology Tools Into Post-COVID Higher Education

Daniel Belanche

ⓘ https://orcid.org/0000-0002-2291-1409

University of Zaragoza, Spain

Marta Flavián

University of Zaragoza, Spain

Sergio Ibáñez-Sánchez

University of Zaragoza, Spain

Alfredo Pérez-Rueda

University of Zaragoza, Spain

ABSTRACT

This chapter examines an innovative learning project in which undergraduate marketing students manage and generate content on an official Instagram profile. The project is designed to provide students with a more active role in the learning process through the application of new virtual technology tools. During the pandemic (course 2020-21), students shared their knowledge about marketing and related topics through storytelling, transmedia, gamification, and virtual/augmented reality via Instagram. The students' perception of the learning outcomes, and their satisfaction, were compared with those of students from three previous courses (2017-20). The findings revealed that students assessed the Instagram activity more highly in the context of the pandemic than in previous years. Interestingly, the students also reported better learning outcomes and improvement in their soft skills and consequently were highly satisfied with the project, which suggests the activity should continue in the future.

DOI: 10.4018/978-1-6684-7123-4.ch032

INTRODUCTION

This book chapter presents a teaching project that uses social media as a paradigmatic new information technologies (ITCs) space to introduce new virtual tools, that is, storytelling, transmedia narrative, gamification, and virtual/augmented reality, into higher education (these terms, along with other key concepts, are defined in the key terms and definitions section at the end of this chapter). The project was undertaken as a part of the Product and Brand Decisions subject of the third year of Marketing and Market Research degree at the University of Zaragoza (Spain); it was based on the students' management of a subject-related Instagram account. The project is one of the several activities assessed in the continuous subject evaluation system. In particular, the activity focusses on the benefits of Instagram as an information and knowledge dissemination channel, and the potential of innovative virtual tools to increase student motivation and engagement.

The project aims to add value to the subject by renewing the pedagogical processes, that is, complementing traditional teaching and theoretical content with active learning based on attractive virtual practical contents (e.g. examples of brand storytelling). The subject "Product and Brand Decisions" is very suitable to the use of Instagram as a learning space because it addresses topics closely related to brand image management and allow the inclusion of virtual tools. This approach is particularly novel because it combines the use of Instagram as a learning space and the implementation of specific innovative virtual tools by students on this channel. In this regard, the project also aims to enhance the students' management of new technologies through the creation of content and critical analysis of brand-generated content. Instagram provides students with an online networking channel for interaction and implementation of innovative virtual tools. Although the project started in the course 2017-18, the teachers considered that in the course 2020-21 this project could be particularly useful to maintain student interest through on-line learning introduced as a result of the Covid-19 pandemic.

The project entails the students creating, and posting, subject-related educational material on social media. Thus, the teaching methodology involves user-generated content (UGC), which encourages students to take a more active role in the learning process as they search for supplementary, updated sources of information. The project tries to take advantage of the virtual tools that can be implemented in social media, and which allow the students to link the subject content with current, more practical aspects (e.g. brand campaigns based on augmented reality) they encounter in their environments, in a simple, appealing way. On the other hand, the classroom-based use of a social network, such as Instagram, as a learning tool, allows students to acquire communication and analytical skills that will be very useful in their professional futures.

An end-of-course survey allowed a comparison of the activity during the pandemic (2020-21) and the three previous courses (2017-20), in terms of students' perceptions (e.g. usefulness), learning outcomes, improvement in soft skills (e.g. team work), and satisfaction. Instagram metrics related to each post and Instagram story published in the account were also analysed to compare the results of the four content categories (storytelling, transmedia narrative, gamification, and innovative virtual tools).

The structure of the chapter is as follows. After this sort introduction, the background is explained. This involves a literature review about the use of Instagram as a learning space in higher education, the benefits of collaborative learning and the presentation of the innovative virtual tools being employed in this project (i.e. storytelling, transmedia narrative, gamification, and virtual/augmented reality). Then, the objectives and the design of the project are described. A specific section explains the methodology and the data collection procedure. The results of self-reported measures (e.g. student's satisfaction) and

Instagram metrics are analyzed in detail. Finally, the findings of the project are discussed; the chapter ends with a conclusion and final remarks about the project.

BACKGROUND

Instagram as a Learning Space

Modern society is immersed in a continuous information exchange, largely due to the advent of the internet and the proliferation of new technologies such as smartphones (Belanche et al., 2017). These advances have had an impact on education, in general, and, specifically, on higher education (Bond et al., 2020). University students can access immediately, from anywhere, small items of information to satisfy their curiosity and can focus on any topic with just a click or a swipe. This change in the way societal members obtain and communicate information, in general, challenges traditional teaching because it can demotivate students (Sánchez-Martínez and Albaladejo-Ortega, 2018). Therefore, it is crucial that higher education professionals apply ITCs which increase students' interest in their academic subjects and learning outcomes (Englund et al., 2017). For example, class activities where students need to use smartphones or virtual reality, computer-generated 3D environment that users can navigate and interact with, resulting in stimulation of the user's senses (Guttentag, 2010, p. 638), have been shown to increase their learning and satisfaction (Belanche et al., 2020; Merchant et al., 2014). This growth in ICT use is due, in part, to the positive relationship between its use in higher education and the learning experience (Orús et al., 2016). ICTs facilitate the combination of content, pedagogy, and technologies that provide higher student engagement, and better learning outcomes, than achieved by more traditional education methods. On the other hand, the lockdowns imposed in many countries due to the Covid-19 pandemic has driven many universities to increase their use of ICTs as tools useful for distance learning. In this new context, it is necessary to examine the digital transformation boosted by the Covid-19 pandemic, and the related barriers and opportunities that the change towards online teaching is creating in the higher education process.

Social networks are a particularly interesting and useful context of communication and interaction to enhance the interrelationship between students and promote learning in the classroom. In fact, social networks allow developing collaborative learning networks (Casaló et al., 2009) specialized in sharing content or information specifically relevant to different groups of students (Lewis et al., 2010). Nowadays, Instagram is one of the most used social networks with over 1 billion of active users (Statista, 2021). Previous literature has highlighted the special interest of Instagram as a learning tool. Sari and Wahyudin (2019) indicated that Instagram positively influences the motivation, engagement and attitudes toward learning the course and as a consequence, it is also an excellent for extending learning beyond the classroom (Aloraini, 2018). Complementarily, Instagram is a social network in which visual aspects are prominent (Casaló et al., 2017), which makes it a particularly interesting tool for sharing photographs to illustrate the subjects studied and even posters or infographics that allow synthesizing the main ideas discussed in a specific lesson.

Collaborative Learning Through Social Media

The educational world has, for years, been looking for ways to overcome the demotivation of some students. In recent years, students have changed the way they learn, and are now demanding new teaching methodologies focused on satisfying their need to be active agents in the learning process (Hortigüela-Alcalá, 2019). In this regard, the integration of social media into higher education allows users to upload and view information in an easy, ubiquitous, and convenient way (Belanche et al., 2020). These capabilities involve active learning and assign new roles to students, who move from being passive to active agents (Orús et al., 2016), and shift the educational model towards a more collaborative-based system focused on the social implications of university learning (Hortigüela-Alcalá, 2019). In consequence, the use of social media as a higher education tool is generating real interest among practitioners and academics (Belanche et al., 2020; Rennie and Morrison, 2013), and it has become to be seen as an excellent, innovative teaching and learning tool (Manca and Ranieri, 2017). Recent studies have confirmed that social media offer efficient mechanisms for communication, inter-student collaboration (Ruleman, 2012), and stimulate the feedback process as a significant part of active (Tess 2013) and collaborative learning (Ricoy and Feliz, 2016).

Instagram represents a powerful tool for use in higher education learning processes because it facilitates information dissemination among peers, such as students in different classes, and the broadcasting of educational material to a wide audience. Instagram has over 1 billion active monthly users, is the most popular social network worldwide, and continues adding new members every day (Statista, 2020). The network is widely used by the young; 63.1 per cent of users are aged between 18 and 34 (Stastista, 2020), so students are familiar with Instagram. On the other hand, from a business point of view, Instagram is widely used by companies to provide information about their values and new products/services. Previous marketing studies have posited that customers and, particularly, active users, perceive that social media are attractive channels that provide added value to marketing actions (Mangold and Faulds, 2009). It has been demonstrated that Instagram generates greater engagement than other social media such as Facebook and Twitter (Casaló et al., 2018). Instagram's hedonic and visual natures are key to explaining the expansion it has experienced in recent years (Belanche et al., 2019). Furthermore, Instagram is a common and valuable transmedia tool that helps companies broadcast information through diverse media. For instance, Instagram is visited daily by millions of users searching for posts published by the brands they follow and product evaluations made by opinion leaders. In a teaching environment, Instagram allows students to acquire very useful communication and analytical skills that will be helpful in their professional futures. Instagram, as a social media learning space, helps students learn about the newest company communication strategies, the virtual tools employed to spread important information, to interact with the target audience, and to design and edit audio-visual content in online contexts.

Collaborative Learning

Collaborative learning is the process in which students form teams to complete tasks together, with learning being promoted through the interpersonal exchanges that occur (Alavi et al., 1995). Collaborative learning is a widely used instructional process in which students form small teams to jointly complete tasks, with teachers acting as facilitators (Kirschner, 2001). In the process, learning is promoted through the exchange of experiences and knowledge within the team and with other learners (Alavi et al., 1995; Aggarwal and O'Brien, 2008). Previous higher education studies have demonstrated that collaborative learning activities promote deeper learning. Linton et al. (2014) suggested that students undertaking collaborative learning activities achieve significantly better conceptual understanding than students undertaking individual activities. In addition, it has been shown that collaborative learning activities have a positive influence on student achievement, effort, persistence, and motivation (Johnson et al., 2007), and provide social skills needed for future professional work. However, collaborative learning is underused in higher education (Nokes-Malach and Richey, 2015). An issue with collaborative learning is that just forming groups is not enough to achieve better learning and motivation (Khosa and Volet, 2013). Some group members adopt free-rider roles due to interpersonal conflicts or logistical issues (Pauli et al., 2008; Scager et al., 2016). In this context, social media are used in higher education to support communication between students, information gathering, and participation in collaborative learning networks based on common interests (Kitsantas et al., 2016). Lambić (2016) suggested that students who use social media are disposed to spend time and effort to connect with other members of their educational communities who share their interests. These points suggest that it is critical to understand how social media can be used to support collaborative learning in higher education settings.

Active Learning

Active learning, as stated in the key terms and definitions section, has been defined as instruction that meaningfully engages students in learning through higher participation in activities (Shekhar et al., 2018), and involves inter-student cooperation (Johnson, Johnson, and Smith, 1998). Active learning encourages students to access subject information outside of the class, and fosters participation (Prober and Heath, 2012). Previous studies into active learning methods have suggested that it has the advantage of increasing the learner's understanding of new concepts and meanings, helps students understand how to do things, rather than to just memorise facts, and supports knowledge transfer from general to specific contexts (Michael, 2006; Prince, 2004). Active-learning processes are user-centred, have reshaped the roles of the teacher and the student, and encourage sharing the responsibility for learning (Belanche et al., 2020). In this way, students see increased value in content and evaluate courses higher (Wright, 2011). In addition, modern technologies and the lockdowns imposed as a result of the Covid-19 pandemic are transforming learning environments in favour of less lecture-based teaching. Some practices, such as filming and archiving online lectures, reduce the incentive for students to attend lecture-based classes (Young 2008). Moreover, the implementation of active-learning processes through social media provides advantages based on the students' higher familiarity with the channel, that is, its simple functioning, free access, and interactive formats (e.g. Instagram stories); these encourage student participation. Various authors have identified particular advantages in the use of social media in active learning; they have been shown to be powerful tools through which students can generate content, enhance their learning (Stanley and Zhang, 2018), skills (Forbes et al., 2016), cross-curricular competences (Orús et al., 2016), and e-leadership (Chua and Chua, 2017).

Learner-Generated Content

Similar to the user-generated content which refers to the content created outside of professional routines and practices (Kaplan and Haenlein, 2010, p. 61), the learner-generated content concept has been widely studied by scholars, and is becoming increasingly used to stimulate collaborative and active-learning processes in higher education (Orús et al., 2016). In particular, some skills often unaddressed in regular courses, such as technological and social abilities, can be improved by establishing student-led content generation systems (Fralinger and Owens, 2009). However, previous studies into the efficacy of learner-generated content have returned contradictory results. On the one hand, some authors have supported ICTs as effective active-learning tools (e.g. Hoogerheide et al., 2016; Lee and Mcloughlin, 2007. It has been demonstrated that when students design, create, and disseminate materials this leads to higher attention and memorisation levels (Clifton and Mann, 2011), better learning outcomes (Kay, 2012), and academic qualifications (Dupuis et al., 2013), and the acquisition of transversal competencies (Orús et al., 2016). On the other hand, other authors have found several difficulties with student-generated educational content (Bennet et al., 2012; Orús et al., 2016). Specifically, some studies have suggested that students do not perceive added value when participating in student-generated content activities (Bennet et al., 2012). In addition, sometimes students have difficulty creating content, express a lack of interest, and try to avoid the activity (Cole, 2009). These results suggest that, to ensure learner-generated content activities have a positive impact on higher education, it will be necessary to further investigate students' perceptions, learning outcomes, and satisfaction related to these activities, which is the basis of this project.

Innovative Virtual Tools for Distance Learning in Higher Education

While the advantages of social media were evident before the eruption of the Covid-19 pandemic, they seem particularly valuable for distance learning in pandemic and post-pandemic eras. Now, more than ever, traditional lessons need to be complemented by virtual tools that students find attractive and convenient. Social media represent open and flexible online spaces in which to apply some of the most innovative higher education learning tools. This project focuses on improving the learning experience by adopting four novel strategies: storytelling, transmedia narrative, gamification, and innovative virtual tools (e.g. virtual/augmented reality).

The selection of these particularly innovative virtual tools is based on the fact that they represent avant-garde technologies which are currently available for students and can be used to arouse their interest and involvement (Loureiro et al., 2020; Çakıroğlu et al., 2017; Sánchez-Martínez and Albaladejo-Ortega, 2018), as well as their motivation and engagement during the classes (Coombs, 2019). These state-of-the-art tools have the power to enhance the learning processes (Ribeiro, 2017; Sánchez-Martínez and Albaladejo-Ortega, 2018) and to improve the overall user experience when interacting in social networks with an inherent visual character, such as Instagram (Flavián et al., 2021). In particular, the importance of the application of these specific innovative virtual tools may be even greater in these times where distance learning is playing a predominant role with the aim of engaging the students (Buckley and Doyle, 2016; Loureiro et al., 2020). In addition, collaborative learning, active learning and learner-generated content processes can be fostered by providing the students with these technologies which allow them to reinforce the contents learned in class by displaying practical examples through innovative tools which they learn to apply through their use. Each of these innovative virtual tools is explained in detail below.

Storytelling

As shown in the key terms and definitions section, storytelling has been defined as the sharing of ideas and experiences through words and actions to communicate and create meaning in one's life and the lives of others (Behmer, 2005, p. 3); and has been described as a collaborative activity focused on the production of a narrative discourse (Mandelbaum, 2013). Storytelling is one of the oldest methods of communicating ideas and learning; it evokes unexpected emotions and ideas, which help transfer knowledge (Ribeiro, 2017). Storytelling has proliferated in various different knowledge areas, such as advertising (Carnevale et al., 2018) and history (Polanyi, 1985). However, some authors have posited that is inappropriate for higher education because of its subjectivity (Ribeiro, 2017). Conversely, some higher education researchers who take a thinking-based approach to education see storytelling as a trigger for reflection and, thus, an interesting teaching tool (Alterio and McDrury, 2003; Wu and Chen, 2020). These authors have suggested that storytelling in higher education helps to establish a solid reasoning path towards the building of knowledge through interpersonal connections, affection, and dialogue (Ribeiro, 2017). In this sense, account must be taken that experiences acquire meaning through stories and, through reflection and interpretation, they become knowledge. In the educational context, social media are playing a crucial role in revolutionising communication, and are changing the way stories are created by combining elements such as images, video, text, and audio to produce effective narratives (Rossiter and Garcia, 2010).

Transmedia Narrative

Transmedia narrative has been defined as different story forms that flow across multiple media channels (Jenkins, 2003). The term transmedia relates to the capacity of a communication message to continue in a medium different to that in which it was initiated (e.g. users continue with the experience on a different device). Previous studies have found that transmedia narrative is interactive, structurally complex, and leads to more participative communication processes aligned with students' own preferences (Sánchez-Martínez and Albaladejo-Ortega, 2018). In addition, other studies have proposed that transmedia environments help students seek out and explore information, aid collaborative learning (Lamb, 2011), and are well suited to social media contexts (Jenkins, 2006).

Gamification

The gamification concept was first documented in 2008 and gained importance in the late 2010s (Deterding, et al., 2011). Taking the definition of Terrill (2008) from the key terms and definitions section, gamification is the application of game mechanics to web properties to increase engagement; in other words, the use of game-design elements in non-game contexts (Deterding et al., 2011). As the definition makes clear, the main purpose of gamification is to increase engagement (Kapp, 2012). Gamification has been shown to evoke positive emotions and increase motivation (Sailer et al., 2017), engagement, and productivity (Buckley and Doyle, 2016; Kim, 2012) during games. For these reasons, gamification has been frequently employed in higher education to fight against the poor engagement and lack of motivation exhibited by some students (Fisher et al., 2014; Subhash et al., 2018).

Innovative Virtual Tools (Virtual/Augmented/Pure Mixed Reality)

Extended reality encompasses virtual reality, augmented reality, and pure mixed reality (Alcañiz et al., 2019). In virtual reality users are fully immersed in a computer-generated environment where they can navigate and, possibly, interact, and where their senses are stimulated and they can achieve a heightened sense of presence (Guttentag, 2010). Augmented reality users are placed in a real environment, and their physical surroundings are modified with superimposed digital elements (Javornik, 2016). In pure mixed reality, users are placed in a real environment which has both real and digital elements integrated into it, and can interact with the elements in real time (Flavián et al., 2019). Previous studies have noted the positive impact that extended-reality technologies have on learning processes. They can: help students be more focused and immersed in educational tasks (Loureiro et al., 2020); increase students' interest and motivation (Sotiriou and Bogner, 2008); help students absorb content in 3D perspectives (Wu et al., 2013); improve students' visualisation of invisible concepts or events (Sotiriou and Bogner, 2008) and; improve learners' engagement during classes (Allcoat and von Mühlenen, 2018; Loureiro et al., 2020). Thus, these technologies are increasingly being applied in educational settings to enhance learning processes, and this development is likely to be accelerated as universities and other institutions convert to distance learning due to the COVID-19 pandemic (Loureiro et al., 2020).

DESCRIPTION OF THE PROJECT

Project Objectives

The project is linked to a compulsory subject, "Product and Brand Decisions", in the third academic year (2020/21) of the Marketing and Market Research Degree of the University of Zaragoza. The project aims to take advantage of the interactive features of Instagram, to learn from the use that companies make of the platform (e.g. for the launch of new products), and to profit from its the intense use by students. The students were tasked to search for, and critically analyse, content uploaded onto this social media by other relevant agents in the brand management and communication process linked to the subject. The students had to create their own content related to the subject and the topics and technologies covered during the academic course and the practical lessons. In particular, the students were asked to focus on any new virtual tools employed by companies that could be used to spread knowledge about the subject content, specifically: storytelling, transmedia narrative, gamification, and innovative virtual tools (virtual/augmented reality).

The project has five main goals:

- First, to renew the pedagogical processes by complementing traditional teaching with active learning via the use of an Instagram account. The activities developed in relation to the account are designed to improve learning outcomes. "Product and Brand Decisions" is a particularly suitable subject for the project because it addresses topics closely related to brand image management (e.g. launching of new products, renewal of brand image, brand positioning) on Instagram.
- Second, the project seeks to increase students' theoretical content understanding and interest and connection with the subject. Accordingly, the project uses Instagram, an attractive and popular external tool. Instagram allows students to relate content covered in the classroom with current and practical aspects they might encounter in their usual environment.
- Third, the project is designed to enhance the students' technological tools' management and collaborative learning through the creation of content and critical analysis of brand-generated content. Instagram provides the student with real-time access to updated information (e.g. following brands or influencers). The use of Instagram as a learning tool allows students to acquire useful (cross-curricular) soft skills for their professional futures, such as teamworking, analysis, creativity, and communication abilities.

- Fourth, Instagram is an additional channel for interaction with the teaching staff and others interested in the same subject (e.g. other Marketing and Market Research Degree students, or students in related degree subjects, such as Management and Business Administration).
- Fifth, to maintain student interest in the subject through on-line teaching introduced as a result of the Covid-19 pandemic.

As previously mentioned, although the project started in 2017-18, the activity seems particularly suitable for improving the learning process in 2020-21, given that the Covid-19 pandemic has resulted in the subject being taught through distance learning. To better address how this form of project might help educators attain their teaching goals in a post-Covid era, the results of the 2020-21 project have been compared with those of the previous three academic courses (2017-20).

PROJECT DESIGN

The research project was carried out over four academic years from 2017-18 to 2020-21. It is based on the management of an Instagram account related to the academic subject @productounizar. The project started with an explanatory session. In this session, an special effort was made to explain to the students how to use an Instagram account for learning purposes, and examples were provided of previously published student-generated content. Specifically, the students were noted that their objective would be to post content on the Instagram account related to the subject in which they had to apply the innovative virtual tools (storytelling, transmedia narrative, gamification, and virtual/augmented reality), which were subsequently explained. In addition, it was clarified that the project is just one of the many activities assessed in the continuous subject evaluation system. The evaluation was based on five aspects of the content published: 1) suitable for the subject; 2) clear and rigorous; 3) visually appealing, using different formats; 4) promotes participation; and 5) current, relevant, and interesting. If the students decided they did not want to take part in this activity they could undertake a complementary exercise in the final exam. More than 75% of the students decided to participate.

Below are the specific steps that the students who participated in the activity followed during the process of managing the Instagram account:

- During the first weeks of the subject, the students filled out a form to register their working group (composed of 4-5 students).
- Each working group was assigned to a specific week during which they would be responsible for creating content to post on, and manage the Instagram account.
- On the first day of the week assigned to them, the instructors issued an email with general guidelines and the data needed (username and password) to access the account.
- The instructions emphasized that students had to adapt and create interesting course-related content. Specifically, students had to search for content about the topics covered in class (e.g., new product launches on the brands' webpages, external news) and, with this information, they had to create and design the posts (e.g., Instagram wall, Instagram stories, reels) during the week linking them to what they had learned in the lessons. To do so, they were encouraged to apply the innovative virtual tools (storytelling, transmedia narrative, gamification, and virtual/augmented reality) in the posted contents.

- Some rules were established that prevented the students from, for example, modifying third-party content or recording in commercial spaces without permission.
  - During that week, the students of the assigned working group were fully responsible for the design of the diverse content (e.g., publications, contests through stories) that was published on the account. To this end, they were encouraged to use certain tools (e.g., Canva) to professionalize their publications.
  - The instructors were available through an email account to answer the students' questions or give advice on how to apply a particular tool.
  - At the end of each week, the instructors evaluated the published content according to the above-mentioned criteria and gave the corresponding working group a numerical score.
  - Every week, at the beginning of the practical sessions, the most relevant publications and/or questions published were discussed in class. Following the methodology used in the practical classes, the teachers presented some of the content that had been published in the Instagram account during that period. The teachers also addressed and analyzed the type of format used (e.g. Instagram wall, Instagram stories, Instagram short videos [reels]), the virtual tools employed, if applicable (e.g. gamification), and the link with the subject syllabus (e.g. creation of a new product, brand positioning, market segmentation).

In the first three academic courses, that is, 2017-18, 2018-19, and 2019-20, regular face-to-face classes were held and students were encouraged to identify content about real brands and products that could be discussed in class. They could use all the Instagram formats (e.g. photos, videos, stories) to publish on the account. For instance, some of the posts were related to company product launches, as in the example at Figure 1.

In 2020-21, due to the Covid-19 pandemic, classes were held online. In addition to the instructions about the material to be posted given in previous years, the teachers encouraged the students to post content about storytelling, transmedia narrative, gamification, and innovative virtual tools, given that these are being used by companies and seem particularly suitable for improving the online-learning process during the pandemic.

At the end of the courses the students completed surveys to assess specific aspects of the project. They were asked to what extent they were satisfied with the activity, their development of soft competences (e.g. creativity, analytical skills), about their perceptions about the activity, and their intentions to continue following the account and to recommend the activity to other students.

METHODOLOGY

The results of the project were empirically analysed. The questionnaire to assess the specific aspects of the project was always hosted in the same platform and used the same scales. The survey was designed by the same team of teachers/researchers and completed by students during the last class of each academic year. This allowed us to compare the results between courses. Specifically, the results of the 2020-21 course and the three previous courses were compared. In addition, the key performance indicators of the publications of the Instagram account (e.g. scope, number of "likes") in relation to the different innovative tools applied in the 2020-21 course were examined.

Figure 1. Content creation by students in the 2018-19 course

After removing invalid and incomplete responses, a total of 245 students answered the questionnaires over the four academic courses, 75 of them in course 2020-21. Of all the respondents of the survey, 62.72% were female and 37.28% male; 88.16% of them were aged between 20-22 years, and 93.47% were Spanish. These demographics are similar to those of students of social sciences studies at the University of Zaragoza (UZ Statistics, 2021). Addressing students in the last years of their degree in Marketing seems particularly adequate because the project aims to link the theoretical contents to more practical virtual tools that could be used by students in their future professional careers.

The students had to give their level of agreement or disagreement to statements about their perceptions, experience of, and satisfaction with, the activity, using Likert-type scales ranging from 1 "Strongly disagree", to 7, "Strongly agree". Specifically, students assessed the ease of use of the activity through the Koufaris scale (2002) (e.g. It was easy to participate in the activity), and interactivity was measured using the scale developed by Blasco-Arcas et al., (2013) (e.g. I think that participating in the activity facilitated interaction with peers). Another block of questions asked the students to assess the usefulness of the activity through the Koufaris (2002) scale (e.g. I think that participating in the activity was useful for me); the learning of the subject was measured using Casaló et al.'s (2011) scale (e.g. Participating in the activity has improved my knowledge about the course). Marketing learning was measured using Casaló et al.'s (2011) scale (e.g. Participating in the activity improved my knowledge about marketing). Soft skills were evaluated using Orús et al.'s (2016) scale, which focuses on communication, social, analytical, creativity and ICT skills (e.g. The activity was useful for developing, presenting, and discussing my ideas in public).

A final block of questions measured the students' satisfaction with the activity; this used Casaló et al.'s (2011) scale (e.g. I am satisfied with the activity). The intention to recommend the activity to other students was measured using Belanche et al.'s (2010) scale (e.g. I will recommend the activity to other students).

As to the key performance indicators of the Instagram account, an analysis was made of the basic Instagram metrics of the content posted as news feeds on the Instagram wall and as stories. Specifically, a comparison between categories was made in terms of their average scope (or reach), average number of views/impressions, and average number of likes received by each publication. The project compared the results of these metrics for the publications related to the four innovative tools (storytelling, transmedia narrative, gamification and virtual/augmented reality tools), and a fifth category, "other contents", covering the remaining publications.

RESULTS

Comparison of Student Perceptions, Learning Outcomes, and Activity Assessments, Between the 2020-21 Course and Previous Courses

This section reports on the comparison between students' responses about the academic course 2020-21, that is, during the Covid-19 pandemic, and about the previous academic courses 2017-20, in terms of their perceptions, learning results, and assessments of the activity. More precisely, we employed IBM-SPSS software to test the differences between the mean value of each group of respondents through the t-test statistic. The differences are graphically represented in Figure 2. In general terms, compared to previous years, students assigned higher values to most of the variables analysed during the academic year 2020-21. Only the ease of use of the Instagram account was scored lower in 2020-21. This may be because the students found it harder to manage the account through distance learning ($M_{2017-20}$=5.43, $M_{2020-21}$=4.92; t(247)=2.898, $p<0.01$). In contrast, interactivity presented little difference over the two periods. The value was slightly higher in the 2020-21 academic course than during 2017-20 ($M_{2017-20}$=4.84, $M_{2020-21}$=5.00; t(246)=0.86, $p>0.10$). Remarkably, the students perceived that the activity was significantly more useful in 2020-21 than during 2017-20 ($M_{2017-20}$=5.02, $M_{2020-21}$=5.78; t(247)=3.72, $p<0.01$).

Better results were obtained for the 2020-21 course for both learning about the subject ($M_{2017-20}$=5.02, $M_{2020-21}$=5.78; t(247)=3.72, $p<0.01$) and learning about marketing issues ($M_{2017-20}$=4.80, $M_{2020-21}$=5.66; t(245)=4.43, $p<0.01$). These particularly positive results highlight the interest that students have in this type of activity, which complements knowledge acquired through other teaching activities.

One of the goals of the activity was to enhance the students' soft skills during the pandemic year, during which, of course, they could not physically interact. In 2020-21 the activity was found to significantly enhance students' soft skills. On average the variable was more than a point higher than in previous years ($M_{2017-20}$=4.42, $M_{2020-21}$=5.65; t(240)=5.89, $p<0.01$). This variable exhibited the greater change over the previous years.

Figure 2. Comparative analysis of student assessment of the activity in 2017-20 and 2020-21 academic courses
Source: Own design

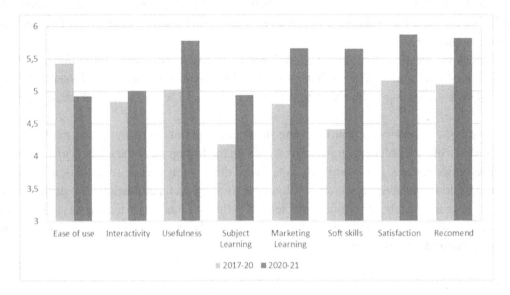

Finally, the students' overall satisfaction with the account management project and their intention to recommend the activity to other students was assessed. Both variables achieved higher values during the 2020-21 academic year than in 2017-20. These higher ratings for satisfaction ($M_{2017-20}=5.16$, $M_{2020-21}=5.87$; $t(246)=3.48$, $p<0.001$) and intention to recommend ($M_{2017-20}=5.10$, $M_{2020-21}=5.82$; $t(246)=3.48$, $p<0.001$) are consistent with the students' overall favourable perception of the activity.

Analysis of the Impact Made by the Different Content Categories

The Instagram stories and posts were classified by the research team into four categories based on their principal content. At least 10 feed post and 30 stories were published in each of the four categories. The categories reflect different types of content with clearly differentiated profiles. The categories include content with various emotional charges, require different cognitive abilities, and motivate interaction between students in different ways. Nevertheless, they can be integrated to further enrich the student learning process.

The categories included in the analysis were:

- Storytelling: The storytelling stories and posts included any type of content linking the consumer to the brand through a story. The stories often highlight the positive qualities of the product/service and, indeed, the brands are sometimes given their own personality as a kind of brand positioning. This category included many posts such as that shown in Figure 3, and many linked Instagram stories. In particular, this posts explained the concept of storytelling for the benefit of other students.

Figure 3. Instagram post with storytelling content

-   Transmedia narrative: These publications attempted, without placing the brand at the centre of the dialogue, to establish links between the brand and the consumers through emotional content. The intent is to focus attention on a conversational topic, not directly related to the brand, via different channels. This allows a direct connection to be established with the audience. The interest generated in, and the connection established with, the viewer allows the dialogue to be redirected towards topics that implicitly and subtly link the brand and the viewer. This category included many posts such as that shown in Figure 4, and many linked stories. This publication shows how the Home Box Office audio-visual company promoted the series Game of Thrones via transmedia narrative. The campaign presented several aspects related to the series, such as restaurant menus, boxes with olfactive sensations, mobiles apps, etc., that helped users to enjoy the Game of Thrones experience through their five senses.

Figure 4. Instagram post with narrative transmedia content

- Gamification: Instagram posts and stories applying game elements to other activities. These posts aimed to engage users and absorb content through playing a game. This category included many posts and related stories, such as that presented in Figure 5. The students of the group managing the account that week created different games. For example, in one of them the users had to link the brand name, the product logos, and the products of the snack-producing company Lacasa (also based in Zaragoza).
- Innovative virtual tools (virtual/augmented reality): The virtual tools included in several Instagram stories and posts involved, in some way, extended-reality technologies such as virtual reality, augmented reality, and mixed reality. These technologies capture the viewer's attention by integrating virtual content into the real world, or by creating completely virtual content that is perceived as very real by the audience. This category included many posts such as that shown in Figure 6; this shows the IKEA app that allows users to view furniture in 3D due to augmented reality. Many stories about virtual/augmented reality were published during the semester.

Figure 5. Instagram reels (short videos) with gamification content

Students' Personal Assessments of the Content Categories

The students also rated their attitude towards, or interest in, the publications, by category. This assessment was made by adapting the attitude scale of Belanche et al., (2019) to a Likert-type 7-point scale (e.g. The gamification content was likeable). The results of the assessment are at Figure 7.

In general, the students' ratings were very positive. In fact, all categories achieved scores higher than 5.6 out of 7. The story categories considered most interesting were "gamification" (M=5.95) and "storytelling" (M=5.92). The categories "virtual reality" (M=5.77) and "Narrative Transmedia" (M=5.67) were also evaluated positively, but with slightly lower ratings.

Figure 6. Instagram post with augmented reality content

Figure 7. Students' assessment of the Instagram publications by category
Source: Own design

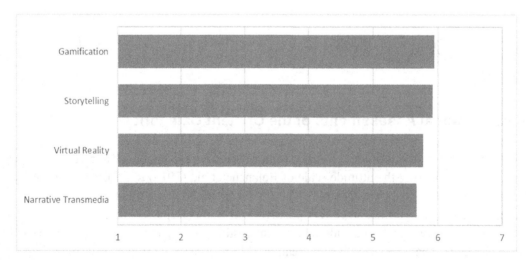

Impact of Different Content Categories

The Instagram account performance indicators were used to measure the impact of each of the content typologies. Specifically, average scope and the average number of views/impressions were used as indicators of the impact of each campaign. The average scope reflects the number of users who have been influenced by content. The number of views/impressions reflects the number of times content is viewed. By definition, the average scope must be equal to, or less than, the number of views/impressions. By definition, all users who were influenced by content will have viewed it at least once. If users influenced by campaigns view the content on several occasions, the average number of views/impressions will be significantly higher than the average scope of the campaign. The number of "likes" was also calculated, that is, the number of followers that clicked on the "heart", or "like", button of posts; however, Instagram stories does not provide this option, thus this metric is not available for that format.

Focusing on the feed post published in the account, Figure 8 shows the average scope achieved by the posts in each of the categories (the range is shown on the left of the figure). The average number of likes achieved in each case is indicated on the right side of the figure. The average number of likes achieved is particularly high for the "storytelling" category, reaching an average of 33.6 likes per post. The average number of likes achieved by the other categories ranged from 26 for the "virtual/augmented reality" category, to 29 for the "gamification" category. The average scope of the different categories also shows notable differences. The range achieved by the "transmedia narrative" category was higher (233.2 users) than the less remarkable values achieved by the "others" category, that is, content unrelated to any other category (e.g. launch of a new product). These values ranged from 171 (users) in the "storytelling" category, to 178.1 in the "gamification" category.

Finally, the relationship between the average scope and the average number of likes received by each category was analysed. This analysis highlighted the particularly high values of the number of average likes achieved by publications in the "storytelling" category (33.6) in contrast to its average scope (171 users). In the opposite direction, the high average scope (233.2 users) achieved by the "transmedia narrative" category contrasts with the limited average number of likes (28) it received.

Figure 9 shows the average scope of the content included in each category, and the average number of views/impressions, for the Instagram stories published in the account. The stories with the greatest scope were in the groups "gamification" (average scope=146.9) and "virtual/augmented reality" (average scope=142.3). The stories with lower average scope were those in the "transmedia narrative" (average scope=103.5) and "others" (average scope=106.9) categories.

As to the relationship between the average scope of the stories and the average number of views/impressions, notable differences were observed between the different groups of stories. The "gamification" group stories had only a slightly higher number of views/impressions than the average scope (average impressions=163.2, average scope=146.9), which means that very few users watched the story more than once. However, many users watched the storytelling content more than once, since the number of views/impressions were 50% higher than the number of users scoped (average impressions=189.3, average scope=126.9). It is probable that these types of stories captured greater audience attention, motivating many of them to view the stories on more than one occasion.

Figure 8. Average likes and average scope of the different categories of Instagram posts for the project activities during the 2020-21 academic course
Source: Own design

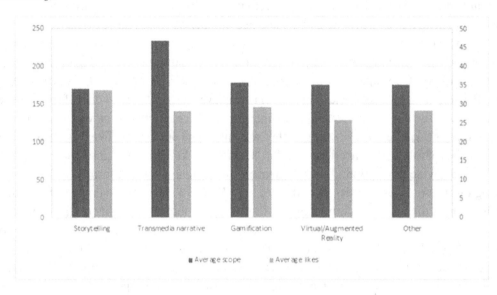

Figure 9. Average scope and impact of the different categories of posts and Instagram stories during the project activity carried out in the 2020-21 academic course
Source: Own design

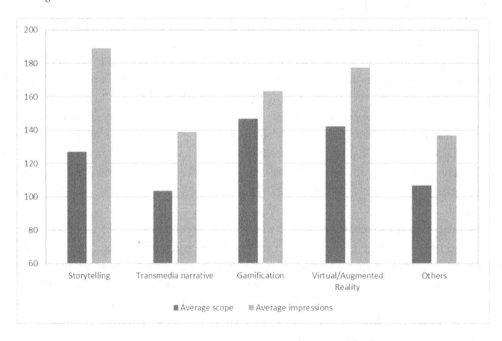

DISCUSSION

This project examines students' management of an Instagram account used as an active learning space in which to implement innovative learning tools. The results showed an overall improvement in students' perceptions of the learning outcomes and assessment of the activity during 20/21 compared to previous years. The integration of strategies such as storytelling, transmedia content, gamification, and innovative virtual tools in the management of the Instagram account particularly enhanced students' evaluations.

The students' perceptions of the usefulness of the activity was significantly higher in 20/21 than in previous years. This may be because encouraging them to apply the strategies previously discussed, and the topics covered, which are very updated, allowed them to identify additional real examples related to the theory taught in the online classes. Similarly, as the students learned how to apply the strategies on social media, they considered that this might be useful for their professional futures. Students' perceptions of interactivity in 20/21 remained at the same (high) levels as in the earlier years, so they did not consider that interaction was facilitated by applying the additional strategies. Ease of use was rated lower than in earlier years. As the course classes were held online, it may have been more difficult for students to discover how to manage the Instagram account, and it required additional effort on their part to search for information to fully understand the concepts and effectively apply them in this context.

Both the learning about the subject (i.e. product and brand related concepts) and practical marketing issues were strongly enhanced by the management of the Instagram account using the new strategies. Apart from the class-based teaching, being able to apply these concepts in a professional situation (the management of an official Instagram account) helped the students engage with them better (Orús et al., 2016). The students, through this opportunity to address these concepts in a way that helped them understand their particular features/value, experienced greater autonomy in the learning process (Chua and Chua, 2017); which, for the students, was enriched as they were able to apply them in a realistic situation. The major improvement in soft skills (e.g. interactive work, developing and presenting ideas in public, synthesising creativity) during the 20/21 course (compared to the previous years) shows that the activity was of great benefit to the students. This is remarkable considering that the students had no physical classroom-based, face-to-face interactions due to the Covid-19 pandemic. Thus, it seems that providing students with specific innovative content categories (i.e. storytelling, transmedia narrative, gamification, and innovative virtual tools), enhanced their overall assessments of the activity and helped improve their soft skills.

In addition, the findings showed that students' satisfaction levels increased due to the activity. Specifically, these strategies, widely used by brands in their social media management, allowed the students to be taught in a more practical way, which fostered their satisfaction with the activity. These results are in line with those found by previous studies on active learning and social media (Forbes et al., 2016; Orús et al., 2016; Stanley and Zhang, 2018). As a consequence of all this, students in the 2020/21 course were more willing to recommend the activity to others than were students in the earlier courses, as they considered it to be helpful and an interesting way to improve their skills.

The results also revealed that the students were highly interested in the storytelling, transmedia, gamification, and innovative virtual tools content. The assessment was slightly more positive for gamification and storytelling. This may be because these categories require higher interaction and, as the story develops, the students' engagement is strengthened (Kapp, 2012; Terrill, 2008). Consequently, the favourable attitude shown towards both activities may have been reinforced. However, it should be noted that the other activities also generated a very positive attitude among the students. The number of likes that each content category received also reflected this, particularly as regards storytelling. In storytelling, the story develops through the content displayed; this can arouse positive emotions among users, who may react directly on Instagram by liking the content. As for the scope, transmedia narrative reached more users, so it seems that they are more prone to seek out and explore the information displayed with this type of content (Lamb, 2011). The results also illustrated that stories in the storytelling category generated more views/impressions per user, so it seems that this type of content catches users' attention, encouraging them to view the content more times. The reason for this may be that, as this type of content aims to provoke emotions, ideas and increase knowledge (Ribeiro, 2017), users feel hooked to the story and view it several times to interpret it better.

CONCLUSION AND FINAL REMARKS

In conclusion, the students had an overall positive evaluation of the activity, and found it useful for enhancing their learning outcomes and soft skills. Consequently, they were very satisfied with the project and would recommend it to other students. The benefits of the project were present in the 2017-20 courses but are particularly valuable and suitable for the 2020-21 course. In particular, Instagram accounts seem perfect social media spaces in which to generate and share content among peers during the pandemic, when face-to-face interaction has not been possible. Thus, the use of social media spaces to apply innovative learning tools (e.g. gamification) in higher education could be particularly fruitful in the post-Covid era.

Finally, the project has limitations that need to be addressed. First, as the students considered that the ease of participating in the account was lower than in previous years, some actions should be taken to overcome this perception. Perhaps, in addition to the initial guidance given, more continuous support should be provided to the students to help them search, design, and publish content. In addition, the activity was focused on Instagram, a social network that is widely used by brands, due to its strong visual character, to show the novelty of their products (Casaló et al., 2017). However, other social networks within this typology might be examined, such as TikTok, which is experiencing growth among the younger generations (Statista, 2020). Furthermore, while the project focused on four content-related strategies (storytelling, transmedia, gamification, and innovative virtual tools), it would be interesting to include other content-generation strategies being widely adopted (e.g. artificial intelligence) to provide students with additional tools to successfully manage the social media accounts of brands in their future professional careers.

REFERENCES

Aggarwal, P., & O'Brien, C. L. (2008). Social loafing on group projects: Structural antecedents and effect on student satisfaction. *Journal of Marketing Education, 30*(3), 255–264. doi:10.1177/0273475308322283

Alavi, M., Wheeler, B. C., & Valacich, J. S. (1995). Using IT to reengineer business education: An exploratory investigation of collaborative telelearning. *Management Information Systems Quarterly, 19*(3), 293–312. doi:10.2307/249597

Alcañiz, M., Guixeres, J., & Bigne, E. (2019). Virtual reality in marketing: A framework, review and research agenda. *Frontiers in Psychology*, *10*, 1530. doi:10.3389/fpsyg.2019.01530 PMID:31333548

Allcoat, D., & von Mühlenen, A. (2018). Learning in virtual reality: Effects on performance, emotion and engagement. *Research in Learning Technology*, *26*(0), 26. doi:10.25304/rlt.v26.2140

Aloraini, N. (2018). Investigating Instagram as an EFL Learning Tool. *Arab World English Journal*, *4*(4), 174–184. doi:10.24093/awej/call4.13

Alterio, M., & McDrury, J. (2003). *Learning through storytelling in higher education: Using reflection and experience to improve learning.* Routledge. doi:10.4324/9780203416655

Behmer, S. (2005). Literature review digital storytelling: Examining the process with middle school students. In *Society for Information Technology & teacher education international conference.* Iowa State University.

Belanche, D., Casaló, L. V., & Flavián, C. (2010). Providing online public services successfully: The role of confirmation of citizens' expectations. *International Review on Public and Nonprofit Marketing*, *7*(2), 167–184. doi:10.100712208-010-0058-1

Belanche, D., Casaló, L. V., Orús, C., & Pérez-Rueda, A. (2020). Developing a Learning Network on YouTube: Analysis of Student Satisfaction with a Learner-Generated Content Activity. In A. Peña-Ayala (Ed.), *Educational Networking* (pp. 195–231). Springer. doi:10.1007/978-3-030-29973-6_6

Belanche, D., Cenjor, I., & Pérez-Rueda, A. (2019). Instagram Stories versus Facebook Wall: an advertising effectiveness analysis. *Spanish Journal of Marketing-ESIC*.

Belanche, D., Flavián, C., & Pérez-Rueda, A. (2017). User adaptation to interactive advertising formats: The effect of previous exposure, habit and time urgency on ad skipping behaviors. *Telematics and Informatics*, *34*(7), 961–972. doi:10.1016/j.tele.2017.04.006

Bennett, S., Bishop, A., Dalgarno, B., Waycott, J., & Kennedy, G. (2012). Implementing Web 2.0 technologies in higher education: A collective case study. *Computers & Education*, *59*(2), 524–534. doi:10.1016/j.compedu.2011.12.022

Blasco-Arcas, L., Buil, I., Hernández-Ortega, B., & Sese, F. J. (2013). Using clickers in class. The role of interactivity, active collaborative learning and engagement in learning performance. *Computers & Education*, *62*, 102–110. doi:10.1016/j.compedu.2012.10.019

Bond, M., Buntins, K., Bedenlier, S., Zawacki-Richter, O., & Kerres, M. (2020). Mapping research in student engagement and educational technology in higher education: A systematic evidence map. *International Journal of Educational Technology in Higher Education*, *17*(2), 1–30. doi:10.118641239-019-0176-8

Buckley, P., & Doyle, E. (2016). Gamification and student motivation. *Interactive Learning Environments*, *24*(6), 1162–1175. doi:10.1080/10494820.2014.964263

Çakıroğlu, Ü., Başıbüyük, B., Güler, M., Atabay, M., & Yılmaz Memiş, B. (2017). Gamifying an ICT course: Influences on engagement and academic performance. *Computers in Human Behavior*, *69*, 98–107. doi:10.1016/j.chb.2016.12.018

Casaló, L. V., Cisneros, J., Flavián, C., & Guinaliu, M. (2009). Determinants of success in open source software networks. *Industrial Management & Data Systems*, *109*(4), 532–549. doi:10.1108/02635570910948650

Casaló, L. V., Flavián, C., & Guinalíu, M. (2011). Antecedents and consequences of consumer participation in online communities: The case of the travel sector. *International Journal of Electronic Commerce*, *15*(2), 137–167. doi:10.2753/JEC1086-4415150205

Casaló, L. V., Flavián, C., & Ibáñez-Sánchez, S. (2017). Antecedents of consumer intention to follow and recommend an Instagram account. *Online Information Review*, *41*(7), 1046–1063. doi:10.1108/OIR-09-2016-0253

Casaló, L. V., Flavián, C., & Ibáñez-Sánchez, S. (2017). Understanding consumer interaction on instagram: The role of satisfaction, hedonism, and content characteristics. *Cyberpsychology, Behavior, and Social Networking*, *20*(6), 369–375. doi:10.1089/cyber.2016.0360 PMID:28570105

Casaló, L. V., Flavián, C., & Ibáñez-Sánchez, S. (2018). Influencers on Instagram: Antecedents and consequences of opinion leadership. *Journal of Business Research*, *117*, 510–519. doi:10.1016/j.jbusres.2018.07.005

Chua, Y. P., & Chua, Y. P. (2017). How are e-leadership practices in implementing a school virtual learning environment enhanced? A grounded model study. *Computers & Education*, *109*, 109–121. doi:10.1016/j.compedu.2017.02.012

Clark, M., Fine, M. B., & Scheuer, C. L. (2017). Relationship quality in higher education marketing: The role of social media engagement. *Journal of Marketing for Higher Education*, *27*(1), 40–58. doi:10.1080/08841241.2016.1269036

Clifton, A., & Mann, C. (2011). Can YouTube enhance student nurse learning? *Nurse Education Today*, *31*(4), 311–313. doi:10.1016/j.nedt.2010.10.004 PMID:21036430

Cole, M. (2009). Using Wiki technology to support student engagement: Lessons from the trenches. *Computers & Education*, *52*(1), 141–146. doi:10.1016/j.compedu.2008.07.003

Coombs, T. (2019). Transmedia storytelling: A potentially vital resource for CSR communication. *Corporate Communications*, *24*(2), 351–367. doi:10.1108/CCIJ-11-2017-0114

Deterding, S., Dixon, D., Khaled, R., & Nacke, L. (2011). From game design elements to gamefulness: Defining "gamification". In *MindTrek'11 proceedings of the 15th international academic MindTrek conference: Envisioning future media environments* (pp. 9–15). Tampere: ACM.

Dumpit, D. Z., & Fernandez, C. J. (2017). Analysis of the use of social media in Higher Education Institutions (HEIs) using the Technology Acceptance Model. *International Journal of Educational Technology in Higher Education*, *14*(1), 5. doi:10.118641239-017-0045-2

Dupuis, J., Coutu, J., & Laneuville, O. (2013). Application of linear mixed-effect models for the analysis of exam scores: Online video associated with higher scores for undergraduate students with lower grades. *Computers & Education*, *66*, 64–73. doi:10.1016/j.compedu.2013.02.011

Englund, C., Olofsson, A. D., & Price, L. (2017). Teaching with technology in higher education: Understanding conceptual change and development in practice. *Higher Education Research & Development, 36*(1), 73–87. doi:10.1080/07294360.2016.1171300

Fisher, D. J., Beedle, J., & Rouse, S. E. (2014). Gamification: A study of business teacher educators' knowledge of, attitudes toward, and experiences with the gamification of activities in the classroom. *The Journal of Research in Business Education, 56*(1), 1–16.

Flavián, C., Ibáñez-Sánchez, S., & Orús, C. (2019). The impact of virtual, augmented and mixed reality technologies on the customer experience. *Journal of Business Research, 100*, 547–560. doi:10.1016/j. jbusres.2018.10.050

Flavián, C., Ibáñez-Sánchez, S., & Orús, C. (2021). User Responses Towards Augmented Reality Face Filters: Implications for Social Media and Brands. In M.C. tom Dieck, T. Jung & S.M.C. Loureiro (Eds.), Augmented Reality and Virtual Reality. New Trends in Immersive Technology (pp. 29-42). Springer.

Forbes, H., Oprescu, F. I., Downer, T., Phillips, N. M., McTier, L., Lord, B., Barr, N., Alla, K., Bright, P., Dayton, J., Simbag, V., & Visserk, I. (2016). Use of videos to support teaching and learning of clinical skills in nursing education: A review. *Nurse Education Today, 42*, 53–56. doi:10.1016/j.nedt.2016.04.010 PMID:27237353

Fralinger, B., & Owens, R. (2009). YouTube as a learning tool. *Journal of College Teaching and Learning, 6*(8), 15–28. doi:10.19030/tlc.v6i8.1110

Guttentag, D. A. (2010). Virtual reality: Applications and implications for tourism. *Tourism Management, 31*(5), 637–651. doi:10.1016/j.tourman.2009.07.003

Hoogerheide, V., Deijkers, L., Loyens, S. M., Heijltjes, A., & van Gog, T. (2016). Gaining from explaining: Learning improves from explaining to fictitious others on video, not from writing to them. *Contemporary Educational Psychology, 44*, 95–106. doi:10.1016/j.cedpsych.2016.02.005

Hortigüela-Alcalá, D., Sánchez-Santamaría, J., Pérez-Pueyo, Á., & Abella-García, V. (2019). Social networks to promote motivation and learning in higher education from the students' perspective. *Innovations in Education and Teaching International, 56*(4), 412–422. doi:10.1080/14703297.2019.1579665

Javornik, A. (2016). Augmented reality: Research agenda for studying the impact of its media characteristics on consumer behaviour. *Journal of Retailing and Consumer Services, 30*, 252–261. doi:10.1016/j. jretconser.2016.02.004

Jenkins, H. (2003). Transmedia Storytelling. Moving characters from books to films to video games can make them stronger and more compelling. *Technology Review*.

Jenkins, H. (2006). *Convergence culture: Where old and new media collide*. New York University Press.

Johnson, D. W., Johnson, R. T., & Smith, K. (2007). The state of cooperative learning in postsecondary and professional settings. *Educational Psychology Review, 19*(1), 15–29. doi:10.100710648-006-9038-8

Johnson, D. W., Johnson, R. T., & Smith, K. (2007). The state of cooperative learning in postsecondary and professional settings. *Educational Psychology Review, 19*(1), 15–29. doi:10.100710648-006-9038-8

Johnson, D. W., Johnson, R. T., & Smith, K. A. (1998). Cooperative learning returns to college what evidence is there that it works? *Change: The magazine of higher learning, 30*(4), 26-35.

Kapp, K. M. (2012). *The gamification of learning and instruction: Game-based methods and strategies for training and education.* Pfeiffer.

Kay, R. H. (2012). Exploring the use of video podcasts in education: A comprehensive review of the literature. *Computers in Human Behavior, 28*(3), 820–831. doi:10.1016/j.chb.2012.01.011

Khosa, D. K., & Volet, S. E. (2013). Promoting effective collaborative case-based learning at university: A metacognitive intervention. *Studies in Higher Education, 38*(6), 870–889. doi:10.1080/03075079.2011.604409

Kim, B. (2012). Harnessing the power of game dynamics why, how to, and how not to gamify the library experience. *College & Research Libraries News, 73*(8), 465–469. doi:10.5860/crln.73.8.8811

Kirschner, P. A. (2001). Using integrated electronic environments for collaborative teaching/learning. *Learning and Instruction, 10*, 1–9. doi:10.1016/S0959-4752(00)00021-9

Kitsantas, A., Dabbagh, N., Chirinos, D. S., & Fake, H. (2016). College students' perceptions of positive and negative effects of social networking. In *Social networking and education* (pp. 225–238). Springer. doi:10.1007/978-3-319-17716-8_14

Koufaris, M. (2002). Applying the technology acceptance model and flow theory to online consumer behavior. *Information Systems Research, 13*(2), 205–223. doi:10.1287/isre.13.2.205.83

Lamb, A. (2011). Reading redefined for a transmedia universe. *Learning and Leading with Technology, 39*(3), 12–17.

Lambić, D. (2016). Correlation between Facebook use for educational purposes and academic performance of students. *Computers in Human Behavior, 61*, 313–320. doi:10.1016/j.chb.2016.03.052

Lee, M. J., & McLoughlin, C. (2007). Teaching and learning in the Web 2.0 era: Empowering students through learner-generated content. *International Journal of Instructional Technology and Distance Learning, 4*(10), 21–34.

Lewis, S., Pea, R., & Rosen, J. (2010). Beyond participation to co-creation of meaning: Mobile social media in generative learning communities. *Social Sciences Information. Information Sur les Sciences Sociales, 49*(3), 351–369. doi:10.1177/0539018410370726

Linton, D. L., Farmer, J. K., & Peterson, E. (2014). Is peer interaction necessary for optimal active learning? *CBE Life Sciences Education, 13*(2), 243–252. doi:10.1187/cbe.13-10-0201 PMID:26086656

Loureiro, S. M. C., Bilro, R. G., & de Aires Angelino, F. J. (2020). Virtual reality and gamification in marketing higher education: a review and research agenda. *Spanish Journal of Marketing-ESIC*.

Manca, S., & Ranieri, M. (2017). Networked scholarship and motivations for social media use in scholarly communication. *The International Review of Research in Open and Distributed Learning, 18*(2), 123–138. doi:10.19173/irrodl.v18i2.2859

Mandelbaum, J. (2013). Storytelling in conversation. In J. Sidnell & T. Stivers (Eds.), *Handbook of conversation analysis* (pp. 492–508). Cambridge University Press.

Mangold, W. G., & Faulds, D. J. (2009). Social media: The new hybrid element of the promotion mix. *Business Horizons*, *52*(4), 357–365. doi:10.1016/j.bushor.2009.03.002

Merchant, Z., Goetz, E. T., Cifuentes, L., Keeney-Kennicutt, W., & Davis, T. J. (2014). Effectiveness of virtual reality-based instruction on students' learning outcomes in K-12 and higher education: A meta-analysis. *Computers & Education*, *70*, 29–40. doi:10.1016/j.compedu.2013.07.033

Michael, J. (2006). Where's the evidence that active learning works? *Advances in Physiology Education*, *30*(4), 159–167. doi:10.1152/advan.00053.2006 PMID:17108243

Nokes-Malach, T. J., Richey, J. E., & Gadgil, S. (2015). When is it better to learn together? Insights from research on collaborative learning. *Educational Psychology Review*, *27*(4), 645–656. doi:10.100710648-015-9312-8

Orús, C., Barlés, M. J., Belanche, D., Casaló, L., Fraj, E., & Gurrea, R. (2016). The effects of learner-generated videos for YouTube on learning outcomes and satisfaction. *Computers & Education*, *95*, 254–269. doi:10.1016/j.compedu.2016.01.007

Pauli, R., Mohiyeddini, C., Bray, D., Michie, F., & Street, B. (2008). Individual differences in negative group work experiences in collaborative student learning. *Educational Psychology*, *28*(1), 47–58. doi:10.1080/01443410701413746

Polanyi, L. (1985). *Telling the American story: A structural and cultural analysis of conversational storytelling*. Ablex.

Prince, M. (2004). Does active learning work? A review of the research. *Journal of Engineering Education*, *93*(3), 223–231. doi:10.1002/j.2168-9830.2004.tb00809.x

Prober, C. G., & Heath, C. (2012). Lecture Halls without Lectures – A Proposal for Medical Education. *The New England Journal of Medicine*, *366*(18), 1657–1659. doi:10.1056/NEJMp1202451 PMID:22551125

Rennie, F., & Morrison, T. (2013). *E-learning and social networking handbook: Resources for higher education*. Routledge. doi:10.4324/9780203120279

Ribeiro, S. P. (2017). Digital storytelling: learning to be in higher education. In *Digital storytelling in higher education* (pp. 207–223). Palgrave Macmillan. doi:10.1007/978-3-319-51058-3_15

Ricoy, M.-C., & Feliz, T. (2016). Twitter as a learning community in higher education. *Journal of Educational Technology & Society*, *19*(1), 237–248.

Rossiter, M., & Garcia, P. A. (2010). Digital storytelling: A new player on the narrative field. *New Directions for Adult and Continuing Education*, *126*(126), 37–48. doi:10.1002/ace.370

Ruleman, A. B. (2012). Social media at the university: A demographic comparison. *New Library World*, *113*(7/8), 316–332. doi:10.1108/03074801211244940

Sailer, M., Hense, J. U., Mayr, S. K., & Mandl, H. (2017). How gamification motivates: An experimental study of the effects of specific game design elements on psychological need satisfaction. *Computers in Human Behavior*, *69*, 371–380. doi:10.1016/j.chb.2016.12.033

Sánchez-Martínez, J., & Albaladejo-Ortega, S. (2018). Transmedia storytelling and teaching experience in higher education. *International Journal of Contemporary Education*, *1*(1), 52–63. doi:10.11114/ijce. v1i1.3077

Sari, F., & Wahyudin, A. (2019). Undergraduate students' perceptions toward blended learning through instagram in english for business class. *International Journal of Language Education*, *1*(1), 64–73. doi:10.26858/ijole.v1i1.7064

Scager, K., Boonstra, J., Peeters, T., Vulperhorst, J., & Wiegant, F. (2016). Collaborative learning in higher education: Evoking positive interdependence. *CBE Life Sciences Education*, *15*(4), 1–9. doi:10.1187/ cbe.16-07-0219 PMID:27909019

Shekhar, P., Prince, M., Finelli, C., Demonbrun, M., & Waters, C. (2019). Integrating quantitative and qualitative research methods to examine student resistance to active learning. *European Journal of Engineering Education*, *44*(1-2), 6–18. doi:10.1080/03043797.2018.1438988

Sotiriou, S., & Bogner, F. X. (2008). Visualizing the invisible: Augmented reality as an innovative science education scheme. *Advanced Science Letters*, *1*(1), 114–122. doi:10.1166/asl.2008.012

Stanley, D., & Zhang, Y. (2018). Student-Produced videos can enhance engagement and learning in the online environment. *Online Learning*, *22*(2), 5–26. doi:10.24059/olj.v22i2.1367

Statista. (2020). *Distribution of Instagram users worldwide*. Retrieved from: https://www.statista.com/ statistics/325587/instagram-global-age-group/

Statista. (2020). *TikTok- Statistics & Facts*. Retrieved from: https://bit.ly/392j8YN

Statista. (2021). *Number of monthly active Instagram users from January 2013 to June 2018*. Retrieved from: bit.ly/36Zes3T.

Statistics, U. Z. (2021). *Estadísticas de Grado y Máster Universitario de la Universidad de Zaragoza*. Retrieved from: https://academico.unizar.es/grado-y-master/estadisticas

Subhash, S., & Cudney, E. A. (2018). Gamified learning in higher education: A systematic review of the literature. *Computers in Human Behavior*, *87*, 192–206. doi:10.1016/j.chb.2018.05.028

Tess, P. A. (2013). The role of social media in higher education classes (real and virtual)–A literature review. *Computers in Human Behavior*, *29*(5), A60–A68. doi:10.1016/j.chb.2012.12.032

Wright, G. B. (2011). Student-centered learning in higher education. *International Journal on Teaching and Learning in Higher Education*, *23*(1), 92–97.

Wu, H. K., Lee, S. W. Y., Chang, H. Y., & Liang, J. C. (2013). Current status, opportunities and challenges of augmented reality in education. *Computers & Education*, *62*, 41–49. doi:10.1016/j.compedu.2012.10.024

Wu, J., & Chen, D. T. V. (2020). A systematic review of educational digital storytelling. *Computers & Education*, *147*, 103786. doi:10.1016/j.compedu.2019.103786

Young, J. R. (2008). The lectures are recorded, so why go to class. *The Chronicle of Higher Education*, *54*(36), 1–4.

ADDITIONAL READING

Babin, J., & Hulland, J. (2019). Exploring online consumer curation as user-generated content: A framework and agenda for future research, with implications for brand management. *Spanish Journal of Marketing-ESIC*, *23*(3), 325–338. doi:10.1108/SJME-07-2019-0053

Belanche, D., Flavián, M., & Ibáñez-Sánchez, S. (2020). Followers' reactions to influencers' Instagram posts. *Spanish Journal of Marketing-ESIC*, *24*(1), 37–54. doi:10.1108/SJME-11-2019-0100

Bilro, R. G., Loureiro, S. M. C., & Angelino, F. J. D. A. (in press). The Role of Creative Communications and Gamification in Student Engagement in Higher Education: A Sentiment Analysis Approach. *Journal of Creative Communications*.

Carpenter, J. P., Morrison, S. A., Craft, M., & Lee, M. (in press). How and why are educators using Instagram*? Teaching and Teacher Education*. PMID:32834464

Casaló, L. V., Flavián, C., & Ibáñez-Sánchez, S. (2020). Be creative, my friend! Engaging users on Instagram by promoting positive emotions. *Journal of Business Research*, *130*, 416–425. doi:10.1016/j.jbusres.2020.02.014

Fraser, B. J. (2014). Classroom Learning Environments: Historical and Contemporary Perspectives. In Handbook of Research on Science Education, Volume II (pp. 118-133). Routledge.

Misseyanni, A., Lytras, M. D., Papadopoulou, P., & Marouli, C. (2018). *Active Learning Strategies in Higher Education*. Emerald Publishing Limited. doi:10.1108/9781787144873

Rodriguez-Illera, J. L., & Castells, N. M. (2014). Educational uses of transmedia storytelling. *Journal of Educational Multimedia and Hypermedia*, *23*(4), 335–357.

KEY TERMS AND DEFINITIONS

Active Learning: Instruction that meaningfully engages students in learning through higher participation in activities (Shekhar et al., 2018).

Augmented Reality: Interactive technology that modifies physical surroundings with superimposed virtual elements. This virtual layer, placed between the physical environments and the user, can add textual information, images, videos, or other virtual items to the person's viewing of the physical environment (Javornik, 2016, p. 253).

Collaborative Learning: Process in which students form teams to complete tasks together, with learning being promoted through the interpersonal exchanges that occur (Alavi et al., 1995).

Extended Reality (XR): A term that encompasses augmented reality, mixed reality, and virtual reality (Alcañiz et al., 2019).

Gamification: Applying game mechanics to other web properties to increase engagement (Terrill, 2008).

(Pure) Mixed Reality: Technology with which users are placed in the real world and digital content is totally integrated into their surroundings, so that they can interact with both digital and real contents, and these elements can also interact with them (Flavián et al., 2019, p. 550).

Storytelling: The sharing of ideas and experiences through words and actions to communicate and create meaning about our lives and the lives of others (Behmer, 2005, p. 3).

Transmedia: Different story forms that flow across multiple media channels (Jenkins, 2003).

User-Generated Content: Content created outside of professional routines and practices (Kaplan and Haenlein, 2010, p. 61).

Virtual Reality: Computer-generated 3D environment – called a 'virtual environment' – that one can navigate within and, possibly, interact with, resulting in real-time stimulation of one or more of the user's five senses (Guttentag, 2010, p. 638).

This research was previously published in the Handbook of Research on Developing a Post-Pandemic Paradigm for Virtual Technologies in Higher Education; pages 188-215, copyright year 2021 by Information Science Reference (an imprint of IGI Global).

Chapter 33
Responding to Contemporary Needs of Learning Communities Through Utilizing Emerging Social Networking Tools

Elif Buğra Kuzu Demir
Dokuz Eylul University, Turkey

Yavuz Akbulut
Anadolu University, Turkey

ABSTRACT

This chapter aims to understand the nature of the learning processes of students who resorted to social networking sites (SNSs) during instructional activities. Throughout the research, a blended learning environment (BLE) involving both SNSs and face-to-face activities was utilized. Frequently used SNSs such as Google+, Twitter, Facebook, and Tumblr were used in accordance with the preferences of the students. Through synchronous, asynchronous, and multimedia supported affordances of SNSs, it was aimed to improve the learning experiences of the students. Explorations revealed that affordances of different SNSs facilitated students' customization of the tools in the BLE for relevant purposes throughout the course. Participants mentioned that they were satisfied with the course, expressed their intention to use contemporary SNSs for their own instructional activities, appreciated the free and flexible learning atmosphere provided by the BLE, and underlined the importance of communication and sharing opportunities among all stakeholders in the classroom.

INTRODUCTION

Contemporary interaction opportunities provided by emerging technologies facilitate our transition from the information age to the interaction age (Butcher & Gibson, 2010; Kaya, 2011). In this regard, individuals' perceptions towards the information available have changed. In the interaction age, individuals

DOI: 10.4018/978-1-6684-7123-4.ch033

place importance on social environments where they are supposed to implement their 21st century skills more effectively such as working collaboratively with others and thinking creatively (Acar, 2013; Nagi & Vate-U-Lan, 2009). The advance and proliferation of Web 2.0 tools accelerate this process, as individuals' socialization practices have been extended through the Internet. That is, the need of interacting with others and maintaining relationships have been facilitated with the help of contemporary Web 2.0 tools.

Among all Web 2.0 tools, online social networking sites (SNS) have become quite widespread as a medium to respond to individuals' socialization needs (Gjoka, 2010; Glynn, Huge & Hoffman, 2012; Hung & Yuen, 2010; Kaya, 2011; Mislove, 2009). The increasing use of these tools among diverse populations has led researchers to work on the utilization patterns and potential impacts of emerging social networking opportunities (Cheung, Chiu & Lee, 2011; Glynn et al., 2012). User statistics of common SNSs reveal that young adults, especially those between the ages of 18-24, frequently use them in their daily lives (boyd, 2010; Mason & Rennie, 2008; Selwyn, 2007). University students are among these tech-savvy individuals, who are also called a variety of different monikers including digital natives, millennium learners, 21st century learners or new millennium learners in different studies.

Numerous features of online SNSs have triggered the transformation of education and training practices. Within a learning-centered framework, learners can create their own content, share and disseminate them, and collaborate with others. These opportunities of online SNSs lead millennium learners to have higher expectations from the schools and the instructional opportunities offered. In this sense, it may be possible to respond to their expectations through integrating the affordances of Web 2.0 tools into educational settings. Thus, many researchers and scholars have emphasized the importance of using such tools for instructional purposes.

Within the scope of this chapter, theoretical background related to the use of online SNSs for educational purposes will be presented along with a mixed-methods research study. The study aimed to investigate and understand the nature of the learning processes of students who resorted to online SNSs during instructional activities. Throughout the research, a blended learning environment was utilized, which was prepared in accordance with the needs reported by the participants (Kuzu & Akbulut, 2013). The research setting involved both social networking sites and face-to-face activities, which lasted 14 weeks. Through the help of qualitative and quantitative data, satisfaction levels of students were explored. Frequently used online SNSs such as Google+, Twitter, Facebook and Tumblr were used in the study in accordance with the preferences of the students. Through synchronous, asynchronous and multimedia supported affordances of online SNSs, it was aimed to improve the learning experiences of pre-service information technology (IT) teachers. Participants were 51 pre-service IT teachers who were senior students at a computer education and instructional technology department. The qualitative data were gathered through activity logs of online SNSs and semi-structured interviews; whereas the quantitative data were gathered through a questionnaire developed by the researchers. While the quantitative data were analyzed with IBM SPSS Statistics, which facilitated the calculation of descriptive statistics and conducting parametric tests, the qualitative data were analyzed through content analysis and inductive coding.

Explorations revealed that affordances of different SNSs facilitated students' customization of the tools in the blended learning environment for relevant purposes throughout the course. For instance, using Facebook more than other SNSs to maintain synchronous and asynchronous exchange of opinions was common. On the other hand, resorting to Tumblr for sharing long-text assignments was another practice. Participants of the process were satisfied with the course, expressed their intention to use contemporary SNSs for their own instructional activities, appreciated the free and flexible learning atmosphere provided by the BLE and underlined the importance of communication and sharing opportunities among all stakeholders in the classroom.

BACKGROUND

Online learning environments have been affected by the developments of Web technologies. As web technologies improve, their use for instructional purposes evolve as well. In the earlier phases, Web 1.0 tools could provide only static pages that were not aesthetically pleasing or interactive, and web pages prepared by only one content provider were available (Murugesan, 2010). Besides, users encountered certain limitations regarding the contribution to contents and interaction on these particular pages (Aghaei, Nematbakhsh & Farsani, 2012). The development of Web 2.0 applications and their increasingly common uses in daily life have enabled users to have two-way interaction with the content (Downes, 2006; Murugesan, 2010; Naik & Shivalingaiah, 2008). Thanks to this transformation, the internet was no longer a one-way passive environment, it started to be considered a participation-based and multi-dimensional activity context (Selwyn, 2012; Solomon & Schrum, 2007).

Web 2.0 is defined in different ways in the literature. Referred to as readable-writable Web, user-centered Web, participatory Web and social Web in different resources, Web 2.0 addresses the ability of users to produce content easily on the internet and make some changes on the existing content (Atıcı & Yıldırım, 2010). In a broader sense, it is defined as a dynamic and interactive platform in which users can easily obtain, produce, share and publish information and cooperate with other users while producing information (Bennet, Bishop, Dalgarno, Waycott, & Kennedy, 2013; Huang, Hood, & Yoo, 2013). In this respect, Web 2.0 consists of web-based applications allowing individuals to use the existing or user-produced content and to edit and share this content when needed. Many studies in the related literature emphasize the fact that it is necessary to see Web 2.0 as an approach leading to wide-range social transformation rather than a pioneering technology (Downes, 2006; Murugesan, 2010). Thanks to its technology, applications and basic features, each user is a participant in Web 2.0. Therefore, it leads to the sustainable social transformation and democratization of the Web.

Creating a social transformation is possible when users are able to form a common understanding and content by using Web 2.0 tools. To achieve this purpose, it is essential to develop Web 2.0 tools that can be used as simply as possible, which is called architecture of participation (Murugesan, 2010). In this regard, the following principles have been suggested for the design and technologies of Web 2.0 tools (Murugesan, 2010, p.5). Web 2.0 tools should

- enable users to work on a flexible web design, to reuse the existing content and to install updates easily,
- provide enriched and sensitive user interface,
- encourage cooperation and the development of a common understanding,
- facilitate editing and cooperative content production for users,
- form social networks for the individuals having common interests,
- enable users to develop new interesting applications by reusing or combining existing applications, or by bringing the data and information from various resources together.

Therefore; by using Web 2.0, any web-literate user can develop applications to publish, share and edit content without having any technical difficulties, and benefits from these applications for effective social interaction and cooperation (Horzum, 2010; Richardson, 2009).

When Web 2.0 and the architecture of participation definitions are considered, it can be concluded that Web 2.0 tools mainly focus on the following issues: bringing individuals with common interests together; ways they can cooperate and learn from each other; and creating communities that enable them to form digital resources (Lee & McLoughlin, 2010). Being user centric, this idea is parallel with a learner-centered approach in the field of education (Berger & Trexler, 2010). Therefore; the use of Web 2.0 tools in educational environments has become a frequently-studied topic. When studies conducted in the field of education are examined, it is observed that the most common Web 2.0 applications used for educational purposes are blogs, wikis, video sharing websites and online social networks (Huang et.al, 2013; Johnson, Levine & Smith, 2008). Many studies in the literature suggest that these applications, which are considered an innovative internet trend, have the potential to structure and improve teaching and learning environments in higher education (Ajjan & Hartshorne, 2008; Bartlett-Bragg, 2006; Huang et al., 2013; Lee & McLoughlin, 2010). Due to the rapid developments of Web 2.0 technologies, which have been a part of daily life for learners, many institutions and educators have started to focus on what can be done to keep up with these new-generation environments and users (Selwyn, 2012).

Educational Use of Social Networking Tools

Among all Web 2.0 tools, online social networks (SNSs) have become very popular as environments meeting the needs of individuals to socialize in the most efficient way (Gjoka, 2010; Glynn et al., 2012; Hung & Yuen, 2010; Kaya, 2011; Mislove, 2009). The fact that SNSs are becoming widespread among individuals with different demographic characteristics has encouraged researchers to conduct studies focusing on the use and effects of this technology (Cheung, Chiu & Lee, 2011; Glynn et al., 2012). SNSs are defined in different ways in the literature. In simplest terms, SNSs refer to socialization-based activities administered by a group of users through online information technologies (Cheung et al., 2011; Hamid, Chang & Kurnia, 2010). Green and Hannon (2007) define SNSs as Web 2.0 tools that provide users with opportunities to connect with other users through their online presence. These online connections refer to social networks and the activities in the network. These connections can be established by joining online groups or through the friends list of other users (Green & Hannon, 2007). Another popular definition of SNSs in the literature has been offered by Boyd and Ellison (2007). They define SNSs as web-based applications which allow people to create a profile that is visible to everybody or to certain individuals, to form a list of connected individuals and to follow others' connections through friend lists. When these definitions are examined, the features of SNSs can be listed as follows:

- SNSs enable users to generate their own social networks through creating a personal profile page.
- SNSs facilitate the interaction among users through providing various services such as e-mail, instant messaging, and video, notes, file and photography sharing.
- Through using SNSs, users can easily find their friends, create groups and share content with those with common interests.
- The majority of SNSs are free of charge.

- Most SNSs improve their services through adding new features and add-ons according to the feedback received. In addition, SNSs provide opportunities for users to create their own applications and share them with other users.
- SNSs enable users to edit privacy and accessibility settings so that they can decide with whom they want to share with or which content they want to share as well.
- SNSs focus on individual-based online communities rather than content- or interest-based online communities (boyd & Ellison, 2007; Mazman, 2009; Özkan & McKenzie; 2008).

These features are the basic ones that any SNSs should have. However; each SNS offers different features to its users depending on why it is developed. The more features an SNS has, the more likely it will be preferred by users. Many features of SNSs have led to certain transformations in educational environments. Students can now produce their own content in a learner-centered structure, share the content and collaborate with other users during content production processes. These educational functions provided by Web 2.0 lead to high expectations by 21st century learners regarding the education offered at schools (Pedró, 2006).

These expectations can be listed as follows:

- Supporting the technological infrastructure of schools through the integration of new technologies,
- Integrating internet technologies such as SNSs, video sharing tools and blogs into courses,
- Being exposed to a learning-centered learning process,
- Working together with other learners in collaborative learning environments,
- Creating social networks with other learners and teachers through SNSs (Kuzu, 2013; Lampert & Gong, 2010; Pedró, 2006; Şahin, 2010).

When we consider the characteristics of 21st century learners, we can see that they match well with the functions offered by Web 2.0 tools. In other words, it is possible to meet the expectations of 21st century learners through integrating Web 2.0 tools into instructional activities as learners frequently use them in their daily lives. Within this context, the importance of using these tools for educational purposes has been emphasized by many scholars. Berger and Trexler (2010, p.6) suggest several reasons why Web 2.0 tools should be used in education.

That is, Web 2.0 tools offer the following:

- Motivate and involve students in learning processes,
- Are in harmony with 21st Century Learner Standards by American School Library Association and National Educational Technologies Standards (NETS),
- Prepare students for real life by helping them to acquire original skills,
- Encourage collaborative learning environments,
- Support learning as a social process,
- Create opportunities for interactive learning,
- Provide real learning communities for learners,
- Provide fun and are free of charge,
- Provide ubiquitous learning environments,
- Enable users to communicate with other learner communities at a global level.

When the educational use of SNSs is concerned, the basic question to be asked is under which conditions this use will contribute to a students' achievement. If carefully selected, applied and combined with innovative educational practice and online communities, SNSs can help learners to develop necessary skills to be successful in the 21st century as well as improving communication and collaborative skills in today's globalized world (Discipio, 2008). SNSs can be considered unfamiliar in terms of education at first; however, many teachers will find a way to use these tools effectively in order to facilitate meaningful learning experiences.

Many SNSs which have been developed for different purposes are available on the internet. Although most of these mainly address daily life activities, their use for academic purposes both by learners and teachers is increasing as time moves on. It is crucial to choose the most suitable SNS for educational purposes. The key point in this selection is to develop a holistic approach regarding accurate tool combinations by taking content and the methods used into consideration. Solomon and Schrum (2010, pp. 11-14) explain the functions provided by Web-based tools such as SNSs with the "8C" framework in which communication, collaboration and creativity components are examined under the "learner skills" dimension, and connectedness and communities of learners under the "teaching skills" dimension. Below, all components of the framework (Kuzu, 2014; Solomon and Schrum, 2010) are discussed briefly along with their potential contribution to current study.

Communication: Students have the opportunities to communicate with other individuals, send them their work and receive comments. As a result, students are able to create better products thanks to the feedback received and the revisions made. In addition, students are able to interact with other individuals from different parts of the world rather than with limited number of people in their daily lives thanks to this communication function.

Collaboration: Student collaboration is a complex process; however, the use of SNSs to support students' collaboration with others makes this process simpler. Students may express their opinions about a specific topic in collaborative learning environments and receive feedback either from other students of from their instructor so that they can create more productive outcomes. In this regard, SNSs outperform other conventional web tools through their synchronous communication opportunities. Instant feedback from other learners increase the possibility for more effective communication and collaboration. In addition, teachers are able to monitor changes throughout the process as well as the contribution of each individual within collaborative learning environments.

Connectedness: Students are able to understand the connectedness nature of individuals. According to students who are 21st century learners, everything is carried out in online environments in their daily life. In this respect, students believe that anything worth learning should be available online. Other individuals in online environments are data sources that contribute to the production of common knowledge.

Communities of learners: While students mainly use SNSs in their daily life to communicate with other individuals, schools make use of these environments to support professional development and students' learning. Communities of learners are online practice groups where learners with a common purpose come together in a digital environment and share their knowledge and experiences. Schools can create online communities of learners where content, project-based studies, other students and teachers are brought together. In addition, it is possible to have real time or asynchronous access to a physically remote student, content or expert opinion thanks to such communities of learners.

Convergence: SNSs make it possible to use content information, teaching skills and technology together. In other words, it refers to the use of content, learning and teaching methods (pedagogy) and technology together (Mishra & Koehler, 2006).

Contextualization: Learning at school differs from real-life learning. At school, students memorize information and use this knowledge in exams as the application area. However, real learning can occur when information learned is given a meaning in a context and later is used in other real-life contexts. Having the capacity to contextualize opinions and contents, SNSs help students to assign meaning to the context and depth of newly learned knowledge.

Cloud Computing: The developments in information technologies affect the demand of schools for data storage. Administrators, teachers and students prefer to have their data on online environments rather than on their computers. Today, it is easier to access this data through mobile technologies. Accessing online applications through SNSs, storing documents online, finding a new course and joining this course online can be given as examples to the innovations brought by cloud computing.

Cost-free Software: The fact that SNSs are free of charge contributes to the increase of their educational use by teachers and students. Instead of using expensive processors and presentation programs, teachers and students prefer these free of charge online applications.

As mentioned in 8C framework, the use of SNSs for educational purposes will bring a lot of advantages to educational institutions, teachers and students; however, the integration of these tools to learning-teaching environments should be carefully realized. The first step to determine students' needs is to determine which content can be blended via SNSs and which methods to be used for an effective application. The most important point to be considered here is to deal with the features of SNSs in a holistic and logical approach. By doing so, it is possible to develop 21st century skills, collaboration skills and creativity in students. In addition, certain solutions can be found to the problems and needs of the students from different socio-economic backgrounds thanks to such features. Moreover, it is necessary not to consider SNSs merely as environments where students can communicate with other students, but they should also be seen as environments where teachers can provide their students with authentic learning experiences through participation in online environments.

MAIN FOCUS OF THE CHAPTER

Although many contemporary learning management systems enable learners to register to the courses they are interested in, they generally do not provide tools for effective communication and personal profile generation (McLoughlin & Lee, 2007). Within this context, SNSs that are frequently used by learners attract more people's attention (Lenhart & Madden, 2007; Selwyn, 2007). In this regard, the current study aims to contribute to the information and practice repertoire to adopt frequently used SNSs for educational purposes. It is believed that certain affordances to support effective communication, effective participation, information and resource sharing, and critical thinking are worth studying (Ajjan & Hartshorne, 2008, Selwyn, 2012)

In this regard, the current study implemented SNSs as Web 2.0 tools to increase instructional effectiveness and to understand the nature of learning process of preservice IT teachers. The aim was to improve learning and teaching experiences of preservice teachers through supplementing online, real-time and multi-dimensional applications of SNSs. Besides, it was expected that teaching practices blended with SNSs could provide collaboration-based learning environments and show potential to increase the quality of teaching. Moreover, thanks to the activities offered within the scope of the current study, preservice teachers could gain knowledge and skills about ways to use SNSs in educational practices prior to their actual job experiences in future.

METHODS

Participants

The participants of the study were determined through convenience sampling which is a purposeful sampling method. The aim of this sampling technique was to facilitate the process by using close and easily accessible cases. Accordingly, the researchers chose the course the first author offered every week so that she could obtain in-depth and detailed information from the students. The course was "BTO426 Project Development and Management II" and was offered in the 2012 Spring term at the Department of Computer Education and Instructional Technology (CEIT) at Anadolu University, Turkey. The researchers collected data from 51 students who were registered to the course. Semi-structured interviews were conducted to obtain in-depth data regarding their satisfaction level regarding the blended learning environment. Participants who were interviewed within the scope of the study were selected randomly among volunteers (n=11, 5 females and 6 males).

Data Collection

The course was structured according to the experiences of the researchers and the information obtained from the literature. Preservice teachers were provided an environment supplemented by SNSs in the course. The main reason for choosing the "Project Development and Management II" was that this course had a content that might enable students to deal with research skills and teaching profession skills together in a holistic way. In order to fulfill the requirements of the course, preservice teachers had to use the majority of skills and knowledge they acquired beginning with the first semester of their undergraduate education. In addition, preservice teachers collaborated with each other in the course while preparing a research project as the final outcome.

The researchers monitored preservice teachers both in face-to-face teaching environment and through SNSs used in the study for 14 weeks. At the end of the application, a questionnaire with two dimensions was administered to explore participants' satisfaction with the online learning environment supported with SNSs. In addition, semi-structured interviews were conducted with 11 preservice teachers.

The Logs of SNS Activities

SNS activities designed and structured on the basis of the expectations and demands of the students were applied in the course. Researchers' experiences and the data obtained from the literature led them to integrate Facebook, Google +, Twitter and Tumblr to instructional activities (Kuzu & Akbulut, 2013). After receiving their consents to participate in the study, students were introduced to these SNSs and they were asked to create an account for each. Later, they were presented teaching activities to address the learning outcomes through SNSs. The logs of these whole-semester online activities for each SNS and for each preservice teacher were recorded. Although these logs differed according to SNS and the corresponding week, the following patterns were observed for each SNS as follows:

- **Facebook:** Contributions of the instructor and preservice teachers (discussion topics, text-based messages such as announcement, multi-media elements such as photographs, sounds, videos and comments about teaching materials).

- **Google+:** Contributions of the instructor and preservice teachers (announcements and text-based messages to inform) and video conferencing logs involving multi users.
- **Tumblr:** Research diaries and the comments involving long-text assignments.
- **Twitter:** Short-text comments and multi-media elements such as photographs, sounds and videos.

Questionnaire for Preservice Teacher Satisfaction

"Online Social Networks Preservice Teachers Satisfaction Questionnaire" with two dimensions was developed to investigate participants' satisfaction levels with the blended learning environment. The first dimension included items written to determine participants' satisfaction levels while the second dimension included the items about demographic information. While writing the items for the questionnaire, several studies were examined in the literature. Following the expert opinion phase, the questionnaire was finalized with 29 items and 7 personal information questions so that it could be administered to preservice teachers. The final version was sent to 51 students who took the course. However; only 43 preservice teachers filled out the questionnaire, which meant 84.4% return rate.

Semi-Structured Interview Form for Preservice Teacher Satisfaction

Semi-structured interviews were conducted to determine the satisfaction levels of preservice teachers about blended learning environment, the educational use of SNSs and the activities introduced via SNSs. Another question asked in the interviews addressed student opinions to see whether they might use SNSs for educational purpose in their future career.

The interviews with preservice teachers were conducted at predetermined times by using hangout (video conferencing) feature of Google +. The researchers asked four questions prepared beforehand and other drill down questions to the participants in a specific order. The codes were used for each preservice candidate for the analysis and reporting of the interviews.

Data Analysis

Quantitative data about the demographic information of preservice teachers were analyzed through descriptive statistics. In addition, the examination of satisfaction level of preservice teachers for blended learning for each specific item were also analyzed through descriptive statistics. In order to determine whether satisfaction level of preservice teachers displayed meaningful differences according to gender, normality tests were applied to the data. According to Kolmogorov-Smirnov test results, satisfaction level, which was the dependent variable, displayed normal distribution ($D(43)=0,124$; $p>.05$) and this result was verified by skewness (.129) and kurtosis (-.634) values (Huck, 2000). Later, one-sample t-test was applied to determine whether there is a meaningful difference between satisfaction level and 3, which is the middle point of the scale range.

Qualitative data obtained from semi-structured interviews and SNS activity logs were analyzed through content analysis method, which is used to determine concepts and relationships that might account for the data obtained from a text or text group (Yıldırım & Şimşek, 2006). In order to ensure reliability and trustworthiness of the research in qualitative dimensions, certain strategies were used such as consensus among coders and direct quotations from the participants.

RESULTS AND DISCUSSION

Weekly Activities on Online Social Networks

In this learning environment supplemented by SNSs, all preservice teachers (N=51) created accounts and joined the personal network of the instructor of the course in study-specific SNSs. Following the first two weeks, which were planned to warm-up the preservice teachers for a blended learning environment, the teaching activities were presented in the third week. It was observed that 42 preservice teachers in average followed the course supplemented by SNSs for 14 weeks regularly. During this period, a total of 30 messages sheltering 119 comments were shared through Facebook. The distribution of the comments for each theme was: discussion topics related to the course ($f=7$), messages to make announcements and inform other participants ($f=5$), sharing teaching materials ($f=3$) and off-the course topics ($f=15$). At the end of 14 weeks, preservice teachers shared a lot of photographs, videos and comments regarding their graduation ceremony. In addition, they used the Facebook account, which was created to communicate among themselves for the current course, when they started to work as teachers. In other words, it can be said that the use of Facebook continued even after their graduation. The researcher shared 37 messages and received 318 comments for these messages in the blended learning environment. The distribution of these messages were as follows: discussion topics related to the course ($f=7$), information about learning process ($f=7$), making announcements and giving information about learning responsibilities ($f=14$) and off-the course topics ($f=9$).

It was found that the feedback sessions between the instructor and the students were more easily structured thanks to the multi-user video conferencing feature of Google+. The instructor allotted 20 minutes on certain weekdays for each project group to provide feedback through video conferencing (Hangouts) feature of Google +, which enabled each preservice teacher to join teleconferencing from their own physical environment. That is, they did not have to be together with the instructor in the same physical environment. The feedback sessions during the application phase (i.e., 12 weeks excluding exams & add-drop week) were carried out with 14 project groups via Google +. Preservice teachers preferred face-to-face feedback sessions for the projects they submitted for the first and second midterm exams.

Tumblr created a suitable environment for students to keep research diary and share of the long-text assignments such as physical observations and research summary. Preservice teachers shared their research diaries via this SNS two times a week before and after they go to schools for research projects, which enabled researcher to follow the process. In addition, the instructor was able to examine the learning process of students in different project groups and provide information about perceived problems, the precautions to be taken and possible solutions. A total of 21 project groups shared their research summary, physical observation and project revision assignments via Tumblr. Each project group submitted three assignments, which meant a total of 63 assignments. Preservice teachers did not make any comments about the assignments, which showed that Tumblr was less preferred in terms of one-to-one communication when compared to Facebook and Google+. The opinions of prospective teachers regarding the reason for this limitation was obtained during the interviews conducted to determine satisfaction levels.

In addition, each preservice teacher shared their research diaries for nine weeks via Tumblr, which corresponded to a total of 477 diaries. The diaries were written twice for each teaching practice day before and after preservice teacher went to schools. They included information about each individual's experiences, the problems they faced and their problem solving skills during this action research process.

This made it possible for both preservice teachers and the course instructor to make detailed evaluations regarding project management processes.

The activities via Twitter did not go beyond making announcements and informing. Only four replies/comments were received for the comments of the instructor regarding supervising activities and of preservice teachers regarding course materials. Participants preferred to express their opinions about the content shared via SNSs mostly via the Facebook course group or teleconferencing via Google +.

In this study, the SNS use behaviors of preservice teachers were observed during the online learning environment designed by using SNSs for the course as well as during face-to-face lessons. According to the observations carried out throughout the semester, the most frequently followed and commented activities were as follows: feedback sessions realized through video conferencing, sharing of project assignments and student diaries, and following the announcements related to the course. Although the supplementary course materials enriched with multi-media environment elements were followed by preservice teachers, the comments about these shares were quite limited in number. This finding may imply that preservice teachers focused on satisfaction on performance and effort expectancy dimensions. The observations made by the instructor revealed that the performance expectancy of preservice teachers for the course was to pass the course successfully. Preservice teachers believed that when they completed the group projects and individual assignments according to the criteria determined by the instructor, they would pass the course with a relatively high grade. Therefore, they tended to follow the topics via SNSs that might affect their grades such as the comments about assignments, feedback sessions and announcements about the exams. In addition, preservice teachers tended to join and use activities which were not likely to bring them any work load. Majority of preservice teachers stated that blended learning environment supplemented with SNSs made them free from time and space limitations during learning process and facilitated instructor-student and student-student interaction.

Online Social Networks Preservice Teachers Satisfaction Questionnaire

Researchers developed the "Online Social Networks Preservice Teachers Satisfaction Questionnaire" (see Appendix 1) which included 29 Likert items. These items were followed by personal information questions to determine preservice teachers' satisfaction levels with the blended learning environment which was supplemented through SNSs. The means of each item in the first part were calculated to find out which items were given more or less importance and summary statistics were provided in Table 1.

In order to determine satisfaction levels of preservice teachers with blended learning environment, the mean for questionnaire items were calculated, and it was found to be 4.06 (*SD*:0.32). In order to determine whether there was meaningful difference between satisfaction levels of preservice teachers and the value "3", which is the middle value between "always" (5) and "never" (1), one sample t-test was applied. It was found that the calculated mean for satisfaction level was meaningfully over the value of 3 ($t_{(42)}$=21.58; p<.001). This finding implied that satisfaction level of preservice teachers for blended learning was high.

The personal information section of the questionnaire (see Appendix 2) included questions about how often students used SNSs in their daily life, in educational activities before the lesson and within the scope of the current course. The responses provided for these questions are summarized in Table 2.

Table 1. Satisfaction of preservice teachers regarding blended learning environment for each item *

Items	X̄	SD
5. following the announcements about the course was easier.	4.63	,54
9. I was able to share information with my friends easily.	4.60	,54
8. I was able to share materials related to the course with my friends easily.	4.53	,67
18. The instructor encourages me to follow social networks for educational purposes.	4.53	,55
25. My (future) students will like this (application).	4.53	,59
1. Communicating with the course teacher was easier.	4.51	,59
12. I was satisfied with the existing communication means (instant messaging, video conferencing etc.).	4.49	,74
16. I was satisfied with the way the course was taught.	4.49	,67
10. I easily shared my experiences related to the course.	4.33	,68
17. I did not face any problems in terms of use.	4.28	,91
13. I was satisfied with the interaction environment.	4.26	,82
3. I benefitted from the instructor more effectively.	4.14	,71
28. This will be one of my future teaching practice applications.	4.07	,91
2. Communication with my classmates was easier.	4.02	,99
19. Other teaching staff encourage us to follow social networks for educational purposes.	4.02	,86
24. My (future) school administration will like this idea.	4.02	,86
15. The contents provided were in harmony with the social network website via which they are presented.	4.00	,82
27. It won't make any difference for me in terms of professional development.	4.00	1,13
4. Following the developments related to my department was easier.	3.93	,96
14. Multimedia environment elements used in the contents were sufficient.	3.86	,97
11. I benefitted from the experiences of my classmates very easily.	3.84	,95
22. Other teaching staff in the field has negative attitude towards the use of social networks for educational purposes.	3.84	,97
23. My close friends encourage me to follow social networks for educational purposes.	3.72	1,08
29. It will bring an advantage in my future job applications.	3.70	1,06
20. The instructor uses social networks in her other courses.	3.65	,84
26. Parents will like that application.	3.56	,77
21. Other teaching staff uses social networks for educational purposes.	3.51	,96
6. I learned more creative ideas related to the content of the course.	3.47	,93
7. I developed more creative ideas related to the course content.	3.30	1,10

*N=43

As the table shows, Facebook was the most commonly used SNS both in daily life and in educational activities. Facebook was followed by Twitter when daily use was taken into account. Twitter was used more frequently than Google + in daily life. However, preservice teachers were more familiar with Google + than Twitter in educational contexts. In addition, preservice teachers' use of SNSs in the course was more common than daily life use due to the blended nature of the course. Besides, the preservice teachers created accounts in these SNSs and had to follow them for a whole semester. The increase in the frequency of SNS use might be a natural outcome of in-class applications. Finally, this finding might imply that preservice teachers used SNSs more often to gain academic benefit from the course.

Table 2. Frequency of SNSs use by preservice teachers

	Daily Life		Educational Activities Before the Lesson		BTÖ426 Project Development and Management II	
	X̄	SD	X̄	SD	X̄	SD
Facebook	4,49	1,01	3,77	1,23	4,67	0,52
Twitter	2,93	1,30	1,84	1,15	2,53	1,18
Google+	2,63	1,23	2,14	1,37	3,98	0,89
Tumblr	1,93	1,13	1,55	0,99	3,44	1,01

*N=43

Preservice teachers were also asked about the time they spent on SNSs for educational purposes as part of the course. More than half of the preservice teachers (52.5%) reported that they spent more than two hours a day, which meant they spent 14 hours or more a week for the course. This course was listed in the curriculum as a four-hour course (i.e., two hours theory & two hours practice). In other words, when a course was supplemented by SNSs, students had the opportunity to access the course content, materials and learning environment throughout the week rather than only in the teaching hours specified in the curriculum.

Semi-Structured Interviews Regarding Student Satisfaction

Semi-structured interviews (see Appendix 1) were conducted with preservice IT teachers in order examine their opinions about their satisfaction with the blended learning environment, the SNSs used, the activities presented via these SNSs, and their intention to use SNSs for educational purposes in future.

In these semi-structured interviews, first of all, the satisfaction of preservice teachers with blended learning environment was examined. At this point, all the participants stated that they were satisfied with this learning environment. As for the reasons of this satisfaction with the blended learning environment, the followings were reported by the participants: providing flexible learning environment (*f*=25), facilitating the communication (*f*=14); supporting different learning styles (*f*=9); sharing (*f*=5); and gaining competence (*f*=5). The participants also reported that blended learning environment provided independence from time, space and technology.

Preservice teachers often stated that a course supplemented with SNSs provided them with a *flexible learning environment*. They also stated that such learning environments eliminated the need for students and the teacher to be in the same place at the same time. That is, teaching and learning processes continued everywhere free from space as long as there was internet access. The participants stated: *"It helped me communicate with you and my classmates. Communicating directly through the internet when we are available instead of meeting at school created a more flexible environment"* (M9). *"I was able to follow 24 hours the latest news, updates, assignments and developments related to the course with my smart phone. It was very convenient for me."* (M5).

Communication sub theme was explained through communication with the instructor and communication with in-class stakeholders. When the responses were examined, it can be stated that communication with the course instructor was often realized to gain academic benefit such as asking some questions about the course content, getting feedback for the assignments and getting firsthand up-to-date information about the course. One participant stated: *"Communication with each other were easier. You know you gave assignments and projects. We did not have to come to school to ask our questions. We contacted you via the internet." (M4).* When the sub theme related to "communication with in-class stakeholders" were examined, we could see that preservice teachers used blended learning environment to gain academic benefit such as sharing with each other up-to-date information about the course, sharing their opinions about the assignments, and giving feedback to each other's assignment. For instance, a participant stated: *"I learned everybody's ideas about assignments, when an assignment was given, I learnt how to do it and when to submit it by reading the comments made under this assignment. My interaction with my classmate was quite good" (M 5).* Preservice teachers mentioned that online communication created a more relaxed environment, which further contributed to their conventional relationships as well. For instance a student stated *"It was useful in terms of time management and not having to go to school. With you. Actually it was useful in terms of relationships. Talking to the instructor face to face like this. I mean... There was a warmer atmosphere online." [M11].* Another participants maintained that online communication was more relaxed and less frustrating since writing was more comfortable than face-to-face talking: *"Communication increased like this. There were friend groups in the school. Everybody was in their own group. When a group member talked, the others did not want to contribute or refute. But, social network was more comfortable. This environment created more communication opportunities." [M7]*

The opinions of preservice teachers about *learning styles* was explained under individual learning, peer-learning and collaboration-based learning styles. Participants were happy to find opportunities to prefer among these alternatives such as: *"Team work was possible through computers and social networks which was ideal for us. We could write our projects, assignments and theses without coming together physically." (M2).*

Similar to statements regarding the support of individual learning preferences, participants were happy with *sharing* opportunities as well. For instance, teacher candidates reported that they had the chance to examine other prospective teacher's projects, give feedback to each other and learn from each other. In addition, they stated that such environments supported collaborative works, their communication with other team members became easier, and they completed the assignments given by the teacher more easily. Direct quotations about this issue can be exemplified as follows: *"We gave feedback to each other (she is talking about other preservice teachers) (M3), "carrying out team work via social network was quite beneficial for us. It helped us to complete our projects, assignments or writing our dissertation without having to come together. (M2)*

Finally, *gaining competence* was mentioned by several participants to address that they were not using current SNSs before the course such as *"I did not know about Google+ to be honest. This course helped me learn it. Same applies to Tumblr. I knew Twitter but did not use actively. I learnt different things to be honest." (M10)*

CONCLUSION

Many scholars in the literature recommend the use of SNSs as a supplement for face to face learning-teaching environments (Hung & Yuen, 2010; Yuen & Yuen, 2008). Accordingly, a blended learning environment supplemented by SNSs was designed for preservice teachers in the current study. The activities in the learning environment were prepared on the basis of the opinions of preservice teachers

(Kuzu & Akbulut, 2013). The SNSs selected to be used in blended learning environment were used for different purposes throughout the 14-week process. First, different activities that might be presented via SNSs and meet different expectations of preservice teachers were selected. All of the activity types were presented to preservice teachers via SNSs first. Later, longitudinal uses enabled the researchers to observe which activity type was adopted for each SNS. It was observed that activities that were appropriate for the technical and social features of SNSs were used more often.

The observations revealed that preservice teachers used Facebook, which is also very popular in daily life, to realize synchronous and asynchronous information sharing between student-student and student-instructor. The fact that Facebook has relatively higher number of features than other SNSs may have contributed to this finding. Therefore, it is suggested that presenting information about course content, explanations about assignments and exams, sharing the experiences of lecturers and creating environment to have discussions about these issues can be realized through Facebook. Similarly, the observations revealed that preservice teachers preferred SNSs, in which a new notification is clearly and noticeably displayed on the main page, to follow multi-environment elements about the course and to make comments. It can be stated that the groups created for these specific courses affected this finding. Group function in SNSs provides a structure separating learning environment from other irrelevant and distractive contents, and facilitates receiving notifications about all the comments made in the group. Contents shared in the group could be displayed as new notifications on the main page of the users and could get students' attention successfully. In this regard, it is recommended that primarily important materials should be shared with course groups via relevant SNSs with such functions.

Following the 14-week implementation, the satisfaction level of preservice teachers regarding the blended learning environment and the activities presented in this environment were explored. Findings revealed that preservice teachers were satisfied with the blended learning practices supported with SNSs. They maintained that they planned to use SNSs in their future teaching practices as well. The frequency of using SNSs for educational purposes and increasing durations of staying online further supported this finding. Preservice teachers stated that they felt freer in a flexible learning environment thanks to blended learning, highlighted that such applications increased the communication and sharing among all stakeholders. At the same time, they reported that a learning environment supplemented by SNSs brought significant benefits in terms of gaining competence about different learning styles and social networking tools. Comparison of the current implementation with other conventional and online settings with regard to communication and collaboration opportunities could be useful for further implementations.

ACKNOWLEDGMENT

The current study is derived from the first author's PhD dissertation, which is supported by Anadolu University Research Fund (Project ID: 1109E133).

REFERENCES

Acar, A. (2013). Attitudes toward blended learning and social media use for academic purposes: An exploratory study. *Journal of e-Learning and Knowledge Society, 9*(3), 107-126.

Aghaei, S., Nematbakhsh, M. A., & Farsani, H. K. (2012). Evolution of the World Wide Web: From Web 1.0 to Web 2.0. International. *Journal of Web & Semantic Technology, 3*(1), 1–10. doi:10.5121/ijwest.2012.3101

Ajjan, H., & Hartshorne, R. (2008). Investigating faculty decisions to adopt Web 2.0 technologies: Theory and empirical tests. *The Internet and Higher Education, 11*(2), 71–80. doi:10.1016/j.iheduc.2008.05.002

Atıcı, B., & Yıldırım, S. (2010). Web 2.0 uygulamalarının e-öğrenmeye etkisi [Effect of Web 2.0 applications on learning]. In M. Akgül, E. Derman, U. Çağlayan, A. Özgit, & T. Yılmaz (Eds.), *Proceedings of XII. Conference of Academic Information* (pp. 369-374). Muğla: Muğla University

Bartlett-Bragg, A. (2006). *Reflections on pedagogy: Reframing practice to foster informal learning with social software*. Retrieved September 10, 2016, from http://matchsz.inf.elte.hu/tt/docs/Anne20Bartlett-Bragg.pdf

Bennett, S., Bishop, A., Dalgarno, B., Waycott, J., & Kennedy, G. (2012). Implementing Web 2.0 technologies in higher education: A collective case study. *Computers & Education, 59*(2), 524–534. doi:10.1016/j.compedu.2011.12.022

Berger, P., & Trexler, S. (2010). *Choosing Web 2.0 tools for learning and teaching in a digital world*. Englewood, CO: Libraries Unlimited.

Boyd, d., & Ellison, N.B. (2007). Social network sites: Definition, history, and scholarship. *Journal of Computer-Mediated Communication, 13*(1), 210-230.

Boyd, d. (2010). Social network sites as networked publics: Affordances, dynamics, and implications. In Z. Papacharissi (Ed.), *Networked Self: Identity, Community, and Culture on Social Network Sites* (pp. 39-58). New York, NY: Routledge.

Butcher, M. F., & Gibson, P. (2010). *Online social networks and their impact on student expectations of university-provided learning technology. OpenStax-CNX module: m35291.*

Cheung, C. M. K., Chiu, P., & Lee, M. K. O. (2011). Online social networks: Why do students use Facebook? *Computers in Human Behavior, 27*(4), 1337–1343. doi:10.1016/j.chb.2010.07.028

Discipio, T. (2008). Adapting social networking to address 21st-century skills. *MultiMedia & Internet @Schools, 15*(5), 10-11.

Downes, S. (2006). E-learning 2.0. *eLearn Magazine, 10*, 1. doi:10.1145/1104966.1104968

Gjoka, M. (2010). *Measurement of online social networks* (Unpublished doctoral dissertation). University of California, Oakland, CA. Retrieved March 10, 2017 from http://www.minasgjoka.com/papers/minasgjoka_thesis.pdf

Glynn, C. J., Huge, M. E., & Hoffman, L. H. (2012). All the news that's fit to post: A profile of news use on social networking sites. *Computers in Human Behavior, 28*(1), 113–119. doi:10.1016/j.chb.2011.08.017

Green, H., & Hannon, C. (2007). *Their space: Education for a digital generation* (E-book). London: Demos. Retrieved March 10, 2017 from http://dera.ioe.ac.uk/23215/1/Their%20space%20-%20web.pdf

Hamid, S., Chang, S., & Kurnia, S. (2009). Identifying the use of online social networking in higher education. In *Proceedings of Ascilite Auckland 2009: Same places, different spaces* (pp. 419–422). Auckland: Melbourne University.

Horzum, M. B. (2010). Öğretmenlerin Web 2.0 araçlarından haberdarlığı, kullanım sıklıkları ve amaçlarının çeşitli değişkenler açısından incelenmesi [Investigating teachers' Web 2.0 tools awareness, frequency and purposes of usage in terms of different variables]. *Uluslararası İnsan Bilimleri Dergisi-Journal of Human Sciences, 7*(1), 603–634.

Huang, W. D., Hood, D. W., & Yoo, S. J. (2013). Gender divide acceptance of collaborative Web 2.0 applications for learning in higher education. *Internet and Higher Education, 16,* 57–65. doi:10.1016/j.iheduc.2012.02.001

Huck, S. W. (2000). *Reading statistics and research* (3rd ed.). New York, NY: Addison Wesley Longman.

Hung, H. T., & Yuen, S. C. Y. (2010). Educational use of social networking technology in higher education. *Teaching in Higher Education, 15*(6), 703–714. doi:10.1080/13562517.2010.507307

Johnson, L., Levine, A., & Smith, R. (2008). *The 2008 horizon report*. Austin, TX: The New Media Consortium.

Kaya, A. (2011). *Öğretmen adaylarının sosyal ağ sitelerini kullanım durumları ve İnternet bağımlılığı düzeyleri* [Teacher candidates' usage of social network sites and internet addiction levels] (Unpublished master thesis). Ege University, Turkey.

Kuzu, E. B. (2014). *Bilişim teknolojileri öğretmen adayları arasında çevrimiçi sosyal ağların öğretim amaçlı kullanımı* [Use of social networks for educational purposes among pre-service it teachers] (Unpublished doctoral dissertation). Anadolu University, Turkey.

Kuzu, E. B., & Akbulut, Y. (2013). Use of online social networking sites among pre-service information technology teachers. *World Journal on Educational Technology, 5*(3), 358–370.

Lampert, J., & Gong, Y. (2010). 21st century paradigms for pre-service teacher technology preparation. *Computers in Schools, 27*(1), 54–70. doi:10.1080/07380560903536272

Lee, M. J. W., & McLoughlin, C. (2010). Social software as tools for pedagogical transformation: Enabling personalization, creative production, and participatory learning. In N. Lambropoulos & M. Romero (Eds.), *Educational Social Software for Context-Aware Learning* (pp. 1–22). Hershey, PA: Information Science Reference. doi:10.4018/978-1-60566-826-0.ch001

Lenhart, A., & Madden, M. (2007). *Social networking websites and teens: An overview*. Washington, DC: Pew Internet & American Life Project. Retrieved March 10, 2017 from http://www.pewinternet.org/~/media//Files/Reports/2007/PIP_SNS_Data_Memo_Jan_2007.pdf.pdf

Mason, R., & Rennie, F. (2008). *E-learning and social networking handbook: Resources for higher education*. New York, NY: Routledge.

Mazman, S. G. (2009). *Sosyal ağların benimsenme süreci ve eğitsel bağlamda kullanımı* [Adoption process of social network and their usage in educational context] (Unpublished master thesis). Hacettepe University, Turkey.

McLoughlin, C., & Lee, M. J. W. (2010). Personalised and self-regulated learning in the Web 2.0 era: International exemplars of innovative pedagogy using social software. *Australasian Journal of Educational Technology, 21*(1), 28–43.

Mishra, P., & Koehler, M. J. (2006). Technological pedagogical content knowledge: A framework for integrating technology in teacher knowledge. *Teachers College Record, 108*(6), 1017–1054. doi:10.1111/j.1467-9620.2006.00684.x

Mislove, A. E. (2009). *Online social networks: Measurement, analysis, and applications to distributed information systems* (Unpublished doctoral dissertation). Rice University, Houston, TX. Retrieved March 10, 2017 from http://www.ccs.neu.edu/home/amislove/publications/SocialNetworks-Thesis.pdf

Murugesan, S. (2010). Web X.0: A road map. In S. Murugesan (Ed.), *Handbook of research on Web 2.0, 3.0 and X.0: technologies, business and social applications* (pp. 1–11). Hershey, PA: Information Science Reference. doi:10.4018/978-1-60566-384-5.ch001

Nagi, K., & Vate-U-Lan, P. (2009). Using emergent technologies for facilitating engaged learning in a virtual learning environment. *International Journal of the Computer, The Internet and Management, 17*(1), 61–66.

Naik, U., & Shivalingaiah, D. (2008). *Comparative study of Web 1.0, Web 2.0 and Web 3.0.* Retrieved March 10, 2017 from http://ir.inflibnet.ac.in/handle/1944/1285

Özkan, B., & McKenzie, B. (2008). Social networking tools for teacher education. In *Proceedings of Society for Information Technology & Teacher Education International Conference* (pp. 2772-2776). Chesapeake, VA: AACE.

Pedró, F. (2006). *The New Millennium Learners: Challenging our views on ICT and learning.* Retrieved March 10, 2017 from https://ideas.repec.org/p/idb/brikps/9228.html

Richardson, W. (2009). *Blogs, wikis, podcasts, and other powerful web tools for classrooms.* Corwin Press.

Şahin, M. C. (2010). *Eğitim Fakültesi öğrencilerinin Yeni Binyılın Öğrencileri ölçütlerine göre değerlendirilmesi* [Evaluation of the education faculty students according to the OECD-New Millennium Learners criteria] (Unpublished doctoral dissertation). Anadolu University, Turkey.

Selwyn, N. (2007, October). *Web 2.0 applications as alternative environments for informal learning - A critical review.* Paper presented at the OECD CERIKERIS International expert meeting on ICT and educational performance, Cheju Island, South Korea.

Selwyn, N. (2012). Social media in higher education. In A. Gladman (Ed.), *The Europa world of learning* (pp. 1–9). London, UK: Routledge.

Solomon, G., & Schrum, L. (2007). *Web 2.0: new tools, new schools* (1st ed.). Washington, DC: International Society for Technology in Education.

Yıldırım, A., & Şimşek, H. (2006). *Sosyal bilimlerde nitel araştırma yöntemleri* [Qualitative research methods in social sciences]. Ankara: Seçkin.

Yuen, S., & Yuen, P. (2008). Social networks in education. In G. Richards (Ed.), *Proceedings of World Conference on E-Learning in Corporate, Government, Healthcare, and Higher Education* (pp. 1408-1412). Chesapeake, VA: AACE.

KEY TERMS AND DEFINITIONS

Blended Learning Environment: A learning environment created by the combination of face-to-face and online learning experiences.

Online Learning Community: A group of people who have common learning interests and objectives and who are seeking a cooperative solution to existing learning problem in online learning environments.

Online Presence: A sense of existence of an individual in an online environment.

Social Networking Tools: Web 2.0 tools that give users the opportunity to create a profile, create a list of the individuals involved, and track their interactions with others.

Pre-Service Teachers: Senior students studying at teacher training departments.

Twenty-First Century Learners: Individuals born in the last decades, growing with new technologies, constantly interacting with new technologies, and making these technologies a part of their lives.

Web 2.0: An interactive platform where users can easily create and modify content on the internet.

Web 2.0 Tools: Web-based applications based on communication and interaction of individuals with common interests.

This research was previously published in Enhancing Social Presence in Online Learning Environments; pages 142-170, copyright year 2018 by Information Science Reference (an imprint of IGI Global).

APPENDIX 1

Online Social Networks Satisfaction Questionnaire

Dear Student:

   This questionnaire aimed to address your satisfaction with the blended learning environment you used in the "BTÖ426 Project Development and Management II". The questionnaire consists of two sections. The first section involves questions regarding your satisfaction with the course whereas the second section has personal information questions. Collected data will be used for scholarly purposes and individual evaluations will not be conducted. In this context, you do not need to write your name. Responding will take ten minutes approximately. Thanks a lot for your contribution.

Elif Buğra Kuzu

Yavuz Akbulut

Student Satisfaction

Questions regarding student satisfaction are given in Table 3.

Table 3.

NO	ITEMS	Strongly disagree				Strongly agree
Through the help of online social networks we used in the course						
1	communicating with the course teacher was easier.	1	2	3	4	5
2	communicating with my classmates was easier.	1	2	3	4	5
3	I benefitted from the instructor more effectively.	1	2	3	4	5
4	following the developments related to my department was easier.	1	2	3	4	5
5	following the announcements about the course was easier.	1	2	3	4	5
6	I learned more creative ideas related to the content of the course.	1	2	3	4	5
7	I developed more creative ideas related to the course content.	1	2	3	4	5
8	I was able to share materials related to the course with my friends easily.	1	2	3	4	5
9	I was able to share information with my friends easily.	1	2	3	4	5
10	I easily shared my experiences related to the course.	1	2	3	4	5
11	I benefitted from the experiences of my classmates very easily.	1	2	3	4	5
Regarding the online social networks we used in the course						
12	I was satisfied with the existing communication means (instant messaging, video conferencing etc.).	1	2	3	4	5
13	I was satisfied with the interaction environment.	1	2	3	4	5
14	multimedia environment elements used in the contents were sufficient.	1	2	3	4	5

continues on following page

Table 3. Continued

NO	ITEMS	Strongly disagree				Strongly agree
15	the contents provided were in harmony with the social network website via which they are presented.	1	2	3	4	5
16	I was satisfied with the way the course was taught.	1	2	3	4	5
17	I did not face any problems in terms of use.	1	2	3	4	5
Regarding people whose opinions I value						
18	the instructor encourages me to follow social networks for educational purposes.	1	2	3	4	5
19	other teaching staff encourage us to follow social networks for educational purposes.	1	2	3	4	5
20	the instructor uses social networks in her other courses.	1	2	3	4	5
21	other teaching staff uses social networks for educational purposes.	1	2	3	4	5
22	other teaching staff in the field has negative attitude towards the use of social networks for educational purposes.	1	2	3	4	5
23	my close friends encourage me to follow social networks for educational purposes.	1	2	3	4	5
Regarding the use of online social networks in my future career						
24	my (future) school administration will like this idea.	1	2	3	4	5
25	my (future) students will like this (application).	1	2	3	4	5
26	parents of my (future) students will like that application.	1	2	3	4	5
27	it won't make any difference for me in terms of professional development.	1	2	3	4	5
28	this will be one of my future teaching practice applications.	1	2	3	4	5
29	it will bring an advantage in my future job applications.	1	2	3	4	5

Personal Information

1. Gender: ☐ Female ☐ Male
2. Age (Please write):………..
3. To what extent did you use the following online social networks before taking "BTÖ426 Project Development and Management II"? (Table 4)

Table 4.

	Social Networks	Never				Always
1	Facebook	1	2	3	4	5
2	Google+	1	2	3	4	5
3	Tumblr	1	2	3	4	5
4	Twitter	1	2	3	4	5

4. To what extent have you used the following online social networks for educational purposes other than the course requirements of "BTÖ426 Project Development and Management II"? (Table 5)

Table 5.

	Social Networks	Never				Always
1	Facebook	1	2	3	4	5
2	Google+	1	2	3	4	5
3	Tumblr	1	2	3	4	5
4	Twitter	1	2	3	4	5

5. To what extent have you used the following online social networks for educational purposes in "BTÖ426 Project Development and Management II"? (Table 6)

Table 6.

	Social Networks	Never				Always
1	Facebook	1	2	3	4	5
2	Google+	1	2	3	4	5
3	Tumblr	1	2	3	4	5
4	Twitter	1	2	3	4	5

6. How much time a day did you spend in these online social networks for activities of the "BTÖ426 Project Development and Management II"?
   ○ Less than half an hour
   ○ Half an hour to 1 hour
   ○ 1 to 1.5 hours
   ○ 1.5 to 2 hours
   ○ 2 to 2.5 hours
   ○ 2.5 to 3 hours
   ○ More than 3 hours
7. How much was your ambition to use online social networks during "BTÖ426 Project Development and Management II"? (Table 7)

Table 7.

	Social Networks	Not at all ambitious				Exteremely ambitious
1	Facebook	1	2	3	4	5
2	Google+	1	2	3	4	5
3	Tumblr	1	2	3	4	5
4	Twitter	1	2	3	4	5

APPENDIX 2

Semi-Structured Interview Questions to Address Student Satisfaction

1. A blended learning environment supported with online social networks have been presented to you during "BTÖ426 Project Development and Management II". What do you think about this method?
   1.1. What were the benefits?
   1.2. What were the problems you experienced?
2. If you evaluate these online social networks one by one, were you happy to use them for instructional purposes? Which ones?
   2.1. Why did you like them?
   2.2. Why did not you like the others?
3. Some activities have been presented to you during the course. Can you evaluate these activities and the accompanying learning environment in terms of
   3.1. Content presented,
   3.2. Sharing,
   3.3. Communication,
   3.4. Scholarly benefits, and
   3.5. Knowledge acquisition?
4. Which of these online social networks you aim to use for instructional purposes in your future career?
   4.1. Why?

Chapter 34
Sparking Engagement:
Translating and Integrating Social Media Into the Literacy Environment

Kamshia Childs

https://orcid.org/0000-0002-6350-9117

Texas A&M University, Commerce, USA

ABSTRACT

The integration of social media, digital literacy, and its elements into the literacy classroom environment is a pairing that is necessary to keep students engaged in order to see the relevance of the skills in which they are learning. Students spend hours taking in popular culture and communicating their perspectives and ideas with the world while taking part in social media, but fail to see that they are learning and using similar skills when they are in the classroom. This chapter will demonstrate how educators can engage students with the skills they develop outside of the classroom, and apply those skills in lessons, tasks, and the classroom environment.

INTRODUCTION

Now, more than ever, technology guides today's students through their everyday world. Even more so, social media serves as a place for them to explore through a social lens when interacting, posting photos, and playing games. Educators could engage students with the skills they develop outside of the classroom in the digital world and apply those skills in lessons and tasks in the classroom environment. Using the connection of academic language and the "language" within the digital realm, teaching practices can be modified to improve the performance and engagement of students. Implementing social media in the classroom does not necessarily mean that an educator creates and uses a specific platform for communication or socialization with the students, but instead begins integrating the terms, features, and communication tasks within social media to teach traditional literacy skills in English Language Arts/ English Language Arts and Reading (ELA/ELAR) classroom settings and lessons.

DOI: 10.4018/978-1-6684-7123-4.ch034

This chapter will seek to:

- Promote and explain how popular culture has an impact on the literacy classroom.
- Give educators new techniques to integrate social media and the teaching of literacy skills.
- Encourage educators to promote a classroom culture that uses various modalities to engage their students.
- Provide examples of how to engage and empower students in various grade levels with elements of social media and popular culture.

The main purpose and focus of this chapter is about recognizing that students are already exposed to language skills and literacy skills that are taught in their everyday lives when they interact with digital tools. It is about the language used and culture that is built in a classroom to reach students. It is about the connection of traditional learning and digital learning. This chapter is not about using social media and its associated apps in the classroom in isolation. This is not a "how to" on using social media to plan lessons. It is about integrating concepts and making connections to use as teaching strategies. This chapter does not exist simply to tell educators to use social media while teaching. It was written to demonstrate that social media's frameworks, purpose, and missions, align with literacy skills that are taught in classrooms.

BACKGROUND

Learning how to transform academic language into the language and culture of today's students is needed in a society that is growing more dynamic and digitally and diverse. Interaction, engagement, and relevance are key in sparking the interest of students. Schools and educators may find that they cannot compete with technology—but may learn to embrace what their students bring culturally, by changing their language, actions, planning, and strategies. Social media is the medium that shapes and shares popular culture. This is such, because, at one point in time, storytelling, reading novels or books, and print materials, such as newspapers and magazines, were the only ways that culture and news within communities were shared. Whether it be politics, music, fashion, art, or sports, with social media, the world now has access to what other societies are doing—and in many cases, in real-time.

Social media has taken over the daily lives of a large population of young people across the globe. Communication is frequently done through messaging apps, formulating thoughts using 280 characters or less, updating status updates with thoughts and feelings, and uploading videos and photos with companioning captions. This has become the norm. These are creative ways of expression and use many of the literacy skills educators use to teach in classrooms every day. However, because social media and popular culture is often focused on in negative aspects, it can be a forgotten language and tool left out of classrooms. Students employ skills such as summarization, paraphrasing, comparing and contrasting, inference, classification, and a variety of traditional literacy skills with the touch of a smart phone or computer, on a daily basis. Due to a disconnect between the classroom and home life, it is necessary to transform and merge academic language with the language and culture of today's students.

Becoming literate involves many skills developed over time, and many of today's students are left disengaged by the direction in which their literacy journey heads once they reach the middle grades in school, or in many cases, before they leave elementary school (Clark, et. al., (2014); Eccles et al., 1991;

Simmons & Blyth, 1987). Engagement in literacy practices and skills taught need a change as they relate to classroom teaching practices. Approximately 25% of teens are online "almost constantly" (Lenhart et al.,, 2015) due to having a smartphone. Students in elementary grades are taught to appreciate literacy through incentive programs—such as computer applications, free food vouchers, class parties, and other enticing things. Later, the level of expectations are raised, and students are expected to take their "fun" journey into an academic world that does not show them how to translate the skills they learned in the past, and extend their knowledge.

Incorporating popular culture shows students that an educator is trying reach out to make a connection, engage, and learn, about their preferences and preferred methods of learning. "Showing children that we see and value all aspects of them—including attributes related to race and culture—is a critical step in helping them feel welcome and connected to their teachers and peers" (Wanless & Crawford, 2016, p. 9). Using technology and using social media are a part of a culture that is often ignored or viewed as useless by educators, but valued by the students that they serve. According to Bolkan (2015), it was found that nine out of ten teachers don't use social media for classroom use, and "Only 44 percent of teachers surveyed said that social media can enhance a student's educational experience" (Bolkan, 2015, p. 1). Due to technology being more prevalent now more than ever, it is likely that educators will have success if they can create an environment where technology is the norm. Incorporating technology does not mean to solely use technology with students, and then they will understand every benchmark and standard they are asked to learn. The effort must be made to meet students halfway and learn to transcend and extend their learning beyond the walls of the classroom.

Benefits and Disadvantages of Using Social Media

Social media often gets "hits" that go viral (widely shared and popular) that range from being positive, comical, inspirational, or offensive. There are those who refuse to use social media, and those who crave the offerings of social media. It is a world that seeks to reflect and broadcast reality, and a world that allows its users to create their own narrative. Researchers such as Hemsley, Jacobson, Gruzd, and Mai (2018), Hou, Xiong, Jiang, Song, & Wang (2019), and Uhls, Ellison, and Subrahmanyam (2017), weigh the benefits of social media in their research. For students and children, social media can be an escape, as well as a non-safe space.

Some perspectives on school-aged children and social media usage as it relates to the benefits and disadvantages:

- **Benefits of Social Media Usage Among Children and Adolescents**
  - Gives access to varying perspectives and cross-cultural exposure
  - Provides comfort and convenience of using technology
  - Gives The ability to freely and creatively express their own voice
  - Gives students the ability touse multimodal ways to communicate
  - Provides appealing content to those with short attention spans
  - Provides opportunities to be a part of a shared culture
- **Disadvantages of Social Media Usage Among Children and Adolescents**
  - Online bullying
  - The risks of inappropriate, offensive, or explicit, content being shared
  - Inaccurate information being learned and spread to others

- ○ The possibility of becoming addicted or over usage
- ○ Potential self-esteem and body image issues due to false expectations created online
- ○ Lack of in-person socialization and personal interactions

It is hoped that the benefits of social media outweigh the disadvantages, but safeguards, such lessons and discussions on bullying prevention and reporting, finding credible and non-credible sources, as well as a plethora of lessons on formal and informal language in communications, need to be in place to share with students and children. The power of having such a resource to use for learning and interaction is beneficial, not just academically, but socially.

INTEGRATING SOCIAL MEDIA INTO THE LITERACY ENVIRONMENT

Traditional Academic Language and the Disconnect

When students enter school, the focus begins with building a literacy foundation. However, before many students ever set foot in a classroom, chances are they have encountered and used a tablet or a smartphone to play a game, use an app, watch a movie, or take part in some form of communication with family. Their experiences with language begin at home, and then they must make an effort to translate their knowledge into the traditional academic standards. Children as young as two years old are able "swipe left" (on phone or computer screens), but the act of literacy and language learning varies from child to child, and their environment and demographics often play a factor in how well they will comprehend the skills needed to be fluent in English language skills. Javaeed, Kibria, Khan, & Ghauri (2020) state that, "New technologies are outpacing the old techniques of education delivery. The 21st century-learner is reliant on new technologies to assist in their learning. Social media can be used to supplement traditional educational methods"(p. 54). The problem and disconnect often begins when the technology to which modern children are exposed and have to learn to manipulate before starting school is not built upon in the classroom when they attend school.

Students move from pre-emergent to early literacy stages, and then eventually the goal is to become fluent in reading, writing, listening, and speaking. As students get older, their exposure to language within and outside of the classroom begins to increase. The literacy skills that students build in an academic sense serves as a foundation and a gateway to other content areas. However, a disconnect between real-world and real-life experiences often cause students to be intimidated by learning traditional English skills that are taught in the classroom. The grammar and conventions that go along with the classroom learning process begin to tell students that the language in which they speak at home is not as valuable or respected.

Being in tune with students' interests and making efforts to embrace and integrate popular culture into instruction comes with its challenges. Not being familiar with technology or social media could cause educators to not be as relevant and engaging. The population that has grown up with social media is used to getting "notifications" which may be seen as a huge distraction by some. Although being notified in a classroom is a distraction, it is also a definite sign that conversations and interactions are taking place—it's just simply conversations and interactions students deem as important.

Social Media's Impact and Influence

Social media does not always get mentioned in a positive light, nor does it get mentioned very often with literacy learning. Internet usage and social media is frequently the culprit of bullying attacks, or often it is the source of comments that are offensive or misinterpreted. And, although students have more technology than ever before, at times students are somewhat limited in how they use the technology that is available—often solely resort to using technology for gaming or social media. There is a gap that exists—which doesn't allow students to fully apply the skills that they are learning, and it is a gap that that could be narrowed with the implementation of social media and popular culture being integrated into literacy learning. In regard to the effects of social media on American students, "A plurality of teens (45%) believes social media has neither a positive nor negative effect on people their age. Meanwhile, roughly 3 in 10 teens (31%) say social media has had a mostly positive impact, while 24% describe its effect as mostly negative." (Anderson & Jiang, 2018, p. 4) The students themselves may have varying opinions about social media, but its influence cannot be denied.

Sites such as Snapchat, YouTube, and Instagram are the most popular among teens today (Anderson & Jiang, 2018). Social media sites allow students to learn and be exposed to a variety of topics and audiences. They provide a platform for anyone with an account to teach, report, and influence. In fact, there are some young "influencers" on sites such as YouTube, who are making over seven figures just by posting videos (Berg, 2019).. If "influencers" can get students engaged enough to be regular viewers, it is possible that educators should look into using some of their strategies to integrate into their lessons in order to engage students. Social media influencers and content creators seek to create content that is:

- Targeted towards a specific audience
- Catchy or engaging to their audience
- Structured with consistent and targeted major points or ideas they want to push
- Relevant

With teaching and learning, educators should seek to implement these same traits when planning their instruction. The connection of traits and skills used in relation to social media and technology use versus those used in a literacy classroom setting are a pair that undeniably will get students to make connections between their classroom learning and everyday life. However, it is up to educators to be willing to take the risk and make the effort to blend students' social learning experiences with their classroom experience.

How to Implement Social Media Into Literacy Classroom Environments

Relevance and Translating the Language

In a society in which high-stakes testing requirements and assessment-driven curriculum is often the driving force, room for creativity in curriculum is often stifled. Educators find that they have to know how to connect the language and skills that they are required to teach--due to local, state, and national standards and in turn be culturally responsive to their students' academic, social, and emotional needs. "Educational policy and curriculum documents have not yet adapted to changes that have occurred with the range of digital media that are becoming embedded in people's lives" (Walsh, 2010, p. 212). Social media is major part of the culture of today's students, and it provides a significant source of news and an outlet of expression.

"Literacy practices are the general cultural ways of utilizing written language, which people draw upon in their lives. In the simplest sense, literacy practices are what people do with literacy" (Barton, Hamilton, & Ivanic, 2000, p. 7). There are ways (See Table 1) to provide a classroom experience that is relevant and engaging. It starts with understanding how elements of social media and popular culture parallel what is being taught in classrooms that focus on local school district and state standards, the Common Core State Standards, and even pulling from guidelines set and resources recommended by national and international organizations, such as the International Literacy Association (ILA), who created specific "Standards for Reading Professionals" (International Literacy Association, 2010) updated and released in 2018. Standard 1 Foundational Knowledge, highlights the importance of understanding major theories of teaching reading and writing and creating learning environments that motivate students to read and write. Standard 2 Curriculum and Instruction, discusses the need to teach from a curriculum that is balanced and integrated, as well as use a collection of traditional print and digital resources that introduce students to an assortment of genres, perspectives, and forms of media that reflect the 21st century.

Table 1. Social media and its literacy connections

Literacy Skill	Apps/Applications/Technology	Literacy Connections to Social Media
Summarizing or Paraphrasing	Twitter, Texts	280 characters on Twitter in which word usage is limited; Texts (creation of acronyms and "stems" to communicate)
Inferring	Instagram; Twitter	Inferring photos or tweets and their accompanying captions
Visualization	Instagram, TikTok, YouTube, Snapchat	All apps provide a means to plan and demonstrate a "theme" of a story or idea.
Sequencing	YouTube, Snapchat, Vlogs (any video platform)	"How To" videos- Create steps to complete a task; Option to tell stories or give directions
Main Idea & Details	YouTube, Snapchat, Vlogs (any video platform)	Developing a plot or theme within a video or event captured
Classification	Facebook, Instagram, Twitter	Using Hashtags, Facebook groups
Mood/Tone	Facebook	Asks for a "status update" or what is on the mind of the user.

In the time that students spend daily on social media, they are using some basic and some advanced literacy skills in which they begin learning early in the classroom setting. For example, when students learn to read, they commonly learn to become more fluent in their literacy journeys through educators teaching lessons that reinforce the Five Pillars of Literacy (National Reading Panel, 2000). These "five pillars" (Comprehension, Phonics, Phonemic Awareness, Fluency, and Vocabulary) create a foundation that later helps students to apply their skills. However, smartphone technology, social media, and apps, have potentially created ways to get users to be comfortable with displaying communication skills—as it is not being assessed, nor does the convenience of an app make it seem like too much effort.

"Literacy practices are as fluid, dynamic, and changing, as are the lives and societies of which they are a part" (Barton, Hamilton & Ivanic 2000, p. 13). As literacies develop, and new forms are being invented, it is the expectation that classroom educators keep up with the changes. Literacy learning (traditional academic literacy, in particular) has been known to have "…connections to power, to social identity, and to ideologies, often in the service of privileging certain types of literacy and certain types of people" (Gee, 1990, p. 67), with a nation of classrooms that are growing more diverse by the day. Whether the student populations are varying in race or ethnicity, wealthy or underprivileged, urban or rural, the challenges of inequities, due to a lack of resources, access (Gee, 2013), or a lack of support at home, can be achieved by differentiation of curriculum and implementing multimodal teaching and learning practices within literacy instruction and the building of students' literacy foundation.

Multimodal learning represents addressing and using two different modes of learning—visual and verbal (Paivio, 1986). In the early 2000s, social media first began to surface. It was primarily for socialization and networking for specialty groups (i.e. colleges, dating, and talent/career). Social media has evolved and is now utilized for communication and as a platform to express, showcase, and become its own culture. It is not just another tool for communication; it is *the* form of communication for younger generations (Wood, Bukowski, & Lis, 2015). Social media allows users to learn using various modes—visually, verbally, listening, and comprehending. It is a form of culture and communication that sparks the interest of its users by making their experience personal, and allowing them to share their own perspectives, as well as view others (Badri, Al-nuaimi, Yang & Rashedi, 2017). With apps that are video focused, some chat focused, and others game focused—social media is a multimodal learning experience. How do educators embody that same energy and level of engagement in their classrooms? They do so by getting connected and integrating the positive concepts of those within the social media culture (Giunta, 2017; Bourke, 2019).

SOCIAL MEDIA AND EARLY LITERACY

When students are in the early stages of literacy learning, they range in grade levels from Pre-Kindergarten to the end of their first-grade year. Within this grade-level range, children are not usually expected to be engaged in using social media inside or outside of the classroom. However, this is a time in which students should be getting experiences being taught using multimodal methods that include using technology as tools to learning. At this age, many students have heard of social media and know how to use Smartphones and tablets. Time should be spent modeling ways that students can use technology to learn—and to instill in them what digital literacies are. Students at this age will be exposed to games and apps to help them learn, but the focus should be to motivating students to become more independent in their technology use beyond playing games.

When developing early literacy skills, the knowledge base among students will vary due to their exposure to literacy skills in their home lives prior to attending school in a formal education setting. This is a crucial point in a student's life that can impact that student's entire educational career. The challenging task to develop new skill sets in students on their journeys to becoming fluent and literate, is complex, and will vary within learning environments and be different depending on the social and behavioral schemas of each student. In the primary grades, the National Reading Panel's (2000) "five pillars" (Fluency, Comprehension, Phonics, Phonemic Awareness, and Vocabulary) become a part of instruction, and is in full swing until students begin to reach fluent levels of reading, writing, listening, and speaking.

Since early literacy learners have so much to learn and have shorter attention spans, there should be significant thought that goes into the planning of lessons and resources. In early childhood education settings, at this stage of academic and literacy development, effective teachers should seek to offer "cognitively stimulating and emotionally supportive interactions" (Hamre, Partee, & Mulcahy, 2017, p. 1). Authentic and relevant experiences are routinely needed to provide a means to engage and inform instruction. Illustrations and visuals (which are heavily used with social media and apps) are a part of teaching letters, vocabulary, and comprehension. Writing is often developed with prompts and response journals. Some examples of how educators can use technology to enhance reflective response journals, stories, and writing prompts, to get students on track to being competent in exploring technology to meet their literacy goals:

- **Making Reflection Journals using *Adobe Spark Video***: Create reflection journals based off of work that has been shared or read in class. The students can also use this resource to create their own writing and accompanying visuals. They can then record their voices to explain or narrate their work and compile it all into a video using the app/website (Adobe Spark, 2020).
- **Creating Stories using *Scribble Press***: Rather than having the students use physical journals, the *Scribble Press* app was made to specifically allow students to write and illustrate their own stories. So, even if student has trouble writing, they can draw their desired narrative (Scribble Press, 2020).
- **Responding to Prompts using *Formative***: The website *Formative*, allows for educators to communicate in real-time, and could be used as a whole group or small group activity. With early literacy learners, this website could be used to answer short writing prompts (even just one sentence or phrase) (Formative, 2020).

Table 2. Apps and resources for primary learners

Apps, Activities, or Resources for Primary Literacy Learners	
Pillar of Literacy	**Resource/Activity**
Comprehension	– Promote reading of ebooks using sites like tumblebooklibrary.com and https://www.storylineonline.net
Fluency	– Use of running record apps (*Record of Reading* App). This is ideal for teacher use.
Phonics	– *Abcmmouse.com 's Early Learning Academy* App – *Articulation Station* App
Phonemic Awareness	– *Partners in Rhyme* App – *Phonemic Bubbles* App
Vocabulary	– *Padlet:* Create classroom (or small group) Word Walls using the *Padlet* App or website. This can be student created or teacher created. Helpful for students, teachers, and parents to interact with and refer to key vocabulary. Easily accessible on a tablet or laptop. – Vocabulary Spelling City

Students at the primary level are exposed to many opportunities to share their knowledge of the books they have read verbally, with an audience. Whether it is through book reports, book talks, or shared reading experiences, apps and websites, such as Flipgrid, iMovie, or Windows Movie Maker, the students are able to work on comprehension and speech. "Children who are routinely read to day in and day out—and immersed in rich talk about books and the various activities in which they are engaged—thrive. And those children with less exposure to books face tougher learning challenges in school and beyond"

(Scholastic, 2013, p. 9; Campbell et al., 2002; Dickinson, McCabe, & Essex, 2006; Neuman & Celano, 2006). Not only is it important to develop oral language with students, but also having discussions should lead to better comprehension (of text, key vocabulary, plot, and sequence of events). By giving emergent students digital tools to aid in conversations about reading that has taken place and literacy skills that are being learned, students are given the green light to be more independent and confident in their literacy journey overall. Table 2. shows resources that help teach early and emergent literacy learners in all areas of the five pillars of literacy.

SOCIAL MEDIA IN MIDDLE AND SECONDARY LITERACY CLASSROOMS

Relevance and real-life experiences are beneficial when working with and teaching fluent literacy learners. As students get older, more specific comparisons need to be made between concepts introduced in the literacy classroom and the students' own schema and prior knowledge, becomes a priority to implement. The applications of skills that have been taught over the elementary years become tested as students grow in their abilities. Being that *"…more than 9 out of 10 teenagers have a social media account" (Benmar, 2015, p. 22), the most logical method of making an effort to connect literacy curriculum to events in students' lives would be to use social media* terminology and the popular culture that surrounds it.

Students need exposure to classroom teaching practices that provide "…continuity between the rich contexts of home and school literacy practices" (Neuman & Roskos, 1997, p. 31). Students spend a substantial amount of time being connected online. Approximately 45% of students in the U.S. say that they are online "almost constantly" (Anderson & Jiang, 2018), and this has increased almost double from a few years ago (2014), at which time 24% of students reported their online usage as being "almost constantly. This shows that students and their engagement with technology are not likely going to decrease. If educators know that technology, social media, and online usage are what students are connected to, it is only fair to get "connected" academically with students a similar manner.

In the primary grades, literacy curriculum is largely composed of hands on activities that give students the ability to engage with their teachers in rich conversations (during small group instruction). There is also a push to promote family literacy within their environments outside of school. In the middle and secondary grades, this engagement declines—as students are thought to be fluent in their literacy skills and require more independence. It is during these years (Middle grades), that the cracks in students' literacy foundation begins to show, and it is at this age in which no one is no longer promoting the importance and need to engage with new texts and types of literacy. At this point, students often see reading and writing as a means to be assessed, and not a means to learn and explore new topics or knowledge.

Educators of students in grades 6 through 12 must be willing to be literacy "influencers" in their classrooms. Himmele and Himmele (2009) noted that, "For teachers to increase exposure to academic language, it's important that they develop a mind-set in which they see almost any verbal interaction as an opportunity for developing academic language" (para. 2). They can reach their students by knowing the power that they hold in further extending a student's literacy skills—it will impact all subjects and academic interactions, if done properly. The proper way is to merge the social culture with academia and give students the opportunity to see that the importance and relevance of their experiences outside of the classroom as having an impact inside the classroom. Table 3 details four components of literacy (reading, writing, listening, speaking) and social media apps or technology that use the indicated skills

Table 3. Four components of literacy in relation to social media

Social Media Apps and Technological Devices that use Literacy Skills	
Reading • Facebook (status updates and chats) • Twitter (tweets, news, hashtags, chats) • Instagram (captions, hashtags, Stories) • Snapchat (stories, chat) • Tumblr (blog posts, reactions) • Blogs (articles, blog, blog feedback) • Smartphones/texting (texts, acronyms, emoji) • Scribd (book clubs) • Goodreads (book clubs, tracking reading) • Wattpad (stories, writing series, anthologies)	**Writing** • Facebook (status updates and chats) • Twitter (tweets, hashtags, chats) • Instagram (captions, hashtags, Stories) • Snapchat (chat) • Tumblr (blog posts, reactions) • Blogs (articles, blog, blog feedback) • Smartphones/Texting (texts, acronyms, emoji) • Wattpad (stories, writing series, anthologies) • YouTube (content and scripts)
Listening • Facebook (creating videos and Facebook Live) • Twitter (videos, live events) • Instagram (videos, stories) • Snapchat (stories) • Smartphones (recording info to playback; FaceTime, video chat) • YouTube (watching videos) • Audible (listening to books) • Spotify (podcasts, music • Apple (music and Apple podcasts/radio shows) • Tidal (music, videos, video series) • Pandora (music)	**Speaking** • Facebook (creating videos and Facebook live) • Instagram (creating videos and stories) • Snapchat (stories) • Smartphones (voice texts; FaceTime, video chat) • YouTube (creating videos) • WhatsApp (voice messages and video)

Table 3 shows the connections that literacy skills have to social media. In reviewing the table, one can see that there is a diverse range of skills and platforms shared. The table even shows emojis as a form of written communication—it technically is a written language, in the sense that it is represented by symbols that have meaning (and in many cases, more than one meaning). One thing to keep in mind is that not all apps represented on the chart (Table 3) are "popular," and some have their own sub-culture (Dupont, 2020) of followers. Some sites also have their negatives sides (as with most social media platforms) and have not always been beneficial to pre-teens and teens (Baccarella, Wagner, Kietzmann, & McCarthy, I, 2018). However, this chart serves as guide and proof that students are engaging in the subjects and skills that are being taught in academic settings.

How can students' language, culture, and schema within their social lives be translated and merged into the use of academic language? Cope and Kalantzis (2009) suggest creating "…a map of the range of pedagogical moves that may prompt teachers to extend their pedagogical repertoires" (p. 186). This map consists of "experiencing," "conceptualizing," "analyzing," and "applying" (pp. 185-186). As it relates to social media and popular culture, perhaps trying to experience students and learn about who they are and what they bring is a good first step for educators. Learning about students' preferences, interactions, and about the genres and topics that interest them will allow for conceptualization about what students already use versus what needs to be introduced. The last two steps become complicated, because not only do educators need to be able to analyze and breakdown concepts in terms that are student friendly, but they also need to be able to teach students how to apply and make connections to the knowledge gained. This is difficult, because students have been told for so long that social media and popular culture have no value inside school, and to try to open minds and see that traditional literacy and its influence is all around, is going in a totally opposite direction.

A few examples of how terminology from social media can be used to describe and enhance the design of traditional literacy assignments:

- **Twitter Connection**: (summaries and paraphrasing) Twitter has elements that mirror several reading and writing skills that are traditionally taught in English Language Arts classrooms. Twitter allows its users to create messages that are up to 280 characters in length.
  - When teaching students to write summaries, they are usually directed to keep their summaries concise and to the point and highlight key points from a piece that they have been presented.
  - Paraphrasing is also a skill that Twitter requires (due to character limitations). In a traditional literacy classroom, paraphrasing is used when teaching students to take notes, as well as when completing research.
- **Instagram Link**: (captions and hashtags) Instagram was originally created to upload photos with a caption to accompany to the photo. As user demands changed, the app allowed for short videos to be shared with the audience of "followers."
  - Captions are a part literacy learning early on, when learning concepts of print and parts of a book. However, it is important to continue to read and interpret captions in order to make sense of visuals. Students encounter captions with every Instagram post, and can make comments based off captions.
  - Users can interact and find other photos with similar topics of interest or locations by using hashtags with their photos. A hashtag serves the purpose of cataloguing and creating a sense of organization. It is very similar to how an index in a book is organized, or how research topics are organized into specific journals.
- **YouTube Videos**: (genre) YouTube is a place to upload and share videos, music, vlogs, and lessons (teaching). What makes the platform unique is that some of the content is heavily edited, and other content is rough and raw footage. That realness or ability to make it appear real is what attracts many young people to vloggers (who often have millions of followers), and the latest updates on music, fashion, sports, etc. It is almost as if it is its own television network that people do not have to audition for. Because of the variety that YouTube offers, the easiest literary element to compare YouTube's platform to is the variety of genres of books and literature that is available. It also incorporates several key literary elements, such as visuals, listening, speaking, and writing/organizing of content (YouTube, 2020).
- **Snapchat**: (storytelling and plots) Snapchat is meant to be a quick way to capture and communicate what are called "stories" and to share them with an audience. Shared experiences in reading and writing are done regularly at the primary level, but this does not always happen in the middle and secondary grades. However, students gain experience using the same skills as they did in the primary grades using Snapchat. The "stories" are usually created about a user's day, or experiences at an event or location (concerts, shopping, school, etc.). Just as users of Snapchat can share sequential events using their cameras and captions, students are told in classrooms to read and give details about plots, settings, and be able to recall themes and the order of events in their classrooms (Snapchat, 2020).
- **Tik Tok**: (sequence and order) Tik Tok is a social media app that allows users to do comedy and lip sync videos and has gained popularity with users due to "challenges" (competitions). The contents of the videos involve movement and dance sequences that are uploaded to the platform.

Although this app requires movement, and it does not necessarily have words, reading, writing, or even speaking, it creates excitement and discussion among teens and users. The movement that is involved requires memorization of choreography, and the videos also address themes. Theme, mood, and tone, are key elements that fluent literacy learners are encouraged to explore in reading and writing within their own skills and abilities, as well as other authors Tik Tok, 2020).

Middle grades and secondary students have exposure to literacy skills, but some fail to see that they are using the very skills they learn in their English/Language Arts class in their social actions—and that is because they have been told to disconnect. The ability is there, but the connection between the two environments must be made. Students in this area in their academic career are still impressionable. Educators have the ability and tools necessary to change the narrative with middle grades and secondary level students.

SOLUTIONS AND RECOMMENDATIONS

Speaking the Same Language

Connecting academic language used in the classroom and social language used in everyday life is possible. Merging these (academic language and social-cultural language) two languages together in the literacy classroom is essential to engage and make learning meaningful. In order to begin to speak the same language as their students, educators should work toward the following goals:

- Learn the culture of students and build relationships that promote independence and personalization in the literacy environment.
- Use multimodal approaches to teach traditional literacy skills in the classroom.
- Further incorporate and introduce various types of digital literacies into the literacy environment.

To begin to make progress towards integrating social media and popular culture into the classroom, educators should analyze their teaching practices and make efforts to connect in ways that students least expect. Media is a form of communication—from the music students listen to, the games which they play, and the platforms that students use to interact—language is weaved throughout. Knowing students' backgrounds (cultural, demographic, academic history etc.) allows teachers to customize instruction to fit their needs. In some students' communities, sports, clothing, and television shows are they topics of conversation in their homes and with their friends. Popular culture determines the language, which often is separated by race, age, or socioeconomic status. The explanations and language used with a student in a rural classroom setting will differ than that of the needs of a student in an urban educational setting. Yet although their surroundings might be different, the manner in which they develop their values and significance of what they see as important is the same—exposure, representation, and access are key. How do teachers know what to teach? How should they make informed decisions about the language and connections to be used when teaching and planning? The following are a few questions that should be considered when determining the culture of what matters and currently impacts students as it relates to social media and popular culture:

Changing the Language: Social Media and Popular Culture Quiz

How well do you know the world in which your students are currently immersed? Answer the following questions to see how much you know:

1. What popular albums were released this week on major music platforms (Apple Music, Spotify, Google Play, Tidal, etc.)?
2. Can you name a current artist in Billboard 100's Top Ten Songs?
3. Which major social media platform allows for students to send messages, photos, and videos, and the contents delete within 24 hours?
4. Which social media platform allows for users to summarize their feelings, thoughts, or opinions in 280 characters?
5. What is the popular online game that is about placing blocks and going on adventures?
6. What are the latest dances/social media challenges within the last six months?

If the answers to the above questions were foreign, that is not by mistake—the quiz was created to show just how culturally distant educators can sometimes be from their students. Methods need to be in place to wake students up and challenge them--studying and applying their interests to the content and resources presented in the classroom is a start. Student voice, motivation, and engagement are essential when teaching literacy skills (Ng, 2018; Wanless & Crawford, 2016). Although language and skills that are used in classrooms by educators appear to be different than what is used in students' social realms, there are numerous commonalties and connections (Greenhow & Gleason, 2012) to traditional literacy curriculums. There are ways to bring the two together. The following list includes ways to motivate students in the area of literacy as it relates to technology and social media:

- *Ensure that classroom lessons utilize technology for teaching tools and as research and learning tools*. This should be the case for formal and informal learning opportunities.
- *Make comparisons to social media and popular culture's link to traditional literacy skills in lesson explanations*. Include the vocabulary interchangeably on assignments and use graphic organizers or class discussions to disseminate between traditional literacies and digital literacies.
- *Assign tasks that allow students to have and make choices*. Use the technologies as a creation tool to write and create new pieces of writing.
- *Designate time to learn technology tools for learning purposes (and not gaming)*. Have students used flipped learning techniques or take the time to use social media as a means to learn about sources (primary, secondary, etc.) and fair use.
- *Create word walls that have academic vocabulary and traditional literacy vocabulary*, as well as create a separate word wall that includes invented spellings, acronyms, appropriate slang, and terms coined by social media or popular culture.

Even with goals and a list of suggested activities, one still might inquire, "What does a social media/ pop culture infused "translated" class look like?" (Translated, refers to the effort to merge the language of popular culture and social media into a traditional literacy classroom experience) A translated class would consider these questions and answers:

- How can you incorporate <u>social media</u> into the learning of traditional literacy skills?
  - ○ Facebook: Use the application as a teaching tool (FB groups); Use the terminology (Status Updates = Authors Purpose, Summary, Point of View) (Facebook, 2020).
  - ○ Twitter: Use the application as a communication tool; Use the terminology (Hashtags are similar to Classification of Genres, Topics); Research (Sources, Credible and non-creditable sources)
  - ○ Instagram: Use the application as a tool (Communication, sharing resources); Use the terminology (Captions are an important part of reading—helps with summary and generalizations; Timeline or Profile- Chronological order, Theme) (Instagram, 2020)
- How can you incorporate <u>movies</u> or <u>television</u>?
  - ○ Use the following as teaching tools to connect with students: Movies, Commercials, TV shows, News, Documentaries/Series. Explore: Plot, setting, comparison and contrast, theme, main idea, gist, genres, imagery, chronological order, sources (primary and secondary, credible and non-credible), Facts/Opinions.
- How can you incorporate <u>music</u>?
  - ○ Music is a form of creative expression (with or without lyrics) …so is writing! *Explore*: Lyrics, Genres, Themes, Tone/Mood, Story, Comprehension, vocabulary choices in songs, and similes/metaphors.
- How can you incorporate <u>sports</u>?
  - ○ Theme, uniformity, and collaboration are key in sports. Rules and order are also necessary. Explore sports when teaching writing and text structure: Reading genres and themes, Rules ("How To" writing and chronological order, timelines).
- How can you incorporate <u>fashion</u>?
  - ○ Use literary terms related to fashion: Mood/Tone, persuasion, characteristics, expression, visuals, imagery, descriptive.
- How can you incorporate <u>slang</u> or <u>inventive language</u>?
  - ○ Have students create a listing/word wall of words that *they* use. Pair it next to their academic vocabulary words.
  - ○ Use slang terms or inventive words to help students understand the makeup and origin of words (Prefixes, suffixes, root/base words).
  - ○ Explore acronyms (Note: WYD and LOL are not the only acronyms around. There are many academic terms that are acronyms DNA, RADAR, LASER, etc.).

FUTURE RESEARCH DIRECTIONS

More conversations need to be had over the need to continue to develop additional frameworks and models of literacy education that are student-centered, purposeful, and innovative. Action should be taken to move beyond the process of sharing with students "how to read" (although very important) and share the value of "why to read." Students are comfortable with using technology (for socialization and entertainment), but have not yet mastered the art of merging technology (Johnson, Jacovina, Russell & Soto, 2016) with gaining academic knowledge in the area of literacy. Potential topics of research and recommendations for support should include but are not limited to:

Using social media for ideas and implementation of literacy education. Students need to know that using the Internet and having access to the world is powerful. Educators need to know that using social media can be an asset to them—as it opens their world to more teaching ideas and a wider network of colleagues. Examples of this would include the creation curriculums that implement technology tools and social media, as well as continued and updated information on access that students have to social media and their usage in various populations and demographics.

Digital literacies and their impact on literacy assessment. Long-term studies and studies with English language learners are needed, -- this is a population that is increasing as the country grows more and more diverse, and with mediums such as music, television, and visuals being important for ELL's literacy development it is only a matter of time that studies be done on social media's impact on language learners.

More training for educators on social media and apps. School districts, consultants, and even publishing companies (textbooks) should work toward training for how to use technology as a tool to teach. Not only is, training for educators to be more comfortable needed, but also providing training to show educators how to empower students to use technology is needed. Trainings currently show educators the benefits of how technology tools (apps, devices, or websites) will make the students respond, but they often lack the direction to enable teachers to feel safe in having students demonstrate knowledge in using these technologies.

Using social media to strengthen parent involvement. Parents often do not have time to devote to physical conferences, and they might be struggling with how to help their children. Social media and technology provide quick access to an educator's resources, and is a way to involve parents in genuine conversations about their child's learning and what is required in the classroom. If a parent sees an educator making the effort to find alternative ways to stay in communication, the respect builds, and hopefully parents will become more empowered to help their children. More research should be done on how many parents use social media, as well as more apps related to parent support and at home education should be developed.

Access and availability to literacy resources (books, videos, news, resources, classes, and webinars) via social media. More studies should be done on literacy access in the U.S. and around the world for marginalized groups, and various demographics to determine how books, resources, and help is needed and received in different areas of the country, as well as the reach to different populations (rural, urban, suburban).

Teaching students to use social media to learn about social justice and teaching students to find their voice though social media. Stimulation and participation in the classroom environment is important (Taylor & Parsons, 2011)—students should not come to school and class only to learn skills and strategies. The goal should be for them is to eventually leave with a set of beliefs that will shape their future and impact their current environment. Teaching students to write gives them a voice but teaching them to share their writing gives them and audience. If we begin to do more research and projects in which students share their voices using social media and technology, the long-term benefits could greatly change society and the way we view education.

Future research should support teaching practices that allow younger learners to understand the benefits of having and using technology to gain knowledge and grow in their abilities. Most importantly, more support should be given to educators to provide engaging and empowering curriculum though grants for action research and partnerships with educational technology companies.

CONCLUSION

To address academic slumps beginning as early as third and fourth grade (Chall, 1983, 1996), and the lack of interest in reading and literacy, educators should explore avenues such as using a deeper integration of technology, social media, and popular culture to parallel and express traditional academic language. Many students are left disengaged by the direction in which their academic literacy journey heads once they reach the middle grades or, in many cases, before they leave elementary school. Though these students might become more disengaged from their academic literacy journey, they are not totally disengaged from literacy interactions altogether.

Social media and popular culture are forgotten languages and are often not used to their full potential in our nation's classrooms—when in fact, these are creative ways of expression and ideas, and use many of the literacy skills taught in classrooms every day.

This chapter addressed traditional literacy terms and skills and intertwined them with technology and social media-based lessons and tasks that integrate and demonstrate the language that students speak today. "We know that the nature of literacy has changed in the digital age, but unfortunately, we do not have decades to catch up to this change" (Hicks & Turner, 2013). Social media is now the cultural medium through which shared values, attitudes, norms, beliefs, and knowledge, are transmitted to the participants of the culture. Social media is the standard, and all other forms of communications only reinforce what is transmitted through social media.

Students often begin their literacy journeys with the hope that they will learn to read, and they are content with that. Over the course of their education, that contentment and spark of hope seemingly fades when personalization of instruction and creativity in lessons ceases. Assessments are frequently taking the place of discussions and talks about text in classrooms and, in many cases, the only time in which students are having discussions about what they read is about what they read on the Internet or social media.

Incorporating social media and merging the literary elements that are traditionally taught in ELA/ELAR classrooms does not mean that all challenges will disappear. Creating a social media account, using associated terminology, and then expecting students to automatically flourish and understand every academic standard is not the end all to getting students to be engaged and accepting of the content being taught (Childs, 2018). Traditional aspects of literacy learning are not to be forgotten or devalued. Social media integration is just one tool that, if used and integrated effectively, can be an instrumental way for educators to connect with students. Educators cannot compete with the important components of what makes up their students' schema—such as popular culture and technology use. "If we truly desire to teach to transform, we must be able to promote and sustain both agency and advocacy" (Samuels, 2018, p. 29). It is essential to learn to translate students' language to reflect the culture of their ever-changing population of students—this starts with the ability to connect and evolve, despite unfamiliarity. Sparking and maintaining students' interest in literacy takes creativity and a fire of ideas, which embers spread and reignite for a lifetime.

REFERENCES

Adobe Spark. (n.d.). https://spark.adobe.com/make/video-maker/

Anderson, M., & Jiang, J. (2018). Teens, social media & technology 2018. *Pew Research Center, 31,* 2018.

Baccarella, C., Wagner, T., Kietzmann, J., & McCarthy, I. P. (2018). Social Media? It's Serious!: Understanding the Dark Side of Social Media. *European Management Journal, 36*(4), 431–438. doi:10.1016/j.emj.2018.07.002

Badri, M., Al-nuaimi, A. H., Yang, G., & Rashedi, A. A. (2017). School performance, social networking effects, and learning of school children: Evidence of reciprocal relationships in Abu Dhabi. *Telematics and Informatics, 34*(8), 1433–1444. doi:10.1016/j.tele.2017.06.006

Barton, D., Hamilton, M., & Ivanic, R. (2005). The new literacy studies. In *Situated Literacies* (pp. 213–224). Routledge. doi:10.4324/9780203984963

Benmar, K. (2015). My favorite teachers use social media: A student perspective. *Journal of Education Week, 34*(28), 22–23.

Berg, M. (2019, December 18). The Highest-Paid YouTube Stars of 2019: The Kids Are Killing It. *Forbes,* 24–26. https://www.forbes.com/sites/maddieberg/2019/12/18/the-highest-paid-youtube-stars-of-2019-the-kids-are-killing-it/#2a36f62938cd

Bolkan, J. (2015, September 2). Research: 9 in 10 Teachers Don't Use Social Media in the Classroom. *The Journal.* https://thejournal.com/articles/2015/09/02/research-9-in-10-teachers-dont-use-social-media-in-the-classroom.aspx

Bourke, B. (2019). Connecting With Generation Z Through Social Media. In H. L. Schnackenberg & C. Johnson (Eds.), *Preparing the Higher Education Space for Gen Z* (pp. 124–147). IGI Global. doi:10.4018/978-1-5225-7763-8.ch007

Campbell, F. A., Ramey, C. T., Pungello, E., Sparling, J., & Miller-Johnson, S. (2002). Early childhood education: Young adult outcomes from the abecedarian project. *Applied Developmental Science, 6*(1), 42–57. doi:10.1207/S1532480XADS0601_05

Childs, K. (2018). Changing the language: Using popular culture and social media to teach traditional literacy skills. *Texas Association for Literacy Education Yearbook, Connections in the Community: Fostering Partnerships through. Literacy, 5,* 72–76.

Clark, D. M., Slate, J. R., Combs, J. P., & Moore, G. W. (2014). A conceptual analysis of grade span configurations for 6-8 and K-8 public schools. *Online Journal of New Horizons in Education, 4*(1), 1–24. Retrieved May 18, 2020 from https://www.tojned.net/journals/tojned/articles/v04i01/v04i01-01.pdf

Cope, B., & Kalantzis, M. (2009). "Multiliteracies": New Literacies, new learning. *Pedagogies, 4*(3), 164–195. doi:10.1080/15544800903076044

Dickinson, D. K., & Neuman, S. B. (2006). Cognitive and linguistic building blocks of early literacy. Handbook of Early Literacy Research, 2.

Dupont, T. (2020). Authentic Subcultural Identities and Social Media: American Skateboarders and Instagram. *Deviant Behavior, 5*(41), 649–664. doi:10.1080/01639625.2019.1585413

Eccles, J. S., Lord, S., & Midgley, C. (1991). What are we doing to early adolescents? The impact of educational contexts on early adolescents. *American Journal of Education*, *99*(4), 521–542. doi:10.1086/443996

Facebook. (n.d.). https://facebook.com

Formative. (n.d.). https://goformative.com/

Gee, J. P. (1990). *Social linguistics and literacies: Ideology in discourses*. Falmer Press.

Gee, J. P. (2013). *The Anti-Education Era: Creating Smarter Students Through Digital Learning*. Palgrave/Macmillan.

Giunta, C. (2017). An Emerging Awareness of Generation Z Students for Higher Education Professors. *Archives of Business Research*, *5*(4), 90–104. doi:10.14738/abr.54.2962

Greenhow, C., & Gleason, B. (2012). Twitteracy: Tweeting as a New Literacy Practice. *The Educational Forum*, *76*(4), 464–478. doi:10.1080/00131725.2012.709032

Hamre, B. K., Partee, A., & Mulcahy, C. (2017). Enhancing the Impact of Professional Development in the Context of Preschool Expansion. *AERA Open*, *1*(4). Advance online publication. doi:10.1177/2332858417733686

Hemsley, J., Jacobson, J., Gruzd, A., & Mai, P. (2018). Social media for social good or evil: An introduction. *Social Media+ Society, 4*(3).

Hicks, T., & Turner, K. (2013). No longer a luxury: Digital literacy can't wait. *English Journal*, *102*(6), 58–65.

Himmele, P., & Himmele, W. (2009). Increasing exposure to academic language by speaking it. *ASCD Express*. Retrieved February 22, 2020 from http://www.ascd.org/ascd-express/ vol5/505-himmele.aspx

Hou, Y., Xiong, D., Jiang, T., Song, L., & Wang, Q. (2019). Social media addiction: Its impact, mediation, and intervention. *Cyberpsychology (Brno)*, *13*(1). Advance online publication. doi:10.5817/CP2019-1-4

Instagram. (n.d.). https://instagram.com

International Literacy Association. (2010). *Standards for reading professionals—revised 2018*. Retrieved on April 24, 2020 from https://literacyworldwide.org/get-resources/standards/standards-for-reading-professionals

Javaeed, A., Kibria, Z., Khan, Z., & Ghauri, S. K. (2020). Impact of Social Media Integration in Teaching Methods on Exam Outcomes. *Advances in Medical Education and Practice*, *11*, 53–61. doi:10.2147/AMEP.S209123 PMID:32021544

Johnson, A. M., Jacovina, M. E., Russell, D. E., & Soto, C. M. (2016). Challenges and solutions when using technologies in the classroom. In S. A. Crossley & D. S. McNamara (Eds.), *Adaptive educational technologies for literacy instruction* (pp. 13–29). Taylor & Francis. doi:10.4324/9781315647500-2

Lenhart, A., Duggan, M., Perrin, A., Stepler, R., Rainie, H., & Parker, K. (2015). Teens, social media and technology overview 2015: Smartphones facilitate shifts in communication landscape for teens. Pew Research Center. *Science & Tech.* Retrieved from http://www. pewinternet. org/files/2015/04/PI_TeensandTech_Update2015_0409151.pdf

National Reading Panel. (2000). *Report of the National Reading Panel—Teaching Children to Read: An Evidence-Based Assessment of the Scientific Research Literature on Reading and Its Implications for Reading Instruction.* National Institute of Child Health and Human Development.

Neuman, S. B., & Celano, D. (2006). Access to print in low-income and middle-income communities: An ecological study of four neighborhoods. *Reading Research Quarterly, 36*(1), 8–26. doi:10.1598/ RRQ.36.1.1

Neuman, S. B., & Roskos, K. (1997). Literacy knowledge in practice: Contexts of participation for young writers. *Reading Research Quarterly, 32*(1), 10–32. doi:10.1598/RRQ.32.1.2

Ng, C. (2018). Using student voice to promote reading engagement for economically disadvantaged students. *Journal of Research in Reading, 41*(4), 700–715. doi:10.1111/1467-9817.12249

Paivio, A. (1986). *Mental representations: A dual coding approach.* Oxford University Press.

Samuels, A. J. (2018). Exploring Culturally Responsive Pedagogy: Teachers' Perspectives on Fostering Equitable and Inclusive Classrooms. *SRATE Journal, 27*(1).

Scholastic. (2013). *Early Literacy. Family and Community Engagement Research Compendium.* Retrieved on February 23, 2020 from http://teacher.scholastic.com/products/face/ pdf/research-compendium/ early-literacy.pdf

Scribble Press. (n.d.). https://app.scribblepress.com/

Simmons, R., & Blyth, D. (1987). *Moving into adolescence: The impact of pubertal changes and school context.* Aldine de Gruyter.

Snapchat. (n.d.). https://snapchat.com

Taylor, L., & Parsons, J. (2011). Improving Student Engagement. *Current Issues in Education (Tempe, Ariz.), 14*(1). http://cie.asu.edu/

TokT. (n.d.). https://tiktok.com

Uhls, Y. T., Ellison, N. B., & Subrahmanyam, K. (2017). Benefits and costs of social media in adolescence. *Pediatrics, 140*(Supplement 2), S67–S70. .2016-1758E doi:10.1542/peds

Walsh, M. (2010). Multimodal literacy: What does it mean for classroom practice? *Australian Journal of Language and Literacy, 33*(3), 211–239.

Wanless, S. B., & Crawford, P. A. (2016). Reading your way to a culturally responsive classroom. *YC Young Children, 71*(2), 8.

Wood, M. A., Bukowski, W. M., & Lis, E. (2016). The Digital Self: How Social Media Serves as a Setting that Shapes Youth's Emotional Experiences. *Adolescent Research Review*, *1*(2), 163–173. doi:10.100740894-015-0014-8

YouTube. (n.d.). https://youtube.com

ADDITIONAL READING

Barton, D., & Hamilton, M. (2012). *Local literacies: Reading and writing in one community*. Routledge.

Blaschke, L. M. (2014). Using social media to engage and develop the online learner in self-determined learning. *Research in Learning Technology*, *22*(1), 1–23. doi:10.3402/rlt.v22.21635

Cahill, M., & McGill-Franzen, A. (2013). Selecting 'app'ealing and 'app'ropriate book apps for beginning readers. *The Reading Teacher*, *67*(1), 30–39. doi:10.1002/TRTR.1190

Cambria, J., & Guthrie, J. T. (2010). Motivating and engaging students in reading. *The New England Reading Association Journal*, *46*(1), 16–29.

Cassidy, J., Valadez, C., & Garrett, S. (2010). Literacy Trends and Issues: A Look at the Five Pillars and the Cement That Supports Them. *The Reading Teacher*, *63*(8), 644–655. Retrieved February 22, 2020, from www.jstor.org/stable/25656175. doi:10.1598/RT.63.8.3

Chall, J. S. (1983). *Stages of reading development*. McGraw-Hill.

Chall, J. S. (1996). *Stages of reading development* (2nd ed.). Harcourt Brace.

Cobb, A. (2010). To differentiate or not to differentiate? Using internet-based technology in the classroom. *Quarterly Review of Distance Education*, *11*(1), 37–45.

Gee, J. P. (2003). What video games have to teach us about learning and literacy. *Computers in Entertainment*, *1*(1), 20–20. doi:10.1145/950566.950595

Gredler, M. E. (2004). Games and simulations and their relationships to learning. Handbook of research on educational communications and technology, 2, 571–582.

Hagood, M. C. (2012). Risks, rewards, and responsibilities of using new literacies in middle grades. *Voices from the Middle*, *19*(4), 10–16.

Ladson-Billings, G. (1995). But that's just good teaching! The case for culturally relevant pedagogy. *Theory into Practice*, *34*(3), 159–165. doi:10.1080/00405849509543675

Ladson-Billings, G. (1995). Toward a culturally relevant pedagogy. *American Educational Research Journal*, *32*(3), 465–491. doi:10.3102/00028312032003465

Low, R., & Sweller, J. (2005). The modality principle in multimedia learning. Cambridge handbook of multimedia learning, 147, 158).

Snow, C. E., Tabors, P. O., Nicholson, P. A., & Kurland, B. F. (1995). SHELL: Oral language and early literacy skills in kindergarten and first-grade children. *Journal of Research in Childhood Education*, *10*(1), 37–48. doi:10.1080/02568549509594686

KEY TERMS AND DEFINITIONS

App: Short for the word "application." An app is a technology program that is meant to perform a certain function, convenience, or service to a consumer or user.

Emoji: A pictorial symbol used in texting and apps to represent emotions, moods, and adjectives.

Five Pillars of Literacy: Comprehension, fluency, vocabulary, phonics, and phonemic awareness.

Hashtag: A symbol that is the pound sign that signifies a category in which the content is categorized under. The symbol is often used on social media to better find topics or areas of interest.

Literacy: Reading, writing, listening, and speaking skills that are pooled together to help a person communicate, interact, and comprehend.

Popular Culture: Elements such as music, media, fashion, sports, and social movements within the society or environment that influence and engage a major population or demographic of people.

Social Learning: Experiences that take place with students outside of the classroom in which they learn from their interactions within the culture that surrounds them (social media, environment, popular culture).

Social Media: Internet websites or smartphone/tablet applications that are created with various purposes for an intended audience (interaction, platform for creating and sharing art, music, writing, expression).

Traditional Academic Language: Language skills and vocabulary that are normally presented in the classroom that are a part of a curriculum that are used when referring to teach a particular subject area.

This research was previously published in Disciplinary Literacy Connections to Popular Culture in K-12 Settings; pages 292-312, copyright year 2021 by Information Science Reference (an imprint of IGI Global).

Chapter 35
Analysing WhatsApp and Instagram as Blended Learning Tools

Alberto Andujar
https://orcid.org/0000-0002-8865-9509
University of Almeria, Spain

ABSTRACT

This chapter explores, from a theoretical point of view, the literature investigating the use of WhatsApp and Instagram applications to foster language learning as well as the outcomes of the studies carried out in these two fields. The possibilities of these two apps to develop blended learning environments are also regarded. The theoretical frameworks in the existing literature for the possible implementation of these social networking tools in classroom contexts are considered. Findings indicate a growing number of studies making use of the WhatsApp application to develop either blended learning models or online tasks in foreign language courses while the research exploring the use of Instagram for language development remains very scarce.

INTRODUCTION

The constant growth of a globalized education model in which information and communication technology (ICT) becomes a fundamental element to carry out ubiquitous teaching and learning processes (Altbach, 2004) has involved changes at all levels. Specifically, at a university level, the need to catch up with the latest educational tools has transformed the learning environment to a context in which technology and in-class tuition coexist. This situation, which is relatively new, has led to the exploration of blended learning processes in which in-class tuition is combined with an online environment in which between 20% to 79% of course contents are delivered online (Arbaugh, 2014). Blended learning becomes a flexible and autonomous environment (Im & Kim, 2015) which need to be investigated from different points of view – technological, educational, and practical among others – in order to develop

DOI: 10.4018/978-1-6684-7123-4.ch035

the most appropriate learning environments to fulfill students' needs. In this context, most of the present literature exploring Computer-assisted Language Learning (CALL) or Mobile-assisted Language Learning (MALL) involves a certain degree of blended learning. The new online environments, in which students normally face a high cognitive load due to their exposure to discourse in a foreign language, have become a support during language learning, in many cases facilitating the learning process (Ball and Lindsay, 2013). Positive effects of this learning model have been found in previous literature (Miyazoe & Anderson, 2010; López-Pérez, Pérez-López & Rodríguez-Ariza, 2011; Law, Geng, & Li, 2019) and different factors such as higher participation or motivation levels and an increase in students' autonomy have been emphasized.

By contrast, it also seems necessary to understand the impact of certain tools in the development of blended learning models and how students' previous knowledge of that tool, the level of engagement generated or its accessibility may entail different outcomes during the development of blended learning processes. In this sense, this chapter will explore from a theoretical perspective, the potential of two of the most common social networking platforms among students, Instagram and WhatsApp. The reason behind this choice has to do with several theoretical and practical considerations. First, the outstanding number of users in each of the applications as of August 2019, WhatsApp with approximately 1.5 billion monthly active users and 1 billion daily active users, and Instagram with 1 billion monthly active users and 600 million daily active users (Stout, 2019). Second, theoretical considerations acknowledged by experts in the field such as Kukulska-Hulme and Shield (2007) who stated that student do not use technology they may consider intrusive or those technological tools and software which may require a long time to master. Thus, from a teacher perspective, it seems necessary to explore how the most used social networking platforms can be used to develop blended learning models and how the existing literature into the two applications can shape teacher practices and course design.

The third reason behind this choice is the growing amount of literature dealing with language learning and social networking platforms. These online environments, normally referred as 2.0 platforms and used for socializing, sharing information or meeting (Boyd, 2014), are visited by a great number of young people (Counts & Fisher, 2010; Dunn, 2013). Interestingly, although the majority of social media platforms have a web version, most of them are accessed from mobile devices (Global Digital Statistics, 2019). This fact needs to be taken into consideration by teachers and institutions willing to implement blended learning models through social networks. Apart from the fact that studies into language learning highlighted differences in students' behavior in computer and mobile environments (e.g. Andujar & Salaberri-Ramiro, 2019), the accessibility and ubiquity of mobile devices becomes a fundamental aspect to guarantee students' engagement during the learning process.

In this context, the chapter aims to shed light on the possibilities of WhatsApp and Instagram to develop blended learning models in which these two social networking platforms can foster language learning development. In order to tackle this aim, the existing literature in each of the two platforms together with researchers' insights for an appropriate implementation of these applications in language learning contexts will be explored.

SOCIAL NETWORKS AND LANGUAGE LEARNING

Social networks have been used in classroom environments since their appearance and for different learning purposes (Mao, 2014). From an early use of Wikis and Blogs (Seaman & Tinti-Kane, 2013) to the use of more widespread social networks such as Facebook, Linkedin, Wechat or WhatsApp among others, social networks have allowed students to interact through new different ways of communication (Mazer, Murphy & Simonds, 2007). This context seems particularly interesting from the language learning perspective as different modes of communication may foster different language abilities such as reading, speaking, listening or writing among others. Moreover, students' social network dependence becomes another factor which needs to be taken into consideration when selecting the best tools for developing blended learning models.

Before mentioning the most relevant studies in the field making use of the social networking platforms investigated in this chapter, it is worth mentioning the most widespread social networks in use as well as a short description so language teachers and practitioners know what to expect from each of them. Table 1 presents the most common ones and their current use.

Table 1. Description of the most common social networking platforms

Nombre	Descripción
Edmodo	Edmodo is an educational webpage that is sometimes used as language management system (LMS) and that shares design with other popular social networking platforms. It provides a safe and easy way of connecting peers and collaborating. Students can also share content and notes as well as access homework and messages from the school or university.
Facebook	An online social network service that was originally designed for secondary students but later extended to the general public. Among the different functionalities found in this platform, it is worth mentioning the possibility of posting pictures, using individual or group chats, commenting on the photos and sharing information.
Google Hangout	This platform takes conversations to real life through pictures, emoticons and even free group calls. Similar to Skype, you can connect with friends through computers, or Android or Apple devices.
GroupMe	GroupMe is a mobile instant messaging application which belongs to Microsoft and is similar to already existing instant messaging applications such as WhatsApp, Wechat, Line, Telegram or KaoTalk.
Instagram	This social network is normally accessed from mobile devices and provides a platform where users can share pictures and videos, giving users the possibility of applying different filters, sharing video stories with other users as well as sharing these contents in other social networks such as Facebook, Twitter, Tumbler and Flickr.
LinkedIN	This social network has similar functionalities to Facebook but it is oriented to the business world.
Pinterest	This tool gathers pictures that people use to compile ideas for their projects and interests. People create and share collections of images called "Pins" that are used to do different things such as planning a trip, organizing events or keeping food recipes.
PodOmatic	This webpage is specialized into the creation of tools and services that help find, create, distribute and foster the listening of audio and video podcasts.
Snapchat	This mobile application allows users to take pictures and create short videos. Its use is very similar to the Instagram "Stories". Users control the visibility of the video and decide when they want the video to disappear.
Twitter	This social and "microblogging" network gives users the possibility of sending short texts with a limit of 140 characters, also called "tweets". Registered users can read and publish tweets from their personal accounts.
Voice Thread	Voice Thread is an interactive tool to share content and collaborate that allows users to add images, documents and videos. Likewise, users can add voice, text, audio files and comments.

As observed in the aforementioned descriptions, some of the social networks may cover a wide spectrum of communication modes that could be exploited from a language learning perspective. By contrast, others such as Twitter or Pinterest may only be used to develop students' writing skills and collaborative work. Thus, it seems necessary to understand the potential of each social networking tool to appropriately develop effective and successful learning environments. These virtual environments may give students the opportunity of interacting using the foreign language, working in groups and improving their linguistic competence (Blattner & Fiori, 2011; Mills, 2011; Blattner & Lomicka, 2012; Farr & Murray, 2016).

Blyth (2008) distinguished between 4 categories to be considered in language learning research: technological, psycholinguistic, sociocultural and ecological. These 4 categories have been part of studies exploring social networks in language learning contexts. In this sense, those studies addressing the technological aspect such as the present book chapter have emphasized the possible benefits of a certain tool that could be useful for other teachers willing to put into practice a particular social network in a language learning environment. Those studies addressing the psycholinguistic aspect are focused on social interaction and can specifically explore the role of social networks as learning tools, emphasizing the connection between peers as a stepping stone towards language development (Lomicka & Lord, 2016). With regard to the sociocultural approach, which lies on Vygotsky's (1978) theory of mediation and zone of proximal development, the role of communication and interaction becomes indispensable for language acquisition and learning. Social networks become a very suitable environment for this type of approach to language learning where interactions with native speakers and non-native speakers favor an environment where language-related episodes (Swain & Lapkin, 1998) can occur. These language related-episodes have been found to be conducive to language development as students reflect on their language productions as well as the language used by their peers (Long, 1996). Likewise, factors such as students' observation and collaborative work are direct consequences of this sociocultural approach as well (Ryberg & Christiansen, 2008). As for those studies using an ecological approach, social networks have not specifically been explored. However, this type of approach which focuses primarily on the quality of learning opportunities, of classroom interaction and of educational experience (Van Lier, 2010), can be applied to any virtual space (Lomicka & Lord, 2016).

Although different studies yielded positive outcomes as result of using social networks for language learning purposes (e.g. Alvarez Valencia, 2016; Andujar & Salaberri-Ramiro, 2019; Donmus, 2010; Stevenson & Liu, 2013), negative aspects have been also found in the literature. Shih (2011) highlighted that the use of social networks for language learning purposes involves an increase in teachers' workload as they have to control the language and contents used. Further aspects pointed out in the literature such as the type of language production which often has an informal character and takes place out of the classroom environment may lead to abbreviations, misspellings or a high number of interventions (Kabilan, Ahmad & Abidin, 2010). However, as stated by Andujar (2016) and Andújar-Vaca and Cruz-Martínez (2017), students who are using a foreign language to interact with their peers through social networks normally aim for accuracy, whether writing or speaking, in order to achieve an understanding. Furthermore, they are not aware of the abbreviations in the target language and thus are unable to put them into practice. Finally, other negative aspects such as privacy issues have been found when implementing social networks for language learning purposes due to the necessary information exchange between peers and between students and teachers (Gettman & Cortijo, 2015; Teclehaimanot & Hickman, 2011). All these issues together with the distractive nature of social networks which are normally associated with informal learning have led to a lack of curricular integration into the course contents at all levels of the educational system. Thus, from a research point of view, it seems necessary to shed light on the possibilities of certain social networks for language development and for developing blended learning processes that can contribute to incorporating technological tools into the classroom environment as well as facilitating the learning process.

TOWARDS A FRAMEWORK FOR INTEGRATING BLENDED LEARNING TOOLS

When making use of technological tools to develop blended learning processes, it seems necessary to understand first the most widespread frameworks for blended learning models in the existing literature. One of these theoretical frameworks is the Revised Community of Inquiry (RCOI) (Shea et al., 2012) that although was not particularly designed for blended models, most of its features such as cognitive presence, learner presence, social presence and teaching presence are relevant to this type of learning environments. Figure 1 presents an example of such model.

Figure 1. The revised community of inquiry framework (RCOI)
Source: Kim, Kim, Kera, and Getman (2014).

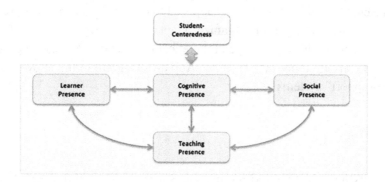

This framework emphasizes communication and collaborative interaction between peers as well as between teachers and students. This type of interaction, from a language learning perspective may lead to foster knowledge building without students' awareness that such learning is occurring. Nevertheless, although this type of learning may be unconscious and unintentional, learners may generate different LREs (Swain & Lapkin, 1998) as well as notice the gap between their current language and the target language (Gass, 2003) which may foster L2 development.

Other blended learning frameworks such as Shea's (2007) pyramid framework or Khan's (2011) octagonal model have explored blended learning from different angles. However, more recent frameworks such as the Complex Adaptative Blended Learning Systems (Wang, Han & Yang, 2015) have attempted to incorporate not only all the elements present in blended learning models but how these elements work individually and with one another in order to offer a more complete picture of the blended learning environment. This system measures the changes brought about by the interaction with new elements in the system as could be the inclusion of any given technological tool. The authors of this framework identified six systems in their framework: the learner, the teacher, the technology, the content, the learning support, and the institution (Wang, Han, & Yang 2015). Within each system there are different subsystems with their own internal characteristics that interact with the rest of the systems to create a blended learning system. Figure 2 shows the different systems in the framework.

Figure 2. The framework of complex adaptive blended learning systems (CABLS)
Source: Wang, Han and Yang (2015)

The systems presented in this framework, as opposed to other frameworks that present a more static nature, are open and dynamic and can self-organize, adapt to and evolve with the different changes happening in the blended model. This type of open theoretical framework seems a solid base to incorporate any potential blended learning tools such as WhatsApp or Instagram to the abovementioned "technology" and "learning support" systems.

WHATSAPP

The number of studies investigating and putting into practice this mobile instant messaging (MIM) application has grown steadily since 2013. Early studies into MIM such as Cavus & Ibrahim's (2009), Kennedy & Levy 's (2008) or Levy and Kennedy's (2007) explored the use of short test messages for language development using SMS to support language learning. However, with the appearance of mobile instant messaging platforms which allow users to maintain individual and group conversations online as well as share videos, voice messages and images, the landscape of MIM changed radically. This change also involved new possibilities for language development due to the various modes of communication available in these platforms which led to a more specific exploitation of MIM functionalities. In this sense, early studies into WhatsApp or other similar MIM platforms such as WeChat, Kaotalk, Line or Telegram explored the potential of these applications from a general point of view, analysing students' perception and reactions to the implementation of these tools in the classroom environment and focusing on the learning potential of these platforms. Some examples are Díaz (2014), Morato-Payá (2014) or Padron (2013) who realized the potential of MIM services for language development and focused on the use of these tools as a complement for their language classes. Subsequent investigations into the field focused on more specific aspects, particularly the development of writing skills which have been one of the main areas under investigation in the WhatsApp literature. In this sense studies such as Castrillo, Martín-Monje and Bárcena's (2014) analysed the responses, attitudes and participation of students of German as well as the meaning negotiation strategies taking place in the application. The researchers in this investigation also highlighted the adequacy of WhatsApp technology to develop students' interactive skills and to promote language learning at early stages of acquisition. Likewise, Andujar's (2016) investigation into the potential of WhatsApp to develop students writing skills explored the interaction in the application of 80 Spanish students taking an intermediate English course. Students' grammatical, lexical and mechanical accuracy as well as syntactic complexity was analysed over six months. An experimental design yielded significant differences between the control and experimental group in favour of the latter in terms of accuracy, but no syntactic differences were found between the two groups. Other studies exploring students' writing development through WhatsApp such as Fattah's (2015) investigation analysed sentence structure, punctuation and generating ideas between two groups, one in which writing was taught through the prescribed book and another in which the application was used. Results yielded significant effects on students' writing as a result of the use of the application.

Although further literature into the use of WhatsApp to foster writing development is sought in order to achieve a better understanding of how to exploit the application for writing purposes, Andujar-Vaca & Cruz's (2017) investigation explored the voice messaging functionality of the app to foster speaking skills. Students' chat conversation took place through voice messages and the samples collected in the application were subsequently analysed to measure the type and triggers of the language-related episodes (LREs) originated. A mixed analysis approach and a temporal axis were used to measure differences between a control and an experimental group. Findings highlighted negotiations of meaning as the most common LREs and phonetic triggers as the most abundant during the interaction. Likewise, factors such as ubiquitous meaning negotiation, students' reflection and evaluation of their own performance and authentic interaction and feedback were emphasized. Students were able to listen several times to their language productions perceiving gaps between their language and the target language. The use of the voice service was also considered by Hsieh, Wu and Marek (2017) who, using a very similar application in this case "Line", investigated oral and written communication in the app to learn English idioms. The application was used to develop a flipped learning model in which 48 students participated during their English training sessions. The questionnaires and interviews carried out revealed that the application had a better perception than the traditional method of tuition and aspects such as motivation, increase knowledge and an improvement of the oral abilities were emphasized.

More recent studies into WhatsApp such as Samaie, Mansouri Nejad, & Qaracholloo's (2018) explored the use of the application for self- and peer-assessments. The attitude of 30 Iranian students towards the two types of assessment were explored through the use of 4 questionnaires before and after the implementation of each assessment type. Results showed that participants adopted negative attitudes towards mobile-assisted assessments through the use of the app. Other recent studies such as Alqahtani, Bhaskar, Vadakalur Elumalai, Abumelha's (2018) explored students' perceptions towards the use of the application as a learning platform which could be used to develop and support their learning skills. 300 students replied to a survey exploring factors related with WhatsApp and language learning. Results yielded positive opinions from participants with regard to the use of WhatsApp to assist students during the learning process. Moreover, students highlighted the necessity of creating courses in which the access to class materials as well as the objectives and outcomes of the course were associated with the use of the app to develop a blended learning model. Finally, Ahmed (2019) investigated the use of the application to foster motivational levels of Yemeni EFL students in order to develop reading and writing abilities. Through the creation of chat group, participants commented on news articles during a period of two months. Pre and post-tests as well as a questionnaire were used to evaluate participants taking part in the chat conversation. Although the findings of this study found the application to be effective to improve students' motivation during the language classes, the difficulty to measure the motivation construct only through the use of a questionnaire poses certain threats with regard to the validity of the results.

Overall, as for the use of WhatsApp in language learning, it seems necessary to develop further studies exploring specific aspects of language development. Many times, the use of the application in the existing literature has been investigated vaguely without carrying out in-depth analysis of language development or exploring factors that are conducive to second language acquisition. Thus, more detailed cross-cultural studies involving higher number of participants are sought in order to obtain relevant and conclusive results that could have an impact on the educational community.

INSTAGRAM

Due to the fact that the social network "Instagram" is a relatively new application which was created in 2010, the number of studies making use of this platform for language learning is very scarce. However, and as aforementioned in the introduction of this chapter, the outstanding popularity of the application has led to the investigation of the possibilities of this application for language development. In this sense, early studies into Instagram and language learning such as such as Al-Ali's (2014) explored the use of the application combining the different functionalities offered by the app. 40 female students had to upload a picture of their vacations that was used as an starting point to develop in-class speaking activities. The second activity involved the exploration of the hashtags in order to find an inspiring picture form which they had to write a story. As for the third activity, students had to take a picture during their school time and publish an Instagram story related to this picture. Although the design of the activities seems to exploit the potential of the application, the research instruments - in this case a questionnaire – and the small number of participants cannot provide conclusive results of the overall experience. Students were satisfied with the use of the app for language learning purposes but several challenges were also found such as privacy issues or students feeling reluctant to upload their homework into their personal profiles.

Other researchers such as Ayuni, Kasuma and Mydin (2017) explored the use of Instagram to develop students' writing abilities. 101 students had to participate in a writing task through the use of the application in which they had to comment on pictures taken by themselves. Different surveys were given to participants in order to explore students' perception of the task carried out. Most of the students indicated that they had improved their language competence and described their Instagram experience as positive. Participants also highlighted that the application could be used for educational purposes. However, challenges were also found such as the distractive nature of the application which led students to different publication from the ones intended and also a certain degree of fear of feeling judged or criticized when writing in a foreign language.

As opposed to previous studies in which the use of Instagram for language learning was focused on the use of images to develop different tasks, Mansor and Rahim (2017) made use of the video service in the app to make students upload presentations that were later commented by their peers. Although the number of students was small (n =20), results indicated an increase in students' motivation towards learning and a higher degree of interaction between peers. Results regarding participation were also significant going from a 50% on the first day to a 95% at the end of the project. More recent investigations into this field are also presented in this book such as Çakmak (2019) who explored the use of Instagram to assess students' oral communication skills. The performance scores of participants on a speaking task delivered through Instagram and in class, and students' scores on the Big Five personality traits were investigated from a statistical point of view. Findings highlighted that the application facilitated students' performance in the oral communication skill and that personality traits are not predictors of students' performance on Instagram.

As aforementioned, the literature regarding the use of Instagram for language learning is still very scarce and although the application provides different options to develop blended learning models and to foster language development, research into this field is almost non-existent.

DISCUSSION

The distinctive nature of mobile devices that allow students to maintain conversations "anytime" and "anywhere" (Traxler, 2009) becomes a fertile environment for language interaction and the development of blended learning models. However, most of the literature which explores the use of technological devices to foster language development is mainly focused on the use of computer devices rather than mobile phones. In this sense, Burston (2014) pointed that the reality of MALL is "still on the fringes" as there is a lack of curricular integration as well as a strong theoretical deficit in studies making use of mobile devices to foster language development. As for the applications tackled in this chapter, the situation is very similar. Studies addressing mobile instant messaging applications are still scarce and there is only a small number of in-depth studies exploring which factors can make a difference when making use of these applications.

In this vein, the possibilities offered by MIM services such as WhatsApp are different from previous chat services and several factors need to be considered: the synchronous and asynchronous nature of mobile chat-based interaction; an easy access to contents; a wider range of chat features that allow teachers to exploit different modes of communication; greater ease when sharing voice, image or text messages; and the availability of using Internet resources anytime and anywhere. These differential characteristics should mark as well the design of blended learning environments in which the affordances of the applications should guide the course design and tasks implemented. MIM apps like WhatsApp or Line can be used to develop blended environments in which the role of the technological devices should shift from a complementary role to a more central one during the language learning process. In other words, MIM services could not only be used as classroom activities but also integrated within the course design to foster autonomous learning outside the class. This has already been carried out by some researchers in the field (e.g. Hew, Tang, Lo, & Zhu, 2018; Hsieh, Wu and Marek, 2017) with very positive results but further empirical studies are sought to better understand and develop successful blended learning environments.

With regard to Instagram, the enormous popularity of the platform has led developers to include many add-ons that allow teachers and language practitioners to use different types of communication. As aforementioned, the literature in this field is very scarce and, as in WhatsApp, the existing studies make use of the application to develop certain tasks instead of taking a more central role during language learning process. An example of this central role could be blended learning processes such as flipped learning (Bergmann and Sams, 2012), which involves a video explanation of the class contents before the start of the lecture while the class time is devoted to collaborative tasks and group work (Hwang, Lai & Wang, 2015). The video contents could be delivered through Instagram instead of using any other platform or LMS students are not familiar with. This may help students' engagement within the blended learning model which has been found to be one of the main challenges in this type of learning environments (e.g. Ancliff and Kang, 2017; Kim, Kim, Khera, and Getman, 2014) as well as decrease truancy (e.g. Yao, 2018).

Furthermore, it also seems necessary to overcome the challenges for the integration of blended learning models using mobile phones, which are not only presented at a classroom level but also at an institutional one as mobile restrictions are still present in many secondary and higher education institutions (Cortesi, Haduong, Gasser, Aricak, Saldaña, & Lerner, 2014). These challenges do not exclusively affect the education system but also the technological development that is still limited in certain parts of the world in which the Internet is not a reality yet. Similarly, in the developing world, the arrival of 5G connectivity may contribute to accelerating technological integration in the classroom as well as increase the possibilities of using mobile phones for language learning.

CONCLUSION

This chapter has attempted to shed light on the current situation of these two social networking tools in the language learning field as well as their possibilities to develop blended learning models. As shown in the literature review carried out for each of the apps, the amount of research is still very scarce and mainly focused on small case studies using experimental designs. Moreover, there is a lack of cross-cultural studies exploring the use of these application and thus, the information presented is usually very limited. In this sense, it seems necessary to further investigate the possibilities of these two apps for language development, particularly Instagram in which the literature seems to be underdeveloped. Likewise, there is a lack of studies using Instagram to carry out blended learning models and only a few using MIM (e.g. Hew, Tang, Lo, & Zhu, 2018; Hsieh, Wu and Marek, 2017). This indicates that the implementation of these technological tools, although interesting from a language development and motivational perspective, has not reached an integration into the course contents and course design. Thus, researchers into CALL and MALL should not exclusively investigate the use of these tools in language learning tasks as a complement to in-class tuition but incorporate them as a relevant element of the blended learning process.

Moreover, due to the fact that these tools are relatively new, there is also a lack of models to follow when making use of these social networking tools as well as certain misunderstanding regarding their use. In this sense, the complex adaptative blended learning systems (CABLS) (Wang, Han, & Yang 2015) framework explained in this chapter becomes a stepping stone towards the development of an open and dynamic blended learning framework that is able to change and evolve, and in which the different systems making up the framework can work individually and with one another. From a theoretical perspective, it is also worth mentioning the importance of Vygotsky's (1978) sociocultural theory that plays a fundamental role when putting into practice social networking tools in language learning environments. Vygotsky's social development theory, which stresses the indispensable role of social interaction in the development of cognition, is very present in social networking platforms. In this sense, as stated by Lantolf and Thorne (2006), individual development cannot be understood without making reference to the social and cultural context of that individual. This theory which supports the idea that higher mental processes have their origin in social processes is directly related with the use of social networking platforms for language development.

With these ideas in mind, it seems necessary to implement technological tools and applications that address the social nature of language and that rely on the interaction to construct knowledge. Social networking tools are a clear example of such tools in which the social element becomes an indispensable part of language development. Thus, together with the development of new technological advances than can contribute to improving the language learning process, researchers into CALL and MALL should also turn their focus towards accessible existing applications and tools that can help foster students' competence and that are still to be explored.

REFERENCES

Ahmed, S. T. S. (2019). Chat and learn: Effectiveness of using whatsapp as a pedagogical tool to enhance EFL learners' reading and writing skills. *International Journal of English Language and Literature Studies, 8*(2), 61–68.

Akhiar, A., Mydin, A. A., & Kasuma, S. A. A. (2017). Students' perceptions and attitudes towards the use of Instagram in English language writing. *Malaysian Journal of Learning and Instruction (MJLI), Special issue on Graduate Students Research on Education*, 47-72.

Al-Ali, S. (2014). Embracing the selfie craze: Exploring the possible use of Instagram as a language mlearning tool. *Issues and Trends in Educational Technology, 2*(2).

Alqahtani, S. M., Bhaskar, C. V., Vadakalur Elumalai, K., & Abumelha, M. (2018). *WhatsApp: An online platform for university-level English language education. Arab World English Journal*, 9. AWEJ.

Altbach, P. G. (2004). Globalisation and the university: Myths and realities in an unequal world. *Tertiary Education and Management, 10*(1), 3–25. doi:10.1080/13583883.2004.9967114

Álvarez Valencia, J. A. (2016). Language views on social networking sites for language learning: The case of Busuu. *Computer Assisted Language Learning, 29*(5), 853–867. doi:10.1080/09588221.2015.1069361

Ancliff, M., & Kang, A. (2017). Flipping an EMI physics class: Implications of student motivation and learning strategies for the design of course contents. *International Journal of Contents, 13*(4).

Andujar, A. (2016). Benefits of mobile instant messaging to develop ESL writing. *System, 62*, 63–76. doi:10.1016/j.system.2016.07.004

Andujar, A., & Salaberri-Ramiro, M. S. (2019). Exploring chat-based communication in the EFL class: Computer and mobile environments. *Computer Assisted Language Learning*, 1–28. doi:10.1080/0958 8221.2019.1614632

Andújar-Vaca, A., & Cruz-Martínez, M. S. (2017). Mobile instant messaging: WhatsApp and its potential to develop oral skills. *Comunicar, 25*(50), 43–52. doi:10.3916/C50-2017-04

Arbaugh, J. B. (2014). What might online delivery teach us about blended management education? Prior perspectives and future directions. *Journal of Management Education, 38*(6), 784–817. doi:10.1177/1052562914534244

Ball, P. & Lindsay, D. (2013). Language demands and support for English-medium instruction in tertiary education. Learning from a specific context. *English-medium instruction at universities: Global challenges, 4466.*

Bergmann, J. & Sams, A. (2012). Flip your classroom: Reach every student in every class every day. *International Society for Technology In Education.*

Blattner, G., & Fiori, M. (2011). Virtual social network communities: An investigation of language learners' development of sociopragmatic awareness and multiliteracy skills. *CALICO Journal, 29*(1), 24–43. doi:10.11139/cj.29.1.24-43

Blattner, G. & Lomicka, L. (2012). Facebooking and the social generation: A new era of language learning. *Alsic. Apprentissage des Langues et Systèmes d'Information et de Communication, 15*(1).

Blyth, C. (2008). Research perspectives on online discourse and foreign language learning. *Mediating discourse online*, 47-70.

Boyd, D. (2014). *It's complicated: The social lives of networked teens*. London, UK: Yale University Press.

Burston, J. (2014). The reality of MALL: Still on the fringes. *CALICO Journal, 31*(1), 103–125. doi:10.11139/cj.31.1.103-125

Çakmak, F. (2019). Social networking and language learning: Use of Instagram (IG) for evaluating oral communication skill. In Andujar (Ed.), Recent tools for computer – and mobile-assisted foreign language learning. Hershey, PA: IGI Global.

Castrillo, M. D., Martín-Monje, E., & Bárcena, E. (2014). *Mobile-based chatting for meaning negotiation in foreign language learning*. International Association for the Development of the Information Society.

Cavus, N., & Ibrahim, D. (2009). m-Learning: An experiment in using SMS to support learning new English language words. *British Journal of Educational Technology, 40*(1), 78–91. doi:10.1111/j.1467-8535.2007.00801.x

Chen Hsieh, J. S., Wu, W. C. V., & Marek, M. W. (2017). Using the flipped classroom to enhance EFL learning. *Computer Assisted Language Learning, 30*(1-2), 1–21. doi:10.1080/09588221.2015.1111910

Cortesi, S., Haduong, P., Gasser, U., Aricak, O., Saldaña, M., & Lerner, Z. (2014, Jan. 15). Youth perspectives on tech in schools: From mobile devices to restrictions and monitoring. *Berkman Center Research Publication*, (2014-3).

Counts, S., & Fisher, K. E. (2010). Mobile social networking as information ground: A case study. *Library & Information Science Research, 32*(2), 98–115. doi:10.1016/j.lisr.2009.10.003

Diaz, J. (2014). *El WhatsApp como herramienta de intervencion didáctica para fomentar el aprendizaje cooperativo* [WhatsApp as a tool of educational intervention to foster cooperative learning]. (Unpublished Paper presented at X Jornadas De Material Didáctica y Experiencias Innovadoras En Educación Superior), Buenos Aires, Argentina. Retrieved from http://eprints.rclis.org/23597/

Donmus, V. (2010). The use of social networks in educational computer-game based foreign language learning. *Procedia: Social and Behavioral Sciences, 9*, 1497–1503. doi:10.1016/j.sbspro.2010.12.355

Dunn, L. (2013). Teaching in higher education: can social media enhance the learning experience? *6th Annual conference of teaching and learning*, University of Glasgow, UK.

Farr, F., & Murray, L. (Eds.). (2016). *The Routledge handbook of language learning and technology.* Routledge. doi:10.4324/9781315657899

Fattah, S. (2015). The effectiveness of using WhatsApp messenger as one of mobile learning techniques to develop students' writing skills. *Journal of Education and Practice, 6*(32), 115–127.

Gass, S. (2003). Input and interaction. In C. Doughty & M. Long (Eds.), *The handbook of second language acquisition* (pp. 224–255). Oxford, UK: Blackwell. doi:10.1002/9780470756492.ch9

Gettman, H. J., & Cortijo, V. (2015). "Leave me and my Facebook alone!" Understanding college students' relationship with Facebook and its use for academic purposes. *International Journal for the Scholarship of Teaching and Learning, 9*(1), 8.

Global Digital Statistics. (2019). Retrieved from https://www.smartinsights.com/social-media-marketing/social-media-strategy/new-global-social-media-research/

Hew, K. F., Tang, Y., Lo, C. K., & Zhu, Y. (2018). Examining a WeChat-supported 5E-flipped classroom pedagogical approach. *International Journal of Services and Standards, 12*(3-4), 224–242. doi:10.1504/IJSS.2018.100217

Hwang, G. J., Lai, C. L., & Wang, S. Y. (2015). Seamless flipped learning: A mobile technology-enhanced flipped classroom with effective learning strategies. *Journal of Computers in Education, 2*(4), 449-473.

Im, J. H., & Kim, J. (2015). Use of blended learning for effective implementation of English-medium instruction in a non-English higher education context. *International Education Studies, 8*(11), 1–15. doi:10.5539/ies.v8n11p1

Kabilan, M. K., Ahmad, N., & Abidin, M. J. Z. (2010). Facebook: An online environment for learning of English in institutions of higher education? *The Internet and higher education, 13*(4), 179–187. doi:10.1016/j.iheduc.2010.07.003

Kennedy, C., & Levy, M. (2008). L'italiano al telefonino: Using SMS to support beginners' language learning. *ReCALL, 20*(3), 315–330. doi:10.1017/S0958344008000530

Khan, B. H. (2001). A framework for web-based learning. In B. H. Khan (Ed.), *Web-based training* (pp. 75–98). Englewood Cliffs, NJ: Educational Technology Publications.

Kim, M. K., Kim, S. M., Khera, O., & Getman, J. (2014). The experience of three flipped classrooms in an urban university: An exploration of design principles. *The Internet and Higher Education, 22*, 37–50. doi:10.1016/j.iheduc.2014.04.003

Kukulska-Hulme, A. & Shield. (2007). An overview of mobile assisted language learning: Can mobile devices support collaborative practice in speaking and listening. In *EuroCALL,* 2007.

Lantolf, J., & Thorne, S. (2006). *Sociocultural theory and the genesis of second language development.* Oxford, UK: Oxford University Press.

Law, K. M., Geng, S., & Li, T. (2019). Student enrollment, motivation and learning performance in a blended learning environment: The mediating effects of social, teaching, and cognitive presence. *Computers & Education, 136*, 1–12. doi:10.1016/j.compedu.2019.02.021

Levy, M., & Kennedy, C. (2007). Learning Italian via mobile SMS. In *Mobile learning* (pp. 92–99). Routledge.

Lomicka, L. & Lord, G. (2016). Social networking and language learning. The Routledge handbook of language learning and technology, 255-268.

Long, M. H. (1996). The role of the linguistic environment in second language acquisition. In W. Ritchie & T. Bathia (Eds.), *Handbook of research on second language acquisition* (pp. 413–469). New York, NY: Academic Press. doi:10.1016/B978-012589042-7/50015-3

López-Pérez, M. V., Pérez-López, M. C., & Rodríguez-Ariza, L. (2011). Blended learning in higher education: Students' perceptions and their relation to outcomes. *Computers & Education, 56*(3), 818–826. doi:10.1016/j.compedu.2010.10.023

Mansor, N., & Rahim, N. A. (2017). Instagram in ESL classroom. *Man in India, 97*(20), 107–114.

Mao, J. (2014). Social media for learning: A mixed methods study on high school students' technology affordances and perspectives. *Computers in Human Behavior, 33*, 213–223. doi:10.1016/j.chb.2014.01.002

Mazer, J. P., Murphy, R. E., & Simonds, C. J. (2007). I'll see you on "Facebook": The effects of computer-mediated teacher self-disclosure on student motivation, affective learning, and classroom climate. *Communication Education, 56*(1), 1–17. doi:10.1080/03634520601009710

Mills, N. (2011). Situated learning through social networking communities: The development of joint enterprise, mutual engagement, and a shared repertoire. *CALICO Journal, 28*(2), 345–368. doi:10.11139/cj.28.2.345-368

Miyazoe, T., & Anderson, T. (2010). Learning outcomes and students' perceptions of online writing: Simultaneous implementation of a forum, blog, and wiki in an EFL blended learning setting. *System, 38*(2), 185–199. doi:10.1016/j.system.2010.03.006

Morato-Paya, A. (2014). El WhatsApp como complemento del aprendizaje en la clase E/LE [WhatsApp as a learning complement in the classroom of E/LE]. Revista Foro De Profesores De E/LE, 10(1), 165-173.

Padron, C. J. (2013). Teaching strategies based on WhatsApp instant messaging application only for phones (mobile learning) and its use to promote collaborative learning. *Revista De Tecnología De Información y Comunicación En Educación, 7*(2), 123–134.

Ryberg, T., & Christiansen, E. (2008). Community and social network sites as technology enhanced learning environments. *Technology, Pedagogy and Education, 17*(3), 207–219. doi:10.1080/14759390802383801

Samaie, M., Mansouri Nejad, A., & Qaracholloo, M. (2018). An inquiry into the efficiency of WhatsApp for self-and peer-assessments of oral language proficiency. *British Journal of Educational Technology, 49*(1), 111–126. doi:10.1111/bjet.12519

Seaman, J., & Tinti-Kane, H. (2013). *Social media for teaching and learning*. London, UK: Pearson Learning Systems.

Shea, P. (2007). Towards a conceptual framework for learning in blended environments. In A. G. Picciano & C. D. Dziuban (Eds.), *Blended learning: Research perspectives* (pp. 19–35). Retrieved from http://elab.learningandteaching.dal.ca/dalblend2013-files/blended-learning-research-perspectives-book.pdf#page=30

Shea, P., Hayes, S., Smith, S. U., Vickers, J., Bidjerano, T., Pickett, A., ... Jian, S. (2012). Learning presence: Additional research on a new conceptual element within the Community of Inquiry (CoI) framework. *The Internet and Higher Education, 15*(2), 89–95. doi:10.1016/j.iheduc.2011.08.002

Shih, R. C. (2011). Can Web 2.0 technology assist college students in learning English writing? Integrating Facebook and peer assessment with blended learning. *Australasian Journal of Educational Technology, 27*(5), 829–845. doi:10.14742/ajet.934

Stevenson, M. P., & Liu, M. (2013). Learning a language with Web 2.0: Exploring the use of social networking features of foreign language learning websites. *CALICO Journal, 27*(2), 233–259. doi:10.11139/cj.27.2.233-259

Stout D. (2019). Retrieved from https://dustinstout.com/social-media-statistics/#whatsapp-stats

Swain, M., & Lapkin, S. (1998). Interaction and second language learning: Two adolescent French immersion students working together. *Modern Language Journal, 82*(3), 320–337. doi:10.1111/j.1540-4781.1998.tb01209.x

Teclehaimanot, B., & Hickman, T. (2011). Student-teacher interaction on Facebook: What students find appropriate. *TechTrends, 55*(3), 19–30. doi:10.100711528-011-0494-8

Traxler, J. (2009). Learning in a mobile age. [IJMBL]. *International Journal of Mobile and Blended Learning, 1*(1), 1–12. doi:10.4018/jmbl.2009010101

Van Lier, L. (2010). The ecology of language learning: Practice to theory, theory to practice. *Procedia: Social and Behavioral Sciences, 3*, 2–6. doi:10.1016/j.sbspro.2010.07.005

Vygotsky, L. (1978). *Mind in society: The development of higher psychological processes.* Cambridge, MA: Harvard University Press.

Wang, Y., Han, X., & Yang, J. (2015). Revisiting the blended learning literature: Using a complex adaptive systems framework. *Journal of Educational Technology & Society, 18*(2), 380–393.

Yao, Z. (2018). Research on flipped classroom teaching mode based on MOODLE. In *Proceedings of the 3rd International Conference on Education & Education Research* (EDUER 2018), 656-660.

This research was previously published in Recent Tools for Computer- and Mobile-Assisted Foreign Language Learning; pages 307-321, copyright year 2020 by Information Science Reference (an imprint of IGI Global).

Chapter 36
Finding Balance:
Social Media Use in Higher Education

Danielle McKain
Beaver Area School District, USA

Julia Bennett Grise
Beaver Area School District, USA

ABSTRACT

Social media use is a complex topic. The type and use of social media presents a variety of formats and creates a multitude of directions for research. Pearson provides research on personal, professional, and teaching social media use in higher education that shows the use of social media in higher education is growing. While this research provides a foundation, it raises many questions. The purpose of this chapter is to provide an overview of common Learning Management Systems or platforms and social media networks that are often used in college courses. This chapter also provides common ways that social media is used outside of the classroom. The chapter concludes with concerns that are raised regardless of the type of social media use, platform, or network.

INTRODUCTION

Social media is prevalent independent of education, race/ethnicity, or health care access (Chou et al., 2009). Cell phones, in the past, were not allowed to be used in many schools; now they are an integral part of teaching and learning. For Generation Z, technology and social media play a role in nearly everything they do, including higher education. Social media use is expected in higher education, but research is needed on effective social media practices (Rowan-Kenyon et al., 2016). While there are many resources for using social media in the classroom, the issue is two-fold. Future employers look for not only strong technology skills, but also effective personal communication skills (Greenhow & Robelia, 2009). Research is showing that these two skills are difficult to maintain simultaneously (Yildirim, 2014).

DOI: 10.4018/978-1-6684-7123-4.ch036

The National Education Association in the United States recently released Preparing 21st Century Students for a Global Society: An Educator's Guide to the "Four Cs". The four Cs are (1) Critical Thinking and Problem Solving, (2) Communication, (3) Collaboration, and (4) Creativity and Innovation. The Educator's Guide to the "Four Cs" emphasizes the need to prepare young people for citizenship and the global workforce, and the ability to work with people of various backgrounds. Communication skills such as clearly expressing thoughts, effectively expressing opinions, providing logical and consistent instructions, and motivating others, are valuable and important for communication in the workplace today (An Educator's Guide to the Four Cs, n.d.).

Many platforms for social media promote communication and collaborative learning. Using the world wide web, content and applications are often continuously altered and expanded by participants in a collaborative way rather than created and published by individuals (Kaplan & Haenlein, 2010). The interaction created by social media supports social learning theories, but there is a lack of research to distinguish between face-to-face collaboration and social media collaboration. Vygotsky's Sociocultural theory of cognitive development was based on the importance of social interactions for cognitive development, but did not consider social media interactions (Slavin, 2018). More recently, Siemens (2005) refers to connectivism theory as a way to explain how social learning takes place through social media use. Learners acquire information through connecting to others knowledge and educators provide students with ways to make connections (Chen & Bryer, 2012).

Social media also serves as a bridge to connect formal and informal learning. Banks et al. (2007) found that the impact of formal learning decreases after high school. Informal learning becomes more important after high school as adults learn through interactions. Yet, the difference between interacting in person versus interacting via social media requires more research. In 2006, Hew and Brush identified the following typical barriers for integrating technology: resources, institution, subject culture, attitudes and beliefs, knowledge and skills, and assessment. Furthermore, they suggested the following strategies to overcome these barriers: having a shared vision and technology integration plan, overcoming the scarcity of resources, changing attitudes and beliefs, conducting professional development, and reconsidering assessments. Social media use is common in informal environments and could be beneficial in formal environments, but research on formal academic use is limited; in addition, it is difficult to implement social network use in formal learning environments due to privacy and security restrictions (Chen & Bryer, 2012).

"Social learning is based on the premise that our understanding of content is socially constructed through conversations about that content and through grounded interactions, especially with others, around problems or actions" (Brown & Adler, 2008, p. 18). Technology is changing faster than ever and there is a growing global demand for continuous learning and the creation of new ideas and skills; furthermore, the internet has the ability to expand and support social learning in various ways (Brown & Adler, 2008).

Keeping up with the current definition of social media along with deciding which platform to use in higher education can be overwhelming for educators. Although aligning curriculum to educational standards and ensuring that students meet each standard is primary in all areas of education, the resources used to assist students with meeting these goals is up to interpretation; therefore, using technology and a variety of social medias in the classroom can be implemented if educators choose to do so. The existing research on social media provides educators with an assortment of websites, applications, and platforms that can potentially be used in the higher education classroom. Although technology is ever-changing, the information presented in this chapter, found in recent literature and shared from practitioner experience, provide readers with a place to start when deciding whether or not to use social media in higher education settings. Additionally, research studies on social media have found common issues and concerns that reoccur regardless of social media platform, application, or website.

The purpose of this chapter is to discuss the existing research on digital participation through the use of social media in higher education settings. Additionally, this chapter will present concerns of digital participation in higher education. Although using social media in the classroom is debatable, educators can benefit from existing research on specially designed technology and social media use that can be used for educational purposes. The objectives of this chapter include:

1. **Social Media Progression:** Providing a description of how complex the term social media is based on the type, aspect, and use.
2. **Different Uses Social Media:** Explaining the differences between personal social media use, professional social media use, and teaching use of social media.
3. **Social Media in the Classroom:** Describing a variety of social media websites and applications.
4. **Social Media Outside the Classroom:** Providing an overview of non-academic uses for social media including student recruitment, communication, and research.
5. **General Social Media Concerns:** Providing an overview of cell phone addiction, privacy, and health concerns that could result from excessive use of mobile devices and/or social media.
6. **Limitations of Current Research and Future Recommendations:** Explaining what research currently lacks in terms of social media in the higher education classroom and providing researchers with suggestions of how to contribute to the literature on social media and higher education.

BACKGROUND: SOCIAL MEDIA PROGRESSION

Social media can be defined in a variety of ways and is often categorized by use and type. Pearson explains that social media is a hazy term due to the fact that it is non-centralized, user created, user controlled, flexible, democratic, and transparent (Moran, Seaman, & Tinti-Kane, 2011). Further emphasizing that content becomes conversation transforming outgoing information into exchanging information leading to individual, industry, societal, and global change. The Education Council of New Zealand describes Social Media as web-based and mobile-based technologies used to facilitate interactive communication between organizations, communities, and individuals (What is Social Media, n.d.). Furthermore, they explain that some of the most common types of social media platforms include collaboration, networking, image-sharing, blogging, and video-sharing.

Golding, Raeymaeckers, and Sousa (2017) consider four aspects of social media: the uncertainty of the term, the scale and speed of the development, the impact on social behavior and sociability, and the financial scale of these technologies. The uncertainty of the term is seen in the various attempts to classify types of social media. Kaplan and Haenlein (2010) present the following six types of social media: collaborative projects, blogs and microblogs, content communities, social networking sites, virtual game worlds, and virtual social worlds. Meanwhile, Schlagwein and Hu (2017) identify the following five different social media use types: broadcast, dialogue, collaboration, knowledge management, and sociability. These examples demonstrate how complex it is just to classify the types of social media. This is further compounded by how these types are used.

Different Uses of Social Media

The British publishing and assessment company, Pearson, began studying social media use in higher education in 2010 when they used a sample of 900 Pearson customers. Over time, the study expanded to over 8,000 higher education faculty. As social media use has changed and expanded, platforms have come and gone and been debated. Faculty use of social media has evolved from simply watching, reading, or listening to interacting and collaborating. The studies strive to make sense of not just how social media is being used or not used, but why.

Pearson produced reports of their social media use in higher education studies in 2011, 2012, and 2013. Each year, overall social media use increased and barriers decreased. The goal of the studies was to reveal how higher education faculty used social media and the value that they saw in using social media for instructional purposes. The three categories for use were: personal, professional (for higher education, but not teaching), and teaching. Teaching included traditional, blended, and fully online courses. Those surveyed included both full-time and part-time faculty, tenured, non-tenured, and adjunct. To allow comparison of results, the wording and presentation of the questions were consistent for the three consecutive years. The social networks, however, did vary from year to year.

Based on the original 2010 data, surveyed faculty response themes emerged concerning social media use in higher education. Faculty viewed social media as a way to extend the classroom, talk to students in the language they were using, break up class, review, and reinforce content; however, social media was not viewed as the primary means of teaching. The social networks presented for the survey were: YouTube, Facebook, Skype, LinkedIn, Twitter, SlideShare, Flickr, MySpace, and Google Wave. As for instructional use, approximately 45% indicated that they had used online videos or podcasts for class, while approximately 10% or less used comments on blogs, wikis, videos, or podcasts (Tinti-Kane, Seaman, & Levy, 2010).

In 2011, the survey included Facebook, Twitter, Myspace, LinkedIn, SlideShare, Flickr, blogs, wikis, video, and podcasts. At that time, 81% of faculty surveyed agreed or strongly agreed that social networks take more time than they are worth, yet 60% indicated that they used social media professionally at least once per month. YouTube and online videos were viewed as the most valuable resources for class, followed by podcasts and wikis. Approximately half of the faculty viewed Facebook and Twitter as having a negative value for class. As for the overall value of social media for teaching, 70% agreed that video, podcasts, blogs, and wikis were valuable tools, and 58% agreed that social media can be valuable for collaborative learning (Moran, Seaman, & Tinti-Kane, 2011).

In 2012, Pearson released blogs, wikis, podcasts, and Facebook, how today's higher education faculty use social media followed by *Social Media for Teaching and Learning* in 2013. The surveys revealed that higher education faculty were much more likely to use social media in their personal lives than academically. Although overall higher education faculty were very aware of social media, they were not as likely to use it for instructional purposes. Facebook was by far the most commonly used social media for higher education, followed by podcasts, LinkedIn, blogs, wikis, and lastly Twitter. Social media use and age revealed a negative correlation, as use declined with age. Video resources showed to be popular among higher education faculty, while many sought out internet video sources, publishers' videos were also commonly used. The main concerns about social media use were privacy and integrity of student submissions. There was also a concern for separating personal and professional accounts and a decline in concern for the time required for social media use.

Social media use consistently increased from 2012 to 2013 in all three categories: personal, professional, and teaching monthly use. Personal social media use increased from 64% to 70%. Professional use increased from 45% to 55% and using social media in teaching increased from 34% to 41%. Social media use continues to grow and transform. Despite the complexity of the various types, uses, and definitions of social media, the ability to share information is consistent. This chapter will use the Oxford dictionary definition for social media: websites and applications that enable users to create and share content or to participate in social networking. Furthermore, the different categories of social media use will be defined based on the Pearson reports of personal, professional, and teaching.

Personal Social Media Use

The first component, personal social media use, asked faculty specifically about their own personal social media use outside of professional or class use. More specifically, this component represented faculty use versus knowledge of social media. The 2013 results found 16.1% did not use social media, 13.6% rarely used social media, and 70.3% used social media at least monthly. Furthermore, when broken down by age, faculty 35 years and younger tended to use social media more. The study also found there was a relationship between social media use and discipline. Humanities and Arts had the highest rate of social media use while Natural Sciences had the lowest rate of social media use. Approximately one-third of faculty expressed that they used social media on a daily basis for personal use, with almost all of them using Facebook.

Professional Social Media Use

The second component, professional social media use found nearly 55% of faculty used social media at least once per month in 2013 (Seaman & Tinti-Kane, 2013). Social media use that supported faculty's professional careers for any aspect other than teaching was considered professional social media use. The same correlation with age was found with professional use as was found with personal use, the older the faculty, the less they used social media. As for the relationship with discipline, it was found that Humanities and Arts, Social Sciences, and Applied Sciences had higher rates than those in the Natural Sciences, Mathematics, and Computer Science. In comparing 2011 results to 2012, LinkedIn professional use increased by 6%, while Facebook use decreased by 11%.

The 2013 report included virtual communities. Pearson defined a virtual community as: "A community of people sharing common interests, experiences, ideas, and feelings over the Internet or other online collaborative networks" (Seaman & Tinti-Kane, 2013, p. 27). Virtual communities take on different forms and may leverage social media, forums, and blogs. Examples include a LinkedIn or Google Group, Message Board, Chat Room, or User Group. When asked if they participated in virtual communities, more faculty reported participation for professional interests (50%) than personal interests (40%). LinkedIn was reported as the most used social media site for professional purposes. When analyzing virtual communities in relation to online courses, it was found that those who teach online courses are more likely to use social media and participate in virtual communities, both professionally and personally.

Teaching/Educational Social Media Use

The third component, teaching use of social media found almost 41% of faculty used social media for teaching within their courses at least once per month in 2013 (Seaman & Tinti-Kane, 2013). Again, similar results were found based on age. Younger faculty were more likely to use social media in teaching. Similarly, it was found again that Humanities and Arts, Social Sciences, and Applied Sciences faculty had higher rates than those in the Natural Sciences, Mathematics, and Computer Science. Blogs and wikis were the most used format for teaching. Facebook and LinkedIn use was much lower compared to personal and professional use. The use of social media in teaching leads to many more questions, as use could simply be directing students to refer to something, or it can be more involved by asking students to post or respond.

A major component of the 2013 survey was how social media was used for assignments. This component was broken down by platform (blogs & wikis, podcasts, Twitter, LinkedIn, and Facebook) and type of assignment (create, add comments, and read, watch, listen). The results showed that faculty were most likely to ask students to individually create a blog or wiki. Twitter, LinkedIn, and Facebook were not commonly used for assignments in any form. These results were almost identical when comparing group assignments to individual assignments (Seaman & Tinti-Kane, 2013).

Videos as Social Media

Higher education faculty video use was found to be very common, with nearly 88% of faculty using videos for class. Again, similar to social media use, it was found that Humanities and Arts, Social Sciences, and Applied Sciences had the highest rate of video use. The most common method for video selection was searching online, yet over half of faculty acknowledged use of publisher's videos and over one-third had created their own video. Some faculty indicated selecting videos based on reviews and ratings, but more commonly, they used recommendations from other faculty members. Video viewing was common in class, while 79% made assignments to view videos outside of class. In addition, 25% assigned students to create videos of their own, with video creation being most common in Humanities and Arts (Moran, Seaman & Tinti-Kane, 2012).

Concerns for Social Media Use in Teaching (vs. General Social Media Concerns)

Concerns for social media use included (presented in order of highest concern): integrity of student submissions, concerns about privacy, separate course and personal accounts, grading and assessment, inability to measure effectiveness, lack of integration with Learning Management System (LMS), too much time to learn or use, and lack of support (Moran, Seaman, & Tinti-Kane, 2012). Although faculty reported these as important concerns, the percentage of concern for each decreased from the previous year. Similar to other findings there was a correlation with level of concern and faculty age. The older faculty members had higher levels of concern.

Simard and Schnackenberg (2006) provide research that acknowledges the value of virtual learning but point out the challenge of bringing interface literacy and online pedagogy together. Furthermore, they point out that classrooms have changed and so must teaching and learning; therefore, synchronous and asynchronous discussion must be carefully implemented. Virtual learning can promote student involvement, collaboration, and interaction.

The 2013 *Social Media in Higher Education* survey revealed that social media use in higher education continued to increase, but there were still concerns. When responding to the statement "the interactive nature of online and mobile technologies can create better learning environments," 13.3% of faculty strongly agreed, 45.9% somewhat agreed, 33.1% somewhat disagreed, and 7.7% strongly disagreed. When asked about "The impact of digital communication has had on your communication with students", 78.9% responded that it increased, 16.6% responded no impact, and 4.4% responded that it had decreased. Over half of faculty members felt that mobile technologies are more distracting than helpful to students for academic work. This is a recurring concern in the Pearson series of research. When presented with the statement, "Online and Mobile Technologies Are More Distracting Than Helpful to Students for Academic Work," 14.8% Strongly agreed, 41.2% somewhat agreed, 34.7% somewhat disagreed, 9.2% strongly disagreed (Seaman & Tinti-Kane, 2013).

Simard and Schnackenberg (2006) explain that university faculty must create engaging learning environments due to the constant growth of online learning and propose that online course facilitation is the new classroom management. Faculty agreed that social media and technology promote digital communication, but with this comes expectations for feedback outside of class and office hours. This was found to extend the day for faculty and was reported as causing stress. Almost half of faculty in this study reported that digital communication had increased their level of stress and over 66% reported longer work hours as a result of digital communication (Seaman & Tinti-Kane, 2013).

Privacy was again revealed as one of the top concerns with social media use for faculty. Thus, Pearson analyzed privacy in more detail. When presented with the following: risks to the personal privacy of faculty, risks to the personal privacy of students, others outside of class should not be able to view class-related content, others outside of class should not be able to view class discussions, and others outside of class should not be able to participate in class discussions, faculty were asked if they strongly agree, somewhat agree, somewhat disagree, or strongly disagree with the statements (Seaman & Tinti-Kane, 2013). Over 80% of the faculty strongly agreed or somewhat agreed with the five statements. The highest level of concern was having non-class members view or participate in class discussions (over 66% strongly agreed). Faculty was then asked to rate each as very important or important. Risks to the personal privacy of faculty was rated the highest as very important (70%). Many of the concerns for social media use in teaching could be addressed through private accounts. Although multiple concerns exist regarding social media us in the classroom, the next section of the chapter will present educational platforms and social media websites that students can use in the classroom.

Educational Platforms and Social Media in the Classroom

The abundance of social media options makes it difficult to decide how to implement use. This section of the chapter will provide examples of social media options that can be used in the classroom and accessed by students through educational platforms or Learning Management Systems. This section will also discuss popular social networks and media sites or applications used around the world. Having students access the particular applications or websites through an approved educational location may help the transition to a social media-based environment while promoting the use of mobile devices inside and outside of the classroom.

According to Hutt (2017), in January 2017 the most popular social networks around the globe were: Facebook, Twitter, Instagram, LinkedIn, QZone, V Kontakte, and Odnoklassniki. A few of these along with other social networks or media are briefly explained in this section.

Facebook

Facebook, a free social media website, founded by Mark Zuckerberg and four other Harvard students, began in 2004. Facebook originated in the United States; however, it is now a global social media and networking site and the most popular social network in the world (Hutt, 2017). Facebook is a way to connect with people, groups, and businesses. It allows users to post a status of written information, video links, or pictures. When users are in a "closed group" only members of that group can view the information posted. Facebook can be used in higher education by instructors and students using the closed group option. Course information and assignments can be posted while group discussions can take place using Facebook. News stations, businesses, and other colleges and universities distribute knowledge to the public using Facebook; this makes it possible for students to gather information and share it directly within a classroom group for others to view.

Facebook is a social media example that students and faculty members may already use personally; therefore, determining creative ways to integrate Facebook into higher education courses will promote the use of using social media for teaching/educational purposes.

Twitter

Another popular global social networking site, Twitter, allows users to post messages, limited to 280 characters. The main use of Twitter is to remain updated about local, global, and international news; however, users can post messages about anything. Embedded within a Twitter message or "tweet" can be a hashtag. If a user hashtags, using the (#) symbol before a word, any person can search the hashtag to read every tweet associated with it. Using a specific hashtag that students can use in a particular class can be helpful.

Many studies have been conducted to determine the appropriate use and benefits of using Twitter in higher education. It has been found that students tend to be more willing to use Twitter on a regular basis and potentially use it in the classroom, as opposed to instructors (Jacquemin, Smelser, & Bernot, 2014); however, a two-year study that consisted of nursing, psychology, and geography students that incorporated Twitter to promote in class discussions and student questioning in larger class sizes found that this social media site improved student perceptions about feeling a sense of belonging and community in their class (Ross, Banow, & Yu, 2015). Twitter can be used in the classroom for discussion purposes, asking or answering questions, and sharing relevant content information and news. Additionally, instructors can share or advertise their students' work and teaching strategies by tweeting images, videos, or brief messages. Additionally, using a specific hashtag with multiple classes can promote collaboration with students who take the same course at a different time or location, and promote communication and collaboration between students in completely different classes. This may emphasize the importance of cross-curricular communication.

These examples will promote the use of social media for teaching and educational purposes; however, Twitter can also be used by faculty members outside of the classroom for professional use. Instructors can use their school Twitter account to connect with professional organizations, other colleagues, and professors and researchers across the globe. This will allow instructors to build their own professional network related to their field, research interests, and teaching agenda.

Instagram

Instagram operates similarly to Twitter but is more commonly used as only a photo or video-sharing platform. Each post can be seen by a users' followers or can be searched by others if the post contains a specific hashtag. Instagram can be used in higher education classrooms by sharing images that promote class discussion, short videos to break up class lecture, or provide images or videos with links or hashtags as the caption that link students to outside articles or media (Al-Bahrani & Patel, 2015). Al-Bahrani & Patel (2015) suggest that Instagram, Twitter, and Facebook can be incorporated into a higher education economics class in two ways: (1) voluntary non-graded assignments or (2) mandatory graded assignments (p. 64). The way in which an instructor incorporates social media into the classroom depends on the content and course design; however, it can promote collaboration, class discussion, and can be an easier and more direct way to communicate with students. As mentioned previously, Instagram, similar to Facebook and Twitter can promote the use of social media in the classroom for teaching/educational and professional use.

YouTube

Mentioned previously in the Different Uses of Social Media section, was the fact that faculty member video use was very common. YouTube is one of the most popular video sharing websites that faculty members could use. YouTube, founded in 2005, is a website that allows users to create an account and upload videos. Without an account, visitors to the website can search and view videos. Instructors can find videos on YouTube that relate to course content and assign students to view the videos either inside or outside of the classroom by accessing the links through the assigned LMS. Class discussions can be sparked through viewing YouTube videos, students can create their own educational videos and upload them to YouTube, or YouTube videos can be used by students as a way to learn or review content material.

Kahoot

Kahoot! launched in 2013 and is a free game-based learning platform designed to make learning fun, inclusive and engaging in all contexts, and can be used by learners who have a mobile device with internet connection. Kahoot! is advertised as being flexible, simple, diverse, and engaging. An account or login is not required; participants can join using a provided pin from an instructor. Kahoot! games can be used to introduce new concepts, take surveys or for a class review. The games can be played individually or as teams to build collaboration. Currently, Kahoot! can be played in real-time with players in over 180 countries. Over 50 million people use Kahoot every month and by early 2017, they had over 1 billion cumulative participating players (What is Kahoot!, 2017).

Instructors can create new Kahoots as a quiz, jumble, discussion, or survey. Videos, images, and diagrams can be added and Kahoot! can be assigned for students to complete on their own time. Although instructors can create their own Kahoots, there are hundreds of premade Kahoots available for use. The Kahoot! site provides a getting started guide, templates, tips and tricks, and video tutorials for first-time users. Instructors and students, of any age, can use Kahoot! as a way to collaborate, communicate, or compete.

VoiceThread

VoiceThread, a learning tool, aims to fill the gap of social presence in online learning. Students and teachers can upload pictures, videos, presentations, or documents into an online collection that mirrors a slideshow. After the media is added, instructors and students can record comments, ask questions, critique ideas, and engage in conversation. VoiceThread allows students to create their work, communicate their work with instructors and peers, and think critically about course content. Participants watching a VoiceThread can write a comment or draw directly on the image or slide in a presentation. A variety of recent research studies show that VoiceThread, as multi-sensory interaction, has a positive impact on learning (VoiceThread, n.d.).

Kahoot! and VoiceThread are social media examples that should primarily be used for teaching or educational use. It is rare that students will have a personal account for either of these; therefore, exploring and experimenting with these two websites prior to having students use them is important for faculty members to recognize. Appropriate use may need to be modeled for classes.

QQ and QZone

QQ and QZone are an instant messaging and social networking website based in China. These social networking options are available in China while other networking sites, such as Facebook and YouTube, are blocked in mainland China. QQ is available in Chinese, English, French, Japanese, Korean, and Spanish while QZone is only available in Chinese.

V Kontakte and Odnoklassniki

V Kontakte, also known as VK, is a social networking website based out of Russia. It is available in over 80 languages but is primarily used by Russian-speaking persons. Odnoklassniki, founded in 2006, is also used by those in the Russian Federation and Soviet Republics and is available in 14 different languages.

Using these social networking sites, similar to Facebook or Twitter, in higher education classrooms around the globe is a way to integrate social media into the classroom. Although more social media and networking sites continue to be created, the ones mentioned in this section have been found to be the most commonly used or those used by the authors of this chapter. In addition to instructors and students using social media to access and create course content, communicate, and collaborate, social media is used by colleges and universities for additional purposed.

Social Media Outside of the Classroom

Although social media can be used by instructors and students for classroom purposes, social media is also present outside of the classroom. Colleges and universities have been using social media accounts on Facebook, Twitter, and Instagram for other reasons: student recruitment, communication, and research. These are examples of how social media is used for personal and professional reasons.

Student Recruitment

Social networks such as Twitter, Facebook, and Instagram are being used by colleges and universities to advertise their academics, sports teams, research projects, awards, etc., as a student recruitment technique. Students who follow specific school accounts or those who stay up-to-date with college and university news or sports, are more likely to view their advertisements via social media. Figure 1 provides an image of five different universities who have Twitter accounts.

Figure 1. Screenshot of five different college or university Twitter accounts

Robert Morris University's Twitter page provides a link to take a virtual tour of their campus along with hashtags related to the school while the Technical University of Munich's page provides a link to their Facebook and Instagram accounts and a YouTube video about the university. Instead of viewing traditional commercials or billboards, social media sites that students use on a regular basis are becoming the new form of advertisement in hopes of recruiting students.

Communication

Aside from using Twitter, Facebook, and Instagram for recruitment purposes, school accounts are used to communicate with the local community and student population. School extracurricular and sporting events, club activities, conferences, crisis or emergency situations, and delays or closures due to weather are only a few examples of important information that can be communicated through social media. Any student who follows their college or university, or searches for specific hashtags, can receive instant alerts about their school. Using social media to remain informed about everyday happenings can be extremely helpful to students. It is vital that students receive immediate notifications if and when an emergency situation occurs; this can be done using school social media accounts.

Research

Another way that colleges and universities are using social media is to inform followers about research projects, conferences, and achievements. Certain universities are known for their research, while others strive to be named a research institute; using social media accounts to share upcoming and innovative research with colleagues, students, and competitors is done easily through a school account. By sharing innovative research and current projects, colleges and universities can find research partners or potential companies or businesses interested in funding such projects.

General Social Media Concerns

While there are a variety of social network options to enhance college courses, there are many concerns that accompany their use. In addition to the faculty concerns from the Pearson reports, the long-term effects of social media use are unknown, and possible concerns include addiction, privacy, and health. Cell phone addiction is a growing concern for children and adults. Privacy continues to be a concern and the impact of social media on health is a critical and timely issue.

Addiction

Research on cell phone addiction is becoming more available and there are now ways to diagnose addiction. Bhise, Ghatule, and Ghatule (2014) used a 10-item questionnaire to conduct a study on mobile addiction among students. The study found that more than 75% of students have mobile addiction. They go on to compare cell phones to cigarettes, classifying it as one of the biggest non-drug addiction of the 21st century. Addiction is clear when an obsession disrupts other things in life such as relationships, school or work (Bhise et al., 2014).

There are five risk factors for Mobile Addiction described by Bhise et al. (2014):

1. **Anxiety Disorders:** Those who suffer from anxiety may use mobile phones to distract them from fear or worry. Obsessive-compulsive disorder may contribute to excessive SMS/MMS checking and compulsive mobile use.
2. **Depression:** Those who suffer from depression may use mobile phones to distract them from feelings of depression. Too much time online can make these feelings worse and further contribute to stress, isolation, and loneliness.
3. **Lack of Social Support:** Those who lack social support may use social networking as a way to establish new relationships and relate to others.
4. **Less Social Activity:** Those who are less mobile or socially active than before due to disability, parenting, or other circumstances that limit leaving home, may turn to mobile use.
5. **Stress:** Those who turn to mobile use to relieve stress. This is usually counterproductive as more time dedicated to mobile use can increase stress.

Yildirim (2014) offers a 20-item questionnaire to determine if one suffers from Nomophobia, the fear of not being able to use your cell phone. His study showed those who score high on the questionnaire may avoid personal interactions and suffer from social anxiety and depression. He further explains that if a person is too dependent on their smartphone, they are decreasing their ability to pay attention. This is a concern for communication in the global workforce.

A study published in the Journal of Media Education found that college students check their digital devices for non-class related content an average of 11.43 times per class (McCoy, 2016). This means that students spend approximately 20% of class time using mobile devices for things that do not related to class. When students were asked if they use their mobile device 10 times or more for non-learning reasons during class, 34% reported yes. Specific reasons for non-class related mobile use included to stay connected and boredom. The consequences for using mobile devices for non-class related things included not paying attention and missing instruction. Thus, 53% of students reported that it would be helpful to have policies that limit non-class related use of mobile devices.

The current studies on cell phone addiction do not distinguish between personal, professional, and teaching or educational use. More research is needed to establish when a student is using social media for things unrelated to class. A student who is actively using social media for class collaboration would increase class communication, but a student who is using social media for personal accounts would decrease class communication. Personal social media use could interfere with intended class collaboration use. Regardless of the type of use, social media can increase virtual interaction, but possibly interfere with or take away from face to face communication.

Privacy

The Pearson reports consistently revealed that higher education faculty were concerned about students' privacy through social media use. Additionally, higher education faculty stated a concern in the lack of integrity in student submissions (Moran, Seaman, & Tinti-Kane, 2012). Parents of adolescents are encouraged to monitor potential problems with bullying, depression, sexting, and inappropriate content (O'Keeffe & Clarke-Pearson, 2011). As young adults transition to higher education, they bring a lot of social media experience.

Another privacy concern is course content. Social media could reveal and expose course content to future students. While many of the platforms only grant access to those with a code or log-in, there is potential for easier access and shared information. When considering privacy as a concern, it is reasonable to consider the category of use as personal, professional, or educational use and the platform that is used. More steps can be taken to separate personal from professional accounts.

Health

Acharya, Acharya, and Waghrey (2013) studied the effects of cell phone use on health among college students. Headaches, irritability, and anger were found as symptoms of cell phone addiction. Mental problems included lack of concentration, poor academic performance, insomnia, and anxiety. Additionally, physical problems included body aches, eye strain, and digital thumb. For a 2013 study through Ottawa Public Health, researchers collected data from 750 teens in grades 7 through 12 concerning social media habits, mental health, and psychological well-being, and mental health support.

The results revealed that teens who use social media for more than two hours per day are more likely to struggle with mental health, psychological distress and suicidal thoughts (Sampasa-Kanyinga & Lewis, 2015).

A study linked Facebook to depressive symptoms due to social comparison. Steers, Wickham and Acitelli (2014) found in a study of 180 people there was a link between time spent on Facebook and depressive symptoms regardless of gender. Another study found an association between online social networking and depression in high school students (Pantic et al., 2012). Pantic et al., (2012) found online social networking was related to depression after interviewing 160 high school students using an anonymous, structured questionnaire and back depression inventory. Another study through the University of Pittsburgh found that young adults who spend more than two hours per day on social media are 2.7 more likely to be depressed. Adults ages 19-32 were surveyed about social media use and depression. Of the 1,787 participants, those who had the highest use of social media had significantly increased odds of depression (Lin et al., 2016).

A study by Twenge, Joiner, Rogers, and Martin (2017) found links to increased new media (means of mass communication using digital technologies such as the Internet) screen time among U.S. adolescents and depressive symptoms, suicide related outcomes, and suicide rates after 2010. In two nationally representative surveys of a total of 506,820 U.S. adolescents in grades 8 through 12, found that adolescents who spent more time on new media were more likely to report mental health issues than those who spent more time on non-screen activities. When compared to national statistics on suicide deaths for ages 13 to 18, from 2010 to 2015, adolescents' depressive symptoms, suicide-related outcomes, and suicide rates all increased. The study concluded that adolescents have spent more time on new media screen activities since 2010 and that may account for the increase in depression and suicide.

A report by the Royal Society for Public Health in the United Kingdom presented the findings of a survey presented to almost 1,500 people between the ages of 14 and 24 concerning how Facebook, Instagram, YouTube, Twitter, and Snapchat made them feel (Young Health Movement, n.d.). The survey consisted of 14 questions about each social media platform. To measure the impact of social media on overall wellbeing, the questions asked participants about their feelings of anxiety, depression, and loneliness, as well as the impact on body image, sleep, bullying, and level of FOMO (fear of missing out), while using or after using each social media platform. All of the social media platforms were associated with poor sleep and tiredness. The results also revealed that Instagram, Snapchat, Facebook, and Twitter all resulted in a worse wellbeing. YouTube was the only platform that slightly improved well-being. Recommendations were to set reminders or trackers to limit social media use, focus on what brings joy, positive content, keep in mind others are not posting their real lives, spend more time posting, liking, and messaging versus simply looking at social media content, and ask why you are looking at social media content.

As with addiction and privacy, when considering health as a concern, current research does not distinguish between personal, professional, or teaching use. Time spent on social media should be further researched to include how the time is spent (personal, professional, or teaching). Perhaps academic social media use would take away from the social pressure that these studies revealed.

Limitations of Current Research

The following research studies provide valuable information, but many lack specific details and direction. Based on the idea that mobile learning has grown informally through individual use more than formal use in education, Hao et al. (2017), analyzed mobile learning as an innovation in higher education. Their comparative study focused on how students in the United States, China, and Turkey perceive mobile learning as an innovation based on relative advantage, compatibility, complexity, trialability, and observability. The survey results showed that students were ready to use mobile learning and many already use a form informally. The survey also revealed student concern for support and infrastructure, but lacks recommendations.

Gikas and Grant (2013) interviewed student focus groups across the United States concerning their perspectives on learning with cellphones, smartphones, and social media. They found that mobile devices and the use of social media allowed interaction and provided opportunities for collaboration. Students shared a fear of technology not working, difficulty typing and concern for distractibility.

A 2005 study found students who used laptops learned more collaboratively, did more project-based learning (PBL), and were more likely to engage in problem-solving (Burns & Polman, 2006). Collaboration was found to be the most popular mobile learning environment in a meta-analysis study that compared collaboration, situated learning, peer-assessment, multidimensional, and PBL to analyze students' critical thinking using mobile technology in the learning environment (Ismail, Harun, Salleh, & Zakaria, 2016).

Casey's (2013) action research study found that when students created an online identity, communicated with peers, reviewed, and assessed through social media platforms, they were active and valued the learning process. A 2015 study compared the use of social networking sites between medical students and medical educators. The results were consistent with Pearson's studies finding that social media use continues to grow in higher education, but with barriers. Educators in the study tended to use social media to post videos, articles, and comments and students indicated a preference in posting quizzes and revision files (Bialy & Jalali, 2015).

The research presented provides a lot of valuable information, yet it is difficult to make specific recommendations and keep up with constantly changing social media. Teens today use completely different social media platforms that were not even mentioned in the Pearson surveys. The most preferred social networks for teenagers in the United States has changed drastically in the past five years. According to Statista (2018), in 2012, Facebook was the most preferred social media among American teenagers (42%). By 2017, Facebook was one of the least favorite among teenagers (9%). Snapchat was one of the least preferred in 2015 (11%) but in 2016 and 2017, was the most preferred among teens, with 47% of teenagers listing it as their most preferred social network. As teens transition into college and social media fads come and go, educators strive to make connections and adapt. Current research is also lacking practical examples or guides on how to incorporate or transition to a social media environment for higher education faculty members.

SOLUTIONS AND RECOMMENDATIONS

Social media use in higher education raises many questions. In addition to the concerns discussed in this chapter, there are many other things to consider. Higher education faculty must be familiar with the social media platform they wish to implement. Additionally, the level and goal of the collaboration must be considered, as well as, the value of formal versus informal learning. There are many aspects of social media in the classroom that can be viewed as advantageous. Social media is part of our everyday lives and creates easy access to information that can be viewed instantly. Research shows that technology is changing the way we learn and that students prefer mobile learning (Benson, 2011). Arokiasamy (2017) notes the flexibility, portability, affordability, and popularity of mobile devices such as iPads, tablets, e-readers, and smartphones as primary reasons for educators to implement their use. Furthermore, he adds that integrating mobile devices into instruction can support digital learners and promote meaningful learning. There are countless ways to use social media in higher education. Providing higher education faculty with research and information on social media can be the first step to allow them to make informed decisions on social media use in their courses. Current research and concerns must be acknowledged to help faculty make informed decisions concerning the use of social media in higher education courses.

Mentioned previously was that students may check their mobile devices, for non-class related information, on average 11.43 times per class (McCoy, 2016). Students stated that this was a result of boredom. The study conducted by Jacquemin et al. (2014) found that using Twitter in the classroom improved the feeling of belonging in the classroom. Noting this, using social media in the classroom will allow students to use their devices during instruction, for educational purposes, which can promote a sense of belonging while potentially diminishing the feeling of boredom or need to use their phone for non-class related purposes.

Battling student phone addiction and personal use in class can raise concerns and may prevent higher education instructors from promoting mobile device and social media in the classroom; however, if a device and social media policy is created, acceptable use is modeled by instructors, and implementation is properly planned and implemented it can change the dynamic of the classroom while allowing students to build the skills for the Four Cs.

FUTURE RESEARCH DIRECTIONS

Most current research on social media use in higher education does not differentiate between personal, professional, and educational use. Future research could be based on personal, professional, and educational use of social media and cell phone addiction and health. Future research could also include social media use in formal and informal learning, social media communication and collaboration, social media use based on discipline, social media use outside of the classroom, and the impact of social media communication on face to face communication.

Many of the studies presented in this chapter could be used as a foundation for further research. Based on the comparative study by Hao et al. (2017), future studies should focus on what form of mobile learning students are most prepared to use and what concerns they have for support and infrastructure.

A follow up to Gikas and Grant's 2013 focus groups could compare social media versus face-to-face interaction and collaboration and ways to handle technology not working and distractibility. Furthermore, a follow up to Casey's (2013) action research study could investigate if students are more active learners when communicating through social media.

Lastly, research currently lacks a "How to Guide" for social media implementation to provide faculty members with practical examples of implementation for multiple age levels and subject areas. Providing a "How to Guide" could provide institutes and instructors with policy suggestions, different types of social media platforms and uses, and suggestions of how to properly implement social media use for teaching and educational purposes. These research suggestions will not only contribute to the literature, but also provide up-to-date references for those hoping to use social media in higher education.

CONCLUSION

Benson (2011) from the Association for the Advancement of Computing in Education explains that social media is changing the way we think and process information. It can be overwhelming for educators to keep up with current social media use and decide which platforms to use. Educational goals should be the first priority. Social media use in higher education could provide benefits through collaboration, communication, and technology skills. As social media use continues to increase, educators must find the most appropriate and effective ways to incorporate social media use into courses. It is nearly impossible to keep up with all of the platforms and predict what social media will be used in the years ahead. Social media choices are constantly changing and the apps that are most used one year can completely change the next. Although the applications presented in much of the research may be used more or less today than when they were studied, the results are valuable in that there are many common issues and concerns regardless of which social media applications are used.

REFERENCES

Acharya, J. P., Acharya, I., & Waghrey, D. (2013). A study on some psychological health effects of cell-phone usage amongst college going students. *International Journal of Medical Research & Health Sciences*, 2(3), 388. doi:10.5958/j.2319-5886.2.3.068

Al-Bahrani, A., & Patel, D. (2015). Incorporating Twitter, Instagram, and Facebook in economics classrooms. *The Journal of Economic Education, 46*(1), 56-67. from http://reddog.rmu.edu:2061/eds/pdfviewer/pdfviewer?vid=3&sid=650d2878-c8d1-4897-8cd7-b53af0f42def@sessionmgr4008

An Educator's Guide to the "Four Cs". (n.d.). *NEA*. Retrieved from http://www.nea.org/tools/52217.htm

Arokiasamy, A. R. (2017). A systematic review approach of mobile technology adoption in higher education. *Economics, Management and Sustainability, 2*(2), 48-55. Retrieved from https://zenodo.org/record/1145854/files/05_Anantha_01.pdf

Banks, J., Au, K., Ball, A. F., Bell, P., Gordon, E., Gutiérrez, K., ... & Valdes, G. (2007). Learning in and out of school in diverse environments. Retrieved from http://life-slc.org/docs/Banks_etal-LIFE-Diversity-Report.pdf

Benson, S. (2011). Social media and the classroom. *AACE Review*. Retrieved from https://www.aace.org/social-media-and-the-classroom/

Bhise, A., Ghatule, A., & Ghatule, A. (2014). Study of mobile addiction among students. *Indian Journal of Research in Management, Business and Social Sciences, 21*(1A), 17-21. Retrieved from http://www.ijrmbss.com/assets/pdf/Vol2Iss1a/5.pdf

Bialy, S.E. & Jalali, A. (2015). Go where the students are: A comparison of the use of social networking sites between medical students and medical educators. *JMIR Medical Education, 1*(2). Retrieved from http://mededu.jmir.org/2015/2/e7/

Brown, J. S., & Adler, R. P. (2008). Minds on fire: open education, the long tail, and learning 2.0. *Educause Review*, 16-32. Retrieved from http://www.oss.net/dynamaster/file_archive/080618/bdb5129a636e9ff-be734351363466c23/Minds%20on%20Fire.%20Open%20Education,%20the%20Long%20Tail,%20 and%20Learning%202. 0%20-%20Brown,%20Adler%20(2008).pdf

Burns, K., & Polman, J. (2006). The impact of ubiquitous computing in the internet age: How middle school teachers integrated wireless laptops in the initial stages of implementation. *Journal of Technology and Teacher Education, 14*(2), 363-385. Retrieved from https://www.learntechlib.org/p/5777/

Casey, G. (2013). Social media in the classroom: A simple yet complex hybrid environment for students. *Journal of Educational Multimedia and Hypermedia, 22*(1), 5-24. Retrieved from https://www.learntechlib.org/p/41333/

Chen, B., & Bryer, T. (2012). Investigating instructional strategies for using social media in formal and informal learning. *The International Review of Research in Open and Distributed Learning, 13*(1). Retrieved from http://www.irrodl.org/index.php/irrodl/article/view/1027/2073?utm_campaign=elearningindustry.com&utm_source=/10-tips-to-effectively-use-social-media-in-formal-learning&utm_medium=link

Chou, W. S., Hunt, Y. M., Beckjord, E. B., Moser, R. P., & Hesse, B. W. (2009). Social media use in the United States: Implications for health communication. *Journal of Medical Internet Research, 11*(4), e48. doi:10.2196/jmir.1249 PMID:19945947

Gikas, J., & Grant, M. M. (2013). Mobile computing devices in higher education: Student perspectives on learning with cellphones, smartphones & social media. *The Internet and Higher Education, 19*, 18–26. doi:10.1016/j.iheduc.2013.06.002

Golding, P., Raeymaeckers, K., & Sousa, H. (2017). Social media – New challenges and approaches for communications research. *European Journal of Communication, 32*(1), 3–5. doi:10.1177/0267323116682801

Greenhow, C., & Robelia, B. (2009). Informal learning and identity formation in online social networks. *Learning, Media and Technology, 34*(2), 119–140. doi:10.1080/17439880902923580

Hao, S., Cui, M., Dennen, V. P., Türel, Y. K., & Mei, L. (2017). Analysis of mobile learning as an innovation in higher education: A comparative study of three countries. *International Journal of Mobile Learning and Organization, 11*(4), 314. Retrieved from http://www.inderscience.com/info/inarticle. php?artid=87080 doi:10.1504/IJMLO.2017.087080

Hew, K. F., & Brush, T. (2006). Integrating technology into K-12 teaching and learning: current knowledge gaps and recommendations for future research. *Educational Technology Research and Development, 55*(3), 223-252. Retrieved from https://www.researchgate.net/publication/225668789_Integrating_technology_into_K-12_teaching_and_learning_Current_knowledge_gaps_and_recommendations_for_future_research

Hutt, R. (2017). The world's most popular social networks, mapped. *World Economic Forum.* Retrieved from https://www.weforum.org/agenda/2017/03/most-popular-social-networks-mapped/

Ismail, N. S., Harun, J., Salleh, S. M., & Zakaria, M. A. (2016). Supporting students' critical thinking with a mobile learning environment: A meta-analysis. In *INTED2016 Proceedings.* Retrieved from https://www.researchgate.net/publication/312940527_SUPPORTING_STUDENTS'_CRITICAL_THINKING_WITH_A_MOBILE_LEARNING_ENVIRONMENT_A_META-ANALYSIS

Jacquemin, S. J., Smelser, L. K., & Bernot, M. J. (2014). Twitter in the higher education classroom: A student and faculty assessment of use and perception. *Journal of College Science Teaching, 43*(6), 22-27. Retrieved from http://reddog.rmu.edu:2061/eds/pdfviewer/pdfviewer?vid=10&sid=df38a0c7-71a8-446d-a62a- 587a3d7c43c6%40sessionmgr4010

Kaplan, A. M., & Haenlein, M. (2010). Users of the world, unite! The challenges and opportunities of Social Media. *Business Horizons, 53*(1), 59–68. Retrieved from http://michaelhaenlein.eu/Publications/Kaplan,%20Andreas%20-%20Users%20of%20the%20world,%20unite.pdf doi:10.1016/j.bushor.2009.09.003

Lin, L. Y., Sidani, J. E., Shensa, A., Radovic, A., Miller, E., & Colditz, J. …Primack, B. A. (2016). Association between social media use and depression among U.S. young adults. *Depression and Anxiety, 33*(4), 323-331. Retrieved from https://www.ncbi.nlm.nih.gov/pmc/articles/PMC4853817/pdf/nihms749957.pdf

McCoy, B. (2016). Digital distractions in the classroom phase II: Student classroom use of digital devices for non-class related purposes. *Journal of Media Education* (7) 5-32. Retrieved on 20 January 2018 from https://digitalcommons.unl.edu/cgi/viewcontent.cgi?referer=https://www.google.com/&httpsredir=1&article=1091&context=journalismfacpub

Moran, M., Seaman, J., & Tinti-Kane, H. (2011). Teaching, learning, and sharing: How today's higher education faculty use social media. Pearson. Retrieved from https://files.eric.ed.gov/fulltext/ED535130.pdf

Moran, M., Seaman, J., & Tinti-Kane, H. (2012). *Blogs, wikis, podcasts And Facebook. Pearson Learning Solutions: how today's higher education faculty use social media.* Pearson. Retrieved from https://www.onlinelearningsurvey.com/reports/blogswikispodcasts.pdf

O'Keeffe, G. S., & Clarke-Pearson, K. (2011). The impact of social media on children, adolescents, and families. *American Academy of Pediatrics, 127*(4). Retrieved from http://research3.fit.edu/sealevelriselibrary/documents/doc_mgr/1006/O'Keeffe_and_Pearson._2011._The_Impact_of_Social_Media_on_Children,_Adolescents,_and_Families.pdf

Pantic, I., Damjanovic, A., Todorovic, J., Topalovic, D., Bojovic-Jovic, D., Ristic, S., & Pantic, S. (2012). Association between online social networking and depression in high school students: Behavioral physiology viewpoint. *Psychiatria Danubina*, *24*(1), 90–93. Retrieved on 20 January 2018 from http://www.hdbp.org/psychiatria_danubina/pdf/dnb_vol24_no1/dnb_vol24_no1_90.pdf PMID:22447092

Ross, H. M., Banow, R., & Yu, S. (2015). The use of Twitter in large lecture courses: Do the students see a benefit? *Contemporary Educational Technology, 6*(2), 126-139. Retrieved from http://reddog.rmu.edu:2061/eds/pdfviewer/pdfviewer?vid=11&sid=df38a0c7-71a8-446d-a62a-587a3d7c43c6%40sessionmgr4010

Rowan-Kenyon, H. T., Alemán, A. M., Gin, K., Blakeley, B., Gismondi, A., & Lewis, J. … Knight, S. (2016). Social media in higher education. *ASHE Higher Education Report, 42*(5), 7-128. Retrieved from http://onlinelibrary.wiley.com/doi/10.1002/aehe.20088/epdf

Sampasa-Kanyinga, H., & Lewis, R. F. (2015). Frequent use of social networking sites is associated with poor psychological functioning among children and adolescents. *Cyberpsychology, Behavior, and Social Networking*, *18*(7), 380–385. doi:10.1089/cyber.2015.0055 PMID:26167836

Schlagwein, D., & Hu, M. (2017). How and why organizations use social media: Five use types and their relation to absorptive capacity. *Journal of Information Technology*, *32*(2), 194–209. doi:10.1057/jit.2016.7

Seaman, J., & Tinti-Kane, H. (2013). *Social media for teaching and learning*. Pearson. Retrieved from http://www.pearsonlearningsolutions.com/assets/downloads/reports/social-media-for-teaching-and-learning-2013-report.pdf#view=FitH,0

Siemens, G. (2005). Connectivism: A learning theory for the digital age. *International Journal of Instructional Technology and Distance Learning (ITDL)*. Retrieved from http://www.itdl.org/journal/jan_05/article01.htm

Simard, D. A., & Schnackenberg, H. L. (2006). Online Course Creation and Facilitation: The New Classroom Management. Department of Special Education SUNY Plattsburgh, New York. Retrieved from http://citeseerx.ist.psu.edu/viewdoc/download?doi=10.1.1.627.422&rep=rep1&type=pdf

Slavin, R. E. (2018). *Educational Psychology: theory and practice*. NY, NY: Pearson.

Statista. (2018). *Most popular social networks of teenagers in the United States from fall 2012 to fall 2017*. Retrieved from https://www.statista.com/statistics/250172/social-network-usage-of-us-teens-and-young-adults/

Steers, M. N., Wickham, R. E., & Acitelli, L. K. (2014). Seeing everyone else's highlight reels: How Facebook usage is linked to depressive symptoms. *Journal of Social and Clinical Psychology*, *33*(8), 701–731. doi:10.1521/jscp.2014.33.8.701

Tinti-Kane, H., Seaman, J., & Levy, J. (2010). *Social media in higher education: The survey*. Pearson. Retrieved from https://www.babson.edu/Academics/Documents/babson-survey-research-group/social-media-in-hi gher-education.pdf

Twenge, J. M., Joiner, T. E., Rogers, M. L., & Martin, G. N. (2017). Increases in depressive symptoms, suicide-related outcomes, and suicide rates among U.S. adolescents after 2010 and links to increased new media screen time. *Clinical Psychological Science*, *6*(1), 3–17. doi:10.1177/2167702617723376

VoiceThread. (n.d.). VoiceThread fills the social presence gap found in online learning interactions. Retrieved from https://voicethread.com/products/highered/

What is Kahoot! (2017). Kahoot. Retrieved from https://kahoot.com/what-is-kahoot/

What is Social Media. (n.d.). Educational Council of New Zealand. Retrieved from https://www.teachersandsocialmedia.co.nz/what-social-media

Yildirim, C. (2014). Exploring the dimensions of nomophobia: Developing and validating a questionnaire using mixed methods research. Retrieved from https://lib.dr.iastate.edu/cgi/viewcontent.cgi?article=5012&context=etd

Young Health Movement. (n.d.). Retrieved from http://www.yhm.org.uk/

ADDITIONAL READING

Basu, B. (2017). Analyzing the perception of social networking sites as a learning tool among university students: Case study of a business school in India. *World Academy of Science, Engineering and Technology International Journal of Educational and Pedagogical Sciences,11*(7), 1683-1689. Retrieved from https://waset.org/publications/10007520/analyzing-the-perception-of-social-networking-sites-as-a-learning-tool-among-university-students-case-study-of-a-business-school-in-india

Bhutia, Y., & Tariang, A. (2016). Mobile phone addiction among college going students in Shillong. *International Journal of Education and Psychological Research*, 5(2), 29–35. Retrieved from http://ijepr.org/doc/V5_Is2_June16/ij6.pdf

Duke, B., Harper, G., & Johnston, M. (2013). Connectivism as a digital age learning theory. *HETL Review*, 4-13. Retrieved from https://www.hetl.org/wp-content/uploads/2013/09/HETLReview2013SpecialIssueArticle1.pdf

Kaplan, A., & Haenlein, M. (2014). Collaborative projects (social media application): About Wikipedia, the free encyclopedia. *Business Horizons*, 57(5), 617–626. doi:10.1016/j.bushor.2014.05.004

Kaplan, A. M., & Haenlein, M. (2012). Social media: Back to the roots and back to the future. *Journal of Systems and Information Technology*, 14(2), 101-104. Retrieved from http://www.michaelhaenlein.eu/Publications/Kaplan,%20Andreas%20-%20Back%20to%20the%20roots%20and%20back%20to%20the%20future.pdf

Misra, S., Cheng, L., Genevie, J., & Yuan, M. (2014). The iPhone effect. *Environment and Behavior, 48*(2), 275-298. Retrieved from https://www.researchgate.net/publication/270730343_The_iPhone_Effect_The_Quality_of_In-Person_Social_Interactions_in_the_Presence_of_Mobile_Devices

Pearson Student Mobile Device Survey 2013. National Report: College Students. (2013). Retrieved from https://www.pearsoned.com/wp-content/uploads/Pearson-Student-Mobile-Device-Survey-2013-National-Report-on-College-Students-public-release.pdf

Pearson Student Mobile Device Survey 2015. National Report: College Students. (2015). Retrieved from https://www.pearsoned.com/wp-content/uploads/2015-Pearson-Student-Mobile-Device-Survey-College.pdf

Przybylski, A. K., & Weinstein, N. (2012). Can you connect with me now? How the presence of mobile communication technology influences face-to-face conversation quality. *Journal of Social and Personal Relationships*, *30*(3), 237–246. doi:10.1177/0265407512453827

KEY TERMS AND DEFINITIONS

Connectivism Theory: Learning theory for the digital age that explains how complex and constantly changing the social digital world is.

Constructivism Learning: Learning through experience, one develops their own understanding and knowledge.

Formal Learning: Structured learning with planned objectives.

Informal Learning: Learning through participation (unorganized, unstructured).

Learning Management System (LMS): A system for educational courses to be delivered, documented, and overseen.

Personal Social Media Use: Social media use unrelated to higher education.

Professional Social Media Use: Social media use for higher education, but not teaching or class.

Problem-Based Learning (PBL): Given a challenging situation, or complex problem, students are given extended time to investigate and work.

Social Learning: Learning from one another through social situations that can include observing, imitating, or modeling.

Teaching Social Media Use: Social media use specifically for teaching or class.

Chapter 37

Instagram as a Tool for Professional Learning:
English Language Teachers' Perceptions and Beliefs

Amir Allan Aghayi
AOI College of Language, USA

MaryAnn Christison
ⓘ https://orcid.org/0000-0003-3760-0619
University of Utah, USA

ABSTRACT

The purpose of the current research is to investigate the potential of a social media tool, known as Instagram, for teacher professional learning. The chapter describes a three-year research project, which used Instagram, to investigate the perceptions and beliefs of 1,500 practicing English language teachers relative to their professional development experiences on Instagram. Six research questions (RQs) framed the study and determined how we viewed and analyzed the data. Qualitative data from six types of activity feeds were analyzed through the processes of open and axial coding. The results indicated that teachers' perceptions and beliefs about Instagram as a tool for professional learning were positive. The professional learning provided teachers with extensive opportunities to work with multimodal texts, create networks and connections with other teachers, and develop their reflective skills.

INTRODUCTION

In recent decades, we have witnessed numerous and dramatic advances in digital technologies. Only a few decades ago, the World Wide Web (hereafter, the Web) was a medium that was used to present read-only text and static factual information and resources, which were predominantly produced by experts. As such, these resources could be viewed by users but could not be changed or added to. Because of steady advances in digital technologies, more software tools, and more powerful computers and mobile

DOI: 10.4018/978-1-6684-7123-4.ch037

devices, the Web has now evolved to include social media websites where individuals can interact with one another, create their own materials, and produce digital content in real time through the use of one of the web browsers. This conceptualization of the Web as a platform for collaborative interaction has been called Web 2.0 and has resulted in the proliferation of social media tools and platforms for facilitating discussion and sharing content through the use of text, audio, video, and images for use on computers and mobile devices. Social media platforms, such as Facebook and LinkedIn, are ubiquitous and have become part of the fabric of daily life for billions of people worldwide. According to the Pew Center (Perrin & Anderson, 2019), 3.1 billion people (42% of the World's population) are social media users.

At the same time, English has become a world language with an estimated 1.75 billion speakers (British Council, 2020), and it is being used increasingly for commerce, science, and technology. With the growth of English has come the demand for more qualified English language teachers. As a result, more English language teachers are seeking online courses that lead to a qualification, such as teaching certificates, endorsements, or degrees and professional learning activities online (Murray, 2013; Murray & Christison, 2017, 2018). Because of the flexibility that online learning affords, the number of opportunities for English language teacher professional development also continues to swell.

In addition, social media has now found its way into educational contexts in both K-12 schools and institutions of higher education and has been used for a number of purposes; for example, to create, share, and receive user-generated content online (Vivakaran & Neelamalar, 2018); to affect student engagement (Abney, Cook, Fox, & Stevens, 2018); to improve writing (Soviyah & Etikaningshik, 2018); to promote peer interaction (Manson & Rahim, 2017); and to increase motivation (Purnama, 2018). In addition, Facebook is now used by teachers to form communities of inquiry (COI) (Arnold & Ducate, 2006), and Google Docs is used by students to connect and complete written projects together online.

The purpose of the current research is to investigate the potential of the mobile assisted, social media tool known as Instagram for teacher professional learning. The chapter describes a three-year research project which investigated the perceptions and beliefs of practicing English language teachers relative to their professional learning experiences on Instagram. Five research questions (RQs) framed the research project and determined how data were viewed and analyzed. The RQs are as follows:

1. Why do English language teachers choose Instagram for professional learning?
2. What do English language teachers hope to gain from their professional learning experiences?
3. What types of activities on Instagram interested teachers the most?
4. What topics interested teachers the most?
5. What are teachers' beliefs about how their professional development and learning experiences on Instagram might ultimately affect their teaching?

BACKGROUND

Theoretical Foundations

Like learning in face-to-face (f2f) classrooms, online learning must also be grounded in theory. Two of the most influential theories for online learning to date are Siemens connectivism (2005) and Downes (2006) distributed learning. *Connectivism* is a theory of learning that explains how internet technologies create opportunities for users to share and learn across the Web. It also provides a theoretical framework for understanding learning in a digital age and emphasizes how internet technologies, such as wiki pages, discussion boards, social networks and the use of multi-media, can create new opportunities for sharing and learning new information. According to connectivism, learning can reside outside of an individual and is a combination of what we know and the abilities we develop for knowing how to share knowledge with others. Connectivism views knowledge as a series of networks. Downes (2006) proposes a framework for learning called distributed learning, and it is consistent with connectivist views because it is based on the notion that human knowledge and cognition are not confined to an individual but are distributed across specific groups of people and the tools they use (Hutchins, 1996), such as across a group of individuals who are social media users.

While social media allows for seemingly endless educational possibilities, it also requires the use of multiliteracies. *Multiliteracies* is a term coined by the New London Group (1996). It is an approach to literacy theory and pedagogy that includes the ability to create meaning across different modalities or forms of communication, for example, visual, oral, musical, and linguistic. A text can be defined as multi-modal when it combines two or more semiotic system. Anstey and Bull (2011) identified five semiotic systems, which are briefly outlined as follows:

1. Linguistic: comprising aspects, such as vocabulary, generic structure, and the grammar of oral and written language.
2. Visual: comprising aspects, such as colour, vectors, and viewpoint in still and moving images.
3. Audio: comprising aspects, such as volume, pitch, and rhythm of music and sound effects.
4. Gestural: comprising aspects, such as movement, speed, and stillness in facial expression and body language.
5. Spatial: comprising aspects, such as proximity, direction, position of layout, and organisation of objects in space. (n.p.)

When a text presents a combination of modalities, such as linguistic and audio, linguistic and visual, or linguistic and spatial systems, it is considered a multimodal text. Most online texts combine different modalities and are similar to picture books for young children, which include prose to tell the story and pictures.

To understand the impact that multimodal texts have on language learning, English language teachers need to have their own experiences with multimodal texts and professional learning opportunities that encourage them to reflect on their experiences and share information with other teachers. These professional learning experiences are particularly important given that literacy is socially constructed, as a sociocultural view of language would suggest (Vygotsky, 1978; Lantolf & Thorne, 2006). Prinsloo and Walton (2008) have also noted the complexity involved in literacy development:

Reading effectively and correctly does not involve just the finding and decoding of words, images, and multi-media screens but also includes the practices of "seeing through" the representational resources of the texts to make sense [of them] in particular ways, which vary across social settings (p. 112).

The study of teachers' beliefs and perceptions and their relationship to classroom teaching practices is rooted in research on teacher cognition (Phipps & Borg, 2007) and is concerned with the unobservable dimension of teaching, in other words, with a focus on what teachers think, know and believe.

It is obvious that what teachers do is directed in no small measure by what they think. To the extent that observed or intended teaching behaviour is "thoughtless," it makes no use of the human teacher's most unique attributes. In so doing, it becomes mechanical and might well be done by a machine. If, however, teaching is done and, in all likelihood, will continue to be done by human teachers, the question of relationships between thought and action becomes crucial (National Institute of Education, 1975, p.1).

Social Media

Charles Babbage and Alan Turing, who have both been credited with inventing the computer, would likely be surprised to find that the computational and analytical machine they envisioned has become a social networking tool (Murray & Christison, 2017). Social media is changing the landscape of human interaction and learning. Due to advances in digital technologies and the increased availability of broadband or high-speed Internet access, social media has grown exponentially. There are now billions of monthly users on Facebook, YouTube, and Instagram (Dreamgrow, 2020), and they spend an average of two hours and 24 minutes each day using social media sites (Education Statistics, 2020), making a little more than half of all online activity tied to social media. Social media is also infiltrating nearly every academic discipline from humanities to the sciences and is being used to network and develop virtual communities of practice. Within social media there is a wide range of tools and platforms, such as blogs and micro-blogs, media sharing, RSS, bookmarking, social networks, and wikis.

In the most general sense, a *blog* is very much like a diary or a web-based journal online. These tools allow users to write about their lives, post pictures and media, and express opinions so that others can view what they have said and even reply. Entries can be made at any intervals that meet the writers' goals. Many individuals blog on a daily basis, especially if they have a large number of followers. Others blog regularly but less often, while some choose to blog irregularly or on special occasions. Blogs can be self-hosted or can be part of a network of bloggers. *Micro-blogs* are like blogs except that writing is limited to brief texts, which are transmitted to readers in real time. The most famous service for micro-bloggers is Twitter.

Media sharing sites such as Flickr, Shutterfly, and YouTube permit users to upload and share multimedia, such as photos, slides, and videos. Uploads can be public or private and can be tagged with comments. YouTube even allows users to have their own channels, which can also be public or private.

Bookmarking tools permit users to bookmark or tag their favorite websites for other users who share their interests. Delicious, Pinterest, and Stumbleupon are websites that offer bookmarking services, which can be public or private. In educational contexts, bookmarking has also been used to develop research-based practices by marking and sharing articles for future discussion or research project.

Social networks sites (SNS) are online communities that are comprised of individuals who come together for share common interests and experiences. Each user has a profile on the network and that profile might include other users and their profiles, depending on with whom they are linked socially. On many sites, users can post photos and videos, write comments, and communicate easily within their networks. Most SNS also provide a means for socially linked users to communicate via email or instant messaging over the Internet. Some of the most popular social network sites are Facebook, LinkedIn, and MySpace.

Really simple syndication or *rich site summary* are both known as RSS feeds. An RSS feed allows users to create customized feeds from their favorite websites and for their favorite topics. Users can subscribe (usually for free) to as many of the feeds of information as they wish. The RSS reader also allows users to manage their feeds. The most popular of these feeds are Digg Reader, Freedreader, and Flow Reader.

Wikis are websites that have been developed collaboratively by a group of users, and they allow individual users to amend, correct, and update sites. The largest wiki is Wikipedia, which is an online encyclopedia. It currently hosts several million articles in over 200 languages.

These social media tools can be grouped into different categories (Rutherford, 2010), depending on their purposes: (a) to connect friends, family, and colleagues; (b) to provide a way to share content; and (c) to provide tools for creating and editing content. Facebook, LinkedIn, Twitter, and Instagram are examples of social networks aimed at making connections. YouTube, Pinterest, and Flickr are examples of social media tools aimed at content sharing, while Wikipedia and Google docs are examples of social media devoted to content creation.

Online Learning

Even before COVID-19, online learning was the fastest growing area of education in the world, and had been for some time (Education Statistics, 2020; Simpson, 2012). For example, in the United States about 6.5 million of the 19.7 million students in higher education chose to study online prior to the COVID pandemic. There has been a surge in online learning since the COVID-19 pandemic hit. In mid-February 2020, about a quarter of a billion K-12 students in China resumed their studies using online platforms. In Wuhan, China, 730,000 K-12 students (about 81% of the total) began to attend classes online. In June 2020, there were about 1.2 billion K-12 children from 186 countries attending classes online (World Economic Forum, 2020). Instruction in institutions of higher education has also been affected by the pandemic. In the United States, 98% of institutions of higher education have been delivering their courses online since April of 2020 (Li & Lalani, 2020). Major universities in the United Kingdom, such as Cambridge University, London College, Oxford University, and University of Edinburgh, moved online in March 2020.

Moving instruction online in response to the COVID-19 crisis seems like an obvious solution to providing instruction during a pandemic, especially for adolescents, who are presumed to be *digital natives* (Prensky, 2001) and, therefore, may not need assistance or instruction in how to access and use online platforms. Nevertheless, the *onlinification* (Weiss, 2020) of educational institutions around the globe has created enormous challenges for both learners and teachers. It is important to remember that for online learning to become an option in educational contexts, users must have access to the Internet. In 1997, only about 6% of the world's population had Internet access compared to 59.6% in 2020 (World Internet Stats, 2020). The increase in access to the Internet represents an impressive growth in a little more than two decades; however, it is also true that the growth in access to the Internet is not equally distributed among the world's population. For example, in North America and Europe, the penetration rate is 94.6% and 87.2%, respectively, while in Africa it is only 39.3% (World Internet Stats, 2019). Even though online education is meant to be an equalizer in terms of making quality educational opportunities available to learners, it often is not the case.

Online Language Teacher Education (OLTE)

Given that online education is the fastest growing area of education, it is no surprise that there would also be an increase in the number of English language teachers who would choose online language teacher education (OLTE) to meet their professional development needs. One of the primary reasons for choosing to study online is because OLTE affords teachers considerable flexibility (Education statistics, 2020; Murray & Christison, 2017), particularly for teachers who reside in different contexts and time zones worldwide.

The term *online* is conceptualized by practitioners and researchers in a number of different ways. For some individuals, it refers to a course in which most of the materials are available online or some of the instructional activities are completed online. For others, it refers to courses that are conducted totally online. The Online Learning Consortium (formerly referred to as the Sloan Consortium) classified courses based on percentage of time spent online. Murray and Christison (2017) took a different approach and categorized online learning based on how the technology was used in the delivery and design of instruction. Table 1 presents the five major types of online options – enhanced, blended/hybrid, flipped, synchronous online, and asynchronous online.

Table 1 Types and characteristics of online courses

Types of OLTE	Key Characteristics
Enhanced	F2f classes are supported by online activity.
Blended or hybrid	F2f classes are supported by online activity and f2f time is reduced.
Flipped	Key content is delivered online; f2f time is devoted to problem-solving activities.
Synchronous online	All instruction and materials are online, and students participate synchronously in online meetings. The time spent in online synchronous meetings varies.
Asynchronous online	All instruction and materials are online and communication among students is asynchronous.

(Adapted from Murray and Christison, 2017, p. 3. Used by permission.)

In their research into the beliefs and perceptions of teacher learners (i.e., teachers enrolled in OLTE) and teacher educators (i.e., instructors of OLTE), Murray and Christison (2017) found that the 309 teacher learners in their study ranked online asynchronous courses as their preferred type of online course. This result is not surprising as pre-service teachers (i.e., teacher learners) also ranked flexibility as the main reason for choosing to study online. Asynchronous online courses provide the most flexibility given that the course can be accessed "anytime, anywhere" (p. 6), and that asynchronous online learning offers high degrees of flexibility to teacher learners in terms of completing assignments. Education statistics (2020) presents similar data, showing that 47% of online learners choose to study online due to the fact that they have competing commitments, such as work and family obligations, thereby making it difficult to attend classes on campus at specific times. The 137 teacher educators ranked the hybrid/blended course as their preferred choice, and this result is also not surprising given that teacher educators ranked opportunities for interaction, group work, and the development of communities of practice (Lave & Wenger, 2002; Wenger, 1998) as the most important characteristics of online learning.

Mobile Assisted Learning

The delivery for OLTE courses and programs has been typically facilitated through computer mediated communication and the use of learning management systems (LMSs), such as Blackboard, Canvas, or

Moodle (Murray, 2013). However, in recent years, the widespread use of mobile devices (Beatty, 2013) has made it possible for teachers to pursue professional development using social media platforms and tools. In fact, "mobile technologies have been heralded as equalizing devices" (Murray & Christison, 2017, p. 20). Eighty-seven percent of individuals who searched for online study programs used a mobile device, and 46% of activities online are now available on mobile devices (Education Stats, 2020).

English language teachers work in diverse global contexts and countries and with diverse groups of learners so that teachers in these contexts may be both isolated and opportunities for teacher professional learning may be infrequent and unpredictable. In addition, English language teaching is often itinerant in nature as teachers move between teaching sites, classrooms and among offices, buildings, and staff rooms, and very often without regular daily teaching schedules or a stable group of students, particularly in adult education with open enrollment courses and adults who have competing agendas relative to work and family. Aubusson, Schuck, and Burden (2016), suggest that "mobile learning would be a most appropriate way for teacher professional learning to occur" (p. 234). They also argue for the need to re-examine teachers' uses of technology as part of their own professional learning, in particular mobile learning. The current research study using Instagram for English language teacher professional development is a response to that call.

Teacher Professional Learning

Ongoing professional learning is essential for English language teachers who operate in today's complex modern world. What constitutes professional learning varies greatly among teachers. Most often educators think of professional learning as what happens when you attend a conference or workshop. However, there are other ways of thinking about one's professional learning or development. Professional learning also happens when you sit down with a colleague to plan a lesson together or discuss a student's work. Professional learning might also include sharing an interesting article with a colleague, giving a piece of advice or offering a teaching tip, reading through one's course evaluations, or watching a video on teaching on YouTube. Professional learning can include any of these activities

It is useful to think of professional learning in three broad categories (a) developing professional awareness, such as learning about new legislation that may affect your students, (b) teaching competencies, such as writing objectives or giving a demonstration lesson; or (c) refining new practices, such as creating demonstration lessons or inviting peers to observe ones teaching.

Professional learning can be any formal or informal learning experiences that are undertaken by teachers to improve their individual professional practice and ultimately the school's collective effectiveness (Cole, 2012). This definition of professional learning brings an effectiveness component into consideration by introducing the expectation that professional learning will bring about a change in teachers' practices, which can ultimately affect student learning and learning outcomes. Even though there is a wide range of professional learning opportunities and activities available for teachers, research into the effectiveness of professional learning is fairly consistent in the view that most professional learning is ineffective in bringing about improvements in teaching and student outcomes.

Studies on effective professional learning have delineated several characteristics found to be related to increased teacher capacity. These characteristics include the fact that effective professional learning needs to be embedded in or directly related to teaching so that professional learning exposes teachers to actual practice rather than to descriptions of practice. Professional learning must also be grounded in the content of teaching with opportunities for observation, critiques of teaching, and reflection. Third, it must be organized around collaborative problem solving and the sharing of ideas. Collaboration is one of the most important components of professional learning (Burbank & Kauchak, 2003) because it promotes critical reflection and acknowledges teachers as active learners and producers of knowledge.

RESEARCH METHODOLOGY

Context

The context for this study was the social-media platform known as Instagram, which is a photo and video sharing social networking service. The designers of Instagram state that it is an entirely visual platform. It is unlike Facebook, which uses both text, photos, and visual art, or Twitter, which relies primarily on text. Instagram has the potential to drive more engaged traffic because of its focus on visual content. Users can edit photos and short videos, add captions and respond to visual images via text or other images.

The Instagram account used in this study was created in September of 2016 with the purpose of sharing knowledge with other English language teachers around the world.[1] After several months, it became apparent that the data Instagram was generating about teacher professional learning was important for us as teacher educators in trying to understand teachers' motivations for professional learning through social media. The decision was made to investigate teachers' beliefs and perceptions and the effectiveness of the tool for facilitating collaboration and reflection among teachers.

Participants

The 1,500 participants in this study were all practicing English language teachers from five different continents (Asia, Europe, The Middle East, North America, and South America) and 17 countries (Canada, Chile, Colombia, Indonesia, Iran, Italy, Malaysia, Peru, Russia, Saudi Arabia, South Korea, Thailand, Turkey, Ukraine, Venezuela, Indonesia, the United States). No other personal data were collected on the users; however, it was clear from the text posts, comments, and the media and photos that were uploaded that the teachers were quite diverse. Although they appeared to be primarily young adults in their 20s or early 30s, they varied in terms of educational background and formal training, English language proficiency, and teaching experience. All participants self-selected to the site, so the assumption was that they joined because of their desire for professional learning and not to participate in a research study. They knew that data would be used for research purposes, but it would be aggregated and individual identifying markers would be removed. Based on the volume of daily traffic to the site, portraying the group of participants as self-motivated would be a precise characterization.

Data Collection

During the initial months of sharing content, the first author of this paper spent time recruiting teachers and searching Instagram for individuals who indicated in their profile that they were ESL teachers. However, interest in the account grew quickly so that within several months of sharing content, the account had reached 1,500 followers, and recruitment was no longer necessary.

In order to manage the volume of data generated, only data from a subset of the total were used to answer the research questions. These data were extracted during the period of time when the account had the most followers. Data were selected according to the volume of traffic and by selecting feeds with no fewer than 130 and no more than 700 responses or likes.

Data Analysis

Through processes of *open coding*, concepts from Instagram feeds were coded and central themes related to teachers' beliefs about teaching and their perceptions of the professional learning activities and practices from the Instagram feeds emerged. Through the process of *axial coding*, examining, comparing, conceptualizing, and categorizing the data, relationships among and between the open codes provided structure to the researchers' notes (Strauss and Corbin 1990). Two researchers read through the data independently and created codes for chunks of data. The coded notes were then compared for similarities and differences. Following the merging data approach (Creswell & Plano Clark 2011), excerpts from the coded observers' notes were selected to answer the research questions.

Data were analyzed and sorted from the six types of activity feeds that constituted the design for professional learning on the Instagram site. These six types of feeds or activities are the following: (1) communicative activities/games, (2) resources, (3) scholars in the field, (4) teaching skills/methodology, (5) teaching tips, and (6) mini-research experiments/sharing opinions. Each of these feeds is briefly described.

Communicative Activities/Games

These feeds reinforced the idea of communicative language teaching (CLT) and were aimed at language learning activities or games that could be used in English as a second language (ESL) or English as a foreign language (EFL) classes. Many could be used in both online and face-to-face (f2f) classes. Each was structured to include the title of the activity, the aim of the activity, the level of proficiency for which the activity was suitable, an explanation of how the activity would fit into a lesson, the required tools, and a description of the procedures to follow to use the activity. Photos that were taken and videos that were made while doing the activity in a real classroom situation were also shared in this feed in order to help teachers better understand how the activity worked.

Resources

This type of activity feed focused on introducing teachers to some resources for English language teaching (e.g., books, websites, apps, articles, upcoming webinars, online conferences, and useful pages from other social media sites). The feed was aimed at familiarizing teachers with key resources that could help them improve their teaching skills, as well as personal skills relative to communication and in order for them become better teachers. This feed also included the topic, a description of the topic, an image (usually a picture of the front cover of the book, the homepage of the website, or the first page of an article of the front cover of a journal) and an explanation as to why the resource was important and could help them as teachers.

Scholars in the Field

This feed aimed at familiarizing teachers and scholars who had made important contributions of English language teaching. These posts included pictures of the scholars, the scholars' profiles, descriptions of their research areas of interest, their fields of expertise, and often pictures of the front covers of their books. Several scholars agreed to participate in short interviews, and the interviews were also included.

Teaching Skills/Methodologies

To understand the importance of this feed, it is useful to compare it to the communicative activities/game feed in terms of the purposes of each. The communicative activities/games were intended to engage teachers initially with activities they could use immediately in their classrooms as many teachers lack resources. The focus was on the implementation of the activities and giving teachers opportunities to see images of the activities in progress. The teaching skills/methodology feeds were aimed at helping teachers gain a more in-depth understanding of the relationship of theory and practice and at introducing teachers to essential ELT theories or methodologies (e.g., communicative language teaching) and improving their pedagogic skills in relationship to the theory or methodology. The prompts were meant to get teachers to reflect on their teaching. The explanations were followed by short videos of experienced teachers in action.

Teaching Tips

Teacher Allan, who was the account designer and teacher educator, was asked numerous questions about teaching, so these posts were aimed at providing answers to questions that the followers asked and responding to ideas that they wanted to share. The responses were directed at providing help in areas in which the followers had determined they needed help.

Mini-research Experiments/Opinion Sharing

This portion of the professional development feed was aimed at collaboration and using the collective knowledge of the teachers to answer a question or address a concern that teachers had. In these posts, the question was posted as a feed or as a story and followers were asked to respond to the questions and share their opinions. The quantitative results were analyzed and shared with the teachers who were asked again to give their opinions and draw conclusions. Their final conclusions were subsequently shared in a separate feed in the form of tips for fellow teachers.

RESULTS

The analysis of the data sought to explicate and interpret participants' views, beliefs, and perceptions, in an effort to understand their professional learning experiences and to determine how these data answer the research questions.

RQ 1. Why do English language teachers choose Instagram for professional development?

The themes that emerged from the teacher data related to RQ1 were efficiency, flexibility, access to a large community of English language teachers, and types of activities. Relative to efficiency, consider the example scenario from the Instagram site.

Imagine that you are an ESL teacher who is going to teach the passive voice tomorrow, and you are looking for ideas and activities to help you do this. How much time do you think you are going to spend reading books or searching through websites in order to find something useful? Now, look at my Instagram pages on "Teaching Passive," look through the ideas and activities. Then, think about the question again from the perspective of Instagram, how much time will you need to spend?

In response to this prompt, many teachers noted how efficient Instagram was and that it took "less time and energy on Instagram to find useful information" (IF1)[2] and "less time to find something related to the topic you are interested in or need help with due to the hashtag feature on Instagram" (IF2), as well as the fact that "most Instagram posts use a cover page with the topic" (IF3). The hashtags and the easy interaction within the broader Instagram community make it one of the most, if not the most, efficient means of getting up-to-date news about webinars, courses, and other relevant information in the field of ESL.

Another reason that teachers chose Instagram was because of the nature of the activities. Instagram feeds use multi-media, so each feed includes pictures and videos, making the feed more attractive to the users than text or prose explanations would be. "Instagram has cool features that are easy to use" (IF5). These features include polls, quizzes, and surveys, which can provide teachers and researchers with large amounts of relevant data in a very short amount of time.

Developing an online network and community was important to the teachers and was one of the main reasons for choosing Instagram for their professional learning. Followers commented on the fact that every Instagram page was not only a workshop but also "a door to a new community of ESL Professionals with whom they could interact and from whom they could learn" (IF6). Instagram is one of the few social media platforms allowing teachers to not only read, watch, and learn but also interact with other professionals from whom they can seek advice. All followers are able to contribute ideas and materials. The communities found on Instagram are larger in size than communities found on other online platforms and, therefore, the site generates more variety in terms of ideas and teaching materials than are found on other platforms (e.g., LinkedIn or Facebook). Instagram stimulated a sense of competition among teachers and motivated some of the teachers to open their own pages, which in turn drove these teachers to look for new ideas to gain more followers.

Teachers also noted that even though they spent quite a bit of time on Instagram, they did so when it was convenient for them. They also mentioned that they liked being able to work on Instagram anytime and anywhere.

RQ2: What do English language teachers hope to gain from the experience?

There were seven top responses to this question. Teacher hoped to do the following:

- expand their community of ESL teachers/professionals,
- learn about a wide range of job opportunities,
- enhance the quality of their teaching by finding new ideas,

- find solutions to the problems they were facing in their classes,
- learn about the contemporary methodologies and current topics in the field,
- gain information about credible degrees, courses, conferences, or webinars, and
- learn about other ESL teachers' professional experiences and learn from them.

RQ 3: What types of activities on Instagram interested teachers the most?

The design of the Instagram site involved about six different types of feeds. Within each of these feeds, there were numerous topics and activity types. For example, in the feed teaching skills/methodology/theory, these topics were included: resolving discipline issues, teaching reading to young learners, classroom management, use of games, error correction, lesson planning, and evaluating a course textbook. For each of these topics, several activities were included. For example, under the topic evaluating a course textbook, teachers were given guidelines for evaluating a textbook, a two-question tool for conducting their own evaluation, and a prompt for sharing their experience with others and what they had discovered.

The activities in which teachers had the most interest mostly fell into the categories of informational and activity posts. Informational posts included guidelines, which were aimed at providing followers with both theoretical and practical information on particular topics. They also appreciated the links to free books, interesting articles, information on and recommendations for books, as well as useful websites with online activities on these topics. The activity posts were aimed at providing followers with resources for immediate use in the classroom.

RQ4. What topics interested the teachers the most?

Based on the number of followers who "liked" a post or an activity, it seems that the topics that were of the most interest to the followers were teaching (1) grammar, (2) vocabulary and (3) writing. Data also revealed that the majority of the followers found it difficult to teach specific aspects of language, such as a grammar rule, and wanted resources and ideas for doing so in ways that were fun for learners and engaging.

RQ5. What are teachers' beliefs about how their professional development experiences on Instagram might ultimately affect their teaching?

Based on analyses of teachers comments and the numbers of likes for each post, it was clear that the teachers believed that the ideas they got from Instagram would help them improve their teaching skills and give their students more enjoyable learning experiences, which in turn would affect the students' perceptions of them as teachers and of their teaching.

SOLUTIONS AND RECOMMENDATIONS

Based on the results of this study, there are several recommendations for professional learning that seem obvious. The first one is related to the fact that the researchers were surprised at the volume of traffic the Instagram account generated in the first few months. This response suggested that for a large number of English language teachers, this type of professional learning met their needs and motivated them to continue advancing in their teaching skills and knowledge of the field. Because Instagram is a social media app that is primarily visual, it seemed to have tapped into the image-based lives of these young adult English language teachers. When the researchers began using short videos to demonstrate activities for the teachers and show examples of actual classrooms, the comments and likes in response to the short videos were almost overwhelming, as the total number of likes jumped from fewer than 200 for most posts and activities to almost 1,000 for video feeds of actual classrooms. It seems that these teachers were keen to connect what they were learning about teaching through the activities to the videos of actual classrooms. Professional learning activities that are intended to engage young adult teachers, need to have a strong visual component and one that is grounded in classroom practice.

The second recommendation for professional learning experiences is that they should be both efficient, allowing teachers to access content quickly and easily, and flexible so that they can access them "anytime, anywhere" (Murray & Christison, 2017, p. 6). Because many English language teachers work in remote contexts and are isolated from other teachers and from sources of input to further their own professional learning, opportunities for online learning are especially important. Mobile assisted learning is meant to be an equalizer, allowing teachers to gain access resources that would not be available to them otherwise.

The third recommendation relates to teachers' desires for interaction and for a community or network of teachers with whom to collaborate and generate new knowledge and understandings. These features of professional learning online are consistent with the primary features of connectivism (Siemens, 2005), which has been suggested as an important theoretical concept motivating online learning. Teachers sometimes have a difficult time on their own knowing how to connect online with other teachers so that they can share experiences, make discoveries, and develop ways of learning from other teachers. The design of the professional learning on the Instagram site for this study provided a structure that encouraged teachers to make connections, such as through the reflective prompts in the activities and the opportunities for posting, replying, questioning, and commenting. Regardless of how professional learning experiences are to be structured, providing opportunities for collaboration should be at the heart of professional learning.

A fourth recommendation for professional learning is that it should promote the development of a reflective practice. The prompts that teachers received were pivotal in moving them in this direction. For example, one activity described three different teachers – the explainer, involver, or enabler. The prompt asked teachers to answer the following questions: Which type of teacher are you? Why do you think this is so?

Another activity focused on lesson planning and on the characteristics of an effective lesson and the tensions that all teachers experience between careful planning and responding to spontaneous in situ teaching moments.

This activity helped me see the difference between what you want to do or think you do and what you actually do in teaching (IF25).

What appears to be a spontaneous lesson is really a well-planned lesson. When a lesson is well planned, it is possible that you can deviate in case you need to (IF22).

Try[ing] to make a good lesson, well, it's complicated. A good lesson is accepted by students, so it can help them reach their aim or purpose (IF12).

These excerpts show that teachers were reflecting on the issues and thinking deeply about how to resolve them.

Instigating professional learning activities that have long terms effects is challenging. Cole (2012) proposed a sequence of professional learning activities that he believes are necessary for professional learning to result in long term change in teachers' behavior. He referred to the sequence of activities as the Funnel of Professional Learning, and the sequence includes the following: (1) introduce a new practice, (2) receive training on the practice, (3) trial the practice in class, (4) reflect on the trailing, (5) add the activity to your repertoire, and (6) help others adopt the activity. If professional learning on Instagram is to result in long-term change, one important question to ask would be how this sequence could be effectively implemented.

FUTURE RESEARCH DIRECTIONS

A logical direction for future research would be to look at the potential of other types of social media for providing effective professional learning. While research on teachers' beliefs and perceptions about professional learning is important, we also want to know how online professional learning experiences affect actual teaching practices and how the knowledge that is learned online and through social media transfers to a face-to-face (f2f) classroom. There is a dearth of research for OLTE (Murray & Christison, 2018).

Teachers in this study had numerous opportunities to work with multimodal texts in almost every professional learning activity to which they were exposed as multimodality texts are a feature of Instagram. More research needs to be done in order to determine how the teachers' experiences with multimodal texts in online professional learning platforms might influence the types of texts they choose for their own learners and the ways in which they prepare their learners for working with these types of texts.

It is generally accepted that professional learning that occurs far away from one's teaching context, such as when teachers attend a rather large conference in another city or country, is less likely to have a long-term impact teaching. In some ways, the professional learning that took place on Instagram could be considered "far away" from teaching as it is not based in a classroom. However, there were also some mitigating factors related to the teachers themselves that must be carefully considered in order determine the effectiveness of this type of professional learning. First, the teachers were highly motivated, were working hard to increase their knowledge based, and were stimulated by the news topics and activities for learning that they received. Given that they self-selected into this type of professional learning, were motivated to learn, and wished to collaborate with their peers, the social media format for professional learning with these teachers may work well over the long term.

CONCLUSION

This chapter presented research on the use of the social media platform, Instagram, as a tool for English language teachers' professional learning. Key theoretical concepts that supported the research were Siemens's (2005, 2006) work on connectivism, which offers a theoretical framework for understanding learning in a digital age and emphasizes how internet technologies create new opportunities for learning and sharing information, the importance of preparing both teachers and English learners to work with multimodal texts which combine two semiotic systems. Qualitative data were analyzed from six different types of feeds in order to answer five research questions. Based on the results, four recommendations for professional development using social media were offered and several directions for future research were provided.

REFERENCES

Abney, A. K., Cook, L. A., Fox, A. K., & Stevens, J. (2018). Intercollegiate social media education ecosystem. *Journal of Marketing Education*. Advance online publication. doi:10.1177/0273475318786026

Anstey, M., & Bull, G. (2006). *Teaching and learning multiliteracies: Changing times, changing literacies*. International Reading Association.

Anstey, M., & Bull, G. (2011). Helping teachers to explore multimodal texts. *Curriculum and Leadership Journal*, *8*(16). Retrieved from www.curriculum.edu.au/leader/helping_teachers_to_explore_multimodaltexts,31522.html?issuesID=12141

Arnold, N., & Ducate, L. (2006). Future foreign language teachers' social and cognitive collaboration in an online environment. *Language Learning & Technology*, *10*(1), 42–66.

Aubusson, P., Schuck, S., & Burden, K. (2016). Mobile learning for teacher professional development: Benefits, obstacles, and issues. *Research in Learning Technology*, *17*(3), 233–247. doi:10.1080/09687760903247641

Beatty, K. (2013). *Beyond the classroom: Mobile learning in the wider world*. https://www.tirfonline.org/wp-content/uploads/2013/12/TIRF_MALL_Papers_Beatty.pdf

British Council. (2020). *The English effect: The impact of English, what it's worth to the UK, and why it matters to the world*. https://www.britishcouncil.org/sites/default/files/english-effect-report-v2.pdf

Burbank, M. D., & Kauchak, D. (2003). An alternative model for professional development: Investigations into effective collaboration. *Teaching and Teacher Education*, *19*(5), 499–514. doi:10.1016/S0742-051X(03)00048-9

Cole, P. (2012). *Linking effective professional learning with effective teaching practice*. Carlton South, Australia: Education Services Australia. https://ptrconsulting.com.au/wp-content/uploads/2018/03/linking_effective_professional_learning_with_effective_teaching_practice_-_cole.pdf

Creswell, J. W., & Plano Clark, V. L. (2011). *Designing and conducting mixed methods research* (2nd ed.). Sage.

Downes, S. (2006, October 16). *Learning networks and connective knowledge*. Instructional Technology Forum: Paper 92. http://it.coe.uga.edu/itforum/paper92/paper92.html

Dreamgrow.com. (2020). https://www.dreamgrow.com/top-15-most-popular-social-networking-sites/

Education Statistics. (2020). *Online education statistics*. https://educationdata.org/online-education-statistics/

Lantolf, J. P., & Thorne, S. L. (2006). *Sociocultural theory and the genesis of second language development*. Oxford University Press.

Lave, J., & Wenger, E. (2002). Legitimate peripheral participation in communities of practice. In R. Harrison (Ed.), Supporting lifelong learning: Volume 1 perspectives on learning (pp. 111-126). Routledge Falmer.

Li, C., & Lalani, F. (2020). *The COVID-19 pandemic has changed education forever*. https://www.weforum.org/agenda/2020/04/coronavirus-education-global-covid19-online-digital-learning/

Mansor, N., & Rahim, N. A. (2017). Instagram in ESL classrooms. *Man in India*, 97(20), 107–114.

Murray, D. E. (2013). *A case for online language teacher education*. http://www.tirfonline.org/wp-content/uploads/2013/05/TIRF_OLTE_Two-PageSpread_May2013.pdf

Murray, D. E., & Christison, M. A. (2017). *Online language teacher education: Participants' perceptions and experiences*. https://www.tirfonline.org/wp-content/uploads/2017/03/TIRF_OLTE_2017_Report_Final.pdf

Murray, D. E., & Christison, M. A. (2018). *Online language teacher education: A review of the literature*. https://aqueduto.com/wp-content/uploads/2018/12/Aqueduto-Murray-Christison.pdf

National Institute of Education. (1975). *Teaching as clinical information processing* (Panel No. 6, National Conference on Studies in Teaching). https://files.eric.ed.gov/fulltext/ED111807.pdf

New London Group (NLG). (1996). A pedagogy of multiliteracies: Designing social futures. *Harvard Educational Review*, 66(1), 60–93. doi:10.17763/haer.66.1.17370n67v22j160u

Perrin, A., & Anderson, M. (2019). *Share of U.S. adults using social media, including Facebook, is unchanged since 2018*. Pew Research Center, FACTTALK. https://www.pewresearch.org/fact-tank/2019/04/10/share-of-u-s-adults-using-social-media-including-facebook-is-mostly-unchanged-since-2018/

Phipps, S., & Borg, S. (2007). Exploring the relationship between teachers' beliefs and their classroom practice. *The Teacher Trainer*, 21(3), 17–19.

Prensky, M. (2001). Digital natives, digital immigrants, part 1. *On the Horizon*, 9(5), 1–6. doi:10.1108/10748120110424816

Prinsloo, M., & Walton, M. (2008). *Situated responses to the digital literacies of electronic communication in marginal school settings*. https://www.researchgate.net/publication/255649993_Situated_Responses_to_the_Digital_Literacies_of_Electronic_Communication_in_Marginal_School_Settings

Purnama, A. D. (2018). Incorporating memes and Instagram to enhance student's participation. *Language and Language Teaching Journal*, 21(1), 94–103.

Rutherford, C. (2010). Using online social media to support preservice student engagement. *Journal of Online Learning and Teaching*, 6(4), 703–711.

Siemens, G. (2005). *Connectivism: Learning as network creation*. http://www.elearnspace.org/Articles/networks.htm

Siemens, G. (2006). *Connectivism: Learning Theory Pastime of the Self-Amused?* http://www.elearns-pace.org/Articles/connectivism_self-amused.htm

Siemens, G. (2008). *Learning and knowing in networks: Changing roles for educators and designers.* Paper 105: University of Georgia IT Forum. http://it.coe.uga.edu/itforum/Paper105/Siemens.pdf

Simpson, O. (2012). *Supporting students for success in online and distance education* (3rd ed.). Routledge.

Soviyah, S., & Etikaningshik, D. R. (2018). Instagram use to enhance ability in writing descriptive texts. *Indonesian EFL Journal, 4*(2), 32–38. doi:10.25134/ieflj.v4i2.1373

Strauss, A., & Corbin, J. M. (1990). Basics of qualitative research: Grounded theory processes and techniques. *Sage (Atlanta, Ga.).*

Vivakaran, M. V., & Neelamalar, M. (2018). Utilization of social media platforms for educational purposes among the faculty of higher education with special reference to Tamil Nadu. *Higher Education for the Future, 5*(1), 4–19. doi:10.1177/2347631117738638

Vygotsky, L. S. (1978). *Mind in society: The development of higher psychological processes.* Harvard University Press.

Weiss, S. (2020). *This is online learning's moment. For universities it's a total mess.* https://www.wired.co.uk/article/university-online-coronavirus

Wenger, E. (1998). *Communities of practice: Learning, meaning, and identity.* Cambridge University Press. doi:10.1017/CBO9780511803932

World Economic Forum. (2020). *The COVID-19 pandemic has changed education forever. This is now.* https://www.weforum.org/agenda/2020/04/coronavirus-education-global-covid19-online-digital-learning/

World Internet Stats. (2020). *Usage and population statistics.* https://www.internetworldstats.com/stats.htm

KEY TERMS AND DEFINITIONS

Communities of Practice: In education, a community of practice (CoP) is a group of professional educators who share a common concern or interest and have a desire to learn more and to want to do something better.

Connectivism: A theory of learning that explains how Internet technologies create opportunities for users to share and learn across the web.

Mobile-Assisted Learning: Learning that is assisted or enhanced through the use of a handheld mobile device.

Multiliteracies: An approach to literacy theory and pedagogy that includes the ability to create meaning across different modalities or forms of communication.

Multimodal Literacy: Literacy development that is focused on two or more semiotic systems, for example, linguistic and visual or visual and audio.

Online Language Teacher Education: A professional development opportunity in education for teachers of English to speakers of other languages (TESOL) where at least 80% of instruction is delivered online.

Onlinification: The process of shifting face-to-face learning to the online environment.

Open Coding: An analytic process by which concepts (i.e., codes) are described, named, and classified in qualitative date analysis.

Professional Learning: Activities in which teachers engage in order to stimulate their thinking and professional knowledge to inform their practice.

Social Media: Websites and applications that are created to assist users in sharing content and participating in social networking online.

Teacher Cognition: A theoretical construct meant to represent the mental lives of teachers, in other words what teachers think, know, and believe.

ENDNOTES

[1]   For more information on the Instagram account or access to the materials used in the current study, please contact the first author, Amir Aghayei @ a_art_20@yahoo.com

[2]   IF1 = Instagram Follower

This research was previously published in CALL Theory Applications for Online TESOL Education; pages 82-99, copyright year 2021 by Information Science Reference (an imprint of IGI Global).

Chapter 38

No Budget, No Barriers:
How Academic Branch Libraries Can Make Twitter Work

Chris Kretz
Stony Brook University, USA

William Blydenburgh
Stony Brook University, USA

ABSTRACT

This chapter provides a roadmap for Twitter use by academic libraries at a branch, remote, or satellite campus. These smaller libraries, operating at a distance from the center of their institution, often face challenges relating to their budget, resources, and status. The use of Twitter can empower a branch to serve their unique populations more effectively, promote engagement within the local community, and establish a presence for the branch within the institution. The authors provide strategies and suggestions for managing Twitter based upon their own experiences while managing the Southampton Campus Library of Stony Brook University Twitter account.

INTRODUCTION

Since Twitter debuted in 2006, it has become a significant part of the popular and cultural landscape. It has been used by a wide range of organizations, businesses, and individuals as a means to further their missions, support their brands, and engage with their communities. Over that time, Twitter has also become a staple of the academic library's social media portfolio. The ease of starting and the simplicity of using this microblogging platform belie its potential impact. Allowing users to post text of up to 280 characters as well as share content in the form of links, images, and videos, Twitter is a potent mechanism for distributing information and building community.

DOI: 10.4018/978-1-6684-7123-4.ch038

Twitter use in academic libraries has also evolved since 2006. Initially seen by many as a one-way broadcasting channel for disseminating library information, Twitter has since been adapted to more innovative and engaging uses. Academic libraries have recognized the platform's power to create community, foster interaction, and extend the reach of their message. Given this, any rationale for using Twitter in an academic library is equally valid for a branch campus library. In fact, Twitter can have an even greater impact for branch libraries. Often located far from the center of their institution with limited staff and budget, branch libraries nevertheless can leverage Twitter to build a network of engaged followers, create compelling content, and interact with their main institution and surrounding community.

This chapter examines ways in which branch campus libraries can overcome barriers to Twitter use, no matter what they might be. The authors will provide supporting rationales for the maintenance of local Twitter accounts at branch libraries as well as strategies and tips for growing, maintaining, and assessing the results. Examples provided are from the experiences of the chapter's authors while operating the Twitter account for the Stony Brook University Southampton campus library in New York, along with research from the field.

Although this chapter uses the term *branch campus library* throughout, there are many similar terms that could be applied. Branch campus is not meant to be exclusive or to denote a specific administrative or conceptual model. It is used here as an umbrella term to describe any academic library within a multi-library system that: a) operates at a geographic location removed from the main library, b) serves a unique patron base, c) maintains a distinct collection development focus, and d) interacts with its own local community. This would include libraries at satellite, remote, and distant campuses. It is hoped that the strategies and tips in this chapter can be applied in numerous library situations, even for branches within a public library system.

BACKGROUND

Many decisions have to be made before establishing a library Twitter account. These range from how the account will be handled, who will contribute content, how they will be trained, and how they will represent the library online (Appleton & Tattersall, 2015; Burkhardt, 2010; Farkas, 2009). Clear assessment goals and expectations should also be formulated at the outset to keep library Twitter use on track (Ramsey & Vecchione, 2014).

It is also important to have a clear sense of mission. Academic libraries have taken to Twitter for a variety of reasons. Some focus on sharing library news, promoting services, and building community (Loudon & Hall, 2010; Vassilakaki & Garoufallou, 2015). Others have centered their efforts on promoting the physical library environment and providing access to content (Harrison, Burress, Velasquez, & Schreiner, 2017).

The intended audience is also a vital element of a Twitter strategy. Students, an obvious choice for academic libraries, may prove the hardest audience to cultivate. Twitter use among people in the typical college-aged demographic, 18-24-year olds, stands at just 45% (Pew Research, 2018). However, college students have also expressed a preference for receiving library information over Twitter (Howard, Huber, Carter, & Moore 2018). For branch campus libraries, which may be serving smaller student populations to begin with, other audiences can be just as valuable. Studies have shown that the most important followers for an academic library are other accounts from within their institution, such as academic departments and administrative units (Kim, Abels, & Yang, 2012; Shulman, Yep, & Tomé, 2015; Stewart & Walker, 2017).

However the audience is defined, engaging with them is critical and yet this engagement is something that academic libraries have at times struggled to do well (Emery & Schifeling, 2015). Built on a network of relationships, Twitter rewards interaction and reciprocity (Mon & Lee, 2015). Following back, responding to comments, and conversing readily with followers are all important activities. To that end, the successful academic library on Twitter will avoid the use of a remote, authoritarian tone in content, favoring instead a more human, even quirky voice when tweeting (Chatten, 2017; Young & Rossmann, 2015).

In addition to the foregoing concerns, Twitter use by branch campus libraries will be impacted by the very nature of a branch campus. Functioning separately yet existing as part of a wider institution, branches have their own specific issues. In terms of identity, the branch campus can be struggling for status, or to define its uniqueness, or address resource disparities (MacDonald, 2013). Varying degrees of branch autonomy can also exist, based on how the campus is organized and administered. This can lead to a number of different strategic approaches that may be taken towards any issues (Dengerink, 2001).

The library on a branch campus faces its own challenges. The fact that each campus provides services to a unique student body can lead to a culture that differs from the main campus library (Knickman & Walton, 2014; Markland, Rempel, & Bridges, 2017). The diverse mix of programs and physical spaces that can exist at different branches often require different approaches to introducing library services (Dryden & Goldstein, 2013). As for staff at branch locations, they face issues of autonomy balanced against the need for inclusion with the main campus, exacerbated by the added logistics of travel (Phinney & Horsman, 2018). Many employees at branch libraries feel a lack of collaboration opportunities (Bottorff, Glaser, Todd, & Alderman, 2008). Additionally, branch campus libraries face the need to engage with their surrounding community and promote the image of the institution (Schneider, 2001). Research into these types of libraries – whether they be referred to as branches, satellite, regional, or distance libraries – is limited (Brandt, Frederiksen, Schneider, & Syrkin, 2005).

Twitter can be used to alleviate many of the above-mentioned issues between a branch and a main campus. While academic libraries have made effective use of other social media platforms like Facebook (Ofili & Emwanta, 2014; Phillips, 2011) and Instagram (Wallis, 2014; Wilkinson, 2018), Twitter provides a ready opportunity for the branch campus library. The relative simplicity and ease of starting a Twitter account make it a great entry point into social media. As will be shown, Twitter can also be a potent vehicle for promoting the branch library's activities and services to the wider institution. Twitter places the branch digitally on the greater campus map, allowing it to participate in conversations through social media and to engage in mutually beneficial support activities with the rest of the institution. The ensuing connections enable relationships to form with people and offices from the main campus that the branch staff may never meet in person.

The authors of this chapter will lay out a framework for developing Twitter at a branch campus library. Examples are drawn from their experiences maintaining the Twitter account of Stony Brook University's Southampton Campus Library (@SBShamptonlib), along with practices drawn from research in the field. Stony Brook Southampton is part of the State University of New York (SUNY). The campus is located within the town of Southampton on the south shore of Long Island. It is the third Stony Brook campus in the region. The Main campus with its Melville Library and the East Campus with its Health Science Library are both located some 40 miles to the northwest in Stony Brook, New York. Southampton is staffed by one full time faculty librarian and two full time staff with varying levels of student assistants. The branch library serves a mix of graduate-level Health Science programs, a Master of Fine Arts (MFA) in creative writing, and a Marine Science research center operated by the School of Marine and Atmospheric Sciences (SOMAS).

As a small branch library facing many of the issues discussed in this chapter, the Southampton Library made a conscious effort to pursue Twitter as its major social media platform due its ease of use and the facility with which the available staff could create content. When the new Head Librarian came on board in October 2016, the library Twitter account had already been established and was growing rapidly. By going through the thought process outlined below and applying many of the strategies mentioned, the authors were able to continue that growth while utilizing Twitter to promote awareness of the branch library throughout the wider institution.

TWITTER IN BRANCH LIBRARIES

Policies

Before establishing a Twitter account, it is important to review existing policy with all of those involved. Most large universities will have social media guidelines to inform and direct any library's social media activity. Typically, these guidelines will cover things like the tone of voice used in posting, how to represent the University, and how to cultivate a positive presence online. In terms of the actual management of a Twitter account, studies have found that a flexible policy works best. Guidelines that empower rather than proscribe help establish a healthy social media presence (Ramsey & Vecchione, 2014). The Southampton Library found that a firm understanding of the overall principles and goals of the Twitter account motivates people to tweet creatively, as opposed to trying to spell out rules for every possible contingency.

Tone/Voice

Social media has produced user expectations of direct and personal interaction with the institutions they follow online. Striking the right tone in these interactions will determine overall success. While this is arguably key to any communication, the stakes are higher in social media. If a message doesn't come off right, the ramifications can haunt an institution to no end. Whether it's attracting an online troll or a local boycott, the perils of tone are just as real as the content one chooses to post. Managing a Twitter account, like any social media account, can be as challenging as it is rewarding. A branch library's Twitter account is representing not just the branch but the institution as a whole.

The more conversational nature of Twitter should also be kept in mind when dealing with things like typos or missed hashtags and the like. Tweets cannot be edited once they are posted but if caught quickly, mistyped messages can be deleted and reposted. However, the longer a tweet has been public and the more impressions it has garnered, the better it is to embrace any minor mistakes with transparency and humor. Rather than deleting it outright, commenting on an original post with a correction and a mea culpa will suffice.

How Often to Tweet

There is no hard and fast rule as to how often one needs to post content. Too many tweets will feel like spam, leading people to unfollow or block an account. Conversely, an account that goes dormant for long stretches is one people will give up on and unfollow. Striking the right balance takes some time, influenced by the number of staff who are involved. In the authors' experience, a key to establishing a social media presence is posting routinely enough to put followers in the habit of checking for the account's content. Estimate a pace of 3 tweets a day to ensure an ideal presence. There are tips and strategies, discussed later, that will help to keep this level of posting on track.

Who Tweets

The act of tweeting involves composing content and posting it through Twitter's app or web page. Having more people involved in tweeting can help alleviate pressure and can lead to a broader range of content (Barnes, 2014). While a single person may often be tasked with starting a Twitter account at a branch library, this does not have to preclude others from participating. Even with limited staff, others can play a role by contributing content offline, monitoring the Twitter timeline, and suggesting strategies. Student workers and interns are other sources of personnel to enlist in maintaining the Twitter account. Use of these workers not only gives the library help from people closer to the potential target audience, it enriches the work experience for the student, giving them new skills in social media management, communications, editing, and writing.

Realistically, not all library staff will be interested in or adept at using social media. The authors have found that it helps to recruit staff who are already familiar with Twitter, who use it themselves, and who recognize the value of the library's use of social media.

No matter who tweets, it is important for the library to have guidelines for how and where it is carried out. Many staff and librarians will have personal Twitter accounts that they use on a daily basis. The line between personal and professional Twitter activity should be delineated as clearly as possible (Farkas, 2009). If those tweeting are using their personal devices with access to the library account, it is important to stay vigilant. Whenever working with personal devices, especially if the person also maintains a personal Twitter account, avoid posting content to the wrong account at all cost.

To avoid this potential confusion, material for posting can be collected offline through a central point – sent by email or uploaded to a shared drive like Google Docs. The administrator would then compose or schedule the tweets from this clearinghouse of content, proofing the text and attaching appropriate links and media files. This approach leads to tighter editorial control but it can also slow down the process and lead to logjams in posting.

A more distributed model for posting would entail multiple people with direct access to the Twitter account posting from an office desktop or laptop in the library. If the branch has a shared mobile device, posting could be done by whoever has the device at the moment, with the Twitter app automatically logged into the account.

Equipment

All that is required to open a Twitter account is a desktop or laptop computer and an internet connection. This minimum initial investment makes Twitter, as a social media platform, ideal for the branch library on a budget. Having said that, however, expanding beyond this basic setup can allow for more flexibility in running the account and increased engagement with the library's content. Specifically, better results can be achieved if one can work with a camera-enabled mobile device. Media, as will be discussed, enhances engagement with content on Twitter. If there is anywhere to allocate money in the social media plan, a device for media production would be it.

The purchase of a camera-enabled tablet or mobile device, readily accessible to the staff involved, can be of great importance. It allows for:

- The capture of high quality photographs
- The ability to record video
- Responsiveness and the ability to react to events and opportunities as they happen in and around the library
- Streamlined access to the library's other social media accounts on the device
- The use of apps (many of which are free) for photo editing
- Accessibility, as the device can be shared among staff

If the outright purchase of a device for the branch is not feasible, look to borrow a camera from a different area of campus such as a communications office or from the main library itself. If need be, plan to have someone come out at specific times of the year and photograph the branch space. With adequate planning, one can amass a stockpile of images that can be used on Twitter throughout the year.

Another option for capturing images and video is the use of a personal device. Mobile phones are ubiquitous and most have camera and video capabilities that are more than adequate for the demands of Twitter. As discussed, there are policy implications when using personal devices and care should be taken to separate library material from personal photos. To alleviate risk, personal devices can be used to gather content that is then forwarded - either by email or to a shared drive - to be posted to the Twitter account at a later date.

The Southampton Library uses a range of approaches. Personal devices are used to capture images and video which are then shared to a centrally located folder for later use. Additionally, periodic visits from the main library's Multimedia Resources Specialist help capture high-quality images using advanced equipment. Cameras from the main library have also been borrowed for periods of time to cover special events and workshops.

Content Creation

The thought of coming up with a constant stream of ideas for content on Twitter can seem daunting, but libraries have proven a source of never-ending ideas. Research has shown that many libraries post content on Twitter revolving around three basic areas: community-building in and around the university, the portrayal of the library as an inviting space, and the sharing of content drawn from archives, collections, and exhibits (Harrison, Burress, Velasquez, & Schreiner, 2017). In a study that analyzed 1,200 tweets from six large academic libraries, Stvilia and Gibradze (2014) found the most frequent categories of tweets focused on: events, resources, community building, operations updates, study support, Q & A, surveys, staffs, and clubs. When surveyed directly about what Twitter content they would be interested in seeing from an academic library, students expressed an interest in campus-wide information and events, research techniques/tips, and library logistics (Brookbank, 2015).

These general topic areas can serve as a foundation of ideas to distinguish one library on Twitter from another.

Using the Physical Space

A branch library's physical space should be a key component of its Twitter activity. As no two libraries are exactly alike, emphasizing the distinct look of the library through visual content is a great strategy. Pictures give followers a sense of the library as place and also present the best image of the institution to the public. Also, the more remote the branch is from other campuses, the more likely that Twitter will be the one consistent window through which others in the institution view the branch.

Aim to highlight as many specific locations in the library as possible. These can range from quiet study areas to group meeting spaces or even favorite study spots suggested by students. Similarly, one can spotlight unique architectural details: vaulted ceilings, floor-to-ceiling windows, balconies, and works of art. All of these can inspire great aesthetic interest. A tighter focus on space can also convey information: whiteboards with interesting messages, or study tables full of students during finals. What seems of no consequence to one person will appeal to someone else. The Southampton Library routinely documents on Twitter the major milestones of its water refilling station. This may seem inconsequential to some, but saving 15,000 water bottles garners a good response from the marine science students.

Look for opportunities to photograph the space in all types of weather conditions. Blizzards and storms raging outside lend an element of drama and also make compelling short video clips. Long shadows across desks, sunsets behind buildings, and glimpses of activity through the book stacks are all ways of capturing the atmosphere and activity of a branch library. Be creative and think of ways to add drama to visuals.

Displays

Any physical display in the library is ready-made for sharing on social media. Presenting photos of the display on Twitter not only documents activity in the library, it also extends the reach of the display. While many visitors will view the display while it is up in the library, sharing it on Twitter along with relevant text and hashtags gives extra life to what is often a time-consuming project to create. Make sure to identify any relevant hashtags or Twitter accounts to mention when posting. Authors will be interested in seeing their books on display and fans of various genres will be a natural audience. Timing displays to particular events or moments in the culture can also increase exposure. Figure 1 shows a display of the Southampton Library's graphic novel collection that ran during the New York City Comicon convention.

The Collection

Do not overlook the value of the physical collection as well. Books can be photographed to highlight new acquisitions, to celebrate literary anniversaries, or to spotlight individual authors. A challenge for academic libraries, visually speaking, will come from working with books stripped of their original dust jackets. As a workaround, try photographing the interior title pages or stack books together and capture their spines. Additionally, mylar-encased book jackets can be difficult to photograph due to their reflectivity. Experiment with locations and camera angles for best effects.

Figure 1. Graphic novel display tweeted with #NYCC hashtag (Southampton Library)
Source: Southampton Library 2018

Many libraries have taken to creating large-scale displays of books that border on book art – volumes stacked into the form of snowmen or jack-o-lanterns, for example. Keep an eye out for such creative ways to repurpose books in photos, even on a small scale. The Southampton Library has become adept at creating spontaneous book art – using items from the physical collection to highlight occasions on Twitter: everything from Valentine's Day to National Pancake Day to S'mores Day. Even a plain black hardcover book can serve as a stand-in for an Oreo on National Cookie Day.

A Social Media Space

To capitalize on the idea of library space as content, try to identify a specific area within the library as a social media production zone. This does not entail any major construction or interior design but simply identifying a space that lends itself to display on a routine basis. Look for areas with shelves suitable for outward-facing books along with plenty of flat surfaces for objects to be photographed. It should be a relaxed space where people tend to gather and engage with communal projects, games, or similar activities. Consider these types of areas as staging grounds or digital store windows, places where the physical meets the digital. A social media space should be fun: ever-changing, creative, and not always making complete sense. Leave random objects in there, such as antiques, 3D-printed objects, old board games, and promotional items.

At the Southampton Library, an open seating area near the main stacks was converted into the Book Lounge. The relaxed atmosphere of this area along with a number of display shelves as well as the library's literary journal collection made it a go-to source for capturing images for Twitter. As an added bonus, a number of metal floor-to-ceiling poles in the space have become perfect spots to hang printed quotations on a rotating basis as seen in Figure 2. Suitable for photographing, they have since been dubbed "the quote pole."

Figure 2. The book lounge at the Southampton Library (Southampton Library)
Source: Southampton Library 2018

Academic Programs

As many branch libraries serve distinct academic programs, Twitter use at these libraries should reflect that fact. Targeting content at students and faculty in specific programs helps build a community of engagement. It also represents an added value proposition for students, an incentive to follow the library's Twitter account. There are several ways the branch can approach this activity.

The most obvious would be tweeting content directly related to specific academic studies: links to library resource guides, databases suggestions, reference sources, or new books in the collection. Also consider retweeting non-library information relevant to each program's field of study. This can be articles from professional and trade organizations, write-ups of new research findings, or reports from important conferences. Part of this work is aided by being aware of prominent hashtags related to each field. Given the nature of programs at Stony Brook's Southampton campus, the Southampton Library habitually tracks occurrences of the hashtags #OT and #PT (occupational and physical therapy) as well as #amwriting for the MFA program. Information that might be of interest to students in those programs gets liked and retweeted. Sharing this content makes the branch library's Twitter feed a type of current awareness service for students. This practice of sharing program-specific content also models Twitter use for students, showing them how Twitter can be used to engage with their profession and enhance their professional development activities.

Branch libraries can also use Twitter to play a part in the life of an academic program. Every program has its yearly routines - recurring assignments, special events, and high-stress periods. Be attuned to what is happening and share related content when the opportunity arises. The Southampton Library routinely documents the activities of the annual Kinesiology Fair on campus, tweeting images of the student-created projects and associated information.

Events

Live events and workshops in academic libraries have become an important outreach and engagement activity. Bringing people together on campus, these activities also attract members of the community and show the library as a vibrant hub of ideas and shared experiences. Twitter can play a number of roles in these events. As part of the initial marketing strategy, Twitter can promote events and create interest among the branch library's followers. Using Twitter to add a real-time element during the event, however, can garner further attention. Live-tweeting in the moment lets those off-campus experience the event on some level and may entice them to attend the next.

If possible, assign the live-tweeting responsibility to a specific person to act like a 'social media DJ'. To start, have them capture the early stages of the event, letting any followers in the area know that there is still time to attend. Without interfering with the speaker, one can also post quotes and updates during the event. Always follow up with a thank you to the speaker and any collaborating organizations, making sure to include any related Twitter accounts and relevant hashtags. This is good practice but also expands the branch library's Twitter posts to the followers of the speakers, their home institutions, and others on Twitter interested in the subject matter.

Twitter-Only Live Events

There are a number of recurring events, often called *tweetchats*, which take place in real time over Twitter. Typically arranged around specific hashtags, they range from live Q & A's with authors and experts to roundtable discussions within a professional organization. Followers must be aware of them and be on Twitter at the right time to participate, although the tweets remain after the fact as a record that can be reviewed later. These events are a unique opportunity that can be explored and developed by branch libraries.

#AskALibrarian is currently live on Twitter every Thursday from 12:00 PM to 1:00 PM Eastern Standard Time. Twitter users from all walks of life ask for reading suggestions from librarians, who respond regardless of geographic location. Mostly engaging public librarians, #AskALibrarian is also a useful exercise for academic librarians to try. Not only does participation in this particular tweetchat help develop reader advisory skills, providing recommendations can raise awareness of the library's Twitter account among new audiences.

#OTTalk is a tweetchat that originated in the United Kingdom. It currently takes place on Tuesday nights, 8:00 PM to 9:00 PM Greenwich Mean Time. The Southampton Library has taken to monitoring this hashtag and promoting it to followers and occupational therapy students as an example of how Twitter can be used for professional development.

As branch libraries build their Twitter presence, they might think of inaugurating their own subject- or location-specific tweetchats. These can be marketed as outreach activities with other areas of the University or community, something along the lines of #AskAboutSouthampton. Similar events could be coordinated with other library branches or areas within the university looking to promote collaboration.

Building a Twitter Network

Much of the power of Twitter lies in its function as a network of relationships. Those followed by and those who follow the library account play an important role in determining how widely any particular tweet is distributed. For branch libraries, who often struggle for recognition and engagement with the greater institution, Twitter is a boon to building relationships. Despite the geographic remove, branches can use Twitter to level the playing field and become a virtual neighbor to departments and groups in other locations. Additionally, the branch can reciprocate by commenting on, retweeting, and similarly engaging with the content of other departments.

Institutional Accounts

At the outset, branch libraries can establish a network by locating and following other accounts from within the university. Likely choices include the main library and the communications office as well as academic departments, service units, and student groups. Not all accounts will be equally active, but most will start following back, helping build the library's follower count. Do not be shy about reaching out and promoting the branch campus to others in the university. A branch campus has the perfect rationale for reaching out - introducing the rest of the institution to branch activities and programs. As the branch library account evolves, a reciprocal relationship among areas will grow, with each account helping to share and amplify the content of the other.

Students

Don't be discouraged if it takes time to build engagement with the student community. As mentioned previously, institutional accounts have been shown to be the most valuable members of the branch library's network. These institutional accounts can act as a conduit through which to reach students. If the library's account is connected to the greater academic community on Twitter, then individual departments, student groups and other service organizations will be sharing the library's content to their own followers. Again, the network effect will amplify the message and distribute it further than the library's account may reach on its own. The reverse is also true. The library can act as an influencer for other areas of campus, spreading their message to members of the library's network that the originating account might not reach.

The branch library can try to gain student followers by appealing to them directly in the real world. Introduce them to the library's Twitter account at orientations, in routine communications, and on campus via bulletin boards and signs throughout the library. When assessing the number of student followers, be mindful that it may not be possible to determine if a follower is a student just by virtue of their profile. School affiliation is not always something people include in their public profile.

Beyond the University

Outside of the university, look to follow accounts of organizations and groups related to the academic programs supported by the campus. In this, Twitter provides a potential new role for libraries: curating and disseminating information from non-library sources on social media. For example, the Southampton Library, cognizant of the MFA program on campus, began following accounts from places such as *Writers Digest*, *Literary Hub*, and the *Paris Review*. The library monitors these accounts for relevant content to like and retweet, things like writing tips, author interviews, new developments in the field, and writing contests.

Outreach to the local community is another key mission of branch libraries and their campuses. As representatives of the main institution, branches have an obligation to represent the face of the university to the area. To that end, the library can follow and engage with local institutions like museums, historical societies, civic groups, and municipal offices.

One can identify accounts to follow by searching keywords on Twitter via the web page or app. There is also an advanced search function at http://twitter.com/search-advanced. Keep in mind that results will depend upon the amount of information that accounts voluntarily supply in their public profiles. If results are coming up short, one can always use the old chain citation trick: identify a valuable account to follow, then check the list of accounts they follow and are followed by. One can also identify accounts by the content they post. Having a list of keywords and hashtags relevant to the library's goals will make it easier to search for accounts that routinely post about those topics. All of these strategies help to build a network of shared interests, overlapping missions, and potential influencers.

Organize With Twitter Lists

Twitter allows for the creation of lists – compiling Twitter accounts into special groups based upon specific criteria. The resulting lists can be made public or private and clicking on them will display the tweets from the accounts involved. This is a handy way of creating a timeline of tweets around a specific topic or theme. One may want a list of peer institutions or of cultural heritage institutions in the local area, or experts in a certain field. The list becomes a resource that can be shared and promoted.

To add someone to a list, navigate to their Twitter profile page. Next to the follow/unfollow button is a small pull-down menu. Select "Add or remove from lists" as shown in Figure 3. A box will appear enabling one to save to an existing list or to create a new list.

Figure 3. Saving a Twitter account to a list (Southampton Library)
Source: Southampton Library 2018

The Southampton Library has created a number of lists to track different constituencies, monitoring the tweets of certain kinds of user groups at once. For example, the library's East End list, made up of accounts from local newspapers, government offices, civic groups and the like, provides a means for keeping up with regional events.

Engaging With Others on Twitter

The goal of a branch library on Twitter is not simply to amass followers. It is to encourage meaningful engagement and to share relevant information. Gaining a follower (or following someone new) is just the beginning. A vital part of the branch library's Twitter activity will be managing the day-to-day interactions of these relationships.

Based on experience, the Southampton Library follows a series of basic principles for engagement:

- Keep a list of institutional accounts to review and potentially interact with each day.
- Retweet content from other accounts from the institution but where possible, add personalized commentary.
- Mention specific university departments and offices when sharing content relevant to their area.
- Retweet any positive mention of the branch -- show that any message that incorporates the library's mission will be boosted.
- Be bold in creating conversations. The Southampton Library, for example, asked SOMAS for its scientific opinion of the movie *Sharknado*. It turned out that they had an article on that very subject ready to share.
- Group like-minded accounts in the same tweet to promote more reciprocal relationships. Is it #MuseumWeek? Mention all the local museums in a single tweet about the great work they do.
- Publicly thank those who follow the branch account.

Weeding the Timeline

The timeline, or home timeline, is what the administrator sees when logging into the branch library's Twitter account. The timeline is made up of content tweeted by the accounts followed, as well as content suggested by Twitter. The timeline gives a broad overview of what the followed accounts are doing and is a source of material to like and retweet. However, it fills up quickly and takes longer to review the more accounts that are followed.

Information overload can be mitigated with a few simple steps.

1. Do not automatically follow everyone who follows the branch account. Review their account first to see if the content is relevant and fits with the library's mission. Follow the rule of reciprocity whenever possible, but accounts that post explicit language or photos or are otherwise contrary to university policy would not warrant a "follow."
2. If a followed account starts to tweet material that is no longer relevant to the library's mission, unfollow them.
3. If there is value in following an account but not in seeing what they are tweeting, the account can be muted. They will still count as a follower, but their posts will not be visible on the home timeline. Additionally, muted accounts do not know they have been muted.

SOLUTIONS AND RECOMMENDATIONS

Time Management Strategies

The time commitment of a Twitter account can feel overwhelming at a branch library, where those who are tasked with managing a social media account often do so as an added duty on top of an already full job description. Keeping up with daily tweeting may seem like an impossible challenge, both logistically and creatively. But running an account does not need to be all-consuming nor does one need to be a wordsmith to keep it going. Two simple steps at the outset will help streamline the process and save time in the day-to-day workflow. A well-planned calendar and a thought-out system of hashtags will help line up posts in advance and keep tweets on track.

The Calendar

Many academic libraries have adopted the idea of a shared spreadsheet for mapping out events in a timeline (Barnes, 2014; Ramsey & Vecchione, 2014). The Southampton Library uses a similar system to create a Twitter calendar with tabs for each month of the year and rows for each day of the month. The spreadsheet is then filled with ideas for things to tweet about: holidays, notable birthdays, events in popular culture, important dates in the academic year, and any other date-specific happening relevant to the library's mission. Google Sheets work well as a collaborative canvas, allowing multiple employees to contribute at the same time.

Consult with appropriate sources to identify key dates and events. The American Library Association's "Celebration Weeks and Promotional Events" will provide valuable help at the outset. This type of planning provides a structure within which to work. Knowing what's coming, even a week or a month at a time, lets one plan content to match. This level of preparation, however, does require the time to research events, populate the calendar, and create content to match. The spreadsheet that Southampton Library uses is shown in Figure 4.

Figure 4. Google Sheet mapping out potential events during the year (Southampton Library)
Source: Southampton Library 2018

A Date	B Month	C Birthdays	D Days	E LitFilm Related events	F Libraries Related
April 1	Poetry Month			Pulitzer Prizes announced	
April 2	National Occupational Therapy Month				
April 3	National Internship Awareness Month	Washington Irving, 1783		F. Scott Fitzgerald marries Zelda	
April 4	Stress Awareness Month	Maya Angelou, 1928	National Walking Day (first Wed in April)		
April 5		Booker T. Washington, 1856			
April 6			Natl Student Athlete Day		
April 7					
April 8					
April 9					National Library Week
April 10			Natl Encourage a Young Writer Day	Great Gatsby published, 1925	
April 11					
April 12					
April 13			Natl Scrabble Day		
April 14					
April 15					

Weekly Hashtags

Use a system of weekly hashtags to plan out content. This provides a great way to organize and sustain a Twitter presence. By assigning content via weekdays, one can stockpile posts beforehand and schedule them to post subsequently. There are a number of established hashtags that can be used to get started and they can be changed as desired. Here is the outline that the Southampton Library often uses with some brief notes on each. Figure 5 provides examples of the hashtags in action.

- **#MondayMotivation:** This hashtag provides uplift at the start of the week, a good time to promote a call to action or advocacy of some sort or a promotion of a service.
- **#TravelTuesday:** Each week, travel bloggers from around the world share pictures, blog posts, and information using this hashtag. Southampton Library applies its own MFA-inspired spin, applying it to travel stories, books with quests in them, or fiction titles set in foreign locales. One can expand into posting pictures or anecdotes from staff and patrons who have traveled abroad or by cross-promoting activities with the Study Abroad office.
- **#WednesdayWisdom:** By hump day, followers may be struggling to cope with the stress of the week. The wisdom in this hashtag can be quotes from historical or cultural figures, something on which to ruminate or thoughts to get followers through it all. For Southampton, this conversation provides a chance to share quotes about issues that define the library's mission - wisdom concerning the value of libraries, writing, research, and literacy. If the quote is from a personality who has a Twitter account, be sure to mention that person!
- **#ThursdayThoughts:** This is a popular and wide-ranging hashtag that spans many topics. While one can share quotes similar to #WednesdayWisdom, it is important to find a way to delineate between the two, either by theme or by content source. The Southampton Library uses Wednesday for quotes from historical and cultural figures while Thursdays are more locally sourced, with thoughts about the library from staff, affiliates, and patrons. The former day takes a broader view, the latter focuses on the particulars of the establishment.
- **#FridayReads:** This is a staple of the Southampton Library's hashtag diet. It is a ready-made vehicle to showcase collections. Photos of books are posted along with any related information about its history or relevance. The selections rotate through staff picks, new acquisitions, literary prize winners, and themed content during events such as Women's History Month, Poetry Month, and Celtic Awareness Month.
- **#SaturdayLibrarian:** A hashtag for the bold. It is library-centric and on the one hand, taps into a sympathetic audience. On the other hand, this hashtag brings with it a sense of humor ranging from sarcastic to sardonic. To put it in perspective, it is largely used by librarians working on the weekends and drinking copious amounts of coffee. That being said, #SaturdayLibrarian has potential to humanize those who work in the library. Post memes, try out some jokes, and interact with patrons in a way more conducive to a weekend vibe.
- **#SundayBlogShare:** Simply put, this is a hashtag used to share blog posts. Most libraries maintain a blog of some sort, discussing library-related news and events as well as recent developments. At the Southampton Library, the blog that is shared contains content from all university libraries. This gives the hashtag the function of a weekly rolling newsletter, giving Southampton followers a look at news from the wider institution.

Figure 5. Examples of weekly hashtags for #MondayMotivatin, #WednesdayWisdom and #FridayReads at the Southampton Library (Southampton Library)
Source: Southampton Library 2018

Scheduling Tweets

Whether tweets are planned weeks in advance or just over the next few days, a scheduling tool will be a boon to the branch library. Combined with weekly hashtags, scheduling will ensure a reliable stream of content in the Twitter feed.

There are a number of free and low-cost software options for scheduling tweets. Many even allow scheduling content to multiple platforms at once - meaning that the same or unique posts can be shared to Twitter as well as Facebook, Tumblr, and elsewhere. Check the settings on each program as some limit the total number of posts one can schedule at a time. As shown in Figure 6, the Southampton Library currently uses the free version of HootSuite to schedule posts to Twitter and Facebook.

Figure 6. Hootsuite dashboard showing posts scheduled for later in the week (Southampton Library)
Source: Southampton Library 2018

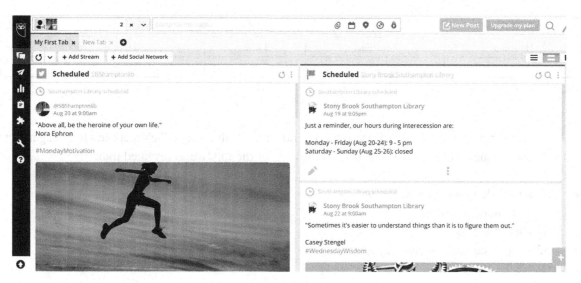

Scheduling tweets lends some peace of mind, knowing that the Twitter account will stay active with at least a minimum of activity over holiday gaps or when one is pulled away by other demands. Other scheduling tools include:

- Buffer
- CrowdFire
- Sendible
- SocialPilot
- TweetDeck

The Recipe for the Perfect Tweet

Much to the frustration of social media managers everywhere, not all tweets are created equal. A carefully crafted message or meme may fail to gain traction while an offhand observation or image will strike a chord and gain thousands of impressions. The difference can hinge on using the right elements at the right time. Some simple strategies and best practices can optimize the chances that users will engage with content when they see it.

The finer details of assessment and Twitter analytics will be discussed later but to illustrate the point, the Southampton Library examined a year's-worth of "top tweets." These were tweets from each month that elicited the most interactions in terms of likes, retweets, and mentions. Further analysis of the distinct elements of these tweets led to a better understanding of what went into an engaging tweet. The resulting "recipe" shown in Table 1, helps to guide construction of new tweets with an eye towards maximizing engagement.

Table 1. The elements in an ideal tweet as derived from a study of high-engagement tweets from 2016-2017 at the Southampton Library (Southampton Library)

Number of:			
Hashtags	**Mentions**	**Links**	**Pictures/Media**
1.86	.9	.28	.76

Source: Southampton Library 2018

The Southampton Library also discovered that no single "silver-bullet" element led to engagement. Rather, results came from a mix of elements. A review of the top tweets revealed that:

- 83% included two or more elements
- 83% included hashtags
- 62% included media
- 52% included hashtags and media

The analysis of Southampton's tweets reinforces other studies of tweet construction that show the prevalent use of media on Twitter (Borruto, 2015). A further discussion of this recipe is a good primer on how to drive engagement.

Hashtags

Of all the elements of a tweet, hashtags are perhaps the most important. In their study of Twitter use at historically black colleges, Stewart and Walker (2017) found that hashtags were a "pathway for library-generated content proliferation well beyond a libraries' follower community" (p. 6).

Hashtags can be defined as user-generated keywords or subject headings. They are words or phrases preceded by a hashtag. When included in a tweet, they become a link to all other tweets using that hashtag. Some hashtags become standards, reused frequently across Twitter by mutual consent. Others rise spontaneously in response to events and can be used to track developing news and reactions across Twitter.

Libraries can identify relevant hashtags in a variety of ways. Twitter displays trending hashtags on the home timeline. In addition, one can search for tweets about a topic, looking for any prevalent hashtags in the results. Conferences, celebrations, and cultural events often create official hashtags to aid communication. By using hashtags, branch libraries can tie their content to ongoing conversations and connect to non-followers interested in similar subject matter.

Figure 7 shows an example of a trending hashtag in use. During one of the many blizzards of the winter of 2018, the Southampton Library was able to spot and participate in #museumsnowballfight. This hashtag had sprung up earlier in the day between two New York City-based institutions as a way to share archival photos featuring blizzards past. The Southampton Library and many other organizations around the country and the world joined in with their own variations, creating a shared conversation that spread well into the next day.

Links

Links are a valuable tool for providing access to the many online resources that academic libraries curate and to content from outside sources.

Some of the most common library content to link to includes:

- Blog posts
- Catalog records
- Databases
- Digital projects
- OERs
- Research guides

Many of the vendors of library systems have customizable social media settings, letting one tie accounts into the administrative interface while embedding "share" buttons on public-facing content. Make sure these functions have been optimized to enable sharing from social media platforms.

Previously, long links were a hindrance to Twitter posts as they ate into character limits. Twitter now automatically shortens all URLs and counts them as 23 characters, regardless of their actual length.

Figure 7. Use of the hashtag #museumsnowballfight (Southampton Library)
Source: Southampton Library 2018

SBU Southampton Library @SBShamptonlib · Jan 4
Replying to @MuseumofCityNY @NYHistory
Can we bring our National Literary Landmark to this #museumsnowballfight ?
Tennessee Williams wrote here and held the strategic high ground

Mentions

Mentions are a powerful tool for communication on Twitter. They are formed by including a Twitter account's user name, such as @SBShamptonlib, within a tweet. The user is notified of the mention and hopefully will engage with it in some way. For branch libraries, mentions can play a key role in attracting followers and increasing engagement. Make sure to mention other accounts in a positive way, whether to highlight an author of a recent acquisition, to thank a speaker, or to engage in conversation with another department or institution. One can search individual names on Twitter to locate their username but keep in mind, the ability to positively identify someone (outside of their photo) is limited by the information they provide in their profiles.

Images and Video

The Southampton Library has found that the use of images and other media such as video and animated GIFs greatly enhances the engagement levels of a tweet. While having a device with a camera for the branch library is ideal for this purpose, there are other ways to include images within tweets without having to expend funds on a camera. These include:

- **Screenshots:** A great budget-saving way to highlight resources. Mine the library's website for sections that can help illustrate resources, guide navigation, and show off the branch.

- **Pixabay:** A free source of royalty free images. The range of content is surprisingly wide and can be used to illustrate or augment plain text content such as quotes, sayings, and announcements. (https://pixabay.com)
- **The New York Public Library Digital Collections:** Much of the public domain portion of their digitized collections are available for free download. (https://digitalcollections.nypl.org/)
- **Library of Congress:** Their Free to Use and Reuse section features public domain images from their collections. (https://www.loc.gov/free-to-use/)
- **Archives & Special Collections:** Work with the home institution's archives and special collections to see if they have digitized content that can be repurposed to augment posts from the branch library.

Image Quality and Size

Most visual content posted on Twitter will be viewed through the small screen of a mobile phone, cutting down on the need to produce high resolution images to start with. It does help, however, to be aware of Twitter's image specifications which are currently:

- Photo size up to 5 MB
- Animated GIFs up to 5MB on mobile devices, up to 15MB on web
- GIF, JPEG, and PNG accepted
- BMP or TIFF not accepted
- Up to four images on one tweet

Image Captioning

Add descriptions to images for the benefit of those using screen readers to access Twitter. To enable this option in Twitter, go to Profile settings and under Accessibility, turn on "Compose Image Descriptions." Thereafter, when adding an image to a tweet from Twitter.com or in the Twitter app on iOS or Android, one will have the ability to enter caption information.

Assessment

Assessment helps determine the success of Twitter activity and a coherent and sustainable assessment plan helps guide and direct that activity. Given the small staffs and budgets at branch libraries, careful thought should be given to what one wants to measure and why. Fortunately, Twitter has one of the most easily accessible statistics platforms providing many ways to retrieve and study Twitter activity.

Twitter Analytics

One can access an account's statistics dashboard by signing in to Twitter Analytics (http://twitter.analytics.com) using the Twitter ID. The home screen will show a 28-day window of activity on the account as well as an overview of each month, including:

- **Top Tweet:** The tweet that received the most impressions for the month
- **Top Mention:** The tweet with the highest impressions that mentioned the library account's @ name
- **Top Follower:** The Twitter account the library is following who has the most followers of their own
- **New Followers:** How many followers were gained over the month

Figure 8 shows an example of one month's top activity at the Southampton Library.

Figure 8. Monthly Twitter analytics for Southampton Library, February 2018 (Southampton Library)
Source: Southampton Library 2018

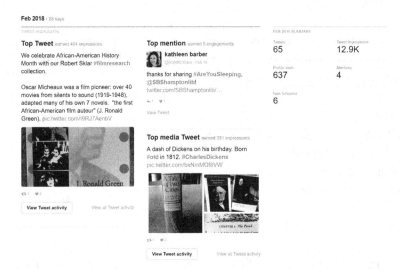

Individual Tweet Statistics

One can also view statistics on any individual tweet from the account, either through the Analytics interface or by clicking the three vertical lines at the bottom of the tweet on Twitter. Figure 9 shows the statistics for a specific tweet. Numbers are shown for impressions, engagements, and the specific types of engagements that occurred.

Cohort Tracking

Measuring the branch library's Twitter account against a cohort of peer institutions is another useful strategy to assess growth and activity. To start, identify what libraries or institutions will make up the cohort. These can be institutions of similar type, size, activity, or from the same geographic area. Just by charting the information available on public profiles, one can see how the branch library's account matches up in terms of number of followers, number of tweets, and number of accounts being followed.

Figure 9. Twitter analytics for a specific tweet (Southampton Library)
Source: Southampton Library 2018

SBU Southampton Library
@SBShamptonlib
Every dog had to start somewhere.
Some RinTinTin puppy facts:

Born on a French battlefield in WWI
Named after a popular pair of French
dolls with his sister Nanette
Spent his first weeks in the US in
Hempstead, LI

From Rin Tin Tin by @susanorlean
#NationalPuppyDay #RinTinTin
pic.twitter.com/sa38wnpOQf

Impressions	7,671
Total engagements	233
Media engagements	196
Likes	25
Link clicks	5
Detail expands	3
Retweets	2
Profile clicks	2

The Southampton Library tracks its performance against a number of SUNY libraries on Twitter, using the metrics of follower growth and number of tweets per month. Compiling all of these library accounts into a Twitter list makes it easier to gather the statistics at the end of each month.

Follower Audit

Knowing who is following the branch library helps in understanding the library's network and in identifying the audience reached. Research has been conducted that breaks down followers into relevant categories for study (Sewell, 2013). For a branch library, the network may break down into students, faculty, and academic departments but there can be a surprising number of outsiders. Knowing the breakdown of follower types can help a branch library determine who they are reaching with their content. If a key audience is not being reached, new campaigns or strategies can be developed to try to reach them.

Surveys

Direct feedback from the current and potential audience is always going to be valuable information to have. Is content reaching them? Is it the type of content they want? Conducting surveys in person or online through Google Forms can garner many useful results. If branch staff do not have the time or resources for surveys, even an informal assessment can garner information. Try leaving a whiteboard and marker out in the library asking students to record their preferences and thoughts.

Analytics Tools

Third party tools will help do even more analysis, from data mining to network mapping. Each of these tools allows one to learn more about various aspects of an account's performance on Twitter. Some are free or freemium, meaning that they provide a certain amount of functionality for free, with more advanced capabilities requiring a paid subscription.

Table 2 in the appendix lists a number of current tools for the branch library that wants to expand Twitter assessment activities.

FUTURE RESEARCH DIRECTIONS

Much research remains to be done on Twitter use at branch campus libraries. A comparison of use and engagement rates between a branch library and its main campus could show the effects of having different populations. Similarly, a poll of main campus users and departments may show what success the branch campus has had using Twitter to raise awareness of its activities.

A closer look at an academic library's following habits – who they choose who to follow - could uncover valuable information on how libraries see their role on Twitter and the level of reciprocity they expect from their network.

Finally, Emery & Schifeling found that "most academic libraries are not communicating with each other through Twitter" (p. 453). A study of interlibrary hashtags, mentions, likes, and retweets could show the level of interaction that exists now, uncover where activity is most prevalent, and suggest reasons why it might not be occurring.

CONCLUSION

Branch libraries can manage their own Twitter accounts without a large outlay of expense. With careful planning and wise use of time and resources, they can overcome logistical barriers to engage with their campus and wider institution while establishing their own presence and influence on Twitter. Keys to success include:

- Establishing flexible policies
- Tweeting with a distinctive voice
- Planning ahead to keep content flowing
- Showing reciprocity within the network
- Using hashtags and mentions to amplify the message and connect with influencers
- Assessing results, using analytics to guide and refine the strategy

Using many of these strategies, the Southampton Library has managed to establish and maintain a strong Twitter presence within Stony Brook University while attracting followers from the community at large. For this campus library located out on the eastern edge of Long Island, Twitter has proven a worthwhile vehicle for keeping in touch with the main campus, establishing an identity for the branch, and promoting awareness of the branch's activities.

REFERENCES

Appleton, L., & Tattersall, A. (2015). How librarians can harness the power of social media for the benefit of their users. *Multimedia Information & Technology*, *41*(4), 23–26.

Barnes, I. (2014). Twitter in special libraries: A distributed social media strategy. *Public Services Quarterly*, *10*(1), 62–65. doi:10.1080/15228959.2014.875789

Borruto, G. (2015). Analysis of tweets in Twitter. *Webology*, *12*(1), 1–11.

Bottorff, T., Glaser, R., Todd, A., & Alderman, B. (2008). Branching out: Communication and collaboration among librarians at multi-campus institutions. *Journal of Library Administration*, *48*(3-4), 329–363. doi:10.1080/01930820802289391

Brandt, J., Frederiksen, L., Schneider, T., & Syrkin, D. (2006). The face of regional campus libraries and librarianship. *Journal of Library Administration*, *45*(1/2), 37–61. doi:10.1300/J111v45n01_03

Brookbank, E. (2015). So much social media, so little time: Using student feedback to guide academic library social media strategy. *Journal of Electronic Resources Librarianship*, *27*(4), 232–247. doi:10.1080/1941126X.2015.1092344

Burkhardt, A. (2010). Social media: A guide for college and university libraries. *College & Research Libraries News*, *71*(1), 10–24. doi:10.5860/crln.71.1.8302

Chatten, Z. (2017). Making social media work: Finding a library voice. *Insights: The UKSG Journal*, *30*(3), 51–61. doi:10.1629/uksg.374

Dengerink, H. A. (2001). Institutional identity and organizational structure in multi-campus universities. *Metropolitan Universities*, *12*(2), 20–29.

Dryden, N. H., & Goldstein, S. (2013). Regional campus learning commons: Assessing to meet student needs. *Journal of Library Administration*, *53*(5-6), 293–322. doi:10.1080/01930826.2013.876822

Emery, K., & Schifeling, T. (2015). Libraries using Twitter better: Insights on engagement from food trucks. *Proceedings of the ACRL 2015 Conference*, 450-458. Retrieved from http://www.ala.org/acrl/sites/ala.org.acrl/files/content/conferences/confsandpreconfs/2015/Emery_Schifeling.pdf

Farkas, M. (2009). Governing social media. *American Libraries*, *40*(12), 35.

Harrison, A., Burress, R., Velasquez, S., & Schreiner, L. (2017). Social media use in academic libraries: A phenomenological study. *Journal of Academic Librarianship*, *43*(3), 248–256. doi:10.1016/j.acalib.2017.02.014

Howard, H., Huber, S., Carter, L., & Moore, E. (2018). Academic libraries on social media: Finding the students and the information they want. *Information Technology and Libraries*, *37*(1), 8–18. doi:10.6017/ital.v37i1.10160

Kim, H. M., Abels, E. G., & Yang, C. C. (2012). Who disseminates academic library information on Twitter? *Proceedings of the American Society for Information Science and Technology*, *49*(1), 1–4. doi:10.1002/meet.14504901317

Knickman, E., & Walton, K. (2014). Branch campus librarianship with minimal infrastructure: Rewards and challenges. *Community & Junior College Libraries*, *20*(3/4), 63–73. doi:10.1080/02763915.2015.1044301

Loudon, L., & Hall, H. (2010). From triviality to business tool: The case of Twitter in library and information services delivery. *Business Information Review*, *27*(4), 236–241. doi:10.1177/0266382110390480

MacDonald, G. (2013). Theorizing university identity development: Multiple perspectives and common goals. *Higher Education*, *65*(2), 153–166. doi:10.100710734-012-9526-3

Markland, M. J., Gascho Rempel, H., & Bridges, L. (2017). Mobile website use and advanced researchers: Understanding library users at a university marine sciences branch campus. *Information Technology and Libraries*, *36*(4), 7–23. doi:10.6017/ital.v36i4.9953

Mon, L., & Lee, J. (2015). Influence, reciprocity, participation, and visibility: Assessing the social library on Twitter. *Canadian Journal of Information and Library Science*, *39*(3/4), 279–294.

Ofili, D. N., & Emwanta, M.-G. (2014). Facebook as an information service delivery tool: Perspectives of library staff at the University of Benin, Nigeria. *African Journal of Library Archives and Information Science*, *24*(2), 195–202.

Pew Research Center. (2018). *Social media use in 2018*. Retrieved from http://www.pewinternet.org/2018/03/01/social-media-use-in-2018/

Phillips, N. K. (2011). Academic library use of Facebook: Building relationships with students. *Journal of Academic Librarianship*, *37*(6), 512–522. doi:10.1016/j.acalib.2011.07.008

Phinney, J., & Horsman, A. R. (2018). Satellite stories: Capturing professional experiences of academic health sciences librarians working in delocalized health sciences programs. *Journal of the Medical Library Association: JMLA*, *106*(1), 74–80. doi:10.5195/JMLA.2018.214 PMID:29339936

Ramsey, E., & Vecchione, A. (2014). Engaging library users through a social media strategy. *Journal of Library Innovation*, *5*(2), 71–82.

Schneider, T. M. (2001). The regional campus library and service to the public. *Journal of Academic Librarianship*, *27*(2), 122–127. doi:10.1016/S0099-1333(00)00184-1

Sewell, R. R. (2013). Who is following us? Data mining a library's Twitter followers. *Library Hi Tech*, *31*(1), 160–170. doi:10.1108/07378831311303994

Shulman, J., Yep, J., & Tomé, D. (2015). Leveraging the power of a Twitter network for library promotion. *Journal of Academic Librarianship*, *41*(2), 178–185. doi:10.1016/j.acalib.2014.12.004

Stewart, B., & Walker, J. (2018). Build it and they will come? Patron engagement via Twitter at historically black college and university libraries. *Journal of Academic Librarianship*, *44*(1), 118–124. doi:10.1016/j.acalib.2017.09.016

Stvilia, B., & Gibradze, L. (2014). What do academic libraries tweet about, and what makes a library tweet useful? *Library & Information Science Research*, *36*(3), 136–141. doi:10.1016/j.lisr.2014.07.001

Vassilakaki, E., & Garoufallou, E. (2015). The impact of Twitter on libraries: A critical review of the literature. *The Electronic Library*, *33*(4), 795–809. doi:10.1108/EL-03-2014-0051

Wallis, L. (2014). #selfiesinthestacks: Sharing the library with Instagram. *Internet Reference Services Quarterly*, *19*(3/4), 181–206. doi:10.1080/10875301.2014.983287

Wilkinson, J. (2018). Accessible, dynamic web content using Instagram. *Information Technology and Libraries*, *37*(1), 19–26. doi:10.6017/ital.v37i1.10230

Young, S. H., & Rossmann, D. (2015). Building library community through social media. *Information Technology and Libraries*, *34*(1), 20–37. doi:10.6017/ital.v34i1.5625

ADDITIONAL READING

Bizzle, B., & Flora, M. (2015). *Start a revolution: Stop acting like a library.* Chicago: ALA Editions.

King, D. L. (2012). Social media. *Library Technology Reports*, *48*(6), 23–27. PMID:22442899

Luo, L., Wang, Y., & Han, L. (2013). Marketing via social media: A case study. *Library Hi Tech*, *31*(3), 455–466. doi:10.1108/LHT-12-2012-0141

Mackenzie, A., & Martin, L. (2014). *Mastering digital librarianship: Strategy, networking and discovery in academic libraries.* London: Facet Publishing.

Mon, L., & Phillips, A. (2015). The social library in the virtual branch: Serving adults and teens in social spaces. *Advances in Librarianship*, *39*, 241–268. doi:10.1108/S0065-283020150000039016

Mon, L. M. (2015). *Social media and library services.* California: Morgan & Claypool. doi:10.2200/S00634ED1V01Y201503ICR040

Palmer, S. (2014). Characterizing university library use of social media: A case study of Twitter and Face-book from Australia. *Journal of Academic Librarianship*, *40*(6), 611–619. doi:10.1016/j.acalib.2014.08.007

Winn, D., Groenendyk, M., & Rivosecchi, M. (2015). Like, comment, retweet: Understanding student social media preferences. *Partnership: The Canadian Journal of Library and Information Practice and Research*, *10*(2), 1–14. doi:10.21083/partnership.v10i2.3449

This research was previously published in Social Media for Communication and Instruction in Academic Libraries; pages 258-284, copyright year 2019 by Information Science Reference (an imprint of IGI Global).

APPENDIX

Table 2. Twitter analysis tools

Name	URL
Buffer	https://buffer.com
Followerwonk	https://followerwonk.com
Keyhole	https://keyhole.co/
Klear	https://klear.com/free-tools/twitter-analysis
ManageFilter	https://www.managefilter.com
NCSU Tweet Visualizer	https://www.csc2.ncsu.edu/faculty/healey/tweet_viz/tweet_app/
Sprout Social	https://sproutsocial.com/features/twitter-analytics/
SumAll	https://sumall.com/
TweetStats	http://www.tweetstats.com/
TweepsMap	https://tweepsmap.com/
Twitonomy	https://www.twitonomy.com

Chapter 39
Twitter as a Language Learning Tool:
The Learners' Perspective

Fernando Rosell-Aguilar
iD https://orcid.org/0000-0001-9057-0565
Universitat Politècnica de València, Spain

ABSTRACT

Studies into the use of Twitter for language learning have mostly been small-scale evaluations undertaken by teachers researching the effectiveness of their own initiatives to use it with their students. To date, there has not been a large quantitative study of how language learners use Twitter autonomously. This paper reports on a large-scale study (n=370) of language learners who use Twitter. It provides a participant profile, their practices, and beliefs about how helpful Twitter is as a tool for language learning. The results provide the first profile of the autonomous user of Twitter as a language learning tool, show very positive attitudes towards the use of Twitter, and provide evidence that learners learn new vocabulary and culturally-relevant information about the areas where the target language is spoken. Many learners engage in production of target language output and make the most of the opportunities Twitter presents to be exposed to target language input and interaction with native speakers, making Twitter a useful tool for their autonomous language learning development.

INTRODUCTION

Computer-Assisted Language Learning has been defined as "the search for and study of applications of the computer in language teaching and learning" (Levy, 1997, p.1). This involves both the development of software and hardware, the use of existing digital tools for language learning purposes, and the study of how the use of these technologies can lead to language acquisition. Utilising social media for language learning purposes falls within the second activity: the use of existing tools, albeit autonomously for the most part. Autonomous learning (in which the learner takes charge of their own learning) is a goal that

DOI: 10.4018/978-1-6684-7123-4.ch039

can be achieved through self-directed learning using learning resources available to the learner, and social media provides a rich source of resources.

Twitter is a Social Networking Site (SNS) that can be accessed from a variety of devices, from desktop computers to mobile phones. Tweets are short messages of up to 280 characters in length (this limit was 140 characters until November 2017). As well as text, users can share hyperlinks, photographs, video, and create polls. Twitter can identify and offer automated translations for 40 different languages. Twitter launched in 2006, and since then has become a hugely popular platform, with enormous impact on the delivery and sharing of news, engagement in politics, promotion of businesses and entertainment, and delivery of education among many other subjects. The use of hashtags within tweets allows topics to be highlighted, and when topics are mentioned in large numbers, they 'trend' on Twitter, drawing attention to the hashtag. Twitter has over 330 million active monthly users, of whom 80% access the tool from mobile devices (Smith, 2020).

Research into Twitter for language learning has so far provided some evidence of engagement between learners and with native speakers, community development, and some language acquisition and improvement in areas such as vocabulary and pronunciation (Hattem and Lomicka, 2016). However, with some exceptions (e.g. Ng, Thang & Noor, 2018) most of this research has been centred on teacher-directed activities in which participants were assigned tasks they would not otherwise have undertaken and, in some occasions, they were prompted to create their Twitter accounts for the sole purpose of the research. In addition, the participants were for the most part university students, a relatively homogenous cohort in terms of age and motivation to learn as part of their studies. As a result, the results from this type of research do not present or evaluate the type of Twitter activities that learners undertake of their own volition as support for their language learning, whether to support formal learning or as part of autonomous learning. They also fail to provide a clear picture of the type of learner that undertakes language learning activity through Twitter. This paper seeks to address those gaps in the research by providing a profile of Twitter users, their practices, and beliefs about using Twitter as a language learning tool.

BACKGROUND

Twitter can provide access to materials that fit with Second Language Acquisition (SLA) theory recommendations, such as those that are authentic (Little, 1997), those that incorporate meaningful and engaging activities (Oxford, 1990), those that offer opportunities to hear modified comprehensible input that allows focus on target features of the second language (Holliday, 1999), and those that are appropriate to the medium used (Furstenberg, 1997).

The potential uses of Twitter as a language learning tool have been explored by many practitioners and researchers (Dickens, 2008; Borau, Ullrich, Feng & Shen, 2009; Craig, 2012; Hattem, 2014). These uses can be summarised under the categories of access to input, output and interaction as presented in Figure 1.

Knowledge, as it is understood from a constructivist point of view, is constructed through active exploration, observation, processing and interpretation (Cooper, 1993). Accessing language learning resources through social media is consistent with this learning process, where the user can access resources and activate knowledge. The social dimension of knowledge construction, following the Vygotskian socio-constructivist perspective, which claims that human development is socially situated and knowledge is

Figure 1. Potential uses of Twitter as a language learning tool (adapted from Rosell-Aguilar, 2018)

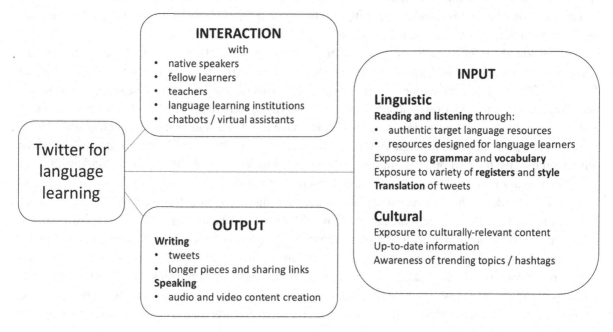

constructed through interaction with others, can be added through the interaction among peers or between tutors and learners that learning environments such as Twitter can afford.

A number of ways for language teaching practitioners to engage learners using Twitter have been suggested, including participating in language tandems (Reinhardt, Wheeler & Ebner, 2012), engaging in language play (Hattem, 2014), posting homework and intercultural information exchanges (Lee & Markey, 2014), and sharing experiences of visiting a target language area (Plutino, 2017).

Whilst these activities can be introduced to the classroom by teachers, there are many independent learners who utilise Twitter autonomously. The use of Twitter for language learning purposes is consistent with the view of learning as something that happens in everyday life outside the classroom, whether intentionally or accidentally, as advocated by theories of informal and lifelong learning (Naismith, Lonsdale, Vavoula, & Sharples, 2004).

Learning languages through social media shifts the focus to the learner and how they use the technology, making it important to research "the ways in which users appropriate the tools, dealing with constraints as well as spaces allowing them opportunities for action" (Lamy and Mangenot, 2013, p. 201). As Reinders and White (2016) point out, tracing the role of social media in contemporary experiences of language learning is a challenge to the field, and more empirical studies are needed which describe how learners use social media for language learning purposes. The use of Twitter undoubtedly facilitates access to language learning resources in an autonomous manner, but to evaluate whether engaging with these resources is a worthwhile activity, more needs to be known about the learners who engage in such activities, what they do, and what they think of the use of Twitter for language learning purposes.

The use of Twitter for language learning has been researched by a number of authors (see Rosell-Aguilar, 2018 for a detailed review). In a review of 17 studies into Twitter for language learning, Hattem and Lomicka (2016) highlight the potential for promoting interaction and communication (among learners, between learners and teachers, and between learners and native speakers), noticing and practising specific language skills and competencies (grammar, pronunciation, focus on form, providing feedback and negotiation of meaning), and community building. The authors also highlight some challenges such as the overwhelming amount of content and activity.

Some studies have found positive effects in their participants' production of output in the target language (TL) and communication with native speakers (Ullrich et al., 2008; Kim, Park & Baek, 2011, Blattner & Dalola, 2018). Others have found positive results in terms of developing a sense of community and encouragement to participation (Antenos-Conforti, 2009) and promoting communication among students and between students and tutors (Kelly, 2019). There have also been studies into the acquisition and improvement of pronunciation through Twitter (Mompean & Fouz-González, 2016; Plutino, 2017) whilst other studies have focused on intercultural exchanges (Lomicka & Lord, 2012; Lee & Markey, 2014).

The character limit on Twitter has provoked discussion among researchers who find it valuable and others who consider it a hindrance, particularly when the limit was set at 140 characters for all languages. Some think that the limit hinders the natural flow of language and can lead to the use of bad grammar (Grosseck & Holotescu, 2008), whilst other researchers propose that the limit encourages more precise thinking, editing and synthesising of language (Dunlap & Lowenthal, 2009, Plutino, 2017). The limit can be more constrictive depending on the language used: for some languages the 280-character limit restricts the message to just a few words, whereas in other languages 140 characters is enough to express much more content, which explains why the character limit remains at 140 for languages such as Chinese, Japanese and Korean.

Some Twitter users identify as language learners on their Twitter biography (the information they include to describe themselves). Looking at these users' Twitter accounts, it is easy to find many examples of varying degrees of engagement, such as retweeting Tweets in their target language, liking Tweets from language learning institutions, interaction with native speakers and with fellow learners, and tweeting in the target language. These are practices are an indication of the type of activity that language learners can undertake to develop their skills using Twitter. Research into this type of informal language learning via Twitter has not been reported so far. Neither has there been an attempt at profiling such a learner. Panter's (2010) concept of 'teaching strangers', coined to describe the challenges that librarians are faced with to support learning by providing suitable resources and advice for students who are unknown to them, is useful here: teachers in a traditional education setting usually know their students: whether they fall into the typical demographic for their institution, their socio-economic background, cultural make-up, learning preferences etc., and they use or design appropriate resources and tasks taking these circumstances into consideration. In a medium such as Twitter, the audience that engages in language learning is unknown: they are 'strangers' with varied levels of target language fluency, with varied backgrounds, educational level, interests and beliefs. The study that this paper reports on focuses on the profiles, practices and beliefs of language learners who use Twitter autonomously rather than because of teacher or researcher intervention, thus 'personalising the stranger' who uses Twitter and providing insight into the type of learner that engages in such online activity.

Research Questions

In order to fill the gaps in the information available about the autonomous use of Twitter as a language learning tool, the main three research questions that this paper reports on are:

1.   Who uses Twitter for language learning purposes?
2.   What practices do Twitter users engage in for language learning purposes?
3.   Can users learn languages using Twitter?

The data obtained serves two purposes: to 'personalise the stranger' and to assess whether the identified potential of Twitter as a language learning tool is indeed perceived as such by the participants of this study.

METHOD

A survey was piloted with ten volunteers known by the researcher to be frequent Twitter users who study languages, as they interact frequently with the Twitter account of the department of Languages at the researcher's institution. The volunteers were approached via Twitter and asked to complete the survey and provide feedback on clarity of questions, time it took to complete, and whether they thought any questions should be added or omitted. Their replies also helped to generate multiple choices for some of the questions that were open in the pilot survey.

The final survey consisted of 30 items: 27 of these were multiple-choice, with some open follow-up questions asking participants to provide examples, further details, or give reasons for their choices, and three standalone open questions. It is available online (Rosell-Aguilar, 2020). The research was approved by the Open University Human Research Ethics Committee. The survey was created using Onlinesurveys.ac.uk, whose servers are in the UK, thus complying with European regulations on data hosting and storage.

Four versions of the survey were written in English, Spanish, French and Italian in an effort to attract a variety of respondents. All versions contained the same questions in the same order. Links to the relevant survey asking potential participants to take part were distributed on Twitter. The researcher also encouraged other language professionals and institutions to retweet the different tweets. The English language tweet obtained the most retweets, followed by the Spanish language tweet, the French tweet and the Italian tweet.

Some participants took the survey in a language other than their first language: 80% of respondents to the Italian survey identified Italian as their first language. For the Spanish survey, the proportion of first language Spanish speakers was 67.9%, and for the English survey 65% of participants indicated that English was their first language. A much smaller proportion of native speakers took the French survey (38.5%), so the majority of respondents to that particular survey took it in a language other than their first language.

The surveys were open for seven months. A total of 401 unique responses were collected: 289 for the English survey, 81 for the Spanish survey, and 26 and five responses respectively for the French and Italian surveys. Participants who had a Twitter account but hardly ever used it, used Twitter mostly as a private communication tool, or had a Twitter account but never use it were removed from the results from this study as it is concerned with users who engage with Twitter on a regular, non-private, manner (n=370).

The survey items which provided data for the first question included questions about gender, age, language(s) they were learning, proficiency level, how long they had studied the language(s) for, and whether they were studying the language(s) formally or informally. They also asked about their Twitter use: how long they had been using it, how often, which devices they used, and the amount of time they normally spent using Twitter at a time. To answer the second question, items in the survey asked participants if they ever tweeted in their target language and why, what language learning activities they engaged with on Twitter, and whether they mostly focused on meaning, form or both when reading tweets in the target language. The items used to provide data for the third question asked participants whether they thought that Twitter could contribute to language learning and why, whether Twitter had helped them learn new vocabulary, grammar, or information about the culture of the areas where the target language is spoken, what they considered most useful about using Twitter to support their language learning, the relationships they had formed with fellow language learners on Twitter, and whether they had any concerns as language learners and Twitter users.

None of the questions in the survey were compulsory, therefore not all questions received the same number of responses. No reward was offered for taking part in the research to avoid a false sense of motivation (Mompean & Fouz-González, 2016).

The results were analysed using the online survey site's own statistics tools. Because the surveys gathered data in four languages, it was decided not to use qualitative data analysis software for the responses to open questions. These were categorised following the thematic analysis process suggested by Braun and Clarke (2006): responses were read three times (once without coding for general impressions, a second time coding and a third time to check the coding), coded depending on the theme by two researchers, and minor discrepancies in categorisation resolved through discussion.

RESULTS

The results are presented here in three sections corresponding to the main research questions.

Who Uses Twitter for Language Learning Purposes?

The user profile presented here is based on the responses from participants in this particular survey. The gender of participants was 63.5% female and 34.6% male. The remaining 1.9% of participants chose not to identify as male or female. Participants between the ages of 25 and 44 made up almost half the respondents. The full breakdown was 1.4% under 18, 17.3% between 18 and 24, 26% between 25-34, 24.4% between 35-44, 21.1% between 45-54, 7.6% between 55-64, and 2.2% over 65.

The main languages that respondents were learning were German (19.9%), Spanish (17.4%), English (15%), and French (11.8%), followed by Welsh (4.5%), Japanese (4.2%), Italian (3.8%) and others. Participants described their language level as beginner (21.5%), intermediate (36.7%), advanced (31%), or near-native (10.9%). Most respondents (58.6%) had studied the language they were learning for over five years, whereas the rest had been studying between three and five years (12.3%), between one and two years (15.1%) or less than one year (14%). In addition, over a quarter of respondents (28.9%) were studying the language formally at school, college or university. A further 48.2% were learning informally with resources such as books, audio and video materials, or apps, and the remaining 22.9% were no longer actively studying but continued to be interested in the language. Most respondents (84.7%) did not currently live in a geographical area where the language they were learning is an official language.

Most respondents (58.6%) had been using Twitter for over three years. A further 28.6% between one and three years, 6.8% between six months and a year, and 5.9% for less than six months. Their use of Twitter varied: 57.3% tweeted regularly and read tweets from accounts they followed, 38.9% rarely tweeted but used Twitter to follow others, and 3.8% tweeted regularly but hardly followed other accounts.

Twitter use among the respondents was very frequent: 81.4% used Twitter at least once every day (16.8% about once a day, 32.4% between two and five times a day and 32.2% over five times a day). The remaining 18.6% used it less frequently (14.3% several times a week, 3.2% about once a week, and 1.1% less frequently than once a week). The types of device that respondents normally used to access Twitter were mostly mobile devices: 69.2% of participants used either a mobile phone (55.7%) or a tablet (13.5%), and the remaining 30.8% used a desktop computer or laptop. The amount of time they normally spent using Twitter at a time was mostly between five and 15 minutes: 14.1% used it for less than five minutes at a time, 21.4% for around five minutes, 24.1% for around 10, 16.3% for around 15 minutes, 14.4% between 16 and 30 minutes, and 9.8% for over 30 minutes.

What Practices Do Twitter Users Engage in for Language Learning Purposes?

Participants were asked if they ever tweeted in the target language. The choice range was 'often' (selected by 16.8%), 'occasionally' (27%), 'rarely' (31.1%) and 'never' (25.1%). A thematic analysis of the reasons given for their choice produced nine main reasons, presented on Table 1. Some participants provided several reasons and other reasons did not appear with enough frequency to be listed on the table, which explains why the percentages within each column do not add up to 100%. For those who do rarely or never tweet in their target language, the main reason is not having any followers who use the language, followed by believing that their language level is not good enough and lack of confidence.

Table 1. Frequency and reasons for tweeting in the target language or not

	Never	Rarely	Occasionally	Often
Lack of confidence	21.62%	23.33%	6.49%	0.00%
Not good enough TL level	21.62%	11.11%	2.60%	0.00%
Cannot see a reason to do it	0.41%	5.56%	1.30%	0.00%
No followers who use TL	24.32%	30.00%	2.60%	0.00%
To communicate with other TL users	0.00%	5.56%	53.25%	42.00%
Fun	0.00%	2.22%	9.09%	4.00%
Language practice	0.00%	6.67%	23.38%	42.00%
Satisfaction / motivation	0.00%	2.22%	10.39%	2.00%
For work or other reasons	0.00%	0.00%	0.00%	14.00%

Seven choices of other language learning activities that users can engage with on Twitter were presented to participants, who could select as many as applicable to them. A total of 1457 responses were recorded from the 370 participants. These were, in order of popularity: Reading tweets in the TL written by native speakers, selected by 78.38% of the respondents; Following native speakers of the TL (68.11%); Following language learning institutions / providers / professionals who tweet LL resources or tips (67.30%); Accessing LL resources (64.32%); Reading tweets in L1 about the TL (52.52%); Following fellow TL learners (31.35%); and Reading tweets in the TL written by other learners (30.81%).

Participants were asked what they mostly focused on when reading tweets in the TL. Of the 330 who responded to this question, 18 (5.5%) selected "the way the language is used", 92 (27.9%) selected "the meaning of the tweet", and 220 (66.7%) selected "both".

Can Users Learn Languages Using Twitter?

Some 369 participants responded to a question about whether they thought that Twitter can contribute to language learning. Of these, 350 (94.9%) replied "yes" and 292 provided reasons for their choice. The vast majority (90.4%) referred to exposure to the target language. Other popular reasons were access to information, news and resources (26%), following people or institutions who tweet in the target language (22.3%), communication and interaction with other users of the target language (13.7%), and the fact that they are exposed to current, authentic, less formal conversational language (8.22%). Some 21 respondents (7.19%) mentioned that the 140-character limit, which still in place when this research was undertaken, was appealing to them as it does not require a long time to read and they can be easily comprehended, as opposed to other resources they find online. Among those who provided a reason why they did not think Twitter could contribute to their language learning, five were sceptical about how this could be achieved, three referred to the 140-character limit as a barrier, a further two mentioned the type of content ("superficial", "not real communication"), and another two mentioned the type of language used on Twitter (abbreviations, "irregular grammar").

Vocabulary, Grammar and Culture

Out of 356 participants who responded to the question "Have you learnt any new vocabulary in the language you're learning that you first noticed in a tweet?", 224 (62.9%) chose "yes" and 132 (37.1%) chose "No". Those who responded in the affirmative were asked to provide an example and 109 did. The examples included nouns, verbs and adjectives in a variety of languages. A further 21 did not provide concrete examples but listed categories such as "technical terms", "slang", or "politics", and the remaining 26 respondents stated that they had learned new vocabulary but could not remember any examples at the time. A few of these made the point that they do not usually remember where they learnt words they had assimilated into their vocabulary.

The next question asked participants if they had learnt any new grammar rules in their TL that they had first noticed in a tweet. Of the 353 respondents who replied to this question, 81 (22.9%) selected "yes" and 272 (77.1%) selected "no". The request for examples elicited 56 responses. Of these, 12 indicated that they did not recall any specific examples, but some noted that the exposure to the target language in the tweets they read had given them an understanding: "Can't think of a specific example at the moment - is mostly just repeated exposure leading to a feeling about what is and isn't correct usage". The remaining replies included examples such as verb conjugations, use of the subjunctive, prepositions, declensions, adjectival agreement, word position within sentences, and forms of the negative.

With regard to learning about the culture of the areas where the TL is spoken, 255 participants (70.8%) claimed that they had learnt new facts about those areas from tweets they had encountered, whereas 105 (29.2%) had not. When those who responded that they had were asked about the subjects that they had learnt about, the most popular category was News / Current affairs with 164 responses (64.3%), followed by Art and Literature (154 / 60.4%), Politics (117 / 45.9%), History (87 / 34.1%), Education (81 / 31.8%), Entertainment (80 / 31.4%), Geography (60 / 23.5%%), Environment (52 / 20.4%), Sport (51 / 20.0%) and Work (50 / 19.6%).

Most Useful Features

Participants were asked what they considered most useful about using Twitter to support their language learning. A total of 241 valid responses were collected. Many of these were coded into more than one category as some of the respondents mentioned several issues within a single response, so the total number of coded responses was 347, which were divided into four main categories: language practice, features and nature of using Twitter, information about the areas where the target language is spoken, and language learning resources. The most popular category was 'Language practice', with 193 responses. This category was divided into two sub-categories: 'Exposure to target language' (125 responses) and 'Access to others / Interaction' (68 responses). In the 'Exposure to target language' category, recurring themes from those who provided further details were the fact that the language is authentic (34 responses), that the language found on Twitter is colloquial in contrast with more formal language they see in books or the press (15 responses), vocabulary (19 responses), and grammar (4 responses): a typical comment was "it's helpful to expose yourself to informal, colloquial internet language as well". In the 'Access to others / interaction', the recurring themes were interaction with native speakers (20 responses), interaction with fellow learners (10 responses), and making friends (2 responses). Another popular category, with 69 responses, referred to the features and nature of using Twitter. These included the fact that information is bitesize (20 responses), its fast nature and immediacy (15 responses), that it is easy to use and convenient (12 responses), the fact that it is not a formal learning environment and something that they use as part of their routine (10 responses), and its 24-hour availability (8 responses): "it's integrated into my wider Twitter use, rather than being something I proactively have to remember to do". The third category was 'information about the areas where the target language is spoken', with 47 responses. Respondents referred to learning about culture, politics and current events. Some 15 respondents specified that they liked the fact that they could personalise their learning by reading tweets that were specific to their own personal interests: "being able to learn through what matters to me, like the teams I support and music I like". The fourth and final category was language learning resources, with 38 responses. Respondents referred to links to resources and activities, language learning tips, and contact with teachers and institutions that teach languages. Five respondents indicated that engaging with Twitter helps their motivation and increases their confidence: "now and again I can see a tweet which I completely understand and it feels like an achievement and that I am getting better".

Relationships with Other Users

Participants were asked to choose one among six options to describe the relationships they had formed with fellow language learners on Twitter. Some 165 respondents (59.8%) chose "I wouldn't say I've formed a relationship with other language learners I follow or who follow me". This was followed by "Members of a community of learners with a joint purpose (language learning) who share ideas, resources and support", selected by 44 respondents (15.9%), "People I can obtain interesting / useful information or resources from", selected by 42 respondents (15.2%), "Acquaintances" (14 respondents, 5.1%), "Friends" (6 respondents, 2.2%), and "other" (5 respondents, 1.8%). These specified that they did not engage with other learners on Twitter; some of them indicated that they use other platforms such as Facebook for more informal contact.

Concerns

Respondents were asked to select from a list what concerns they may have as language learners and Twitter users, if any. Of these, 123 respondents (33.2%) indicated that they did not have any concerns. The concerns of the remaining 247 participants were split as follows: making mistakes if they tweet in the language they are learning (98 responses, 39.7%), concerns that tweets may contain information that is inaccurate / just opinion rather than fact (62, 25.1%), concerns about learning incorrect use of language from fellow learners (48, 19.4%), and exposure to abuse / negative tweets (10, 4%). A further 10 respondents (4%) chose 'other'. The 'other' concerns included use of abbreviations and acronyms in tweets which make them difficult to understand, advertising, the 140-character limit, and not making connections with native speakers. One respondent wrote "People don't follow me so I can practice my bad Italian on them".

Overall Assessment for Language Learning Purposes

Finally, participants were asked to what extent they agreed with two statements. The Likert-scale options ranged from 1=strongly disagree to 5=strongly agree. The first statement was "using Twitter has improved my knowledge of the language I'm learning". A total of 358 responses were collected and the mean average was 3.61. The second statement was "using Twitter has improved my knowledge of the areas where the language I'm learning is spoken". A total of 357 responses were collected and the mean average was 3.77.

Discussion

The results are discussed here first in relation to the three research questions and then to assess whether the potential of Twitter as a language learning tool as identified by previous research is perceived as such by the participants of this study.

The respondent profile provides a picture of autonomous users who utilise Twitter to support their language learning, unreported so far. This picture helps to 'personalise the stranger', one of the aims of the study. The larger proportion of female users corresponds with the general picture across most language learning institutions, where female students tend to outnumber male students. The age of respondents also fits with the average age of Twitter users in general. Respondents were learning a variety of languages, but these were among the most-commonly studied languages in the world and also among the most-used languages on Twitter. This suggests that Twitter may be of less use to learners of less commonly-taught languages. Since most previous studies of Twitter users had been carried out by researchers within an educational setting, the fact that only 28.9% of respondents were formally studying a language makes the cohort very different from those surveyed in previous research and provides a realistic picture of the characteristics of autonomous language learners on Twitter. Given the large number of participants, this provides reliability to the data gathered.

The practices recorded capture an image of experienced, long-term users who utilise Twitter frequently, mostly from mobile devices, and for relatively short periods of time. Almost three quarters of respondents have tweeted in the target language (even if for some this is a rare occurrence), which shows a high proportion of participants engaging with target language production (similar to findings by Kim, Park & Baek, 2011). Unsurprisingly, those learners who tweet in the target language most often reported the highest proportion of useful language learning activity such as language practice and communicating with target language users. The other practices that users engaged with also showed useful strategies for autonomous language learning such as reading authentic material in the target language and accessing resources. Learners clearly showed a preference for interacting with native speakers rather than fellow learners. The respondents also showed preference for focusing on meaning ('the meaning of the tweet') rather than form ('the way the language is used'), although the largest proportion indicated that they focused on both. Whereas almost two thirds of participants indicated that they had noticed new vocabulary and almost half of these were able to produce examples, over three quarters of respondents indicated that they had not noticed any new grammatical features and only just over 10% of the total number of respondents were able to provide an example. With over 70% of respondents reporting that they had learnt something new about the cultures of the areas where their target language is spoken, Twitter can be recognised as a source of knowledge in a variety of subjects about these areas in a way that is personalised to the learner.

The beliefs about Twitter as a language learning tool showed that the vast majority of respondents (94.9%) believed using it can contribute to their language learning for a variety of reasons, exposure to the target language being the most popular. Similarly, the results produced very positive statements about improvement of language ability and knowledge of the target language cultures, which matches previous research by Ullrich at al. (2008). Despite concerns about the 140-character limit expressed by previous research (Lee & Markey, 2014), only three users mentioned this as a negative feature whereas 21 mentioned it as a positive. The affordances of Twitter as an environment to foster a community between language learners (Antenos-Conforti, 2009; Lomicka & Lord, 2012), however, do not appear to be important to most of the respondents. The fact that a third of respondents did not have any concerns about using Twitter as a language learning tool was positive, as was the fact that the concerns reported by those who had them focused on linguistic issues rather than any of the negative features that are often reported by the media relating to bullying and negativity (which was mentioned by a low 10 respondents). The linguistic concerns, such as making mistakes or worrying about the accuracy of the language they encountered, were typical of language learners in any environment.

In terms of revisiting the potential of Twitter as a language learning tool, the results provide evidence of Twitter being used as a social environment (Vie, 2007) where learners are exposed to target language and immersed in an environment where they encounter comprehensible input, produce output and engage in interaction (Hattem, 2014). This research takes that further by demonstrating that for many users that exposure to the target language and its speakers is the main reason and perceived benefit of using it. Learners find opportunities to navigate across languages, identities and cultures, as Chen (2013) had argued, and learn about a variety of topics in current affairs, politics and culture, as proposed by Reindhart, Wheeler & Ebner, (2012). The positive attitudes reported by Lin, Warschauer & Blake (2016) are also evidenced in this research. Although engagement with fellow learners was not perceived as being part of a community by most of the participants, there is evidence that users benefit from the social interactions with and output from native speakers in their Twitter network. This evidence supports the claim by Craig (2012) that Twitter can provide linguistic, cultural and social benefits.

LIMITATIONS, FURTHER RESEARCH AND CONCLUSION

Limitations

A number of limitations affect this study. The data collected is self-reported, and therefore affected by issues such as time limitation, credibility, inaccuracy or memory (Paulhus & Vazire, 2007). It was also collected online, which adds anonymity and can sometimes lead to non-serious responses (Gosling, Vazire, Srivastava & John, 2004). Whilst these limitations exist, self-report is an established method any non-serious responses to the survey were easily identified and removed. In addition, gathering data through a link within a tweet is consistent with ethnographic research into the use of Twitter and brings the data collection method within the users' environment. This does however bring another limitation, which is the validity of the sample. The call for participants to take part was shared by followers of the researcher's own Twitter account and those who in turn follow them. There could be an argument that the sample is therefore restricted and not representative. Whilst this cannot be avoided, the fact that many of those who shared the link to the survey were language learners or involved in language teaching helped the survey find the right audience. Both the self-report and online nature of the survey can also lead to responses being short and superficial. Although most responses were short and some could be described as superficial, many of the responses provided useful information and insight – it could be argued that brevity is not a barrier to conveying meaning among Twitter users, who are used to condensing thoughts into short messages.

The research has also been limited to quantitative methods so far, which fits this exploratory stage and provides the opportunity to obtain reliability through the large numbers of responses gathered.

Further Research

The study would be easy to replicate, which may be a useful activity at a later point as this would allow a comparison between data sets. Because of the nature of the respondents as autonomous users, it is not possible to correlate their responses with actual language gains. However, a replication of this study within the context of a teacher / researcher-led activity could include targeted exposure to tweets within a certain topic and semantic field and pre-and post-tests could be carried out to explore vocabulary gains and recollection, for example.

CONCLUSION

Online applications and tools appear and disappear, evolve into massively-popular environments or go out of fashion, making it harder to choose which ones to evaluate and research beyond the initial possible potential for learning activity. As the purpose of some tools becomes broader - Twitter was not designed as a language learning and teaching tool - the impact of social environments with massive user numbers on teaching and learning must continue to be part of the research agenda.

The research presented in this paper advances the knowledge in the area of Twitter for language learning by providing a profile of the autonomous language learner and Twitter user, their practices and beliefs. It is also the first large-scale study into Twitter for language learning outside the confines of teacher-led activity. Such evaluations of learning tools are scarce, but they provide insights that would not be available otherwise and help create a picture of how tools are utilised in a more ethnographic way. It could be argued that many of the results found in this study are unsurprising. The fact that the users who use Twitter most often are the most likely to find it useful for learning, or that the main gain for language learning is vocabulary acquisition could have been easily hypothesised, but up to this point there was no evidence to support these hypotheses. What this research has found is that many language learners use Twitter as part of their daily routine, that using Twitter as a language learning tool is integrated into their wider Twitter activity, and it has become one of the range of activities they undertake to support their autonomous language learning, regardless of whether they are formal or informal learners. As such, the use of Twitter can be included in the range of activities that language learners can undertake as a means to access exposure to input in the target language, information about the cultures where it is spoken, and a platform for production of input and interaction.

This paper has focused on the autonomous activities that language learners engage in on Twitter. Many of these are likely to be replicated on other microblogging tools such as Instagram or Weibo. Practitioners wishing to incorporate Twitter into their teaching practice can use some of the activities carried out in the previous research reported above such as tasks that promote noticing and practising specific language skills and competencies, production of output and interaction with native speakers, or taking part in intercultural exchanges. These activities, however, can be time-consuming to prepare and make students use their personal social media for specific task - which they may be reluctant to do. Also, activities initiated by teachers may not lead to learners incorporating social media into their lifelong learning repertoire. The results from this paper show that learners can use microblogging autonomously with positive results, and teachers may wish to simply demonstrate to their students some of the activities that learners can engage in on social media to support their independent language learning, leading perhaps to more individualised, motivating and successful use.

REFERENCES

Antenos-Conforti, E. (2009). Microblogging on Twitter: Social networking in intermediate Italian classes. In L. Lomicka & G. Lord (Eds.), *The Next Generation: social networking and online collaboration in foreign language learning* (pp. 59–90). CALICO.

Blattner, G., & Dalola, A. (2018). I Tweet, You Tweet, (S)He Tweets: Enhancing the ESL Language-Learning Experience Through Twitter. *International Journal of Computer-Assisted Language Learning and Teaching*, 8(2), 1–19. doi:10.4018/IJCALLT.2018040101

Borau, K., Ullrich, C., Feng, J., & Shen, R. (2009). Microblogging for language learning: Using twitter to train communicative and cultural competence. In *Advances in Web Based Learning–ICWL 2009* (pp. 78–87). Springer Berlin Heidelberg. doi:10.1007/978-3-642-03426-8_10

Craig, D. (2012). *Twitter for Academic Writing*. Retrieved from http://www.danielcraig.com/2012/09/06/twitter-for-academic-writing-2/

Cooper, D. P. (1993). Paradigm shifts in designing instruction: From behaviourism to cognitivism. *Educational Technology*, 33(5), 12–19.

Dickens, S. (2008, April 29). Twitter – microblogging. *Digitalang*. Retrieved from http://www.digitalang.com/2008/04/twitter-microblogging/

Dunlap, J. C., & Lowenthal, P. R. (2009). Tweeting the night away: Using Twitter to enhance social presence. *Journal of Information Systems Education, 20*(2), 129–135.

Furstenberg, G. (1997). Teaching with Technology: What is at Stake? *ADFL Bulletin, 28*(3), 21-25. Retrieved from https://www.mla.org/adfl/bulletin/v28n3/283021.htm

Gosling, S. D., Vazire, S., Srivastava, S., & John, O. P. (2004). Should we trust web-based studies? A comparative analysis of six preconceptions about internet questionnaires. *The American Psychologist, 59*(2), 93–104. doi:10.1037/0003-066X.59.2.93 PMID:14992636

Grosseck, G., & Holotescu, C. (2008, April). *Can we use Twitter for educational activities.* In 4th international scientific conference, eLearning and software for education, Bucharest, Romania.

Hattem, D. (2014). Microblogging activities: Language play and tool transformation. *Language Learning & Technology, 18*(2), 151–174.

Hattem, D., & Lomicka, L. (2016). What the Tweets say: A critical analysis of Twitter research in language learning from 2009 to 2016. *E-Learning and Digital Media, 13*(1-2), 5–23. doi:10.1177/2042753016672350

Holliday, L. (1999). Theory and research: Input, interaction, and CALL. In J. Egbert & E. Hanson-Smith (Eds.), *CALL environments: Research, practice, and critical issues* (pp. 181–188). TESOL.

Kelly, O. (2019). Assessing language student interaction and engagement via Twitter. In New Case Studies Of Openness In And Beyond The Language Classroom (pp. 129-143). Research-publishing. net. doi:10.14705/rpnet.2019.37.971

Kim, E.-Y., Park, S.-M., & Baek, S.-H. (2011). Twitter and implications for its use in EFL learning. *Multimedia-Assisted Language Learning, 14*(2), 113–137. doi:10.15702/mall.2011.14.2.113

Lamy, M.-N., & Mangenot, F. (2013). Social media-based language learning: insights from research and practice. In M.-N. Lamy & K. Zourou (Eds.), *Social networking for language education* (pp. 197–213). Palgrave Macmillan. doi:10.1057/9781137023384_11

Lee, L., & Markey, A. (2014). A study of learners' perceptions of online intercultural exchange through Web 2.0 technologies. *ReCALL, 26*(03), 281–297. doi:10.1017/S0958344014000111

Levy, M. (1997). *Computer-assisted language learning: Context and conceptualization.* Oxford University Press.

Lin, C.-H., Warschauer, M., & Blake, R. (2016). Language learning through social networks: Perceptions and reality. *Language Learning & Technology, 20*(1), 124–147.

Little, D. (1997). Responding authentically to authentic texts: a problem for self-access language learning? In P. Benson & P. Volley (Eds.), *Autonomy and Independence in Language Learning* (pp. 225–236). Longman.

Lomicka, L., & Lord, G. (2012). A tale of tweets: Analyzing microblogging among language learners. *System, 40*(1), 48–63. doi:10.1016/j.system.2011.11.001

Long, M. H. (1996). The role of the linguistic environment in second language acquisition. In W. C. Ritchie & T. K. Bhatia (Eds.), *Handbook of research on language acquisition. Vol. 2: Second language acquisition* (pp. 413–468). Academic Press. doi:10.1016/B978-012589042-7/50015-3

Mompean, J. A., & Fouz-González, J. (2016). Twitter-based EFL Pronunciation Instruction. *Language Learning & Technology*, *20*(1), 166–190.

Naismith, L., Lonsdale, P., Vavoula, G., & Sharples, M. (2004). Literature Review in Mobile Technologies and Learning. *FutureLab Report 11*. http://www.futurelab.org.uk/resources/ documents/lit_reviews/ Mobile_Review.pdf

Ng, L. S., Thang, S. M., & Noor, N. M. (2018). The Usage of Social Networking Sites for Informal Learning: A Comparative Study Between Malaysia Students of Different Gender and Age Group. *International Journal of Computer-Assisted Language Learning and Teaching*, *8*(4), 76–88. doi:10.4018/ IJCALLT.2018100106

Oxford, R. (1990). *Language learning strategies: What every teacher should know*. Newbury House.

Panter, M. E. (2010). Collaborative Teaching: Teaching Strangers. *Library Media Connection*, *28*(6), 34–35.

Plutino, A. (2017). Teachers as awakeners: a collaborative approach in language learning and social media. In C. Álvarez-Mayo, A. Gallagher-Brett, & F. Michel (Eds.), Innovative language teaching and learning at university: enhancing employability (pp. 115-125). Research-publishing.net.

Reinders, H., & White, C. (2016). 20 years of autonomy and technology: How far have we come and where to next? *Language Learning & Technology*, *20*(2), 143–154. http://llt.msu.edu/issues/june2016/ reinderswhite.pdf

Reinhardt, W., Wheeler, S., & Ebner, M. (2010). All I need to know about twitter in education I learned in kindergarten. In *Key Competencies in the Knowledge Society* (pp. 322–332). Springer Berlin Heidelberg. doi:10.1007/978-3-642-15378-5_31

Rosell-Aguilar, F. (2018). Twitter as a formal and informal language learning tool: from potential to evidence. In Innovative language teaching and learning at university: integrating informal learning into formal language education (pp. 99-106). Research-publishing.net. doi:10.14705/rpnet.2018.22.780

Rosell-Aguilar, F. (2020). *Survey on the use of Twitter as a language learning tool* (Version 1). doi:10.6084/ m9.figshare.12382778.v1

Smith, K. (2020). *60 Incredible and Interesting Twitter Stats and Statistics*. Retrieved from https://www. brandwatch.com/blog/twitter-stats-and-statistics

Swain, M. (2005). The output hypothesis: Theory and research. In *Handbook of research in second language teaching and learning* (pp. 495–508). Routledge.

Ullrich, C., Borau, K., Luo, H., Tan, X., Shen, L., & Shen, R. (2008). Why web 2.0 is good for learning and for research: principles and prototypes. In *Proceedings of the 17th international conference on World Wide Web* (pp. 705-714). ACM. 10.1145/1367497.1367593

This research was previously published in the International Journal of Computer-Assisted Language Learning and Teaching (IJCALLT), 10(4); pages 1-13, copyright year 2020 by IGI Publishing (an imprint of IGI Global).

Chapter 40

Perception of Stakeholders on the Use of Social Networking Tools for Classroom Instruction in School Environment:
Use of Social Network Tools for Classroom Instruction

Ogunlade Bamidele Olusola
iD https://orcid.org/0000-0002-1029-3383
Veritas University Abuja, Nigeria

ABSTRACT

Social networking platforms are becoming the most important tools for interaction among people, where everybody can share, exchange, comment, discuss, and create information and knowledge in a collaborative way. The aim of this chapter is to examine the perception of stakeholders on the use of social network tools for classroom instruction in school environment in Ibadan North Local Government of Oyo State. Based on literature and experiences carried out by the researcher in Ibadan metropolis, it also explores the impact of the social networking platforms applications on personal, teaching, and learning uses among secondary students, teachers, and parents. Based on these, it is recommended that, if social networking platforms are effectively used, it will develop positive attitude towards learning as well as enhancing academic achievement among secondary school students.

INTRODUCTION

Social networking is difficult to define because it is constantly changing as technologies grow and transform. Webster's Dictionary (2013) defines social networking, social networking, or social technologies simply as, "Forms of electronic communication through which users create online communities to share

DOI: 10.4018/978-1-6684-7123-4.ch040

information, ideas, messages, and other content." It frequently refer to the implementation of social networking as a campaign because it represents a connected series of operations designed to reach a set of specific goals (Webster, 2013). Each social networking platform, such as YouTube, Twitter and Facebook, offer users different tools for sharing information and ideas through news articles, photos, videos and information or personal posts with friends and online communities.

Social networking are internet applications that rely on openly shared digital content that is authored, critiqued and re-configured by a mass of users. Social networking applications therefore allow users to converse and interact with each other; to create, edit and share new forms of textual, visual and audio content; and to categorize, label and recommend existing forms of content. Perhaps the key characteristic of all these social networking practices is that of 'mass socialization'—i.e. harnessing the power of the collective actions of online user communities rather than individual users (Shirky, 2008).

Eke, Omekwu and Odoh, (2014) noted that social networking sites are fast becoming very popular means of both interpersonal and public communication in Nigeria. They further defined it as modern interactive communication channels through which people connect to one another, share ideas, experiences, pictures, messages and information of interest. Boyd and Ellison (2007) define social networking sites as web based services that allow individuals to construct a Public or semi public profile within a bounded system, articulate a list of other users with whom they share a connection and view and traverse their list of connections and those made by others within the system. Also, Ahn (2011) define SNS as online community of internet users who want to communicate with other users about areas of mutual interest. They are also sites built on web 2.0 which allows users to generate and transfer contents to peers, friends and relatives. These sites like facebook, BlackBerry Messenger (BBM), 2go, myspace, and WhatsApp among others have become an established part of the online environment that enables individuals, institutions and organizations to maintain and visualize their social networks. They have become global phenomenon's that have attracted extensive population from different ages, cultures, and educational levels (Mazman & Usluel, 2011).

In recent time, the world has witnessed what could be referred to as communication evolution through 'technological advances and increased use of the Internet' (Moqbel, 2012). This communication revolution, as well as the more technologically empowered lifestyle of individual users, has changed the way people communicate and connect with each other (Coyle, 2008; O'Murchu, Breslin & Decker, 2004). Social networking sites are a recent trend in this revolution. Social networking sites are created to take care of variety of human needs and could be classified using that format. For instance, Ellison, Steinfield, and Lampe (2007) classified SNSs into: work-related contexts (*LinkedIn*.com), romantic relationship initiation (*Friendster*.com), connecting those with shared interests such as music or politics (*MySpace*.com), or the college student population (*Facebook*). It should however be noted that the examples mentioned above were based on the original intentions of founders of the SNSs, though these intentions have been taken to another level by users. This is why latter classification of SNSs takes somewhat different approach and put different factors into consideration. To Fraser and Dutta (2008), SNSs should better be classified into the following five categories- egocentric/identity construction social networking sites such as *Facebook* and *MySpace*; opportunistic social networking sites for business connections such as LinkedIn; community social networking sites representing cultural or neighborhood groups; media-sharing social networking sites such as YouTube and Flickr; and Passion-centric social networking sites for sharing common interests such as Dogster.

Folorunso, Vincent, Adekoya and Adewale (2010) reviewed that, in Africa, social networking sites are becoming widely spread than it has ever been before, and it appears that people's Perception of this technology is diverse. The emergence of the Internet and the development of wireless communications technology have enabled the presentation of education in various methods without limitations of time and place. Along with these changes, usage of diverse Social Networking Services (SNS) such as Facebook, Twitter, Line, and others have been invigorated. Especially, as Internet usage by portable mobile devices has increased due to the development of wireless communications technology, SNS has become a part of daily life for the younger generation (Eke, Omekwu & Odoh, 2014).

Though there is an argument that excessive use of SNS interferes with learning in youth, considering the fast growth of SNS as a daily communication tool, it is better to encourage meaningful educational applications than to prevent its use. Public education, the fruit of communication and interaction among teacher, students, and learning contents, can be promoted by the proper application of media that helps communications such as SNS. While past education focused on face-to-face communication between teacher and students or knowledge acquisition through books, recent education has evolved by adapting various media including e-books and smart devices. Highly advanced networks and the spread of smart devices enable more comfortable and diverse applications of SNS as a new educational communication tool (Lim, Kang, & Shin, 2012; Weber, 2012).

More also, due to the ability of social networking to enhance connections by making them easily accessible, social networking can yield many benefits for the students, including providing a virtual space for them to explore their interests or problems with similar individuals, academic support, while strengthening online communication skills and knowledge. "Students who may be reluctant to speak up in class are participating in book discussion blogs and writing for real audiences. There are new Web tools emerging all the time that are On the other hand, social networking sites have caused some problems for their users, individuals, families, groups and students. Most of their users, these days, prefer to communicate via the sites rather via face-to-face contact or oral communication, thus, making social network their preferred socializing forces. This Benniger (1987) opined "has gradually replaced interpersonal communication." "According to Sherry Turkle, the founder and director of MIT initiative on Technology and self, via wikipedia (2011), stated that, networked, we are together, but so lessened are our expectations of each other that we feel utterly alone. And there is the risk that we come to see each other as objects to be accessed and only for the parts that we find useful, comforting or amusing.

Ahmed (2011) reported that one of the dangers of social networks ; cyber or E crime encourages copyright infringement which has always remain a serious case in dealing with social Networking sites especially about the video clips for instance in the YouTube. Users without considering the terms can easily upload download or watch any kind of video clip. YouTube for instance was sued several times on these issues. For example Viacom sued YouTube claiming one billion dollar for uploading 160 thousand videos belonging to Viacom without their permission as did the French independent labels collecting society. Another drawback to social networking is that some users simply share too much information; people can lose their jobs or a friendship over leaking information on social networking. Even if a user of a social site has her privacy settings of highest level, their information can still be passed on by someone on their friends list. It doesn't take much for an angry follower to copy and paste a status or download a picture if they are looking for revenge. On the following note there are a number of scammers on social networks who may try to steal or use your personal information; information that can be used for potential crime such as identity theft or fraud.

Furthermore, there has been a recent spike in phishing attacks associate with social networking sites Fisher (2011). Many people view social networking sites on cell phones or other mobile devices. This makes it harder to distinguish real and fake web sites. Additionally, social networking enables attackers to send phishing messages that appear to come from someone that the victim knows. Having obtained long information for a few accounts, scammers will then send out messages to everyone connected to the compromised accounts, often with an enticing subject line that suggests familiarity with the victim Baker (2009).

Additionally, social networking sites like Facebook and Twitter create the illusion of familiarity and intimacy on the internet. The result is that people may be inclined to share information on which they would have preferred to keep private. Again, cross site request forgery (CSRF) is an attack which causes an end user's web browser to execute actions of the attacker's choosing without the user's knowledge. By embedding a malicious link in a web page or sending a link via email or chat, an attacker may cause the users of a web application to perform unwanted actions. More specifically, the attack causes the user's browser to make requests to a web site to which it has been authenticated, without the users or the web sites knowledge. These actions may result in compromised end user data operations, or even an entire server or network.

Therefore, it is necessary to examine the Perception of stakeholders on the use of social network tools for classroom instruction in school environment in Ibadan North Local Government of Oyo State. A study like this shall help to ascertain whether teacher and students use of the social networking for teaching/learning purposes could be allowed and regulated or not in the academic environment.

STATEMENT OF THE PROBLEM

Social networking is such a prevalent part of modern society most especially the adolescents and students. The issue has led many schools to ban the use of phones and mobile devices during school days, social networking websites such as Facebook, WhatsApp, and Twitter etc. have been blocked on schools' computers because of the negative influences it has on the students moral and academic. However, schools and educators are beginning to take a different approach by introducing social networking into the educational system because of its perceived opportunities and advantages such as helping parents, teachers and students be on the same page; sharing resources quickly; useful for homework, increase students' participation and collaboration among others. This phenomenon has led to series of argument among stakeholders and educators at all levels, it is on this note that this research intends to examine the perspective of stakeholders (students, teachers and parents) on the use of social networking in classroom instruction in school environment.

RESEARCH QUESTIONS

The study is designed to answer the following research questions:

1.   What is the level of familiarity of stakeholders in social networking use?
2.   What are the various categories of social networking sites use by stakeholders?

3. Do parents' religious beliefs influence their perception on the use of social networking tools in classroom instruction?
4. Do parents' socio-technological backgrounds affect their perception of the use of social networking tools in classroom instruction?
5. Do students' religious beliefs influence their perception toward the use of social networking tools in classroom instruction?
6. Do teachers' socio-technological backgrounds affect their perception on the use of social networking tools in classroom instruction?

RESEARCH DESIGN

The descriptive survey research design will be used for this study because descriptive survey method helps to obtain information regarding the prevalence, distribution, determinants and interrelationship of variables within a population. It could be used to collect information on people's action, knowledge, awareness, opinions, intention, attitude and values.

SAMPLE AND SAMPLING TECHNIQUE

For the purpose of adequate spread of the study within Ibadan-North Local Government a random sampling technique will be used to select three hundred respondents from student's parents and teachers were randomly selected, which are: 200 students, 50 parents and 50 teachers within the study area.

RESEARCH INSTRUMENT

The instrument for data collection for the research was questionnaire which would be divided into two sections, the first section covers the information on respondents' bio data and some personal information, and their background of social networking tools for classroom instruction. The questionnaire was testing perceptions of stakeholders (in-service teachers, students and parents) on the use of social networking tools for classroom instruction, their experience on social networking tools for classroom instruction, the usefulness to designing the use of social networking for classroom instruction and views on religious and technology use of social networking for classroom instruction.

VALIDITY AND RELIABILITY OF INSTRUMENTS

To ensure validity of the instruments, a draft of the questionnaire was presented to the expert's educational technology for constructive criticisms. Necessary corrections was effected before the administration of the instruments in order to improve face and content validity. However, to determine the reliability of the instrument, the validated version of the questionnaire was administered on 25 students, 15 teachers and 20 parents making 60 all together from Ibadan South Local Government Area. Which was not part of the population for the study but share the same characteristics with the population of the study.

Responses of participants were subjected to Cronbach Alpha analysis and a reliability coefficient of 0.754 was obtained.

Results

Research Question One: What is the level of familiarity of stakeholders in social networking use?

Table 1. Level of familiarity of stakeholders in the social networking use

S/N	Item	SA (%)	A (%)	D (%)	SD (%)	No Response	Mean	STAND. DEV.
1	**PARENTS:** My knowledge of technological tools help in the constructive raising of the children	106 (53.0)	70 (35.0)	17 (8.0)	7 (3.5)		3.39	0.79
2	**STUDENTS:** I interact with my friends on various social networking platforms and therefore find it useful for learning purposes	100 (50.0)	99 (49.5)	00 (0.0)	1 (0.5)		3.49	0.53
3	**TEACHERS:** I have a good knowledge of the use of social networking for learning purposes	76 (38.0)	82 (41.0)	13 (6.5)	29 (14.5)		3.03	1.01
	Weighted Average						**3.30**	

Table 1 shows that the parents have the knowledge and familiar with the use of technological tools as 53.0% and 35.0% of them strongly agreed and agreed respectively to item one which says my knowledge of technological tools help in the constructive raising of the children, while only 3.5% of them strongly disagreed to the notion. Also almost all the students are familiar with the social networking tools with item 2 indicating 3.49 mean and 50% and 49.5% strongly agreed and agreed to the item. More so, teachers of the study area are familiar with social networking site with item 3 showing 38% and 41% of the respondents strongly agree and agree respectively to the item that says I have a good knowledge of the use of social networking for learning purposes.

Based on the interpretation of results above coupled with calculated weighted average of 33 mean, it can be concluded that the level of familiarity of stakeholders in social networking use is relatively high.

Research Question Two: What are the various categories of social networking sites use by stakeholders?

Table 2 showed the social networking tools used by the respondents (parents, students and parents) 46.8% of the respondents know how to use Facebook, 31.5% of the respondents were WhastApp users, 10% uses blogs networking, 5.8% and 4.2% respondents are users of 2go/Instagram and Wikis respectively while 1.7% of the respondents does not use any of the social networking tools. Based on the analysis, it can be concluded that various categories of social networking sites use by stakeholders include Facebook, WhatsApp, 2go/Instagram, blogs and wiki according to their popularity among the respondents.

Table 2. Social networking Tools used by stakeholders

Social Networking Tools	Frequency	Percentage (%)
Wikki	25	4.2
Blogs	60	10.0
Facebook	281	46.8
Whatsapp	189	31.5
2go/instagram	35	5.8
None	10	1.7
TOTAL	**600**	**100.0**

Research Question Three: Do parents' religious beliefs influence their perception on the use of social networking tools in classroom instruction?

Table 3. Comparison of parents' religious belief and social networking

S/N	Item	SA (%)	A (%)	D (%)	SD (%)	No Response	Mean	STAND. DEV.
1	The doctrine of my religion does not permit children to make use of social networking	24 (12.0)	9 (4.5)	44 (22.0)	123 (61.5)		1.67	1.02
2	Usage of social networking has been an avenue for initiating children into wrong religious views	26 (13.0)	38 (19.0)	59 (29.5)	77 (38.5)		2.07	1.05
3	Religion and technology are two parallel lines	28 (14.0)	57 (28.5)	72 (36.0)	43 (21.5)		2.35	.97
4	Social networking expose children to areas of religion that would develop them positively	86 (43.0)	92 (46.0)	7 (3.5)	11 (5.5)	4 (2.0)	3.29	.79
	Weighted Average						**2.345**	

Table 3 illustrates the comparison of how parents' religion belief influence their perception of the use of social networking tools in classroom instruction. It could inferred from the table under item 4 with mean 3.29 which showed that social networking exposes children to areas of religion that would develop them positively. This is contrary to the belief that social networking aid evil perpetration as 43% of the total respondents strongly and 46% agree respectively that social networking expose children to areas of religion that would develop them positively. The item 3 with mean 2.35 depicts that religion and technology were not two parallel lines since 36% of the respondents disagree and 21.5% strongly disagree respectively with the item which says religion and technology are two parallel lines. It could also been seen in item 2 which has mean 2.07 revealed that usage of social networking has never been an avenue for initiating children into wrong religious view as item's percentile affirmed with 29.5% of the respondents disagree and 38.5% strongly disagree respectively. The research item 1 with mean 1.67 noted that the doctrine of parents' religion permit their children to make use of social networking as 22% of the respondents disagree and 61.5% strongly disagree with item that the doctrine of parents does not allow children to make use of social networking.

Based on the interpretation of results above coupled with calculated weighted average of 2.345, the research questions which ask; do parents' religious belief influence the perception on the use of social networking tools in classroom instruction is therefore answered that parents' religious belief influence their perception of the use of social networking tools in classroom instruction.

Research Question Four: Do parents' socio-technological backgrounds affect their perception of the use of social networking tools in classroom instruction?

Table 4. Comparison of parents' socio-cultural background and social networking

S/N	Item	SA (%)	A (%)	D (%)	SD (%)	No Response	Mean	STAND. DEV.
1	My knowledge of technological tools help in the constructive raising of the children	106 (53.0)	70 (35.0)	17 (8.5)	7 (3.5)		3.38	**.79**
2	The relevance of wikis makes me recommend it for learning purposes in the classroom	95 (47.5)	94 (47.0)	6 (3.0)	5 (2.5)		3.40	.67
3	Blogs have immense benefit when used for leaning purpose	109 (54.5)	69 (34.5)	15 (7.5)	3 (1.5)		3.45	.70
4	Social networking sites can be acceptable platform for learning purposes when properly used	113 (56.5)	76 (38.0)	11 (5.5)	00 (0.0)		3.51	.60
5	The use of social networking sites will expose my children negatively to social ills	27 (13.5)	50 (25.0)	76 (38.0)	47 (23.5)		2.29	.97
6	I would allow my child to use social networking for instruction if I use such social networking	76 (38.0)	58 (29.0)	27 (13.5)	39 (19.5)		2.86	1.13
	Weighted Average						**3.15**	

Table 4 illustrates the comparison of how parents' socio-technological background influences their perception on the use of social networking tools in classroom instruction. It could inferred from the table under item 4 which has mean 3.51 showed that social networking sites can be an acceptable platform for learning purposes when properly used. The item's percentile affirmed that since 56.5% out of the total respondents strongly agree and 38% agree with research item that social networking sites can be an acceptable platform for learning purposes. The item 3 which has mean 3.45 revealed that blogs have immense benefits when used for learning purposes since 54.5% of the total respondents strongly agree and 34.5% agree respectively with the research item. The item 2 with mean 3.40 depicts that the relevance of wikis makes parents recommend it for learning purpose in the classroom since 47.5% of the parents strongly agree and 47% agree with the research item. This was an attestation that wikis were effective social networking tools to impart knowledge. The item 1 which has mean 3.38 shows that parents' knowledge of technological tools help in the constructive raising of the children as 53% of the respondents to the research item strongly agree and 35% agree respectively. This is contrary to the belief that social networking aid evil perpetration as 43% of the total respondents strongly and 46% agree respectively that social networking expose children to areas of religion that would develop them positively. The parents also strongly agree with item 6 which has the mean 2.86. It reveals that parents would allow their child to use social networking for instruction if they used such social networking since

38% of parents strongly agree and 29% agree in the item's percentile. Based on the interpretation of results above coupled with calculated weighted average of 3.15, the research questions which ask; do parents' socio-technological background affect their perception of the use of social networking tools in classroom instruction is therefore answered that socio-technological background influence their perception of the use of social networking tools in classroom instruction.

Research Question Five: Do students' religious beliefs influence their perception toward the use of social networking tools in classroom instruction?

Table 5. Comparison of students' religious beliefs and social networking

S/N	Item	SA (%)	A (%)	D (%)	SD (%)	No Response	Mean	STAND. DEV.
1	The doctrine of my religion does not permit me to make use of social networking	6 (3.0)	16 (8.0)	62 (31.0)	114 (57.0)	2 (1.0)	1.57	.77
2	Usage of social networking have been an avenue for initiating children to wrong views	18 (9.0)	17 (8.5)	55 (27.5)	109 (54.5)	1 (0.5)	1.72	.96
3	Social networking expose students to more areas of religion that would develop them positively	25 (12.5)	35 (17.5)	54 (27.0)	86 (43.0)		1.20	1.05
4	The use of social networking in the classroom is a welcome development as long as it is not used to abuse my religious belief	83 (41.5)	80 (40.0)	10 (5.0)	24 (12.0)	3 (1.5)	3.13	.97
5	I see no reason social networking should not be used in the classroom since it's also used in various religious institutions	102 (51.5)	80 (40.0)	00 (0.0)	17 (8.5)	1 (0.5)	3.34	.86
6	Though my religious belief does not permit the use of technology at home. I would not like it to be used in the classroom	93 (46.5)	65 (32.5)	25 (12.5)	17 (8.5)		3.17	.95
7	Social networking expose students to areas of religion that could develop them negatively	122 (61.0)	55 (27.5)	16 (8.0)	6 (3.0)		3.47	.77
	Weighted Average						**2.51**	

Table 5 showed the comparison of how students' religious beliefs influence their perception towards the use of social networking in classroom instruction. It is evident in item 7 which has mean 3.47 from the table reveals that social networking expose students to areas of religion that could develop them negatively since 61% and 27.5% of the students strongly agree and agree respectively. Item 5 in the table with the mean 3.34 reveals that students see no reason why social networking should not be used in the classroom since it is also used in various religious institutions since the item's percentile of the research item shows that 51% of the total respondents strongly agree and 40% agree as well. Item 6 which has mean 3.17 depicts that despite the fact that their religious belief did not permit the use of technology at home, they would not like it to be used in the classroom since 46.5% of the respondents strongly agree and 32.5% agree respectively. Item 4 of the research item with mean 3.13 reveals that the use of social networking in the classroom is a welcome development as long as it is not used to abuse their religious institutions. Item's percentile affirmed to this, as 41.5% and 40% of the respondents strongly agree and agree respectively. Item 2 which has mean 1.72 indicated that usage of social networking was not an avenue for initiating children into wrong views since the item's percentile showed that 43% and 27% of the respondents strongly disagree and disagree respectively with the research item. Item 1 with the mean of 1.57 shows that the doctrine of student religion permits them to make use of social networking as 57% and 31% of the respondents strongly disagree and disagree with the research item. The item 3 with mean 1.20 reveals that social networking does not expose students to more areas of religious that would develop positively as item's percentile indicated that 43% of the respondents strongly disagree and 27% disagree with the research item. Based on the interpretation of results and calculated weighted average of 3.50, the research questions which ask; do student's socio-technological background influence their perception towards the use of social networking in classroom? Is therefore answered that students' socio-technological background influence their perception towards the use of social networking in classroom instruction.

Research Question Eight: Do teachers' socio-technological backgrounds affect their perception on the use of social networking tools in classroom instruction?

Table 6. Comparison of teachers' socio-technological background and social networking tools

S/N	Item	SA (%)	A (%)	D (%)	SD (%)	No Response	Mean	STAND. DEV.
1	The relevance of wikis makes me recommend social networking for learning purposes in the classroom	117 (58.5)	65 (32.5)	9 (4.5)	9 (4.5)		3.45	.78
2	Blogs have immense benefits when used for learning purposes	80 (40.0)	96 (48.0)	16 (8.0)	8 (4.0)		3.24	.77
3	I have a good knowledge of the use of social networking for learning purposes	76 (38.0)	82 (41.0)	13 (6.5)	29 (14.5)		3.03	**1.01**
4	Social networking sites can be viable for learning purposes when properly used	114 (57.0)	86 (43.0)	00 (0.0)	00 (0.0)		3.57	.50
5	Use of social networking would promote collaboration among my students	102 (51.0)	84 (42.0)	10 (5.0)	2 (1.0)	2 (1.0)	3.44	.64
6	Social networking can affect the moral values of my students	32 (16.0)	78 (39.0)	36 (18.0)	53 (26.5)	1 (0.5)	2.44	1.05
7	Students tend to misuse the opportunity if a social networking sites is used to teach for classroom instruction	92 (46.0)	87 (43.5)	11 (5.5)	8 (4.0)	1 (0.5)	3.33	.76
	Weighted Average						**3.21**	

Table 6 shows the comparison of teachers' socio-technological background and social networking Tools. The table under item 4 which has mean 3.57 indicates that social networking sites can be viable for learning purposes when properly used since item's percentile confirmed this as 57% of the total respondents strongly agree and 43% agree respectively. Item 1 which has mean 3.45 showed that the relevance of wikis to teaches make them recommend social networking for learning purposes in the classroom since 58.5% out of the total respondents strongly agree and 32.5% agree respectively with the research item. The research item 5 with the mean 3.44 reveals that the use of social networking teachers would promote collaboration among their students since item's percentile showed that 51% of respondents strongly agree and 42% agree respectively. Item 7 with the mean 3.33 affirmed that students tend to misuse the opportunity if a social networking sites is used to teach for classroom instruction as 46% of the respondents strongly agree and 43.5% agree with the item. Item 2 which has mean 3.24 depicts that blogs have immense benefits when used for learning purposes, it could be deduced from item's percentile as 48% agree and 40% strongly agree respectively. Item 3 with them mean 3.03 connotes that teachers have good knowledge of the use of social networking for learning purpose since item's percentile showed that 41% of the respondents agree and 38% strongly agree with the research item. Item 6 with the mean 2.44 revealed that social networking can affect the moral values of students since 39% out of the total respondents agree and 16% strongly agree respectively. Based on the interpretation of results above couple with calculated weighted average of 3.21, the research questions which ask; do teachers' socio-technological background affect their perception of the use of social networking tools in classroom instruction? Is therefore answered that teachers' socio-technological background influence and affect their perception of the use of social networking tools in classroom instruction.

DISCUSSION OF FINDINGS

The findings revealed that the level of familiarity of stakeholders in social networking use is relatively high. The finding of this study is in line with the assertion of Awake (2011) that ''social networking has become hugely popular among all the population. Similarly, it took 38 years for radio to reach 50 million users, 13 years for television to attract the same number and 4 years for the Internet to do so, but it took Facebook 12-month only to gain 200 million users. Social networking sites provide various interactive platforms based on the intentions of their founders. There are for instance, social, political, academic, businesses, sports, romantic and religious platform. In other words, the social networking site by their nature has the capabilities of educating, informing, entertaining and inflaming the audience. Onomo (2012) also acknowledged that ability of the media by remarking that social networking sites has become ''a widespread tool for communication and exchange of ideas, helping individuals and organizations with just causes to reach a phenomenally vast audience that could hitherto not be reached by traditional media.

Concerning the various social networking used by the stakeholders, the finding of the study revealed that various categories of social networking sites use by stakeholders include Facebook, WhatsApp, 2go/Instagram, blogs and wiki according to their popularity among the respondents. The result of the finding is in agreement with the report on Wikipedia (2011) documents that, the major social networking sites includes academic.edu. Asian Avenue, Ahtlinks, Audiomated, Black planet, Blogster, Bolt.com, cate-mom, care2, cellufun, blogs, wikkis, whatsapp, instagram, Daily booth, Dol 12 Day, Explore, facebook faceparty, face.com, flister, friends, frienster, Gather.com, Google Buzz, linkedin, MEET, in my space, Netlog, Orku, Pingsta, Twitter, Yoruneo, Xing. One of the most recently added social network is 2go. It is a mobile social network founded by a South African, Michaels. Egan, in 2008. Jenkins, (2006) also, sums it up by asserting that "social networking sites are classified based on the nature of their communities. "in his own eyes, these networks include social news, social measuring, micro blogging, social Q&A, video, sharing, photo sharing, professional networks, niche communities, social E-mail, comment communities, broadcasting communities, blog networks, product-based, networks, presentation sharing and review and recommendation sites.

Moreover the study revealed that stakeholders' (parents, students and teachers) religious belief influence their perception on the use of social networking tools in classroom instruction. The finding corroborate the assertion of Oblinger and Oblinger, (2005) that SNSs are widely embraced by all population in respective of their age, socio-economic status, religious affiliation, educational background and other differences. This could be as a result of the fact that SNSs break down barriers at different levels, such as private and public space, learning spaces and social spaces, and informal and formal communication modes. The affordability of social networking sites gadgets like mobile phones and computers further enable communication among broad circles of contacts, locally and globally, and permit the combination of activities of e-mail, messaging, website creation, diaries, photo albums and music or video uploading and downloading. Vance (2012) also reported that, Facebook reigns supreme as the social networking site where an individual, group, or agency can use multiple media tools including content, video, and photo sharing to advance information. In October 2012, Facebook had officially registered one-seventh of the world's population when they hit their one-billionth user. Furthermore, one study found that of all of the time that Americans spend on personal computers connected to the internet, seventeen percent is spent using Facebook (Nielsen, 2012).

Finally, the study established that that teachers' socio-technological background influence and affect their perception of the use of social networking tools in classroom instruction. This is in line with the findings of Asabere (2012) that current ICT trends are providing accessibility to online services such as social networks and these enable collaboration amongst students and contribute a lot to social learning activities. Students of tertiary institutions in Nigeria are keying into the limitless opportunities. The rapid growth of this technology has improved and enabled collaborative and learning activities especially because of its high level of interactivity, accessibility and affordability. Majias (2005) also observed that people use social networking sites for analyzing and sharing information, reflection, establishing and maintaining spontaneous social contacts and relationships and supporting informal learning practices. Social networking sites are considered to play an active role in younger generation's daily lives.

CONCLUSION

Based on the findings of the study, it is revealed that the level of familiarity of stakeholders in social networking use is relatively high, and the commonest social networking used among the stakeholders include; Facebook, WhatsApp, 2go/Instagram, blogs and wiki according to their popularity among the respondents. It is also concluded that stakeholders' (parents, students and teachers) religious belief and socio-technological background influence their perception of the use of social networking tools in classroom instruction. It is concluded that there is significant relationship between the introduction of social networking tools for classroom instruction in school environment and the involvement of teachers and students to make use of it. It is also concluded that it could be used to develop the country in the modern age because a country who is not developing technologically might be left behind among the globe.

SOLUTIONS AND RECOMMENDATIONS

Based on the findings of the study, the following recommendations were made:

1.   There should be further research which will incorporate other stakeholders such as government, administrator and curriculum planner on the issue of social networking use in classroom environment.

2.   Those that are using it already or planning to use it should take necessary precaution to avoid the negative effects of the tools on the side of the students. This will help to reduce the abuse of it by the students.

3.   If government will adopt the use of social networking in schools, then, there should be proper planning, orientation, maintenance and management in other to avoid the negative effect of the social networking on the academic achievement.

4.   There should be trained teachers and adequate facilities should be provided in other to ensure technological development in the school environment. ;

5.   Respondents should be made to understand that the main purpose of introducing the use of social networking in the classroom is for nation building.

REFERENCES

Ahmed, A. (2011). *An Assessment of the Vulnerability of the UK to the Dangers Inherent in the use (and mis-use) of Social networking.* Policy brief is conducted on behalf of a private consultant to the UK government.

Ahn, J. (2011). The effect of Social Network Sites on adolescents' social and academic Development: Current theories and controversies. *Journal of the American Society for Information Science and Technology, 62*(8), 1435–1445. doi:10.1002/asi.21540

Asabere, N. Y. (2012). *A research analysis of online social networking sites (SNSs) and social behaviour at University of Ghana (UG).* Legon, Accra, Ghana. *International Journal of Science and Technology.*

Awake. (2011, July). *What Should I know social networking? Part 1.* Retrieved from https://wol.jw.org/en/wol/d/r1/lp-e/102011250

Baker, A. (2009). Phishing Scams Continue to Plague Social networking Sites. *Wise Bread.* Retrieved April 22, 2011, from http://www.wisebread.comphishing-scams-continue-to-plague-social-media-sites

Benniger, K. (1987). *Understanding Network centric warfare.* Retrieved from https://books.google.com.ng/books?

Coyle, C. L., & Vaughn, H. (2008). Social networking: Communication revolution or evolution? *Bell Labs Technical Journal, 13*(2), 13–17. doi:10.1002/bltj.20298

Eke, H. N., Omekwu, C. O., & Odoh, J. N. (2014). The Use of Social Networking Sites among the Undergraduate Students of University of Nigeria, Nsukka. *Library Philosophy and Practice (e-journal).* Paper 1195. Retrieved from http://digitalcommons.unl.edu/libphilprac/1195

Ellison, N. B., Steinfield, C., & Lampe, C. (2007). The benefits of Facebook "friends": Social capital and college students' use of online social network sites. *Journal of Computer-Mediated Communication, 12*(4), 1143–1168. doi:10.1111/j.1083-6101.2007.00367.x

Fisher, D. (2011). Phishing, Social Networking Attacks on the Rise. *Threat Post*.

Folorunso, O., Vincent, R. O., Adekoya, A. F., & Adewale, O. O. (2010). Diffusion of innovation in social networking sites among university students. International Journal of Computer Science and Security, 4(3), 361-372.

Fraser, M., & Dutta, S. (2008). *Throwing sheep in the boardroom: How online social networking will transform your life, work and world* (1st ed.). Wiley Publisher.

Jenkins, H. (2006). *Confronting the challenges of participatory culture: Media education for the 21st century*. Chicago: The John D. and Catherine T. MacArthur Foundation.

Lim, K., Kang, M. S., & Shin, S. W. (2012). The Study on Experts' Perceptions on Usage Elements of SNSs and the Investigation on the Priority of the Elements for SNSs' Educational Use through Importance-Performance Analysis. *Journal of Educational Technology*, 28(4), 925–952. doi:10.17232/KSET.28.4.925

Mazman, G., & Usluel, Y. K. (2011). The usage of social networks in educational context. *Computers & Education, 55*(2010), 444-453. Retrieved from https://www.researchgate.net/publication/282701525

Mejias, U. (2005). *Nomad's guide to learning and social software*. Retrieved 19.05.2008, from. http://knowledgetree.flexiblelearning.net.au/edition07/download/la_mejias.pdf

NIELSEN. (2012). *Buzz in the Blogosphere: Millions More Bloggers and Blog Readers*. Retrieved from http://www.nielsen.com/us/en/newswire/2012/buzz-in-the-blogosphere-millions-morebloggers-and-blog-readers.html

Oblinger, D. G., & Oblinger, J. L. (2005). *Educating the net generation*. Retrieved from www.educause.edu/educatingthenetgen

Onomo, A. A. (2012, January 15). People power 15 social networking. *The Guardian*, p. 38.

Vance, A. (2012). Facebook: The Making of 1 Billion Users. *Bloomberg Businessweek*. Retrieved from http://www.businessweek.com/articles/2012-10-04/facebook-the-making-of-1-billion-users

Webster. (2013). *Social networking*. Retrieved from Webster: http://www.merriam-webster.com/dictionary/social%20media

Wikipedia. (2011). *List of social networking websites*. Retrieved February from www.en.wikipedia.org/wiki/social-networking-service

ADDITIONAL READING

Aduwa-Ogiegbaen, S. E., & Iyamu, E. O. S. (2005). Using Information and Communication Technology in Secondary schools in Nigeria: Problems and Prospects. *Journal of Educational Technology & Society*, 8(1), 104–112.

Inyanng-Abia, M. E. (2015a). Essentials of Educational Technology: A handbook for Teachers and Media practitioners. (Third Edition) Calabar: Excel Publishers

Sturges, M. (2012). Using Facebook as a teaching tool in higher education setting: Examining potentials and possibilities from http://www.conference.pixel-online-net/edu

KEY TERMS AND DEFINITIONS

Application: Most of the existing social networking are not interoperable with existing application and they limit the addressable to those willing to write new application from the scratch.

Network Teaching Platform: Social network is internet-based development and use of computer technology, whereby dynamically scalable and often virtualized resources are provided as a service over the internet.

Personalized Learning: Social Networking affords opportunities for greater student choice in learning using an internet connected devices, students can accept a wide array of resources and software tools that suit their learning styles and interest.

Support Teacher: Social network platform can support teachers in professional development and in developing quality work. Teachers can prepare teaching portfolio, presentation materials and a manuscript to be submitted for publication.

User Friendly: This new facility is user friendly and no need to worry about the compulsory. It is easy to understand and operate.

This research was previously published in Open and Social Learning in Impact Communities and Smart Territories; pages 64-83, copyright year 2019 by Information Science Reference (an imprint of IGI Global).

Chapter 41
Impact of Facebook as a Learning Tool on Learning Outcomes, Technology Acceptance, and Attitude

Manal Abdo Farhan Saif
Virtual University of Tunis, Tunisia

Ahmed Tlili
LaTICE Laboratory, Kairouan, Tunisia

Fathi Essalmi
University of Tunis, Tunis, Tunisia

Mohamed Jemni
Research Laboratory of Technologies of Information and Communication and Electrical Engineering, Tunis, Tunisia

ABSTRACT

While several studies have investigated learners' opinions toward using Facebook in learning, limited attention has been paid to examine the effectiveness of Facebook as a learning tool in classrooms. Thus, this article proposes a newly designed Facebook learning tool that is used in a public Tunisian university to learn the "game development" course. It then investigates its impact on the learners' level of knowledge and motivation compared to the traditional learning method. This article also investigates the impact of this tool on the learners' technology acceptance and attitudes. The experimental results showed that the Facebook learning tool can significantly improve the learners' level of knowledge. In addition, learners who learned with this tool revealed a high degree of perceived usefulness, security, and intention to use the Facebook learning tool again. Furthermore, these learners reported a favorable attitude towards the Facebook learning tool. In addition, a set of recommendation is found that researchers and educators should consider while using Facebook in their classrooms.

DOI: 10.4018/978-1-6684-7123-4.ch041

1. INTRODUCTION

With the rapid spread of social network technologies worldwide, many fields (e.g., business and education) took advantage of them. In particular, Web 3.0 applications, such as social network sites (SNSs), offer new ways of communication and information exchange. Paul, Baker and Cochran (2012) reported that academic institutions and faculties are increasingly using social networking sites, such as Facebook and LinkedIn, to connect with students and to deliver instructional contents. Facebook has particularly grabbed the attention of educators due to its popularity among individuals, including learners. In this context, Facebook claims that, as of March 2018, 1.45 billion on average are daily active users (Zephoria, 2018). Learners are particularly using Facebook on a daily basis (Kirschner & Karpinski, 2010; Roblyer, McDaniel, Webb, Herman & Witty, 2010). Junco (2012) stated that universities have an opportunity to enhance learners' learning experiences by helping them use Facebook.

On the other hand, other studies highlighted several limitations which may limit the use of Facebook as a learning environment. For instance, Prescott, Wilson, and Becket (2013) stated that the fear of behaving unprofessionally on Facebook makes the learners not prefer to use Facebook in formal learning. Weeden, Cooke and McVey (2013) pointed out that social networks, including Facebook, may easily distract learners which affect their learning performances negatively. Rap and Blonder (2017) found that the use of Facebook for academic and learning purposes is not well investigated. Therefore, this study explores the potential of using Facebook in classrooms. Specifically, this study explores separately the effects of Facebook on learning outcomes, namely the level of knowledge and motivation. Additionally, it evaluates the students' attitude and technology acceptance of using Facebook in classrooms.

The rest of the paper is structured as follows: Section 2 presents related work about the use of Facebook in education. Section 3 presents the proposed Facebook learning environment. Section 4 describes the conducted experiment, while the findings are presented in section 5. Section 6 discusses these results and presents recommendations, from this practical experience, on how to use Facebook as a learning environment in classrooms. Finally, section 7 concludes the paper.

2. RELATED WORK

Many studies highlighted the efficiency of using social networks, specifically Facebook, as a learning environment (Greenhow & Askari, 2017; Guzmán-Simón, García-Jiménez, & López-Cobo, 2017; Manca & Ranieri, 2017; Saif, Tlili, Essalmi & Jemni, 2017; Mufidah & Bin-Tahir, 2018). For instance, Kurniawan, Jingga and Prasetyo (2017) investigated the effect of Facebook as a learning environment on students' learning motivation in an information system course. Results showed that Facebook has a positive effect on student learning motivation. In another study, Yang (2018) investigated the effect of Facebook activities, such as peer collaboration, on language acquisition of college students from an Asian university through experimental studies. Students who experienced learning languages using Facebook showed more engagement and participation, and they gained more self-confidence in learning English. Mufidah and Bin-Tahir (2018) also examined the efficiency of Facebook in increasing students' Arabic language acquisition. The obtained results showed that the use of Facebook groups can positively affect students' ability to write in the Arabic language. Furthermore, Din and Haron (2018) showed that Facebook can be a useful environment to support information retrieval as well as self-learning for students who have a high level of self-directed learning characteristic.

On the other hand, Greenhow and Askari (2017) argued that social network sites have the potential to support collaborative knowledge construction, such as contributing to the hybridization of expertise, academic help-seeking and accessing specialized just-in-time information, however, this can also pose challenges to learning. Moghavvemi, Salarzadeh and Janatabadi (2018) pointed out that Facebook can be used only as a complementary learning environment by offering learners useful links and materials when they are online. Rap and Blonder (2017) investigated students' attitude toward using Facebook groups for learning chemistry. Their results showed that only students in active Facebook groups found that Facebook contributed to their learning experience. Cartledge, Miller and Phillips (2017) also investigated students' perception of Facebook as a distance learning tool in the medical education field. The findings showed that despite the feasibility of using Facebook, no impact was seen on the learners' level of knowledge. Based on a literature review, Yang, Wang, Woo and Quek, (2011) found that learners' attitudes toward the idea of using Facebook in formal learning are mixed, some learners prefer this idea while others do not. Manca and Ranieri (2013) found many obstacles that may limit the full adoption of Facebook as a learning environment, such as cultural issues and teacher and student pedagogies.

Furthermore, despite the popularity of Facebook for personal use, only a small percentage of students and faculties use them for academic practice (Lenhart, Purcell, Smith & Zickuhr, 2010; Abdulahi, Samadi & Gharleghi, 2014). Rap and Blonder (2017) have also mentioned that the use of Facebook for academic and learning purposes is still rather limited. Therefore, this study contributes to the extant literature by further investigating the importance of Facebook as a learning environment in classrooms compared to the traditional learning method, namely lectures. Specifically, this study aims to answer the following research questions:

1. Does the designed Facebook learning environment significantly increase the learners' level of knowledge in comparison with the traditional learning method, namely lectures?
2. Do the learners who learn with the Facebook learning environment show significantly higher learning motivation than those who learn with the traditional learning method, namely lectures?
3. Does using the Facebook learning environment show high technology acceptance degree in terms of perceived usefulness, perceived security while learning and perceived intention to use this environment again?
4. Do the learners who use the Facebook learning environment report a favorable attitude towards this environment?

3. PROPOSED FACEBOOK LEARNING ENVIRONMENT

The proposed Facebook learning environment in this study aims to teach learners the "game development" course. This course aims to help learners gain knowledge regarding game genres, elements and design. It also aims to help learners gain technical skills about developing games using a particular game engine. In this context, the instructor started first by creating a private Facebook closed group where only him can accept or decline the requests of joining this group. The motivation behind choosing Facebook groups instead of pages is because in Facebook groups it is easier to moderate who can join in and see the content of the group. This can make learners feel safer to learn in this environment since no outsiders can see their posted information or details. May & Sébastien (2011) pointed out that security and privacy protection are crucial in e-learning systems. Additionally, to avoid cyber bullying which is a common problem in most online learning systems (Irwin, Ball, Desbrow & Leveritt, 2012) and to encourage collaboration and support while learning, the instructor posted as a video the rules within the proposed Facebook learning environment which mainly focus on respecting and helping each other.

Furthermore, the instructor used several Facebook elements to make the learning process interactive. For instance, he used Emojis to gamify the learning content, where the number of "likes" on an answer represents the score that learner got on that answer. As shown in Figure 1, the first learner had five likes on his answer which means that he had a score of 5 points. Also, the instructor used Facebook posts to pose questions regarding several parts of the course, where learners answer them by commenting under each posted question. The instructor then goes through the given comments and interacts with the learners to help them find the correct answer. Furthermore, the instructor used the Facebook live functionality to invite external experts in the field of game development to interact with the learners and share their ideas and expertise with them and answer their questions. This has further helped learners to learn from these experts and enhance their knowledge regarding game development.

The next section presents the experimental method to validate the above described Facebook learning environment.

Figure 1. An example of using Facebook posts during the learning process

4. METHOD

4.1. Participants

The researchers conducted a pilot experiment, with sixty learners, in a public Tunisian University for two months after the Institutional Review Board (IRB) approval. All these learners were enrolled in the game development course.

4.2. Research Instruments

The research instruments used in this study are as follows: a pre-test, a post-test, a pre-motivation questionnaire, a post-motivation questionnaire, a technology acceptance questionnaire and interviews. An experienced instructor developed the pre-test and post-test. Learners took the pre-test before the start of the learning process. The aim of the test is to assess the learners' prior knowledge about game development. It consisted of eight multiple choice questions and two open-ended questions, with a maximum score of 20. The post-test was taken after the learning process (after two months) and it aims to assess the learners' gained knowledge about game development.

The pre and post-motivation questionnaires are the same (see Appendix A). They are a five point Likert scale questionnaires which aim to assess the learners' motivation towards learning the game development course before and after the learning process respectively. The motivation questionnaires were modified from the measure developed by (Hwang & Chang, 2011; Hwang, Yang & Wang 2013).

The technology acceptance questionnaire is a five point Likert scale questionnaire (see Appendix B). It covers three variables, namely usefulness, intention to use and security, which are presented in the Technology Acceptance Models (TAM) of Davis (1989) and Alloghani, Hussain, Al-Jumeily and Abuelma'atti (2015). From the usefulness perspective, three items are proposed which investigate if the learners found the new proposed Facebook learning environment useful and helped them in gaining new knowledge regarding game development. From the intention to use perspective, three items are also proposed which investigate if the learners want to use the environment again to learn. From the security perspective, four items are proposed which investigate if the learners felt safe while learning using this environment after applying the security strategies by the instructor.

The conducted interviews were unstructured where the learners had to freely speak about their attitudes towards the learning experience using the proposed Facebook learning environment. Interviews are used because they allow learners to be more forthcoming in their answers. They were used in the literature to evaluate various newly designed learning tools and models (Tlili, Essalmi & Jemni, 2016; Tlili, Essalmi, Ayed, Jemni & Kinshuk, 2016).

4.3. Procedure

The learners were randomly assigned into two groups: (1) Control group learns the game development course using lecture teaching method; and (2) Experimental group learns the same game development course using the designed Facebook group. The two teaching methods (using lectures and Facebook) were given by the same teacher and using the same learning content. In particular, the instructor prepared the learning content for the control group in the form of lectures and workshop sessions. He also prepared the same content for the experimental group in the form of video tutorials, links, etc., which was then uploaded to the proposed Facebook learning environment.

As shown in Figure 2, the control and the experimental group started by answering a pre-test and a pre-motivation questionnaire. After the two months learning process, the two groups answered the post-test and post-motivation questionnaires, in order to assess the impact of the proposed Facebook learning environment on the motivation and knowledge levels of the learners in comparison to lectures. Besides, the experimental group answered a technology acceptance questionnaire and conducted short interviews regarding technology acceptance and attitudes towards this proposed Facebook learning environment.

Figure 2. Experimental procedure

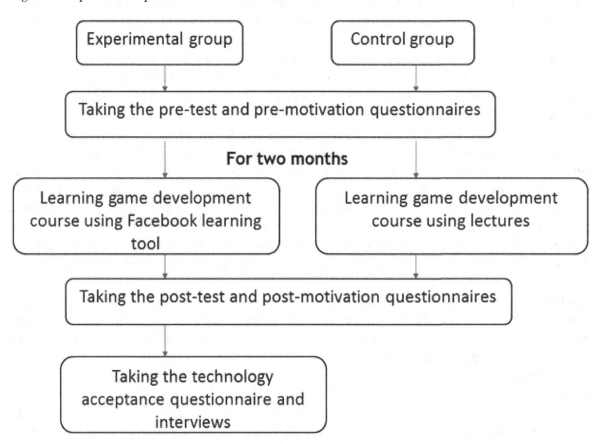

5. RESULTS

Learners who had missing answer(s) in any of the questionnaires were excluded from the experiment. Consequently, only thirty-five (among 60) learners were included in the experiment, eighteen of them were from the experimental group and seventeen were from the control group. The learners' collected data was then analyzed to answer the above presented research questions (in section 2).

5.1. Analysis of Level of Knowledge

The pre and post-test questionnaire score of both the control and experimental group were first analyzed separately using the paired t-test method. This method is appropriate in this context because the same group of learners answered both questionnaires (pre and post). This can help to separately assess the effects of learning using the Facebook learning environment and lectures on the level of knowledge of both groups, as shown in Table 1.

Table 1. Results of paired t-test group statistics

	Paired Differences					t	Sig. (2-Tailed)
	Mean	Std. Deviation	Std. Error Mean	95% Confidence Interval of the Difference			
				Lower	Upper		
Pair1: **Control group**	1.79	1.40	0.37	0.39	1.40	2.18	0.01*
Pair 2: **Experimental group**	4.33	1.25	0.21	-0.92	1.00	1.71	0.00*

*p < .05

As shown in Table 1, learning using the proposed Facebook learning environment and lectures have significantly enhanced the level of knowledge of both the experimental group (p is equal to 0.00 and less than 0.05) and the control group (p is equal to 0.01 and less than 0.05). Furthermore, to investigate if the learners who learned using the Facebook learning environment show significantly higher learning achievement than those who learned using the traditional method, the pre and post-test scores of both groups were analyzed. Specifically, the pre-test scores were analyzed using the t-test method, as presented in Table 2.

Table 2. Results of t-test for the level of knowledge pre-tests

Group	N	Mean	Std. Deviation	t	Sig.
Control	17	6.47	2.29	33	0.51
Experimental	18	6.97	2.19		

As shown in Table 2, the pre-test mean scores of the students' game development achievement for the experimental group taught by the Facebook learning environment was 6.97 (SD = 2.19), and that for the control group taught by the traditional method was 6.47 (SD = 2.29). Results indicated no statistically significant difference between the pre-test mean scores of the control and experimental group, since p was equal to 0.51 and less than 0.05. Consequently, it is evident that the two groups of learners had equivalent prior knowledge before the learning activity. Finally, the post-test scores were analyzed using the independent t-test, as shown in Table 3.

Table 3. Results of t-test for the level of knowledge post-tests

Group	N	Mean	Std. Deviation	t	Sig.
Control	17	8.26	4.37	33	0.03*
Experimental	18	11.30	3.73		

*p < .05

As shown in Table 3, the post-test mean scores of the students' game development achievement for the experimental group taught by the Facebook learning environment was 11.30 (SD = 3.73), and that for the control group taught by the traditional method was 8.26 (SD = 4.37). Table 3 shows that the mean score for the experimental group (M = 11.30) was greater than that for the control group (M = 8.26). The difference between these two post-test mean scores was significant p = 0.03 (less than 0.05) in favour of the experimental group, which revealed that the performance of the experimental group was significantly better than the control group. As such, the Facebook learning environment positively affects students' game development achievement.

5.2. Analysis of Motivation

The motivation questionnaire results were first separately analyzed using the paired t-test method. This method is appropriate in this context because the same group of learners answered both questionnaires (pre and post). This can help investigating separately the impact of learning using the Facebook learning environment lectures on the motivation of the experimental and control group, as shown in Table 4.

Table 4. Results of paired t-test group statistics

	Paired Differences					t	Sig. (2-Tailed)
	Mean	Std. Deviation	Std. Error Mean	95% Confidence Interval of the Difference			
				Lower	Upper		
Pair1: Control group	0.12	1.79	0.37	0.73	1.60	1.18	0.59
Pair 2: Experimental group	0.19	1.25	0.21	0.66	1.15	1.51	0.51

As shown in Table 4, both the Facebook learning environment and the traditional learning method do not significantly improve the motivation level of the experimental group, where p is equal to 0.51 and greater than 0.05, and the control group, where p is equal 0.05 to 0.59 and greater than 0.05. Furthermore, to investigate if the learners who learned with the Facebook learning environment show significantly higher learning motivation than those who learned using the traditional method, the pre and post-motivation questionnaires' scores of both the control and experimental group were analyzed and compared. In particular, the pre-motivation questionnaire scores were analyzed using the t-test method, as presented in Table 5.

Table 5. t-test results of the pre-motivation questionnaires

Group	N	Mean	Std. Deviation	t	Sig.
Control	17	3.87	0.93	-0.78	0.43
Experimental	18	4.12	0.88		

As shown in Table 5, the obtained pre-motivation questionnaire scores (before the learning process) of both the control and experimental group are almost the same. Also, it is seen that there is no significant difference between the pre-motivation questionnaire scores (of both control and experimental groups) since the obtained p value is equal to 0.43 and above 0.05. This implies that the two groups had equivalent learning motivation before participating in the learning activity. After finishing the learning process, the post-motivation questionnaire scores of both groups were also analyzed using the independent t-test, as shown in Table 6.

Table 6. t-test results of the post-motivation questionnaires

Group	N	Mean	Std. Deviation	t	Sig.
Control	17	3.75	1.12	-0.52	0.6
Experimental	18	3.93	0.93		

As we can see in Table 6, the experimental group has slightly higher motivation than the control group and the difference was not large enough to be statistically significant, since the obtained p value is above 0.05 (p = 0.6). This implies that both the proposed Facebook learning environment and lectures can enhance motivation equally well.

5.3. Analysis of Technology Acceptance

As shown in Table 7, the Cronbach's alpha values of the three variables are above 0.7. This implies that the questionnaire is reliable. To minimize individual response bias, the standard z-score was computed. Learners with $z > 0$ were considered as learners with high level of technology acceptance, while learners with $z < 0$ were considered as learners with low level of technology acceptance. In our case, no learners were found with $z = 0$. As shown in Table 7, most learners have found the proposed Facebook learning environment useful. They also wanted to keep using it in the future. Furthermore, all the learners who used the proposed Facebook learning environment felt safe while using it.

Table 7. Technology acceptance questionnaire results

Variables	Inter-Items	Cronbach's Alpha	% of Students With High Level of Technology Acceptance	% of Students With Low Level of Technology Acceptance
Security	4	0.91	72.22%	27.78%
Usefulness	3	0.88	83.33%	16.67%
Intention to use	3	0.78	61.11%	38.89%

5.4. Analysis of Attitude

The collected learners' attitudes, via short and unstructured interviews, were qualitatively analyzed. Attitude is a psychological construct that represents an individual's degree of like or dislike for something. According to Jung (1971), the four major components of attitude are: (1) Affective which highlights emotions or feelings; (2) Cognitive which highlights belief or opinions held consciously; (3) Conative which highlights inclination for action; and (4) Evaluative which highlights positive or negative response to stimuli. The first step was coding, through several rounds, the given attitudes of the learners. Table 8 lists the used codes and their definitions during the coding process.

Table 8. Used codes and their definitions

Number	Code	Definition	When to Use
1	Feelings	Negative or positive feelings towards the learning experience	Use this code for all the references which illustrate positive or negative expressed feelings towards the learning experience or the Facebook learning environment.
2	Feedback	Feedback on the learning experience	Use this code for all the references which illustrate appreciation, suggestions or other feedback about the learning experience or the Facebook learning environment.
3	Knowledge	Changes in knowledge	Use this code for all references which illustrate any changes in the knowledge of learners that was directly brought about by learning with the Facebook learning environment.
4	Interaction	applied interactions	Use this code for all references which illustrate any interactions made during the learning experience within the Facebook learning environment.

As a second step, similar codes were grouped together to create categories where each category was labeled. Table 9 presents the obtained categories, their definitions and the grouped codes in each category.

Table 9. Labeled categories

Category	Definition	Grouped Codes
Facebook learning environment impact	This category investigates the impact of the learning experience with the proposed Facebook learning environment on the learners.	Feelings, Knowledge
Behavior of learners	This category investigates the behavior of learners while learning with the Facebook learning environment.	Interaction
Feedback regarding Facebook learning environment	This category investigates the reported recommendations, suggestions or improvements.	Feedback

These categories are finally used to better understand the findings from the learners' attitudes and draw conclusions, as follows:

- **Facebook learning environment impact:** From this category, it is seen that the Facebook learning environment made a positive impact on the learners' feelings and knowledge, regardless of their gender (male or female). For instance, some learners reported that this environment increased their motivation levels to study the game development course, while others reported that this environment made them competitive. In addition, other learners reported that the environment helped them gain new information regarding game development, as this quotation demonstrates: "Facebook is a new technology which made learning easy compared to the traditional learning method and helped me gain new knowledge on how to develop games;"

- **Behavior of learners:** From this category, it is seen that the Facebook learning environment made learners, regardless of their gender (male or female), more active while learning by interacting with each other and with the instructor online;
- **Feedback on the Facebook learning environment:** From this category, it is seen that the learners, regardless of their gender (male or female), found the Facebook learning environment useful and they were satisfied with this learning experience. Besides, the learners wished that other instructors and universities would start using the Facebook learning environment to teach other subjects. Finally, some of them showed even further interest in this environment and suggested to improve the Facebook live functionality, as this quotation demonstrates: "The sound was not synchronized with the video during the live presentation, please fix it."

To conclude, the qualitative analysis of the learners' attitudes showed that the learners reported a very favorable attitude towards the Facebook learning environment. In particular, the findings did not highlight any negative attitudes reported by learners during this learning experience, except few suggested enhancements regarding the Facebook live functionality.

6. DISCUSSION

The obtained results (presented in the previous section) showed that the proposed Facebook learning environment has had a significant impact on the learners' level of knowledge compared to lectures. These results are consistent with the results from Kazi, Saxena and Vinay (2016) where they found that learners who used Facebook showed better learning performance compared to the lecture method. These results are also consistent with the results from Shih (2011; 2013) where he also used pre and post-tests as an instrument to evaluate the impact of Facebook on the learners' level of knowledge. He found that the use of Facebook has a positive impact on the development of English writing skills.

Additionally, the findings showed that the proposed Facebook learning environment and lectures have had no significant impact on the learners' motivation. This can be explained with the learners, regardless of the learning method (Facebook or lectures), were very excited and motivated from the beginning to learn about game development. This is further highlighted in Table 5 where the learners' pre-motivation questionnaire scores are very high. In this context, Levine (2008) stated that nowadays learners are considered as the gamer generation, thus the learners were already motivated and eager to learn about games, regardless of the used learning method. For instance, Tlili, Essalmi, Jemni and Kinshuk (2017) found that the rate of learners attending the game development course in classrooms, which was newly added to the curriculum, is very high compared to other courses. Therefore, further investigation is needed to better understand the effect of the proposed Facebook learning environment on the learners' motivation.

Moreover, the learners reported a high perceived usefulness, intention to use and security towards the proposed Facebook learning environment. This is because learners were learning using technologies which are familiar with and accepted by their generation (Oradini & Saunders, 2008). In particular, according to the final statistics provided by Facebook, the instructor declined the requests of forty two unknown persons who wanted to join the designed Facebook learning environment (group). This helped keep the learner's privacy, including their posts and discussions, secured while learning. Additionally, no learner has reported that he was in an uncomfortable situation while learning using the Facebook learning environment. Thus, it can be deduced that the applied learning and security strategies applied by the instructor (see section 3), such as the chosen "closed" privacy settings, helped overcome two major problems found in online learning, including Facebook, namely privacy and cyber bullying (Irwin et al., 2012). Moreover, the instructor did not approve one post from a learner because he considered it not relevant to the course. This kept the proposed Facebook learning environment useful.

On the other hand, learners encountered some difficulties while learning using the proposed Facebook learning environment. For instance, the posted learning contents (videos, posts, etc.) were disorganized and not sorted in chronological order. This made learners confused about the learning content they should start with. Furthermore, during the live Facebook, learners had problems with the streamed video, such as the audio was not synchronized with the video. Jarrett (2016) found that the use of Facebook live in classrooms is interesting, but requires good and stable Internet, which is not the case in most universities.

Finally, a set of recommendations was drawn, from this practical experience, which researchers, teachers and practitioners should consider while using Facebook in classrooms, as follows:

Recommendation 1: Teachers should use private Facebook groups as a learning environment instead of pages. This will help them control who can and cannot join in to this group, hence keep learners' privacy and written information secured while learning.

Recommendation 2: Teachers should make learners sign a code of conduct paper which highlights the rules that the learners must respect while learning using Facebook. This will make them aware of the consequences of any misbehavior and be more responsible. Besides, teachers should post a video explaining the rules of the Facebook group, such as more support and interaction and no bullying or making fun of others. This will encourage learners to participate in the learning process and create a safe environment for them to learn without disrespecting each other.

Recommendation 3: Teachers should post the outline of a give course for learners while learning using Facebook or use numbers to order the posted learning content (e.g., video1, video2, etc.). This can help learners know which learning content was uploaded and should read first, since the posted content cannot be sorted in chronological order.

Recommendation 4: Facebook live is a very interesting functionality to use in learning, but it requires a very good and stable Internet connection.

7. CONCLUSION, LIMITS AND FUTURE DIRECTIONS

This study investigated the effects of using Facebook as a learning environment in classrooms, on learners' learning outcomes. The obtained results, based on a pilot experiment, highlighted that the proposed Facebook learning environment has significantly enhanced only the learners' level of knowledge in comparison with lectures. Additionally, the learners reported a favorable technology acceptance and attitude towards the designed Facebook learning environment.

7.1. Practical Managerial Significance

This study is also important for practical managerial significance. It can benefit the educators who want to use Facebook in their classrooms by identifying the key success factors to consider while using Facebook as a learning environment. The findings of the study, especially the provided recommendations, can also serve as a guide for future efficient design of Facebook in classrooms.

This research also has implications for educational institutions that had already been using Facebook in classrooms, but failed to achieve the desired learning outcomes. They may also use the findings of this study to enhance their Facebook-based learning. The outcomes of the study can also push researchers and practitioners to further investigate the importance of using Facebook in classrooms, since it is still in its infancy.

7.2. Limitation and Future Direction

It should be noted that this study has several limitations that should be acknowledged and further investigated. For instance, the sample size was small. Hence, more participants from different universities and majors (e.g., economics) will be included in our future experiments to generalize the obtained results. Additionally, this study did not investigate the relationship between the addressed factors (motivation, level of knowledge, attitude and technology acceptance) while learning using the Facebook learning environment. Furthermore, this study did not explore the potential of Facebook as a collaborative learning environment.

Future directions could focus on further investigating the above mentioned limitations. In addition, since many research studies highlighted the importance of considering individual differences in computer-based learning, such as personality and cognitive load (e.g., see Tlili, Essalmi, Jemni, Kinshuk & Chen, 2016), future directions could also focus on exploring the impact of these individual differences on the adoption of Facebook as a learning environment.

REFERENCES

Abdulahi, A., Samadi, B., & Gharleghi, B. (2014). A study on the negative effects of social networking sites such as Facebook among Asia Pacific university scholars in Malaysia. *International Journal of Business and Social Science*, 5(10).

Alloghani, M., Hussain, A., Al-Jumeily, D., & Abuelma'atti, O. (2015). Technology Acceptance Model for the Use of M-Health Services among health related users in UAE. *Proceedings of the International Conference on Developments of E-Systems Engineering (DeSE)*, 213-217. 10.1109/DeSE.2015.58

Cartledge, P., Miller, M., & Phillips, R. (2017). Can Facebook be used to administrate distance-learning module of evidence-based medicine? An observational study. *Rwanda Medical Journal*, 74(1), 14–18.

Davis, F. D. (1989). Perceived usefulness, perceived ease of use, and user acceptance of information technology. *Management Information Systems Quarterly*, *13*(3), 319–340. doi:10.2307/249008

Din, N., & Haron, S. (2018). Information Retrieval, Self Directed Learning and Academic Performance among Facebook Users. *Journal of ASIAN Behavioural Studies*, *3*(7), 49–58. doi:10.21834/jabs.v3i7.257

Greenhow, C., & Askari, E. (2017). Learning and teaching with social network sites: A decade of research in K-12 related education. *Education and Information Technologies*, *22*(2), 623–645. doi:10.100710639-015-9446-9

Guzmán-Simón, F., García-Jiménez, E., & López-Cobo, I. (2017). Undergraduate students' perspectives on digital competence and academic literacy in a Spanish University. *Computers in Human Behavior*, *74*, 196–204. doi:10.1016/j.chb.2017.04.040

Hwang, G. J., & Chang, H. F. (2011). A formative assessment-based mobile learning approach to improving the learning attitudes and achievements of students. *Computers & Education*, *56*(4), 1023–1031. doi:10.1016/j.compedu.2010.12.002

Hwang, G. J., Yang, L. H., & Wang, S. Y. (2013). A concept map-embedded educational computer game for improving students' learning performance in natural science courses. *Computers & Education*, *69*, 121–130. doi:10.1016/j.compedu.2013.07.008

Irwin, C., Ball, L., Desbrow, B., & Leveritt, M. (2012). Students' perceptions of using Facebook as an interactive learning resource at university. *Australasian Journal of Educational Technology*, *28*(7). doi:10.14742/ajet.798

Jarrett, N. (2016). *Using Facebook 'Live' In The Classroom Is A New, Exciting Learning Tool*. Accessed 9 Mai 2017 from https://edtech4beginners.com/2016/05/12/using-facebook-live-in-the-classroom-is-a-new-exciting-learning-tool/

Junco, R. (2012). The relationship between frequency of Facebook use, participation in Facebook activities, and student engagement. *Computers & Education*, *58*(1), 162–171. doi:10.1016/j.compedu.2011.08.004

Jung, C. (1971). *Psychology of the Unconscious: A Study of the Transformations and Symbolisms of the Libido. A Contribution to the History of the evolution of thought*. New York: Moffat, Yard and Co.

Kazi, M. M., Saxena, R., & Vinay, V. (2016). Use Of Facebook As Teaching Method In Learning Microbiology For Second Year BDS Students. *National Journal of Integrated Research in Medicine*, *7*(3), 97–100.

Kirschner, P. A., & Karpinski, A. C. (2010). Facebook® and academic performance. *Computers in Human Behavior*, *26*(6), 1237–1245. doi:10.1016/j.chb.2010.03.024

Kurniawan, Y., Jingga, F., & Prasetyo, A. (2017). The Impacts of Social Media Facebook as Learning Media towards Learning Motivation for Students (A Case Study Approach). *Proceedings of the International MultiConference of Engineers and Computer Scientists*, *1*.

Lenhart, A., Purcell, K., Smith, A., & Zickuhr, K. (2010). *Social Media & Mobile Internet Use among Teens and Young Adults. Millennials*. Pew internet & American Life Project.

Levine, J. (2008). The gaming generation. *Library Technology Reports*, *42*(5), 18–23.

Manca, S., & Ranieri, M. (2013). Is it a tool suitable for learning? A critical review of the literature on Facebook as a technology-enhanced learning environment. *Journal of Computer Assisted Learning*, *29*(6), 487–504. doi:10.1111/jcal.12007

Manca, S., & Ranieri, M. (2017). Implications of social network sites for teaching and learning. Where we are and where we want to go. *Education and Information Technologies*, *22*(2), 605–622. doi:10.100710639-015-9429-x

May, M., & Sébastien, G. (2011). Privacy concerns in e-learning: Is using tracking system a thread. *International Journal of Information and Education Technology (IJIET)*, *1*(1), 1–8. doi:10.7763/IJIET.2011.V1.1

Moghavvemi, S., & Salarzadeh Janatabadi, H. (2018). Incremental impact of time on students' use of E-learning via Facebook. *British Journal of Educational Technology*, *49*(3), 560–573. doi:10.1111/bjet.12545

Mufidah, N., & Bin-Tahir, S. Z. (2018). Arabic Acquisition through Facebook Group Learning. *Ijaz Arabi Journal of Arabic Learning*, *1*(1).

Oradini, F., & Saunders, G. (2008). The use of social networking by students and staff in higher education. *iLearning Forum*, 4-5.

Paul, J. A., Baker, H. M., & Cochran, J. D. (2012). Effect of online social networking on student academic performance. *Computers in Human Behavior*, *28*(6), 2117–2127. doi:10.1016/j.chb.2012.06.016

Prescott, J., Wilson, S., & Becket, G. (2013). Facebook use in the learning environment: Do students want this? *Learning, Media and Technology*, *38*(3), 345–350. doi:10.1080/17439884.2013.788027

Rap, S., & Blonder, R. (2017). Thou shall not try to speak in the Facebook language: Students' perspectives regarding using Facebook for chemistry learning. *Computers & Education*, *114*, 69–78. doi:10.1016/j.compedu.2017.06.014

Roblyer, M. D., McDaniel, M., Webb, M., Herman, J., & Witty, J. V. (2010). Findings on Facebook in higher education: A comparison of college faculty and student uses and perceptions of social networking sites. *The Internet and Higher Education*, *13*(3), 134–140. doi:10.1016/j.iheduc.2010.03.002

Saif, M. A. F., Tlili, A., Essalmi, F., & Jemni, M. (2017). Facebook as a learning tool in classrooms: A case study. *IEEE/ACS 14th International Conference on Computer Systems and Applications (AICCSA)*, 509-514. 10.1109/AICCSA.2017.97

Sánchez, R. A., Cortijo, V., & Javed, U. (2014). Students' perceptions of Facebook for academic purposes. *Computers & Education*, *70*, 138–149. doi:10.1016/j.compedu.2013.08.012

Shih, R. C. (2011). Can Web 2.0 technology assist college students in learning English writing? Integrating Facebook and peer assessment with blended learning. *Australasian Journal of Educational Technology*, *27*(5), 829–845. doi:10.14742/ajet.934

Shih, R. C. (2013). Effect of Using Facebook to Assist English for Business Communication Course Instruction. *The Turkish Online Journal of Educational Technology*, *12*(1), 52–59.

Tlili, A., Essalmi, F., Ayed, L. J. B., & Jemni, M., & Kinshuk. (2016). Towards a generic UML model to support designing educational role playing games. *Proceedings of the 16th International Conference on Advanced Learning Technologies (ICALT)*, 153-157. 10.1109/ICALT.2016.133

Tlili, A., Essalmi, F., & Jemni, M. (2016). Improving learning computer architecture through an educational mobile game. *Smart Learning Environments*, *3*(1), 7. doi:10.118640561-016-0030-6

Tlili, A., Essalmi, F., Jemni, M., & Kinshuk. (2017). Towards Applying Keller's ARCS Model and Learning by doing strategy in Classroom Courses. *Innovations in Smart Learning*, 187-196.

Tlili, A., Essalmi, F., Jemni, M., Kinshuk, & Chen, N.-S. (2016). Role of personality in computer based learning. *Computers in Human Behavior*, *64*, 805–813. doi:10.1016/j.chb.2016.07.043

Weeden, S., Cooke, B., & McVey, M. (2013). Underage children and social networking. *Journal of Research on Technology in Education*, *45*(3), 249–262. doi:10.1080/15391523.2013.10782605

Wise, L. Z., Skues, J., & Williams, B. (2011). Facebook in higher education promotes social but not academic engagement. Changing demands, changing directions. *Proceedings of ASCILITE Hobart*, 1332-1342.

Yang, P. L. (2018). Promoting EFL College Learners' Language Learning Strategies Through Facebook Interaction. *Expand Your Interests*, 211.

Yang, Y., Wang, Q., Woo, H. L., & Quek, C. L. (2011). Using Facebook for teaching and learning: A review of the literature. *International Journal of Continuing Engineering Education and Lifelong Learning*, *21*(1), 72–86. doi:10.1504/IJCEELL.2011.039695

Yu, C. H. (2001). An introduction to computing and interpreting Cronbach Coefficient Alpha in SAS. *Proceedings of 26th SAS User Group International Conference*, 22-25.

Zephoria. (2018). *The Top 20 Valuable Facebook Statistics – Updated May 2017*. Accessed 9 Mai 2017 from https://zephoria.com/top-15-valuable-facebook-statistics/

This research was previously published in the Journal of Cases on Information Technology (JCIT), 21(4); pages 46-61, copyright year 2019 by IGI Publishing (an imprint of IGI Global).

APPENDIX A: MOTIVATION QUESTIONNAIRE

This questionnaire is modified from the measure developed by (Hwang and Chang, 2011; Hwang, Yang, & Wang, 2013), as mentioned in the manuscript.

Table 10. Motivation questionnaire

Statements	Strongly Disagree		Neutral		Strongly Agree
	1	2	3	4	5
I think learning game development is interesting and valuable.					
I would like to learn more about game development.					
It is worth learning those things about game development.					
It is important for me to learn the game development course well.					
I find it motivating to learn game development.					
I will actively search for more information and learn about game development.					
It is important for everyone to take the game development course.					

APPENDIX B: TECHNOLOGY ACCEPTANCE QUESTIONNAIRE

Statements 1, 4, 5 and 10 are related to the security variable (4 statements). Statements 2, 6 and 7 are related to the usefulness variable (3 statements). Statements 3, 8 and 9 are related to the intention to use variable (3 statements).

Table 11. Technology acceptance questionnaire

Statements	Strongly Disagree		Neutral		Strongly Agree
	1	2	3	4	5
I felt that my privacy information was safe within the Facebook learning group.					
The Facebook functionalities did not help me learn game development.					
I will frequently use the Facebook learning group to learn.					
The rules proposed by the instructor in the Facebook learning group made me feel safe.					
The Facebook learning group supported respecting and encouraging each other.					
The Facebook functionalities used during learning game development are useful.					
The Facebook functionalities enriched learning game development.					
I intend to use the Facebook learning group again in the future.					
I do not plan to use Facebook again in learning game development.					
The Facebook learning group was unprotected which made me feel uncomfortable.					

Chapter 42
Opinion Mining of Twitter Events using Supervised Learning

Nida Hakak

Maharshi Dayanand University, Haryana, India

Mahira Kirmani

Maharshi Dayanand University, Haryana, India

ABSTRACT

Micro-blogs are a powerful tool to express an opinion. Twitter is one of the fastest growing micro-blogs and has more than 900 million users. Twitter is a rich source of opinion as users share their daily experience of life and respond to specific events using tweets on twitter. In this article, an automatic opinion classifier capable of automatically classifying tweets into different opinions expressed by them is developed. Also, a manually annotated corpus for opinion mining to be used by supervised learning algorithms is designed. An opinion classifier uses semantic, lexical, domain dependent, and context features for classification. Results obtained confirm competitive performance and the robustness of the system. Classifier accuracy is more than 75.05%, which is higher than the baseline accuracy.

1. INTRODUCTION

Opinion mining is used to refer to the task of automatically determining the opinion expressed in text, phrases, sentences or any piece of writing. However, more generally it is used to determine one's attitude towards a particular event or reaction to an event. Here, attitude means qualitative opinion, feeling or reaction to some situation that triggered the event. Opinion measurement and sentiment analysis for Twitter data are attracting much research both in academia and industry. Millions of users of Twitter are posting tweets about their daily life, write opinions on a variety of issues. Twitter is easily accessible through smartphones and other web services and thus is a preferred media for communication. Hence internet users are shifting from traditional communication tools like blogs and mailing lists to twitter.

DOI: 10.4018/978-1-6684-7123-4.ch042

More specifically, as Twitter users are expressing their opinions about several issues including religious matters, political views, and reviews of e-services, products or even movie reviews twitter has become a viable source for opinion measurement and detection. Such data is extremely potent for the industry for feedback and political parties to frame their policies and strategies.

Dey, Babo, Ashour, Bhatnagar & Bouhlel (2018) presented a detailed implementation of strategies and challenges to social network intelligence in their study. Twitter posts are 240 characters long messages called tweets. Java, Song, Finin & Tseng (2007) in their study suggest that users use Twitter for following reasons (1) for information source (2) to be in touch with family and friends and (3) seeking information about trends happing worldwide. Opinion mining involves data mining and Natural Language Processing (NLP) techniques to uncover hidden information and opinions from social web's substantial textual sources. Opinion mining from the text written in natural languages is challenging as it requires a deep understanding of explicit and implicit, regular and irregular, syntactic and semantic rules of language. Therefore, opinion mining is a challenge for NLP researchers for taking utilizing tools of NLP for efficient and effective opinion mining systems and thus leading to substantial practical impact.

Most of the companies are using opinion mining systems to create and automatically maintain reviews written by their customers for their popular products. Opinion mining can also be used by companies to improve customer relationship. Opinion mining also finds its applications in the recommender systems used by e-commerce sites. Moreover, opinion mining can play an essential part in the anti-spam policy drafting. Political parties also use opinion mining to know if the people support their decisions and programs or not and use feedback to frame their policies and strategies for future.

Opinion mining involves tracking users perception towards the brand or an event so as to capture mood of the public towards the brand or some political movement. Automatic opinion mining uses the NLP tools and machine learning techniques to effectively extract sentiments in text. Several studies exist in literature which have used machine learning to automatically detect the opinion like (Mohammad, Zhu, Kiritchenko & Martin, 2015; Yan, Turtle & Liddy, 2016; Gore, Diallo & Padilla, 2015). Pak & Paroubek (2010) used multinomial Naïve Bayes classifier with linguistic features to perform opinion analysis of collected twitter corpus. Grigori Sidorov (Sidorov, Miranda-Jiménez, Viveros-Jiménez, Gelbukh, Castro-Sánchez, Velásquez, & Gordon, 2012) used several machine learning algorithms for automatic detection of opinions in a Spanish language Tweet corpus.

In this paper, we discuss opinion mining of Twitter event done used state-of-art NLP techniques and machine learning tools. We show how to use Twitter for the corpus of opinion detection system. We have collected a corpus of 4,928,436 tweets about event namely Kashmir Unrest 2016 downloaded from the twitter from 10, July 2016 to 31, December 2016. We then preprocess tweets cleaning noise and performing other text transformations. Then the state-of-art linguistic analysis is performed using NLP techniques and then built an opinion classifier using supervised learning algorithms. We have also developed a rich opinion corpus using crowd-sourcing.

1.1. Contribution

The contributions of our research are:

1. We present a method for efficient preprocessing of text for removing and replacing slangs and to correct misspelled words.
2. We have built a vibrant opinion mining corpus for supervised learning algorithms.

3. We have used state-of-art NLP techniques for linguistic analysis of text to uncover explicit and implicit, regular and irregular, and syntactical and semantic language rules.

4. Built a supervised opinion classifier capable of mining opinions in Twitter.

5. Performed evaluation experiments that confirm competitive performance and robustness of our system.

6. Crowd-sourcing is used to create the opinion corpus where each tweet was labeled with five judgments and then majority voting was chosen and label agreed by at least three judges is given to the tweet.

2. RELATED WORK

Since the growth of social media, research in the field of opinion mining and sentiment analysis has grown many folds. Opinion mining is done at two levels: document level opinion mining and sentence level opinion mining. Pang and Lee (2008) presented a survey of existing approaches an techniques for opinion mining in textual systems. In their survey the authors present the detailed survey of the existing techniques and approaches of information retrieval using opinion analysis.

Another approach employed by Go, Bhayani and Huang (2009) uses machine learning algorithms to opinion detection in textual data streams. Their approach uses Twitter as a platform to collect the data for training. Training set is created using distant supervision. They used positive and negative emoticons for automatically creating dataset. Das, Borra, Dey and Borah (2018) presented movie recommendation system with good results. Turney (2002) used the average semantic orientation of phrases to calculate documents polarity. He used point wise mutual similarity to compute semantic orientation between documents and extracted phrases. Turney and Littman (2003) used cosine similarity and Latent semantic analysis at document level for opinion analysis. Dave, Lawrence and Pennock (2003) used term frequencies on uni-gram, bi-gram, and tri-gram to classify reviews on Amazon. Das and Chen (2001) used financial documents to classify sentiment polarity. Pang, Lee and Vaithyanathan (2002) used state-of-art machine learning algorithms to classify movie reviews for their sentiment polarity. They also used subjectivity with minimum graph cuts along with machine learning to detect sentiment in movie reviews as document-based opinion classification. Pang and Lee (2004) work is entirely different from these approaches as they have used sentence level opinion classification with state-of-art machine learning algorithms using feature classifiers. Kamal, Dey, Ashour, Ripon, Balas and Kaysar (2017) designed an automated system for monitoring Facebook data. Lan, Wang, Fong, Liu, Wong and Dey (2018) presented a survey of data mining and deep learning in bioinformatics. Zhuang, Jing and Zhu (2006) used sentence level classification using high-frequency keywords and high-frequency opinion keywords for classification of movie reviews. They used dependency graphs to identify feature-opinion pairs, along with a fixed set of keywords and thus their system was limited. Kouloumpis, Wilson and Moore (2011), Saif, He and Alani (2012), Sarlan, Nadam and Basri (2014), Balabantaray, Mohammad and Sharma (2012) based strategies, however, do not produce satisfactory results when used for opinion mining at the sentence level. Several works have suggested extending emotion lexicons with distribution semantic algorithms like Word2Vec (Mikolov, Chen, Corrado, & Dean, 2013) for classification (Canales, Strapparava, Boldrini & Martnez-Barco, 2016).

All these works focus on sentiment analysis, opinion mining or emotion detection at the fine-grained or coarse-grained level, however, and they lack subjectivity and domain dependent features. Domain dependent features describe the opinion that is currently being mined. All the work in the literature are general in nature and miss the crucial aspect of the current opinion being mined. The novelty of this work is that the domain dependent features are being introduced for the task of emotion mining. We capture the domain dependent features by creating an initial seed set by the domain experts. The opinions that are to mined require subject experts for identification of opinion terms; that act as the initial seed set for lexicon creation. The lexicon is then used by the automatic classifier for the opinion classification.

In this work, we will be using domain dependent features and show how they help in improving the efficiency of the classifier. Also, we have built an opinion corpus that can be used by other classifiers.

3. METHODOLOGY

In this section, a novel opinion classifier is proposed built using supervised classifier. The supervised classifier is built using lexical, contextual, semantic, domain dependent and morphological features. We have used pre-processing to normalize the dataset by reducing noise and correct misspelled words. Our classifier clarifies tweeter feed into six opinion classes viz; anti-India, pro-India, anti-Kashmir, pro-Kashmir, anti-Pakistan, pro-Pakistan and neutral depending on the opinion described in the tweet. We have built an opinion corpus of 9818 tweets that is useful for several opinion related tasks.

4. DATASET

We used twitter streaming API[1] and twitter4j[2] to download our dataset for opinion mining task. Dataset was downloaded to automatically for mining opinion during Kashmir unrest 2016[3]. Violent protests erupted in the Kashmir valley (J&K India) during summer of 2016 due to the killing of Hizbul Mujahidin commander, Burhan Wani. Burhan got killed on 8th July 2016. On 12th July 2016, we started downloading the tweets about the event until 31st December 2016. The dataset had 4,928,436 tweets. The downloaded dataset has non-English tweets as well we removed them and kept English only tweets, re-tweets were also discarded. Figure 1 show timeline of event where the frequency is plotted against date. Table 1 shows a sample of tweets downloaded.

5. AUTOMATIC OPINION CLASSIFICATION

Our automatic opinion classifier is developed using supervised classifier. We have used multiclass Support Vector Machine ($SVM_{multiclass}$) (Joachims, Finley & Yu, 2009). Our automatic classification algorithm consists of following parts:

1. Twitter scrapping module
2. Pre-processing
3. Lexicon generation
4. Feature selection
5. Generation of opinion corpus
6. Automatic classifier

7.   Proposed Algorithm.

We discuss each of the sub-processes in following subsections. Figure 2 shows overall functioning of our system.

Figure 1. Time series of the event

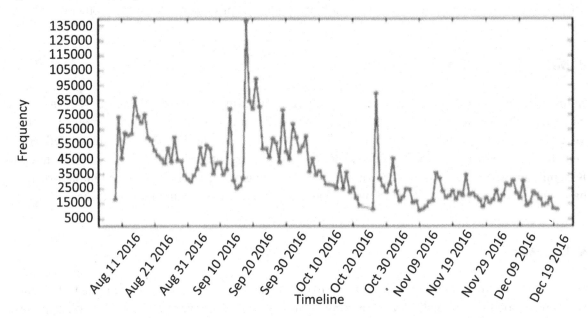

Table 1. Sample Tweets

Serial number	Tweet
1	createdAt:Wed Oct 26 14:28:10 CEST 2016, location: Bangalore, tweet: RT @Username: 19 schools burnt down in Kashmir in 3 months. Dear @username, pls confirm if schools were useless because they didn't have a\u2026", lang: en, rtweet: true, tid:791255097766350849, username: username
2	createdAt:Wed Oct 26 14:28:11 CEST 2016, location: India, tweet: Burning schools is new way of celebrating \#Diwali \#kashmir, lang: en, rtweet:false, tid:791255101570555905, username: username
3	createdAt: Wed Oct 26 14:28:12 CEST 2016, tweet: RT @maulinshah9: @username During the unnatural alliance of \#PDP_BJP in the state and NDA in the Center, \#Kashmir has faced maximum days of \u2026, lang: en,rtweet: true, tid:791255105563570176, username: username
4	{"tweet":"@saysdiyanag @CatchNews This one statement made me worry more about his wife than the jawans in Kashmir. So much power", "tid":791255101570556914}
5	{"tweet":"@TimesNow i get stunned when u still trying to get consensus over Kashmir..it is never going to take place..the Q is why gov. (1)", "tid":763044533558874113}
6	{"tweet":"Anyone watching Times Now?Better not. Hell break loose over Kashmir & la ilaaha illalla.Where are these debates taking us2. Shameful indeed.","tid", 763046521180790784}

Figure 2. Overall working of the System

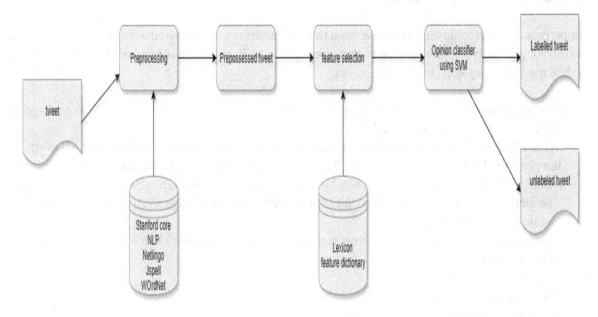

5.1. Twitter Scrapping Module

We made a scraper for collecting tweets related to the unrest. Scrapper was developed using twitter4j and twitter streaming API. Figure 3 shows the architecture of our scrapping module.

Our scrapping module receives a set of query string words which are probed to twitter for retrieving relevant tweets.

Figure 3. Scrapping module architecture

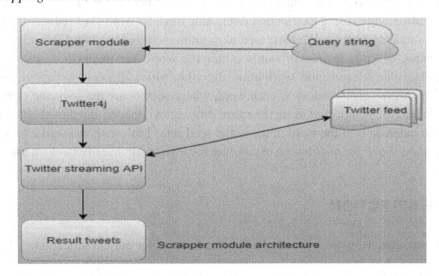

6. PREPROCESSING MODULE

Our preprocessing module removes noise from tweets. Tweets are unstructured a noisy which need to be cleaned for processing before passing to the supervised classifier for classification. Our preprocessing module use following steps to clean the tweet.

1. Stanford core NLP (Manning, Surdeanu, Bauer, Finkel, Bethard & McClosky, 2014) package is used to tokenize tweets into words.
2. We use English dictionary modules to remove slangs and abbreviations from the tweet. All words of the tweet are feed to dictionary module for retrieving their meaning. All words that have no proper meaning returned are passed to the word replacer module for replacement with proper meanings. The dictionary module is used WordNet (Miller, 1995) and Jspell. The word replacer module uses Netlingo and urban dictionary.
3. Stemming from each word in the tweet is done using potter stemmer (Van Rijsbergen, Robertson & Porter, 1980).
4. Stop words removed.
5. Usernames and URL's removed.
6. The case of tweet changed to lowercase.

7. LEXICON GENERATION

We built an opinion lexicon for feature extraction to be used by the opinion classifier. The lexicon contains seed words representing opinion mined. For all the classes of opinion that are to be mined in the Twitter dataset, we built the lexicon. Lexicon was initially developed using initial seed seeds for all classes and later on extended by using distributional semantic similarity models like Word2vec [Mikolov, T., Chen, K., Corrado, G., & Dean, J. (2013)]. The initial seed set is created using domain experts who choose the seed words belonging to the different opinions to be mined. The seed set is then extended to capture the domain specific features using distributional semantic models. Word2Vec reduces the bias that may creep into the annotation process. We have used Skip-gram model of the Word2Vec algorithm. To this model entire dataset given as lemmas of words to train the Word2Vec model.

Word2vec algorithm is a semantic distribution algorithm which allows us to capture domain dependent features. Word2vec gives vectors of each word, where vectors are the semantic extensions of the word probed. Word2vec was trained using the entire dataset downloaded and thus enabled us to capture domain-specific extensions of the word in the initial seed sets. Table 2 shows seed words in the initial seed set and Table 3 shows the distribution of words in the lexicon after seed extension using Word2Vec.

8. FEATURE SELECTION

Features were extracted using java. We used following features for our classification:

1. **Unigrams**: Unigrams are nouns, adjectives, noun verbs from the corpus.
2. **Bigrams**: bigrams are the randomly selected two unigrams.

3. **Trigrams**: Trigrams are the three words. The word after and before the middle word depends on the middle word. The middle word is chosen from the seed set, after reading the tweet if the seed word exists there we choose words before and after the seed word in the tweet to form the trigram.
4. **Adjective**: Adjectives are extracted from the corpus using the Stanford NLP toolkit
5. **POS-Bigrams**: using the same NLP toolkit we extracted adjectives and proper nouns from the corpus to generate the POS-bigrams.
6. **Opinion lexicon**. We use opinion lexicon as a domain dependent features. The opinion lexicon serves as a domain dependent features as they are related to the mining of opinion directly and are more correlated with the opinion to be mined.

Table 2. Seed words in lexicon

Class	Seed words	# seed words
O1	Kashmir, prison, war, school, burn, pellet, blind, kill, child, grave, crpf, beat, force, human, right, violate, blood, fire, gun, curfew, Muslim, injury, force, occupy, shell, child, police, India	29
O2	education, effect, mask, youth, damage, problem, young, terrorist, religion, separatist, stone, pellet, throw, Geelani, unrest, want, state, Kashmir, militant, evacuate, dirty, illiterate, direction, dismiss, local	26
O3	Pakistan, ceasefire, violate, Nawaz, Taliban, isis, terrorist, Balochistan, illegal, fuel, unrest, terror, state, train, camp., pok, blackday, destabilize, claim, Kashmir, bomb, unrest, Nawaz, trouble	25
O4	Kashmir, referendum, dispute, territory, uno, resolve, issue, protest, separatist, love, silent, Burhan, hero, martyr, demand, freedom, Kashmir, develop, Congress, Abdullah, Azadi, Nehru, support, Burhan, Geelani	28
O5	Pakistan, valley, beauty, flag, banayaga, love, zindabad, support, Pakistani, fake, strike, China, support, Kashmiri, Jinnah, Jeeva, zindabad, Muslim, raise, issue, peace, peaceful, Islamic, poster	26
O6	part, India, Kashmir, with, celebrate, Diwali, legal, accession, army, job, accede, home, protect, love, Modi, PDP, Indian, Hindustani, discipline, win, bjp, Modi, game	26

Table 3. Distribution after extension

Class	# seed words after extension
O1	231
O2	137
O3	97
O4	225
O5	40
O6	98

9. OPINION CORPUS

Any corpora annotations are reliable only when we have multiple annotations for the same tweet by multiple judges. We used five annotators to annotate our corpus. A total of 12,000 tweets randomly selected from the dataset were chosen for annotation. Annotators did not receive any training but were shown samples to make them understand what kinds of annotation were required. Each annotator has to label a tweet with a category among the six opinion classes namely: O1, O2, O3, O4, O5, O6 or Neutral if no opinion is found. Thus, an opinion corpus has seven labels, six opinion classes plus neutral. From the 12,000 tweets, we choose only those tweets where at least three annotators have agreed, and thus our opinion corpus has 9,818 tweets. Table 4 shows the distribution of opinion classes in the opinion corpus. Figure 4 shows the percentages of opinion classes in manually annotated opinion corpus.

Table 4. Distribution of opinion classes in the manually annotated corpus

Class	# of instances in manually annotated opinion corpus
O1	2544
O2	1638
O3	1562
O4	2534
O5	171
O6	837
neutral	532
Total	9818

Figure 4. Percentages of opinion classes in manually annotated opinion corpus

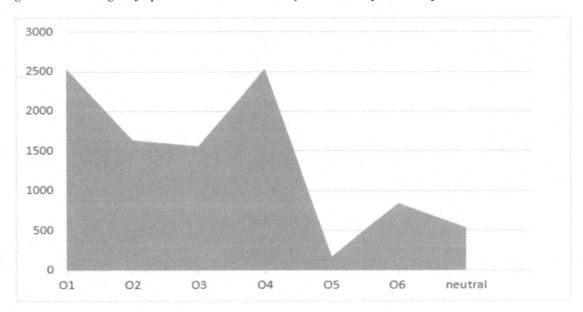

10. AUTOMATIC CLASSIFIER

Our automatic opinion classifier uses Support vector machine ($SVM^{multiclass}$) for classification. It processes input as vectors in a feature weight combination. We transform features generated in the preceding phase into vectors for classification. We have used different combinations of features to test our classification.

$SVM^{multiclass}$ uses multiclass formulization described in [22], but it optimizes it with an algorithm that is fast in linear case For a training set (x1, y1) ... (xn,yn) with labels yi in [1..k], it finds the solution of the following optimization problem during training.

min 1/2Σi=1..k wi*wi +C/n Σi=1..n ξi

for all y in [1..k]: [x1 • wyi] >= [x1 • wy] + 100*Δ(y1,y) - ξ1

for all y in [1..k]: [xn • wyn] >= [xn • wy] + 100*Δ(yn,y) - ξn

C is the usual regularization parameter that trades off margin size and training error. Δ(yn,y) is the loss function that returns 0 if yn equals y, and 1 otherwise.

The opinion classifier takes as input the set of tweets and the set of labels which are opinions that are to be mined and returns the set of tweets labelled with the opinion classes. The pinion classifier uses the features for opinion extraction and creates a model using $SVM^{muticlass}$ based on the features and then the model is used for inference of opinion for the unknown test examples.

10.1. Proposed Algorithm

The algorithm of the opinion classifier is as follows:

1. Use domain experts to generate seed words for the opinion classes.
2. Train Word2Vec model using the corpus for which mining is to be done.
3. Extend the seed set generated in step (a) with the trained Word2Vec model to obtain the extended seed set to obtain the opinion lexicon
4. Preprocess the training corpus generated using crowd-sourcing to obtain the preprocessed training corpus.
5. Generate the features for opinion mining.
6. Convert features into numbers for the $SVM_{muticlass}$ training.
7. Preprocess, generate features and convert them into numbers of the test set for classification.

11. EVALUATION AND RESULTS

Our opinion classifier takes as input the set of tweets and six opinion classes named 01,02, ...O6 and the output of the classifier is the tweet along with the opinion label for the tweet or Neutral otherwise. We tested our classifier on the opinion corpus and got the accuracy of **75**.05% with macro-average of 72.32%, 67.72% and 68.71% for precision, recall and f1-score respectively.

Confusion matrices, accuracy, F_1- score, precision, and recall were used to evaluate the proposed opinion classifier. Confusion matrices are a good indicator of measuring the efficiency of the multi-class classifier. The general structure of a confusion matrix is shown in Table 5. The diagonal elements represent the true positives (correctly classified) of the classification process, represented by tp in the table and other elements in the corresponding row represent the false positives. Elements of the corresponding column represent the false negatives. Misclassifications are both false positives and false negatives.

Table 5. General structure of confusion matrix

		Predicted class			
		A	B	C	D
Known class	A	tp_A	eAB	eAC	eAD
	B	eBA	tp_B	eBC	eBD
	C	eCA	eCB	tp_C	eCD
	D	eDA	eDB	eDC	tp_D

Precision is the ratio of true-positives to the sum of false negatives and true positives. Mathematically, the precision of class A is defined as:

$$Precison\ A = \frac{tpA}{tpA + fpA}$$

Where tp_A is the true positives of class A and fp_A is the false positives of all classes corresponding to class A. The recall is the ratio of true positives to the sum of true positives and false negatives. Mathematically, recall of class A is defined as

Where tp_A is the true positives of class A and fn_A is the false negatives of all classes corresponding to class A.The harmonic mean of both precision and recall gives F-score of the classifier. Mathematically F_1-score of classifier is

$$F1 - score = 2*\frac{precision * recall}{precision+recall}$$

Accuracy is the ratio of correct classifications to the total classifications. Mathematically,

$$Accuracy = \frac{tpc}{total}$$

There tpc is the sum of all true positives and total is the total no of classifications. We used leave one out validation for the evaluation purpose.

Table 6 shows the confusion matrix and results of our classifier. Figure 5 shows the graph of our precision, recall and f-score for different opinion classes classified by our classifier.

Table 6. Confusion matrix and evaluation

	Confusion matrix							Results		
	O1	O2	O3	O4	O5	O6	Neutral	Precision	Recall	F1-score
O1	1658	56	220	119	10	26	19	66.23	75.52	70.57
O2	49	1008	65	108	0	102	12	64.53	75.56	69.41
O3	139	0	1102	0	0	180	17	67.27	76.63	71.64
O4	63	192	74	810	0	220	19	96.77	58.70	73.13
O5	21	14	0	5	110	9	0	64.32	67.90	66.06
O6	493	209	73	15	13	1623	23	64.04	66.27	65.13
Neutral	80	97	84	15	12	185	442	83.08	53..21	65.09
Macro-average								72.32	67.72	68.71
Accuracy								75.05%		

Figure 5. Precision, recall and F1-score of different opinion classes

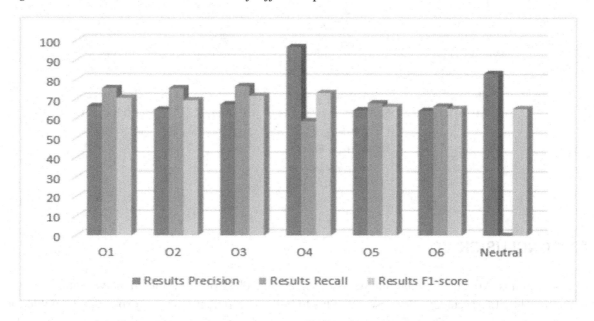

12. DISCUSS AND COMPARATIVE ANALYSIS

In this section, we will discuss results of our algorithm and compare our proposed approach with other similar techniques. We have achieved accuracy of 75.05% with macro-average of 72.32%, 67.72% and 68.71% for precision, recall and f1-score respectively. While the agreement between results of our proposed algorithm and manual annotation was found to be having accuracy of 75.05%. Using initial seed set as starting point, which was created by domain experts, the domain specific word extension was done using word2vec algorithm. Table 7 and Figure 6 compares the results of our opinion classifier with the similar studies results.

Table 7. Comparative analysis

Technique	Accuracy
Proposed algorithm	75.05%
Canales, Strapparava, Boldrini & Martnez-Barco, 2016	59.5%
Mikolov, Chen, Corrado & Dean, 2013	65.2%
Balabantaray, Mohammad, & Sharma, 2012	73.05%

Figure 6. Comparative analysis of different techniques

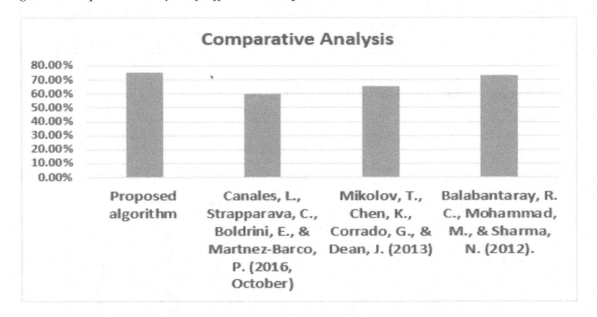

13. CONCLUSION

This research is about the opinion mining using supervised classifiers, use of extensive features to improve the classifier accuracy. This research aims to build an efficient opinion corpus that is usable for opinion mining purpose. The supervised classifier is trained on well-crafted opinion corpus, and results confirm the competitive performance and robustness of the system. Our proposed algorithm achieved an overall accuracy of 75.05%. With the micro-average precision of 72.32%, recall of 67.72% and f1-score of 68.71% which is higher than the baseline accuracy.

In our future work, we will use more lexicographical, and topic modulation features to improve the performance of our supervised classifier. Usage of Glove for lexicon building will also be explored.

REFERENCES

Agarwal, A., Xie, B., Vovsha, I., Rambow, O., & Passonneau, R. (2011, June). Sentiment analysis of twitter data. In *Proceedings of the workshop on languages in social media*(pp. 30-38). Association for Computational Linguistics.

Balabantaray, R. C., Mohammad, M., & Sharma, N. (2012). Multi-class twitter emotion classification: A new approach. *International Journal of Applied Information Systems*, *4*(1), 48–53. doi:10.5120/ijais12-450651

Canales, L., Strapparava, C., Boldrini, E., & Martnez-Barco, P. (2016, October). Exploiting a bootstrapping approach for automatic annotation of emotions in texts. In *2016 IEEE International Conference on Data Science and Advanced Analytics (DSAA)* (pp. 726-734). IEEE. 10.1109/DSAA.2016.78

Das, N., Borra, S., Dey, N., & Borah, S. (2018). Social Networking in Web Based Movie Recommendation System. In *Social Networks Science: Design, Implementation, Security, and Challenges* (pp. 25–45). Cham: Springer. doi:10.1007/978-3-319-90059-9_2

Das, S., & Chen, M. (2001, July). Yahoo! for Amazon: Extracting market sentiment from stock message boards. In *Proceedings of the Asia Pacific finance association annual conference (APFA)* (Vol. 35, p. 43).

Dave, K., Lawrence, S., & Pennock, D. M. (2003, May). Mining the peanut gallery: Opinion extraction and semantic classification of product reviews. In *Proceedings of the 12th international conference on World Wide Web* (pp. 519-528). ACM. 10.1145/775152.775226

Dey, N., Babo, R., Ashour, A. S., Bhatnagar, V., & Bouhlel, M. S. (2018). Social Networks Science: Design. In Implementation, Security, and Challenges From Social Networks Analysis to Social Networks Intelligence.

Go, A., Bhayani, R., & Huang, L. (2009). Twitter sentiment classification using distant supervision. CS224N Project Report, Stanford, 1(12).

Gore, R. J., Diallo, S., & Padilla, J. (2015). You are what you tweet: Connecting the geographic variation in America's obesity rate to twitter content. *PLoS One*, *10*(9). doi:10.1371/journal.pone.0133505 PMID:26332588

Hall, M., Frank, E., Holmes, G., Pfahringer, B., Reutemann, P., & Witten, I. H. (2009). The WEKA data mining software: an update. *ACM SIGKDD explorations newsletter, 11*(1), 10-18.

Java, A., Song, X., Finin, T., & Tseng, B. (2007, August). Why we twitter: understanding microblogging usage and communities. In *Proceedings of the 9th WebKDD and 1st SNA-KDD 2007 workshop on Web mining and social network analysis* (pp. 56-65). ACM. 10.1145/1348549.1348556

Joachims, T., Finley, T., & Yu, C. N. J. (2009). Cutting-plane training of structural SVMs. *Machine Learning*, *77*(1), 27–59. doi:10.100710994-009-5108-8

Kamal, S., Dey, N., Ashour, A. S., Ripon, S., Balas, V. E., & Kaysar, M. S. (2017). FbMapping: An automated system for monitoring Facebook data. *Neural Network World*, *27*(1), 27–57. doi:10.14311/NNW.2017.27.002

Kouloumpis, E., Wilson, T., & Moore, J. D. (2011). Twitter sentiment analysis: The good the bad and the omg! *Icwsm*, *11*(538-541), 164.

Krammer, K., & Singer, Y. (2001). On the algorithmic implementation of multi-class SVMs. In *Proc. of JMLR* (pp. 265-292).

Lan, K., Wang, D. T., Fong, S., Liu, L. S., Wong, K. K., & Dey, N. (2018). A Survey of Data Mining and Deep Learning in Bioinformatics. *Journal of Medical Systems*, *42*(8), 139. doi:10.100710916-018-1003-9 PMID:29956014

Manning, C., Surdeanu, M., Bauer, J., Finkel, J., Bethard, S., & McClosky, D. (2014). The Stanford CoreNLP natural language processing toolkit. In *Proceedings of 52nd annual meeting of the association for computational linguistics: system demonstrations* (pp. 55-60). 10.3115/v1/P14-5010

Mikolov, T., Chen, K., Corrado, G., & Dean, J. (2013). Efficient estimation of word representations in vector space. arXiv:1301.3781

Miller, G. A. (1995). WordNet: A lexical database for English. *Communications of the ACM*, *38*(11), 39–41. doi:10.1145/219717.219748

Mohammad, S. M., Zhu, X., Kiritchenko, S., & Martin, J. (2015). Sentiment, emotion, purpose, and style in electoral tweets. *Information Processing & Management*, *51*(4), 480–499. doi:10.1016/j.ipm.2014.09.003

Nakov, P., Ritter, A., Rosenthal, S., Sebastiani, F., & Stoyanov, V. (2016). SemEval-2016 task 4: Sentiment analysis in Twitter. In *Proceedings of the 10th International Workshop on Semantic Evaluation (SemEval-2016)* (pp. 1-18). 10.18653/v1/S16-1001

Pak, A., & Paroubek, P. (2010, May). Twitter as a corpus for sentiment analysis and opinion mining. In LREc (Vol. 10, pp. 1320-1326).

Pang, B., & Lee, L. (2004, July). A sentimental education: Sentiment analysis using subjectivity summarization based on minimum cuts. In *Proceedings of the 42nd annual meeting on Association for Computational Linguistics* (p. 271). Association for Computational Linguistics. 10.3115/1218955.1218990

Pang, B., & Lee, L. (2008). Opinion mining and sentiment analysis. *Foundations and Trends in Information Retrieval*, *2*(1–2), 1-135.

Pang, B., Lee, L., & Vaithyanathan, S. (2002, July). Thumbs up?: sentiment classification using machine learning techniques. In *Proceedings of the ACL-02 conference on Empirical methods in natural language processing* (Vol. 10, pp. 79-86). Association for Computational Linguistics. 10.3115/1118693.1118704

Popescu, A. M., & Etzioni, O. (2007). Extracting product features and opinions from reviews. In *Natural language processing and text mining* (pp. 9–28). London: Springer. doi:10.1007/978-1-84628-754-1_2

Saif, H., He, Y., & Alani, H. (2012, November). Semantic sentiment analysis of twitter. In *International semantic web conference* (pp. 508-524). Springer. 10.1007/978-3-642-35176-1_32

Sarlan, A., Nadam, C., & Basri, S. (2014, November). Twitter sentiment analysis. In *2014 International Conference on Information Technology and Multimedia (ICIMU)* (pp. 212-216). IEEE. 10.1109/ICIMU.2014.7066632

Sidorov, G., Miranda-Jiménez, S., Viveros-Jiménez, F., Gelbukh, A., Castro-Sánchez, N., Velásquez, F., . . . Gordon, J. (2012, October). Empirical study of machine learning based approach for opinion mining in tweets. In *Mexican international conference on Artificial intelligence* (pp. 1-14). Springer.

Turney, P. D. (2002, July). Thumbs up or thumbs down?: semantic orientation applied to unsupervised classification of reviews. In *Proceedings of the 40th annual meeting on association for computational linguistics* (pp. 417-424). Association for Computational Linguistics.

Turney, P. D., & Littman, M. L. (2003). Measuring praise and criticism: Inference of semantic orientation from association. *ACM Transactions on Information Systems, 21*(4), 315–346. doi:10.1145/944012.944013

Van Rijsbergen, C. J., Robertson, S. E., & Porter, M. F. (1980). *New models in probabilistic information retrieval*. London: British Library Research and Development Department.

Yan, J. L. S., Turtle, H. R., & Liddy, E. D. (2016). EmoTweet-28: a fine-grained emotion corpus for sentiment analysis. In *Proceedings of the 10th International Conference on Language Resources and Evaluation. LREC* (pp. 1149-1156).

Zhuang, L., Jing, F., & Zhu, X. Y. (2006, November). Movie review mining and summarization. In *Proceedings of the 15th ACM international conference on Information and knowledge management* (pp. 43-50). ACM.

ENDNOTES

[1]   https://dev.twitter.com/streaming/overview
[2]   http://twitter4j.org/en
[3]   https://en.wikipedia.org/wiki/2016-17-kashmirunrest

This research was previously published in the International Journal of Synthetic Emotions (IJSE), 9(2); pages 23-36, copyright year 2018 by IGI Publishing (an imprint of IGI Global).

Chapter 43
I Tweet, You Tweet, (S)He Tweets:
Enhancing the ESL Language–Learning Experience Through Twitter

Geraldine Blattner

Florida Atlantic University, Boca Raton, USA

Amanda Dalola

University of South Carolina, Columbia, USA

ABSTRACT

This study seeks to further the research on online language learning by examining the level at which intermediate ESL students understand and process sociopragmatic information in their second language (L2) in globally networked environments like Twitter. In this semester-long study, L2 English learners from a variety of first languages (Chinese, Spanish, Arabic) analyzed authentic English-language tweets produced by well-known native speakers, with a focus on abbreviations, hashtags and tweeter mood. Results revealed that high intermediate ESL students relied most heavily on word choice when making sense of English tweets, demonstrating that a majority were able to extract significant meaning from common abbreviations, prosified hashtags, indices of tweeter mood and the tweet's larger context. This investigation highlights Twitter's status as an authentic and dynamic L2 setting that facilitates the cultural enrichment of learners and enhances their socio-pragmatic awareness, while developing their multiliteracy skills in an L2.

INTRODUCTION

The popular microblogging tool, Twitter, which debuted in 2007 and currently reports over 500 million users (Semiocast, 2012; Oreskovich, 2015), is one of the ten most visited websites worldwide (Fitzgerald, 2012). Twitter is viewed as a prominent method for information gathering and propagation, and is commonly used by teenagers, adults and celebrities (athletes, politicians, singers, etc.) (Greenhow &

DOI: 10.4018/978-1-6684-7123-4.ch043

Gleason, 2012). The growing popularity of this social media has transformed literacy perspectives by highlighting everyday vernacular practices (Lankshear & Knobel, 2006). Jones (2016) recently underscored the fact that digital technology has altered the way people use language. Preston (2012) further argued that digital literacy is becoming a required skill for active members of the workforce. The ability to search for and critically evaluate information online, to construct meaningful reading paths through hypertext documents, to comment on the online writing of others in appropriate ways and to construct knowledge collaboratively through a variety of online platforms have become essential aspects of our daily interactions. Despite this recent communicative evolution, current research continues to document how foreign language textbooks lack authenticity by failing to introduce current linguistic norms, instead focusing on grammatical rules and cultural simplifications. Studies have shown that speakers' identity of the target language is often framed in terms of static national culture and standard language (Cole & Meadows 2013; Dervin & Liddicoat 2013). Such a nationalist frame promotes, as Cole & Meadows call it, an 'essentialist trap' (p.30), where perspectives of language and culture result in the spreading of stereotypes. Consequently, language learners frequently display the understanding of language and culture in terms of static codes through frequent linguistic and cultural generalizations, even though L2 teaching and learning should challenge this monolithic representation (Blyth, 2015), by allowing students to experience "the language of the speech community in terms of content, frequencies of that content and the mappings of form to functional interpretation" (Ellis, 2002a, p. 167). Vellenga (2004) explained that the omission of authentic linguistic samples in language textbooks results in the lack of a reliable source of (sociopragmatic) input, which restricts learners in their ability to notice valuable input and learn implicitly (Ellis, 2002a; 2002b). This conscious oversight prevents language learners from acquiring digital literacy, as such a skill cannot be intuited, but rather is developed via the analysis of naturally occurring language samples. Numerous scholars have documented language educators' view of textbooks as inadequate in terms of providing 'nontraditional' and authentically grounded pedagogical tasks (Bardovi-Harlig, 2001; Hassal, 2008; Uso-Juan, 2007; Vellenga, 2004; among others). It is possible for dedicated language instructors to overcome these shortcomings by providing learners with pragmatically appropriate input, but it requires the creation of additional activities that reflect language in its current uses and forms. Likewise, digital opportunities for learners to use foreign languages in authentic ways extracurricularly are evident and accessible albeit avoided if learners do not feel like competent members of the online communities. The challenge of 21st century language instructors thus reveals itself as one of designing environments and pedagogical methods to guide students through activities that promote a greater awareness of the forms and functions of social media, and encapsulate general practices in digital literacy, which encourage the discovery of new linguistic forms in the target language and eventually trigger a restructuring of the learner's interlanguage system (Schmidt, 1990). The present study offers one way to use the microblogging tool Twitter to provide students with linguistic input, following a method that allows them to notice and experience the authentic forms commonly used by native speakers, but which are not often formally presented in traditional foreign language textbooks. Our goal is to highlight the importance of non-traditional input through electronic media, by establishing it as a complementary linguistic source that is capable of enriching L2 competence via the overt noticing of different language types (abbreviations, acronyms, slang, etc.) typically used in Twitter.

LITERATURE REVIEW

Twitter in ESL and Foreign Language Classes

The last decade has witnessed a plethora of studies investigating the power of social media in foreign language learning, capitalizing on learners' new technological habits. A wide range of electronic tools and tasks have been the focus of pedagogically oriented studies, mostly in non-immersion contexts (Abraham & Williams, 2009; Antenos-Conforti, 2009; Blattner, Dalola & Lomicka 2015, 2016a; 2016b; Blattner & Fiori, 2011; Blattner & Lomicka 2012; Hanna & de Nooy, 2003; 2009; Lomicka & Lord, 2012; Perrifanou, 2009). Digital literacy practices tend to be marginalized in mainstream ESL classrooms, where instruction remains primarily focused on a curriculum that exclusively promotes the language skills required to operate in print-based environments or unmediated face-to-face settings (Hafner, Chick, & Jones, 2013). Research on the use of social media in ESL classes in higher education is still limited, as are studies focusing on the potential of microblogging tools (i.e. Twitter) to allow learners to notice authentic input (Schmidt, 1993). This trend is perplexing, given that language learners in immersive contexts are the ones most likely to be confronted with sociopragmatically charged language in a digital milieu.

Hattem (2012) investigated the use of Twitter among advanced ESL learners over one year, by asking them to use the site to practice grammar forms learned in class (i.e. the passive voice) in contexts relating to their own lives. He concluded that microblogging both helps learners process new grammatical constructions and consolidate new ones in long-term memory.

In a follow-up study, Hattem (2014) analyzed the tweets of ESL learners and their instructor in an advanced language grammar course where students practiced complex grammatical constructions and received corrective feedback from the instructor via Twitter. Results found that despite the academically motivated nature of the task, participants played with language in a variety of ways during their microblogging experiences, which created an expansive learning context.

Focusing on ways of improving output production, Mompean and Fouz-González (2016) conducted a study with ESL learners to determine whether Twitter can foster online participation or have a positive effect on the pronunciation of words commonly mispronounced by EFL students. The students were sent tweets on a daily basis, each of them containing a pronunciation of a word considered to be difficult, due to unusual sound-spelling correspondences, lexical stress or the presence of silent letters. Results showed that instructive tweets had a positive effect on the students' pronunciation of the target words and increased their active engagement.

The benefits reported from these studies are evident, however, one key question must be raised: can language educators claim to exploit an authentic setting when they 'force' students to use social media for a class activity? It can and should be argued that such activities which restrict students' interaction to just the teacher or other non-native users of a similar level remove the underlying authenticity offered by digital technologies. In some cases, production tasks of this sort have also been reported as overwhelming by students (Gao et al., 2012) because the initial unfamiliarity with the tool may prevent them from being able to immediately engage. For this reason, many educators have argued for preparing language learners to use these electronic social venues in their natural and uncontrived contexts, thereby respecting the original objectives of social media and encouraging autonomous learner exploration outside of class (Jones, 2016) as a means to develop an awareness of tweeting practices, or 'Twitteracy' (Greenhow & Gleason, 2012). This approach goes hand in hand with Schmidt's (1993) proposal that the subjective experience of noticing is a necessary condition leading to the transformation of input to intake in

L2 acquisition. To acquire new vocabulary or develop pragmatic awareness, a learner must notice both linguistic forms and the relevant contextual features. Following this thought, a series of recent studies were conducted in various university-level French classes, which investigated how French learners interpreted tweets from French-speaking celebrities. Blattner, Dalola & Lomicka (2015) argued that Twitter is a valuable platform for exposing language learners to L2 invisible culture because it allowed early learners to cultivate an ability to notice relevant L2 pragmatic features during a six-week period. Overall, the early learners had difficulty correctly interpreting English borrowings and identifying and interpreting abbreviations to which they had never been exposed. The presence of this difficulty, despite the high frequency of those forms in electronic social and news media, indicates that language learners must be exposed more regularly to frequently used language, in order to both enhance their sociopragmatic understanding of authentic language and reinforce their multilingual communicative repertoire.

Blattner, Dalola & Lomicka (2016a) found comparable results with first and second semester French learners in an investigation of how early learners analyzed abbreviations and the use of English words in French-language tweets. Results demonstrated that both groups were permissive of English borrowings in French tweets, but that second semester learners were better able to understand false cognates. Consistent with previous research, the learners were able to identify but not interpret high-frequency abbreviations and novel English borrowings in French, despite their high frequency. The authors argue that the incorporation of cross-cultural pragmatic elements is necessary for the development of intercultural communicative competence, and that Twitter is an effective method for exposing early learners to such invisible elements, because it provides them with authentic and dynamic culture and linguistic input that encourages the development of L2 digital literacy.

In a follow-up study, Blattner, Dalola & Lomicka (2016b) analyzed intermediate French language learners' ability to understand and interpret hashtags in French tweets. Results revealed that, overall, intermediate learners were able to parse and make sense of hashtags to understand the general meaning of a tweet, however, they were also visibly driven by the 'new' conventions of fast-paced online media (Kramsch, 2014) because they often only glanced at hashtags superficially to get the gist of a tweet and notice new linguistic forms (Schmidt 1993; 1995). These findings indicate that learning about and understanding hashtags in the target language can, in fact, stimulate the learner's development of cultural references, especially because the use of hashtags has spread to other social media involving both personal and professional ventures.

More recently, Hattem and Lomicka (2016) analyzed 18 studies in which Twitter was used in the context of language learning and teaching. They explained that integrating Twitter in foreign language classes is not always done without the frustration of certain students, especially those who are less familiar with microblogging systems and have not adopted them as part of their daily life. They revealed that some learners reported feeling overwhelmed by having to check or write tweets regularly. Overall, however, the studies highlighted the many benefits of incorporating Twitter in L2 learning for its ability to develop L2 digital literacy. The present study aims to extend this line of research by exploring how exposure to native speaker tweets can culturally and linguistically enhance the immersion experience of ESL learners living in the US, by encouraging them to notice (Schmidt, 1993) nontraditional authentic input forms. In other words, our goal is to see if educators can promote 'Twitteracy' and make language learners 'more tweetsmart' in their L2, by integrating activities that do not revolve around formal print-based documents, as a means to fully establish them in the new L2 e-culture.

Present Study

The present study adds to the existing body of literature by examining how Twitter can enrich the language and culture learning experience of intermediate ESL learners in an immersion setting, by exposing them to authentic input and guiding them to notice new linguistic forms and patterns that will develop their sociopragmatic understanding of popular culture and hone their linguistic awareness of contemporary features of the English language. This investigation focuses on the understanding of abbreviations and the interpretation of hashtags and tweeter mood, all essential paralinguistic elements for understanding microblogging messages and becoming multiliterate (Kern, 2000). These parameters were chosen for examination because of their salience and high frequency in Twitter exchanges and, in the case of abbreviations and hashtags, the reported difficulty low-level L2 learners have in reliably interpreting them (Blattner, Dalola & Lomicka, 2015; 2016a; 2016b).

Research Questions

The research questions of the present study are the following:

1. What features in English-language tweets qualify as markers of abbreviations, hashtags and tweeter mood?
2. Can high intermediate ESL learners correctly identify and interpret these features in English language tweets written by native speakers? Do they do so at similar rates?
3. What is the nature of any observed errors?

Methods

Participants

25 participants were recruited on a voluntary basis from two levels (high intermediate) of a pathway program (which grants conditional college admission for academically qualified international students who need access to English language and other academic and social preparation for success in a US university setting; courses use communicative methodology in an immersion setting) at a southeastern university in the United States during the fall semester of 2015. They came from a variety of ethnic backgrounds, with first languages encompassing Arabic (n = 7), Chinese (n = 6), Spanish (n = 6), Portuguese (n = 3), Turkish (n = 1), Kazakh (n = 1) and French (n = 1). Fifteen participants were male; ten were female. Ages ranged from 19 to 37, with a mean age of 23.48 years (SD = 5.64). Participants ranged in terms of their exposure to the English language, from 20 months to 324 months, with a mean exposure time of 46.44 months (SD = 86.61 months). They also ranged in years of prior Twitter experience, from 0 to 7, with a mean of 2.12 years (SD = 2.60).

Procedure

Participants completed guided questionnaires (see Appendix A) composed of short modules of questions that directed their attention to and inference of three target pragmatic features—abbreviations, hashtags and indices of tweeter mood—as represented by the words, characters and accompanying media contained in each tweet (adapted from Blattner et al. 2015, 2016a, 2016b to be level-appropriate for more advanced learners by including a different array of components and fewer vocabulary-based questions). The questionnaire used open boxes to allow participants to input both their qualitative and quantitative answers as necessary, e.g. Can you identify Parameter X in the tweet? If YES, what is it? What words, punctuation, capitalization, hashtags, etc. helped you to identify Parameter X? Participants began by following a combination of three Anglophone personalities of their choosing in the categories of "Entertainment" and "Newsgroups" and selecting two tweets per week for individual analysis with the questionnaire. A suggested list of popular Anglophone personalities/groups known to be active on Twitter was provided in each category (so that those not familiar with Anglophone culture could still participate), but participants were also allowed and encouraged to choose figures not appearing on the list (see Table 1 for complete list of followed personalities). Participants took a screenshot of each tweet they chose for close analysis and submitted it with their questionnaire answers. A total of 450 questionnaires were completed during the course of the task (25 participants X 2 questionnaires/week X 9 weeks), 29 of which were excluded from the analysis due to incompleteness or rater discrepancy. Information on the participants' demographics, linguistic history and previous experience with social media was solicited via a separate background survey (see Appendix B). A post-task survey elicited open-ended written feedback from participants on their satisfaction and language-learning experience in this task (see Appendix C).

Table 1. Suggested Anglophone Twitter Personalities

	Entertainment	**Newsgroups**
Comedians	EllenDeGeneres: @TheEllenShow Jimmy Fallon: @jimmyfallon Jon Stewart: @TheDailyShow	CNN: @CNN Fox News: @FoxNews The Today Show: @TODAYshow Rachel Maddow MSNBC: @maddow
Sports Figures	LeBron James: @KingJames Serena Williams: @serenawilliams Lindsey Vonn: @lindseyvonn	
Musicians	Bruno Mars: @BrunoMars Justin Timberlake: @jtimberlake Kim Kardashian: @KimKardashian Rihanna: @rihanna	
Additional Personalities Selected by Participants	Taylor Swift: @taylorswift13 Hugh Jackman: @RealHughJackman Selena Gomez: @selenagomez Kobe Bryant: @kobebryant Brad Paisley: @BradPaisley Adam Levine: @adamlevine	CNN Breaking News: @cnnbrk

Data and Analysis

Two L1-English researchers independently examined each of the 421 English-language tweets for the target parameters of interest (abbreviations, hashtags and indices of tweeter mood) and then compared their expert results to those given by the participants. Cases of discrepancy among the raters (3/450) were excluded from the analysis. Token counts and percent correctness were then tabulated for each of the parameters, and instances of over-, under- and misidentification were then examined qualitatively.

Results

General Tweet Comprehension

Before delving into specifics pertaining to the various pragmatic and linguistic variables, the guided questionnaire asked participants to rate their initial overall comprehension of the tweet on a scale of 1 "no comprehension at all" to 7 "complete comprehension." This allowed the researchers to locate contexts of weakened comprehension before considering answers about particular parameters. The breakdown of overall tweet comprehension is presented in Figure 1 below.

Figure 1. General Tweet Comprehension

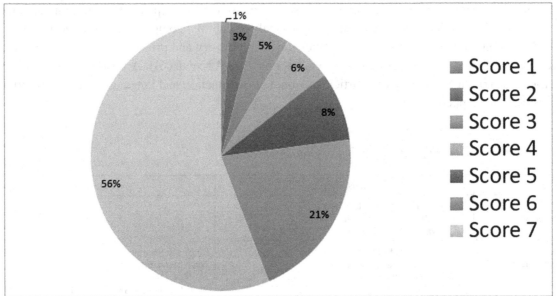

Of interest is the 56% of tweets for which participants rated their comprehension as 7 (complete) and the combined 29% of tweets for which they assessed it to be 5 or 6 (better than average, near-complete). Participants awarded less than 10% of tweets scores of 1, 2 and 3 (no, very little and marginal understanding). Because overall comprehension in an L2 is often dependent on metaphorical competence and language- and culture-specific references, the tweets receiving low ratings were inspected to see what had triggered the participant's comprehension difficulty. Two example tweets receiving low comprehensibility ratings are presented in Figures 2 and 3 below.

In the case of Figure 2, the participant stated that he did not understand why the tweeter was talking about Valentine's Day and chalk together in the same message, and proposed, based on his knowledge of the genre of tweets posted by this particular personality, that it was likely "some kind of prank where you make people eat chalk." This reveals the problematic element as being the participant's lack of cultural knowledge surrounding Valentine's Day traditions in the US, namely the exchange of small candy hearts with a chalky texture. The example in Figure 3, however, presents an error of another sort, that is, one that is both cultural and linguistic—the case of the idiomatic expression. When asked to explain the meaning of the tweet, the participant proposed, "The comedian Ellen DeGeneres made a joke about a lazy woman named Susan." While she understood that it was meant as a joke (identifiable to her by the phrase "just think"), she did not understand why a human being's movement would be described with the verb "spin," nor what it had to do with indicating a winning table in the competition referred to by Ellen. As such, her self-comprehension rating is quite just—on one hand, she is able to extract the strict denotative sense of the words, but on the other, she is unable to make them all make sense together, since she lacks knowledge of the American English idiomatic expression, "lazy susan," which is used to describe a revolving tray.

Figure 2. A misunderstood tweet: Participant rating of 1 (no understanding)

Figure 3. A misunderstood tweet: Participant rating of 2 (very little understanding)

Abbreviations

Abbreviations present a special challenge to comprehension in an L2 context, largely because they may be context-, culture- and/or individual-specific. In this study, we define abbreviations as any shortened form of a longer word, including truncations (e.g. *cray* for *crazy*), acronyms (e.g. *RIP* for *Rest In Peace*) and sms-speak (e.g. *thx* for *thanks*). A total of 116 abbreviations were observed in 111/421 (23.37%) tweets, of which participants identified 108/116 (93.10%). The breakdown of overall abbreviation comprehension is presented in Figure 4 below.

Figure 4. Abbreviation Identification Rates

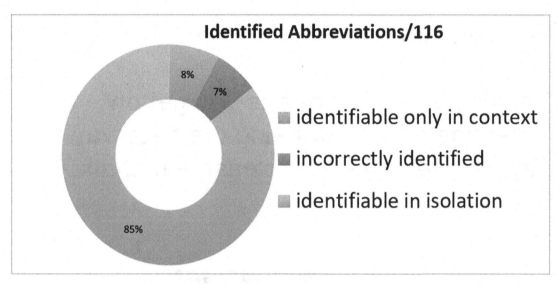

Participants' ability to understand the meaning of abbreviations was assessed via two direct questions in the abbreviations module (Appendix A: Questions #4, #5) which asked if they were: able to recognize any abbreviations in the tweet without looking them up or inferring their meaning from information given elsewhere in the tweet, or able to figure out the meaning of any abbreviations unknown to them, using just the larger context of the tweet. To be sure participants were accurate in their reporting of what they were able to recognize and what they had inferred/looked up, their answers to these questions were crosschecked with their answers to Question #5, which asked at the beginning of the questionnaire to report which words/expressions they had to look up in order to fully understand the tweet. Cases of discrepancy, i.e. where a participant cited looking up an abbreviation in Question #5, but then listed it as recognizable in isolation in Question #9, totaled 7 items in the dataset, which were excluded from the analysis. The answers to these questions allowed researchers to sort the nature of their comprehension into the above categories, shown in Figure 4. By far, the largest subgroup (99/116 or 85.34%) includes items that participants were able to identify in isolation. This category included all three types of abbreviations attested in the dataset: truncations, e.g. *gov* for *government*, acronyms, e.g. *RIP* for *Rest In Peace* and sms-speak, e.g. *Btw* for *By The Way*. Examples from this category can be found in Table 2 below. The next largest subgroup (9/116 or 7.75%) includes items that participants correctly identified, but only with the help of the larger context presented by the tweet. This category included only two of the three attested abbreviation types: acronyms, e.g. *SNL* for *Saturday Night Live* and sms-speak, e.g. *tmrw* for *tomorrow*, with the vast majority belonging to the acronym category. See Table 2 for more examples. Similar in size was the group of incorrectly identified abbreviations (8/116 or 6.89%), which contained only one type of abbreviation (acronyms, e.g. *HBO* for *Home Box Office*) and an item that was not an abbreviation, but that a participant mistook for one because it was written in all capital letters, e.g. *BOI* for *boy*. See Table 2 for more examples.

Table 2. Abbreviation Types

Category	Examples
Identifiable in isolation	[Truncations]: *B-day* (Birthday), *gov* (government) [sms-speak]: *S/O* (Shout Out), *BFF* (Best Friends Forever), *Btw* (by the way) [Acronyms]: *LA* (Los Angeles), *RIP* (Rest In Peace), *RV* (Recreational Vehicle), *U.N.* (United Nations)
Identifiable only in context	[Truncations]: none [sms-speak]: *tmrw* (tomorrow), *F/w* (Fashion Week) [Acronyms]: *SNL* (Saturday Night Live), *HBD* (Happy Birthday), *NLCS* (National League Championship Series)
Incorrectly identified	[Truncations]: none [sms-speak]: none [Acronyms]: *HBO* (Home Box Office), *GOP* (Grand Old Party), *S.C.* (South Carolina), *Bts* (Behind the scenes) [Other]: *BOI* (boy)

Hashtags

Hashtags also present a unique challenge to L2 comprehension because they require the reader to not only know the meaning of the words they contain, but also where one word ends and the next begins, e.g. #FATALBERT may be parsed as "Fat Albert" or "Fatal Bert." In this study, we define hashtags as any string of text attached to the symbol #, including single words, e.g. #weekend, short phrases, e.g. #mondaymotivation, and full sentences, e.g. #icanteven. The 421 tweets in our corpus contained 174 hashtags, 162 of which participants correctly identified (=93.10%). Of the 162 correctly identified, some 123 of them were correctly parsed and understood by participants for meaning (=70.69%). The hashtags that were identified but not understood fell into four main categories: cultural references, pop cultural references, idiomatic expressions and puns. A percentage breakdown is visualized in Figure 5 below.

The largest group of hashtag identification errors was that which contained cultural references to the United States (19/51 or 37.25%). These items included the names of American traditions, e.g. #trickortreat, American political events, e.g. #demdebate, and national social movements, e.g. #Selma50. See Table 3 for more examples. A similarly large error category was that involving pop culture references (16/51 or 31.37%). This contained the names of American films, e.g. #OurBrandIsCrisis, games from American television shows, e.g. #ThankYouNoteFriday (Jimmy Fallon), social media phenomena, e.g. #mcmonday (Man Crush Monday) and punchlines from American commercials, e.g. #DrinkGoodDoGood (Naked Juice). See Table 3 for more examples. Another well represented category of errors featured the use of collocations or idiomatic expressions (14/51 or 27.45%). Items in this category represented commonly used phrases, e.g. #onamission, as well as more figurative expressions, e.g. #keepyourcool. See Table 3 for more examples. The smallest error category featured puns or word play on colloquial and commonly used phrases (2/51 or 3.92%). These examples included the hashtag #MugLife (play on #ThugLife) to accompany a picture of two comedians celebrating National Coffee Day and the hashtag #AwwHellSnow (play on #AwwHellNo) to accompany a comedian's call for tweeter participation in sharing weird stories about winter.

Figure 5. Hashtag Identification Error Rates

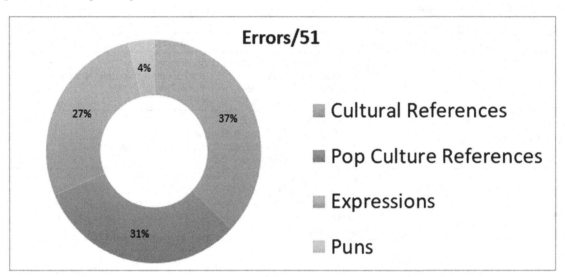

Table 3. Hashtag Error Types

Category	Examples
Cultural References	#Selma50 (voting rights), #demdebate, #2Degrees (climate change), #christmasfail (holiday mishaps), #VeteransDaySalute (holiday), #trickortreat (holiday), #SuperbowlSunday (sports event)
Pop cultural references	#Today9 (news channel), #CMAawards (awards show), #OurBrandIsCrisis (movie), #KUWTK (Keeping Up With The Kardashians tv show), #mcmonday (Man Crush Monday), #tbt (Throwback Thursday), #DrinkGoodDoGood (Naked Juice commercial), #nolimesneeded (Timberlake tequila commercial)
Collocations & Idiomatic expressions	#onamission, #keepyourcool, #gitterdone, #icanteven, #attheendoftheday, #potmeetkettle, #HighHorse, #tothenines, #OnYourSoapbox
Puns	#MugLife, #AwwHellSnow

Tweeter Mood

Indices of tweeter mood, or the expressed emotional state of the tweeter in his tweet, present a unique challenge to L2 comprehension because they may be indexed via multiple independent, sometimes extralinguistic features, making them easy to spot and parse, or they may require readers to decode written words with an attention to nuance, sarcasm or figurative speech that may be culture- and/or individual-specific. Participants correctly identified tweeter mood in 127 of the 421 tweets (30.17%), via one or a combination of various linguistic, indexical or visual clues. A breakdown of these strategies is visualized in Figure 6.

Figure 6. Strategies for Understanding Tweeter Mood

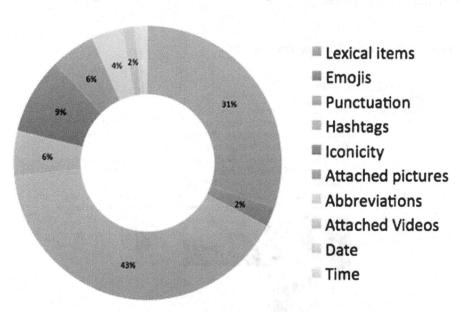

Strategies for Understanding Tweeter Mood

- Lexical items
- Emojis
- Punctuation
- Hashtags
- Iconicity
- Attached pictures
- Abbreviations
- Attached Videos
- Date
- Time

Participants' ability to understand tweeter mood was assessed via a direct question at the end of the mood module which asked them to list all features of the tweet they referred to when deciding on their assessment of the tweeter's mood. Their answers to this question allowed researchers to sort the nature of their comprehension into the above categories. For every answer, participants reported having consulted at least two features. The following results report raw counts for each strategy, which is why the total number of reported strategies outnumbers the number of tweets in which these strategies were reported. The feature that participants made use of most frequently when making sense of tweeter mood (43% of the time) was punctuation, e.g. repeated strings of exclamation points, questions marks, ellipses or combinations thereof. The next most frequent strategy (31% of the time) was emotionally charged lexical items of various grammatical categories: nouns, e.g. *love/luv*, verbs, e.g. *like*, adjectives, e.g. *awesome*, and exclamations, e.g. *congrats*. A much larger gap separates the two most common strategies from the remaining eight. The most frequent category in this group of lesser-used strategies (9% of the time) was iconicity, or the correspondence between visual representation and meaning, e.g. capital letters to indicate anger or excitement or the use of unparsable symbols for expletives, e.g. *This game is AWESOME* (index of intensity of word represented in capital letters), *B!@#$ better have my trophy* (index of comical anger in word represented by unreadable symbols). The next most common strategies were hashtags, e.g. *#SoSeriousOnSet* (index of seriousness/professionalism), and reference to pictures that had been included in the tweet, e.g. a picture of shirtless male strippers who predicted the World Series winners with the color of their uniforms (index of joviality). Following these was reference to abbreviations (4% of the time), e.g. *U* for 'you', *w* for 'with', emojis (2% of the time), e.g. (laughing until crying) emoji in response to an event that the tweeter found extremely funny, attached videos (2% of time), e.g. a video of the tweeter laughing at an audience member jumping up and down uncontrollably (index of joviality), a date mentioned in tweet/that tweet was posted (1% of the time), e.g. 9/11 (index of sadness), and a particular moment in time mentioned in tweet/that tweet was posted (1% of the time), e.g. 12 midnight (index of excitement for the kick-off of important days). See Table 4 for a more examples, ordered top to bottom from most to least common.

Table 4. Strategies for Making Sense of Tweeter Mood

Category	Examples
Punctuation	!!!, !!!!!!!!!!!!!!!!, ??, ??????????, ?!, …
Lexical Items	Nouns: tragedy, love/luv, Verbs: celebrate, love/luv, like, scream, dance, cry, can't wait Adjectives: awesome, amazing, best, sad, happy, honored, excited Exclamation: congrats, wow, thanks, yahoo, yaassss Intensifiers: totes, forreals/forrill
Iconicity	This game is AWESOME, I NEED!!!!! TO !!!! CALM DOWN!!!!, UNREAL., B!@#$ better have my trophy
Hashtags	#christmasfail, #SoSeriousOnSet, #WeAreInThisTogether, #icanteven, #keepyourcool, #OnYourSoapbox, #keepWalking, #soexcited, #Blessed
Attached Pictures	
Abbreviations	lol/lolololol (laugh out loud), nm (nevermind), btw (by the way), ffs (for f--- - sake), stfu (shut the f--- up), idgaf (I don't give a f----), wtf (what the f---)
Emojis	(smiling), (laughing until crying), (sad), (shocked), (mad), (whatever), (in love), (meh/unimpressed), (good job/agreement)
Attached Videos	Video of tweeter smiling, video of tweeter laughing and dancing, video of two guests on tweeter's talkshow dancing
Date	9/11 (commemoration of US attacks)
Time	12 midnight (to kick off beginning of birthdays/holidays/special events), 4:20 (code term for a common hour of marijuana consumption)

DISCUSSION

The linguistic items under investigation are commonly used in everyday exchanges in English. However, our results indicate that English learners at a high intermediate level, although overwhelmingly able to interpret the global meaning of tweets in English, still show gaps in their comprehension of linguistic variables with a cultural, pragmatic or figurative component. In this series of tasks, they performed best at interpreting the meaning of abbreviated forms in English, even to the point of being able to sight-read abbreviations in isolation and outside of the narrowed context of the tweet. Situations of inaccessible abbreviations did arise in just under 10% of identifications, and were triggered by either the presence of an uncommon abbreviation or a lack of awareness of the cultural phenomenon to which it referred. Although participants reported being able to make sense of the vast majority of abbreviations without the larger context of the tweet, they also reported explicitly using that context when faced with less frequent abbreviations or forms they had no previous experience with. This was not surprising considering traditional textbook material is often narrow and decontextualized, which limits any further pragmatic inferring from the part of the learners. Next in terms of decodability for these learners was hashtags. While the rate of hashtag understandability hovered at around 70%, areas of comprehension breakdown emerged in contexts requiring cultural awareness of American traditions and present-day media-based phenomena. We also found evidence of figurative language in the form of idiomatic expressions and puns creating hindrances in learners' comprehension. The most difficult parameter for learners at this level was, by far, tweeter mood (~30% correct). They most commonly relied on punctuation as a visual cue to the tweeter's mood, followed by emotionally charged lexical items, most of which were high-frequency. When they were unable to make sense of the lexical items contained in the tweet, they then reverted to using other visual strategies, including iconicity, attached videos and pictures and emojis, which also often mislead them when tweeters were speaking figuratively or ironically. We did, however, find evidence that they were able to access some of the lexical content involved in emotional expression, unlike what Blattner, Dalola & Lomicka (2016b) found in beginning French learners interpreting tweeter mood in French-language tweets. This finding supports Schmidt (1993), who noted that factors such as expectation, frequency, saliency, skill level and task demands all influence the ability that learners have to notice input. In their open-ended responses, Participants #7, 9, 14, 19, 21 and 24 mentioned several items, such as "on your soapbox," "high horse" and "forrill/forreals" as examples of lexical items/expressions they had not previously encountered before this task. In addition, over 80% of participants reported abbreviations to be the most interesting feature type to learn on account of their prevalence in electronic discourse, revealing their understanding of the role of such linguistic elements in everyday interactions. As such, these findings served to reinforce the students' interest in the task because it assisted them in discovering new words in authentic and relevant contexts, which they could forecast themselves using them in their own language production in the future.

As educators we see these results as a call to integrate more activities that focus on developing learners' ability to notice input that is unavailable in traditional textbooks. In particular, it is in high intermediate language courses taught in an immersion context that learners must engage in tasks that do not simply emphasize the development of grammar and communicative knowledge, but rather focus on sociopragmatic elements, which represent a ubiquitous dimension of language use that is often viewed as cumbersome or peripheral to L2 acquisition (Hashemian & Talebi Nezhad, 2013). In addition, it is essential for students to notice and understand the differences in terms of linguistic norms that microblogging tools and other electronic media offer. To be considered proficient in a foreign language, learners must nowadays be able to function in the world of social media. Following daily news and events requires a certain mastery of the twittersphere. Dissemination and retrieval of information via social media have become normalized, but seemingly not enough to be included in language textbook material. Consequently, incorporating activities comparable to the one described in this study has become a needed addition for serving language learners on the road to becoming active members of a second language society. Williams (2009) rightfully describes the need for language learners to have access to and understand the linguistic norms associated with a particular technology, before developing the ability and linguistic skills to use electronic platforms adequately and following conventional norms. While the ability to decode metaphors, idioms or puns in a foreign language might not appear as essential skills of self-expression, with social media and the linguistic playfulness it encourages in full expansion, we argue that it has become a necessary linguistic ability, not only for correct interpretation, but also for authentic language production. In addition, the conceptual appropriateness that typifies native speakers is one of the integral traits of native-speaker competence that language learners often perceive as the ultimate goal of language acquisition.

CONCLUSION

This study was conducted in order to determine how ESL learners understand short microblogging posts focusing on certain elements specific to microblogging spheres like Twitter, as well as to determine this social media's suitability for noticing new types of input that are absent from traditional teaching material. The results showed that the linguistic task assigned to the participants provided them with exposure to cultural and linguistically relevant input not present in traditional language textbooks. This suggests that language instructors may benefit from incorporating similar noticing activities involving Twitter, since the skill is necessary for implicit learning (Ellis, 2002a; 2002b), (conceptual) fluency, and fulfilling the knowledge gap in the use of L2 (idiomatic) language. In this guided observation task, participants were able to notice input that is not salient in foreign language textbooks, and, as noted by Hattem (2014), would unlikely be acquired *sans intervention* (p. 42). Such input allowed exposure to linguistic forms influenced by pop culture references and current events, as well as hashtag use, a widespread indexing system that has migrated to other social media platforms. Furthermore, uncommon forms in the tweets prompted the learners to investigate the meaning of English acronyms, abbreviations and truncations. Similarly, learner difficulty in reliably interpreting idiomatic/metaphorical expressions in authentic contexts highlights the need for a more inclusive curriculum in regard to pragmatic instructions (Kasper, 1997). As explained by Ellis (2002a, 2002b), regular or repeated exposure to similar input reinforces students' current knowledge and allows them to implicitly defer the meaning of new lexical items, such as abbreviations or idiomatic expressions, typically encountered in online social media. Finally, developing L2 digital literacy is an indispensable asset for a 21st-century language learner, not just for academic success, but for their future professional career(s) (Preston, 2012). As Hafner, Chik and Jones (2013) highlighted, it is evident that the communication that occurs in digital media demands a different set of skills from those traditionally taught in foreign language classrooms. The ESL learners who took part in this study were guided via the progressive questioning in the questionnaire to notice features of authentic input which allowed them to become familiar with the sociopragmatic norms of Twitter, and interact with unknown elements in L2 digital communication more generally. Over time, these opportunities can promote autonomous learning (Little, 2015), which allows students to discover new L2 venues and communities of practice outside the classroom context. We, therefore, argue that complementing L2 curricula with digitally-based activities improves L2 learners' ability to evaluate perspectives and practices on their own, and ultimately enhances their understanding of L2 online social media. The development of social literacy, or Twitteracy, is arguably an essential skill for the next generation of language learners, as it is via social media that they are the most likely to inform and express themselves in an L1 or L2. There is nothing stagnant about electronic social media and as it continues to evolve, and similar studies are, no doubt, underway which will further reveal the full potential of using microblogging tools in a culturally constructive way in foreign language classes at every level.

REFERENCES

Abraham, L., & Williams, L. (2009). The discussion forum as a component of a technology-enhanced Integrated Performance Assessment. In L. Abraham, & L. Williams (Eds.), Electronic Discourse in Foreign Language Learning and Teaching (pp. 291-317). Series: Language Learning & Language Teaching. Amsterdam: John Benjamins. doi:10.1075/lllt.25.21abr

Antenos-Conforti, E. (2009). Microblogging on Twitter: Social networking in intermediate Italian classes. In L. Lomicka & G. Lord (Eds.), *The next generation: Social networking and online collaboration in foreign language learning* (pp. 59–90). San Marcos, TX: CALICO.

Bardovi-Harlig, K. (2001). Empirical evidence of the need for instruction in pragmatics. In K. Rose & G. Kasper (Eds.), *Pragmatics and language teaching* (pp. 13–22). Cambridge, UK: Cambridge University Press. doi:10.1017/CBO9781139524797.005

Blattner, G., Dalola, A., & Lomicka, L. (2015). Tweetsmarts: A pragmatic analysis of well-known native speaker Tweeters. In Researching language learner interactions online: From social media to MOOCs (E. Dixon and M. Thomas, Eds.) (pp. 213-236). San Marcos, TX: Computer Assisted Language Instruction Consortium.

Blattner, G., Dalola, A., & Lomicka, L. (2016a). Twitter in foreign language classes: Initiating learners into contemporary language variation. In Handbook of Research on Learning Outcomes and Opportunities in the Digital Age (pp. 769–797). Hershey, PA: IGI Global. doi:10.4018/978-1-4666-9577-1.ch034

Blattner, G., Dalola, A., & Lomicka, L. (2016b). Mind Your Hashtags: A Sociopragmatic Study of Student Interpretations of French Native Speakers' Tweets. In Handbook of Research on Foreign Language Education in the Digital Age (pp. 33–58). Hershey, PA: IGI Global. doi:10.4018/978-1-5225-0177-0.ch003

Blattner, G., & Fiori, M. (2011). Virtual social network communities: An investigation of language learners' development of socio-pragmatic awareness and multiliteracy skills. *CALICO*, *29*(1), 24–43. doi:10.11139/cj.29.1.24-43

Blattner, G., & Lomicka, L. (2012). Facebook: The Social Generation of Language Learners. *Apprentissage des Langues et Systèmes d'information et de communication, 15*(1), 1-36.

Blyth, C. (2015). Exploring the complex nature of language and culture through intercultural dialogue. In D. Koike & C. Blyth (Eds.), *Dialogue in Multilingual and Multimodal Communities* (pp. 139–165). Philadelphia, PA: John Benjamins. doi:10.1075/ds.27.05bly

Cole, D., & Meadows, B. (2013). Avoiding the essentialist trap in intercultural education: Using critical discourse analysis to read nationalist ideologies in the language classroom. In F. Dervin & A. Liddicoat (Eds.), *Linguistic for Intercultural Education* (pp. 29–47). Amsterdam, Netherlands: John Benjamins. doi:10.1075/lllt.33.03col

Ellis, N. (2002a). Frequency effects in language processing: A review with implications for theories of implicit and explicit language acquisition. *Studies in Second Language Acquisition*, *24*(2), 143–188. doi:10.1017/S0272263102002024

Ellis, N. (2002b). Reflections on frequency effects in language processing. *Studies in Second Language Acquisition*, *24*(2), 297–339.

Fitzgerald, B. (2012, August 8). The 17 most-visited websites in the world. *The Huffington Post*. Retrieved from http://www.huffingtonpost.com/news/most-visited-websites

Gao, F., Luo, T., & Zhang, K. (2012). Tweeting for learning: A critical analysis of research on microblogging in education published in 2008-2011. *British Journal of Educational Technology*, *43*(5), 783–801. doi:10.1111/j.1467-8535.2012.01357.x

Gee, J., & Hayes, E. R. (2011). *Language and learning in the digital age*. New York, NY: Routledge.

Greenhow, C., & Gleason, B. (2012). Twitteracy: Tweeting as a New Literacy Practice. *The Educational Forum*, *76*(4), 464–478. doi:10.1080/00131725.2012.709032

Hafner, C., Chik, A., & Jones, R. H. (2013). Engaging with digital literacies in TESOL. *TESOL Quarterly*, *47*(4), 812–815. doi:10.1002/tesq.136

Hanna, B. E., & de Nooy, J. (2003). A funny thing happened on the way to the forum: Electronic discussion and foreign language learning. *Language Learning & Technology*, *7*(1), 71–85.

Hanna, B. E., & de Nooy, J. (2009). *Learning Language and Culture via Public Internet Discussion Forums*. New York, NY: Palgrave Macmillan. doi:10.1057/9780230235823

Hassal, T. (2008). Pragmatic performance: what are learners thinking? In E. Alcon Soler & A. Martinez Flor (Eds.), *Investigating pragmatics in foreign language learning, teaching and testing* (pp. 72–93). Buffalo, NY: Multilingual Matters. doi:10.21832/9781847690869-006

Hattem, D. (2012). The Practice of microblogging. *The Journal of Second Language Teaching and Research*, *1*(2), 38–70.

Hattem, D. (2014). Microblogging activities: Language play and tool transformation. *Language Learning & Technology*, *18*(2), 151–174.

Hattem, D., & Lomicka, L. (2016). What the tweets say: A critical analysis of Twitter research in language learning from 2009-2016. *E-Learning and Digital Media*, *13*(1-2), 5–23. doi:10.1177/2042753016672350

Jones, R. (2016). Digital literacies. In E. Hinkle (Ed.), *Handbook of research into second language teaching and learning* (Vol. III, pp. 286–298). London: Routledge.

Kasper, G. (1997). The role of pragmatics in language teaching education. In K. Baardovi-Harlig & B. Hartford (Eds.), *Beyond Methods: Components of Second Language Teacher Education* (pp. 113–136). New York: McGraw-Hill.

Kern, R. (2000). *Literacy and language teaching*. Oxford: Oxford University Press.

Kramsch, C. (2014). The challenge of globalization for the teaching of foreign languages and cultures. *Electronic Journal of Foreign Language Teaching*, *11*(2), 2249–2254.

Lankshear, C., & Knobel, M. (2006). New literacies: Everyday practices and classroom learning (2nd ed.). Milton Keyes: Open University Press.

Little, D. (2015). Language learner autonomy, Vygotsky and sociocultural theory: Some theoretical and pedagogical reflections. In K. Schwienhorst (Ed.), *Learner autonomy in second language pedagogy research: Challenges and issues* (pp. 5–28).

Lomicka, L., & Lord, G. (2012). A tale of tweets: Analyzing microblogging among language learners. *System*, *40*(1), 48–63. doi:10.1016/j.system.2011.11.001

Mompean, J., & Fouz-Gonzalés, J. (2016). Twitter based EFL pronunciation instruction. *Language Learning & Technology*, *20*(1), 166–190.

Oreskovic, A. (2015). Here's another area where Twitter appears to have stalled: Tweets per day. *Business Insider*. Retrieved September 10, 2016 from http://www.businessinsider.com/twitter-tweets-per-day-appears-to-have-stalled-2015-6

Perifanou, M. A. (2009). Language micro-gaming: Fun and informal microblogging activities for language learning. *Communications in Computer and Information Science*, *49*(1), 1–14.

Preston, J. (2012, February 29). If Twitter is a work necessity. *The New York Times*. Retrieved from http://www.nytimes.com/2012/03/01/education/digital-skills-can-be-quickly-acquired.html

Schmidt, R. (1990). The role of consciousness in second language learning. *Applied Linguistics*, *11*(2), 129–158. doi:10.1093/applin/11.2.129

Schmidt, R. (1993). Awareness and second language acquisition. *Annual Review of Applied Linguistics*, *13*, 206–226. doi:10.1017/S0267190500002476

Schmidt, R. (1995). Consciousness and foreign language learning: A tutorial on attention and awareness in learning. In R. Schmidt (Ed.), *Attention and awareness in foreign language learning* (pp. 1–63). Honolulu, HI: University of Hawaii, National Foreign Language Resource Center.

Schmidt, R. (2001). Attention. In P. Robinson (Ed.), *Cognition and second language instruction* (pp. 3–32). Boston: Cambridge University Press. doi:10.1017/CBO9781139524780.003

Semiocast. (2012, July 30). Twitter reaches half a billion accounts more than 140 million in the U.S. Retrieved from http://semiocast.com/en/publications/2012_07_30_Twitter_reaches_half_a_billion_accounts_140m_in_the_US

Uso-Juan, E. (2007). The presentation and practice of the communicative act of requesting in textbooks: Focusing on modifiers. In E. Alcon & M. P. Safont (Eds.), *Intercultural language use and language learning* (pp. 223–244). Amsterdam: Springer. doi:10.1007/978-1-4020-5639-0_12

Vellenga, H. (2004). Learning pragmatics from ESL and EFL textbooks: How likely? *TESL-EJ8*(2). Retrieved from http://www.tesl-ej.org/wordpress/issues/volume8/ej30/ej30a3

Williams, L. (2009). Navigating and interpreting hypertext in French: New literacies and new challenges. In L. B. Abraham & L. Williams (Eds.), *Electronic Discourse in Language Learning and Language Teaching* (pp. 43–64). Amsterdam: John Benjamins. doi:10.1075/lllt.25.05wil

This research was previously published in the International Journal of Computer-Assisted Language Learning and Teaching (IJCALLT), 8(2); pages 1-19, copyright year 2018 by IGI Publishing (an imprint of IGI Global).

APPENDIX A: QUESTIONNAIRE

Questionnaire for each tweet

1.   Please rate on a scale of 1 (not at all) to 7 (completely) how well you understood this tweet.
2.   Which word(s)/expression(s) did you need to look up in order to fully understand the tweet? If none, type NA.
3.   Are there any abbreviations in this tweet? If YES, which one(s)?
4.   Can you recognize any abbreviations without looking them up or inferring their meaning from information given elsewhere in the tweet? If YES, please indicate which ones here.
5.   Are you able to figure out any abbreviations that are unknown to you using the larger context of the tweet? If YES, please indicate which ones here.
6.   Can you write the full corresponding word(s) and meaning(s) of all included abbreviations? If YES, please write them here.
7.   Do you use equivalent abbreviation(s) in your L1? If YES, please write them here.
8.   Are there any hashtags in this tweet? If YES, which one(s)?
9.   Examine each of the hashtags. Are any of them written in the same way as words in other languages?
10. If YES, look at how others have tagged them (by clicking on the hashtag and examining the list of tweets it appears in). Are all of the speakers tagging it also speaking English?
11. Does the tag indicate the same thing as in your original tweet?
12. Why do you think the tweeter has included this hashtag / these hashtags in the tweet?
13. Can you guess the mood of the tweeter? If YES, what is it?
14. What words, punctuation, capitalization, hashtags, etc. helped you identify the mood?
15. Now imagine you have a friend sitting nearby who speaks English as a second language, but isn't as experienced with it as you are. In the space below, translate this tweet for him/her into basic English (i.e. being careful to avoid slang, abbreviations, etc.). Pay attention not only to the language, formality, mood and content, but also to the cultural concepts mentioned therein.

APPENDIX B: BACKGROUND SURVEY

1.   Please type your initials below.
2.   What is your age?
3.   What is your gender?
4.   What do you consider your first language?
5.   What do you consider your second language?
6.   Do you speak any other languages? Please indicate them below.
7.   How long have you been exposed to the English language?
8.   How old were you when you first used Twitter?
9.   How old were you when you first used Facebook?
10. How old were you when you first used Instagram?
11. On average, how many hours per week do you spend on Twitter?
12. On average, how many hours per week do you spend on Facebook?
13. On average, how many hours per week do you spend on Instagram?

14. What kinds of people and groups do you follow and interact with on Twitter in your FIRST LANGUAGE?
15. What kinds of people and groups do you follow and interact with on Twitter in ENGLISH?
16. What kinds of people and groups do you follow and interact with on Twitter in ANY OTHER LANGUAGES you speak?
17. What kinds of people and groups do you follow and interact with on Facebook in your FIRST LANGUAGE?
18. What kinds of people and groups do you follow and interact with on Facebook in your ENGLISH?
19. What kinds of people and groups do you follow and interact with on Facebook in ANY OTHER LANGUAGE you speak?
20. What kinds of people and groups do you follow and interact with on Instagram in your FIRST LANGUAGE?
21. What kinds of people and groups do you follow and interact with on Instagram in your ENGLISH?
22. What kinds of people and groups do you follow and interact with on Instagram in your ANY OTHER LANGUAGE you speak?
23. Have you previously used social media in ENGLISH?
24. If you use it or have used it in English, is it a PASSIVE use (i.e. reading, liking other posts) or an ACTIVE use (i.e. posting, commenting)?
25. Rate the social networks from your preferred (1) to your least preferred (3).
26. Do you use any other social networks?

APPENDIX C: POST-TASK SURVEY

Thank you for your participation in the ESL Twitter project! Please rate the statements below on a scale of 1 to 7 (where 1 is "not at all" and 7 is "completely") based on your experience in this project. This survey should take 5 minutes or less to complete. We welcome all feedback.

1. Please indicate your initials below.
2. I liked participating in this Twitter project in English.
3. I have a better understanding of abbreviations in English because of my participation in this project.
4. I have a better understanding of hashtags in English because of my participation in this project.
5. I have a better understanding of tweeter mood in English because of my participation in this project.
6. Of abbreviations, hashtags and tweeter mood, which feature did you find the most interesting to study? Why?
7. What new words and expressions did you learn during this task? Give a few examples.
8. I think Twitter is a worthwhile place for learners to study the English language.
9. I used Twitter regularly (in any language) before this project.
10. I will use Twitter regularly (in any language) after this project.
11. I will continue to follow the same English speakers that I followed for this project now that this project is over.
12. I will follow other English speakers on Twitter now that this project is over.
13. Please leave any additional comments you have about this experience here.

Chapter 44
Social Networking and Language Learning:
Use of Instagram (IG) for Evaluating Oral Communication Skill

Fidel Çakmak
https://orcid.org/0000-0002-3285-7661
Alanya Alaaddin Keykubat University, Turkey

ABSTRACT

This chapter gives a brief overview on the use of social network sites (SNSs) for language learning and presents an empirical study of the use of Instagram (IG), one of the most popular SNSs, to assess learners' oral communication skills in the foreign language classroom. Several studies have mainly revealed the perceptions and preferences of learners in regards to using SNSs for learning grammar, vocabulary, L2 writing, reading, and speaking. In the current study, the performance scores of participants on an oral communication speaking task delivered both on IG and in class, as well as their scores on the Big Five personality traits as measured by the Quick Big Five Personality Test (QBFPT), were examined statistically. The results demonstrate IG facilitated students' performance in oral communication skill significantly and that personality traits do not predict the performance on IG, but the extroverted and conscientious are highly likely to achieve high scores in classroom.

INTRODUCTION

The world has become increasingly interconnected as people use devices and social platforms to form communities, at the same time mobile phones and tablets can also increase isolation as multiple political, ideological and cultural contexts both within and across communities intrude and place demands upon our attention and time. Today's era has marked itself by not only increasing the speed of information exchange dramatically but also increasing interconnectedness of people via mobile technologies. Digital tools and social media (often referred as social networking sites) are premised upon emergent mobile

DOI: 10.4018/978-1-6684-7123-4.ch044

technologies that have made feasible a whole new potential ecology for language learning. When well-configured, these SNSs can provide immersive connections between individuals even when they in fact exist in disparate spaces. In the first decade of the 2000s, Web 2.0 was introduced and enhanced the experience of active social media participation. It enhanced social connections and interaction with one another by introducing liking, posting, connecting, and blogging through the use of various platforms such as blogs, wikis. This enhanced experience increased user participation and social networking sites became commonplace. Over time the idea of mobility has evolved from initially referring to the devices to gradually include the mobility of people and shared exposure to the data underpinning different forms of digital social networks and media. This has allowed users of mobile media to become collaborative and interactive content sharers. Activities such as blogging, wikis, pod/screen casting, multimedia sharing have evolved as ways to stay connected with others (Zeng, 2018). By the end of the first decade of 2000s the social dimension of CALL got the attention of CALL scholars with two publications: The Handbook of Research on Web 2.0 and Second Language Learning by IGI Global, and The next generation: Social networking and online collaboration in foreign language learning by CALICO (Reinhardt, 2019). A volume of articles on the social impact of teaching resources employing Web 2.0 technologies and platforms for digital communication, information sharing and digital collaborations also emerged. This emergence of the social web has created an opportunity for learners to move from data acquisition to data creating and sharing and to connect to other people digitally. Since 2009, social network sites (SNSs) have attracted the attention of researchers and practitioners in the field of language teaching and there has been explosive growth in research publications on social media use in learning (Mao, 2014). This growth has been accelerated by the continued technological advancement in mobile devices, mobile network bandwidth and increasing mobile internet penetration in our lives. The research has explored effectiveness in regards to the learning outcomes, perceptions of learners as users, illuminated design issues and considerations when using social media tools for language learning. However, there has been less emphasis on theoretical and empirical studies on learning in general (Merchant, 2011) and a lack of experimental or longitudinal studies of the use of SNSs specifically (Ellison & Boyd, 2008; Lomicka & Lord, 2016). This chapter aims to provide a brief review on the use of Instagram (IG) as one of the most popular social networking sites for language learning and presents an empirical study of the use of IG to assess learners' oral communication skills in the foreign language classroom.

BACKGROUND

SNSs are online environments where people create a profile on public display and get connected to other people in the same environment for self-representation and data acquisition through personal connections (i.e., followers, friends, etc.). Additionally, the profiles display posts (self-representation data) marking users' connections, and popularity and appreciation data achieved through social activity in the SNS (Zourou, Potolia, & Zourou, 2017). The interactive experience of posters with their audience forms connections and can provide a feeling of attachment in the social world (Merchant, 2011). In another broad definition, SNS refers to "web-based services that allow individuals to (1) construct a public or semi-public profile within a bounded system, (2) articulate a list of other users with whom they share a connection, and (3) view and traverse their list of connections and those made by others within the system. The nature and nomenclature of these connections may vary from site to site." (Ellison & Boyd, 2008, p. 211). Such services encourage individuals to make visible connections among people who may be strangers but who share similar tastes, hobbies, and interests, and could actually be socially connected through mutual acquaintances, and encourages users to communicate with individuals in their social network. The presence of SNSs in our daily life has increased tremendously. From 2010 to 2018 the number of social media users worldwide increased from 0.97 billion to 2.46 billion, and foreseen growth is 2.9 billion by 2020 (Statista, 2017). The popularity of SNSs can be partly attributed to a desire to meet new people, exchange opinions, and to keep in touch with friends and other people that are already in our social circle (Lomicka & Lord, 2016). There can be powerful motives for staying tuned in to online networks for interaction and self-expression (Thorne, 2010). Social interaction and self-expression are two key functions of SNSs that are also necessary for language acquisition; therefore, integration of SNSs into language learning could create a context where language learning can occur (Brick, 2012; Huang & Su, 2018; McBride, 2009; Thorne, 2010) through interactions between digitally connected people and through self-expression (Greenhow, Robelia, & Hughes, 2009; Hwang & Cho, 2018). With this SNS integration, learners can be actively involved in more authentic social and communicative behavior than would be the case in classrooms (Brick, 2012; Chen, Lambert, & Guidry, 2010; Lomicka & Lord, 2009; McBride, 2009; Sun et al., 2017). This puts forward sociocultural approaches advocating for integration of SNSs into learning. Since the sociocultural approach focuses on learning through social interaction within a community of individuals, SNSs are particularly well-suited to the approach. They enable learners to interact with and observe other 'citizens' in the digital community, and to express and exchange opinions through social media sites. This fosters a sense of belonging, confidence in being a member of digital communities, and satisfies the need for self-expression (Doleck, Bazelais, & Lemay, 2017; Greenhow & Robelia, 2009) or presentation of identity (Leier, 2018; Lomicka & Lord, 2016; Reinhardt, 2019). Along similar lines, Haythornthwaite (2019) articulates the kinds of relations built within social networks and interaction where a "learning tie" between actors is established through interaction (p. 29). She remarks that empirical examination of connections between users is of importance since it can form a basic premise for social learning and an input for the design of learning environments. Hamid, Waycott, Kurnia and Chang (2015) clarify in what forms interactions can take place and identified three main interactions in online social network for learning 1) student-student 2) student-teacher 3) student content interactions. This mapping of interaction shows actors in the sites but it is important to bear in mind that SNSs are open to public view unless users have strict privacy, so exceptions to these interactions might also occur, there is always the possibility for unexpected connections with others to occur in addition to these enumerated actors.

INSTAGRAM (IG) AND LANGUAGE LEARNING

Language learning via IG has been explored in several studies. Some highlight the usability of IG in language classrooms due to its specific technical and social features. The majority of existing research is about the perception of the experience when language learners use IG to practice language skills. IG's navigational tools to edit posts, to add location, friends and keywords (hashtags), to tag photos or videos shared, as well as the exchange of opinions with other followers or "friends" through comments/posts (Handayani, 2016) all contribute to improving engagement. These features can help to retain the attention of scholars and practitioners in the educational field, as well as that of visual learners who benefit from the situated contextualized visual data presented in posts and videos. In addition to this, IG can enable users to take part in community building outside the classroom environment (Al-Ali, 2014) where they can enjoy their learning experience (Handayani, 2016). Last but not least, of the SNSs that are popular among the youth such as Facebook, IG and Twitter, IG has gained popularity quickly and is one of the most commonly used among young people (Al-Ali, 2014; Handayani, 2016) ages18 to 29 (Smith, 2015). It is suitable to utilize at most higher education institutes (HEI). Recently several studies have been published which look at the effects of Instagram use as a platform to facilitate language learning.

Yadegarfar and Simin (2016) investigated the effects of IG on grammatical accuracy of word classes among 92 Iranian TEFL students and also explored their perceptions of using IG for learning grammar accuracy for word classes. The experimental group was taught grammatical accuracy for word classes in sessions where English lessons and example sentences focusing on grammar accuracy of the word classes were provided via IG. The control group was exposed to face to face classroom teaching of the same material. Researchers found that the experimental group outperformed the control group in terms of grammatical accuracy of the presented word classes. Moreover, based on the students' responses showing their perceptions on using IG, the researchers noted that the experimental group had positive perceptions towards the use of IG for developing accuracy in relation with context and that IG served well for focusing on both interaction and linguistic content. A study relevant to linguistic structures was carried out by AlGhamdi (2018). In the research design, he set up an account named "i_english_m" which was followed by more than 48000 learners and uploaded English language content comprised of American English expressions and translations from Arabic to English. The posts lasted one minute in duration every day for two weeks. The content had two levels of difficulty: simple and complex. The researcher tracked the responses to each post, and the numbers of likes and views, and then evaluated satisfaction and preference toward the levels of structures. The result showed that the simple posts received the most likes and interactive attention from learners. This indicates that they preferred to engage with simple structures. This preference could be also be explained by the underlying philosophy of an Instagram account which is that users snap posts and connect people "in the moment" to grasp what is going on right now (Abbott, Donaghey, Hare, & Hopkins, 2013, p. 3). The study indicated that daily simple linguistic content might facilitate learners' motivation for language learning. This is a notable observation since the benefits of IG application use in language classes is also mentioned in association with increased motivation for learning echoes observations from other studies (Al-Ali, 2014; Kurniawan and Kastuhandani, 2016; Listinai, 2016; Munday, Delaney, & Bosque, 2016; Wulandari, 2019), supporting the rationale for using IG for classes. What was interesting in this case was that the followers were self-selected. Participation was open to anyone in the Arab world and others living in different countries. Since the account was anonymous, some learners and also family members tagged their friends and other family members to follow the account and take a note of the content. Getting the attention of others and making the learning circle grow highlights the potential for fast growth in an online language learning community.

Morshidi, Embi and Hashim (2019) explored the use of IG to promote reading among 11 young learners (4th graders) in an urban school in Meleka, Malaysia. The pupils were assigned a reading activity mixed with 2 week- reading activities in class followed by a 3-week series of IG video posts. The findings from interview, questionnaire, and observation notes show that IG was fun to integrate when teaching classes for young learners' and that the students were keen on reading in front of the cameras to post the videos on IG. They indicated that they appreciated likes and comments, which boosted their enthusiasm to make more posts on IG. This study's implication is in line with the practical application mentioned in Blattner and Lomicka's (2012) study which claims that SNS can work beyond classroom environment, and enable language progress in a fun environment wherever students feel like connecting.

Although this study shows positive outcomes from the data, there are areas for concern; specifically, the participants' profile of being young pupils. Their age leaves them especially vulnerable to potential online safety threats such as cyberbullying, offensive or vulgar language use in the comments, and exposure to nudge techniques such as likes on IG, allowing the service to track their personal data for marketing aims. These risks must be balanced against the benefits of the platform and ensuring privacy and appropriate moderation could be challenging in such context. Additionally, how reading skills are assessed could be improved during the process. Although it is claimed that respondents' positive perceptions of using mobile SNSs affect performance with an increase in learning experiences (Wong, Tan, Loke, & Ooi, 2015; Yang, 2013), a quantitative metric of increased performance rather than self-reported responses to a questionnaire would provide a more meaningful assessment of the actual effects of integrating IG when teaching reading. Munday, Delaney and Bosque (2016) highlighted the potential of IG to develop language use and cultural awareness by partaking in a challenge of describing a daily prompt (words or grammar phrases in Spanish). Students of Spanish were called to take part in the challenge with photos uploaded, hashtags and quotes added and then tagged with the word given on that day as #InstagramELE. The challenge provided an enhanced opportunity for practicing grammar studied in during those weeks in the month. Students learning Spanish in over 50 classes and in collaboration with over 70 teachers uploaded 32.000 pictures from all around the world. This project was an example of an online community coming together for language learning and provided interpersonal communication opportunities within that community through the posting of comments and/or responding comments. The teachers participated in the challenge by uploading photos for the showcase of culture and provided contextual explanations for words (lexical variations). The researchers concluded from the project that structured IG use in Spanish classes with activities such as the challenge were advantageous in attracting young adults for learning, providing both autonomous learning and cooperative learning opportunities, encouraging intrinsic motivation, and promoting skills growth for strategic and digital competence. Although these advantages of IG were not empirically evaluated in the project, the researchers suggested that the practitioners take privacy issues, the tracking of comments and an improved assessment of the participation in learning into consideration. The taking part in language project shows IG could be a useful digital authentic tool for imbuing students with enthusiasm (Leier, 2018) and promoting cooperation for learning out of the classroom environment and ultimately facilitate the learner becoming an engaged community member actively responsible for learning (Akbari, Naderi, Simons, & Pilot, 2016). Along similar lines, Kessler's (2013) study mentions that new forms of language have been welcomed in a social media context where learners and teachers are given opportunities to partake in meaningful language learning practice:

The digital landscape that we are immersed in not only provides us with access to information, but it also requires that we play an active role in the ongoing exchange of information. After all, it is a participatory culture that is being co-constructed. We are not only surrounded by potential corpora of authentic linguistic input, but we are expected to engage with one another around the construction of new forms of language in the realm of social media. This linguistically dense realm offers English teachers and learners unlimited opportunities to interact around meaningful, authentic, and diverse instances of language practice. (p. 616)

Another study on vocabulary and grammar use by Aloraini (2018) investigated the effect of Instagram posts (vocabulary or grammar) on the amount of EFL learners' production, accuracy of that production and the amount of feedback the user obtained. The findings showed vocabulary posts got more comments and had more errors than grammar posts with a small size effect. As for the accuracy of posts and amount of feedback received, these were not affected by the types of the posts. What this research concluded was that although there might be variation in the amount of posts as output, there was no variation in the quality of data. This would lead us to pay attention to the improvement of the output quality irrespective of the linguistic classification of posts. A study by Sukri, Mustapha, Othman, Aralas, and Ismail (2018) presented an example on the integration of IG in EFL classes. It showcased four students from a Malaysian context with a low proficiency who partook in a classroom activity presenting a short story entitled 'Tanjong Rhu' by Minfong Ho. The students were expected to upload a photo they liked to associate with their favorite character in the story, and then explain why they used that picture to depict their favorite character. The posts made were discussed in successive classroom sessions. This integration, though the procedures and outcome analysis were not refined, highlights how IG and combined language skills: in this case writing and speaking skills could be worked into English classes. In her paper, Handayani (2016) introduced effective simple implementations of IG in skills teaching in a descriptive way. Speaking exercises, posting field trip memories, role plays, review of a famous historical figure and pronunciation practice were all suggested as beneficial IG activities. For reading, sharing reading recommendations was suggested, however, this activity does not target language practice in reading but promotes practical literacy development through likes and suggestions. For writing, descriptive captioning with attention to grammatical structure and word choice based on photo inspiration and writing comments on a post were suggested to improve writing skills, notably creative writing. As for the listening skill, listening to posts of native speakers of English was suggested. This might be questionable since we are well aware of that there are other forms of English such as International English and English as Lingua Franca. In a follow-up study, Handayani (2017) investigated how eight students taking a Paragraph Writing course perceived descriptive captioning and photo inspiration writing activities on IG. When asked how they perceived the use of IG for their writing classes, expectedly, the students reported highly positive attitudes towards the use of Instagram in teaching writing. As a remark, the activities suggested by Handayani (2016; 2017) sound like they would be easily implementable, although their usefulness needs to be quantified and scientifically verified. IG when implemented in a classroom setting should result in an observable improvement in skills which can be verified with quantifiable data. Otherwise, the use of SNSs in the classroom cannot be viewed as anything more than a mere list of additional class activity suggestions. Another paragraph writing activity through IG was investigated by Hopkyns (2017). It had a similar research design, asking for student perceptions of IG both pre class and after two writing tasks on topics of their choice. Topics included observations of fellow university students, siblings, favorite artist and so forth. In association with the pictures posted participants were asked to make a short movie about the subjects and to present a narrative in four paragraphs with several associated pictures. The researcher found that students were well engaged in the activities and felt that these activities enabled the students to improve their writing and speaking skills as well as identify and take joy in the improvement in their writing. Another research focus of IG integration in language classes had to do with the perceptions of students towards use of IG in language classes. Akhiar, Mydin and Kasuma (2017) examined 110 university students' perceptions and attitudes towards the use of Instagram in English language writing classes. The students enrolled in English courses were given a descriptive writing activity based on the photos of people, locations, and various objects posted on IG. They then responded to the questionnaire and took part in group discussions. The findings show that the students perceived that collaboration and cooperation occurred during the writing activity and noted that they had improved communication between their peers and the teachers. Additionally, the students thought they improved their language proficiency. As for the writing activity, the students were very positive about their overall engagement in using IG. What was interesting among the findings is that although the students enjoyed experiencing learning through IG, the majority of them (%67) preferred the face to face lessons over the ones on IG. This indicates that students might consider IG as a supplementary learning tool in support of face to face classrooms, and use it to facilitate teaching and learning processes with fun self-exposure to ideas.

Kurniawan and Kastuhandani (2016) also mentioned effective uses of IG for creative writing activities such as acrostic poem writing and writing captions for past vacation pictures with a brief description of the procedures. Based on the observational notes they claimed that the students could develop creative ideas for their writing tasks and that students were actively involved in the tasks, strengthening their motivation for learning. Additionally and similarly, Shazali, Shamsudin and Yunus (2019) conducted an action research with 25 secondary school students to investigate the use of IG for developing writing ability and the students' attitudes towards IG. Before posting on IG, students were given a self-descriptive writing activity imagining what they would publish on an online website. Students' performance was graded with CEFR grading system and then students were assigned to partake in five writing tasks on IG to elicit feedback from peers in the comment section. Their performance was graded by teachers and when the tasks were completed, students were asked to describe their experience and later filled out a questionnaire about their perception of use of IG in the writing class. The findings showed that students' CEFR level increased and that they adopted positive attitudes towards the use of IG in writing classes. The study's finding in regards to attitudes towards the use of IG is expected, however, the research design lacks generalizable features and the clarification on the writing tasks, and how each of them were to be evaluated could have been more explicit for the practitioners. Another study from a secondary school context was conducted by Sirait and Marlina (2018) in which the researchers explored how students could use IG for peer-review activities when writing descriptive texts. Students were given a list of steps such as opening up an Instagram account, sending the essays to the admin of the group class account and giving feedback and comments. They were then asked to list advantages and disadvantages of IG. Technical features of IG such as captioning, commenting, responding, and editing were mentioned as advantages; while the affordability of connectivity and mobile devices were mentioned as disadvantages. Similar to other research focused on the effect of IG use on descriptive writing skills, yet with a different research design than the ones above mentioned, Soviyah and Etikaningsih (2018) conducted an experimental research designed to investigate the effects of the use of IG on the students' performance in writing descriptive texts. 50 students in a private high school in Yogyakarta, Indonesia were assigned to one of two groups: experimental and control. While the experimental group received the treatment of writing tasks involving using Instagram, the control group received traditional classroom teaching. Both groups received the same material and took a writing test before and after the treatment. Based on the statistical analysis of the pre and post-tests, the researchers found that there was a statistically significant difference between the writing performance of students who used IG and the students who didn't. They concluded that Instagram could serve as an effective educational tool for teaching how to write descriptive texts. Like Soviyah and Etikaningsih (2018), Listiani (2016) also investigated the effect of IG on students' writing summaries of a text. 40 students with high and low motivation were assigned to experimental and control group. The experimental group used Instagram as a teaching technique, whereas the control group received teacher centered writing. Results based on pre and post-test analysis indicated that students using Instagram outperformed their counterparts in writing summary texts, which supports the conclusion that IG can serve as an effective tool in language classrooms. Khalitova and Gimaletdinova (2016) carried out a case study of using IG in teaching English to 50 advanced level students studying at HEI in Russia. They explored students' perception of the mobile- assisted language learning activities and investigated whether using IG in English classes improved listening comprehension. Students were randomly assigned to experimental and control group, where the former were supposed to watch videos (n=34) of 20 seconds each with their mobile phones, and the latter did not receive the treatment. Based on the analysis of results, the findings also indicated that IG improves students' listening comprehension skills especially in the ability to understand opinions and find specific information in speech.

Practicing speaking skills through SNSs has not been examined much in the research of SNSs and language learning. The notable studies were a study by Hitosugi (2011), where Ning, an SNS for the Japanese context, was found to enable students to work in cooperation and provide feedback to each other on their oral communication projects in Japanese. Another study by Sun et al. (2017), in which improvement in speaking skill was observed in the performance of two first grade young learner groups from an urban public elementary in Beijing, China. The experimental group (n=37) who utilized mobile SNSs for speaking practice showed greater improvement when compared to a control group (n=35) who did not use mobile SNSs. The application used by the experimental group was Papa, which is a Chinese audio streaming platform where users can interact for sharing audio files and posting pictures, and also make recordings and comments through their profiles. Oral language improvement was found as an outcome of the combination of classroom activities with the mobile SNS *Papa*. It is suggested that activities promoting social interaction and task-based activities such as information providing or interactive reasoning could be carried out by the integration of a mobile SNS. In line with these studies and their research focus on speaking improvement, Azlan, Zakaria, & Yunus (2019) investigated how integrating Instagram into task-based speaking tasks affected learning and explored pupils' motivation when using IG. Eight low proficiency pupils (four from pre-school and four from primary school) from Negeri Sembilan, Malaysia were selected. The findings from the research showed that IG helped pupils improve their speaking skills and at the same time, motivated them to be involved in task-based learning. Additionally, it made them feel connected with family and friends when sharing their activities. Students also felt excitement about being exposed to the IG integration in speaking classes. Leier (2018) notably indicated that the use of IG helped learners to build online relationships consciously and allowed them to be responsible for curating them. Wulandari (2019) also investigated whether IG Video Blog (Vlog) facilitated EFL's speaking ability. It also examined students' perceptions on the implementation. 28 students taking a Speaking 1 course were assigned an IG Vlog every two weeks, which entailed uploading an Instagram post of their 1-3 minute-long video. They took pretests before the treatment and posttests after the treatment. The findings showed that the integration of IG Vlog into the speaking classes improved the learners' speaking skills in regards to pronunciation, fluency, vocabulary, syntax, the target language use as well as an increase in motivation. With a qualitative research study design, Rahman (2018) investigated students' perspectives on posting photos on IG and how the integration of social media related to boosting their confidence for speaking English. She found that posting on IG did increase their confidence about speaking in that: a) they were less anxious on IG compared to the classroom b) IG boosted reported confidence in speaking c) the students used the platform to collaborate with peers for feedback.

When it comes to the concerns related to the use of IG in the educational environment, the first and major one is related to privacy. Language learning environments on SNSs are open to others publicly and can be archived. Learners (users) should be well aware of the responsibility of their own posts, likes, or comments, which may create risks in future. The online content of any materials should serve primarily as an educational tool for the learning community. Learners should be informed about the code of conduct, and educated as to how to behave in such socially networked platforms (Lomicka & Lord, 2009). Additionally, the terms of service (especially age limitations for opening an account in the country of residence), privacy policies and security of student data should be taken into account when integrating IG use into language learning. Learners' rights and privacy should be protected so that they are inhibited to the least degree when giving their own responses (Aloraini, 2018; Ellison & Boyd, 2008; Erben, Ban, & Castañeda, 2009; Kukulska-Hulme, Lee, & Norris, 2017; Leire, 2018; Lomicka & Lord, 2009; van Dijk, 2006). Additionally, students may not have SNSs accounts or may think participating in SNSs is a waste of time and be unwilling to partake in the use of SNSs as a part of their learning (Abbott, Donaghey, Hare, & Hopkins, 2013; Taşkıran, Gümüşoğlu, & Aydın, 2018). We cannot force students to open an account just for learning, as such could be an imposition. The learners must be willing to use IG for their own learning. Also, assessment of the data for learning outcomes is crucial when using IG for learning. Teachers need to specify how learners can partake in such social network sites for learning and also inform students as to how their participation is going to be assessed beforehand. (Sukri et al., 2018). Learners must be informed about feedback and how feedback can be received both peer to peer, and teacher to learner. (McBride, 2009) Policies should specify the expected outcomes for learning, manage the language data set, and encourage students to avoid any violations of codes of conduct with regards to privacy, shyness, social exclusion, or cyberbullying (Griffith & Liyanage, 2008; Thomas, Reinders, & Warschauer, 2013). Fostering this awareness could be done by training for networking for language learning. The abovementioned studies rarely mentioned the necessity of training for SNS participation and setting expectations for acceptable rules of interaction. If learning is to be facilitated through SNSs, then expectations should be shared before any treatment so that participants know the boundaries in advance and how to appropriately show their presence in the digital community. It is vital to afford time for student to absorb the implications of new technology before they are assigned any learning tasks through (Erben et al., 2009) speaking in the context of SNSs. They should be guided as they negotiate appropriate use of the SNS and make a tangible transition from seeing them as a fun familiar network into a learning zone. This line of thinking, that the training of learners prior to being socially connected on SNS, and giving them time to understand the new treatment, is beneficial has its justification in the research. Laghos and Nisiforou (2018) conclude that students need time to develop success in effectively communicating while learning in web-based groups through planned activities. Students require time to get to know their peers, and then effectively contribute and collaborate with them on the SNS. In other words, students need time to get to know one another and interact with each other in order to build a sense of community. The accumulation of interactions over time leads to on-topic productivity in terms of language learning and discussions being more topic or course related. To conclude, there is a timeline in which we start with a wide open zone, get to know one another, build ties between us and then move on to engage in productive interactions in L2 through sustained network connections.

PERSONALITY

Personality has been viewed in a variety of different ways in social science as a predictor of behavior patterns both socially and academically (Johnson, Krueger, Bouchard, & McGue, 2002). The impact of personality has long been one of the subjects on the language research agenda (Biedroń, 2016). Now that language learners with their individual features are a focal point in designing materials and teaching activities tailored to the learner, cognitive styles and personality can be taken into account as a predictor not only of information processing but also (Messick, 1994) to predict what a learner is "likely to do" (Sharp, 2008, p. 18). In conjunction with predicted behavior, personality is regarded as having an influential impact on second language learning (Lightbrown & Spada, 2006). There are several studies showing the relationship between personality differences as measured by various indicators such as Eysenck Personality Questionnaire (EPQ) (Eysenck & Eysenck, 1985), The Myers Briggs Type Indicator (MBTI) (Myers, McCaulley, Quenk, & Hammer, 1998) and the Five Factor Model (FFM) (e.g., Goldberg, 1992; McCrae & Costa, 2003) and learning strategies and outcomes. Some of the existing research found a direct observable relationship (Griffith, 1991, Li & Quin, 2006) and some did not (Carrell, Prince, & Astika, 1996; Sharp, 2008) between the personality of learners and the strategies they adopt for language learning.

Of the personality indicators mentioned above, The Five Factor Model (FFM) is a more recent and popular personality scale providing "a good representation of the central features of personality" (Dörnyei, 2005, p. 14) in five key categories- *Openness to Experience, Conscientiousness, Extraversion, Agreeableness and Neuroticism*. Dörnyei (2005) discusses personality more within the borders of personality psychology rather than the Big Five model's integration of cross-situational factors. He views personality as a construct involving a more eclectic structure of personality taking situational factors and processes in particular contexts into consideration. Additionally, the research on personality portrays individual differences, though not universally, since the FFM is not valid for all people yet covers a large majority of them (Allik, Hrebíčková, & Realo, 2018). However, the investigation of the development of personality with environmental and biological factors taken into consideration could be complementary to explain these traits properly. Dörnyei (2005) describes five broad personality dimensions with a list of adjectives reflecting the high scorers and low scorers on its scales (p. 15).

- Openness (to experience): High scorers are imaginative, curious, flexible, creative, moved by art, novelty seeking, original, and untraditional; low scorers are conservative, conventional, down-to-earth, unartistic, and practical.

- Conscientiousness: High scorers are systematic, meticulous, efficient, organized, reliable, responsible, hard-working, persevering, and self-disciplined; low scorers are unreliable, aimless, careless, disorganized, late, lazy, negligent, and weak-willed.

- Extraversion: High scorers are sociable, gregarious, active, assertive, passionate, and talkative; low scorers are passive, quiet, reserved, withdrawn, sober, aloof, and restrained.

- Agreeableness: High scorers are friendly, good-natured, likeable, kind, forgiving, trusting, cooperative, modest, and generous; low scorers are cold, cynical, rude, unpleasant, critical, antagonistic, suspicious, vengeful, irritable, and uncooperative.

- Neuroticism: High scorers are worrying, anxious, insecure, depressed, self-conscious, moody, emotional, and unstable; low scorers are calm, relaxed, unemotional, hardy, comfortable, content, even tempered, and self-satisfied.

As SNSs provide opportunities to present identity (Leier, 2018; Lomicka & Lord, 2016; Mehdizadeh, 2010; Reinhardt, 2019), a user can utilize this opportunity to express an identity she or he holds for various motives such as seeking a feeling of belonging, popularity or ambition to take part in a particular community. Personality traits in relation to second language learning has garnered research attention. The relationship between personality traits and specific topics of language learning such as speaking confidence (Khany & Ghoreyshi, 2013), the academic achievement of prospective English as a Foreign

Language (EFL) teachers (Kırkağaç & Öz, 2017), communicative competence (Verhoeven & Vermeer, 2002), attitudes towards foreign language learning (Pourfeiz, 2015), and learning strategies (Asmalı, 2014; Sharp, 2008) has been investigated. As for the studies on the relationship between SNSs use and personality traits, differing results as to the direction of the relationship being either positive or negative have been found. De Zúñiga, Diehl, Huber, and Liu's (2017) study demonstrated that extraversion, agreeableness, and conscientiousness are positive predictors of SNS use while emotional stability and openness are negative predictor of the SNS use. Wehrli (2008) investigated the effect of personality traits on online social networking behavior and found a positive effect for neuroticism, a negative influence for conscientiousness, and no effects for openness and agreeableness. (Correa, Hinsley, & Zúniga, 2010) found that the use of SNS and extroversion and openness were positively correlated; while, the use of social networks and neuroticism was negatively correlated.

MAIN FOCUS OF THE CHAPTER

Research Context

We surely have been on the move from Social CALL 1.0, where we were just getting to know what digital contexts were available for getting connected which started with opening up accounts on Facebook WhatsApp and Twitter (inclusion literacy), to Social CALL 2.0 where we began to be a part of the online community by using these social sites and actively engaging in those communities (participatory literacy). The more we get active, the more we are inclined to stick to one SNS according to our individual experiences and how much we think a given platform fits our needs. Social CALL 2.0 has moved from introducing people to SNS in order to connect with others, even strangers, with common tastes or interests, to a point where the connecting means also being invested in SNSs because the platform itself is a reflection of certain preferences and identity traits that can place us where we want to be as a user of SNSs. SNSs are very much the subject of recent research under the tag of social CALL. Instagram in particular has been commonly used for online photo or video sharing but has been less empirically researched when compared with Facebook or Twitter (Leier, 2018). The current research has been conducted to contribute to the existing studies, most of which lack quantitative design and evaluation of learning outcomes. The focus of the research is oral communication skill, which is the practice of speaking to communicate in English as a Foreign Language. The research interest in the use of IG has come with the idea of providing a learning zone through a channel with which students are already familiar and already use when using their mobile phones. The author (also a researcher in the context) developed a research question on whether the formal learning environment (classroom) can affect young adult learners' oral performances. Specifically, whether or not IG, which is assumed to be among the mostly frequently used SNSs by young adults, when integrated as a learning tool for temporary period of time affects oral performance. The researcher also explored whether the learners' personality traits would serve as a reliable predictor of their performance on IG and in-classroom. The current study is premised on the quantitative research method and aims to explore whether oral communication performance in two different contexts (classroom and IG) differs significantly, as well as how personality traits affect performance in the two contexts. The study addresses the following research questions:

1. Is there any significant difference between students' oral performance in a classroom context and on Instagram?
2. Do personality traits predict performance in the classroom context and on Instagram?

The hypothesis for the research questions is that students will perform better on IG (Azlan, Zakaria & Yunus, 2019; Rahman, 2018; Sun et. al, 2017; Wulandari, 2019) and that the students who are high scorers in personal trait dimensions such as openness to experience, agreeableness and extraversion, and being open to new experiences will have high scores in their performance in both contexts (de Zúñiga et al., 2017; Raad & Mlačić, 2015; Wehrli, 2008).

Setting and Participants

The research was conducted in a state university during the 2018-2019 winter semester in Turkey. The participants were freshmen students with ages ranging from 18 to 20 who are studying in the program of Teaching English as a Foreign Language. A total of 88 students registered to the course. However, 2 of them were with A1 and C2 proficiency, even though they were involved in the activities, their scores were not counted in this research statistically to avoid any possible outliers. Also 6 of the students did not want to participate in the SNS-natured study. This resulted in 8 participants being excluded from the study. 80 ELT students with B2 level of proficiency did voluntarily participate in the study. 30 of the participants had completed one year of English Language Preparatory Program prior to the treatment. Their level of English was evaluated before the treatment to assess whether or not they had similar language proficiency by employing the Oxford Placement Test (Allen, 2004).

Data Collection Tool

This research consisted of two measurements:

Table 1. Assessment grid for spoken language use of the CEFR B2 level (Council of Europe, 2018)

Range: *Has a sufficient range of language to be able to give clear descriptions, express viewpoints on most general topics, without much conspicuous searching for words, using some complex sentence forms to do so.* *---/20pts*
Accuracy: *Shows a relatively high degree of grammatical control. Does not make errors which cause misunderstanding, and can correct most of his/her mistakes.* *---/20pts*
Fluency: *Can produce stretches of language with a fairly even tempo; although he/she can be hesitant as he or she searches for patterns and expressions, there are few noticeably long pauses.* *---/20pts*
Interaction: *Can initiate discourse, take his/her turn when appropriate and end the conversation when he / she needs to, though he /she may not always do this elegantly. Can help the discussion along on familiar ground confirming comprehension, inviting others in, etc.* *---/20pts*
Coherence: *Can use a limited number of cohesive devices to link his/her utterances into clear, coherent discourse, though there may be some "jumpiness" in a long contribution.* *---/20pts*
Total: ---/100

Oral Communication performance was assessed by a grid which has five qualitative aspects of spoken language use of Common European Framework of Reference for Language (CEFR 3.3) (Council of Europe, 2018): Range, accuracy, fluency, interaction and coherence. Each of these aspects is 20 points maximum with a total possible of 100 point aggregate in the five aspects.

The grid was used for assessing students' oral performances in both contexts: classroom and IG. Two raters assessed the performance independently. The scores were compared and measured to ensure reliability. The inter-rater reliability of oral communication performance is 0.88. The discrepancies were resolved in agreement between the raters.

The Quick Big Five Personality Test (QBFPT)

To measure the personality traits, QBFPT, the revised and short form of Goldberg's (1992) 100 descriptions of personal traits were utilized. Each of the five broad personality dimensions is represented with 6 adjectives totaling up a list of 30 adjectives in the test (Verlmuts & Geris, 2005). The test was translated into Turkish and included a 7-point Likert scale from "completely correct" (7) and "completely wrong" (1). The minimum scores of each dimension 1 and maximum is 7. The Cronbach's alphas of the scale were reported. 81 for extraversion, .86 for conscientiousness, .80 for agreeableness, .73 for openness to experience and .78 for neuroticism in the validity and reliability study of the test in Turkish by Morsünbül, (2014). Cronbach`s alphas were .87 for extraversion, .84 for conscientiousness, .72 for agreeableness, .72 for openness to experience, and for neuroticism .79.

Procedures

Oral Communication Skills 1 includes a variety of communication-oriented activities such as discussions, debates, individual and group presentations, informative and persuasive presentations, and interviews. It is a compulsory course in the departmental program where students gain speaking practice. Preparation for the integration of IG use for the oral communication classes started with a simple questionnaire to ascertain whether or not students were active on IG at the beginning of the semester. The mean time for experience of use for IG was 3 years 3 months. 92% of participants reported using IG more than Facebook or Twitter and the mean of active time on IG was 2 hours 10 minutes per day. This data indicated that the students were already active on IG and were not required to open up an account just for the assigned task. The students added the researcher (instructor of the course) to their friend list when the course started by voluntarily accepting her friend request. The intervention started in week of 7 of the 14-week-fall-semester and ended in the 9th week. The instructor talked about movie analysis theories and the students did a classroom-activity involving watching parts of the movie *The Man called Ove*. They then discussed it in class as pair work in relation to the types of movie analysis introduced the 6th week. The task assigned on the 7th week was to watch a suggested movie and then work in groups of three to talk about it. In the 8th week, students in group had approximately 1-2 minutes per person to briefly talk about the movie on IG.

The two raters assessed students' oral performances in the class using the grid (See Table 1). For the following week, the instructor elicited the consent forms from students about the IG assignment. Their assignment was to post a brief review of the movie using the principles of analysis introduced in class on their IG. Six of the students did not want to post their video of this assignment on IG but instead submitted the assignment as an audio file, therefore, their data were excluded from the study. 80 students posted their videos where they talked about the movie they had watched from a critical point of view for 59 seconds in English (See Figure 1). They received likes and comments either in Turkish or English. The raters assessed the posts with the same grid used to assess students' in-class oral performances.

Figure 1. Student's video on IG for movie analysis
Image used with consent

Results

Descriptive statistics for the scores are provided in Table 2. The data indicates that students' performance in IG context was scored higher than their in-classroom performance. In terms of QBFPT scores, they scored highest in the openness dimension while they scored lowest in the extraversion dimension.

A paired-samples t-test was conducted to compare students' oral communication performance in classroom context and on IG. It revealed that there was a significant difference in the scores for students' performance in the classroom context (M=73,12), SD=9,94) and on IG (M=75,43, SD=9,18); t (79) = -2.46, p< .01.

Table 2. Descriptive statistics for scores

	N	M	SD	Min	Max
In-classroom	80	73,12	9,94	50	95
IG	80	73,43	9,18	50	90
Openness	80	32,55	4,58	23	42
Conscientiousness	80	26,86	7,58	9	42
Extraversion	80	26,51	7,45	7	42
Agreeableness	80	24,27	7,05	18	41
Neuroticism	80	24,27	7,05	10	40

As to how well personality traits predict oral communication performance in-classroom and on IG, multiple regression analysis was performed. Regression analysis results indicated that the personality traits significantly predict oral communication performance in the classroom context ($R = .41$, $R2 = .16$, $F = 3.00^*$ $p < .05$). This finding suggests that independent variables accounted for 16% variance of oral communication performance in the classroom context. It was found that extraversion ($\beta = .30$, $p<.05$) and conscientiousness ($\beta = 32$, $p<.05$) significantly predicted oral communication performance in the classroom context. As for the prediction of oral communication performance on IG, the results showed that the personality traits didn't significantly predict oral communication performance on IG ($R = .29$, $R2 = .08$, $F = 1.38$ $p > .05$).

The results indicated that the participant's performance on IG was significantly higher in terms of oral communication skills compared to their performance in the classroom context, suggesting that IG facilitated their performance in oral communication skills. Additionally, the hypothesis was confirmed in terms of increased performance in oral communication skills on IG since the participants performing oral communication skills on IG had significantly higher means than they did in the classroom context. It is not that surprising that students performed more uniformly on the IG assignment. It might be much less stressful and much more fun to record a video, especially if students have the opportunity to only post their best effort, rather than having to make an on the spot presentation in class.

Additionally, the results demonstrated that learners whose personality traits score high for extraversion and conscientious are highly likely to achieve high scores in oral communication skills in a classroom context since they might feel confident in their speaking abilities whereas on IG personality traits do not serve as significant predictors for the oral communication performance on IG. This shows us that the personality traits are not good predictors for the oral communication performance on IG and they cannot reliably predict language performance.

CONCLUSION

This study has reviewed the current developments in SNSs as they relate to language learning, reporting gained language benefits by integrating the use of IG in language teaching. As most previous studies have focused on the perceptions about SNS use in the classroom, and taking note of the few experimental studies on using IG for skill teaching, the author designed the research study to assess whether the use of IG in an Oral Communication Skill courses led to improvements in oral communication skills. The study also examined whether the Big Five Personality Model could predict student oral communication performance. While it found that the model did not work as a predictor for performance on IG, the dimensions such as extraversion and conscientious are significant predictors of the oral communication performance in class. The current study contradicts with the study by de Zúñiga et al. (2017) and Raad & Mlačić (2015). It partially confirms the findings of Öz's (2016) study where he found that openness to experience and extraversion were the strongest predictors of academic motivation-if we regard the term as willingness to take part in learning in an academic environment. It also partially supports the observation in the study by Khany and Ghoreyshi (2013) where extroversion was found to be the most powerful predictor of a students' foreign language speaking confidence and the study by Karadağ and Kaya (2019) which found that there is a significant relationship between willingness to communicate and Big Five personality trait dimensions such as extraversion, openness to experience and conscientiousness. This implies that students' personality does not help us predict significantly whether they would improve language skills or outperform on IG. The study confirms the studies that advocate for the use of IG in language classes but does not support the finding of the studies by Correa, Hinsley and Zúniga (2010), de Zúñiga et. al (2017) and Wehrli (2008). The emerging trend shows us that SNSs have pushed the boundaries of what is learning and how learning can occur outside the confines of constructed zones such as classrooms. The popularity of SNSs brings up the question in an opportunistic mind as to whether they could be used for learning too. As long as precautions such as privacy policies and proper security of student data, as well as careful planning to ensure interactions and feedback are appropriate and the expected language use for interactions are specified, it is worth experimenting in integrating SNSs into language learning and skill practice. This will likely empower 21st century learners with competencies such as experiential learning, digitally collaborative and unorthodox practices of learning and help them develop an identity as global citizens and learners in the SNS context. The integration of SNSs might be partial as users might not want to use it exclusively for learning language, but rather partake in it from time to time and as a supplement to take their learning beyond the classroom context. Further research is warranted on how the effects of learner personality characteristics, learners' learning styles, and visual and verbal ability levels come into consideration as possible predictors of performance in language learning through SNSs, as such performance may be more directly related to other factors in the multimedia environment itself.

ACKNOWLEDGMENT

This research received no specific grant funding from any agency in the public, commercial, or non-profit sectors. Dr. Fidel Çakmak gratefully thanks Madlen Ma for always her being there, providing companionship, constant emotional support, and occasionally equipment to conduct research in the field of language learning.

REFERENCES

Abbott, W., Donaghey, J., Hare, J., & Hopkins, P. (2013). An Instagram is worth a thousand words: An industry panel and audience Q&A. *Library Hi Tech News*, *30*(7), 1–6. doi:10.1108/LHTN-08-2013-0047

Akbari, E., Naderi, A., Simons, R. J., & Pilot, A. (2016). Student engagement and foreign language learning through online social networks. *Asian-Pacific Journal of Second and Foreign Language Education*, *1*(1), 1–22. doi:10.118640862-016-0006-7

Akhiar, A., Mydin, A. A., & Kasuma, S. A. A. (2017). Students' perceptions and attitudes towards the use of Instagram in English language writing. *Malaysian Journal of Learning and Instruction* [Special Issue], 47–72.

Al-Ali, S. (2014). Embracing the selfie craze: Exploring the possible use of Instagram as a language m-learning tool. *Issues and Trends in Educational Technology*, *2*(2), 1–16. doi:10.2458/azu_itet_v2i2_ai-ali

AlGhamdi, M. A. (2018). Arabic learners' preferences for Instagram English lessons. *English Language Teaching*, *11*(8), 103–110. doi:10.5539/elt.v11n8p103

Allen, D. (2004). *Oxford placement test*. Oxford, UK: Oxford University Press.

Allik, J., Hrebícková, M., & Realo, A. (2018). Unusual configurations of personality traits indicate multiple patterns of their coalescence. *Frontiers in Psychology*, 1–14. PMID:29515499

Aloraini, N. (2018). Investigating Instagram as an EFL learning tool. *Arab World English Journal*, *4*(4), 174–184. doi:10.24093/awej/call4.13

Asmalı, M. (2014). The relationship between the Big Five personality traits and language learning strategies. Balıkesir University Journal of Social Sciences Institute, 17(32), 1–18.

Azlan, N. A. B., Zakaria, S. B., & Yunus, M. M. (2019). Integrative task-based learning: Developing speaking skill and increase motivation via Instagram. *International Journal of Academic Research in Business and Social Sciences*, *9*(1), 620–636. doi:10.6007/IJARBSS/v9-i1/5463

Biedroń, A. (2016). Personality factors as predictors of foreign language aptitude. *Studies in Second Language Learning and Teaching*, *1*(4), 467–489. doi:10.14746sllt.2011.1.4.2

Blattner, G., & Lomicka, L. (2012). Facebooking and the social generation: A new era of language learning. *Apprentissage Des Langues et Systèmes d'Information et de Communication*, *15*, 1–32.

Brick, B. (2012). How effective are web 2.0 language learning sites in facilitating language learning? *Compass: The Journal of Learning and Teaching*, *3*, 57–63.

Carrell, P. L., Prince, M. S., & Astika, G. G. (1996). Personality types and language learning in an EFL context. *Language Learning*, *46*(1), 75–99. doi:10.1111/j.1467-1770.1996.tb00641.x

Chen, P. S. D., Lambert, A. D., & Guidry, K. R. (2010). Engaging online learners: The impact of web-based learning technology on college student engagement. *Computers & Education*, *54*(5), 1222–1232. doi:10.1016/j.compedu.2009.11.008

Correa, T., Hinsley, A. W., & de Zúñiga, H. G. (2010). Who interacts on the web? The intersection of users' personality and social media use. *Computers in Human Behavior*, *26*(2), 247–253. doi:10.1016/j.chb.2009.09.003

Council of Europe. (2018). Qualitative aspects of spoken language use - Table 3 (CEFR 3.3): Common reference levels. Retrieved from https://www.coe.int/en/web/common-european-framework-reference-languages/table-3-cefr-3.3-common-reference-levels-qualitative-aspects-of-spoken-language-use

De Zúñiga, H. G., Diehl, T., Huber, B., & Liu, J. (2017). Personality traits and social media use in 20 Countries: How personality relates to frequency of social media use, social media news use, and social media use for social interaction. *Cyberpsychology, Behavior, and Social Networking, 20*(9), 540–552. doi:10.1089/cyber.2017.0295 PMID:28922034

Doleck, T., Bazelais, P., & Lemay, D. J. (2017). Need for self-expression on Instagram: A technology acceptance perspective. In *3rd International Conference on Computational Intelligence & Communication Technology (CICT)*, 1-3. IEEE. Retrieved from https://ieeexplore.ieee.org/stamp/stamp.jsp?arnumber=7977305

Dörnyei, Z. (2005). *The psychology of the language learner individual differences in second language acquisition*. Mahwar, NJ: Lawrence Erlbaum.

Ellison, N., & Boyd, D. M. (2008). Social network sites: Definition, history, and scholarship. *Journal of Computer-Mediated Communication, 13*, 210–230.

Erben, T., Ban, R., & Castañeda, M. (2009). *Teaching English language learners through technology*. New York, NY: Routledge.

Eysenck, H. J., & Eysenck, M. W. (1985). *Personality and individual differences*. New York, NY: Plenum. doi:10.1007/978-1-4613-2413-3

Goldberg, L. R. (1992). The development of markers for the Big-Five factor structure. *Psychological Assessment, 4*(1), 26–42. doi:10.1037/1040-3590.4.1.26

Greenhow, C., Robelia, E., & Hughes, J. (2009). Web 2.0 and classroom research: What path should we take now? *Educational Researcher, 38*, 246–259. doi:10.3102/0013189X09336671

Griffith, R. (1991). Personality and second language learning: theory, research and practice. In E. Sadtonom (Ed.), *Language acquisition and the second/foreign language classroom*. Singapore: SEAMEO.

Griffith, S., & Liyanage, L. (2008). An introduction to the potential of social networking sites in education. In I. Olney, G. Lefoe, J. Mantei, & J. Herrington (Eds.), *Proceedings of the Second Emerging Technologies Conference 2008* (pp. 76–81). Australia: University of Wollongong. Retrieved from http://ro.uow.edu.au/etc08/9

Hamid, S., Waycott, J., Kurnia, S., & Chang, S. (2015). Understanding students' perceptions of the benefits of online social networking use for teaching and learning. *Internet and Higher Education, 26*, 1–9. doi:10.1016/j.iheduc.2015.02.004

Handayani, F. (2016). Instagram as a teaching tool? Really? In *Proceedings of the Fourth International Seminar on English Language and Teaching (ISELT-4)*, 320-327. Atlantis Press.

Handayani, F. (2017). Students' attitudes towards using Instagram in teaching writing. *Journal of Educative Studies, 2*(1), 23–29.

Haythornthwaite, C. (2019). Learning, connectivity and networks. *Information and Learning Science*, *120*(1-2), 19–38. doi:10.1108/ILS-06-2018-0052

Hitosugi, C. I. (2011). Using a social networking site in Japanese class. In E. Forsythe, T. Gorham, M. Grogan, D. Jarrell, R. Chartrand, & P. Lewis (Eds.), *CALL: What's your motivation?* (pp. 72–83). Nagoya, Japan: JALT CALL SIG.

Hopkyns, S. (2017). The Instagram identity project: Improving paragraph writing through social media. In *10th International Conference on ICT for Language Learning Conference Proceedings*, 224–228. Libreria Universitaria.

Huang, Y.-T., & Su, S.-F. (2018). Motives for Instagram use and topics of interest among young adults. *Future Internet*, *10*(77), 1–12.

Hwang, H. S., & Cho, J. (2018). Why Instagram? Intention to continue using Instagram among Korean college students. *Social Behavior and Personality*, *46*(8), 1305–1315. doi:10.2224bp.6961

Johnson, W., Krueger, R. F., Bouchard, T. J. Jr, & McGue, M. (2002). The personalities of twins: Just ordinary folks. *Twin Research*, *5*(2), 125–131. doi:10.1375/twin.5.2.125 PMID:11931690

Karadağ, Ş., & Kaya, Ş. D. (2019). The effects of personality traits on willingness to communicate: A study on university students. *Manas Sosyal Araştırmalar Dergisi*, *8*(1), 397–410.

Kessler, G. (2013). Teaching ESL/EFL in a world of social media, mash-ups, and hyper-collaboration. *TESOL Journal*, *4*(4), 615–632. doi:10.1002/tesj.106

Khalitova, L. & Gimaletdinova, G. (2016). Mobile technologies in teaching English as a foreign language in higher education: A case study of using mobile application Instagram. In *ICERI2016 Proceedings*, *1*, 6155-6161. IATED.

Khany, R., & Ghoreyshi, M. (2013). The nexus between Iranian EFL students' Big Five personality traits and foreign language speaking confidence. *European Online Journal of Natural and Social Sciences*, *2*(2), 601–611.

Kırkağaç, Ş. & Öz, H. (2017). The role of Big Five personality traits in predicting prospective EFL teachers' academic achievement. *International Online Journal of Education and Teaching (IOJET)*, *4*(4), 317-328. Retrieved from http://iojet.org/index.php/IOJET/article/view/243/174

Kukulska-Hulme, A., Lee, H., & Norris, L. (2017). Mobile learning revolution: Implications for language pedagogy. In C. A. Chapelle & S. Sauro (Eds.), *The handbook of technology and second language teaching and learning* (pp. 217–233). Oxford, UK: Wiley & Sons. doi:10.1002/9781118914069.ch15

Kurniawan, A. & Kastuhandani, L. A. (2016). Utilizing Instagram for engaging students in their creative writing. In Proceedings of Indonesia Technology Enhanced Language Learning, 4–7. Salatiga, Indonesia: Satya Wacana University Press Universitas Kristen Satya Wacana

Laghos, A., & Nisiforou, E. (2018). Computer assisted language learning social networks: What are they talking about? *Social Networking*, *7*(3), 170–180. doi:10.4236n.2018.73014

Leier, V. (2018). Using Instagram in a tertiary German language course: Students' perception and approaches. *The New Zealand Language Teacher, 44*, 77–90.

Li, J., & Qin, X. (2006). Language learning styles and learning strategies of tertiary level English learners in China. *RECL Journal, 37*, 67–89.

Lightbrown, M. P., & Spada, N. (2006). *How languages are learned.* Oxford, UK: Oxford University Press.

Listiani, G. (2016). The effectiveness of Instagram writing compared to teacher centered writing to teach recount text to students with high and low motivation. *Journal of English Language Teaching, 5*(1), 1–8.

Lomicka, L., & Lord, G. (2009). Introduction to social networking, collaboration, and Web 2.0 tools. In L. Lomicka & G. Lord (Eds.), *The next generation: Social networks and online collaboration in foreign language learning.* San Marcos, TX: CALICO.

Lomicka, L., & Lord, G. (2016). Social networking and language learning. In F. Farr & M. Murray (Eds.), *The Routledge handbook of language learning and technology* (pp. 255–268). New York, NY: Routledge.

Mao, J. (2014). Social media for learning: A mixed methods study on high school students' technology affordances and perspectives. *Computers in Human Behavior, 33*, 213–223. doi:10.1016/j.chb.2014.01.002

McBride, K. (2009). Social networking sites in foreign language classes: Opportunities for re-creation. In L. Lomicka & G. Lord (Eds.), *The next generation: Social networking and online collaboration in foreign language learning (CALICO Monograph Series)* (pp. 35–58). San Marcos, TX: CALICO.

McCrae, R. R., & Costa, P. T. Jr. (2003). *Personality in adulthood: A Five-Factor Theory perspective* (2nd ed.). New York, NY: Guilford. doi:10.4324/9780203428412

Mehdizadeh, S. (2010). Self-presentation 2.0: Narcissism and self-esteem on Facebook. *Cyberpsychology, Behavior, and Social Networking, 13*(4), 357–364. doi:10.1089/cyber.2009.0257 PMID:20712493

Merchant, G. (2011). Unravelling the social network: Theory and research. *Learning, Media and Technology, 37*(1), 4–19. doi:10.1080/17439884.2011.567992

Messick, S. (1994). The matter of style: Manifestations of personality in cognitive, learning and teaching. *Educational Psychologist, 29*(3), 121–136. doi:10.120715326985ep2903_2

Morshidi, A., Embi, M. A., & Hashim, H. (2019). Instagram application: An active tool in cultivating reading behavior. *Journal of Information Systems and Technology Management, 4*(11), 95–106.

Morsünbül, U. (2014). The validity and reliability study of the Turkish version of Quick Big Five personality test. *Düşünen Adam, 27*(4), 316–322. doi:10.5350/DAJPN2014270405

Munday, P., Delaney, Y., & Bosque, A. (2016). #InstagramELE: Learning Spanish through a Social Network. *Languages Faculty Publications.* Retrieved from http://digitalcommons.sacredheart.edu/lang_fac/57

Myers-Briggs, I., McCaulley, M. H., Quenk, N. L., & Hammer, A. L. (1998). *MBTI manual: A guide to the development and use of the Myers Briggs type indicator.* Palo Alto, CA: Consulting Psychologists Press.

Öz, H. (2016). The importance of personality traits in students' perceptions of metacognitive awareness. *Procedia: Social and Behavioral Sciences, 232*, 655–667. doi:10.1016/j.sbspro.2016.10.090

Pourfeiz, J. (2015). Exploring the relationship between global personality traits and attitudes toward foreign language learning. *Procedia: Social and Behavioral Sciences, 186*, 467–473. doi:10.1016/j.sbspro.2015.04.119

Raad, B., & Mlačić, B. (2015). Big Five factor model, theory and structure. In J. D. Wright (Ed.), *International encyclopedia of the social & behavioral sciences* (pp. 559–566). Oxford, UK: Elsevier. doi:10.1016/B978-0-08-097086-8.25066-6

Rahmah, R. E. (2018). Sharing photograms on Instagram boosts students' self-confidence in speaking English. *Pedagogy Journal of English Language Teaching, 6*(2), 148–156. doi:10.32332/pedagogy.v6i2.1335

Reinhardt, J. (2019). Social media in second and foreign language teaching and learning: Blogs, wikis, and social networking. *Language Teaching, 52*(1), 1–39. doi:10.1017/S0261444818000356

Sharp, A. (2008). Personality and second language learning. *Asian Social Science, 4*(11), 17–25.

Shazali, S. S., Shamsudin, Z. H., & Yunus, M. M. (2019). Instagram: A platform to develop student's writing ability. *International Journal of Academic Research in Business and Social Sciences, 9*(1), 88–98. doi:10.6007/IJARBSS/v9-i1/5365

Sirait, J. B., & Marlina, L. (2018). Using Instagram as a tool for online peer-review activity in writing descriptive text for senior high school students. *Journal of English Language Teaching, 7*(1), 291–302. Retrieved from http://ejournal.unp.ac.id/index.php/jelt/article/view/9771/pdf

Smith, A. (2015). *U.S. Smartphone use in 2015*. Retrieved from http://www.pewinternet.org/files/2015/03/PI_Smartphones_ 0401151.pdf

Soviyah, S., & Etikaningsih, D. R. (2018). Instagram use to enhance ability in writing descriptive texts. *Indonesian EFL Journal, 4*(2), 32–38. doi:10.25134/ieflj.v4i2.1373

Statista. (2017, September). *Number of daily active Instagram users*. Retrieved from https://www.statista.com/statistics/657823/number-of-daily-active-instagram-users/

Sukri, H. I. M., Mustapha, L., Othman, M., Aralas, D., & Ismail, L. (2018). Social media: Engaging language learning. *International Journal of Academic Research in Business and Social Sciences, 8*(12), 287–294. doi:10.6007/IJARBSS/v8-i12/5013

Sun, Z., Lin, C. H., You, J., Shen, H. J., Qi, S., & Luo, L. (2017). Improving the English-speaking skills of young learners through mobile social networking. *Computer Assisted Language Learning, 30*(3–4), 304–324. doi:10.1080/09588221.2017.1308384

Taşkıran, A., Koral-Gümüşoğlu, E., & Aydın, B. (2018). Fostering foreign language learning with Twitter: Reflections from English learners. *Turkish Online Journal of Distance Education-TOJDE, 19*(1), 100–116. doi:10.17718/tojde.382734

Thomas, M., Reinders, H., & Warschauer, M. (Eds.). (2013). *Contemporary Computer-Assisted Language Learning*. New York, NY: Continuum.

Thorne, S. L. (2010). The 'intercultural turn' and language learning in the crucible of new media. In F. Helm & S. Guth (Eds.), *Telecollaboration 2.0 for Language and Intercultural Learning* (pp. 139–164). Bern, Switzerland: Peter Lang.

van Dijk, J. (2006). *The network society: social aspects of new media.* Thousand Oaks, CA: Sage.

Verhoeven, L., & Vermeer, A. (2002). Communicative competence and personality dimensions in first and second language learners. *Applied Psycholinguistics, 23*(3), 361–374. doi:10.1017/S014271640200303X

Vermulst, A. A., & Gerris, J. R. M. (2005). *QBF: Quick Big Five personality test manual.* Leeuwarden, The Netherlands: LDC Publications.

Wehrli, S. (2008). Personality on social network sites: An application of the Five Factor Model. *ETH Zürich Sociology Working Paper 7,* 1–16.

Wong, C.-H., Tan, G. W.-H., Loke, S.-P., & Ooi, K.-B. (2015). Adoption of mobile social networking sites for learning? *Online Information Review, 39*(6), 762–778. doi:10.1108/OIR-05-2015-0152

Wulandari, M. (2019). Improving EFL learners' speaking proficiency through IG Vlog. *LLT Journal: A Journal on Language and Language Teaching, 22*(1), 111–125.

Yadegarfar, H., & Simin, S. (2016). Effects of using Instagram on learning grammatical accuracy of word classes among Iranian undergraduate TEFL students. *International Journal of Research Studies in Educational Technology, 5*(2), 49–60. doi:10.5861/ijrset.2016.1572

Yang, S. (2013). Understanding undergraduate students' adoption of mobile learning model: A perspective of the extended UTAUT2. *Journal of Convergence Information Technology, 8*(10), 969–979. doi:10.4156/jcit.vol8.issue10.118

Zeng, S. (2018). *English learning in the digital age-Agency, technology, and context.* Singapore: Springer. doi:10.1007/978-981-13-2499-4

Zourou, K., Potolia, A., & Zourou, F. (2017). Informal social networking sites for language learning: Insights into autonomy stances. In T. Lewis, A. Rivens Mompean, & T. Cappellini (Eds.), CALICO monograph "Learner autonomy and Web 2.0", 141–167.

This research was previously published in Recent Tools for Computer- and Mobile-Assisted Foreign Language Learning; pages 110-131, copyright year 2020 by Information Science Reference (an imprint of IGI Global).

Chapter 45
Reinforcement Learning in Social Media Marketing

Patrik Eklund

iD https://orcid.org/0000-0003-3965-2834

Umea University, Sweden

ABSTRACT

In this chapter, the authors describe an architecture for reinforcement learning in social media marketing. The rule bases used for action selection within the architecture build upon many-valued (fuzzy) logic. Action evaluation and internal learning is based on neural network like structures. In using variables measuring the effect of advertising, we must understand direction of influence between advertiser, owning the content of the advertisement, and advertisee, as the target of an advertisement, and as facilitated by social media marketing. Examples are drawn from Facebook marketing.

INTRODUCTION

Social media marketing (SMM) is a special form of marketing using combinations of various media channels. General marketing AI principles are relevant, but the underlying information structures need to be specific to SMM, and are further specified within particular SMM media e.g. like in Facebook.

Given advertiser objectives and expected outcomes, including return of investment (ROI) expectations, the advertiser specifies the overall campaign budget, and other investments related to the execution of the marketing campaign.

Various constraints are provided, many of which fall outside the scope of the way the campaign is handled and executed.

In the end, ROI depends on conversion, even if conversions alone are not sufficient to calculate the ROI of a campaign. Further, ROI can be seen as static and global with respect to the campaign as a whole, or as dynamic and local given conversion frequency appearing during a campaign.

An important part of advertiser objectives relates to customer relations and its management (CRM), which embraces management of social media marketing audiences. Audience and CRM modelling is continuously on the agenda among marketing technology providers, but underlying structure, phenom-

DOI: 10.4018/978-1-6684-7123-4.ch045

ena and dynamics is not always fully understood. This leads to approaches like those involving social media marketing campaigns, where a recorded dialogue between campaign and audience improves the understanding of the relation between the advertiser (or its brand), and the advertisee.

The objectives of this chapter is to show how reinforcement learning involving fuzzy logic rule bases can provide SMM ROI optimization.

BACKGROUND

An Ad conveys a message, and is represented by keywords and the content of the Ad, containing text, images and video, annotated with links and objects (like buttons) enabling and inviting the Advertisee to interact with the Ad, and become influenced by the Ad. An Ad is like an expression presented (syntactically), and perceived (semantically) by the Advertisee. That perception depends on the Advertisee profile and behaviour. Ads with video content are either digital video Ads or as based on programmatic video advertising.

The content of that Ad can be dynamically modified, and the characteristics of the Ad should be described as fine-granularly as possible. A coarse-granular description of the Ad leaves less room for subjecting the Ad itself to modification during optimization of the campaign.

Ads are part of Ad sets, and a set of Ad sets constitutes a Campaign. This means that Advertisers must deal not just with the fine-granular description of respective Ads, but also consider the characteristics of the Ad sets, and the structure of the Campaign.

Facebook generates cost related to Ads, so that costs of Ad sets are aggregated costs. A campaign cost is the accumulation of all costs incurred by specific Ads and Ad sets.

Bidding and Facebook's Ads auction is not only price related, i.e., the highest monetary bid does not necessarily win, but the winner is the Ad that creates the most overall value. The mechanism for calculating that "overall value" is hidden. Apart from the Advertiser Bid, being manual or automatic, Ad quality and relevance comes into play. An auction takes place whenever someone is eligible to see an Ad. Manual bidding influences reinforcement learning differently as compared to automatic bidding.

Ad performance can be measured e.g. by engagement and brand lift. Engagement with the Ad, can be measured either by hovering, scrolling or interaction with an extension, scroll velocity as a proxy for attention, how long a native Ad is viewed (even if not clicked), average time reading or watching, and so on. Brand lift can be measure e.g. by shares, followings, and email subscriptions.

There is a continuously on-going debate about performance metrics, but the *What* of measuring seems not properly connected with the *Why* of measuring. Metrics has been focused on outcome and performance, but the trend is to focus more also on Ad content. Formal terminology and nomenclatures, and as based on formal logic [Eklund et al 2014], for classifying Ad content is largely missing in marketing.

Performance metrics include

- Actions
- Clicks
- CTR
- Impressions
- Relevance score

CTR (Click-Through Rate) is the ratio of ad clicks to impressions (not ad clicks to reach, where reach is the number of unique impressions). Low CTR means Advertisees are not inspired to click on Ad and visit landing page. High CTR alone does not mean success, in particular in a combination with high CTR and low conversion. CTR is also related to keyword targeting and calculations of expected CTR. With CTR reasonably high, overly focus on keywords may not be needed. The importance of CTR may be different in comparison between Ad content and Campaign types, e.g. as in video campaigns. Impression can be measured at least by rate (%) and time (seconds). Impression is important for Advertisers that want to be top ranked in search for keywords in their business areas. CTR thereby measure engagement within impression, which is the first step towards conversion.

The Relevance score improves as Advertisees respond positively to Ad, e.g. by sharing it or going to the landing page. The score is oppositely affected by negative responses like "I don't want to see this ad". The score is updated as Advertisees interact with and engage with the Ad. The score may further include conversions and video views. The Relevance score there makes sense for CPC Ads rather than CPM Ads.

For Advertiser data related to objectives and constraints, and Ads characteristics as data, including relevance and feedback obtained from Facebook and its Audience, and other input values used in order to reinforce the Campaign, respective variables x as such are important, but also changes (differentials), Δx, and durations (integrals) $\int x$ of values in these variables. Variables and their differentials as part of the input variables in the Action Selection of the reinforcement loop are expectedly more important than duration variables. Using variables including their derivatives (and integrals) over time makes campaign optimization a fine-tuning of a control system, where the underlying dynamic system is extremely hard to model. Therefore, modelling and optimization has its focus on the controller, rather than on the system. In conventional control systems, the dynamic system is modelled as accurately as possible, and then the controller can be optimized given that system model. Obviously, the behaviour of an audience in Facebook cannot accurately be modelled. However, we can continuously record that behaviour, even if we cannot describe it. Recorded data is used to fine-tune the controller using unsupervised reinforcement learning.

Advertisee and Audience profile structures are defined within Facebook. All Advertisees obviously do not provide all information, which makes targeting and audience selection subjected Advertisee attributed provided. Relations, e.g. as Friends structures, between Advertisees is also partly subjected Advertisee actions within Facebook.

The Facebook pixel has a number of standard events that are useful for both building audiences and tracking your website conversions back to your Facebook ads. A good fit between the Ad message and the Audience profile potentially leads to favourable interaction between Ad and Audience, in terms of PPC (pay per click), whereas the interaction between Advertiser and Advertisee is measured in terms of PPA (pay per acquisition).

Figure 1. Return of investment

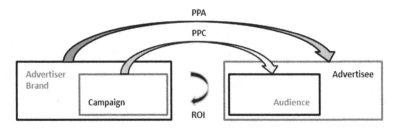

Shallow and broad targeting increases the size of the audience and jeopardizes ROI. Further, careful targeting aiming at minimizing PPC (pay per click) without reducing PPA is not the same as maximizing PPA without increasing PPC.

Ad content typically includes topics to click, and from AIDA (Awareness/Attention, Interest, Desire, Action) point of view, clicks could be classified as "awareness clicks" (read more ...), "interest clicks" (download), "desire clicks" (enrol) and "action clicks" (purchase).

The standard view of Facebook bidding is related to awareness raising, i.e., focusing on PPC rather than PPA. Conversion tracking is therefore focused on A-to-I rather that I-to-D or D-to-A in the AIDA funnel.

For detail and historical perspective on the AIDA funnel, see [Barry, 2012; Strong, 1925; Sheldon, 1911].

SOCIAL MEDIA MARKETING

In using variables measuring the effect of advertising we must understand *direction of influence* between **advertiser** (owns the content of the advertisement) and **advertisee** (as the target of an advertisement), as facilitated by **Social Media Marketing** e.g. through Facebook.

Figure 2. AIDA as related to Facebook's Awareness-Consideration-Conversion

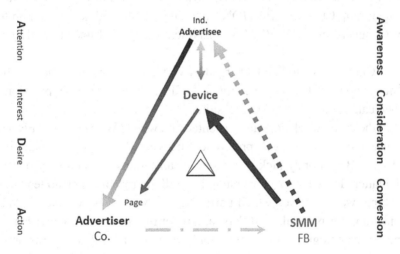

Choice of variables is expectedly different in brand awareness, traffic and conversions. Awareness related outcome measures describes the SMM-Advertisee relation, whereas conversion related measures is more about advertisee action on advertiser pages.

Spend per action and action per spend then comes into play.

Does bidding make any sense? Facebook aims to apply their bidding strategies and auctions based algorithms to every advertiser and every campaign everywhere and at all time. Facebook explains on a general level how this works, e.g. saying that a higher bid does not necessarily lead to paying that much. Facebook, of course, never reveals anything about the distribution of the numbers 'pay/bid'. Some "experts" say it can be much lower than 100%, and we can certainly experience surprisingly low values. Facebook monitors all this, but must clearly be very careful not to reveal it, and obviously so that advertiser cannot estimate it more precisely. Given the billion+ monthly users it is also clear that the objective to satisfy everybody or to be algorithmically complete and consistent with all advertises is impossible to meet. Therefore, in quite a number of cases, the advertisers pay the amount of the bid. This should mean that a rule base focused on using the 'pay/bid' proportion as a control value may sometimes go "off track". Clearly, in the case of Facebook bidding for the advertiser, different internal algorithms will apply. In these cases, a rule base providing suggestions for stop/continue concerning a campaign will focus more on its input variables aiming at being used to optimize decision points. In this situation, the importance of creative content and its structure increases. Changing content on-the-fly may become more important than focusing on winning in auctions.

Budget & schedule contains several options, and increasing the automation degree in advertising inevitable requires making specific choices concerning the attributes of the campaign. **Optimization for Ad Delivery & Bid Strategy** requires to choose between AWARENESS ('awareness' is the most typical subselection), CONSIDERATION ('traffic' is the most typical subselection) or CONVERSION ('conversions' is the most typical subselection), where bid strategy is lowest or target cost. **Ad Scheduling & Delivery type** involved running ads all the time or on schedule, in a standard or accelerated fashion.

The basic principle is to avoid spending large budgets on campaigns that fail to deliver. Facebook seems to suggest Lifetime over Daily, as Lifetime is more unconstrained and invites to "leave it to us to spend".

- Brand awareness (in supergroup AWARENESS), typical variables: Reach, Spend, CTR, CPC.
- Traffic (in supergroup CONSIDERATION), typical variables: Link Clicks, Landing Page Views.
- Conversions (in supergroup CONVERSION), typical variables: Link Clicks, Landing Page Views.

Opting for 'Link Clicks' leads to being charged by CPC, always when someone clicks a link in the Ad. Opting for 'Impression' leads to being charged by CPM, every time an impression of Ad is shown, and the price is then calculated per 1000 impressions.

If running ads all the time, which ones are presented and when? Who decides? FB decides, randomly rotating, or otherwise, the ads. FB uses no preferences between the ads, because that information is not available to FB. Does FB randomly pick over time for all targets, or randomly pick as presented for targets? Maybe the latter? If we have a conversion, FB will not reveal which ad lead to that conversion.

Generally speaking, we do not see which particular ad "works" better than another ad, otherwise than comparing spending for particular Ad Sets, and recording how particular Ads might be activated and paused during the campaign. Ads can potentially be ranked, so that there is an "order" between them. This order can be used to incorporate the on-the-fly modification of ad status into the rule base.

Machine learning (ML) in social media marketing is quite scattered. Approaches like those e.g. in [Jaakonmäki et al, 2017], and [Dhaoui et al, 2017], respectively, on content features and user engagement identify relations, and on automated sentiment analysis, use using ML techniques, but they do not cover reinforcement into the marketing campaign. These approaches are therefore not directly related to the approach in this paper, but their approaches can be compared with our approach.

THE ROLE OF VARIABLES AND HOW TO COMBINE THEM

There is a wide range of Facebook variables (metrics), and availability of these variables depends on the choice of optimization for Ad delivery and bid strategy. The largest amount of variables are available under CONSIDERATION/Traffic and CONVERSION/Conversions.

It is important to understand

1. the role of a variable in a chosen optimization strategy
2. the way a variable in fact is a *combined* or *transformed* variable

'Reach', as one of the few variables being available in all optimization strategies, is related to 'impressions', which may include multiple views of your ads by the same people, but is different in that it is the number of people who saw your ads at least once.

'Reach' will actually **reach the Advertisee**, whereas 'Impressions' only **reaches the device** on which the Advertisee may be using

Figure 3. Devices forwarding social media content to advertisees.

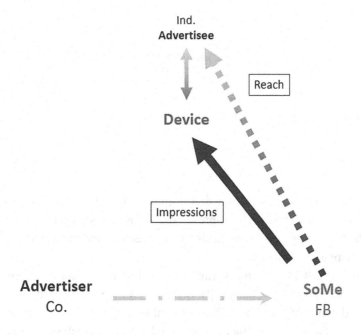

According to Facebook, 'Reach' is an estimated variable, i.e., Facebook estimates it using sampling or modelling. Estimated metrics can provide directional insights for outcomes that are hard to precisely quantify. They may evolve as Facebook gathers more data. This may be a problem if used in generated and reinforced rule bases. If a variable unexpectedly evolves, rule base parameters become side-stepped.

It may seem more natural to use 'Reach' for AWARENESS, but as a CONVERSION it may seem doubtful to use 'Reach' only without variables that actually show how Advertisees click e.g. to land on Advertiser pages.

'Link Clicks' and 'Landing Page Views', on the other hand, are true Conversions. 'Landing Page View' more so, as a 'Link Click' from the Advertisee's device does not necessarily mean that the landing page is actually loaded back to the device. There may be delays so that the Advertisee's will not wait until the page has been completed loaded into the browser of the device.

Figure 4. Devices reinforcing advertisee actions back to social media marketing platforms.

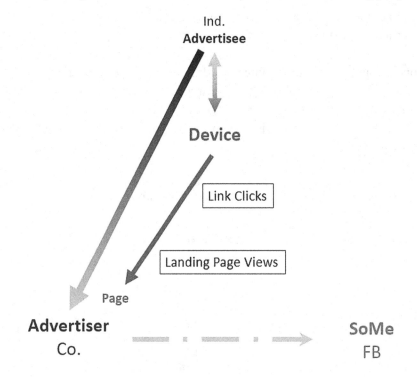

'CTR' combines 'Link Clicks' and 'Impressions', calculated as a click divided by impressions. It proportionalizes link clicks with respect to impressions. 'CTR' could also be seen as the "cost" of a link click measured in the "currency" of impressions. It may seem more natural and appealing to increase impressions than to increase the budget.

'CPC' again is different. 'CPC', as the average cost for link clicks (for each link click), is calculated as the total amount spent divided by clicks (all). So it's a *cost per action* type variable. For rule bases involving template and generated rule base files, the value scope of variables needs to be normalized. CPC is non-normalized, but can be further transformed into a normalized variable when the overall budget is included in the transformation formula. Note how 'CTR' is kind of an *action per cost* in the "currency of impressions".

Average values

$$\frac{f\left(t_0\right) + \ldots + f\left(t_n\right)}{n+1} \approx \frac{1}{n+1} \int_{t_0}^{t_n} f\left(t\right) dt$$

are based on summations, so they are essentially ***integral*** values.

If t_n is *present* time, that integral is based in *past* values. **Derivative** (differential) values are future predicting. The **first derivative** is then more for near future, whereas the **second derivative** may be seen as predicting at least somewhat beyond just near future. This is true in particular under the assumption that increasing curves are convex or concave. They most usually are, and they are also typically both, i.e., something may first be convex and later on turning to concave. In this case the inflexion point (second derivative changes from positive to negative!) is an interesting focus. If the derivative at the inflexion is higher, we may want to proceed with whatever we are doing at least a bit beyond that inflexion point. On the other, if the derivate, even if still positive, is smaller at the inflexion point, we would probably take action.

Figure 5. Negative and positive acceleration.

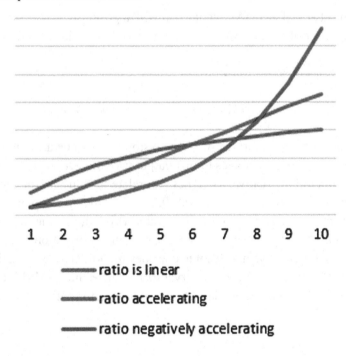

The role of gradient descent in solution subspaces has also been reported by researchers at Facebook [Gur-Ari et al, 2018].

Note how derivation "cancels" or "reverses" integration, i.e., $D\!\int\!f = f$, and also how derivation of speed (derivation of position) is acceleration.

- Mean of past positions (or integral) $\sim \int\!f$
- Present position $f(t_n)$
- Speed at present position $\sim \left(f\left(t_n\right) - f\left(t_{n-1}\right) \right)$
- Acceleration at present position $\sim \left(\left(f\left(t_n\right) - f\left(t_{n-1}\right) \right) - \left(f\left(t_{n-1}\right) - f\left(t_{n-2}\right) \right) \right)$

Facebook variables are mean or present values, but using the Facebook Marketing API, combined and constructed variables for represent speed and acceleration values can be included into the rule base. **Facebook does not do that for you in any way**. Why? Because Facebook does not manage historical data for you as you do yourself. Technically, Facebook could do it, but they won't or actually can't since it would breech rules they have to obey. With your own data you can do whatever you want, beyond what Facebook is allowed to do for you.

A positive acceleration should in most situations mean to go ahead with the campaign, whereas a negative acceleration means that the campaign in slowing down.

First and second derivatives may be more useful in optimization than simply using present positions and mean values.

In itself, Reinforcement Social Media Marketing (RSMM) algorithms do not assume anything concerning the computational aspect of variable transformations based on variables and metrics in Facebook's Business Manager.

A template rule base executes as a function

RSMM_template_rule_base: InputSpaceVariable$_1$ ×···× InputSpaceVariable$_n$ → Output

If the output variable aims to support the decision to stop or continue a campaign, there is typically no input variables carrying value that relates to that output variable. On the other hand, if the output is a variable related e.g. with bid or creative, its values will relate to values in the input space.

In RSMM, all values appear in the unit interval [0,1], so if *InputSpace$_i$* would be an interval [*a,b*], then the solution provides the boundaries of that interval to RSMM, and the transformation τ: [a,*b*] → [0,1] is performed within the RSMM Class Library. Linear transformation is typical and appears in RSMM Class Library 1.0. Later on we may want to consider sigmoidal transformations [Eklund, 1994].

Ideally, [*a,b*] in RSMM would be the unit interval [0,1], where the RSMM internal transformation $\tau R_{SMM:}$ [0,1] → [0,1] then is linear or sigmoidal. The external transformation $\tau es_{t:}$ [a,*b*] → [0,1] is linear only, i.e.,

$$\tau_{ext}\left(x\right) = \frac{x-a}{b-a}$$

An additional aspect, easily implementable, will come into play, namely, that the rule base must contain only **one** interval. This makes the internal Min-Max interval in the xml file to become [0,1]. For example, with two variables x and Δx, respectively, for actual and differential values, the external system (web application) must transform actual x and Δx values, respectively, from [min_x, max_x] and [min_Δx, max_Δx] to [0,1].

This transformation formula can simply be the linear transformation

$$f\left(x\right) = \frac{x - \min\_x}{\max\_x - \min\_x}$$

As quickly seen, $f(min\_x)=0$ and $f(max\_x)=1$, as it should be. The transformation for the differential is similarly

$$g\left(\Delta x\right) = \frac{\Delta x - \min \_ \Delta x}{\max \_ \Delta x - \min \_ \Delta x}$$

Note that this is not the whole story, since for x and Δx values outside those intervals, we must 'truncate' them into the interval.

Algebraic methods for managing many-valued truth typically uses structures like quantales [Eklund et al, 2018] instead of the unit interval. AI techniques used in marketing can be compared to AI used in other domains, like e.g. in health care [Eklund et al, 1995].

THE REINFORCEMENT ALGORITHM

Reinforcement learning is unsupervised learning. In this chapter we use form of a reinforcement learning algorithm [Sutton et al, 2018], described in [Berenji et al, 1992].

Figure 6. The overall RSMM systems architecture.

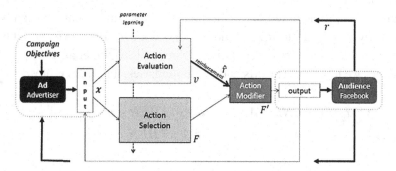

Action Selection is provided by a parameterized function f_{AS} taking input representing data from the current state of the Campaign and producing a 'force' F as an output.

$F = f_{AS}(current\ state\ input)$

The Action Selection function must be differentiable, so that parameters can be adjusted using gradient descent techniques. This function can be a black box as typically represented by neural networks, or it can be a rule base as a differential function.

This force carries the action through the Action Modifier to become the output to the Campaign system. The modified action is thereby the actual output changing data in the updated state of the Campaign. This output then affects the system and the resulting output and feedback from the Audience includes a failure signal r, which in combination with the output v of the Action Evaluator

$v = \mathrm{f}A_{E(}current\ state\ input)$

is used to calculate the reinforcement $\hat{r}$ as a function of r and v.

The Action Modifier f_{AM} is a stochastic modifier representing the present quality of the Action Selection. The role of the Action Evaluation f_{AE} is to evaluate the selected action and to reinforce the Action Modifier with an internal reinforcement $\hat{r}$ in order to enable an appropriate update also its own parameters representing the quality of the selection. Thus, the Action Evaluator additionally provides a self-evaluation. The Action Modifier uses the internal reinforcement $\hat{r}$ and the force F to update its perturbation, and then uses F as a mean, and with $\hat{r}$, to define a standard deviation to produce the action F', which is the actual input to the system.

The Action Evaluation network is based on weighted sums and weights p are trained by gradient descent. The Action Selection network is a set of many-valued rules including parameters, similarly trained by gradient descent.

Facebook's Automated Rules is based on bivalent predicate logic with conventional if…then rules

If <condition> then <action> rules
If <condition_1> AND … AND <condition_n> then <action> rules

The conditions typically specify cut-offs or boundaries so that values make conditions true or false. Tuning cut-offs is not straightforward.

The use of many-valued logic based rules is useful, e.g., since historical data can be used to initiate the rule base with many-valued clustering techniques, e.g., using the fuzzy c-means clustering technique [Bezdek, 1981] and its related rule base generation technique [Sugeno et al, 1993].

In many-valuednes we have soft cut-offs and soft boundaries, and rules represent uncertain states

$R_1:$ *IF x_1 is A_{11} AND x_2 is A_{12} AND… AND x_m is A_{1m} THEN u is U_1*

$R_2:$ *IF x_1 is A_{21} AND x_2 is A_{22} AND… AND x_m is A_{2m} THEN u is U_2*

$\vdots$

$R_n:$ *IF x_1 is A_{n1} AND x_2 is A_{n2} AND… AND x_m is A_{nm} THEN u is U_n*

where "x_j is A_{ij}" is the truth value $A_{ij}(x_j)$ in the set of truth values. This can be feedback {low, medium, high}, relevance {0,1,2,3,4,5,6,7,8,9,10}, the unit interval [0,1], or some other structure, where logical operation can be defined and handled.

The output $F=F_p(x)$ of the rule base with input $x=(x_1,\ldots,x_m)$ is given by

$$F = F_p\left(\boldsymbol{x}\right) = f_{AS}\left(current\ state\ input\right) = defuzz\left(DISJ\left(\varphi\left(CONJ_j\left(A_{ij}\left(x_j\right)\right),U_i\right)\right)\right)$$

where *CONJ* is the many-valued logical conjunction over all $A_{ij}(x_j)$, φ represents logical implication, *DISJ* computes the resulting function U from all Ui.s, and defuzz(ification) is applied to provide the final output F of the Action Selection function. A simplification is allowing U_i to be a constant ui or a vector ui of constants. In this case

$$\varphi(CONJ_j(A_{ij}(x_j)),\ U_i) = \alpha_i \Delta u_i \text{ where } \alpha_i = CONJ_i(A_{ij}(x_j)).$$

The output is then

$$F = \frac{\sum_{i=1}^{n} \alpha_i u_i}{\sum_{i=1}^{n} \alpha_i}$$

Where parameters in p reside in functions for logical connectives $CONJ_j$ and in the membership functions A_{ij}.

The logical conjunction is not unique as in bivalent logic, and is selected to fit the application. The whole expression must be differentiable, and the A_{ij} function can be represented by the Gaussian function

$$G\left(x; \mu, \beta\right) = e^{-\left(\frac{x-\mu}{\beta}\right)^2}.$$

For α=0.5 and μ=0.25, G has the following shape providing uncertainty representation of "medium" values:

Figure 7. Typical gaussian membership function for "medium".

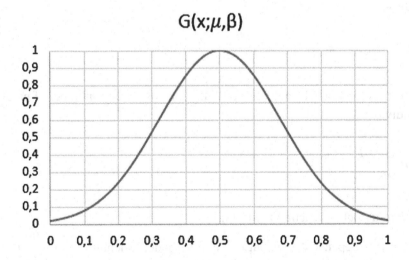

Smaller μ will narrow the shape, larger will widen it. The μ value represents the midpoint of the distribution.

For $\alpha=0$ and $\mu=0.25$, G is the left-hand side "shoulder" providing uncertainty representation of "low" values.

Figure 8. Typical gaussian membership function for "low".

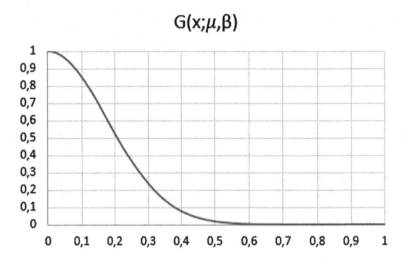

It turns out that addition

$$+ = R \times R \rightarrow R$$

extended, using the Extension Principle [Zadeh, 1965], to fuzzy addition $\tilde{+}$ of Gaussian functions will satisfy the condition

$$G\left(x_1; \mu_1, \beta_1\right) \tilde{+} G\left(x_2; \mu_2, \beta_2\right) = G\left(x_1 + x_2; \mu_1 + \mu_2, \beta_1 + \beta_2\right).$$

The output v is thus computed by a differential function containing a number of parameters p, which can be trained individually according to

$$\Delta p = \mu \frac{\partial v}{\partial p} = \mu \frac{\partial v}{\partial F} \frac{\partial F}{\partial p}$$

where the force F as a stochastic action modifier.

Clearly, F is directly dependent of p, but v is indirectly dependent of F, so $\frac{\partial v}{\partial F}$ has to be approximated by a differential using values in consecutive steps in the outer loop of the reinforcement.

The selection and arrangement of input $x=(x_1,...,x_m)$ depends on both objectives as well as placement and platform. Individual variables are e.g. of form x or Δx, or both, and represent a selection of variables made available by Facebook and Audience generated variables x_{fb}, Advertiser variables x_{adv}, Ad variables x_{ad}, Ad set variables x_{adset}, and Campaign variables $x_{campaign}$ (Ad Set and Campaign Insights).

Brand awareness campaign using Facebook desktop feed may use a different set of variables as compared video viewing using Facebook mobile feed.

As typical input to Action Selection and Evaluation, common to many campaign types, we may have variables like x_{ctr}, Δx_{ctr}, $x_{relavance\_score}$ and $\Delta x_{relevance\_score}$.

Training of parameters in Action Evaluation must ensure stability, and cover changes reflected both by parameter updates as well as changes caused by the system. The following is one way of ensuring that stability.

$$y_j\left(t, t+1\right) = g\left(\sum_{i=1}^{n} a_{ij}\left(t\right) x_i\left(t+1\right)\right)$$

$$g\left(s\right) = \frac{1}{1+e^{-s}}$$

Given variables x_{ctr}, Δx_{ctr}, $x_{relevance\_score}$, typical rules in Action Selection are of the form

Rule 1: IF x_{ctr} is *high* AND Δx_{ctr} is *negative* AND $x_{relevance\_score}$ is *medium* THEN u_1
Rule 2: IF x_{ctr} is *medium* AND Δx_{ctr} is *zero* AND $x_{relevance\_score}$ is *high* THEN u_2
Rule 3: IF x_{ctr} is *low* AND Δx_{ctr} is *positive* AND $x_{relevance\_score}$ is *medium* THEN u_3

where *low, medium, high, negative, zero* and *positive* are represented by Gaussian functions, e.g., as $G(\Delta x_{ctr}; \mu_{low}, \beta_{low})$. The output value can be an update related to bidding and/or a quantification for a modification of the Ad creative.

The Stochastic Action Modifer uses F and $\hat{r}$ to produce F', using a Gaussian random variable with F as the mean and $\sigma\left(\hat{r}\left(t-1\right)\right)$ as standard deviation, with σ as a suitable non-monotonically decreasing function, e.g. $\sigma(t)=e$-t The internal reinforcement $\hat{r}$ is given by

$$\hat{r}\left(t+1\right) = \begin{cases} 0 & start \\ r\left(t+1\right) - v\left(t,t\right) & failure \\ r\left(t+1\right) + \gamma v\left(t, t+1\right) - v\left(t,t\right) & otherwise \end{cases}$$

The fundamental idea of using ranking and order is that a campaign starts to establish a stable ranking (order), without using any information on how much higher ranked candidates win over lower ranked candidates.

The meaning of "*stable ranking*" or "*order apparently no longer changing*" is taken as a sufficiently high standard deviation of candidate observables, and that the differential of that standard deviation is not decreasing.

In the following we provide an example rule base.

If x is LOW & Δx is LOW Then add proof to RED

If x is LOW & Δx is MEDIUM-to-HIGH Then add proof to YELLOW

If x is MEDIUM-to-HIGH & Δx is MEDIUM-to-HIGH Then add proof to GREEN with related parameters

The RSMM output appears in the unit interval [0,1], with RED, YELLOW and GREEN set as in Table 2 when using the Takagi-Sugeno [Takagi et al, 1985] inference mechanism. The compositional rule of inference will aggregate the output from all three rules, given the input match with each rule. That aggregated output will again appear in the unit interval [0,1] (in fact within the interval [0.1,0.9] in this particular case.

Table 1. Gaussian membership function parameter values for "low" and "medium-to-high".

Gaussian Function	μ	β
LOW	0.25	0.25
MEDIUM-to-HIGH	0.666	0.33

Table 2. Parameter values for the output function.

Gaussian Function	u
RED	0.1
YELLOW	0.5
GREEN	0.9

In our second example, we make use of the second derivative. The fundamental idea in this example is the use action/cost or cost/action and one base variable for a constructed variable, for which the adjusted differential and adjusted double differential are used as input to the rule base.

Input variables are $\Delta_{adj}x$ and $\Delta^2_{adj}x$, where x typically is *link_click_per_spend* or *landing_page_view_per_spend*.

Output is the recommendation either to stop campaign, monitor the campaign more intensively and in detail also by means of external criteria, or allow campaign to continue.

Rules:

- Red flag: Negative $\Delta_{adj}x$ in combination with negative $\Delta^2_{adj}x$ speaks clearly against having satisfactory campaign outcome, and the campaign should be stopped.

- Yellow flag: Approximately zero $\Delta_{adj}x$ in combination with approximately zero $\Delta^2_{adj}x$ indicates that the campaign is neither gaining more conversions nor declining in number of conversion, and the campaign can continue but should be closely monitored

- Green flag: Positive $\Delta_{adj}x$ in combination with Positive $\Delta^2_{adj}x$ shows that the campaign has increasing and accelerating numbers of conversions, and the campaign should definitely continue.

- Green flag: Close to zero $\Delta_{adj}x$ in combination with positive $\Delta^2_{adj}x$ shows conversion increase is in the making, and the campaign should be allowed to continue.

- Green flag: Positive $\Delta_{adj}x$ in combination with close to zero $\Delta^2_{adj}x$ shows constantly increasing conversions even if without acceleration, and the campaign should be allowed to continue.

The rule base a bit more formally:

If $\Delta_{adj}x$ is NEGATIVE & $\Delta^2_{adj}x$ is NEGATIVE Then add proof to RED

If $\Delta_{adj}x$ is ZERO & $\Delta^2_{adj}x$ is ZERO Then add proof to YELLOW

If $\Delta_{adj}x$ is POSITIVE & $\Delta^2_{adj}x$ is POSITIVE Then add proof to GREEN

If $\Delta_{adj}x$ is ZERO & $\Delta^2_{adj}x$ is POSITIVE Then add proof to GREEN

If $\Delta_{adj}x$ is POSITIVE & $\Delta^2_{adj}x$ is ZERO Then add proof to GREEN

with related parameters

The RSMM output appears in the unit interval [0,1], with RED, YELLOW and GREEN set as in Table 4.

Again when using the Takagi-Sugeno inference mechanism for aggregating the output from all five rules, given the input match with each rule. That aggregated output will again appear in the unit interval [0,1].

Table 3. Gaussian membership function parameter values for "low" and "medium-to-high".

Gaussian Function	μ	β
NEGATIVE	0.3	0.25
ZERO	0.5	0.33
POSITIVE	0.7	0.25

Table 4. Parameter values for the output function.

Gaussian Function	u
RED	0.1
YELLOW	0.5
GREEN	0.9

Aggregation of values inside expressions involves a hidden "flattening" of hierarchical expressions. This situation is not all that complicated when involving numerical values only. However, when including symbolic values, where expressions are typed, and expressions appear as terms over a signature, and further as appearing in a many-valued setting [Eklund et al, 2014], that "flattening" is achieved by a multiplication in a corresponding monad. This is very technical, yet necessary, when expressions become richer in content and may need to appear in various extension structures [Gahler et al, 2000]. Such extensions will be needed also when attributes used in social media marketing are not just variables but indeed expressions.

FUTURE RESEARCH DIRECTIONS

RSMM has been implemented as a library, which is integrated into a web application using Facebook's Marketing API for developers, and as used in Facebook marketing campaigns. The objective is to increase the degree of automation in social media marketing campaigns.

Next steps include development of a fully automatized SMM architecture, and the involvement of discrete levels of uncertainties based on algebraic foundations of many-valuedness.

REFERENCES

Barry, T. E. (2012). The Development of the Hierarchy of Effects: An Historical Perspective. *Current Issues and Research in Advertising*, *10*(1-2), 251–295.

Berenji, H. R., & Khedkar, P. (1992). Learning and tuning fuzzy logic controllers through reinforcements. *IEEE Transactions on Neural Networks*, *3*(5), 724–740. doi:10.1109/72.159061 PMID:18276471

Bezdek, J. C. J. C. (1981). Pattern Recognition with Fuzzy Objective Function Algorithms. Plenum Press.

Dhaoui, C., Webster, C. M., & Tan, L. P. (2017). Social media sentiment analysis: Lexicon versus machine learning. *Journal of Consumer Marketing*, *34*(6), 480–488. doi:10.1108/JCM-03-2017-2141

Eklund, P. (1994). Network size versus preprocessing. In R. Yager & L. Zadeh (Eds.), *Fuzzy Sets, Neural Networks and Soft Computing* (pp. 250–264). Van Nostrand Reinhold.

Eklund, P., & Forsström, J. J. (1995). Computational intelligence for laboratory information systems. *Scandinavian Journal of Clinical and Laboratory Investigation*, *55*(222), 21–30. doi:10.3109/00365519509088447 PMID:7569742

Eklund, P., Galán, M. A., Helgesson, R., & Kortelainen, J. (2014). Fuzzy terms. *Fuzzy Sets and Systems*, *256*, 211–235. doi:10.1016/j.fss.2013.02.012

Eklund, P., Gutiérrez García, J., Höhle, U., & Kortelainen, J. (2018). *Semigroups in complete lattices: Quantales, modules and related topics. Developments in Mathematics 54*. Springer. doi:10.1007/978-3-319-78948-4

Gähler, W., & Eklund, P. (2000). Extension structures and compactifications. Categorical Methods in Algebra and Topology. *CatMAT*, *2000*, 181–205.

Gur-Ari, G., Roberts, D. A., & Dyer, E. (2018). *Gradient Descent Happens in a Tiny Subspace*. arXiv:1812.04754v1 [cs.LG]

Jaakonmäki, R., Müller, O., & vom Brocke, J. (2017). The Impact of Content, Context, and Creator on User Engagement in Social Media Marketing. *Hawaii International Conference on System Sciences, HICSS-50*. 10.24251/HICSS.2017.136

Sheldon, A. F. (1911). *The Art of Selling*. The Sheldon School.

Strong, E. K. (1925). *The Psychology of Selling and Advertising*. McGraw-Hill.

Sugeno, M., & Yasukawa, T. (1993). A Fuzzy-Logic-Based Approach to Qualitative Modeling. *IEEE Transactions on Fuzzy Systems*, *1*(1), 7–31. doi:10.1109/TFUZZ.1993.390281

Sutton, R. S., & Barto, A. G. (2018). *Reinforcement learning* (2nd ed.). The MIT Press.

Takagi, T., & Sugeno, M. (1985). Fuzzy identification of systems and its Applications to modeling and control. *IEEE Transactions on Systems, Man, and Cybernetics*, *15*(1), 116–132. doi:10.1109/TSMC.1985.6313399

Wierenga, B., & van der Lans, R. (Eds.). (2017). *Handbook of Marketing Decision Models*. Springer. doi:10.1007/978-3-319-56941-3

Zadeh, L. A. (1965). Fuzzy sets. *Information and Control*, 8(3), 338–353. doi:10.1016/S0019-9958(65)90241-X

ADDITIONAL READING

Richard, S., Sutton, R. S., & Barto, A. G. (2018). *Reinforcement Learning: An Introduction* (2nd ed.). MIT Press.

Wierenga, B., & van der Lans, R. (Eds.). (2017). *Handbook of Marketing Decision Models*. Springer. doi:10.1007/978-3-319-56941-3

KEY TERMS AND DEFINITIONS

Fuzzy Logic: A logic language involved many-valued truth.

Neural Network: A supervised learning algorithm, based on layers of weighted sums, suitable for classification.

Reinforcement: An unsupervised learning algorithm.

Social Media Marketing: Marketing using media channels provided by social media like Facebook, Instagram, etc.

This research was previously published in the Handbook of Research on Applied AI for International Business and Marketing Applications; pages 30-48, copyright year 2021 by Business Science Reference (an imprint of IGI Global).

Chapter 46
Usage of Social Media Among LIS Students in India

S. Thanuskodi

Alagappa University, India

ABSTRACT

Social media has become a popular method for students to share information and knowledge and to express emotions. They enable students to exchange videos files, text messages, pictures, and knowledge sharing. They provide an opportunity for students to improve social networking and learning processes, which promotes knowledge in society. This study examined the use of social media among LIS students of selected universities in India. The main objectives of the study are to find out the reasons why LIS students use social media, to identify students' perception of social media, and to find out the frequency of social media usage. The study used a questionnaire in order to discover the use of SNS. Well-structured questionnaires were distributed among 400 LIS students in India. Out of the 400 questionnaires distributed, 360 were completely filled and returned, giving a return rate of 90%.

INTRODUCTION

The transformation in the technology of information and communication generation, processing, storage and dissemination witnessed in the 21st century unprecedentedly opened-up new media platforms unmatched in history in terms of interconnectedness, interactivity, multiplicity and accessibility (McQuail, 2005, p. 38). During the last two decades the world, in general and India, in particular has witnessed for remarkable changes in Information Technology (IT). The advancement in IT led to the emergence of Social Networking Sites (SNS). SNS are currently being used regularly by millions of people. The usage of SNS has been so widespread that they have caught the attention of academics worldwide. SNS are now being investigated by numerous social science researchers. An increasing number of social scientists are developing interest in studying SNS, because of its impact on society. Further, the usage of Social Networking Sites (SNS) among the people of India is evidently increasing, particularly among the Indian college students (Manjunatha, 2013).

DOI: 10.4018/978-1-6684-7123-4.ch046

Social Media are media that allow users to meet online via the Internet, communicate in social forum like Facebook, Twitter, etc., and other chat sites, where users generally socialise by sharing news, photo or ideas and thoughts, or respond to issues and other contents with other people. Common examples of social media are the popular social networking sites like *Facebook*, *Myspace*, *Youtube*, *Flicker*, etc. Social Media is an interactive media format that allows users to interact with each other as well as send and receive content from and to each other generally by means of the Internet.

The first noteworthy trend has been the evolution of the Internet. The modern Internet is often called "Web 2.0". The central components of Web 2.0 are the different social media and social web communities. Invented by Tim O'Reilly in 2005, the term "Web 2.0" is just a name for the evolution of Internet-based communications, and it shows that networking and electronic interaction have advanced to the next level. The quick development of mobile technology and different mobile terminals has been important for the creation and use of social media. A modern, well-equipped Smartphone can be a pocket-sized mega-studio. The applications and services of information and communications technology are merging together more and more. An ubiquitous presence, the different hardware and services we use now contain a new kind of "intelligence", where these machines and services communicate with each other without any particular action by the user.

Use of Social Media as an Educational Tool

Social media instead of sending messages should be used for educational purpose. Students should be taught different ways to use social media which can help them to enhance their knowledge. Students should be engaged in doing practical work like writing blogs. It will help them to get vast knowledge on a topic and to apply various techniques while solving problems. Teachers should control an online environment of the students which can help them to gather information, to socialize and to build a personality. Students should be made aware about the positive aspects of social media. They should be taught that it is one of the very powerful mediums by which they can get connected to the professionals. With the advent of latest applications like what's App, educational institutes should try to gauge the students in more productive work.

Over the past few years social media or social networking sites (SNS) have been more popular than any other sites, especially among students and young population. SNS allow individuals to be visible to others and establish or maintain connections with others. These sites can be used for work-related issues, personal issues, romantic relationships, and shared interests such as music, arts, sports, or politics. Facebook, for example, allows its users to have online profiles and invite others to be their "friends" so they can view each other's profiles and post comments on each other's pages. Facebook members can also join virtual groups based on their common interests, see what interests they have in common, and learn about each other's interests, hobbies, and relationship status by viewing their profiles (Ellison et al., 2007).

REVIEW OF LITERATURE

Har Singh and Anil Kumar (2013) in their paper entitled 'Use of Social Networking Sites (SNSs) by the research scholars of Punjab University, Chandigarh: A study' explored to study the activities and purposes for using SNSs by the scholars of Punjab University, Chandigarh. The findings of their study shows that majority of the respondents were found to be aware and making use of such applications in their research work. Their study also reveals that facebook is the most popular SNSs by all categories of researchers.

According to Thanuskodi (2011), there are lots of web 2.0 websites which is used by library organization for effective and efficient services. Web 2.0 technology and social media applications such as social networking sites, blogs, wikis etc. they all assure an extra vibrant, social participatory internet.

Noa Aharony (2013) in his paper entitled "Facebook use by Library and Information Science students" The findings of the study revealed that personality characteristics as well as gender, level of education and age influence both LIS students' patterns of Facebook use, and their perceptions about Facebook.

According to Thanuskodi (2011), students have to read books other than textbooks to improve thinking and other cognitive activities. An individual's interests are determined to a considerable extent by the amount of textual materials consumed and the intensity with which he will pursue his reading activity. By reading books, one gets confirmation or rejection of one's own ideas, which in turn increases the knowledge level of the reader. In addition, reading provides people with a sense of values, which enable them to discriminate between what is acceptable in the society and what is not.

Bennett et al (2004) also analysed in their study on physicians' internet information-seeking behaviors. The purpose of this study was to begin to shape a theory base for more fully describing physicians' information-seeking behaviors as they apply to internet use for effectively support learning. For this purpose, a structured survey questionnaire was distributed regarding internet use. The study comes with the results that almost all physicians have access to the internet, and most believe it is important for patient care. The most frequent use is in accessing the latest research on specific topics, new information in a disease area, and information related to a specific patient problem. Electronic media are viewed as increasingly important sources for clinical information, with decreased use of journals and local continuing medical education (CME). Barriers to finding needed information include too much information, lack of specific information, and navigation or searching difficulties.

Chew et al. (2004) have studied on using diffusion of innovations theory to understand doctor's internet use. This study used "diffusion of innovations" theory to identify strategies for increasing Internet use by family physicians. For this purpose, conducted a mail survey of 58 family physicians in a midsized North eastern metropolitan area in the US to assess internet use. The study brings the results that internet use begins when physicians are not constrained by a heavy patient volume and are able to learn about and observe the benefits of internet use. They concluded the study with the findings that the internet use by family physicians might be increased by providing them time to learn about how to use it and to experience its benefits. Integration of continuing medical education courses created for the purpose of developing and enhancing internet usage skills into their schedule may be a workable solution. Also found that demographic factors such as gender and training regency have no influence on internet use by family physicians.

Miller & Sim, (2004) conducted a study on physicians' use of electronic medical records. The electronic medical record (EMR) is an enabling technology that allows physician practices to pursue more powerful quality improvement programs than is possible with paper-based records. However, achieving quality improvement through EMR use is neither low-cost nor easy. This study identified key barriers to physicians' use of EMRs. The authors suggested some policy interventions to overcome these barriers, including providing work/practice support systems, improving electronic clinical data exchange, and providing financial rewards for quality improvement.

Peterson et al. (2004) have studied in their paper on medical students' use of information resources. In 2001, the authors monitored second-year medical students' use of a unique digital textbook, Up To-Date, as they transitioned from preclinical to clinical years at the University of Iowa Roy J. and Lucille A. Carver College of Medicine. In 2002, at the end of their third year, students were surveyed about their preferred clinical information resources. This study results that the medical students rapidly adopted Up To-Date as a clinical resource during their clinical clerkship as evidenced by a rapid growth in the electronic textbook's use. They also reported using the information resources on a daily basis and requiring less than 15 minutes to answer most of their clinical questions. In conclusions, this study clearly demonstrates that medical students embrace and use electronic information resources much more than has been reported among practicing clinicians. The authors also noted that the current generation of students may be the leaders in a medical culture shift from paper to electronic resources.

Baker et al. (2003) also conducted a survey study regarding use of the Internet and e-mail for health care information in national level. This study aims to measure the extent of Internet use for health care among a representative sample of the US population, to examine the prevalence of e-mail use for health care, and to examine the effects that internet and e-mail use has on users' knowledge about health care matters. For this study purpose, a survey conducted among a sample drawn from a research panel of more than 60000 US households developed and maintained by Knowledge Networks. The results of the study are, approximately 40% of respondents with internet access reported using the internet to look for advice or information about health or health care. Six percent reported using e-mail to contact a physician or other health care professional. This study comes with conclusions from the findings that although many people use the internet for health information, use is not as common as is sometimes reported.

Harris et al. (2003) has discussed in their study about whether women physicians are early adopters of on-line continuing medical education. This paper studied the actual use of several different on-line CME programs within three different groups of physicians. The on-line programs were developed as part of research studies funded by the National Institutes of Health, with no relationship to commercial interests. This study compared the characteristics of physicians who chose to use these on-line programs with demographic data from larger populations representing the groups from which these users originated. This study came with the results from the findings that physicians who used these on-line CME programs were younger than average and, importantly, more likely to be female than expected. The data suggest that the growth of on-line CME is most likely occurring in diffusion networks dominated by relatively new medical school graduates and, possibly, women physicians. These results provide valuable insight to those who seek to develop and market on-line CME and those who seek to reach women physicians with CME programs.

Powell, et al. (2003) has conducted a study regarding the doctor, the patient and the world-wide web and to know how the internet is changing healthcare. This study aimed to understand individual use of the internet and its impact on individuals, communities and societies is a challenge that is only beginning to be addressed. This study concludes that the internet is having profound impacts on health and healthcare. It has the potential to improve the effective and efficient delivery of healthcare, empower and educate consumers, support decision-making, enable interaction between consumers and professionals, support the training and revalidation of professionals, and reduce inequalities in health.

Patt, Madhavi et al. (2003) has conducted a study on doctors who are using e-mail with their patients. This study aims to survey physicians currently using e-mail with their patients daily to understand their experiences. For this purpose in-depth phone interviews conducted among 45 physicians currently using e-mail with patients were audio taped and transcribed verbatim. This study ends with the results that the most consistent theme was that e-mail communication enhances chronic-disease management. They conclude the study as these physician respondents did perceive benefits to e-mail with a select group of patients. Several areas, such as identifying clinical situations where e-mail communication is effective, incorporating e-mail into office flow, and being reimbursed for online medical care/communication, need to be addressed before this mode of communication diffuses into most practices.

Murray et al. (2003) has conducted a national survey study among 1,050 US physicians regarding the impact of health information on the internet on health care and the physician-patient relationship. For this purpose, a cross-sectional survey of a nationally-representative sample of United States physicians was conducted. The study brings the results that eighty-five percent of respondents had experienced a patient bringing internet information to a visit. They concluded the study as, the quality of information on the internet is supreme, accurate relevant information is beneficial, while inaccurate information is harmful. A minority of physicians feels challenged by patients bringing health information to the visit; reasons for this require further research.

Casebeer et al (2002) have conducted a study regarding physicians' internet medical information seeking and on-line continuing education use patterns. The purpose of this study was to examine physician medical information–seeking behaviors and their relevance to continuing education (CE) providers who design and develop on-line CE activities. For this purpose, a survey concerning internet use and learning was administered by facsimile transmission to a random sample of 2,200 U.S. office-based physicians of all specialties. The findings of the study are, nearly all physicians have access to the Internet, know how to use it, and access it for medical information. Barriers to use included too much information to scan and too little specific information to respond to a defined question. Access to on-line continuing medical education must be immediate, relevant, credible, and easy to use. The roles of the CE provider must be reshaped to include helping physicians seek and construct the kind of knowledge they need to improve patient care.

Arroll et al (2002) discussed in their paper on use of information sources among New Zealand family physicians with high access to computers. This study aims to characterize the information sources used by family physicians in a half day of practice with particular emphasis on computerized sources. For this study purpose, a written questionnaire was administered and distributed. The findings of the study are, books were the most common source of answers, followed by colleagues. They concluded this study as, despite great expectations that computers will be used to solve the information needs of family physicians, this study demonstrated that, currently, family physicians rarely use electronic sources to gather clinical information. Further work is needed to make computerized information more accessible to family physicians and to accustom family physicians to using computers at the time of an office visit.

Gjersvik et al. (2002) also conducted a combined study on use of the Internet among dermatologists in the United Kingdom, Sweden and Norway. For this survey study purpose, questionnaires distributed to 1,291 members of the dermatological societies of the United Kingdom, Sweden, and Norway. Seventy-nine percent used the World Wide Web for medical updating and other professional purposes. Sixty-two percent found medical databases on the Internet and 25% believed the internet version of medical journals to be important for their continuing medical education. This study shows that a large proportion of dermatologists, especially younger doctors, use the internet for medical and educational purposes. But internet use has not yet replaced traditional ways of obtaining continuing medical education.

Cullen (2002) also analysed in his study on family practitioners' use of the internet for clinical information. The aim of the study was to determine the extent of use of the internet for clinical information among family practitioners in New Zealand. For this purpose, a random sample of members of the Royal

New Zealand College of General Practitioners was surveyed to determine their use of the internet as an information source and their access to MEDLINE. The study brings the results that up to 10% of patients bring information from the Internet to consultations. They concluded the study as the practitioners urgently need training in searching and evaluating information on the Internet and in identifying and applying evidence-based information. Portals to provide access to high-quality, evidence-based clinical and patient information are needed along with access to the full text of relevant items.

Kalsman and Acosta (2000) conducted a pilot study on use of the internet as a medical resource by rural physicians. This pilot study reviews rural physicians' usage patterns of the internet as a medical resource and examines the barriers that might preclude rural providers from using this technology. This study undertook a questionnaire survey of rural providers in Wyoming, Montana, and Idaho. A background MEDLINE search was performed using the MeSH headings "internet," "medical informatics" and "rural health." In conclusions although the findings of this survey suggest that, compared with broader physician populations, rural physicians are using the internet with the same frequency; their scope of use might be much more limited. Barriers to using the internet are difficult to determine, but lack of time, hard- ware, and a sense of need appear to be important factors.

Kassirer (2000) also conducted a study on patients, physicians, and the internet. In this study the author pointed out that the patients will have access to vast information sources of variable validity. Many physician organizations are preparing for the electronic transformation, but most physicians are unprepared, and many are resistant. The author of the study recommended few points to transform care will require new, sophisticated soft- ware that permits unconstrained interaction with computers by voice, that incorporates patient information from disparate electronic sources, that unerringly solves clinical problems, and that makes information searching reliable, focused, and fast.

Thanuskodi (2012) carried out a survey on awareness of library 2.0 applications among library and information science professionals at Annamalai University, India, which indicated that majority 37 (61.66%) of the respondents needed training on Web 2.0 technologies and tools. The study found that 20 (33.33%) of the respondents considered workshops as important for using blogs. When asked about workshop on using wikis, only a very few respondents (15.55%) agreed to it.

Samir N. Hamade (2013) in his paper entitled "Perception and use of social networking sites among university students" The results showed a heavy use of Twitter and Facebook among university students who were viewing their sites more frequently than posting. The most positive impacts were better relation with family, relatives, and friends and more involvement in social, political and cultural activities. Neglecting study/work and the time consumed are the two major drawbacks.

Kumar Anil and Kumar Rajinder (2013) in his paper entitled "Using Social Networking Sites by the Post Graduate students and research scholars of Maharishi Dayanand University, Rohtak, India. The findings of the study shows that majority of the respondents to be aware and making use of such applications in their research work. The study also reveals that Facebook is the most popular SNSs among the all categories of students and research scholars.

Mansour (2012) assessed the role of SNS in the latest Egyptian revolution. He found that SNS have played a central role in the events known collectively as the Arab Spring. Their importance as a source of non-governmental information and as a means of informing the external and internal communities of internal events is highlighted by all participants.

Thanuskodi, S (2011) had a survey to understand and sketch a framework of information literacy level of library professionals of fifteen major engineering colleges in the state of Tamil Nadu. Professionals with right ICT skills and expertise will have plenty opportunities in future and will be crucial to the management of technology intensive libraries. He concluded that 95.12 percent of professionals have knowledge in computer fundamentals, 81.07 percent in Internet, 42.68 percent in multimedia and only a very few professionals 29.26 percent have knowledge in computer programming.

Al-Fadhli and Al-Saleh (2012) investigated the political impact of Facebook on Kuwaiti college students. Their sample consisted of 297 students at Kuwait University. The findings indicate positive relationship between Facebook use and students political engagement in Kuwait. Facebook appears to be a powerful tool for political change.

Another study in India was conducted by Kumar (2012), who investigated the perception and use of SNS among Sikkim University students. The study showed that a good number of university students use SNS for academic purposes in addition to entertainment. Facebook was the most used social networking site followed by Orkut and Twitter.

Park (2010) studied the differences among university students and faculties in their perception and use of social networking. He found that most undergraduate students regard SNS as an entertainment feature, and most faculty members were not active users of this technology. He suggested making social networking site-based services tailored to them and the benefits emphasised to them in order to attract them to get involved in these activities. In the same year, Kanagavel and Velayutham (2010) studied the impacts of social networking on college students in India and The Netherlands. They found that Indian students spend more time in these sites than Dutch students but they were mostly passive. Dutch students, on the other hand, participate more actively than Indian students by posting to these sites.

In Kuwait, Al-Daihani (2010) explored the use of social software by master of library and information science students at Kuwait University as compared to those at the University of Wisconsin-Milwaukee in the USA. He found that the majority of students from the two schools were aware of social software applications and their use. Their perceptions about online activities, their use of social software and the obstacles in using them were not significantly affected by institutional affiliation. However, institutional affiliation exhibited significant differences for their perceptions of social software applications in education.

OBJECTIVES OF THE STUDY

The main objectives of the study are as follows:

- To know the use of Social Networking sites among LIS students in India;
- To find out the usefulness of social networking sites by the LIS students;
- To know purposes using SNSs;
- To know the specific uses, preferences, and specialized academic SNSs;
- To find out benefits and affects of using SNSs;
- To know the problems being faced by the users while using SNSs; and
- To find out the most visited social networking sites.

METHODOLOGY ADOPTED

This study of the research used questionnaire- based survey method. A detailed and well structured questionnaire was designed and distributed to the Library and Information Science (LIS) students of selected universities in India. Out of 400 respondents 360 questionnaires were returned duly filled in by the LIS students in India with over all response rate was 90%. The questionnaire contained both open ended and close-ended questions. The collected data were classified, analyzed and tabulated by using statistical methods. The study was limited to use of social media by LIS students in India.

ANALYSIS OF DATA

Analysis of data is the ultimate step in research process. It is the link between raw data and significant results leading to conclusions. This process of analysis has to be result oriented.

Population Study

Table 1 shows the list of selected twenty universities in India considered for the study.

Table 1. General Information about Universities under study

Sl. No.	Name of the University
1	Alagappa University
2	Annamalai University
3	Banaras Hindu University
4	Bangalore University Burdwan University
5	Burdwan University
6	Delhi University
7	Gulburga University
8	Kashmir University
9	Kerala University
10	Kurukshetra University
11	Madurai Kamaraj University
12	Mysore University
13	Nagpur University
14	Osmania University
15	Pune University
16	Punjabi University
17	Rajasthan University
18	Sardar Patel University
19	Sri Venkateswara University
20	Vikram University

Table 2 shows that out of 360 respondents, 107 (34.62%) were male and 253 (70.27%) of respondents were female.

Table 2. Gender wise distribution of respondents

Gender	Respondents	Percentage
Male	107	29.73
Female	253	70.27
Total	360	100.00

Table 3. Status wise distribution of respondents

Status	Respondents	Percentage
UG Students	96	26.67
PG Students	264	73.33
Total	360	100.00

The Table 3 furnished above gives a brief account of the basic information of the respondents covered under the study. Here it is seen that out of 360 respondents 73.33% are PG students and remaining 26.67% are UG students.

Table 4 presents the age wise distribution of respondents. The data shows that majority of the 122 (33.89%) of respondents fall between the age group of 22-24, 104 respondents (i.e.28.88%) fall between the age group of 25-27, 69 respondents (19.17%) of respondents fall between the age group below 22 whereas 65 (i.e. 18.06%) of respondents are the age group of above 27, who used SNSs.

Table 4. Age wise distribution of respondents

Age	Respondents	Percentage
Below 22	69	19.17
22 – 24	122	33.89
25 – 27	104	28.88
Above 27	65	18.06
Total	360	100.00

Table 5. Experience in using Social Networking Sites

Variables	Respondents	Percentage
Below 1 year	156	43.34
1 to 2 year	95	26.39
2 to 3 year	64	17.77
More than 3 years	45	12.50
Total	360	100.00

Table 5 shows the duration period, for which the respondents used SNSs. It indicates that 156 respondents (i.e. 43.34%) were using the SNSs from below 1year, 95 respondents (i.e. 26.39%) were using from 1-2 years, whereas 64 (17.77%) of respondents were using from 2-3 years and 45 (12.50%) of respondents were using more than 3 years.

Sources of Knowledge

Table 6 shows that majority 218(60.56%) of the students got information about SNSs from guidance of their friends. There are 61 students representing 16.95% learnt about the social networking sites by the guidance of the teachers. There are 47 (13.05%) students who got information about social networking sites through external courses. There are 34 (9.44%) of students through trial and error method.

Table 6. Sources of knowledge about social networking websites

Variables	Respondents	Percentage
Guidance from friends	218	60.56
Trial and error Method	34	9.44
Through external courses	47	13.05
Guidance from Teachers	61	16.95
Total	360	100.00

There are different types of social networking sites, which are used by the user's community. The important social networking sites used by the LIS students of India are given in Table 7. It was found that majority of the students i.e. 208 (57.77%) use Facebook. A good number of the students use Wikipedia 132 (36.66%) and Blogs 110 (30.55%). There are 103 (28.61%) of students use Google+ and 98 (27.22%) of students use the YouTube. A less number of students use LinkedIn 76 (21.11%), followed by Delicious 64 (17.77%), Orkut 57 (15.83%), Flickr 46 (12.77%) and Slideshare 35 (9.72%). The above result shows that majority of the students were using Facebook and Wikipedia on a regular basis.

Table 7. Use of social networking websites regularly

Variables	Respondents	Percentage
YouTube	98	27.22
Google+	103	28.61
Wikipedia	132	36.66
Facebook	208	57.77
Orkut	57	15.83
Delicious	64	17.77
LinkedIn	76	21.11
Blogs	110	30.55
Flickr	46	12.77
Slidshare	35	9.72

Note: Total sample exceeds the required size since the questions are multiple choices

Frequency of Using Social Networking Sites

The table 8 shows that majority of LIS students i.e., 134 (37.22%) visit the SNSs daily. There are 92 (25.56%) LIS students who visit the SNSs weekly and 75 (20.84%) of them visit the SNSs twice in a week. Further, there are 33 (9.16%) students who visit the SNSs occasionally, 17 (4.72%) of them visit the SNS fortnightly and 9(2.50%) of them visit the SNSs monthly.

The table 9 shows that out of 360 students, 168 (46.67%) students spend less than one hour in using social networking sites, 82 (22.78%) of them spend 1-2 hours, 73 (20.28%) of them spend 2-3 hours and a few students 37 (10.27%) spend above 3 hours in using social networking sites.

Table 8. Frequency of visit to social networking sites

Frequency	Respondents	Percentage
Daily	134	37.22
Twice in a week	75	20.84
Weekly	92	25.56
Fortnightly	17	4.72
Monthly	9	2.50
Occasionally	33	9.16
Total	360	100.00

Table 9. Time Spent on social networking sites

Frequency	Respondents	Percentage
Less than 1 hour	168	46.67
1-2 hours	82	22.78
2-3 hours	73	20.28
Above 3 hours	37	10.27
Total	360	100.00

Table 10 shows the friendship nature of the respondents of the study on Social Networking Sites. The data depicts that 123 respondents (34.17%) have 101-200 friends on SNSs, 84 respondents (23.34%) have less than 50 friends, 67 respondents (18.61%) have 200-300 friends, 60 respondents (16.66%) have 50-100 friends and only 26 respondents (7.22%) have above 300 friends on Social Networking Sites. The data emphasized that SNSs can be a good platform for finding new friends.

Table 10. Friends in social networking sites

Friends	Respondents	Percentage
Less than 50	84	23.34
50-100	60	16.66
101 – 200	123	34.17
200 – 300	67	18.61
Above 300	26	7.22
Total	360	100.00

Purpose of Using Social Networking Sites

The table 11 shows that majority of the students i.e. 194 (53.88%) use social networking sites to find seminar / conferences, 165 (45.63%) use these sites to updating profile information and 148 (41.11%)

students use these sites to uploading photos. There are 142 (39.44%) user who use these sites to share photos, files, music and videos, 103 (28.61%) students use these sites to find information. Each there are 95 (26.38%) students who use these sites to meet new people and entertainment. There are 67 (18.61%) of students who use these social networking sites to feedback to friends and 54 (15.00%) use these sites to participating in discussion. Only 49 students (13.61%) used SNSs for Instant message and 38 (10.55%) other purposes like making friends.

Table 11. Purpose of using Social Networking Sites

Variables	Respondents	Percentage
To meet new people	95	26.38
Sharing photos, files, music & videos etc.	142	39.44
Instant message (chat)	49	13.61
To find information	103	28.61
Participating in discussion	54	15.00
Seminar / conferences	194	53.88
Updating profile information	165	45.83
Uploading photos	148	41.11
Entertainment	95	26.38
Feedback to friends	67	18.61
Any other	38	10.55

Note: Total sample exceeds the required size since the questions are multiple choices

Table 12 shows that respondents have less difficulty while using these sites. The data shows that only 24 respondents (6.67%) feels it is very difficult to use these sites while 34 respondents (9.44%) found them moderately difficult, 60 respondents (16.66%) feels average, on the other hand 78 respondents (21.67%) felt it is moderately easy and finally 164 (45.56%) of respondents found them very easy to use Social Networking Sites.

Table 12. Flexibility with social networking sites

Flexibility	Respondents	Percentage
Very easy	164	45.56
Moderately easy	78	21.67
Average	60	16.66
Very difficult	24	6.67
Moderately difficult	34	9.44
Total	360	100.00

Problems Faced While Using Social Networking Sites

The table 13 depicts the various problem faced by the respondents in using SNSs. The majority of the respondents 167 (46.38%) expressed poor internet connectivity, 102 (28.33%) respondents feel that unwanted attention from others. There are 83 (23.05%) respondents that they are not facing any problem while using SNSs except 'Lack of Time', 59 respondents (16.38%) feel that it is lack of privacy and 35 respondents (9.72%) feel that lack of privacy. Only 24 (i.e. 26.67%) of respondents said that SNSs are not user friendly.

Table 13. Problems faced while using social networking sites

Problems	Respondents	Percentage
Not user friendly	24	6.66
Poor internet connectivity	167	46.38
Lack of privacy	59	16.38
Lack of security	35	9.72
Lack of time	83	23.05
Unwanted attention from others	102	28.33

Note: Total sample exceeds the required size since the questions are multiple choices

The table 14 shows that 136 (37.78%) students opined that they became addict to social networking sites, 79 (21.95%) students opined that they were unable to concentrate on study, 68 (18.88%) students expressed that they stay up and lack sleep using SNSs and 52(14.45%) students opined that use social networking sites have affecting their academic performance. Only 25(6.94%) students opined that they found these as waste of time.

Table 14. Effects of social networking sites on students

Variables	Respondents	Percentage
Affecting academic performance	52	14.45
Unable to concentrate on study	79	21.95
Waste of time	25	6.94
Stay up and lack sleep	68	18.88
Addiction to SNSs	136	37.78
Total	360	100.00

Table 15 shows the respondents' view regarding the reliability of the information available on SNSs. The majority of the respondents 187 (51.95) show that the information found on SNSs is reliable. Out of 360 respondents, 115 (31.94%) respondents replied that information is partially reliable and 58 (16.11%) of respondents think that information found on SNSs are not reliable.

Table 15. Reliability of social networking sites

Reliable Information	Respondents	Percentage
Reliable	187	51.95
Partially reliable	115	31.94
Not reliable	58	16.11
Total	360	100.00

Ratings of Social Networking Sites

Table 16 presents the satisfaction level of respondents using SNSs. Out of 360 respondents, 138 (38.33%) of respondents remarked that it is highly satisfied, 102 (28.34%) respondents have mentioned as satisfied, 87 (24.16%) of respondents have remarked partially satisfied and only 33 (9.16%) of respondents mentioned that they are not satisfied while using SNSs. However, the majority of the respondents indicated that they are satisfied with SNSs.

Table 16. Satisfaction level of social networking sites

Variables	Respondents	Percentage
Highly satisfied	138	38.33
Satisfied	102	28.34
Partially satisfied	87	24.16
Not satisfied	33	9.16
Total	360	100.00

Major Findings of the Study

- The gender wise distribution indicates that out of 360 respondents 70.27% are female students and remaining 29.73% are male students.
- The findings of the age wise distribution reveals that majority of the 122 (33.89%) respondents fall between the age group of 22-24.
- Majority of the 156 respondents (i.e. 43.34%) were using the SNSs from below 1year experience.
- The study shows that majority 218(60.56%) of the students got information about SNSs from guidance of their friends.
- The study result shows that majority of the students were using Facebook and Wikipedia on a regular basis.
- The study shows that majority of LIS students i.e., 134 (37.22%) visit the SNSs daily.
- Out of 360 students, 168 (46.67%) students spend less than one hour in using social networking sites, 82 (22.78%) of them spend 1-2 hours.

- Out of 360 respondents, 123 respondents (34.17%) have 101-200 friends on SNSs, 84 respondents (23.34%) have less than 50 friends. The data emphasized that SNSs can be a good platform for finding new friends.

- Majority of the students i.e. 194 (53.88%) use social networking sites to find seminar / conferences, 165 (45.63%) use these sites to updating profile information and 148 (41.11%) students use these sites to uploading photos.

- The study shows that only 24 respondents (6.67%) feel it is very difficult to use these sites and 164 (45.56%) of respondents found them very easy to use Social Networking Sites.

- The findings of problems faced while using Social Networking Sites reveal that majority of the respondents 167 (46.38%) expressed poor internet connectivity, 102 (28.33%) respondents feel that unwanted attention from others.

- Majority of the respondents 187 (51.95) show that the information found on SNSs is reliable.

- Out of 360 respondents, 138 (38.33%) of respondents remarked that it is highly satisfied, 102 (28.34%) respondents have mentioned as satisfied with SNSs.

CONCLUSION

The present study was focus on the use of Social Networking Sites by the LIS students in India. SNSs provide the various ways to the students to interact with each other. Student keep themselves updated by surfing profile of each other, posting of messages, videos and photos, share professional and personal information at international online platform. In the present era, SNSs have become one of the largest online platforms in the world for sharing real time information. To implement the fourth law of Dr. S.R. Ranganathan "Save the Time of the Users" SNSs is becoming the interest area of libraries, documentation centers, information centers, for implementing new services in libraries and informing their clientele in short time period.

The main problem students are seen using the SNS even in the class hours. There is need for students to learn time management and to allocate, to each task, a specific timeframe. LIS students and young adults should always make out special time for using the SNSs and not to devote all their available time to it. Furthermore, parents, guardians, tutors, religious leaders, etc. should monitor their wards on how they use these sites and what they use the sites for. They should also encourage them (youths) to engage the tools pro-actively and profitably. The youths should be encouraged to use the websites more creatively to their advantage and the benefit of the society. Finally, this study provides an in-road for future studies that could draw comparisons for gender, institution, race, and length of use to ascertain further results that might lend insight into social media network usage and preferences among different groups of people.

REFERENCES

Aharony, N. (2013). Facebook use by Library and Information Science students. *Aslib Proceedings*, *65*(1), 19–39. doi:10.1108/00012531311297168

Al-Daihani, S. (2010). Exploring the use of social software by master of library and information science students. *Library Review*, *59*(2), 117–131. doi:10.1108/00242531011023871

Al-Fadhli, S., & Al-Saleh, Y. (2012). The impact of Facebook on the political engagement in Kuwait. *Journal of Social Sciences, 44*(4), 11–23.

Arroll, B., & ... . (2002). Use of information sources among New Zealand family physicians with high access to computers. *The Journal of Family Practice, 51*(8), 706.

Baker, L., Wagner, T. H., Singer, S., & Bundorf, M. K. (2003). Use of the Internet and e-mail for health care information: Results from a national survey. *Journal of the American Medical Association, 289*(18), 2400–2406. doi:10.1001/jama.289.18.2400 PMID:12746364

Bennett, N. L., Casebeer, L. L., Kristofco, R. E., & Strasser, S. M. (2004). Physicians' Internet Information-Seeking Behaviours. *The Journal of Continuing Education in the Health Professions, 24*(1), 31–38. doi:10.1002/chp.1340240106 PMID:15069910

Casebeer, L., Bennett, N., Kristofco, R., Carillo, A., & Centor, R. (2002). Physician Internet Medical Information Seeking and On-line Continuing Education Use Patterns. *The Journal of Continuing Education in the Health Professions, 22*(1), 33–42. doi:10.1002/chp.1340220105 PMID:12004639

Chew, F., Grant, W., & Tote, R. (2004). Doctors On-line : Using Diffusion of Innovations Theory to Understand Internet Use. *Family Medicine, 36*(9), 645–650. PMID:15467942

Cullen, R. J. (2002). In search of evidence : Family practitioners' use of the Internet for clinical information. *Journal of the Medical Library Association: JMLA, 90*(4), 370–379. PMID:12398243

Ellison, N., Steinfield, C., & Lampe, C. (2007). The benefits of Facebook 'friends': Social capital and college students' use of online social network sites. *Journal of Computer-Mediated Communication, 12*(4), 1143–1168. http://jcmc.indiana.edu/vol12/issue4/ellison.html RetrievedDecember52014. doi:10.1111/j.1083-6101.2007.00367.x

Gjersvik, P. J., Nylenna, M., & Aasland, O. (2002). Use of the Internet among dermatologists in the United Kingdom, Sweden and Norway. *Dermatology Online Journal, 8*(2), 1. PMID:12546756

Hamade, S. N. (2013). Perception and use of social networking sites among university students. *Library Review, 62*(6/7), 388–397. doi:10.1108/LR-12-2012-0131

Harris, J. M. Jr, Novalis-Marine, C., & Harris, R. B. (2003). Women physicians are early adopters of on-line continuing medical education. *The Journal of Continuing Education in the Health Professions, 23*(4), 221–228. doi:10.1002/chp.1340230505 PMID:14730792

Kalsman, M. W., & Acosta, D. A. (2000). Use of the Internet as a Medical Resource by Rural Physicians. *Journal of the American Board of Family Medicine, 13*(5), 349–352. PMID:11001005

Kanagavel, R., & Velayutham, C. (2010). Impact of social networking on college students: A comparative study in India and The Netherlands. *International Journal of Virtual Communities and Social Networking, 2*(3), 55–67. doi:10.4018/jvcsn.2010070105

Kassirer, J. P. (2000). Patients, Physicians, And The Internet. *Health Affairs, 19*(6), 115–123. doi:10.1377/hlthaff.19.6.115 PMID:11192394

Kumar Anil & Kumar Rajinder. (2013). Use of Social Networking Sites (SNSs): A study of Maharishi Dayanand University, Rohtak, India. *Library Philosophy and Practice*. Retrieved from http://digitalcommons.unl.edu/libphilprac/1000

Manjunatha, S. (2013). The Usage of Social Networking sites Among the College Students in India. *Int. Res. J. Social Sci.*, *2*(5), 15–21.

Mansour, E. (2012). The role of social networking sites (SNSs) in the January 25th revolution in Egypt. *Library Review*, *61*(2), 128–159. doi:10.1108/00242531211220753

McQuail, D. (2005). *McQuail's Mass Communication Theory* (5th ed.). SAGE Publications Ltd.

Miller, R. H., & Sim, I. (2004). Physicians' Use Of Electronic MedicalRecords: Barriers And Solutions. *Health Affairs*, *23*(2), 116–126. doi:10.1377/hlthaff.23.2.116 PMID:15046136

Murray, E., Bernard, L., Pollack, L., Donelan, K., Catania, J., Lee, K., & Turner, R. (2003). The Impact of Health Information on the Internet on Health Care and the Physician-Patient Relationship: National U.S. Survey among 1.050 U.S. Physicians. *Journal of Medical Internet Research*, *5*(3), e17. doi:10.2196/jmir.5.3.e17 PMID:14517108

O'Reilly, T. (2005). *What is Web 2.0? - Design Patterns and Business Models for the Next Generation of Soft ware*. Retrieved December 2, 2014, from http://oreilly.com/web2/archive/

Park, J. (2010). Differences among university students and faculties in social networking site perception and use: Implications for academic library services. *The Electronic Library*, *28*(3), 417–431. doi:10.1108/02640471011051990

Patt, M. R., Houston, T. K., Jenckes, M. W., Sands, D. Z., & Ford, D. E. (2003). Doctors Who Are Using E-mail With Their Patients: A Qualitative Exploration. *Journal of Medical Internet Research*, *5*(2), e9. doi:10.2196/jmir.5.2.e9 PMID:12857665

Peterson, M. W., Rowat, J., Kreiter, C., & Mandel, J. (2004). Medical Students ' Use of Information Resources : Is the Digital Age Dawning? *Academic Medicine*, *79*(1), 89–95. doi:10.1097/00001888-200401000-00019 PMID:14691004

Powell, J. A., Darvell, M., & Gray, J. A. M. (2003). The doctor, the patient and the world-wide web: How the internet is changing healthcare. *Journal of the Royal Society of Medicine*, *96*(2), 74–76. doi:10.1177/014107680309600206 PMID:12562977

Singh, H., & Kumar, A. (2013). Use of social networking sites (SNSs) by the research scholars of Panjab University, Chandigarh: A study. *58th International Conference on: Next Generation Libraries: New insights and Universal Access to Knowledge,* 682-691.

Thanuskodi, S. (2011). WEB 2.0 Awareness among Library and Information Science Professionals of the Engineering Colleges in Chennai City: A Survey. *Journal of Communication*, *1*(2), 69–75. doi:10.1080/0976691X.2010.11884772

Thanuskodi, S. (2011). ICT Literacy among Library Professionals in the Engineering College Libraries of Tamil Nadu: An Analytical Study. *International Journal of Digital Library Services*, *1*(2), 131–141.

Thanuskodi, S. (2011). Reading Habits among Library and Information Science Students of Annamalai University: A Survey. *International Journal of Educational Sciences, 3*(2), 79–83. doi:10.1080/09751 122.2011.11890011

Thanuskodi, S. (2012). Awareness of library 2.0 applications among library and information science professionals at Annamalai University, India. *International Journal of Library Science, 1*(5), 75–83. doi:10.5923/j.library.20120105.02

ADDITIONAL READING

Rowe, B. H., & ... . (1995). First-Year Family Medicine Residents Use of Computers: Knowledge, Skills and Attitudes. *Canadian Medical Association Journal, 153*, 267–272. PMID:7614442

Russel, MP (1980): Education and training of the medical librarian in Great Britain.

Santhi, L., & Radhakrishnan, N. (2014). Usage Pattern of Electronic Resources among the Research Scholars in Anna University of Technology, Coimbatore and Its Affiliated Colleges. *IOSR Journal of Humanities and Social Science, 19*(7), 23–26. doi:10.9790/0837-19742326

Schalnus, R., Aulmann, G., Hellenbrecht, A., Hägele, M., Ohrloff, C., & Lüchtenberg, M. (2010). Content quality of ophthalmic information on the internet. *Ophthalmologica, 224*(1), 30–37. doi:10.1159/000233233 PMID:19684426

Selltiz, C., & ... . (1962). *Research Methods in Social Relations*. New York: Holt, Rinehart and Winston.

Sharma, Chelan (2009). Use And Impact of e-Resources at Guru Gobind Singh Indrapratha University (India): A case study *Electronic Journal of Academic and Special Librarianship* Vol. 10 (1): 1 – 8.

Singh, K. P., & Gill, M. S. (2012). Use of E-Journals by Medical Professionals : A Study of Indian Council of Medical Research (ICMR) Libraries in Delhi. *Library Philosophy and Practice (e-Journal)*.

Smith, R. P., & Edwards, M. J. (1997). *The Internet for Physicians*. New York, NY: Springer New York. doi:10.1007/978-1-4757-6744-5

Thanuskodi, S. (2013). *Challenges of Academic Library Management in Developing Countries* (pp. 1–348). Hershey, PA: IGI Global; doi:10.4018/978-1-4666-4070-2

Thanuskodi, S. (2015). *Handbook of Research on Inventive Digital Tools for Collection Management and Development in Modern Libraries* (pp. 1–422). Hershey, PA: IGI Global; doi:10.4018/978-1-4666-8178-1

Thanuskodi, S. (2015). ICT Skills among Library Professionals: A Case Study of Universities in Tamilnadu, India. In S. Thanuskodi (Ed.), *Handbook of Research on Inventive Digital Tools for Collection Management and Development in Modern Libraries* (pp. 1–20). Hershey, PA: IGI Global; doi:10.4018/978-1-4666-8178-1.ch001

Thanuskodi, S., & Alagu, A. (2015). Awareness and Use of Social Media: A Case Study of Alagappa University. In A. Tella (Ed.), *Social Media Strategies for Dynamic Library Service Development* (pp. 263–278). Hershey, PA: IGI Global; doi:10.4018/978-1-4666-7415-8.ch014

Thanuskodi, S., & Revathi, C. (2015). Expectation of Research Scholars and Students on Library Resources and Services: A Case Study of Alagappa University, India. In S. Thanuskodi (Ed.), *Handbook of Research on Inventive Digital Tools for Collection Management and Development in Modern Libraries* (pp. 190–207). Hershey, PA: IGI Global; doi:10.4018/978-1-4666-8178-1.ch012

KEY TERMS AND DEFINITIONS

Facebook: Currently Facebook is the fifth most trafficked site on the internet worldwide and second most trafficked social media site on the world. It was first founded by Mark Zuckerberg in 2004. These are interactive allowing visitors to leave comments, message each other via widgets on the blogs and it is the interactivity that distinguishes them from other static websites. It has affected the social life and activity of people in various ways.

Library and Information Science (LIS): (Sometimes given as the plural library and information sciences) or as "library and information studies" is a merging of library science and information science. The joint term is associated with schools of library and information science (abbreviated to "SLIS"). In the last part of the 1960s, schools of librarianship, which generally developed from professional training programs (not academic disciplines) to university institutions during the second half of the twentieth century, began to add the term "information science" to their names.

Modern Society: Modern society is based on the differentiation of social roles. In modern society, human beings act in different capacities in different social roles.

Social Network: Social network is a broad term used to denote the blogs, user created videos and wikis. A social networking is an online service, platform or site that focuses on building and reflecting of social network or social relations among people who share interests and activities.

Social Networking Sites: Social networking site functions like an online community of internet users. People use social networking sites for communication personally as well as professionally to contact with others. Social networking sites like Facebook provides new venues for young LIS Professionals to express themselves and to interact with one another.

This research was previously published in Literacy Skill Development for Library Science Professionals; pages 1-24, copyright year 2019 by Information Science Reference (an imprint of IGI Global).

Chapter 47
The Use of Social Media in Knowledge Sharing Case Study Undergraduate Students in Major British Universities

Motteh Saleh Al-Shibly
Amman Arab University, Amman, Jordan

ABSTRACT

This study aims to investigate how the social media tools can help the exchange of knowledge between university students to build a knowledge sharing culture. The purpose of this study is to examine the influence of individual and organizational factors, social media technologies (SMT) and knowledge sharing factors, thus predicting the online user behavior towards social media knowledge-sharing. Different methods such as (PLS) were used to analyze the study results in order to consider the influence of all constructs on the framework simultaneously. Therefore, a (157) online questionnaires were collected from undergraduate students in major British universities. The results reveal that knowledge sharing behavior had five positive factors: mutual trust, reciprocity, eWOM quality, perceived usefulness and perceived online attachment motivation. Practical implications, limitations and directions for future research are also discussed.

INTRODUCTION

"Knowledge is Power", Knowledge element is acknowledged as the fundamental resource that can provide sustained competitive advantage. Hernaez and Campos (2011) defined Knowledge as "Justified true belief that increases an entity's capability for effective animation" (p. 225). The importance of Knowledge in an organizational context can refer to the increase of its awareness, understanding, perceiving and discovering new territories thus leads to increase its ability to create and innovate in its global dynamic environment.

DOI: 10.4018/978-1-6684-7123-4.ch047

"Social Media" is used as a communication apparatus where students will be able to participate in knowledge sharing (Jones, Temperley & Lima 2009). Social media technologies (SMT) and tools have provided new opportunities to the world, it supports the procedure of knowledge sharing in institutions as it allows easy and prompt communication.

In academic fields, SMT is a powerful type of communication system that provides a platform for knowledge sharing which is essential to attract the attention of both students and faculty members (Anari, Asemi et al., 2013). Moreover, people are adept to make use of social media tools in order to increase and richen their networks and collect information by integrating social media into their business processes (Gaál et al., 2014).

According to Brown (1988) students are expected to be responsible of their education proactively by learning with both individual responsibility and communal sharing. This concept determines the importance and value of knowledge sharing through students.

The purpose of this study is to study the role played by social media in disseminating knowledge in universities with the individual and organizational factors and their impact on improving the educational system by studying the intensive targeting of students in universities. This study also offers proposals that contribute to the improvement and development of the educational and academic level, thereby achieving a competitive advantage.

LITERATURE REVIEW AND HYPOTHESES DEVELOPMENT

So far there has been no research on how social media tools can help to share knowledge between students and faculty at universities. So, we tried to include some researchers relevant to the subject of our study.

The effectiveness of social networks in organizations was investigated by Van Zell (2009). The study aimed to educate information technology, business decision makers, knowledge workers and others about the various applications, benefits and risks associated with social networking. It concluded that the application of this type of Web 2.0 toolkit in enterprises would help individuals to engage in knowledge management.

Kong, Ogata et al. (2009) investigate factors affecting the exchange of knowledge among students. Covering individual factors, classrooms, and technological aspects. A questionnaire was used to collect data, assigning that technology supports the student's ability to participate and compete with colleagues and influence the exchange of knowledge for students respectively.

Damoffek, Bottgit and Mernes (2012) realized the trends of social media technology in Nielsen to find out how these techniques can help create a culture of knowledge sharing. The study indicates that respondents had a positive attitude to share knowledge with each other through the use of social media tools.

Fatima Anari, Asifah Asmi et al. (2013) define the use of interactive social media tools such as social networking tools, social networking tools (SAT) and image tools or video sharing tools (EVISHT) to expand knowledge and information among university librarians.

Faculty members can use social media to create e-learning experiences. More importantly, students can use social media in ways that can help their learning experience (Jonavithola and Trityakov, 2012).

Need for Knowledge Sharing

Sharing knowledge is helping others to learn, joining with others to solve problems, develop new ideas, or implement operations (Cummings, 2004).

There are several reasons for focusing on knowledge sharing because it may lead to improved innovation capacity and thus a sustainable competitive advantage (Foss, Hastid & Michelova, 2010).

Knowledge is valuable and intangible assets to create and sustain competitive advantages within institutions, especially educational institutions (Miller & Chamsey, 1996), as mentioned above, three results related to knowledge sharing have been extracted as shown in Figure 1.

Figure 1. Knowledge sharing outcomes. Source: conceptual Model.

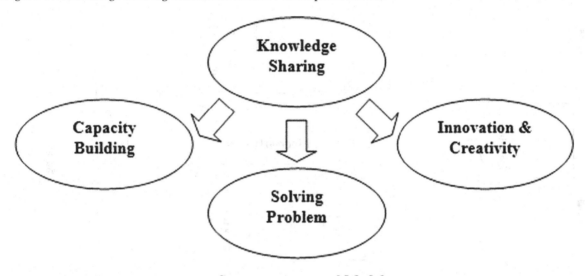

Source: conceptual Model

Knowledge sharing is a social phenomenon linked to interpersonal relations and social interactions (Lin, Wu & Andlo, 2012.) Unfortunately, people have different reasons for not sharing knowledge in all circumstances as their organizations wish (Cho, Li, & Sue, 2007). (Reg, 2005) however, sharing knowledge is a difficult task that requires time and effort and requires students to be persistent and willing to interact with each other (Ghadirian et al., 2014).

Social Media Tools for Effective Communication

Many definitions of social media, such as computer tools that allow people or companies to create, exchange or exchange information, functional interests, ideas, images and videos in virtual communities and networks (Bitner, 2016), the idea is that social media have the ability to bring people together Very broad definition. This definition suggests that telegraph and telephone are social means of communication - not technology scientists intend to describe them. (Schuster, Tiroche, 2015)

SMT tools provide facilities and opportunities for students that can be used as a means to advance their education. As an example, image and video sharing tools can be used to introduce resources and services, to teach information literacy and to provide a rich archive of photographs and films related to various conferences, seminars and lectures. (Anari Al, 2013)

In recent decades, the world has witnessed a quantum leap in technological development, particularly with the advent of the Internet, which has facilitated the easier and faster transfer of information and data through various means. (Such as Facebook), video sharing (e.g. YouTube), sharing presentations (such as SlideShare), social networking services (such as Facebook and LinkedIn), instant messaging (like Skype) and group programs (like Google Docs), (Anderson, 2007) (Figure 2).

Figure 2. Social media technologies. Source: conceptual Model.

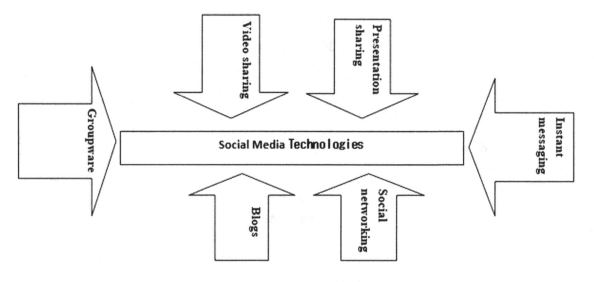

Source: conceptual Model

Figure 3 shows the world's leading social networks as of January 2017, ranked by the number of active users (in millions), and these social networks are usually available in multiple languages and enable users to communicate with people across geographical, political or economic areas. Nearly 2 billion Internet users are using social media networks, these numbers are still expected to grow as the use of mobile devices and mobile social networks increasingly gain (Statista, Statistical Portal, 2016).

Development of Hypotheses

The literature suggests that additional communication and coordination practices can lead to greater organizational innovation and enhanced coordination and collaboration (Mishra et al., 2012), a new and powerful type of communication system that provides a good platform for knowledge sharing (Reyzai, 2014), and makes it possible to share ideas Between students and create an appropriate context for sharing knowledge and information online (Anari, Assemi, et al., 2013).

*Figure 3. Leading social media networks worldwide as of January 2017 Retrieved from https://www.
statista.com/statistics/272014/global-social-networks-ranked-by-number-of-users/*

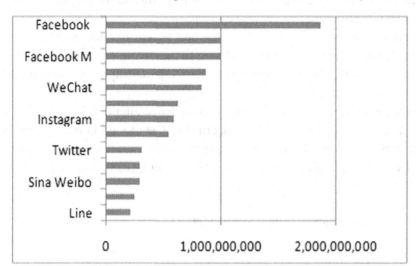

**Source: Statista. The Statistics Portal "Leading global social networks 2017 | Statistic"
(https://www.statista.com/statistics/272014/global-social-networks-ranked-by-number-of-users/)**

For this study the type of information process and flow of knowledge among students may vary depending on individual factors, organizational factors and social media techniques.

Figure 4 shows the factors that affect this process and its effect on its results as follows:

1. Individual Factor: The desire to share it will depend on: Reciprocity. Davenport and Brusack (1998) and Sealandini (2006) define reciprocity as a social norm, and people must pay, in kind, what others have given them. (The definition is unclear or something is missing)

2. Organizational factors: They will be classified as values of internal culture, beliefs and work systems that can promote knowledge sharing (Ganz and Prasarvanic, 2003), collective which is defined as "the degree of encouragement of institutions and community institutional practices and reward collective distribution of resources and teamwork" P. 30). Trust is also important for sharing knowledge. Studies on sociology have indicated that trust is not only related to people's belief in others, but their desire and desire to use knowledge to influence future actions (e.g. Lehmann, 1979; Lewis & Weigert, 1985). The trust aspect is very important for most knowledge processes, and for the transparency, utilization and sharing of knowledge (e.g., 2013).

3. Social communication technologies: Technology is a facilitator to encourage and support knowledge exchange by making it easier and more effective (Reg, 2005). Therefore, we used the word "eum" (Boom), the perceived commitment to online relationships, and perceived ease of use, and perceived benefits (BO) as factors for measuring the impact of social media tools and technology-based systems in knowledge exchange and online knowledge sharing behavior.

When searching for reviews online, the amount of om makes reviews more obvious and reading many reviews can reduce anxiety when making a decision. (Cheung & Thadani, 2010) A few studies have examined the drivers of online knowledge sharing behavior (Ghadirian et al., 2014). The concept of committed online relationships describes other behavioral motivations. Ma and Yuen (2011) define the perceived online motivation facility (Boam) as

"The ability of the individual to improve his social interaction and sense of communication with others on the online learning platform." Moreover, the commitment to the online relationship (Burke) was identified as "the individual believes that he can continue to have a relationship with others on the learning platform across The Internet "(p. 213).

The Internet has influenced the education sector in lectures and students' attention in recent years (Alexey, 2016.) One of the most serious social networking concerns has been found in its application (Rowlands, 2011); many researchers have found that perceived ease of use and perceived utility Significant influence on the individual's behavioral intention to use e-learning systems (Liu, Liao, Pratt, 2009).

Figure 4. The knowledge sharing process. Source: conceptual Model.

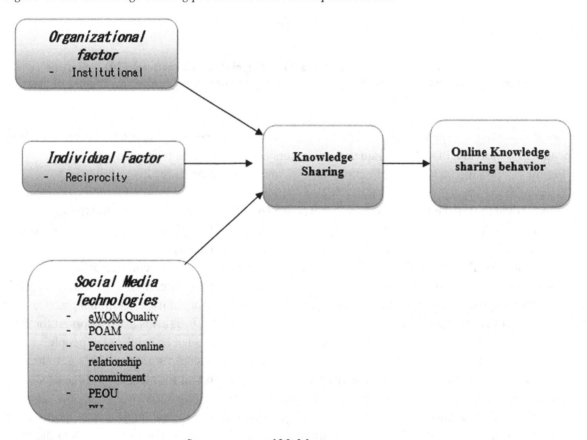

Source: conceptual Model

As a result, it is hypothesized that:

H1. Institutional collectivism would be significant in determining knowledge sharing.
H2. Mutual trust would be significant in determining knowledge sharing.

H3. Reciprocity would be significant in determining knowledge sharing.

H4. Quality of online word of mouth (eWOM) would be significant in determining knowledge sharing.

H5. Perceived online attachment (POAM) would be significant in determining knowledge sharing.

H6. Perceived Online Relationship Commitment would be significant in determining knowledge sharing.

H7. Perceived ease of use would (PEOU) be significant in determining knowledge sharing.

H8. Perceived usefulness (PU) would be significant in determining knowledge sharing.

H9. Knowledge sharing significantly and positively predicted the online user behavior towards social media knowledge sharing

METHODOLOGY

The current research uses a quantitative approach to test the study's model. Among the different quantitative data collection methods, a self-completion and a cross-sectional survey instrument was utilized to assess the key factors influencing customer knowledge sharing in an online context. As pointed out the main purpose of this study is improving educational system through the use of SMT, thus the targeted population of this study was defined as students pursuing any courses of study in major British universities (Kong, Ogata, et al., 2009). Similar to previous research, non-probability convenience sampling was employed to collect the required data for the study. Originally, 378 questionnaires were collected and 56 were excluded due to partial completeness or early exit, resulting in 222 usable questionnaires for the final analysis.

Questionnaire Design and Measurement Scales

In the current study, the survey was designed and organized to assure the clarity and the accuracy of the questions. The questionnaire design was divided into two sections. The first section holds scale questions which are used to measure the independent and dependent variables related to the research model. The second section was designed to take up the respondents' profiles (i.e. demographics data) using multiple-choice questions. To achieve the clarity of the survey, each type of questions was separated from other types. Thus, the scale questions were placed first, followed by the demographic questions. A pre-test of the questionnaire involved three phases: the first with business and marketing professors who have large experiences with surveys; the second with master's degree students; the third with 50 social media users. They suggested only little changes, which we performed.

Measurements

Previously validated scales were used to measure the study's constructs. Some items were utilized with the original wording, while others were reworded to fit the context of the study. The final structured questionnaire consisted of 42 statements. All the statements were evaluated on a seven-point Likert scale, ranging from strongly disagree, to strongly agree. Institutional collectivism was measured using five items from C. Grove (2005). Mutual trust was measured using six items from Hsu, Ju, Yen, and Chang (2007) and William (2006). Reciprocity was measured using a nine-item scale from Gee-Woo, Young-Gul Kim, and Robert W. Zmud (2005). Electronic word-of-mouth (EWOM) quality was measured using six items from Awad and Ragowsky (2008) and Chiu, Hsu, and Wang (2006). Perceived Online Attachment

Motivation (POAM) was measured using five items derived from (Ma & Yuen, 2011). Perceived Online Relationship Commitment was measured using five items from Ma and Yuen (2011). Perceived ease of use was measured using three items from Davis (1989) and perceived usefulness was measured using four items from Davis (1989). Knowledge sharing was measured using multiple items from Kankanhalli et al. (2005). Online knowledge sharing behavior was measured using items from Ko et al. (2005).

DATA ANALYSIS AND RESULTS

Results

PLS method was used to test the study's hypotheses. It is worth noting that PLS is considered more rigorous when assessing a model compared with regression analyses (Mintu-Wimsatt and Graham, 2004). It also allows for testing the structural relationships between latent constructs in one model simultaneously (Harris et al., 2011). When testing a model using PLS, three issues need to be reported: path coefficients (β); R^2 values (0.67, 0.33 and 0.19 for endogenous constructs, which are regarded as legend, moderate and weak, respectively) (Henseler et al., 2009), and t-values (> 1.96- < 2.58 suggest a significance level of 0.05, > 2.58- < 3.26 suggest a significance level of 0.01, and > 3.26 suggest a significance level of 0.001) (Chin, 1998). However, it should be noted that the decision of whether to accept/reject hypotheses depends on the significance level (t-values) of the path coefficients. PLS estimation requires ten times the largest number of structural paths directed at a particular construct in the model (Chin, 1998; Gefen et al., 2000). The sample in our study met the necessary conditions for using PLS (Figure 5).

Measurement Model

Tables 1 and 2 present the measurement model results. PLS was used to assess Cronbach's alpha (α) and composite reliability (CR). The results of (α) ranged from 0.820 to 0.955, and all scales exceeded the threshold value of 0.70 Table 3 (Nunnally, 1978). On the other hand, CR ranged from 0.852 to 0.925, and all scales were above the cut-off-point of 0.80 (Table 3) (Crossley et al., 2002). However, only one construct 'PEOU' showed low AVE score (.382) and low reliability (Alpha = 0.091) which are both below the acceptable level, as highlighted in the same table (Table 2). This result supports the decision of excluding this construct from the study.

Convergent Validity (CV) was assessed via average variance extracted (AVE), which measures the level of variance captured by a construct versus the level due to measurement error (Farrell, 2010). Table 3 shows that the AVE of the seven scales exceeded the cut-off-point of 0.50 (Fornell & Larcker, 1981; Hair et al., 2012; Henseler, Ringle, & Sinkovics, 2009). However, three items: MT01, PEOU02 and REC08 were found with low loadings: (0.184), (0.229), and (0.282) respectively. Therefore, as recommended by Hair et al. (2012), these items were eliminated from this study and were not involved in further analysis. Additional testing of the quality and the scales was conducted, which established the construct's validity and reliability. The AVE, CR, and Alpha values are higher than the recommended thresholds of 0.500, 0.700, and 0.700 respectively (Bagozzi & Yi, 1988; Gefen, Straub, & Boudreau, 2000; Nunnally, 1978).

Table 1. Individual item reliability and construct validity

Construct	Factor	Loadings	AVE	Composite Reliability	Cronbach's Alpha
Institutional collectivism	INC01 INC02 INC03 INC04 INC05	.812 .915 .948 .887 .789	.552	.905	.881
MUTUAL TRUST	MT01 MT02 MT03 MT04 MT05 MT06	.184 .769 .719 .898 .910 .895	.600	.891	.852
RECIPROCITY	REC01 REC02 REC03 REC04 REC05 REC06 REC07 REC08 REC09	.743 .912 .930 .901 .928 .718 .672 .229 .545	.599	.926	.903
EWOM	EWOM01 EWOM02 EWOM03 EWOM04 EWOM05 EWOM06	.636 .848 .915 .742 .730 .843	.619	.906	.882
PEOU	PEOU01 PEOU02 PEOU03	.910 .282 .588	.382	.603	.091
PU	PU01 PU02 PU03 PU04	.884 .903 .896 .919	.811	.945	.925
SMT RELATIONSHIP COMMITEMENT	RELCOM01 RELCOM02 RELCOM03 RELCOM04 RELCOM05	.772 .915 .924 .878 .735	.728	.927	.901
PERCEIVED ONLINE ATTACHMENT MOTIVATION (POAM)	POAM01 POAM02 POAM03 POAM04 POAM05	.801 .825 .656 .715 .655	.539	.852	.820
KNOWLEDGE SHARING	KS01 KS02 KS03 KS04 KS05	.912 .901 .893 .807 .910	.784	.948	.930
ONLINE KNOWLEDGE SHARING	OKS01 OKS02 OKS03 OKS04 OKS05	.897 .936 .910 .915 .943	.847	.965	.955

Source: developed for the current research

Finally, discriminate validity was tested based on the square root of AVE for each construct should be greater than the correlations with all constructs (Boudreau, Gefen, & Straub, 2001; Fornell & Larcker, 1981). In Table 1, it can be seen that the square root of AVE is higher than the correlation between constructs.

Table 2. Latent variable correlations

INC	.742							
MT	.462	.772						
REC	.648	.716	.759					
EWOM	.664	.652	.739	.787				
PU	.656	.658	.717	.789	.900			
RELCOM	.693	.714	.797	.814	.825	.848		
POAM	.492	.718	.672	.713	.684	.726	.734	
KS	.475	.641	.716	.637	.729	.657	.608 .885	
OKS	.713	.738	.725	.818	.887	.873	.681 .672.920	

Structural Model

In the structural equation model, the causative relationships were hypothesized between institutional collectivism, mutual trust, reciprocity, eWOM quality, POAM, PORC, PU, knowledge sharing and online knowledge sharing behavior .For the assessment of the model, the path coefficients, their significance via bootstrap resampling method (Henseler et al., 2009), with 500 iterations of resampling (Chin, 1998),and the R^2 values were estimated. The results, as summarized in Table 3, show that of the eight paths, seven were significant and supported, while the remaining two hypotheses were insignificant and not supported according to the obtained t-values and p-values. The knowledge sharing explained 72% of variance from its antecedents while online knowledge sharing behavior explained 48% of the variance.

Table 3. Partial least squares results for the theoretical model

Predicted Variable	Predictor Variable	Hypotheses	Path	R Squared	Critical Ratio	
KNOWLEDGE SHARING	INC	H1	-.099	.718	1.029	Rejected
	MT	H2	.324		2.631	Supported
	REC	H3	.541		3.199	Supported
	EWOM	H4	.045		1.987	Supported
	PU	H5	.574		4.028	Supported
	PORC	H6	-.484		3.802	Supported
	POAM	H7	.079		2.113	Supported
ONLINR KNOWLEDGE SHARING	KS	H9	.673	.476	7.719	Supported

In summary, the results of these tests showed that knowledge sharing behavior had five positive antecedents: mutual trust, reciprocity, eWOM quality, perceived usefulness, and perceived online attachment motivation. Perceived usefulness had the strongest effect, followed by mutual trust. As shown in Table 3, relationship between perceived online relationship commitment and knowledge sharing behavior was found to be negative. The PLS results, as shown in Table 3, indicate that institutional collectivism had no significant effect on knowledge sharing behavior (ß = -0.099, t = 1.029), thereby, rejecting H1. Mutual trust, as suggested in H2, had a significant and positive effect on knowledge sharing behavior (β = 0.324; t = 2.631, p < 0.01), emerge as the third strongest relationship in the model supporting H2. This implies that users who have trust with others member using social media technologies would be more likely to share knowledge.

Figure 5. Research model with PLS results

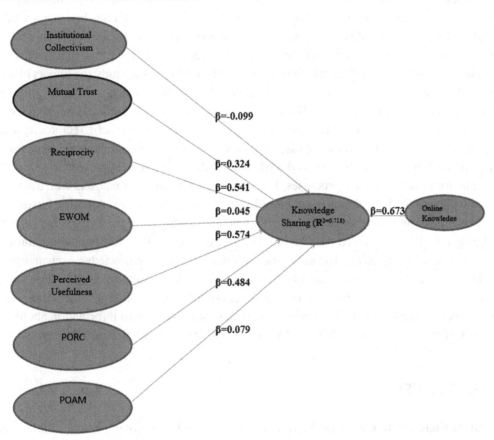

Consistent with H3, reciprocity had the second strongest significant positive effect on knowledge sharing (β = 0.541; t= 3.199, p < 0.01); hence H3 was supported. eWOM quality was positively related to knowledge sharing behavior (β = 0.045; t = 1.987, p < 0.10); thus H4 was supported, suggesting that the quality of online word of mouth may increase users' behavior towards sharing knowledge Likewise, perceived online attachment motivation was significantly and positively related to knowledge sharing behavior (β = 0.79; t = 2.113, p < 0.01); thus H7 was supported. Consistent with H5, perceived usefulness had the strongest positive impact on users' behavior towards knowledge sharing ($\beta = 0.574$, t = 4.028, p < 0.01), thereby providing support to H5. The data supports H6 concerning the negative effect of perceived online relationship commitment on knowledge sharing ($\beta = 0.484$; t= 3.802, p < 0.01). As expected, knowledge sharing significantly and positively predicted the online user behavior towards social media knowledge sharing ($\beta = 0.673$; t = 7.719, p < 0.01). Thus, H9 was supported.

CONCLUSION AND FUTURE RESEARCH

Social media is no longer a negligible phenomenon; tools like Facebook, Twitter, Instagram, or sudden chat have taken the world into a storm. Social media became a modified personal relationship that allowed individuals to contribute to a number of issues and create new possibilities and challenges to facilitate partnerships. Organizations need to focus not only on innovation in new products and services, but also pay special attention to the sharing of effective knowledge, which has become a vital tool for their success. The advantages of embracing and implementing social media are huge. This study aimed at identifying how social networking tools can help to exchange knowledge among British university students in order to build a culture of knowledge exchange. The purpose is to study the impact of individual (reciprocity), regulatory factors and Social Media Technologies (SMT) such as: (quality of Om, Boam, commitment to online relationship, Bio, Bo) to share knowledge and thus predict online user behavior towards knowledge sharing social media. It has been shown that perceived benefit, reciprocity and mutual trust have had the strongest impact on the exchange of knowledge among students, respectively. People are seeking methods that enable them to work faster and make their lives easier, as well as confidence is very important for most knowledge processes, Use and Share This means that users who trust with other members using social media techniques are more likely to share knowledge. All other factors have also had a positive impact on the behavior of online knowledge sharing (online word quality of the mouth, perceived online facility, perceived ease of use, knowledge sharing) while the institutional collective and online facility seen has no significant impact on online behavior Knowledge exchange, its impact proved to be negative. This research could be expanded as it is interesting to compare knowledge sharing practices and the use of social media tools in other countries or in other service sectors, as well as research on separate platforms on social networks, which can reveal more information about The roles of each platform plays and how it affects the behavior of sharing knowledge online from individuals.

ACKNOWLEDGMENT

Mohammad Al Khasawneh of Princess Sumaya University for Technology, Amman, Jordan and Reem M. Alrefai, Independent Researcher, Amman, Jordan were involved in the research for this paper.

REFERENCES

Adamovic, D., Potgieter, A., & Mearns, M. (2012). Knowledge sharing through social media: Investigating trends and technologies in a global marketing and advertising research company. *South African Journal of Information Management*, *14*(1). doi:10.4102ajim.v14i1.514

Ahed, A.W. (2015). Higher education in Jordan — who to blame and how to improve. The Jordan Times. Retrieved from http://www.jordantimes.com/opinion/ahed-al-wahadni/higher-education-jordan

Anari, F., Asemi, A., Asemi, A., & Abu Bakar, M. (2013). Social Interactive Media Tools and Knowledge Sharing: A Case Study.

Anderson, J., & Gerbing, W. (1988). Structural equation modeling in practice: A review and recommended two stage approach. *Psychological Bulletin, 27*(1), 5–24.

Anderson, P. (2007), What is Web 2.0? Ideas, technologies and implications for education. JISC reports. Retrieved from http://www.jisc.ac.uk/media/documents/techwatch/tsw0701b.pdf

Auh, S., & Menguc, B. (2005). Top management team diversity and innovativeness: The moderating role of interfunctional coordination. *Industrial Marketing Management, 34*(3), 249–261. doi:10.1016/j.indmarman.2004.09.005

Awad, N. F., & Ragowsky, A. (2008). Establishing trust in electronic commerce through online word of mouth: An examination across genders. *Journal of Management Information Systems, 24*(4), 101–121. doi:10.2753/MIS0742-1222240404

Bagozzi, R. P., & Yi, Y. (1988). On the evaluation of structural equation models. *Journal of the Academy of Marketing Science, 16*(1), 74–94. doi:10.1007/BF02723327

Boudreau, M. C., Gefen, D., & Straub, D. W. (2001). Validation in information systems research: A state-of-the-art assessment. *Management Information Systems Quarterly, 25*(1), 1–16. doi:10.2307/3250956

Brown, A. L. (1988). Motivation to learn and understand: On taking charge of one's own learning. *Cognition and Instruction, 5*(4), 311–321. doi:10.12071532690xci0504_4

Buettner, R. (2016). Getting a Job via Career-oriented Social Networking Sites: The Weakness of Ties. In *49th Annual Hawaii International Conference on System Sciences*, Kauai, HI. IEEE. 10.1109/HICSS.2016.272

Business dictionary. (2016). Knowledge definition. Retrieved from http://www.businessdictionary. com/definition/knowledge.html#ixzz4AzyxjhZL

Grove, C.N. (2005). Worldwide Differences in Business Values and Practices.

Cheung, C. M. K., & Thadani, D. R. (2010). The effectiveness of electronic word-of-mouth communication: A literature analysis. In *Proceedings of the 23rd Bled eConference eTrust: Implications for the Individual, Enterprises and Society.*

Chin, W. W. (1998). The Partial Least Squares Approach for Structural Equation Modeling. In G.A. Marcoulides (Ed.), Modern Methods for Business Research (pp. 295-336). London: Lawrence Erlbaum Associates.

Chiu, C.-M., Hsu, M.-H., & Wang, E. T. G. (2006). Understanding knowledge sharing in virtual communities: An integration of social capital and social cognitive theories. *Decision Support Systems, 42*(3), 1872–1888. doi:10.1016/j.dss.2006.04.001

Cho, N., Li, G. Z., & Su, C.-Z. (2007). An empirical study on the effect of individual factors on knowledge sharing by knowledge type. *Journal of Global Business and Technology*, *3*(2), 1–15.

Cialdini, R. (2006). *Influence: The Psychology of Persuasion* (Revised ed.). Harper Business.

Cummings, J. N. (2004). Work groups, structural diversity, and knowledge sharing in a global organization. *Management Science*, *50*(3), 352–364. doi:10.1287/mnsc.1030.0134

Davenport, T. H., & Prusak, L. (1998). *Working Knowledge: How Organizations Manage What They Know*. Boston: Harvard Business School Press.

Davis, F. D. (1989). Perceived usefulness, perceived ease of use, and user acceptance of information technology. *Management Information Systems Quarterly*, *13*(3), 319–339. doi:10.2307/249008

Elkaseh, A. M., Wong, K. W., & Fung, C. C. (2016, March). Perceived Ease of Use and Perceived Usefulness of Social Media for e-Learning in Libyan Higher Education: A Structural Equation Modeling Analysis. *International Journal of Information and Education Technology*, *6*(3), 192–199. doi:10.7763/IJIET.2016.V6.683

Fornell, C., & Larcker, D. (1981). Structural equation models with unobservable variables and measurement error. *JMR, Journal of Marketing Research*, *18*(1), 39–50. doi:10.1177/002224378101800104

Foss, N. J., Husted, K., & Michailova, S. (2010). Governing knowledge sharing in organizations: Levels of analysis, governance mechanisms and research directions. *Journal of Management Studies*, *47*(3), 455–482. doi:10.1111/j.1467-6486.2009.00870.x

Gaál, Z., Szabó, L., & Obermayer-Kovács, N. (2014). Personal knowledge sharing: Web 2.0 role through the lens of Generations. In *ECKM 2014 – Conference Proceedings, 15th European Conference on Knowledge Management*, Santarem (pp. 362-370).

Gaál, Z., Szabó, L., Obermayer-Kovács, N., & Csepregi, A. (2015). Exploring the role of social media in knowledge sharing. *Electronic Journal of Knowledge Management*, *13*(3), 185–197.

Gee-Woo, Y.-G. K., & Zmud, R. W. (2005). Behavioral intention formation in knowledge sharing: Examining the roles of extrinsic motivators, social-psychological forces, and organizational climate. *Management Information Systems Quarterly*, *29*(1), 87–111. doi:10.2307/25148669

Gefen, D., Straub, D. W., & Boudreau, M.-C. (2000). Structural Equation Modeling and Regression: Guidelines for Research Practice. *Communications of the Association for Information Systems*, *4*(7), 1–70.

Ghadirian, H., Ayub, A. F. M., Silong, A. D., Bakar, K. B. A., & Zadeh, A. M. H. (2014). Knowledge sharing behaviour among students in learning environments: A review of literature. *Asian Social Science*, *10*(4), 38–45. doi:10.5539/ass.v10n4p38

Ghadirian, H., Ayub, A. F. M., Silong, A. D., Bakar, K. B. A., & Zadeh, A. M. H. (2014). Knowledge sharing behaviour among students in learning environments: A review of literature. *Asian Social Science*, *10*(4), 38. doi:10.5539/ass.v10n4p38

Hair, J. F., Sarstedt, M., Ringle, C. M., & Mena, J. A. (2012). An assessment of the use of partial least squares structural equation modeling in marketing research. *Journal of the Academy of Marketing Science*, *40*(3), 414–433. doi:10.100711747-011-0261-6

Henseler, J., Ringle, C. M., & Sinkovics, R. R. (2009). The use of partial least squares path modeling in international marketing. *Advances in International Marketing*, *20*, 277–320.

Hernáez, O. R., & Campos, E. B. (2011). Handbook of Research on Communities of Practice for Organizational Management and Networking: Methodologies for Competitive Advantage. Hershey, PA: IGI Global.

House, R. J., Hanges, P. J., Javidan, M., Dorfman, P. W., & Gupta, V. (Eds.). (2004). *Culture, Leadership and Organizations: The GLOBE Study of 62 Societies*. Thousand Oaks, CA: Sage.

Hsu, M.-H., Ju, T. L., Yen, C.-H., & Chang, C.-M. (2007). Knowledge sharing behavior in virtual communities: The relationship between trust, self-efficacy, and outcome expectations. *International Journal of Human-Computer Studies*, *65*(2), 153–169. doi:10.1016/j.ijhcs.2006.09.003

Janz, B. D., & Prasarnphanich, P. (2003). Understanding the antecedents of effective knowledge management: The importance of a knowledge-centered culture. *Decision Sciences*, *34*(2), 351–384. doi:10.1111/1540-5915.02328

Jones, B., Temperley, J., & Lima, A. (2009). Corporate reputation in the era of Web 2.0: The case of Primark. *Journal of Marketing Management*, *25*(9), 936. doi:10.1362/026725709X479309

Jonnavithula, L., & Tretiakov, A. (2012). A model for the effects of online social networks on learning. *Presented at Ascilite Conference*.

Kankanhalli, B. C. Y. T., & Wei, K. (2005). Contributing knowledge to electronic knowledge repositories: An empirical investigation. *Management Information Systems Quarterly*, *29*(1), 113–143. doi:10.2307/25148670

Khesal S., Samadi B, Andira H, Musram M, Zohoori M. (2013). The Impact of Trust on Knowledge Sharing. *Interdisciplinary Journal of Contemporary Research in Business*, *5*(2).

Ko, D.-G., Kirsch, L. J., & King, W. R. (2005). Antecedents of knowledge transfer from consultants to clients in enterprise system implementations. *Management Information Systems Quarterly*, *29*(1), 59. doi:10.2307/25148668

Lewis, D. J., & Weigert, A. (1985). Trust as a social reality. *Social Forces*, *63*(4), 967–985. doi:10.1093f/63.4.967

Lin, T. C., Wu, S., & Lu, C. T. (2012). Exploring the affect factors of knowledge sharing behavior: The relations model theory perspective. *Expert Systems with Applications*, *39*(1), 751–764. doi:10.1016/j.eswa.2011.07.068

Liu, S.-H., Liao, H.-L., & Pratt, J. A. (2009). Impact of media richness and flow on e-learning technology acceptance. *Computers & Education*, *52*(3), 599–607. doi:10.1016/j.compedu.2008.11.002

Looi, C. K., Milrad, M., Mitrovic, A., Nakabayashi, K., Wong, S. L., & Yang, S. J. H. (Eds.). (2009). *Proceedings of the 17th International Conference on Computers in Education [CDROM]*. Hong Kong: Asia-Pacific Society for Computers in Education.

Luhmann, N. (2018). *Trust and power*. John Wiley & Sons.

Ma, W. W. K., & Yuen, A. H. K. (2011). Understanding online knowledge sharing: An interpersonal relationship perspective. *Computers & Education*, *56*(1), 210–219. doi:10.1016/j.compedu.2010.08.004

Miller, D., & Shamsie, J. (1996). The resource-based view of the firm in two environments: The Hollywood film studios from 1936 to 1965. *Academy of Management Journal*, *39*(5), 519–543. doi:10.2307/256654

Mishra, D., Mishra, A., & Ostrovska, S. (2012). Impact of physical ambiance on communication, collaboration and coordination in agile software development: An empirical evaluation. *Information and Software Technology*, *54*(10), 1067–1078. doi:10.1016/j.infsof.2012.04.002

Polányi, M. (1966). The Tacit Dimension. London: Routledge & Kegan Paul.

Rezaei, S., & Ismail, W. K. W. (2014). Examining online channel selection behaviour among social media shoppers: a PLS analysis. *Int. J. Electronic Marketing and Retailing, 6*(1).

Riege, A. (2005). Three-dozen knowledge-sharing barriers managers must consider. *Journal of Knowledge Management*, *9*(3), 18–35. doi:10.1108/13673270510602746

Rowlands, I., Nicholas, D., Russell, B., Canty, N., & Watkinson, A. (2011). Social media use in the research workflow. *Learned Publishing*, *24*(3), 183–195. doi:10.1087/20110306

Schejter, A. M., & Tirosh, N. (2015). "Seek the meek, seek the just": Social media and social justice. *Telecommunications Policy*, *39*(9), 796–803. doi:10.1016/j.telpol.2015.08.002

Statista. (n.d.). Leading global social networks 2017. Retrieved from https://www.statista.com/statistics/272014/global-social-networks-ranked-by-number-of-users/

Williams, D. (2006, August). On and off the Net: Scales for social capital in an online era. *Journal of Computer-Mediated Communication*, *11*(2), 593–628. doi:10.1111/j.1083-6101.2006.00029.x

This research was previously published in the International Journal of Online Marketing (IJOM), 9(4); pages 19-32, copyright year 2019 by IGI Publishing (an imprint of IGI Global).

Chapter 48
Usage of Social Media Among Information Technology Students of Alagappa:
A Case Study

A. Alagu
Alagappa University, India

ABSTRACT

In this study, Alagappa University is used to analyze social media applications among many information technology students. One hundred sixty-three questionnaires were collected from computer science, computer application, library and information science, and computational logistics department students. ANOVA test, chi-square, and independent t-test were used to test hypotheses. ANOVA t-test analysis showed that the frequency of using social media relationship with the department at the rate of f= 5.192, statistical significant level P=0.002. This study reveals that students are using social media sites such as Whatsapp, YouTube, Facebook, Instagram, etc. Information technology students often use social media for their educational activities.

INTRODUCTION

Social involvement is a life process and an important part of whose success in life. It supports independent life, social experience and relationship. To enhance the social interaction process, technologies such as the Internet and social media are now being introduced and widely used as a new way of social communication amongst people. These are the methods of communication, education, career development and technologies that are successful in life. A post-graduate student has been given a survey to identify the size of social media usage. There is a wide range of social media applications that benefit students in many ways. Research sources have suggested that access opportunities for graduate studies for social media sites increase the quality and efficiency of their social affairs, develop meaningful mutual growth

DOI: 10.4018/978-1-6684-7123-4.ch048

and reduce the sense of loneliness. Today's students spend their time to recognize a good communication stream. Social media can play an important role in supporting the empowerment and participation of individuals and groups by enabling networking, improving self-esteem (Moreno & Kolb, 2012), and enabling online campaigning among marginalized groups such as disabled people (Bowker&Tuffin, 2002). Research has shown that peoples can be supported to use the internet within their normal lives. There has been lot of developmentsin social media services specifically for students. The social media is increasingly using sites including blogs, forums, Facebook, YouTube, Twitter, WhatsApp and Instagram etc.

REVIEW OF LITERATURE

Weber, Alan S (2012) expressed that SNSs are winding up progressively universal, they are likewise ending up increasingly complex and many work on a free administration show dependent on publicizing incomes. The instructive uses have by and large been the consequence of the innovative adjustment of SNSs by instructors and application developers. Consequently some difficult issues of information protection, trust, and security have emerged since both the instructive, medicinal, and therapeutic training domains work in the U.S. under strict information insurance laws, for example, HITECH, HIPAA, FERPA, and COPPA. Notwithstanding, the plans of action of numerous SNSs as basically advertising stages and as methods for following on the web practices which can be adapted (with non-straight forward strategies of data collection and maintenance) raise some key worries for instructors.

Marisol Gomez Aguilar (2012) featured that the new mechanical devices (social networks, online journals, video stages, and so on) have given them the opportunity and capacity to share, make, educate and convey and have turned into an augmentation of their lives'. The Social Networking sites have various measurements and implications in the general public.

Chakraborty (2012) in her paper entitled Activities and reasons for using Social Networking Sites by the research scholars in NEHU: A study on Facebook and Research Gate' endeavours to contemplate the movement and purposes behind utilizing SNSs by the examination researchers of North Eastern Hill University. The discoveries of the examination demonstrates that the vast majority of the specialists from social science foundation utilized SNSs for instruction and research perspective and researchers from pure science deduce that Social Networking sites has nothing to do with education and research.

Leitch, S (2011) referenced about earlier research which was directed at an Australian University into the structure of internet instructing and taking in frameworks from a student's point of view and uses these results to center and preliminary the utilization of two social networking advancements in a tertiary training establishment.

Singh and Gill (2011) in their paper entitled 'Utilization of Social Networking Sites by the exploration researchers: An investigation of Guru Nanak Dev University, Amritsar' decided the utilization and viability of such applications and research by the examination researchers. Their examination uncovers that greater part of the respondents were observed to know and making utilization of such applications in their exploration undertakings. The discoveries of the investigation likewise uncovered that Facebook is the most well known SNSs by the all field of research scholars

Brady, Kevin P (2010) assessed to a great extent about unexplored educational advantages of SNSs and studied alumni students selected in separation training courses utilizing Ning in Education, a training based SNS, in light of their frames of mind toward SNSs as gainful online devices for educating and learning. The investigation proposed that education based SNSs can be utilized most viably in separation training courses as an innovative device for enhanced online interchanges among students in higher distance education courses.

James, L et.al (2010), Social Networking websites, for example, Facebook and LinkedIn have risen quickly. The utilization of Facebook by higher education students is particularly keen on social occasion scholastic data. New advancements in the mechanical world have made the web an imaginative route for people and families to convey. Social media networks have made a wonder on the web that has picked up prevalence in the course of the most recent decade. Individuals utilize social media sites, for example, Facebook, Twitter, and My space to establish and maintain relationships with others. Spending time on social networking sites has all the earmarks of being a part of daily activities of young adults.

Yoo and Gretzel (2010) accentuated that it is important to look at the ramifications of identity with regards to social media since it has been observed to be an imperative factor affecting a wide assortment of human practices and decisions.

Kaplan and Haenlein (2010) characterized social media as "a gathering of Internet-put together applications that work with respect to the ideological and innovative establishments of Web 2.0, and that permit the creation and trade of User Generated Content". Kaplan and Haenlein then ordered social media into six noteworthy sorts dependent on a lot of hypotheses, which are media explore (media extravagance hypothesis and social presence), and social procedures (self-introduction and self-revelation), in particular cooperative activities, sites, content networks, social networking sites, virtual amusement universes and virtual social universes. Kaplan and Haenlein even recognized social media from Web 2.0 and user-generated content

Taylor and Kent (2010) opined that social media instruments incorporate intelligent social networking sites, and also blogs, digital recordings, message boards, online recordings and picture albums, and cell phone cautions. In addition, social media are viewed as easy to use, modest, adaptable web and versatile based advances that take into consideration the sharing of user-generated materials.

Curtis et al. (2010) considered the selection of social media by PR professionals in the non-profit organizations by utilizing the Unified Theory of Acceptance and Use of Technology (UTAUT). Their survey estimated social media reception with relations to execution anticipation, exertion hope, social impact, encouraging conditions, and wilfulness of utilization, self-viability and anxiety. They found that social media apparatuses are getting to be gainful techniques for correspondence for PR experts and associations with characterized PR divisions are bound to receive social media advancements and use them to accomplish their authoritative objectives. Nevertheless, PR professionals are bound to utilize social media devices on the off chance that they discover them realistic.

Mahajan (2009) in the paper entitled Use of social networking in a linguistically and literally rich India' investigated the use, effect and issues identified with Social Networking sites and their effect on the social and cultural ethics of India. It also described the top most social networking websites of India alongside their awful and great elements.

Eyrich, Padman and Sweetser (2008) viewed social media to comprise of various tools like intranets, blogs, podcasts, photo sharing, video sharing, social networks, gaming, wikis, virtual universes, micro blogging/presence applications, content informing, video conferencing, PDAs, text talk, social occasion/logbook frameworks, social bookmarking, news total/RSS and email.

Tiffany et al., (2008) a large number of contemporary youthful grown-ups utilize social networking sites. Nonetheless, there is little awareness about why and how they utilize these sites. In this examination, 92 students evaluated every day for seven days, reporting day by day time use and reacting to an exercises agenda to evaluate their utilization of the popular social networking site, Facebook. Toward the week's end, they additionally finished a subsequent study. Results showed that students use Facebook roughly 30 min for the duration of the day as a component of their day by day schedule. Students conveyed on Facebook utilizing a one-to-many style, in which they were the makers scattering substance to their companions. All things considered, they invested more energy watching content on Facebook than really posting substance. Facebook was utilized regularly for social association, principally with companions with whom the students had a pre-set up relationship offline. Notwithstanding great character markers of developing adulthood, for example, religion, political philosophy, and work, youthful grown-ups likewise utilized media inclinations to express their personality. Ramifications of social networking site use for the advancement of character and friend connections are talked about.

Lau (2017) stated that upshot of social media use and social media performing various tasks impact the scholarly execution of university students. The exploration found that utilizing social media for scholarly reasons for existing was not an imperative indicator of educational execution as estimated by total review point normal, though utilizing social media for non-academic purposes (video gaming specifically) and social media performs multiple tasks essentially adversely anticipated academic performance.

Mahadi, Jamaludin, Johari and Fuad (2016) directed an examination on the effect of social media on Art students' frame of mind from Art and Design Faculty in University Technology Mara, Perak campus. The result uncovers that the greater part of students are progressively associated with social media and they understood the effect of social media in their day by day life and also their demeanour.

Alwagait, Shahzad and Alim (2015) inspected the effect of inordinate social media use on scholastic execution. They also decide out which social network site is the most popular and liked among Saudi students, the thing that students thought about their social media utilization and factors other than social media use which contrarily influence academic performance. The result is invertebrate that there was no direct connection between social media use in a week and GPA score. Students hued that also social media use; time the executives is an angle which influences students 'considers contrarily. The discoveries of the investigation can be utilized to propose the viable plans for enhancing the scholarly execution of the students so that equalization in the unwinding, data trade and scholastic execution can be kept up.

Cookingham and Ryan (2015) in their evaluation on the "impact of social media on the sexual and social wellness of adolescents" portrayed the job of social media in the advancement of social standards, to represent how online movement can contrarily affect youthful confidence and add to high-hazard pre-adult practices, to explain how this action can result in genuine outcomes with long lasting outcomes, and to give direction in regards to social media use for the individuals who care for young people. They detailed that health care service providers for adolescents were vital supporters of this new field of study and should set out to remain educated and to connect with this best in class age on the advantages and dangers of social media use. Social media has likewise negatively affected the social health of a significant number of its immature clients.

Kanagarathinam (2014) demonstrated that students utilized a greater amount of Facebook, Skype, WhatsApp and YouTube, anyway Google+ and LinkedIn were the minimum utilized among the respondent. Google is a generally acknowledged vehicle for looking through all or any kind of data through Internet; one can make singular gatherings for point by point discourses identifying with all fields of study. Facebook is a prevalent social networking site, and furthermore a helpful instructive device because of its structure and various employments. It furnishes clients with learning openings by method for sharing premiums, trading data, sharing thoughts and talking about points. While sites such as Facebook and Twitter draw in expansive crowds who socialize. LinkedIn and tribe.net are business situated sites that pull in expert businesspeople who share business thoughts together. The utilization of social media sites by students have both constructive and antagonistic repercussion on the lives of students showed that SNS began as a side interest for some PC proficient individuals, recently it has turned into a social standard and lifestyle for individuals from everywhere throughout the world. Besides his discoveries uncovered, that about 61% of the respondents utilized social networking sites for downloading music, posting photographs and visiting. While about, 39% utilized the systems administration for research, submitting of task and articles. The vast majority of these students concurred on the way that these sites helped them scholastically in getting instructive materials for their assignments and ventures and for research work. He further clarified that about 26% of the respondents demonstrated that they use SNSs for scholastic purposes like speaking with their lecturers and supervisors (8%), directing scholarly related exchanges (9%), and speaking with companions for scholarly interests (9%), which is not exactly the time they spend on different activities disconnected to scholastic issues.

Li and Sakamoto (2014) stated how aggregate conclusion may impact the apparent honesty and the sharing probability of wellbeing related articulations on social media. It was exposed that, when surveying the unwavering quality of an announcement, members embraced the mutual honesty rating associated with the announcement. In like manner, experimentation two demonstrated that the probability that members would share an announcement pursued the aggregate sharing opportunity associated with the announcement. These social effects were boundless, occurring for explanation suspected as questionable, true and false. This result contributed new experiences into how individuals perceive and share data on social media and in addition how aggregate conclusion may influence the nature of data on social media.

Salvation and Azharuddin (2014) opined that Social system sites (SNS) draws in impressive consideration among adolescents and youthful grown-ups who will in general associate and offer basic intrigue. The investigation was structured in approaches to break down the effect of social system sites on students' scholastic execution in Malaysia, utilizing a theoretical methodology. The investigation presumed that more students incline toward the utilization of Facebook and twitter in scholarly related exchanges in supplementing ordinary classroom instructing and learning process.

Maria F. Paramo, et al., (2014), dissected the degree to which diverse sources and subjective/emotional parts of apparent social help anticipated explicit regions of change in an example of 300 first-year Spain University students. The example achieved the Social Support Questionnaire (SSQ), the Perceived Acceptance Scale (PAS) and the Student Adaptation to College Questionnaire (SACQ). Relapse examination uncovered that apparent social help was a decent indicator of change to school. The affiliation was tough for companions bolster than family bolster once University section review point normal and gender were controlled for. The association between the quantity of accessible others when required and the fulfilment with accessible help with modification was intermediated by apparent feeling of acknowledgment.

Tayseer et al., (2014) in their examination analyzed the impact of use of social networks on students' commitment in both scholarly and social viewpoints. The examination uncovered that students utilize social networks for social purposes more than the scholastics. Students consider social media as amusement networks and it lessens pressure and influences them to disregard scholastics.

Mahat, S (2014) Lot of writing is accessible now days on the social networking sites and their effect on the youth of any country, youngsters, adolescence and families as amid the most recent 5 years, utilization of such sites has expanded among preadolescents and teenagers. Out of 75% of young people owning mobile phones, 25% use them for social media, 24% use them for texting and 54% use them for messaging. Positive out originates from these advances as employments found through LinkedIn or political activities sorted out by means of Facebook.

Geetanjali Naidu &Sunil Agrawal (2013) described that in the present situation social media turned into an exceptionally valuable apparatus in purchasing conduct basic leadership. It is impacting client/shopper in a dynamic way. Presently client/purchaser is taking help of social media with respect to buying of any item. Social media like Facebook, Twitter and Skype will assume an essential job in purchaser/client purchasing conduct basic leadership. Presently in the present situation social media like Blogs, LinkedIn, Facebook, Twitter, Skype, and so on are assuming an imperative job in decision making process of customers' buying behaviour indirectly or directly. In ongoing pattern of development in the management social media turns out to be amazing and cost free way to deal with elevate item to customer. According to the study result India's 75% youth are utilizing social media for sharing their idea and perspectives and remark in various zone of nation.

Al-Rahmi and Othman (2013) investigated the Impact of Social Media use on Academic Performance among college students. The exploration was done so as to underline the possibilities of social media in the scholarly foundation by community learning and enhance the students' scholastic execution. The Study demonstrated that common adapting totally and broadly with intelligent with friends, intuitive with teachers and commitment which affect the students' scholastic execution.

De Andrea, Ellison, LaRose, Steinfield and Fiore (2012) gave an account of a student focused social media site intended to improve students' view of social help preceding their landing on grounds. Result demonstrated that site utilization enlarged students' discernments that they would have assorted social encouraging group of people amid their first semester at college.

Jahan and Zabed Ahmed (2012) considered view of scholarly utilization of social networking sites (SNSs) by the students of University of Dhaka, Bangladesh. That review shows an uplifting demeanour towards scholarly utilization of SNSs by the students. In spite of the fact that there are a few contrasts as far as students' assessments on scholarly uses of SNSs, these distinctions are to a great extent because of the way that the utilization of these sites in scholastic settings is not all around characterized. The higher scholastic establishments need to devise fitting arrangements and methodologies on how they can use social networking sites to help training and learning past the classroom.

Kindi & Alhasmi (2012) lead an investigation "Use of Social networking among Shinas college of Technology students in Oman". The investigation found that the significant purposes behind incessant utilization of SNSs are discovering data and sharing news. The investigation demonstrated that absence of experience and lacking time and IT abilities are viable variables of not utilizing SNSs. At long last, the examination found that Google Groups, Facebook and Yahoo! 360 are the most well known SNSs utilized by SHCT students.

Yan Zhang (2012) investigated undergrads' utilization of social networking sites for wellbeing and health data. Thirty-eight undergrads were met. The meeting transcripts were dissected utilizing the subjective substance investigation strategy. Generally, members were incredulous about the nature of data. In light of the outcomes, a model of students' acknowledgment of social networking sites for wellness and health data was proposed and suggestions for planning social stages to all the more likely help wellbeing request were talked about Using social networking sites for wellbeing and health data is certifiably not a famous conduct among college students in this investigation.

Petter Bae Brandtzaeg and Jan Heim (2009) in their examination express that there are various persuasive clarifications behind using Social Networking Sites among people and students particularly. Brandtzaeg and Heim draw their revelations, after the examination on society's abstract inspirational purposes behind using Social Networking Sites, by playing out a quantitative substance examination for 1,200 emotional responses from Social Networking Sites customers. Further, the examination influenced a couple of undertakings to appreciate the choice, to use, scattering, choice and affirmation of Social Networking Sites among students.

Pempek, T. A., Yermolayeva, Y. An., and Calvert, S. L. (2009), presumed that Millions of current youthful grown-ups utilize social networking sites. However, unassuming is thought about how much, why, and how they utilize these sites. In this investigation, 92 students finished a journal like process every day for seven days detailing day by day time to assess their utilization of the prominent social networking site, Facebook. Results showed that students use Facebook around 30 min for the duration of the day as a component of their everyday propensity. Students imparted on Facebook utilizing a one-to many style, in which they were the makers dispersing substance to their companions. All things being equal, they invested more energy watching content on Facebook than in truth redistribution content. Facebook was utilized regularly for social correspondence, principally with companions with whom the students had a pre- perceived relationship disconnected. Notwithstanding conventional personality markers of rising adulthood, for example, religion, political thoughts, and work, youthful grown-ups additionally utilized media inclinations to explain their character.

Nicole Ellison (2008) on Social Networking Sites gives particularly fascinating bits of information. As demonstrated by this examination, 85% of the respondents use somewhere around one long range casual correspondence goals. The level of the usage of Social Networking Sites has extended definitely in the past two years and the utilization of Social Networking Sites additionally shifts essentially by age. A huge part of the respondents developing 18 and 19 years old use Social Networking Sites (95%), yet simply 37% developing 30 years or more uses these frameworks organization districts. The larger part including 18 and 19 years old, have in excess of 200 colleagues while those developed at least 30 have basically 25 or lesser allies on these districts. Subsequently Facebook is the most by and large used Social Networking Site, with MySpace as the second choice. It was furthermore found that about bit of these customers utilize just a single Social Networking Site, having only a solitary profile, and share in one to five get-togethers inside Social Networking Sites. Profiles of Social Networking Sites are truly consistent, with most respondents changing them month to month or less routinely. The majority of the customers of Social Networking Sites consume 5 hours or less consistently. More young respondent reports contributing more vitality than progressively settled respondents. It moreover underscored that most students (87%) put get to restrictions on their profiles. Progressively energetic respondents and females are well while in transit to do all things considered.

Coyle and Vaughn (2008) in their examination dissected the composition on Social Networking Sites and coordinated a survey on how students are possessed with long range casual correspondence. They found that the basic inspiration driving using Social Networking Sites is to remain in contact with friends. They furthermore exhibit that these are used for just insignificant correspondence with friends. These regions are basically new sort of correspondence that is creating after some time with the guide of development.

Sebastián Valenzuela (2008) this study looks Facebook, as a standout amongst the most famous social system sites among youthful grown-ups in the US, satisfies the guarantee of municipal news coverage: to start frames of mind and practices that improve open life and community activity. Utilizing information from an irregular web review of undergrads in Texas, We discover moderate, positive connections between force of Facebook use and students' life fulfilment, social trust, urban interest and political commitment. The relationship between Facebook utilization and students' social capital are distinguishable notwithstanding when taking statistic, financial and socialization factors into record. These discoveries feature vital exercises for columnists and media keen on reconnecting people, particularly youthful grown-ups, to society and open life.

Goodman (2007) breaks down how students associate with advancement mostly that required in Social Networking Sites. He explores how students use Social Networking Sites, which Social Networking Sites and ventures they find more captivating than others and moreover endeavours to grasp the noteworthy purposes behind the extending utilization of Social Networking Sites among students. He fittingly raised "Informal communication Sites are not some segment of students' lives these days, truly they are their lives". Young people are not simply the early adopters of by far most of the new developments yet they are among the most progressive customers.

STATEMENT OF THE PROBLEM

The present study aims to analyse the usage of social media among information technology Students of Alagappa University in various departments in the students.

OBJECTIVES OF THE STUDY

- To know the category-wise distribution of respondents
- To analyze the level of social mediausage.
- To find the reason to prefer the social media sites
- To study the frequency of using Social media by respondents.
- To know the preferred location of access social media by respondents.
- To examine the purpose of using Social media by respondents
- To study the problem in using social media by respondents.

HYPOTHESIS

- There is no significant difference between the location of using social media and gender and nativity of the respondents;
- There is no significant difference between the tools for using social media and gender and nativity of the respondents;
- There is no significant difference between the purpose of using social media and the gender of the respondents
- There is no significant difference between the reason for using social media and the gender of the respondents
- There is no significant difference between the frequency of usage of social media sites and department of the respondents
- There is no significant difference between problems of using social media and nativity of the respondents

NEED FOR THE STUDY

This study aims to determine the level of usage and purpose of Alagappa university information technology students towards the use of social media sites. Eleven chosen social media sites for this study include Facebook, LinkedIn, Twitter, MySpace, YouTube, Whatsapp, Instagram, RSS Feeds, Blog, Subject Online Forum and Wikis were taken for this study as it suits the practice of using social media sites in Alagappa University. Also, the level of usage and purpose of university information technology students towards the use of social media sites would be measured by examining the study they use the tool, their purposes of using the social media tools and their opinion on the strengths of the tools.

METHODOLOGY

A comprehensive research method was used in this study. The study was conducted with the focus of the use of social media for information technology students at Alagappa University. The population of the study covered 4 departments in the students, as per the university records, there are 371 postgraduate information technology students doing a study in the university. The study adopted a random sampling method for collecting the primary data. A questionnaire method was used for collecting the data. The Raosoft software was used to calculate how many students should be selected from the total students. A total number of 189 questionnaires were distributed each department to the postgraduates students and 163 duly filled in the questionnaire were received back, making the respondents rate 86.24%. The study used frequency counts; the percentages mean score and standard deviation were systematically organized, tested and analyzed with SPSS. Research questions designed based on the rating criteria proposed by Likert Scale method.

DATA ANALYSIS AND INTERPRETATION

A total of 189 of the questionnaire were distributed to the students and retrieved 163 from the respondents. The data obtained from this was organized and analyzed using mean average simple percentage and statistical method ANOVA test and t-test chi-square which are presented in the table as follows:

Population Study

Table 1 shows that the mean value is 1.85 and std deviation is 0.355. Overall population (n=163) based on gender, there are 139 female respondents with a percentage of 85.3% as compared to 24 Male respondents with 14.7%. The majority of the respondents were female and the numbers of male respondents are comparatively less.

Table 2 shows that the mean value range is 1.88 and std deviation range is 0.489. Out of 163 respondents, 30 of respondents (18.4%) are in the age group of below 20, followed by 122 of the respondents (74.8%) are 21-24 category and 11 of respondents (6.7%) are in the age group of above 25.

Table- 3 shows that the 163 of the respondents (100%) have in the use of the social media application and Zero percent respondents do not use it.

Table 1. Gender-wise distribution

Gender	Respondents	Percentage	Mean Value	Std. Deviation
Male	24	14.7		
Female	139	85.3	1.85	0.355
Total	163	100.0		

Table 2. Distribution of respondents by age

Age	Respondents	Percentage	Mean	Std. Deviation
below 20	30	18.4		
21-24	122	74.8	1.88	.489
above 25	11	6.7		
Total	163	100.0		

Table 3. Social media application

Social Media	Respondents	Percent
Yes	163	100.0
No	0	0
Total	**163**	**100.0**

Table 4 shows that the respondents received from the students in four departments. The mean value of the category range is 1.90 and std deviation range is1.038. Out of 163 respondents, 77 (47.2%) are Computer science, and 44(27%) are Computer Application, 23(14.1%) are Computational Logistics, 19 (11.7%) are Library and information science are selected as sample.

Table 4. Department wise distribution of respondents

Department	Respondents	Percentage	Mean	Std. Deviation
Computer Science	77	47.2		
Computer Application	44	27.0		
Computational Logistics	23	14.1	1.90	1.038
Library and Information Science	19	11.7		
Total	**163**	**100.00**		

Table 5 reveals that the data collected from the details of respondents to nativity wise distribution. It has also found that 62 of respondents (38%) are from the rural area, 43 of respondents (26.4%) are from semi-urban, 58 of respondents (35.6%) are from the urban area, the majority of the respondents are from the rural area, with mean value 1.98 std deviation value 0.860.

Table 5. Nativity wise distribution of respondents

Nativity	Respondents	Percentage	Mean	Std. Deviation
Rural	62	38.0		
Semi-Urban	43	26.4	1.98	0.860
Urban	58	35.6		
Total	**163**	**100.00**		

The table 6 shows that majority 130 of the respondents (79.8%) are using social media sites their home. It followed by 13 of respondents (8%) are using social media in their department and equal 13 responses (8%) are using the social media sites in the library. Fewer of the respondent 7 (4.3%) are using social media sites in cybercafé.

Table 6. Location wise distribution of respondents

Location	Respondents	Percentage	Mean	Std. Deviation
Library	13	8.0		
Department	13	8.0		
Cybercafé	7	4.3	3.56	0.943
Home	130	79.8		
Total	**163**	**100.00**		

The table 7 shows that a majority of 91 of respondents (55.8%) are pursuing II year students. It is followed by 61 of respondents (37.4%) are pursuing I year students, and 11 respondents (6.7%) are III year students there is a computer application department only, with a mean value is 1.69 and standard deviation value is 0.591.

Table 7. Pursuing wise distribution of Respondents

Nativity	Respondents	Percentage	Mean	Std. Deviation
I Year	61	37.4		
II Year	91	55.8	1.69	0.591
III Year	11	6.7		
Total	**163**	**100.00**		

Table 8 shows that the majority 133of respondents (81.6%) likely usesa smartphone and 10of respondents (6.1%) are useDesktop, 15 of respondents (9.2%) are use tools in a laptop, less than number 5of respondents (3.1%) are use of tools in a tablet.

Table 8. Tools wise distribution of respondents

Location	Respondents	Percentage	Mean	Std. Deviation
Desktop	10	6.1		
Laptop	15	9.2		
Tablet	5	3.1	3.60	0.893
Smart Phone	133	81.6		
Total	**163**	**100.00**		

Table 9 analyses the level of using social media sites among students. The opinion ranges do not know about it, Heard about it but never used it, rarely used and frequently are used for the study. From the opinion of social media sites for Blogs 117(71.8%), RSS feeds 116(71.2%), MySpace 100(61.3%), LinkedIn 89(54.6%), Subject Online Forum 78(47.9%), Wikis 57(35%), Twitter 43(26.4%), Facebook 30(18.4%) are do not know about it. The respondents have given first priority for using social media sites Whatsapp 112 (68.7%), second, third and fourth priority for YouTube 86(52.8%), Facebook 51(31.3%), Instagram 47(28.8%) are frequently used.

Table 9. Level of use associated with specific online social media

S. No	Social Media Sites	Do Not Know About It	Heard About It but Never Used It	Rarely Used	Frequently Used
1	Face book	30(18.4%)	27(16.6%)	55(33.7%)	51(31.3%)
2	LinkedIn	89(54.6%)	47(28.8%)	19(11.7%)	8(4.9%)
3	Twitter	43(26.4%)	73(44.8%)	34(20.9%)	13(8%)
4	MySpace	100(61.3%)	22(13.5%)	18(11%)	23(14.1%)
5	You Tube	12(17.4%)	18(11%)	47(28.8%)	86(52.8%)
6	Whatsapp	13(8%)	15(9.2%)	23(14.1%)	112(68.7%)
7	Instagram	35(21.5%)	39(23.9%)	42(25.8%)	47(28.8%)
8	RSS feeds	116(71.2%)	17(10.4%)	17(10.4%)	13(8%)
9	Blogs	117(71.8%)	19(11.7%)	20(12.3%)	7(4.3%)
10	Subject Online Forum	78(47.9%)	28(17.2%)	35(21.5%)	22(13.5%)
11	Wikis	57(35%)	27(16.6%)	57(35%)	20(12.3%)

CHI-SQUARE TEST VALUE FOR VARIOUS VARIABLES

H1: There is no significant difference between the location of using social media and gender and nativity of the respondents.

Table 10. Location of using social media vs gender and nativity

Demographic Data	Location of Using Social Media		
	Chi-Square Value	df	Sig.
Gender	1.587	3	0.662
Nativity	33.854	6	0.001

Since it is found in the above table in term of Gender, the chi-square value when calculated is 1.587, the degree of freedom = 3 and p= 0.662 which is more than 0.05. It accepted the null hypothesis. This means that there is no significant difference between the gender and location of using social media of the respondents.

In term of nativity, the chi-square value when calculated is 33.854 degree of freedom = 6 and p= 0.001 which is less than 0.05. It rejected the null hypothesis. This means that there is a significant difference between the locations of using social media and nativity of the respondents

H2: There is no significant difference between the tools for using social media and gender and nativity of the respondents.

Table 11. Tools for using social media vs gender and nativity

Demographic Data	Tools for Using Social Media		
	Chi-Square Value	df	Sig.
Gender	2.765	3	0.429
Nativity	10.011	6	0.124

It is found from the above table that the in term of Gender, the chi-square value when calculated is 2.765, the degree of freedom = 3 and P= 0.429 which is more than 0.05. It accepted the null hypothesis. This means that there is no significant difference between the gender and tools for using social media of the respondents.

In term of nativity, the chi-squarevalue when calculated is 10.011, the degree of freedom = 6 and P= 0.124 which is more than 0.05. It accepted the null hypothesis. This means that there is no significant difference between the tools for using social media and nativity of the respondent.

Independent Sample T-Test

H3: There is no significant difference between the purpose of using social media and the gender of the respondents

To verify the above hypothesis the respondents are classified into two groups namely, male and female. Further, the purposes of using social media which consist of nine statements were concatenated using the compute variable option in SPSS into a single factor. To find out the significant difference, the Independent t-test is applied, and the details are presented in the Table 13.

Table 12. A test of significant difference in the test of significant difference in the purpose of using social media and gender of the respondents

Group Statistics				
Gender	N	Mean	Std. Deviation	Std. Error Mean
Male	24	33.7083	4.01605	.81977
Female	139	34.7664	4.72830	.40397

Table 13. Independent samples test

Purpose of Using Social Media	Levene's Test for Equality of Variances		t-Test for Equality of Means					95% Confidence Interval of the Difference	
	F	Sig	t	df	Sig. (2-tailed)	Mean Difference	Std. Error Difference	Lower	Upper
Equal variances assumed	.105	.746	-1.032	159	.304	-1.05809	1.02499	-3.08244	.96626
Equal variances not assumed			-1.158	35.176	.255	-1.05809	.91390	-2.91308	.79690

As p-valueLevene's test for the purpose of using social media .746 is more than 0.05, it accepted the null hypothesis and concludes that the variance in the purpose of social media of male is not significantly different between female. It can accept that the population variances are relatively equal.

The two-tail significance for purpose of using social media shows that the p-value of 0.304 is more than 0.05, it accepted the null hypothesis. However, there is a 95 percent chance that the population means difference falls somewhat between -3.08244 and .96626. The confidence interval includes zero, which mean that there is no difference. Thus, the t-test concludes that there is no significant difference between the purpose of using social media and the gender of the respondents are equal.

H4: There is no significant difference between the reason for using social media and the gender of the respondents

The table 12 reveals that the sinceP-value is less than 0.001 the null hypothesis is rejected at 1% level. Hence there is a significant difference among age group and frequency and reason for using social media. Based on the Duncan multiple range test (DMRT) the age group of below 25 and 21-24 is significantly differ with above 25. From the following statistics and ANOVA tables as shown in tables 14, the p-value for all the given purposes of using social media is 'write and read blog posts Comment on other blogs' p =0.057, 'Comment on newspaper articles' p = 0.63, 'upload and view pictures and videos' p= 0.001, less than 0.001 the null hypothesis is rejected at 1% level. Thus, age-wisestudents, there is a significant between age and upload and view pictures and videos. 'Use discussion forums' p = 0.366, 'Play Online Games' p =0.35.

Table 14. Test whether significant difference among gender with the reason for using social media

Group Statistics				
Gender	N	Mean	Std. Deviation	Std. Error Mean
Male	24	13.9167	5.25784	1.07325
Female	139	11.6259	4.40565	.37368

Table 15. Independent samples test

Purpose of Using Social Media	Levene's Test for Equality of Variances		t-Test for Equality of Means					95% Confidence Interval of the Difference	
	F	Sig	t	df	Sig. (2-tailed)	Mean Difference	Std. Error Difference	Lower	Upper
Equal variances assumed	1.839	.177	2.284	161	.024	2.29077	1.00293	.31018	4.27135
Equal variances not assumed			2.016	28.844	.053	2.29077	1.13645	-.03407	4.61561

ONE WAY ANOVA TEST

H5: There is no significant difference between the frequency of usage of social media sites and department of the respondents

Table 16. Test whether significant difference among department with the frequency of using social media

One Way ANOVA and Post Hoc Test (Duncan Test)					
ANOVA					
	Sum of Squares	df	Mean Square	F	Sig.
Between Groups	305.941	3	101.980	5.192	.002
Within Groups	3103.670	158	19.643		
Total	3409.611	161			
Post Hoc Test (Duncan Test)					
Duncan.b					

Departments	N	Subset for alpha = 0.05	
		1	2
Library & Information Science	19	17.6842	
Computational Logistics	22	17.8636	
Computer Science	77	18.2338	
Computer application	44		21.1364
Sig.		.655	1.000

903

The table 16 reveals that the One way ANOVA was conducted by taking alpha level =.05, to study is there any significant difference in the frequency of using social media among four groups of students pursuing PG courses at Alagappa University. The results suggested that the Library and Information Science students (17.68), Computational Logistics students usage of social media (17.86),and Computer science students usage of social media (18.23), Computer application students usage of social media (21.13) are with F value= 5.192, df=3and p = 0.002.

One way ANOVA test was conducted to see the difference between the four groups is there any mean difference. The results failed to reject the null hypothesis F=5.192, df =3,less than 0.05 meaning that there is a difference in their usage of social media among the four groups

H6: There is no significant difference between problems of using social media and nativity of the respondents

The table 17 reveals that the study has been analyzing the problems in using social media among students in the university. One way ANOVA testis used for this tableand the conducted by taking alpha level =.05, f-test value along with p-value, to study is there any significant difference in the problem of using social media in response to respondents. Comparing the f-test values and significance values, it has made clear that the ANOVA comparisons the acceptance of the null hypothesis. Note that the significance values are more than 0.05 in the variable. If null hypothesis is accepted, one way ANOVA can not be used for Post Hoc Test (Duncan Test). The results suggested that the Rural, Semi-Urban,and Urban are three groups of students is there any mean difference. The results failed to reject the null hypothesis F=5.192,df=3,less than 0.05 meaning that there is a difference in their usage of social media among the three groups.

Table 17. Test whether significant difference among nativity and problem with using social media sites of the respondents

One-way ANOVA					
	Sum of Squares	df	Mean Square	F	Sig.
Between Groups	3.321	2	1.661	.052	.949
Within Groups	5080.298	160	31.752		
Total	5083.620	162			

CONCLUSION

The conclude that the use of social media sites among Alagappa university students. Social media support, upgrade and research will be very helpful. The majority of students receive the aim of social media research and expert information to get new ideas. However, the use of social media has given priority to the use of social media sites, showing that Whatsapp follows YouTube, Facebook and Instagram. There is a significant nativity difference in the use of social media among students.

ACKNOWLEDGMENT

This article has been written with the financial support of RUSA – Phase 2.0 grant sanctioned vide Letter No. F.24-51 / 2014-U, Policy (TNMulti-Gen), Dept. of Edn. Govt. of India, Dt.09.10.2018

REFERENCES

Acquisti, A., & Gross, R. (2006). Imagined communities: Awareness, information sharing, and privacy on the Facebook, In *International workshop on privacy enhancing technologies* (pp. 36-58). Springer. 10.1007/11957454_3

Ahmed, Q. (2011). http://californiawatch.org/dailyreport/social-networkinghelpsstudents-perform-better-professor-says-12292

Ahn, J. (2011). The effect of Social Network Sites on Adolescents' Social and Academic Development: Current Theories and Controversies. *Journal of the American Society for Information Science and Technology, 62*(8), 1435-1445.

Ahn, J. (2012). Teenagers' experiences with social network sites: Relationships to bridging and bonding social capital. *The Information Society, 28*(2), 99–109. doi:10.1080/01972243.2011.649394

Banquil, K., & Chua, N. A. (2009). Social Networking Sites affects one's academic Performance adversely. *UST College of Nursing*, 1-42. Retrieved from http// www.Scribd. Com/ doc/2891955

Baro, E. E., Edewor, N., & Sunday, G. (2014). Web 2.0 tools: A survey of awareness and use by librarians in university libraries in Africa. *The Electronic Library, 32*(6), 864–883. doi:10.1108/EL-11-2012-0151

Barry, S. (2014). *Searching for value in social media marketing.* www.cmswire.com/cms/customer-experience/searching-for-value-in-socialmediamarketing-024548.php35T

Bhatt, R. K. (2014). Student opinion on the use of social networking tools by libraries. *The Electronic Library, 32*(5), 594–602. doi:10.1108/EL-09-2012-0110

Boyd, M. (2007). Why youth (heart) social network sites: The role of networked publics in teenage social life. In D. Buckingham (Ed.), Youth, identity, and digital media (pp. 119– 142). Academic Press.

Chakraborty, N. (2012). *Activities and reasons for using social networking sites by research scholars in NEHU: A study on Facebook and Research Gate.* 8th Convention Planner. Sikkim University Gangtok.

Chao, C., & Keung, N. (2017). Predicting social capital on Facebook: The implications of use intensity, perceived content desirability, and Facebook-enabled communication practices. *Computers in Human Behavior, 72*, 259–268. doi:10.1016/j.chb.2017.02.058

Charnigo, L., & Barnett-Ellis, P. (2007). The Impact of a Digital Trend on Academic Libraries. *Information Technology and Libraries, 26*(1), 23–33. doi:10.6017/ital.v26i1.3286

Chen, D. Y. T., Chu, S. K. W., & Xu, S. Q. (2012). How do libraries use social networking sites to interact with users. *Proceedings of the American Society for Information Science and Technology, 49*(1), 1–10. doi:10.1002/meet.14504901286

Deb, P. K. (2012). The buzz of viral marketing-viral marketing encourages to pass along company-developed products and services or audio, video or written information to others online. *Indian Management, 51*(6), 91–92.

Di Gennaro, C., & Dutton, W. H. (2007). Reconfiguring friendships: Social relationships and the Internet. *Information Communication and Society, 10*(5), 591–618. doi:10.1080/13691180701657949

Dwyer, C., Hiltsz, S. R., & Widmeyer, G. (2008). Understanding development and usage of social networking sites, The social software performance model. In *Hawaii International Conference on System Sciences, Proceedings of the 41st Annual* (pp. 292-292). IEEE. 10.1109/HICSS.2008.476

Eleanor, Y. S. (2011). http://californiawatch.org/dailyreport/social-networkinghelpsstudents-perform-better-professor-says-12292

Ellison, N., Steinfield, C., & Lampe, C. (2007). The benefits of Face book "friends:" Social capital and college students' use of online social network sites. *Journal of Computer-Mediated Communication, 12*(4), 1143–1168. doi:10.1111/j.1083-6101.2007.00367.x

Gemma, N., & Angel, B. (2013). Use of social networks for academic purposes: A case study. *The Electronic Library, 31*(6), 781–791. doi:10.1108/EL-03-2012-0031

Gennaro, C. D., & Hargittaii, E. (2007). Whose space? Differences among users and non-users of social network sites. *Journal of Computer-Mediated Communication, 13*(1), 14.

Globerson, A., Chechik, G., Pereira, F., & Tishby, N. (2007). Euclidean Embedding of Co-Occurrence Data. *Journal of Machine Learning Research, 8,* 2265–2295.

Goodman, J. (2007). Click first, ask questions later: Understanding teen online behaviour. *Australasian Public Libraries and Information Services, 20*(2), 84.

Hamat, A., Embi, M. A., & Hassan, H. A. (2012). The Use of Social Networking Sites among Malaysian University Students. *International Education Studies, 5*(3), 56–66. doi:10.5539/ies.v5n3p56

Hargittai, E. (2008). Whose Space? Differences among Users and Non-Users of Social Network Sites. *Journal of Computer-Mediated Communication, 13,* 276–297.

Helou, A. M. (2014). The Influence Of Social Networking Sites On Students' Academic Performance In Malaysia. *International Journal of Electronic Commerce Studies, 5*(2), 247–254. doi:10.7903/ijecs.1114

Hendricks, D. (2014). *3 ways social media is driving a business revolution.* www.forbes.com/sites/drewhendricks/2014/02/25/3-ways-social-media-isdriving-a business-revolution/35T

Kenchakkanavar, A. Y. (2015). Facebook and Twitter for Academic Libraries in the Twenty First Century, International Research. *Journal of Library and Information Science, 5*(1), 163–173.

Kindi, S., &Alhashmi, S. M. (2012). Use of Social Networking Sites among Shinas College of Technology Students in Oman. *Journal of Information & Knowledge Management, 11*(1), 1250002-1-1250002-9.

Kuppuswamy, S., & Narayan, P. (2010). The Impact of Social Networking Websites on the Education of Youth. *The Impact of Social Networking Websites on the Education of Youth International Journal of Virtual Communities and Social Networking, 2*(1), 67–79. doi:10.4018/jvcsn.2010010105

Li, H., & Sakamoto, Y. (2014). Social impacts in social media: An examination of perceived truthfulness and sharing of information. *Computers in Human Behavior, 41,* 278–287. doi:10.1016/j.chb.2014.08.009

Loving, M., & Ochoa, M. (2011). Facebook as a classroom management solution. *New Library World, 112*(3/4), 121–130. doi:10.1108/03074801111117023

Madge, C., Meek, J., Wellens, J., & Hooley, T. (2009). Facebook, Social Integration, and Informal Learning at University: It is more for socializing and talking to friends about work than for actual doing work. *Learning, Media and Technology, 34*(2), 141–155. doi:10.1080/17439880902923606

Madhavan, N. (2012). As if by magic. *Business Today (Norwich), 21*(7), 24–26.

Mahadi, S. R. S., Jamaludin, N. N., Johari, R., & Fuad, I. N. F. M. (2016). The Impact of Social Media among Undergraduate Students: Attitude. *Procedia: Social and Behavioral Sciences, 219,* 472–479. doi:10.1016/j.sbspro.2016.05.022

Mahajan, P. (2009). Use of social networking sites in a linguistically and culturally rich India. *The International Information & Library Review, 41*(3), 129–136. doi:10.1080/10572317.2009.10762807

Mahajan, P., Singh, H., & Kumar, A. (2013). Use of SNSs by the researchers in India. *Library Review, 62*(8/9), 525–546. doi:10.1108/LR-11-2012-0119

Mahat, S. (2014). Impact of social networking Sites (SNS) on the youth. *National conference on Innovations in IT and Management,* 978-81.

Mamic, L. I., & Almaraz, I. A. (2013). How the larger corporations engage with stakeholders through Twitter. *International Journal of Market Research, 55*(6), 851–873. doi:10.2501/IJMR-2013-070

Nicole Ellison, C. S. (2008). *Social Networking Sites. Students and Information Technology.* Educause Center for Applied Research.

Paul, J. A., Baker, H. M., & Cochran, J. D. (2012). Effect of Online Social Networking on Student Performance. *Computer in Human Behaviors, 28*(B).

Pempek, T. A., Yermolayeva, Y. A., & Calvert, S. L. (2009). College Students' Social Networking Experiences on Facebook. *Journal of Applied Developmental Psychology, 30*(3), 227–238. doi:10.1016/j.appdev.2008.12.010

Pherwani, S. (2012). How social are you? *Business India,* (889), 98.

Ruleman, A. B. (2012). Comparison of student and faculty technology use. *Library Hi Tech News, 29*(3), 16–19. doi:10.1108/07419051211241877

Saluja, S. (2014). The digital challenge. *Business India,* (935): 83.

Salvation & Adzharuddin. (2014). The Influence of Social Network Sites (SNS) upon Academic Performance of Malaysian Students. *International Journal of Humanities and Social Science, 10*(1).

Schneider, F. M., Vorderer, P., & Krömer, N. (2016). Permanently online permanently connected: Explorations into university students' use of social media and mobile smart devices. *Computers in Human Behavior, 63*, 694–703. doi:10.1016/j.chb.2016.05.085

Scott, K. (2012). Social technology: The next frontier. *Financial Executive, 28*(4), 40–45.

Steiner. (2012). *Social Media Instruction In Journalism And Mass Communications Higher Education.* Philip Merrill College of Journalism.

Stelzner, M. (2014). *Social media marketing industry report.* https://www.socialmediaexaminer.com/tag/social-media-study/

Stollak, M. J., Vandenberg, A., Burklund, A., & Weiss, S. (2011). Getting Social: The Impact of Social Networking Usage on grades Among College Students. *ASBBS, 18*(1), 859–865.

Subhash. (2013). Social circuit. *Business World, 32*(48), 24.

Subrahmanyam, K., & Lin, G. (2007). Adolescents on the Net: Internet Use and Well-Being. *Adolescence, 42*(168), 659–677. PMID:18229503

Subramani, R. (2015). The Academic Usage of Social Networking Sites by the University Students of Tamil Nadu. *Online Journal of Communication and Media Technologies, 5*(3), 162–175. doi:10.29333/ojcmt/2522

Thanuskodi S (2009). The Environment of Higher Education Libraries in India. *Library Philosophy and Practice (e-journal).* Paper 278.

Thanuskodi, S. (2016). Gender differences in internet usage among college students: A comparative study. *Library Philosophy and Practice, 2016*, 1–12.

Thanuskodi, S. (2019). *Information literacy skills among library and information science professionals in India. Library Philosophy and Practice, 2019.* Retrieved from Scopus.

Thanuskodi, S., & Alagu, A. (2014). Awareness and use of social media: A case study of alagappa university. In Social Media Strategies for Dynamic Library Service Development (pp. 263–278). doi:10.4018/978-1-4666-7415-8.ch014

Tiffany, A. (2009). College students' social networking experiences on Facebook. *Journal of Applied Developmental Psychology, 30*(3), 227–238. doi:10.1016/j.appdev.2008.12.010

Timothy, H. J. (2013). Online social networking: Relationship marketing in U.K. Hotels. *Journal of Marketing Management, 29*(324), 393–420.

Valkenburg, P. M., Peter, J., & Schouten, A. P. (2006). Friend Networking Sites and Their Relationship to Adolescent's Well-Being and Social Self-Esteem. *Cyberpsychology & Behavior, 9*(5), 584–590. doi:10.1089/cpb.2006.9.584 PMID:17034326

Vassilakaki, E. & Garoufallou, E. (2014). The impact of Facebook on libraries and librarians: a review of the literature, Program: *Electronic Library and Information Systems, 48*(3), 226 – 245.

Weber, A. S. (2012). Considerations For Social Network Site (SNS) Use in Education. *International Journal of Digital Information and Wireless Communications*, *2*(4), 306–321.

Yan, Z. (2012). College students' uses and perceptions of social networking sites for health and wellness information. *Information Research*, *17*(3), 3.

Yoo, K.-H., & Gretzel, U. (2010). Influence of personality on travel-related consumer generated media creation. *Computers in Human Behavior*, *27*(2), 609–621. doi:10.1016/j.chb.2010.05.002

Zohoorian-Fooladi, N., & Abrizah, A. (2014). Academic librarians and their social media presence a story of motivations and deterrents. *Information Development*, *30*(2), 159–171. doi:10.1177/0266666913481689

ADDITIONAL READING

Alagu, A., & Thanuskodi, S. (2018b). *Awareness and use of ICT among undergraduate students of rural areas in Dindigul district: A study. Library Philosophy and Practice, 2018*. Retrieved from Scopus.

Alagu, A., & Thanuskodi, S. (2018c). User perception of electronic information resources: A case study of Alagappa College of Arts and Science, Tamilnadu, India. *Library Philosophy and Practice, 2018*. Retrieved from Scopus.

Balamurugan, T., & Thanuskodi, S. (2019). Use of social networking sites among the college students in Tamil Nadu, India. *Library Philosophy and Practice, 2019*. Retrieved from Scopus.

Muthuvennila, S., & Thanuskodi, S. (2018). *Impact of open access resources on library and information science students in India. Library Philosophy and Practice, 2018*. Retrieved from Scopus.

Muthuvennila, S., & Thanuskodi, S. (2019). User perception on open access resources among college students in India: A survey. *Library Philosophy and Practice, 2019*. Retrieved from Scopus.

Thanuskodi, S. (2013). *Challenges of Academic Library Management in Developing Countries*. Hershey, PA: IGI Global. doi:10.4018/978-1-4666-4070-2

Thanuskodi, S. (2015). *Handbook of Research on Inventive Digital Tools for Collection Management and Development in Modern Libraries*. Hershey, PA: IGI Global. doi:10.4018/978-1-4666-8178-1

This research was previously published in Challenges and Opportunities of Open Educational Resources Management; pages 103-123, copyright year 2020 by Information Science Reference (an imprint of IGI Global).

Chapter 49
Using Social Media to Improve Peer Dialogue in an Online Course About Regional Climate Modeling

Morgan B. Yarker
Yarker Consulting, Cedar Rapids, USA

Michel D.S. Mesquita
Uni Research, the Bjerknes Centre for Climate Research, Bergen, Norway & Future Solutions, Bømlo, Norway

ABSTRACT

Recent technology advancements provide worldwide information exchange that has been invaluable for the scientific community, particularly for issues surrounding global climate change. Many online learning spaces have developed which are often repositories of information rather than a space of knowledge construction. Classroom dialogue is shown to be an important component for effective learning, therefore it should be developed online as well. This article explores how social media can support dialogue in e-learning. Interactions were studied in two online courses about regional climate modeling. The first used traditional forums and the other promoted a Facebook group for online interactions. Qualitative results indicate that the Facebook group showed improvement because elements of dialogue began to emerge, including open-ended questions and episodes of peer discussion. Quantitative findings suggest the Facebook interactions were perceived as more informal and participants posted, responded, and interacted with their peers more significantly than traditional forums.

DOI: 10.4018/978-1-6684-7123-4.ch049

INTRODUCTION

One of the biggest challenges facing society is our ability to mitigate and adapt to a changing climate. This creates an important challenge in education because it is imperative that knowledge, skills, and trainings about the earth system are made available not only to scientists, decision makers, and leaders of developing countries but everyone else as well. In a paper submitted to COP17, Mesquita, Veldore, Yarker, and Lamadrid (2011) highlight the challenges and potential solutions to make professional development accessible to weather and climate model users in developing countries. For many, limited funds and available resources make it difficult to adequately assess the challenges their region of the world faces in light of a changing earth system. Traveling to facilities is extremely costly and limits the time participants can interact with the instructor (most sessions lasting only a week). Additionally, there can be political constraints, including restrictions on who can travel to what country as well as the number of participants allowed per country. Finally, with short, in-person professional developments (i.e., instructors and students travel to the same physical space), follow up with the instructor as the participants attempt to apply their new knowledge to their region can be lost completely. Prior research suggests that participants who are able to follow up with their instructor regularly after a professional development are better able to adequately apply the new information to their own setting (Penuel et al., 2009). Therefore, knowledge and resources need to be readily available whenever possible.

An online course that can effectively teach professional scientists how to set up and run weather and/ or climate models can provide a cost-effective solution to many of these issues, because each scientist can take the course on their own schedule from anywhere in the world. However, utilizing an online environment to construct knowledge comes with its challenges. In particular, how best practice educational theory can be applied to maximize learning, rather than to be a static online repository of information. Some strides have been made to address this issue (e.g., Walton, Yarker, Mesquita, & Otto, 2016), but the role peer-to-peer dialogue plays in online learning has yet to be extensively studied. While forums are commonly used to facilitate discussion in online spaces, we found that they were generally underutilized, thus peer-to-peer discussion was not occurring. Many of our participants would introduce themselves on a forum post (requested as part of the first assignment), but after that rarely posted again, seeming to prefer emailing the instructor directly. We hypothesize that forums may be problematic because 1) they are not an integral part of student's day-to-day life (like the way email is) so they are not regularly checked, and 2) may be intimidating because they may be perceived as a formal tool within a formal learning setting. Therefore, it was necessary to explore alternative tools for online discussion.

There is emerging research that suggests that social media can be an effective learning tool. Kotecha (2017a) states that "the contribution of Facebook to promoting inclusive education, student interaction, and collaborative learning [is] highly significant." We believe that social media (as part of many people's everyday life) maybe checked more frequently and may be perceived to be a less formal (though still "public") space for discussing course content over forums.

Learning Pitfalls in Climate and Weather Modeling

Climate projections and weather predictions are used more and more in impact studies and policymaking. However, in order for individual communities to better mitigate and adapt to climate change, global climate projections need to be scaled down to more localized, regional projections (i.e., regional climate modeling). Since new models can take years to be fully developed, the fastest way to generate regional climate data is to utilize already existing fine scale weather models. Due to their more detailed parameters, weather models can provide more detailed long-range forecasts for a smaller region than global-scale climate models are capable of doing (Liang et al., 2012). For example, engineers use regional climate modeling to develop infrastructure that can withstand future weather extremes, politicians plan for future economies, and health organizations prepare for future disease outbreaks. Therefore, having reliable climate and weather information is vital. One consequence of climate change is that regional planners need to plan for the future, so there is pressure on scientists to provide downscaled climate information through the use of regional climate models. Since these models are open access, anyone who has access to a supercomputer with a regional climate model installed on it can follow rote instructions and get it to run. However, there is increasing concern of the quality of information from models, as many may be using them mechanistically and with very limited understanding of the models (Warner, 2011) thereby producing unreliable results. Walton et al. (2016) refers to this phenomenon as the Warner-effect.

While it is common for novice climate and weather modelers to start running the model right away in order to familiarize themselves with Linux/Unix and the model's coding language and syntax, it is better to conceptually understand the model's framework before trying to run it. Mesquita et al. (2011) argues that novice modelers who have successfully run a computer model still view them as a metaphorical "black box", where data is generated with little understanding of the input data, parameters, and domain settings that drive the model. As a result, the participant cannot properly reason through model outputs or the model's limitations (Werner, 2011).

Additionally, climate and weather models function under the understanding that the various earth system interact and operate as one entity (i.e., water, ice, earth, atmosphere interactions), which is a good representation of reality. However, most students learn about each system separately and not as a whole system, which is a detriment when they begin to run climate and weather models. Students must understand that the system has temporal and spatial characteristics and that continuous or dynamic disturbances in one system may cause changes throughout the whole system (Ben-Zvi & Orpaz, 2010), which can make them better modelers. Doing so requires a change in students' conceptual framework, or conceptual change (Posner, Strike, Hewson, & Gertzog, 1982). Becoming a systems thinker takes a long time to develop, which limits the effectiveness of short in-person climate and weather modeling professional development courses (Mesquita et al., 2011). However, the limitation of online courses is that it is difficult to generate effective peer-to-instructor and peer-to-peer interactions. Additionally, it is important to note that while weather, climate, and regional climate models serve very different purposes with regard to atmospheric processes, the framework and conceptual processes required to run these models are actually the same (Warner 2011).

Currently, there is only one other online course in regional climate modeling where the students learn about the model framework and science content that drives it, but do not run it as part of the course (Met Office, 2011). The course discussed in this paper is the first to provided participants with hands-on experience running a regional climate model. Therefore, the creation of the course poses a unique challenge because, at the time of development, there was no framework to teach atmospheric modeling in an online environment.

Since argument-based inquiry has been shown to be an effective approach for teaching science content in in-person learning environments (e.g., Driver & Oldham, 1986; Driver, Newton, & Osborne, 2000; Duschl & Osborne, 2002; Hand, Norton-Meier, Staker, & Bintz, 2009; Keys, Hand, Prain, & Collins, 1999; Osborne, Erduran, & Simon, 2004), it makes sense to apply this approach in an online setting as well. In-person classrooms that utilize argument-based inquiry teach science content through authentic science inquiry with particular attention paid to the dialogue generated by the instructor and students throughout the learning process (Benus et al., 2009). Applying some aspects of inquiry in an online learning environment can be relatively easy to do (such as asking questions, designing an experiment, deriving evidence, and making a claim), however generating the online dialogue that occurs as a result of written questions, claims, and evidence (argumentation) between peers is much more difficult to achieve; not just in an online setting, but for in-person classrooms as well (Benus, Yarker, Hand, & Norton-Meier, 2013). As a result, assessing opportunities to engage in dialogue becomes one important component to evaluating the effectiveness of online courses, and is the focus of this study.

Social Media in Education

Tess (2013) reviewed the literature about using social media sites as a tool in higher education and concluded that there is limited evidence (outside of self-reported survey and questionnaires) to indicate how to effectively implement social media into in-person learning environments. Online learning environments present different sets of challenges that social media could potentially support. For example, Ledimo and Martins (2016) argue that in distance, open-ended courses social media can be a great way to connect participants and support collaboration. It also allows students to connect with the content in different ways, as well as easily create and share digital content (Ledimo & Martins, 2016). One pitfall found in our previous online, open-ended courses is that participants rarely access forums, thus they are generally underused. In an effort to improve interactions between participants as well as with the course material, we decided to try using social media, since it is already implemented into many people's daily lives and is currently being used by some educators with promising results (e.g., C. Rice, 2014; Kotecha, 2017b).

In higher education classrooms, Kotecha (2016) argued that Facebook could improve student engagement, promote dialogue, and provide an online space for collaborative research. Moreover, Kotecha (2017b) reports that Facebook study groups lowered student anxiety about mathematics and statistics content in her introductory courses. These findings suggest that a social media platform may be a less intimidating way for students to post questions, comments, or responses to the learning community. Since the forums were vastly underutilized in the first course, simply increasing the number of participant posts and responses in the second course would be an important step towards encouraging more dialogic interaction.

This study seeks to answer two driving research questions. First, can Facebook improve peer dialogue during online courses? And second, is Facebook a better tool than forums to facilitate peer discussion? The next section will discuss the theoretical framework used throughout the study, followed by the methodology that will describe the course, participants, and data analysis. The results and a discussion of the results will review the findings in light of the theoretical framework, and finally implications and limitations to the study will be reviewed.

THEORETICAL FRAMEWORK

While the course structure and set up will be discussed in the Methodology section, the reason why the course was developed (Mesquita et al., 2011) and the learning theory used to construct the course (Walton et al., 2015) will not be discussed at length in this paper. Since the goal is to identify if Facebook, a popular social media site, is a better tool than traditional online forums to facilitate dialogue between students in an online course, the framework for the study is based on use of technology in education, argument-based inquiry, writing-to-learn approaches, and characteristics of effective dialogue.

Technology as a Learning Tool and Modeling as Part of Science Instruction

While there is a variety of research that highlights various tools that can support student learning, it is important to note that if constructed properly, technology can be a motivational tool, support the building of new knowledge, and support students as they organize and connect new knowledge into their conceptual framework through application and reflection (Edelson, 2001). In particular, students should have the opportunity to explore openly, which is in opposition to the strategy where there is one correct outcome. Open exploration with technology can be an effective way to develop understanding of the content (Windschitl & Andre, 1998).

The field of science education has a variety of definitions for models (e.g., Gilbert, 2011; Gilbert, Boulter, & Elmer, 2000; Harrison & Treagust, 1998; Harrison & Treagust, 2000; Schwarz et al., 2009), there is general consensus that models range from simple (such as concrete, physical representations of reality) to complex (depicting a group of concepts or multiple processes). Since climate and weather models are mathematical simulations of a variety of earth processes as described by many scientific theories and laws, they would be considered one of the more complex kinds of models. As a result, it takes time and a focused approach to effectively support students to use and understand these kinds of complex models (Yarker, 2013). In the case of the courses used in this study, students learn science content through the use of computer modeling in an approach to model-based inquiry.

Research in model-based inquiry indicates that it is important that the students not just use the model, but also construct and evaluate it (Coll, France, & Taylor, 2005; Schwarz, et al., 2009). In the case of complex computer models, that means having students design their own experiment based on a topic of their own choosing that is of interest to them, choosing model parameters, and establishing initial conditions; rather than having them run a pre-determined simulation with expected results. Research indicates that utilizing science models in this manner not only improves student understanding of the model as well as the nature of science, but also the physical properties that the model represents (Schwarz & White, 2005). Once students have a handle on the logistics of generating a simulation, the process of experimenting with it is enhanced learning (Hsu & Thomas, 2002) and can increase problem-solving skills (Faryniarz & Lockwood, 1992). In other words, the process of having students design an experiment, set up the model and run it not only helps them understand the model, but also the entire earth system (earth, atmosphere, and ocean processes) which drives the model. Generally, students are taught about these processes in a very disciplined, individual approach (Ben-Zvi & Orpaz, 2010), which makes learning the model difficult. One way to help students connect concepts is to encourage deep, peer-to-peer discussions in order to problem solve and think critically about the concepts (i.e., through argument-based inquiry).

Argument-Based Inquiry and Writing-to-Learn

Argumentation is considered to be a discourse process (Osborne et al., 2004) that is about evaluating and critiquing the construction of scientific claims (Duschl, Schweingruber, & Shouse, 2007). According to Fischer (1995), authentic science is a socially constructed knowledge base centered upon argumentation. No individual scientist can exist without a community of other scientists in which to share ideas, critique ideas, and construct a better understanding of the world around us. In essence, science is based entirely on the process of sharing, critiquing, and constructing knowledge (Fischer, 1995; Kuhn, 1992; Lemke, 1990).

The importance of dialogue in classroom learning has been widely studied through an approach to inquiry known as argument-based-inquiry. There have been numerous studies on the use of argument to help students construct scientific knowledge (e.g., Driver & Oldham, 1986; Driver et al., 2000; Duschl & Osborne, 2002; Hand et al., 2009; Keys et al., 1999; Osborne et al., 2004). The purpose of argument-based inquiry approaches is to emphasize the communication element of inquiry (Next Generation Science Standards, 2013; National Research Council, 1996). While the focus of argument-based inquiry is generally on spoken dialogue (Benus, et al., 2009; Benus, et al., 2013;), there have been many studies that utilize argument-based inquiry through writing-to-learn strategies, such as the Science Writing Heuristic (e.g., Hand, Wallace, & Yang, 2004; Hand, 2006; Hand et al., 2009; Keys et al., 1999; Prain & Hand, 1996).

Writing can be a useful language tool to enhance student learning (Prain & Hand, 1996; Dlugokienki & Sampson, 2008). It is a form of problem solving, and with all production of text comes thinking and learning (Galbraith, 1999; Prain & Hand, 1996). This approach is referred to as writing-to-learn (Dlugokienki & Sampson, 2008). Additionally, giving students the opportunity to write informally about a concept (beyond the typical science protocol, such as formal lab reports) allows for deeper appreciation for the role science plays in society (Bricker, 2007; Hohenshell & Hand, 2006).

Components of Dialogue

Since dialogue is the driving force behind successful implementation of argument-based inquiry, it is important to define dialogue (as opposed to discussion or talk) by exploring its unique components.

Two studies provide several characteristics of dialogue that can be applied to the online environment. Schein (1993) describes dialogue as a building of mutual trust, confronting own and other assumptions, thinking and feeling as a group, convincing and advocating, exploring oppositions, and resolving by logic. Benus et al. (2013) found whole-class in-person dialogue to be an important factor in the implementation of an approach to argument-based inquiry. The authors developed a progression of dialogue that included five specific categories: complexity of question, depth of idea exchange, classroom interactions, evidence-based ideas, and conversation patterns. Each category can elicit effective dialogue depending on the level of dialogic interaction. For each category, the level of dialogic interaction ranges from Level One (low to no dialogical interaction) to Level Three (high level of dialogical interaction). For the purposes of this study, we are not concerned about the level of dialogical interaction; we are only interested in whether or not any of these factors of dialogue exist in the online discussions. Therefore, we have summarized the categories from Benus et al. (2013, Table 1) in the following way:

- **Complexity of Questions:** Questions that attempt to elicit explanation and justification are characteristics of high levels of dialogue. Therefore, questions that ask "why" or "how" are indicators of effective dialogue;
- **Depth of Idea Exchange:** In high levels of dialogue, discussion exists for many turns of talk about a focused topic between the students. Therefore, students responding to initial posts and asking relevant follow up questions about a clear topic is an indicator that effective dialogue may be occurring;

- **Classroom Interactions:** At the highest levels of dialogue, students ask follow up questions that challenge each other and elicit explanations from each other. Therefore, student responses to questions and asking for explanations are an indicator that effective dialogue may be occurring;
- **Evidence-Based Ideas:** Extensive discussion of evidence to support claims occurred during high dialogical interaction. Therefore, dialogue may be occurring if students present evidence to support their argument during discussion;
- **Conversational Pattern:** Conversation moves beyond a question/answer type format to become more integrated and with very lengthy discussions. Therefore, long discussions between several students may be an indicator of dialogue.

Since classroom discussion can be very different from online discussion, it is reasonable to assume that some of the characteristics observed in the study by Benus et al. (2013) will not be applicable in an online environment. Also, unlike the previous studies, the goal of this paper is not to define specific characteristics of dialogue in an online environment. Rather, we are looking for any emergence of characteristics that indicate that some level of effective dialogue is occurring in online discussions.

METHODOLOGY

This is a mixed methods study of the differences in student dialogue between two nearly identical online capacity building courses about regional climate modeling. This section will review a description of the courses, participants, data collected and data analyzed.

Course Description and Participant Demographics

Two virtually identical courses were developed as part of two, independent capacity building programs with the goal to make atmospheric modeling more accessible to practicing scientists, particularly those from developing countries. Thus, participants for the study were a sample of convenience (McMillian, 2008), from those who voluntarily registered for the courses as a result of each of the capacity building projects. Both courses utilized the Weather Research and Forecasting (WRF) model, which is a state-of-the-art weather and regional climate model that can be run in high horizontal and vertical resolution for a specified area (city, state, country, continent, or even global scale; Skamarock et al., 2005). Each course was given a title to describe the goals of the corresponding project: a) Regional Climate Modeling Using WRF; and b) WIMEA-ICT e-learning: WRF Training for Africa.

Regional Climate Modeling Using WRF was developed with the goal to teach WRF to professionals around the world (493 participants). While this course was open to anyone to take, the majority of registered participants were graduate students and early career researchers (78% of post-course survey respondents). The majority of participants were from India (160 participants), Brazil (41 participants), and Cuba (34 participants); the rest were scattered throughout the rest of the world. Participants had discussions via forms that were internal to the course platform.

WIMEA-ICT e-learning: WRF Training for Africa was run by the University of Bergen, Norway, where students from Africa would learn how to run the WRF model (127 participants). This course was open to anyone to take, however, the majority of registered participants were graduate students and early career researchers (82% of post-course survey respondents). Additionally, all participants were from economically developing countries, with the most represented being Uganda (26 participants), Ethiopia (24 participants), Tanzania (21 participants), and Rwanda (15 participants); the rest were scattered throughout the rest of Africa. The course content and structures were identical to the first course, including topics covered, delivery of content, activities, assignments, and course outcomes. The only exceptions were: 1) real-world examples utilized for activities were drawn from events of particular interest to regions of Africa (rather than globally with the first course), and 2) participants were given the opportunity to discuss aspects of the course in a Facebook group called WRF Regional Climate Modeling.

The courses were taught via the m2lab.org website, created by the authors in response to ideas developed in Mesquita et al. (2011) and utilizes an approach to both model and argument-based inquiry. The website runs on Moodle (2011), a web-based platform for creating and teaching distance learning courses. The aforementioned online forum is one of the resources provided in Moodle. The courses were divided into eight parts, each of which brought the following contents:

- **Reading Assignments:** These were based on the book 'Numerical Weather and Climate Prediction' (Warner, 2011), which the students were supposed to study and ask questions about. These assignments provided the theoretical background needed to understand how the WRF model works;
- **Tutorials:** These were given in the form of Moodle books, which are delivered one page at a time. The books are interactive, in the sense that they include hyperlinks to navigate from one content to the next. Also, throughout the books, we included several links to external scientific content. The books contained step-by-step activities, which allowed the students to follow through the running process of the WRF model on their computers;
- **Assignments:** These were given so as to provide extra practice from what the students learned in the Tutorials. The activities were personal, so that they asked participants to conduct model experiments for their own cities and countries.

Each of the aforementioned course parts was based on the Personal Reinforcement of Technology and Content (PRTC), described in detail in Walton et al. (2015). In summary, the PRTC framework reinforces content by having participants practice working with the model and formulating scientific questions through a number of cycles. These cycles are also built into the tutorials in such a way that participants receive questions to reflect on, they have the opportunity to make their own assumptions, and then they receive feedback on the questions. Two types of feedback were given, immediate and interactive: participants were given immediate feedback from answers given in the Tutorials, but they could also receive feedback through the interaction with the Tutors and peers in the Forums and/or on Facebook (depending on the course). In the WIMEA-ICT Africa course, PRTC combined with Facebook and forums that helped to create more cohesive and persistent opportunities for public and private interactions by participants and tutors.

Also, in parts 3 and 4 of each course, students were supposed to submit a reflective learning piece on their learning process. Tutors used these pieces to follow the progress of each student and to provide feedback when needed. Through these pieces, students also had the opportunity to see what they had studied so far and they could make plans for their progress ahead. A few questions were given to guide the reflective process. Additionally, participants had a midterm exam, called Computer Marked Assessment (CMA), which was based on their reading of Warner (2011); and a final exam called End of Course Assignment where participants had to answer essay style questions about their learning experience, a model simulation they had performed, and how they thought their career would benefit from the course.

Due to the complex task of installing the WRF model on a Linux-based machine, we have circumvented this task through the use of e-WRF, WRF for Educational Purposes (Mesquita, 2013), developed by the authors and described in Walton et al. (2015) and Yarker, Kelsey, and Mesquita (2015). e-WRF is the same, open-source WRF model, but packed as one file, or a virtual hard disk, which participants can open and read on any computer platforms (Windows, Mac, or Linux). e-WRF is an achievement in science education for weather and regional climate modelers, as it helps participants to focus on the learning process and not on the frustrations of installing a model or struggle to locate and pay for computational time from a supercomputer. Because participants experience fewer technical hurdles, they focus more on the framework that fosters a better understanding of the model (Warner, 2011). Additionally, participants are better able to achieve course goals (as stated in earlier sections) to become an experienced, knowledgeable, critical thinker of weather and regional climate models.

Components of Dialogue, Data Collection, and Analysis

Since the courses were offered at different times and have no defined end dates, the data was collected for the first six months of both courses, when student activity was at its maximum. All forum and Facebook posts were collected for qualitative analysis. Additionally, feedback surveys for both courses were anonymously collected for analysis. The feedback survey was created on the Moodle platform (Moodle, 2011) and is made up of 24 statements that students responded to using a Likert scale. The survey is provided in Table 3 in the Appendix.

In order to make sense of the forum and Facebook posts, an approach to qualitative coding was used. Forum and Facebook posts were collected and qualitatively coded using a constant comparative method (Merriam, 1998) and then categorized based upon emerging trends as well as the analytical framework outlined in Table 1. Since the goal of this project was to improve dialogue between students, it was also necessary to identify whether the initial discussion post was the instructor or a student and whether an instructor or another student posted responses. After the initial round of coding, a round of qualitative categorizing was performed through a lens that includes the components of effective dialogue as outlined in the theoretical framework (Charmaz, 2001).

Ultimately, each post was identified based on the following characteristics: when students were asked to explain, if students provided feedback to other students, the complexity of the question asked, and the number of replies to each post. Some categories were common between the forum and the Facebook cohorts, which included participants asking technical questions, students asking a clarifying question, students asking a conceptual question, and instructor-prompting question. However, there were a few categories that emerged from the Facebook analysis that did not occur on the forums. Facebook included participants sharing their results, students sharing a resource, instructor providing motivational comments, and instructor sharing a resource. Finally, a quantitative frequency of occurrence for each category was determined for both groups.

The feedback survey was designed to gain insight from the participants about how they think the course structure and design is working for them, which was created and provided by the Moodle platform, used to create the course (Moodle, 2011). Participants were asked a series of statements and asked to report the extent to which they agree or disagree with the statement using a Likert scale response system. The survey was designed to test six major areas of interest, which included the relevance of the course material, opportunities for reflective thinking, student interaction with peers and instructor, level of instructor support, level of peer-to-peer support, and the extent to which ideas were interpreted by peers and instructor. Since the focus of this project was on dialogue, the categories of most interest to this study are interaction, peer support, and interpretation. Table 1 highlights how each category from the Moodle survey aligns with components of dialogue as discussed in the theoretical framework. Note that relevance of topic is not considered to be a dialogue component, but is part of the survey itself. Also, complexity of questions is a component of dialogue not addressed in the survey, thus is only analyzed through Facebook and Forum posts.

Table 1. Description of how Moodle survey categories relate to elements of dialogue as described in the theoretical framework. Also serves as the analytical framework for the qualitative data analysis of Forum and Facebook posts.

Moodle Feedback Survey	Benus et al., 2013	Schein, 1993
Topic Relevance	N/A	N/A
Tutor support	Conversation Pattern	Building Mutual Trust
Peer support		
Interpretation	Depth of idea exchange	Confronting own and other assumptions
Interaction	Interaction	Thinking and feeling as a group
		Convincing and advocating
Reflective Thinking	Evidence-based ideas	Exploring Oppositions
		Resolving by logic
N/A	Complexity of questions	N/A

The mean value for each response was calculated among all participants who took the survey and statistical significance was tested. For a more robust analysis, two statistical tests were used: Student's t-test (J. A. Rice, 2006) and the nonparametric Mann-Whitney test (Mann & Whitney, 1949). Although t-tests are often used for this type of analysis, due to its flexibility when it comes to sample size, it assumes that the data are normally distributed. However, this is not always the case. Thus, in addition to the t-test, a nonparametric test was also chosen, as it does not assume any distributions, to assess the statistical significance.

Here, the null hypothesis tested is that the difference d between the forum and Facebook cohorts for each category. More formally, for each category $c(i)$, where i= 1, 2, ..., n the null and alternative hypotheses are: a) H_0: $d_{c(i)} = 0$; and b) H1: $d_{c(i)} \neq 0$, respectively.

RESULTS AND DISCUSSION

The results of this study will be presented in terms of common themes that emerged from the qualitative and quantitative analysis. Frequency charts from the Facebook and forum posts are reported as well as statistical analysis from the feedback surveys taken by both groups. Everyone enrolled in both courses were asked to take the feedback survey. There were 51 respondents for the WRF Regional Modeling (i.e., forum) course and 31 respondents for the WRF WIMEA-ICT (i.e., Facebook) course. The summary of the six categories reported by the feedback survey indicates that the most statistically significant differences between the forum and Facebook groups are the three categories that relate to dialogue (interaction, peer support, and interpretation) and are most directly applicable to this study (Figure 1). The three remaining categories do not relate to the study and do not have statistically significant differences, therefore will not be reported.

Figure 1. Responses from student surveys that report the mean values for all six categories measured by the feedback survey for the Facebook group and Forum group. Categories where the difference is statistically significant, for t-test (t) and/or Mann-Whitney test (M-W), are shown at the bottom of the plot. Whiskers show 95% confidence intervals.

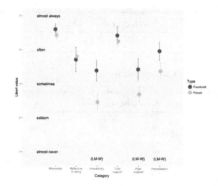

The Facebook Group Had More Posts Across a Broader Range of Topics Than the Forum Group

Using qualitative coding strategies, the Facebook and Forum posts fell into a number of emerging categories. Student posts fell into the following categories: seeking solutions to technical problems (including a variety of model set up questions and error messages), asking questions to clarify assignments or specific course content, asking conceptual questions that seek further understanding of the content and the model's characteristics, sharing results of the model set up and output for feedback and/or motivational support, and sharing additional resources that they found helpful. While the instructors almost always responded to student posts on both Facebook and the forums, they also posted their own topics, including prompts for group discussion, motivational posts to congratulate the group on their progress, and/or to share helpful resources. For examples, see Table 2.

The frequency of each post by topic is summarized in Figure 2. While the Facebook group posted significantly more often than the forum group (p value <0.005), it is also important to note that only the Facebook group shared their results as well as resources with the class. There were no instances of these topics occurring with the forum group. In addition, the instructors posted more frequently on Facebook than on the forums, usually as a way to share new information and resources (rather than through email as done previously). It is likely that the increased instructor activity influenced the increased activity of the students, however it is also important to note that students began sharing resources and their results on the Facebook without any prompting from the instructors, indicating some level of comfort and/or motivation on Facebook that the forum group did not have (Towner & Muñoz, 2011). Also, the instructor was not on Facebook prior to teaching this course, therefore was not familiar with using it on a daily basis. Many posts in the Facebook group had peer responses shortly after posting, before the instructor even saw it. Additionally, while email notifications were sent to instructors and students for all forum posts, there is an inertia in this process such that it may be perceived as less cumbersome to send an email directly to the instructor rather than click through the website and log into the forums. Facebook is generally something people use as an informal social tool that they are persistently logged into. Additionally, posts are embedded in their feed with updates from the rest of their social network. It is easy to quickly read the topic, comment before moving on, and/or click the "like" button. These affordances lead to fast feedback and can motivate participants and the instructor.

Table 2. List of Facebook and Forum post categories and corresponding examples

Post Topic Category	Example
Student asks technical question	"I am getting the following error message. Please advise."
Student asks a clarifying question	"How do I submit the assignment?"
Student asks a conceptual question	"What are the differences between the MM5 model and WRF model?"
Student shares their results	"My domain configuration: [image attached]. Comments welcome."
Student shares a resource	"I am pleased to see an updated version of [software]. You can download it [at this web address]."
Instructor prompts discussion	"In your opinion, are models perfect?"
Instructor motivates the students	"Congratulations to those of you who recently completed the course!"
Instructor shares a resource	"There have been wonderful questions asking about how to analyze WRF output. There is great software for that! [link to web address]."

In addition to forum posts, students responded to each other significantly more often on Facebook than they did on the traditional forums (p value <0.005). For the six months that data was collected for each group, students using forums posted a total of 48 times with 137 responses. Of the responses that were answering a specific question relating to the course, only 7 were students responding to other student questions. Conversely, students using Facebook posted a total of 257 times with 799 responses. Of the responses that were answering a specific question relating to the course, 86 were students responding to other students. Having students respond to each other's questions is an extremely important component of successful dialogue because peer-to-peer conversation can generate ideas and promote learning (Benus et al., 2013; Dewey, 1971; Schein, 1993) and has been shown to increase critical thinking skills (Taylor, Chanlen, Therrien, & Hand, 2014).

Additionally, the idea that Facebook is a more comfortable and motivational space can be an important contribution (Towner & Muñoz, 2011). From the perspective of the participant, forums may feel like a space that belongs to the instructor, which may hinder interaction. It is comparable to talking to a professor during a class lecture, a space where people don't often ask questions. However, Facebook is a public space similar to an off-campus café, where participants and the instructor can discuss things informally.

Figure 2. Categorical frequency chart of topics discussed on Facebook and on the forums

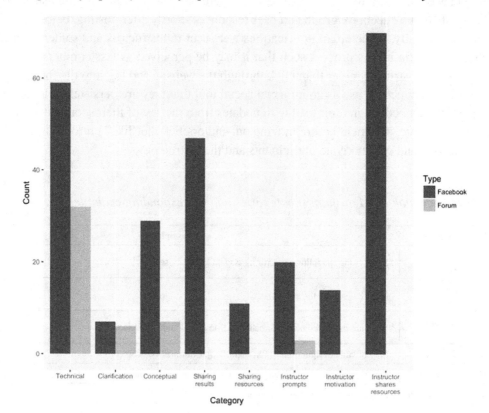

Students Report Being More Interactive on Facebook Than on the Forums

One important aspect of effective dialogue is for students to interact with each other while learning new material (Driver & Oldham, 1986; Driver et al., 2000; Duschl & Osborne, 2002; Hand et al., 2009; Keys et al., 1999; Osborne et al., 2004). In particular, if student have the opportunity to explain their ideas to each other, conceptual understanding is reinforced. Students responded to a series of questions on a Likert scale with a value of 0 indicating that they completely disagree with the statement and a value of 5 indicating that they completely agree with the statement, and the results are summarized in Figure 3. Results of the student interactivity portion of the survey indicates that students reported being asked to explain things and asking others to explain things more in the Facebook group than the forum group. Additionally, students reported a statistically significant increase in explaining their ideas and having other students respond to them in the Facebook group than the forum group (p value <0.05).

Students Report That They Provided Each Other With More Support on Facebook Than on the Forums

Peer support is an important component of dialogue because if students do not relate to their peers, it can cause barriers for the development of more complex characteristics of effective dialogue, such as explanations, interactions, and asking more complex questions (Benus et al., 2013). Responses to student surveys regarding peer support are reported in Figure 4. There was no discernable difference in how students felt they empathized with each other, however there was an increase in students reporting that their peers praised them. There is also a statistically significant increase in students reporting that their peers encouraged them and that they felt valued by the other students (p value <0.05).

One advantage to Facebook over forums is the "like" feature. On Facebook, students have the opportunity to like posts and responses, which allows them to be publicly interactive with the content without having to formulate a specific response to the original post. During the six months that data was collected for the Facebook group, there were a total of 673 "likes" on original posts. Responses of any kind can motivate students to continue working on the content and interacting with the group. Additionally, "liking" posts is an alternative way for peers to motivate and support each other (Schein, 1993; Towner & Muñoz, 2011).

Figure 3. Responses from student surveys that report how interactive they felt they were while taking the course for the Facebook group and Forum group. Topics where the difference is statistically significant, for t-test (t) and/or Mann-Whitney test (M-W), are shown at the bottom of the plot. Whiskers show 95% confidence intervals.

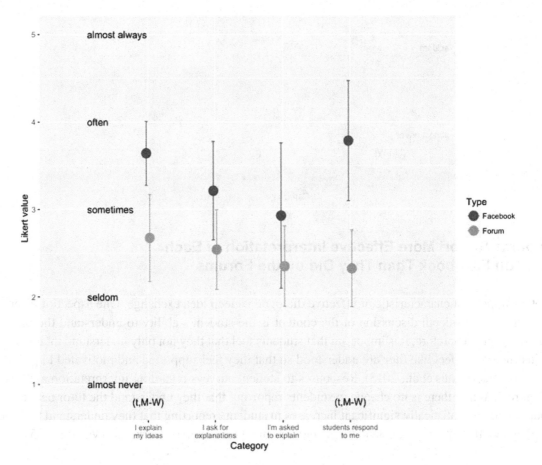

Figure 4. Responses from student surveys that report how supportive peers were to each other while taking the course for the Facebook group and Forum group. Topics where the difference is statistically significant, for t-test (t) and/or Mann-Whitney test (M-W), are shown at the bottom of the plot. Whiskers show 95% confidence intervals.

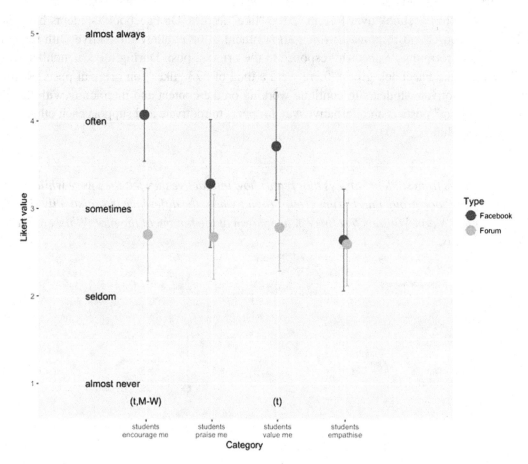

Students Report More Effective Interpretation of Each Other on Facebook Than They Did on the Forums

Another important characteristic of effective dialogue is deep idea exchange. One aspect of discussion that can hinder in-depth discussion of the content is the student's ability to understand the instructor and their peers. Therefore, it is important that students feel that they not only understand their peers and the instructor, but feel like they are understood so that they feel supported and motivated to participate in discussions (Benus et al., 2013). Responses to student surveys regarding interpretation are reported in Figure 5. While there is no change in students reporting that they understand the tutor between each group, there are statistically significant increases in students reporting that they understand their peers, that they feel their peers understand them, and that the tutor understands them (p value <0.05).

Figure 5. Responses from student surveys that report how well students and instructors understood each other while taking the course for the Facebook group and Forum group. Topics where the difference is statistically significant, for t-test (t) and/or Mann-Whitney test (M-W), are shown at the bottom of the plot. Whiskers show 95% confidence intervals.

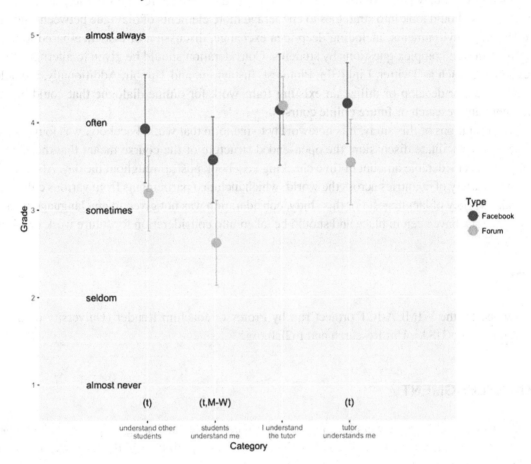

CONCLUSION AND IMPLICATIONS

As a tool to facilitate discussion, the data suggest that Facebook is a better option than the traditional forums. Students using Facebook posted more frequently over a variety of topics than the students using forums. Students from the Facebook group were more interactive with each other, were asked to explain their ideas more, understood their peers better, and felt understood and supported by their peers. As a result, students were more motivated to continue with the course and talk to each other throughout the process, which aligns with prior findings that social media study groups can reduce student anxiety in statistics and mathematics classes (Kotecha 2017a, 2017b). In addition, the use of the "like" feature allowed students to participate in the discussion without having to formulate a response. Findings from this study indicate that peer-to-peer interaction and the complexity of questions asked improved for the Facebook group over the Forum group. However, all other characteristics of dialogue were not evident in either group, therefore there is still need to improve dialogical interactions in online learning environments.

This study found Facebook to be a useful social media platform. However, Facebook is constantly being modified and updated with new features and services. Privacy settings, access issues, and choice of social platform are in constant flux by students. Therefore, we encourage future studies to carefully consider using what they perceive to be the best social media platform for their participants.

Future work should look into strategies to encourage more elements of dialogue between students in online learning environments, including deep idea exchange, discussion of evidence-based ideas, and further initiation of complex questions by students. Consideration should be given to alternative forms of social media, such as Twitter, LinkedIn, Pinterest, Instagram, and Tumblr. Additionally, it would be beneficial to either develop or utilize an existing framework for online dialogue that could drive the development and research of future online courses.

For the limitations of this study, it is noteworthy to mention that while Facebook was found to be an effective tool to facilitate discussion, the open-ended structure of the course meant that the instructor had to spend a considerable amount of time checking Facebook posts throughout the day. Also, students were from a variety of countries across the world, which included participants from various cultures and who speak a variety of languages. For this study, consideration was not given to any language or culture barriers that may have been in place and should be taken into consideration for future work in this area.

FUNDING

Partly funded by the WIMEA-ICT project run by Professor Joachim Reuder (University of Bergen), Yarker Consulting (USA), Uni Research and m2lab.org.

ACKNOWLEDGMENT

We thank the anonymous reviewers for their thoughtful comments and suggestions. We also thank Dr. Matthew J. Benus, Dr. Meena Kotecha, and Dr. Peter Walton for their fruitful discussions and contributions throughout the development of this project.

REFERENCES

Ben-Zvi, O., & Orpaz, I. (2010). The "Life at the Poles" study unit: Developing junior high school students' ability to recognize the relations between earth systems. *Research in Science Education, 40*(4), 525–549. doi:10.100711165-009-9132-2

Benus, M. J., Jang, J. Y., Kingir, S., Stecklein, J. J., Yarker, M. B., & Hand, B. (2009, December). An exploration of discourse patterns in argument-based inquiry science classrooms using the Science Writing Heuristic (SWH) approach. *Poster presented at the Iowa Educational Research and Evaluation Association Annual Conference*, Ames, IA.

Benus, M. J., Yarker, M. B., Hand, B. M., & Norton-Meier, L. A. (2013). Analysis of discourse practices in elementary science classrooms using argument-based inquiry during whole-class dialogue. In M. Khine & I. Saleh (Eds.), *Approaches and strategies in next generation science learning* (pp. 224–245). Hershey, PA: IGI Global. doi:10.4018/978-1-4666-2809-0.ch012

Bricker, P. (2007). Reinvigorating science journals. *Science and Children, 45*(3), 24–29. Retrieved from http://common.nsta.org/resource/?id=10.2505/4/sc07_045_03_24

Charmaz, K. (2001). Qualitative interviewing and grounded theory analysis. In J. Gubrium & J. Holstein (Eds.), *Handbook of interview research: Context and method* (pp. 675–694). Thousand Oaks, CA: Sage Publications, Inc.

Coll, R. K., France, B., & Taylor, I. (2005). The role of models and analogies in science education: Implications from research. *International Journal of Science Education, 27*(2), 183–198. doi:10.1080/0950069042000276712

Dewey, J. (1971). *How we think*. Chicago, IL: Henry Regnery Company.

Dlugokienski, A., & Sampson, V. (2008). Learning to write and writing to learn in science: Refutational texts and analytical rubrics. *Science Scope, 32*(3), 14–19. Retrieved from http://www.nsta.org/store/product_detail.aspx?id=10.2505/4/sc08_032_03_14

Driver, R., Newton, P., & Osborne, J. (2000). Establishing the norms of scientific argumentation in classrooms. *Science Education, 84*(3), 287–312. doi:10.1002/(SICI)1098-237X(200005)84:3<287::AID-SCE1>3.0.CO;2-A

Driver, R., & Oldham, V. (1986). A constructivist approach to curriculum development in science. *Studies in Science Education, 13*(1), 105–122. doi:10.1080/03057268608559933

Duschl, R. A., & Osborne, J. (2002). Supporting and promoting argumentation discourse. *Studies in Science Education, 38*(1), 39–72. doi:10.1080/03057260208560187

Duschl, R. A., Schweingruber, H. A., & Shouse, A. W. (Eds.). (2007). *Taking science to school: Learning and teaching science in grades K-8*. Washington, D.C.: National Academies Press.

Edelson, D. (2001). Learning-for-use: A framework for the design of technology-supported inquiry activities. *Journal of Research in Science Teaching, 38*(3), 355–385. doi:10.1002/1098-2736(200103)38:3<355::AID-TEA1010>3.0.CO;2-M

Faryniarz, J. V., & Lockwood, L. G. (1992). Effectiveness of microcomputer simulations in stimulating environmental problem solving by community college students. *Journal of Research in Science Teaching, 29*(5), 453–470. doi:10.1002/tea.3660290503

Fischer, R. (1995). Science, argumentation and organization. In V. Shen & T. Van Doan (Eds.), *Philosophy of science and education: Chinese and European views* (Vol. 9, pp. 41–54). Washington, D.C.: The Council for Research in Values and Philosophy.

Galbraith, D. (1999). Writing as a knowledge-constituting process. In M. Torrance & D. Galbraith (Eds.), *Knowing what to write: Conceptual processes in text production* (pp. 139–159). Amsterdam: Amsterdam University Press.

Gilbert, J. K., Boulter, C. J., & Elmer, R. (2000). Positioning models in science education and in design and technology education. In J. K. Gilbert & C. Boulter (Eds.), *Developing models in science education* (pp. 3–17). Springer Netherlands. doi:10.1007/978-94-010-0876-1_1

Gilbert, S. (2011). *Models-based science teaching*. Arlington, VA: NSTA Press.

Hand, B. (2006). Using the Science Writing Heuristic to promote understanding of science conceptual knowledge in middle school. In R. Douglas, M. P. Klentschy, K. Worth, & W. Binder (Eds.), *Linking science & literacy in the K-8 classroom* (pp. 117–126). Arlington, VA: NSTA Press.

Hand, B., Norton-Meier, L., Staker, J., & Bintz, J. (2009). *Negotiating science: The critical role of argument in student inquiry*. Portsmouth, NH: Heinemann.

Hand, B., Wallace, C. S., & Yang, E. M. (2004). Using the Science Writing Heuristic to enhance learning outcomes from laboratory activities in seventh grade science: Quantitative and qualitative aspects. *International Journal of Science Education*, 26(2), 131–149. doi:10.1080/0950069032000070252

Harrison, A. G., & Treagust, D. F. (1998). Teaching science effectively with analogies: An approach for pre-service and in-service teacher education. *Journal of Science Teacher Education*, 9(2), 85–101. Retrieved from http://www.jstor.org/stable/43156184 doi:10.1023/A:1009423030880

Harrison, A. G., & Treagust, D. F. (2000). A typology of school science models. *International Journal of Science Education*, 22(9), 1011–1026. doi:10.1080/095006900416884

Hohenshell, L. M., & Hand, B. (2006). Writing-to-learn strategies in secondary school cell biology: A mixed method study. *International Journal of Science Education*, 28(2-3), 261–289. doi:10.1080/09500690500336965

Hsu, Y.-S., & Thomas, R. A. (2002). The impact of a web-aided instructional simulation on science learning. *International Journal of Science Education*, 24(9), 955–979. doi:10.1080/09500690110095258

Keys, C. W., Hand, B., Prain, V., & Collins, S. (1999). Using the Science Writing Heuristic as a tool for learning from laboratory investigations in secondary science. *Journal of Research in Science Teaching*, 36(10), 1065–1081. doi:10.1002/(SICI)1098-2736(199912)36:10<1065::AID-TEA2>3.0.CO;2-I

Kotecha, M. (2016, January 11). Addressing anxiety in the teaching room: Techniques to enhance maths and stats education [Blog post]. Retrieved from https://blog.oup.com/2016/01/addressing-anxiety-teaching-mathematics/

Kotecha, M. (2017a). *Beyond teaching excellence*. Retrieved from http://eprints.lse.ac.uk/83554/

Kotecha, M. (2017b). Reducing Statistics Anxiety via Social Media. *Presented at RSS Annual Conference*. Glasgow, Scotland: Royal Statistical Society.

Kuhn, D. (1992). Thinking as argument. *Harvard Educational Review*, 62(2), 155–178. doi:10.17763/haer.62.2.9r424r0113t670l1

Lemke, J. (1990). *Talking science: Language, learning and values*. Norwood, NJ: Ablex.

Liang, X.-Z., Xu, M., Yuan, X., Ling, T., Choi, H. I., Zhang, F., ... Michalakes, J. (2012). Regional climate–weather research and forecasting model. *Bulletin of the American Meteorological Society*, *93*(9), 1363–1387. doi:10.1175/BAMS-D-11-00180.1

Lidemo, O., & Martin, N. (2016, July). The implementation of social media in an open distance learning context. In C. Bernadas & D. Minchella (Eds.), *Proceedings of the 3rd European Conference on Social Media Research.* (pp. 162-167). Reading, UK: Academic Conferences and Publishing International Limited.

Mann, H. B., & Whitney, D. R. (1947). On a test of whether one of two random variables is stochastically larger than the other. *Annals of Mathematical Statistics*, *18*(1), 50–60. Retrieved from http://www.jstor.org/stable/2236101 doi:10.1214/aoms/1177730491

McMillan, J. H. (2008). *Educational research: Fundamentals for the consumer* (5th ed.). Boston, MA: Pearson Education Inc.

Merriam, S. B. (1998). *Qualitative research and case study applications in education.* San Francisco, CA: John Wiley & Sons, Inc.

Mesquita, M. D. (2013). WRF for Educational Purposes [computer software]. Retrieved from m2lab.org

Mesquita, M. D., Veldore, V., Yarker, M. B., & Lamadrid, A. (2011). Long-Term E-Capacity Building (LEAD): A new approach for climate science research. *Paper presented at Conference Of the Parties (COP)*. New Delhi: TERI Press.

Met Office. (2011). *PRECIS user support.* Retrieved from http://www.metoffice.gov.uk/precis/support

Moodle.org. (2011). *About Moodle.* Retrieved from http://moodle.org/about/

National Research Council. (1996). *National science education standards.* Washington, D.C.: National Academies Press.

Next Generation Science Standards. (2013). *Next Generation Science Standards: For states, by states.* Washington, DC: National Academies Press.

Osborne, J., Erduran, S., & Simon, S. (2004). Enhancing the quality of argumentation in school science. *Journal of Research in Science Teaching*, *41*(10), 994–1020. doi:10.1002/tea.20035

Penuel, W. H., McWilliams, C., McAuliffe, A., Benbow, C., Malby, C., & Hayden, M. (2009). Teaching for understanding in earth science: Comparing impacts on planning and instruction in three professional development designs for middle school science teachers. *Journal of Science Teacher Education*, *20*(5), 415–436. doi:10.100710972-008-9120-9

Posner, G. J., Strike, K. A., Hewson, P. W., & Gertzog, W. A. (1982). Accommodation of a scientific conception: Toward a theory of conceptual change. *Science Education*, *66*(2), 211–227. doi:10.1002ce.3730660207

Prain, V., & Hand, B. (1996). Writing for learning in secondary science: Rethinking practices. *Teaching and Teacher Education*, *12*(6), 609–626. doi:10.1016/S0742-051X(96)00003-0

Rice, C. (2014). *Social media transforms the textbook lesson.* Retrieved from http://www.bbc.com/news/technology-25888737

Rice, J. A. (2006). *Mathematical statistics and data analysis* (3rd ed.). Belmont, CA: Duxbury.

Schein, E. H. (1993). On dialogue, culture, and organizational learning. *Reflections: The SoL Journal*, *4*(4), 27–38. doi:10.1162/152417303322004184

Schwarz, C., & White, B. (2005). Metamodeling knowledge: Developing students' understanding of scientific modeling. *Cognition and Instruction*, *23*(2), 165–205. doi:10.12071532690xci2302_1

Schwarz, C. V., Reiser, B. J., Davis, E. A., Kenyon, L., Acher, A., Fortus, D., ... Krajcik, J. (2009). Developing a learning progression for scientific modeling: Making scientific modeling accessible and meaningful for learners. *Journal of Research in Science Teaching*, *46*(6), 632–654. doi:10.1002/tea.20311

Skamarock, W. C., Klemp, J. B., Dudhia, J., Gill, D. O., Barker, D. M., Wang, W., & Powers, J., G. (2005). *A description of the Advanced Research WRF Version 2* (NCAR. Technical note NCAR/TN-468+STR). doi:10.5065/D6DZ069T

Taylor, J. C., Chanlen, N., Therrien, W. J., & Hand, B. (2014). Improving low achieving students' critical thinking skills through an argument-based inquiry approach to science. *Academic Exchange Quarterly*, *18*(1), 77–84. Retrieved from https://www.researchgate.net/publication/280938636_Improving_low_achieving_students'_critical_thinking_skills_through_an_argument-based_inquiry_approach_to_science

Tess, P. A. (2013). The role of social media in higher education classes (real and virtual) – A literature review. *Computers in Human Behavior*, *29*(5), A60–A68. doi:10.1016/j.chb.2012.12.032

Towner, T. L., & Muñoz, C. L. (2011). Facebook and education: A classroom connection? In C. Wankel (Ed.), *Educating Educators with Social Media*. Bingley, UK: Emerald Group Publishing Limited. doi:10.1108/S2044-9968(2011)0000001005

Walton, P. J., Yarker, M. B., Mesquita, M., & Otto, F. (2016). Helping to make sense of regional climate modeling: Professional development for scientists and decision makers anytime, anywhere. *Bulletin of the American Meteorological Society*, *97*(7), 1173–1185. doi:10.1175/BAMS-D-14-00111.1

Warner, T. (2011). *Numerical weather and climate prediction*. Cambridge: University Press.

Windschitl, M., & Andre, T. (1998). Using computer simulations to enhance conceptual change: The roles of constructivist instruction and student epistemological beliefs. *Journal of Research in Science Teaching*, *35*(2), 145–160. doi:10.1002/(SICI)1098-2736(199802)35:2<145::AID-TEA5>3.0.CO;2-S

Yarker, M. B. (2013). *Teacher challenges, perceptions, and use of science models in middle school classrooms about climate, weather, and energy concepts* [Doctoral dissertation].

Yarker, M. B., Kelsey, E., & Mesquita, M. d. (2015, January). A hybrid approach to online and traditional learning during a boundary layer meteorology course. *Paper presented at the 95th American Meteorological Society Annual Meeting*, Phoenix, AZ.

This research was previously published in the International Journal of Online Pedagogy and Course Design (IJOPCD), 8(4); pages 1-21, copyright year 2018 by IGI Publishing (an imprint of IGI Global).

APPENDIX

Table 3. Feedback survey that participants completed. Survey constructed and provided by Moodle (2011). Each question informed a category, which were used in the analysis of this study

Category	Question	Almost Never	Seldom	Sometimes	Often	Almost Always
Relevance	My learning focuses on issues that interest me.	1	2	3	4	5
	What I learn is important for my professional practice.	1	2	3	4	5
	I learn how to improve my professional practice.	1	2	3	4	5
	What I learn connects well with my professional practice.	1	2	3	4	5
Reflective Thinking	I think critically about how I learn.	1	2	3	4	5
	I think critically about my own ideas.	1	2	3	4	5
	I think critically about other students' ideas.	1	2	3	4	5
	I think critically about ideas in the readings.	1	2	3	4	5
Interactivity	I explain my ideas to other students.	1	2	3	4	5
	I ask other students to explain their ideas.	1	2	3	4	5
	Other students ask me to explain my ideas.	1	2	3	4	5
	Other students respond to my ideas.	1	2	3	4	5
Tutor Support	The tutor stimulates my thinking.	1	2	3	4	5
	The tutor encourages me to participate.	1	2	3	4	5
	The tutor models good discourse.	1	2	3	4	5
	The tutor models critical self-reflection.	1	2	3	4	5
Peer Support	Other students encourage my participation.	1	2	3	4	5
	Other students praise my contribution.	1	2	3	4	5
	Other students value my contribution.	1	2	3	4	5
	Other students empathize with my struggle to learn.	1	2	3	4	5
Interpretation	I make good sense of other students' messages.	1	2	3	4	5
	Other students make good sense of my messages.	1	2	3	4	5
	I make good sense of the tutor's messages.	1	2	3	4	5
	The tutor makes good sense of my messages.	1	2	3	4	5
Uncategorized	How long did this survey take you to complete?					
Uncategorized	Do you have any other comments?					

Chapter 50

Social Media and Networks for Sharing Scholarly Information Among Social Science Research Scholars in the State Universities of Tamil Nadu

C. Baskaran

https://orcid.org/0000-0002-2990-958X
Alagappa University, India

Pitchaipandi P.

Alagappa University, India

ABSTRACT

The study examines the impact and utilization of social networks and media for disseminating scholarly information among social science research scholars in south universities of Tamil Nadu, India. The study analyzed the respondent coverage from the universities: University of Madras, Bharathiar University, Bharathidasan University, Madurai Kamaraj University, Alagappa University, Manonmaniam Sundaranar University, and Periyar University. An aggregate of 520 polls appropriated to the respondents out of eight universities in Tamil Nadu and 501 (96.34%) of the filled survey got from the respondents in the social science departments of the universities for the examination. The task of research has taken effort to collect the data to find out usefulness and impact of the social media and networks among the respondents in the selected state universities of Tamil Nadu.

DOI: 10.4018/978-1-6684-7123-4.ch050

1. INTRODUCTION

Research includes the generation, use and utilization of data and information. The examination world has developed various systems intended to encourage the exchange of information between specialists. These incorporate academic diaries and gatherings, and quality confirmation components like arrangement boards, peer audit, distribution and survey. We may speak to this in a diagrammatic structure as follows:

In this model we have four phases (ID, creation, quality affirmation and scattering) which are supported by an assortment of social associations and types of joint effort. Joint effort is characterized extensively here to incorporate crafted by every one of the individuals who may be associated with explore including scientists, administrators, funders and the overall population. Each stage is imperative to the exploration network's capacity to deliver information and gain from crafted by others. Social apparatuses can possibly contribute something to every one of these stages. Be that as it may, they likewise can possibly challenge the manners by which research is finished. We subsequently talk about every one of these phases thus and inspect how online life can challenge and upgrade current thoughts and practice.

Wan Roslina Wan Othman, Ziti Fariha Mohd Apandi and Nurul Haslinda Ngah discussed that the social media has dominated their communications with friends and family, which give the influence of students' self-concepts. Considering the wide usage of the social media, it is hoped that this study has given new insights to understand the potential value of social media on college students. Applications/ Improvements: Further studies should be conducted with a focus on the use of this media for academic purposes, realizing the implications of social media on student's performance (Wan et al., 2016).

Shafawi and Hassan have discussed that research the components that drive users" commitment with online life and genuine library use from the two clients and librarians" viewpoints. The discoveries showed that Information Quality, Perceived Interactivity, and Perceived Net Benefit have exactly demonstrated to be noteworthy indicators of clients. The outcomes show that couple of library clients connected with online networking through a few exercises, for example, preferring, remarking, and perusing, sharing, after and watching web-based social networking content gave by the library. It has inspected and the outcomes found that the data quality saw intuitiveness and saw net advantages were seen as a significant indicator of clients commitment with library online networking (Shafawi & Hassan, 2018). Levula and Harré made the analysis that informal organization estimates do add impressive logical capacity to MH with social segregation (SI) having the most noteworthy impact ($\beta=-0.198$, p<0.001) trailed by social associations (SCs) ($\beta=0.141$, p<0.001) and afterward social trust (ST) ($\beta=0.071$, p<0.001). The AIC best fit model incorporated all the interpersonal organization indicators anyway it rejected physical working which contributed practically nothing (Levula & Harré, 2016). Josserand, Schmitt and Borzillo talked about the exploration discoveries are two-crease. To start with, and in spite of earlier investigations, the creators find that people's social capital adds to both investigation and misuse at the specialty unit level. Second, creating and utilizing people's outer social capital requires a particular hierarchical setting at the specialty unit level that enables representatives to create and sustain their private issue associations with customers (Josserand et al., 2017). Littman, Chudnov, Kerchner, Peterson and Tan examined the examination disclose to proceeding and create and improve Social Feed Manager (SFM), an open source application helping researchers gathering information from Twitter's API for their exploration. Web filing networks and other potential clients of internet based life assortments. The provenance metadata as required by analysts. As antiquarians and different analysts use web files, their encounters add to future prerequisites (Littman et al., 2018). Liu, Zhang and Ye emphasized the dissemination of SNs utilized by 112 libraries in Chinese colleges under the "211 task". The circulation of SNS s utilized by virtual networks, portable application, customized administration and application stage was directed in the wake of examining library sites of 112 Chinese "211 Project". It was investigated the components identified with smaller scale websites, for example, number of adherents, utilized in posts and distributed articles(Liu et al., 2018). Meenakshi, Sivakumar & Ilango, examined that There are eight items used including response efficacy and behaviour efficacy to report about the target audience on social media for health campaigns. The target audience are identified using age or ethnicity. Implementing a social marketing approach through social media to initiate interest and engagement for a web-based software package is both hands-on and reliable with the way young individuals practice the media to share ideas and promote them, thus the intervention was considered a central focus of a greater campaign (Baskaran, 2019). Baskaran reported that larger part 73 (32.0%) of the respondents recorded from Alagappa University, while 44 (19.3%) of them male and 29 (12.7%) of them female. The investigation exposures that more respondents 54(18.8%) of respondents in the age bunch between 26-35 at Alagappa University. It is seen that out of 228 respondents were reacted from four Universities, among them significant bit 146 (64.0%) of respondents are Unmarried when contrasted with (36.0%) of them Married classes (Meenakshi et al., 2017). Baskaran investigated that 11,941 all out records on informal organizations and media recovered from Web of Science database during the time of study. The investigation found that in excess of 10 distributions contributed by an individual region out of 11,941 records during period. Liu Y has contributed 37 (0.31%) of the distributions as top positioned creator in the exploration (Baskaran, 2020). Fai. M. Bin Salamh analyzed that total of 382 Kuwaiti citizens initially approached for responses, which were then analyzed for research. The results revealed that the majority of the respondents (82%) are at least sometimes affected by news and information available on social media, while 87% believe that social media is a successful tool in maintaining the reputation of a company. 65% of respondents indicated that social media plays a significant role in the development of companies, and 58% are influenced by abusive comments showing up on social media in relation to the companies' reputation (Fai, 2019).

2. OBJECTIVES OF THE STUDY

1. To investigate the use of various sorts of SNs among the respondents in the State Universities of Tamil Nadu.
2. To look at the utilization of Devices of SNs among the respondents and Place where use SNs and Media among the respondents.
3. To discover the Time inclination to utilize SNs by the respondents in a day and Period of involvement with use SNs and Media among the respondents.
4. To find out the utilization of SNS /Media Modules by the respondents in the State Universities of Tamil Nadu.
5. To analyze the kinds of motivations to utilize SNs and Media and inclination of Research Reference Management Software (RRMS).
6. To explore the utilization of research ID devices for SNs among the respondents.
7. To evaluate the inclination of Research Citation Indexes (RCI) and instruments for Contents and Texts through SNs.
8. To investigate the inclination of SNs for sharing examination data and Preference of research interpersonal organizations (RSN) among respondents.

3. HYPOTHESES

H1: There is no noteworthy distinction between the respondents from Selected State Universities and shared academic Contents in the State Universities in Tamil Nadu.

H2: There is a noteworthy distinction between the respondents from Selected State Universities and they utilized SNs for Citations.

H3: There is a noteworthy distinction between the respondents from Selected State Universities and they utilized SNs for tweeting the examination thoughts in the State Universities of Tamil Nadu.

4. METHODOLOGY

The present investigation has intended to disseminate and gather the information among the exploration researchers as Respondents from eight State Universities in Tamil Nadu by utilizing an organized poll. This investigation has taken with the assistance of different wellsprings of reports online databases and so forth. The investigation endeavors to dissect the information by conveyance and gathered from the respondents in the chose state Universities in Tamilandu. The number of inhabitants in the present examination incorporates just full time Ph.D inquire about researchers engaged from chosen State Universities in Tamilandu. The Universities are University of Madras, Annamailai University, Bharathiar University, Bharathidasan University, Madurai Kamaraj University, Alagappa University, Manonmaniam Sundaranar University and Periyar University. An aggregate of 520 surveys circulated to the respondents out of eight Universities in Tamil Nadu and 501 (96.34%) of the filled poll got from the respondents in the Social Science Departments of the Universities for the investigation. So as to portray and abridge information gathered from the respondents. Further, the endeavor to investigate Percentage instrument is utilized to discover most of utility on specific factors, chi-Square test, one way 'ANOVA' tests were utilized for examination of the components considered between the factors.

5. RESULTS AND DISCUSSION

5.1. Research Areas Wise Respondents in State Universities

Table 2 explains that Research territories insightful respondents reacted from chosen State Universities of Tamil Nadu. The investigation is seen that Total no of 501 respondents reacted to this examination, out of which 73 (14.6%) of them reacted from Alagappa University. It followed by Bharathidasan University 51 (10.2%), Bharathiar University 62 (12.4%), University of Madras 42 (8.4%), Periyar University 70(14%), Annamalai University 87 (17.4%), Madurai Kamaraj University 50 (10%) and Manonmaniam Sundaranar University 66 (13.2%) of the respondents.

5.1.1. Alagappa University

The investigation uncovers that dominant part 27 (5.4%) of there from Education/Physical Education. It followed Management/trade under (8%) of the respondents of Education/Physical Education. (1.4%) of them respondents from library and Information Science, and Others the investigation affirmed that under (1%) of the respondents were accounted for from Economics (.8%) Sociology/Social work (0.4%) and History/Geography (.6%).

5.1.2. Bharathidasan University

The investigation found that over one Percent of the respondents from Management/Commerce (2.2%), Sociology/Social work (3.4%) and History/Geography (1.6%). Then again, under (1%) of them detailed from Education/Physical Education (2%), Library and Information Science (.8%) and others (.2%).

5.1.3. Bharathiar University

The examination detailed that in excess of two Percent of the respondents were partaken from Education/Physical Education (2.8%), Management/Commerce (2.4%), Economics (2.2%), Above one Percent of them from human science/social work (1.8), Philosophy/Psychology (1.8%), the investigation could locate that less them one Percent of the respondents where announced from library and Information Science (.4%), History/Geography (.4%) and Others (.6%).

5.1.4. University of Madras

Information presents into investigate territories insightful responders of the examination was embraced in University of Madras. The investigation found that above (1%) of the respondents from Economics (1.6%), Education/Physical Education (1.4%), Management/trade (1.4%), and Sociology/Social work (1.0%).

5.1.5. Periyar University

Over one Percent of the Respondents who under so the Research territories of these, Management/Commerce (4.6%), Economics (2.0), Library and Information Science (1.8%), Philosophy/Psychology (1.6%), Education/Physical Education (1.4%), Journalism and Mass communications (1.4%).

5.1.6. Annamalai University

The examination shows the abovementioned (2%) of the respondents who experience investigate regions from Management/Commerce (4.2%), History/Geography (4.0%), Philosophy/Psychology (2.2%) and Education/Physical instruction (2.0%) then again, the investigation reacted that more than one Percent of the respondents from library and Information Science (1.8%) of them took an interest.

5.1.7. Madurai Kamaraj University

The examination found that above (1%) of the respondents partook from the exploration territories Economics (2.2%) Sociology/social work (2.0%). The Dept. of Commerce (1.4%) and Library and Information Science (12%) of the respondents. Then again, the examination could be accounted for that (32%) of the respondents took part short of what one Percent from four research territories for example Dept. of Physical, Philosophy/Psychology, Journalism and Mass Communication.

5.1.8. Manonmaniam Sundaranar University

The examination territories shrewd respondents of the respondents from MKU, the investigation reports that more than one Percent of the detailed of entire (83%) of them out of 66, those from Education/ Physical Education (2.0%), Management/Commerce (4.6%), History/Geography (2.6%) and Journalism and Mass correspondence (1.8%) Further, the examination revealed that respondents that fest of 16.6% of the respondents announced short of what one Percent of the respondents were taken part.

Table 1. Research areas wise respondents in State Universities

S.No	Research area	Alagappa University	Bharathidasan University	Bharathiar University	University of Madras	Periyar University	Annamalai University	Madurai Kamaraj University	Manonmaniam Sundaranar University	total
1	Economics	4 (.8)	9 (1.8)	11 (2.2)	8 (1.6)	10 (2.0)	-	11 (2.2)	1 (.2)	54 (10.8)
2	Education/Physical Education	27 (5.4)	1 (.2)	14 (2.8)	7 (1.4)	7 (1.4)	10 (2.0)	4 (.8)	10 (2.0)	80 (16.0)
3	Management/ Commerce	23 (4.6)	11 (2.2)	12 (2.4)	7 (1.4)	23 (4.6)	21 (4.2)	7 (1.4)	23 (4.6)	127 (25.3)
4	Sociology/ social work	2 (.4)	17 (3.4)	9 (1.8)	5 (1.0)	3 (.6)	1 (.2)	10 (2.0)	3 (.6)	50 (10.0)
5	Library and Information Science	7 (1.4)	4 (.8)	2 (.4)	1 (.2)	9(1.8)	9 (1.8)	6 (1.2)	3 (.6)	41 (8.2)
6	History/ Geography	3 (.6)	8 (1.6)	2 (.4)	-	2(.4)	20 (4.0)	-	13 (2.6)	48 (9.6)
7	Philosophy/ Psychology	-	-	9 (1.8)	1 (.2)	8 (1.6)	11 (2.2)	4 (.8)	1 (.2)	34 (6.8)
8	Public Administration	-	-	-	1 (.2)	-	2 (.4)	-	-	3 (.6)
9	Anthropology/ Criminology	-	-	-	3 (.6)	-	-	-	3 (.6)	6 (1.2)
10	Journalism and Mass Communication	-	-	-	2 (.4)	7 (1.4)	-	2 (.4)	9 (1.8)	20 (4.0)
11	Political Science	-	-	-	1 (.2)	-	12 (2.4)	3 (.6)	-	16 (3.2)
12	Others	7 (1.4)	1 (.2)	3 (.6)	6 (1.2)	1 (1.2)	1 (.2)	3 (.6)	-	22 (4.4)
		73 (14.6)	51 (10.2)	62 (12.4)	42 (8.4)	70 (14.0)	87 (17.4)	50 (10.0)	66 (13.2)	501 (100.0)

Figure 1. Research areas wise respondents in state universities

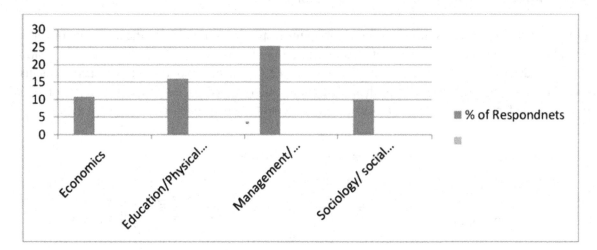

5.2. Use of Various Types of SNs Among the Respondents

The respondents knew and use of various kinds of SNs and Media for looking through academic data among the respondents in the State Universities in Tamil Nadu. Table 3 shows that there are seven kinds of informal organizations are recorded and respondents they thought about them Social Media and Networks.

1. **Face Book:** The respondents announced that they were utilized SNs in the chose Universities in Tamil Nadu. Greater part 52 (10.4%) of them utilized" face book from Annamalai University and Bharathidasan University. It followed by 50 (10%) of the respondents utilized Social Networks and Media from Periyar University.
2. **Twitter:** The greater part 21 (4.2%) of the respondents structure Alagappa University and Bharathiar University, they utilized '' Twitter''. It has been seen that rest of 103 (20.1) of them utilized ''Twitter'' from Madurai Kamaraj University, Annamalai University, Bharathidasan University, University of Madras and Manonmaniam Sundaranar University.
3. **You Tube:** Majority 56 (11.2%) of them utilized from Periyar University and 10.6% of the re-spondents from Alagappa University, 10.2% and 9.8% of them utilized by the respondents from Bharathiar University and Annamalai University.
4. **Tumblr/Messenger:** most of them detailed that "Not utilize" this Social Networks, it estimates 45.4% of them higher than utilized Tumblr/Messenger. Consequently this Tumblr/Messenger is a not well known one and offers infrequently data through Social Networks.
5. **Whatsapp:** The dominant part 86.2% of the respondents answered that they were "Use" WhatsApp, since this Social Media is generally famous among all classification of individuals, in like manner the respondents disperses the academic data sharing the insightful substance by means of this. It is presuming that when think about the "Non-use" class respondents 72.4% not as much as that "Utilization" of WhatsApp.
6. **Google +:** The respondents utilization of Google + Social systems larger part 288 (57.5%) of them announced "Use" in the chose State Universities of Tamil Nadu. Just 15.2% of the respondents sees that to be a higher than "Non-use" this Social Network.

7. **Instagram:** the lion's share 367 (73.3%) of the respondents were referenced ''Not Use'' Instagram, though, 36.6%. of the "Utilization" respondents not as much as that "Non-use" class.
8. **Others:** Above recorded seven informal communities prominently known and utilized by the respondents in the chose Universities of Tamil Nadu. It is noticed from Figure 3, "Others" sorts of Social Networks uncovered that bars above recorded seven interpersonal organizations. It reasoned that that greater part 86.0% of the respondents is answered "Non-use" of this classification.

Table 2. Usage of different types of SNs among the respondents

S.No	Name of Social Media & Networks	Alagappa University	Bharathidassan University	Bharathiar University	University of Madras	Periyar University	Annamalai University	Madurai Kamaraj University	Manonmaniam Sundaranar University	Total
1	Face Book	46 (9.2)	40 (8.0)	52 (10.4)	37 (7.4)	50 (10.0)	52 (10.4)	42 (8.4)	36 (7.2)	355 (70.9)
2	Twitter	21 (4.2)	16 (3.2)	21 (4.2)	16 (3.2)	20 (4.0)	18 (3.6)	19 (3.8)	14 (2.8)	145 (28.9)
3	You Tube	53 (10.6)	37 (7.4)	51 (10.2)	35 (7.0)	56 (11.2)	49 (9.8)	44 (8.8)	45 (9.0)	370 (73.9)
4	Tumblr/Messenger	23 (4.6)	11 (2.2)	25 (5.0)	13 (2.6)	24 (4.8)	18 (3.6)	12 (2.4)	11 (2.2)	137 (27.3)
5	Whatsapp	63 (12.6)	45 (9.0)	55 (11.0)	41 (8.2)	60 (12.0)	67 (13.4)	45 (9.0)	56 (11.2)	432 (86.2)
6	Google +	47 (9.4)	24 (4.8)	41 (8.2)	25 (5.0)	38 (7.6)	53 (10.6)	28 (5.6)	32 (6.4)	288 (57.5)
7	Instagram	17 (3.4)	13 (2.6)	27 (5.4)	19 (3.8)	17 (3.4)	17 (3.4)	15 (3.0)	9 (1.8)	134 (26.7)
8	Others	18 (3.6)	4 (.8)	9 (1.8)	8 (1.6)	8 (1.6)	5 (1.0)	10 (2.0)	8 (1.8)	70 (14.0)

Figure 2. Use of different types of SNs among the respondents

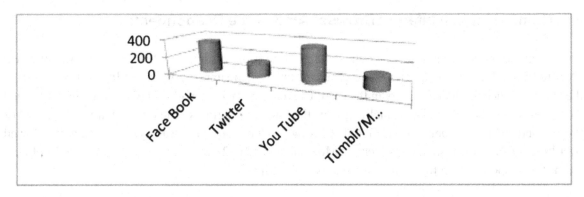

Table 3. Opinion on use internet browser among the respondents

S. No	Types of Internet Browser	State Universities								Total
		Alagappa University	Bharathidasan University	Bharathiar University	University of Madras	Periyar University	Annamalai University	Madurai Kamaraj University	Manonmaniam Sundaranar University	
1	Mozilla	25 (5.0)	18 (3.6)	19 (3.8)	9 (1.8)	21 (4.2)	11 (2.2)	17 (3.4)	19 (3.8)	139 (27.7)
2	Internet explorer	18 (3.6)	8 (1.6)	16 (3.2)	12 (2.4)	16 (3.2)	14 (2.8)	20 (4.0)	17 (3.4)	121 (24.2)
3	Google Chrome	68 (13.6)	49 (9.8)	60 (12.0)	40 (8.0)	67 (13.4)	81 (16.2)	46 (9.2)	58 (11.6)	469 (93.6)
4	Any others	7 (1.4)	1 (.2)	6 (1.2)	3 (.6)	2 (.4)	3 (.6)	6 (1.2)	5 (1.0)	33 (6.6)

Figure 3. Opinion on use internet browser among the respondents

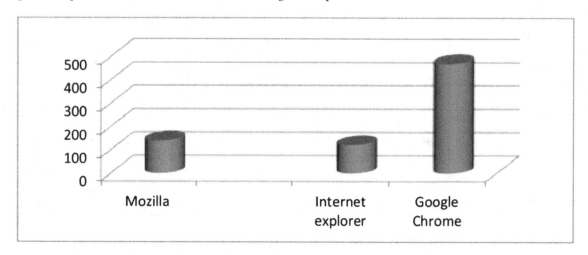

5.3. Opinion on Use Internet Browser Among the Respondents

The researcher's achieving academic data as far as composing research analysis, for reporting the new ideas to the exploration. It clarifies the respondents about their supposition on use Internet Browsers by the social science research scholars in the State Universities in Tamilnadu. The investigation examined that the respondents selected their inclination us the Internet programs. The major share 469 (93.6%) of the respondents favored being used "Google Chrome" to look through the analyzed the data. It followed by 139 (27.7%) of the respondents picked "Mozilla" and 121 (24.2%) of them use "Internet Explorer" out of 501 respondents in the State Universities in Tamilnadu.

Table 4. Use of research identification tools for SNs among the respondents

S.No	Types of Research ID tools	State Universities								Total
		Alagappa University	Bharathidasan University	Bharathiar University	University of Madras	Periyar University	Annamalai University	Madurai Kamaraj University	Manonmaniam Sundaranar University	
1	Researcher ID	58 (11.6)	36 (7.2)	41 (8.2)	22 (4.4)	48 (9.6)	63 (12.6)	35 (7.0)	49 (9.8)	352 (70.3)
2	ORCID ID	17 (3.4)	9 (1.8)	6 (1.2)	6 (1.2)	7 (1.4)	4 (.8)	2 (.4)	3 (.6)	54 (10.8)
3	Any others	16 (3.2)	9 (1.8)	16 (3.2)	16 (3.2)	16 (3.2)	21 (4.2)	11 (2.2)	12 (2.4)	117 (23.4)

5.4. Use of Research Identification Tools for SNs Among the Respondents

The study analyzed that the respondents they use of SNs for them also research Identification of their publications identity gets through research resources indexed in Google scholars, Scopus and web of science. Table 5 shows that use of SNs also have the Research Identification tools such as "Research ID" and "ORCID ID", the majority 352 (70.3%) of the respondents preferred "Research ID". Further, about 54 (10.8%) of them opted "ORCID ID" and others Research identification tools used respectively.

5.5. Preference of Research Citation Indexes (RCI) Among the Respondents

The exploration researchers of sociology typically concentrate to distribute the papers in different Journals, where as they wouldn't fret about reference Index and h-Index. Table 6 shows that there have been recorded six 'Exploration reference Indexes (RCI)". It is recorded that over 80% of the respondents among 492(98.2%) and 431 (86.0%) of them Stated "Get CITED" and "Google Scholar" individually. The examination additionally explicit that over 20% of them 146 (29.1%) and 115 (23.0%) of the respondents recorded "Scopus" and "Web of science" separately. Further, the investigation talked about that under 10% of them among 21 (4.2%) and 9 (1.8%) of the respondents recommended non famous reference Indexes are "Refer to Cite Seer" and "Math Scinet" individually the respondents likewise have recognized "EBSCO" and "Pro Quest" information based on both reference Indexes joined together 15.4% of the respondents unmistakably given as 53 (10.6%) and 24 (6.8%) of them stated " Pro Quest" and "EBSCO" individually recorded in the investigation.

5.6. The Respondents vs Shared Scholarly Contents through Social Networks and Medias in the State Universities in Tamil Nadu

The investigation examined from table 7 relates that common insightful Contents in the State Universities in Tamil Nadu. It has seen from the investigation FR is 2.9509 and FP is 49. Henceforth, it is dissected the examination that ''Null Hypothesis'' is acknowledged from over the investigation. There is no huge distinction between the respondents from Selected State Universities and shared insightful Contents in the State Universities in Tamil Nadu.

Table 5. Preference of Research Citation Indexes (RCI) among the respondents

S.No	Research Citation Indexes	State Universities								Total
		Alagappa University	Bharathidasan University	Bharathiar University	University of Madras	Periyar University	Annamalai University	Madurai Kamaraj University	Manonmaniam Sundaranar University	
1	Google Scholar	68 (13.6)	45 (9.0)	57 (11.4)	36 (7.2)	66 (13.2)	65 (13.0)	42 (8.4)	52 (10.4)	431 (86.0)
2	Cite Seer	6 (1.2)	1 (.2)	2 (.4)	2 (.4)	3 (.6)	1 (.2)	1 (.2)	5 (1.0)	21 (4.2)
3	Get CITED	1 (.2)	1 (.2)	2 (.4)	-	1 (.2)	87 (17.4)	50 (10.0)	62 (12.4)	492 (98.2)
4	Math Scinet	1 (.2)	-	2 (.4)	-	1 (.2)	2 (.4)	2 (.4)	1 (.2)	9 (1.8)
5	Scopus	19 (3.8)	18 (3.6)	18 (3.6)	15 (3.0)	30 (6.0)	19 (3.8)	10 (2.0)	17 (3.4)	146 (29.1)
6	Web of science	16 (3.2)	16 (3.2)	11 (2.2)	10 (2.0)	16 (3.2)	19 (3.8)	10 (2.0)	17 (3.4)	115 (23.0)
7	EBSCO	1 (.2)	4 (.8)	7 (1.4)	1 (.2)	3 (.6)	-	5 (1.0)	3 (.6)	24 (4.8)
8	Pro Quest	4 (.8)	5 (1.0)	14 (2.8)	6 (1.2)	8 (1.6)	8 (1.6)	4 (.8)	4 (.8)	53 (10.6)
9	Others	10 (2.0)	3 (.6)	17 (3.4)	9 (1.8)	11 (2.2)	18 (3.6)	9 (1.8)	13 (2.6)	90 (18.0)

Table 6. The respondents Vs. shared Scholarly Contents in the State Universities in Tamil Nadu

Source	D.F	Sum of squares	Mean Squares	F Ratio	F Prob.
Between Groups within Groups	7 493	34.1573 815.236	4.8796 1.6536	2.9509	49
Total	500	849.393			

Table 7. The respondents Vs. they used SNs for Tweeting the Research ideas in the State Universities in Tamil Nadu

Source	D.F	Sum of squares	Mean Squares	F Ratio	F Prob.
Between Groups within Groups	7 493	62.0412 875.4958	8.8630 1.7759	4.9909	.0000
Total	500	937.5369			

Table 8. The respondents Vs. they have Blogs on research in the State Universities in Tamil Nadu

Source	D.F	Sum of squares	Mean Squares	F Ratio	F Prob.
within Groups	7 493	15.6750 986.4807	2.2393 2.0010	1.1191	.3495
Total	500	1002.1557			

5.7. The Respondents vs They Used SNs for Tweeting the Research Ideas in the State Universities in Tamil Nadu

Table 9 discussed that respondents from Selected State Universities in Tamil Nadu and they utilized SNS for references. It is noticed from the examination FR is 3.973 and FP is .0003. Consequently, it is examined that ''Null Hypothesis'' is dismissed from over the investigation. There is a noteworthy contrast between the respondents from Selected State Universities and they utilized SNs for tweeting the exploration thoughts in the State Universities of Tamil Nadu.

6.8. The Respondents vs They Have Blogs on Research in the State Universities in Tamil Nadu

Table 10 investigated that respondents from Selected State Universities in Tamil Nadu and they make Blogs on look into. It is seen from the examination FR is 1.1191 and FP is .3495. Henceforth, it is examined that ''Null Hypothesis'' is acknowledged from over the examination. There is no noteworthy contrast between the respondents from Selected State Universities in Tamil Nadu and they make Blogs on examine.

6. CONCLUSION AND RECOMMENDATION

The study discussed above the respondents observes the useful and impact of sharing Social Networks (SNs) media in the selected eight state Universities of Tamilnadu. The study could remain the analysis would embark thoroughly justified based on the survey undertaken in the selected Universities. Total no of 501 respondents reported in this study, the analysis made that larger section 87 (17.4%) of them respondents from Annamalai University. The Study found that over 14% of the respondents from Alagappa University (14.6%) and Periyar University (14%). The analysis seen that Total no of 501 respondents responded to this assessment, out of which 73 (14.6%) of them responded from Alagappa University. It followed by Bharathidasan University 51 (10.2%), Bharathiar University 62 (12.4%). The respondents reported that they were used SNs in the picked Universities in Tamil Nadu. The major section 52 (10.4%) of them used" face book from Annamalai University and Bharathidasan University. The larger share 21 (4.2%) of the respondents structure Alagappa University and Bharathiar University, they used '' Twitter''. The significant offer 469 (93.6%) of the respondents favored being utilized "Google Chrome" to glance through the corresponding to the study. the larger share 352 (70.3%) of the respondents favored "Research ID". Further, around 54 (10.8%) of them picked "ORCID ID" and others Research distinguishing proof apparatuses utilized individually.

The study concentrates quantitative information from the respondents in the Selected State Universities in Tamil Nadu. The examination centers the respondents achieve the Scholarly Information through Social Networks significance of Social Science in the chose five Universities in Tamil Nadu. The investigation made it clear and finds that the analysts need to have cell phone for Research applications establishment in wording make specialists bunch inside and off the limits of the Universities. The examination could find that Whaatsapp, YouTube and Facebook were utilized dominatingly contrast with other Social Networks in Selected five State Universities in Tamil Nadu. Consequently specialists typically share their exploration data and are watching current data from YouTube too. The University must give free Wi-Fi availability to utilize the SNs. The investigation find that greater part of the respondents were utilizing SNs in their home contrast with other spot, it find that the analyst may get all the more extra time separated from working hours at the Institutions. Most of the respondents increasingly favored Ref. works, End Note and Mendeley Reference the executives Software, so as to the reference the board exceptionally needful to deal with the assets where incorporate the Citations utilizing different Citation style needful and surveys in their exploration. By and by, the specialists are more enthusiasm to check their Citations on their exploration work and h-Index on the motivation behind Google Scholar is essential one it tends to be enlisted effectively by each analyst. The investigation broke down that more respondents' exceptionally favored Google researcher for examinations their h-Index, Citations and research effect of the Publications of sociology Scholars.

REFERENCES

Baskaran, C. (2019). Disseminating Scholarly Information Access through Social Networks (SNs) and Media by the Social Science Research Scholars in Selected State Universities of Tamil Nadu. *Journal of Advances in Library and Information Science.*, *8*(3), 124–131.

Baskaran, C. (2020). Research Patterns on the Social Networks and Media: A Scientometric Portrait. Handbook of Research on Emerging Trends and Technologies in Library and Information Science. doi:10.4018/978-1-5225-9825-1.ch014

Fai, M. (2019). Protecting Organization Reputations during A Crisis: Emerging Social Media in Risk and Crisis Communication. *Indian Journal of Science and Technology*, *12*(18). doi:10.17485/ijst/2019/v12i18/144603

Josserand, E., Schmitt, A., & Borzillo, S. (2017). Balancing present needs and future options: How employees leverage social networks with clients. *The Journal of Business Strategy*, *38*(1), 14–21. doi:10.1108/JBS-01-2016-0003

Levula, A., & Harré, M. (2016). Social networks and mental health: An egocentric perspective. *Mental Health Review (Brighton)*, *21*(3), 161–173. doi:10.1108/MHRJ-10-2015-0029

Littman, J., Chudnov, D., Kerchner, D., Peterson, C., Tan, Y., Trent, R., Vij, R., & Wrubel, L. (2018). API-based social media collecting as a form of web archiving. *International Journal on Digital Libraries*, *19*(1), 21–38. doi:10.100700799-016-0201-7

Liu, L., Zhang, L., & Ye, P. (2018). Research on the application of SNS in university libraries: A case study of micro blogs in Chinese "211 project" universities. *The Electronic Library, 36*(2), 369–386. doi:10.1108/EL-05-2016-0120

Meenakshi, Sivakumar, & Ilango. (2017). Effective Health Promotion Interventions for Targeted Audience using Social Networking Sites: A Systematic Review. *Indian Journal of Science and Technology, 10*(36). doi:10.17485/ijst/2017/v10i36/86994

Shafawi, S., & Hassan, B. (2018). User Engagement with Social Media, Implication on the Library Usage: A Case of Selected Public and Academic Libraries in Malaysia. *Library Philosophy and Practice (e-journal).* https://digitalcommons.unl.edu/libphilprac/1820

Wan, R. W. O., Ziti, F. M. A., & Ngah, N. H. (2016). The uses of Social Media on Student's Communication and Self Concepts among TATIUC Students. *Indian Journal of Science and Technology, 9*(17). Advance online publication. doi:10.17485/ijst/2016/v9i17/88730

This research was previously published in the International Journal of Social Media and Online Communities (IJSMOC), 13(2); pages 58-70, copyright year 2021 by IGI Publishing (an imprint of IGI Global).

Chapter 51
Use of Social Media Platforms for Increased Access and Visibility by the Botswana National Archives and Records Services

Tshepho Lydia Mosweu
https://orcid.org/0000-0002-2144-7544
University of Botswana, Botswana

ABSTRACT

This chapter discusses the use of social media platforms for increased access and visibility by the Botswana National Archives and Records Services (BNARS). A qualitative research approach is used to illuminate efforts to use social media for marketing archival services by BNARS, and to closely analyze the benefits and challenges embedded in the use of social media for marketing and outreach by archival institutions. This chapter also draws inferences from the study and proffers recommendations. Primary data was collected through interviews of archivists who manage BNARS social media pages while secondary data was derived from documentary and content analysis. The study reveals that while BNARS was visible to users and potential users online, the legal and policy framework was found to be lacking. Challenges associated with the use of social media pertained to issues of privacy, security, data management as well as policy and the legal framework. The chapter adds literature on advocacy, promotion, and public programming by archival institutions in the digital era.

INTRODUCTION

The use of social media platforms has nowadays been shown to be a more dominant way to reach out to potential customers as acknowledged by Bountouria and Giannakopoulosa (2014) that social media is a tool that has been widely used by the cultural heritage institutions. In the context of archival agencies,

DOI: 10.4018/978-1-6684-7123-4.ch051

this allows access to services without having to physically visit the institution. Currently the Botswana National Archives and Records Services (BNARS) does not have a website of its own and consumers of archival services have to physically visit to get service. This is despite the report by Ngoepe and Keakopa, (2011, p.156) that the Department had a web page within the Ministry's (Ministry of Youth empowerment, sport and culture development) web site, which was supposed to be used to post publications and other informational materials. The Ministry's website has been defunct for some years now. The placement of the BNARS under this Ministry has compromised the transversal regulatory role of its services as the exercising of authority by the Director of BNARS is diminished and frustrated by bureaucracy and adherence to hierarchical controls (Ngoepe & Keakopa, 2011, p.157). Crymble (2010) has argued that social networking services, if used effectively by archives can be an engaging aspect of an archives' outreach programme.

The advent of social media platforms affords archival institutions an opportunity for wider publicity and outreach. The conceptual foundation of this chapter is that archival institutions need to adopt new technologies for increased access as argued by Saurombe and Ngulube (2016) that getting more people interested in the archives requires public archival institutions to be more creative and innovative. As is the norm with other national archival institutions, the Botswana National Archives and Records Services (BNARS) has an outreach programme, which it uses to market its services through, workshops, public lectures, media adverts and radio interviews, school and public educational tours and exhibitions (in-house and trade shows) and publications in the form of newsletters (Ngoepe & Keakopa, 2011, p. 516).

CONTEXTUAL SETTING

Archival institutions are essentially information resource providers. They provide access to archives and records that show the economic, political and social development of their nations. As one of such institutions, the Department of Botswana National Archives and Records Services (BNARS) holds records that depict the development of the country from the colonial era to the post- independence elected government of the people. The records that captured the activities of the colonial power are now used for reference purposes by the public. Part II, Section 3A of the National Archives and Records Services Act of 1978 as amended in 2007 gives the National Archives and Records Services the mandate to provide records and information management service to government agencies; and to collect, preserve and make access to the nation's documentary heritage (National Archives and Records Services Act 1978).

Public programming activities form part of archives work as the collection the archival institutions hold need to be publicized for users to know about them and use them. Ngulube, Sibanda and Makoni (2013, p. 124) posit that providing access to primary data contained in archives as constituted in the documents, housed in archival buildings, and managed by a requisite archival institution is an important component of archives administration. A study done by Maphorisa and Jain (2013) to investigate the perceptions of BNARS Archivists and administrative personnel towards marketing revealed that though BNARS personnel confused marketing to mere promotional activities, the organization appreciated the importance and relevance of marketing in Archives Administration. BNARS has been using social media platforms for increased visibility and access as alluded to by Phologolo (2015), Pule (2015) and Simon (2016). In Botswana, the government is committed to providing internet accessibility and connectivity in the country as reported by Batane (2011, p. 117) that through the Ministry of Communication Science and Technology, the government has developed an Information and Communication Technology

Policy which provides a roadmap that drives technology implementation in the country. According to Statistics Botswana (2014) survey, of the more than 90% of households in Botswana which had access to ICT through mobile cellular telephones, most internet users (78.4 percent) used it to participate in social networks. Garaba (2012, p. 11) posits that cellular technology, the telephone and video screen are relatively affordable for the majority of archival institutions within ESARBICA and these need to be exploited fully in order to make the heritage available to the public.

Social media has been defined as an online environment where content is created, consumed, promoted, distributed, discovered or shared for purposes that are primarily related to communities and social activities rather than to functional, task-oriented objectives (Gartner, 2018). Although Washburn et al., (2013, p. 6) posit that the interest in using social media by libraries and archives has been a topic of interest, investigation, and experimentation for some time, the literature reviewed in this study showed limited published research in Africa, hence the need for this study to specifically explore the use of social media for increased visibility by the Botswana National Archives and Records Services.

PROBLEM STATEMENT

The increased use of social media platforms by most organizations has seen archival institution also using these platforms for outreach purposes (Bosch, 2018; Washburn, Eckert, & Proffitt, 2013; Duff, Johnson, & Cherry, 2013; Theimer, 2011). BNARS has also jumped into the bandwagon of public agencies by using social media to market its services but how it deals with associated issues such as data management, privacy and policy issues is yet to be determined. The chapter explores usage of social media for outreach by BNARS including challenges and benefits of using social media platforms. Bertot, Jaeger and Hansen (2012) argue that the interaction by government through social media introduces new challenges related to privacy, security, data management, accessibility, social inclusion, governance and other information policy issues. BNARS Facebook page shares the rich documentary heritage within its repositories such as photographs, letters and extracts from minutes of reports as well as major events (Pule, 2015) and in doing so it is important to be aware of both benefits and challenges. Hence this study is appropriate in that it highlights issues archival institutions should be aware of as they adopt and use social media platforms for marketing and outreach purposes.

Objectives of the Study

- To determine efforts to use social media for marketing archival services by BNARS.
- Analyze the benefits and challenges embedded within the use of social media for marketing and outreach by archival institutions.
- Assess the impact of social media platforms for marketing and outreach of archives services.

SCOPE AND RESEARCH METHODOLOGY

This section provides the research methods employed in this study to explore the use of social media platforms for increased access and visibility by BNARS. The study uses a qualitative research approach which is an approach for exploring and understanding the meaning individuals or groups ascribe to a social or human problem (Creswell, 2014, p. 32). Although quantitative data yields specific numbers that can be statistically analyzed, can produce results to assess the frequency and magnitude of trends, and can provide useful information if you need to describe trends about a large number of people, qualitative data, such as open-ended interviews that provide actual words of people in the study, offer many different perspectives on the study topic and provide a complex picture of the situation (Creswell, 2012, p. 535). Data was collected using interviews (See Appendix) and content analysis. The qualitative data collected in this study is analyzed according to themes from the study objectives. Out of a total of seven archivists at BNARS, five were purposively selected as the researcher believed they had the information wanted for the study (Greener, 2008, p. 49). The study participants were all administrators of BNARS social media pages. Other BNARS staff members were not included in the study as they did not have inside information of managing the department's social media pages.

SOCIAL MEDIA AND ARCHIVAL INSTITUTIONS

Social media platforms have been increasingly used by archival institutions for marketing and outreach purposes (Garaba, 2012; Bosch, 2018; Washburn, Eckert, & Proffitt, 2013; Duff, Johnson & Cherry, 2013; Theimer, 2011). Notably, for archives this is comparatively a new phenomenon (Bountouria & Giannakopoulos, 2014) as for libraries and museums, the platform has been used for some time to disseminate a variety of information to the wider public (Rogers 2009; Whelan 2011). As archives exist to be accessed and used, promotion of the national heritage is of paramount importance (Kamatula, Mnkeni-Saurombe & Mosweu, 2013). Access to archives held by archival institutions is paramount as Mnjama (2008) posits that access to archives affords citizens an opportunity to hold their governments accountable for its decisions. The literature shows that unlike in the developed world, most archival institution in Africa have been slow in adopting the use of social media platforms for outreach purposes. A study by Kamatula et al. (2013) revealed that by 2013 none of the national archival institutions in Botswana, Tanzania and South Africa used social networking sites to promote their collections, despite more and more people in those countries having access to social networks through mobile technologies. In a study done by Maphorisa and Jain (2013), when respondents were asked on how they learnt about BNARS archival reference services majority (64%) of them indicated that they learnt about BNARS archival reference services through friends (colleagues). Maphorisa and Jain (2013, p. 39) concluded that BNARS promotional activities (use of television, radio, workshop, newsletters, tours and newspapers) were not reaching the intended audience thus were ineffective. The proliferation of the use of social media has become an opportunity for archival institutions to be widely known as they are able to effortlessly interact with their customers.

BENEFITS OF SOCIAL MEDIA USE FOR PROMOTING ARCHIVAL SERVICES

The literature shows that the field of records and archives management has not yet fully utilized the benefits that came with social media usage (Sinclair, 2012, Bountouria & Giannakopoulosa, 2014; Saurombe & Ngulube, 2016). Theimer (2011, p. 62) puts it in a more clear perspective that whereas in the past, many archives were confident that their predefined audience of professional historians, genealogists, and "hobbyist" researchers would find their way to the archive, with a philosophy summed up as, "if we describe it, they will come," in today's world an appropriate philosophy is, "go where your users are" through making digital collections available in online spaces such as social media platforms. Although Sinclair (2012, p. 1) argues that in the early work of archives the main focus was on the functions of appraisal, arrangement and description with little attention to the outreach function, an exploratory study done to investigate the extent to which Web 2.0 features have been integrated into archival digitization projects by Samouelian (2009) suggests that a number of archival professionals were moving towards embracing technology to remain vital and essential to current and future users in the digital era.

Getting more people interested in the archives requires public archival institutions to be more creative and innovative (Saurombe & Ngulube 2016, p. 31). A research survey done by Bountouria and Giannakopoulosa (2014) amongst archival services in order to see how they were using these platforms revealed that 88% of them believe that social networking has provided them with greater visibility for their organization and more direct contact with their users. As social media has transformed the interaction and communication of individuals throughout the world (Edosomwan et al., 2011, p. 2), it has a potential and impact in strengthening relationships with the user community and with other institutions, creating new access points and increasing the visibility of collections, promoting the reputation of the institution or department, and advocating for the value of the archives' resources and services (Mason 2014, p. 158; Garaba, 2012, p. 26; Edosomwan et al., 2011, p. 8; Bountouria & Giannakopoulosa, 2014, p. 511).

The use of social media enables users across the globe to be aware of archival services offered by national archival institutions. Some international researchers have been able to enter their enquiries through social media platforms and got assisted. Clough (2013) argues that because of the open access ethic of libraries and archives, it was natural to use social media platforms to make their information and knowledge available to users whereby by the end of 2011, almost 90 percent of American libraries reported using Facebook and almost half were using Twitter to promote their services, provide user updates, and reach potential new users. A survey of library staff members in the U.S. to determine how libraries, which are similar to archives in many ways, are employing Web 2.0 and social networking tools to promote library programs and services found that many libraries use social media for various reasons. According to survey respondents, libraries are using social media tools to provide "technical instruction/how-to at the library/Skype with authors," and "advocacy", as well as "recruiting and managing volunteers." Some libraries are using social media as a "reminder of special resources available to academic community" and as a tool for "reference transactions, receiving/resolving complaints, building community" (Curtis, 2012).

In archives, it has been revealed by Crymble (2010) that archival institutions overwhelmingly used social media services to promote content they have created themselves, whereas archivists promote information they find useful though in both cases, more frequent posting did not correlate to a larger audience. The study concluded that for individual archivists, social networking services can be enriching tools for individual professional development while for archives, social networking services can be an engaging aspect of an archives' outreach program which can be used to reach a large, targeted audience with little or no cost to the archives (Crymble, 2010, p. 147). A survey done by Bountouria and Giannakopoulosa (2014) among various archival services revealed, among others, an extended use of Facebook, YouTube and blogs by the archival services. The study concluded that even though social media was a new and remarkable trend of the internet, it had many benefits such as the promotion of archives' image to the public and, hence, improves their public relations though lack of financial and human resources could hamper the effective exploitation of the benefits of social networking.

CHALLENGES IN THE USE OF SOCIAL MEDIA FOR PROMOTING ARCHIVAL SERVICES

Even though the use of social media comes with all these benefits, there are some challenges archival institutions need to be aware of. Social media technologies raise a large number of information management issues mainly concerning privacy, security, accuracy, and archiving, spanning major issues such as personally identifiable information, security of government data and information, and the accuracy of publicly available data (Bertor et al., 2012, p. 32). Therefore, in using social media to publicize archival holdings, archival institutions must be mindful of these issues and how they may be addressed. In other words, these issues have an impact on the use of social media platforms by archival institutions to promote archives services. In their project report on an assessment of Privacy-Preserving and Security Techniques for Records Management in Cloud Computing, InterPARES Trust (2016) argued that the major obstacle to adopting cloud-based technologies, which social media platforms fall under, in the public sector, is a lack of trust in sufficient security and privacy protection. These issues call for clear spelt-out policies on the use of social media for outreach and marketing purposes by archival institutions.

In Botswana, BNARS has the legal mandate as directed by the National Archives and Records services (NARS) Act of 1978 as amended in 2007 to direct policies with regards to the management of records and archives in the country. But it has been argued by Ngoepe and Keakopa (2011, p. 155) as well as Mosweu (2012, p. 78) that despite the amendments made in 2007, the act still fell short in strengthening BNARS role in the management of digital records. It has also been argued by Goh (2014, p. 56) that presently the records-related and archival legislation does not effectively address the creation, processing, and preservation of records and data in a cloud environment such as in social media. This challenge is further highlighted by Franks and Smallwood (2014, p. 268) who argue that the two main risks associated with the use of social media in an organization are lack of a social media policy and the risk of employees who may unintentionally expose information that may not be meant for public consumption. Social networking sites, such as Facebook, encourage people to provide personal information that they intend to be used only for social purposes which call for government organizations that use social media platforms to have rules and regulations in place on how such information can be used (United States Government Accountability Office, 2011).

RESEARCH FINDINGS AND DISCUSSIONS

This section presents the findings and presentation of data collected through interviewing archivists who manage BNARS social media pages as well as content analysis of BNARS social media pages to illuminate efforts by BNARS in using these social media platforms for marketing and outreach purposes. The survey responses do not show much difference from other studies done on the use of social media by archival institutions across the world. The results of the survey showed that BNARS was actively using social media platform for outreach and marketing purposes. BNARS started using social media platforms in 2014. The pages are updated twice a week. Other activities include sharing and re-tweeting posts on national interest especially from the Botswana government social media pages. Despite the available different social media platforms such as LinkedIn, Google +, YouTube, Pinterest, Instagram, blogs, wikis, BNARS used Facebook and twitter for its outreach and marketing purposes. This chapter would mainly present the findings from the BNARS Facebook page named Botswana National Archives and Records Services on Facebook as it is the most active. The BNARS twitter account, @archivesbw, mainly shows what was shared from the Facebook pages as the two accounts are connected. The BNARS Facebook page had 16000 likes as compared to their twitter account which had a mere 39 followers by 23 July 2018.

The benefits and challenges of using social media for outreach and marketing purposes as well as the impact social media had on BNARS outreach programme are also presented as part of the findings. The results showed that despite that active use of social media by BNARS, there was no staff solely dedicated to manage and run social media pages for the department. The pages were managed by archivists on part-time basis as they were also engaged with other archives duties. It was also evident that the archivists were just roped in to run the pages without the requisite skills as indicated by one respondent who gave an example of failure to protect the archival documents shared on social media to deal with data theft.

EFFORTS IN SOCIAL MEDIA USE FOR MARKETING ARCHIVAL SERVICES BY BNARS

The survey responses revealed different reasons for BNARS to use social media. The participants indicated that the Department adopted the use of social media to increase awareness on archival holdings and the department as a whole, to reach out to the youth who might be lazy to physically visit the department for research, the need to broaden the scope of users as well as to harness technology in their outreach programme. According to Phologolo (2015), Pule (2015) and Simon (2016) BNARS has been using social media platforms for increased visibility and access. BNARS' newsletter reports indicate that through the use of social media, the department has become more visible to the public (Phologolo, 2015; Pule, 2015; Simon, 2016). The department has even received donations of private archives from abroad by the descendants of non-Batswana people who worked in the country during colonial times (Simon, 2016). Figure 1 shows engagements and level of reach on BNARS Facebook posts.

It has been revealed by Phologolo (2015) that for increased access to archival documents and visibility, BNARS vigorously marketed its services in the late 1990s through what we can term the traditional methods of publicity such as newsletters, exhibitions and workshops. As information and communication technologies advanced, BNARS realized the need to tap into newer methods of reaching out to the public. The Department joined other government departments in Botswana and embraced the use of social media platforms in 2014 to reach out to as many people as possible (Pule, 2015). Through the use of social media, BNARS' archival services have become visible as depicted in Figure 1.

The Kind of Information Shared on BNARS Social Media Platforms

The participants were questioned on the kind of information that BNARS shares with the public, and they had the following responses in Table 1.

Figure 2 shows the kind of information shared by BNARS on social media.

A look into BNARS Facebook page shows that people engaged more on photograph updates than on other status updates as shown by Figure 2. A photograph could have an average reach of 13, 404 while a status reached 1388.

Figure 1. BNARS Facebook showing engagements and level of reach on posts published
(BNARS Facebook page, 2018)

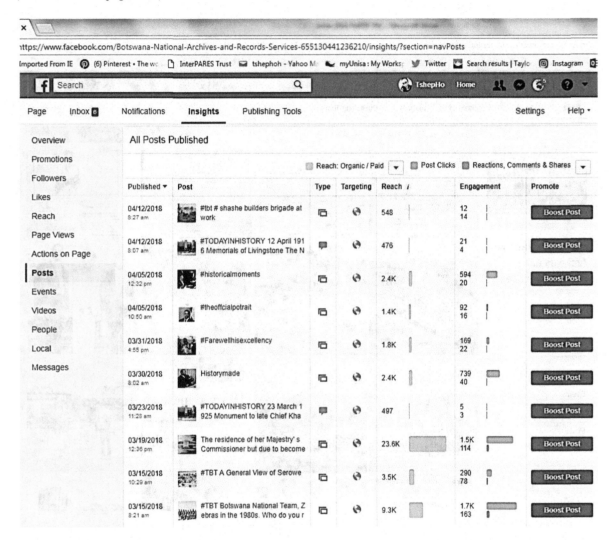

Table 1. Information shared on social media by BNARS

Participant	Response
Participant A	We share historical information (textual and pictorial) on our social media platforms.
Participant B	We share information that might be interesting to our followers. This information concerns events that happened in Botswana in the past in the form of photographs or texts.
Participant C	Our social media platforms share photographs on our archival holdings, quotable quotes, events that happened on a particular day of the past and events that will take place at BNARS. We also share government of Botswana social media posts as well as posts by historians who interact on social media platforms.
Participant D	We share bits and pieces of our archival collection.
Participant E	We share information that could be deemed interesting by our users.

Figure 2. Screenshot of recent BNARS Facebook page showing information shared on social media (*BNARS Facebook page, 2018*)

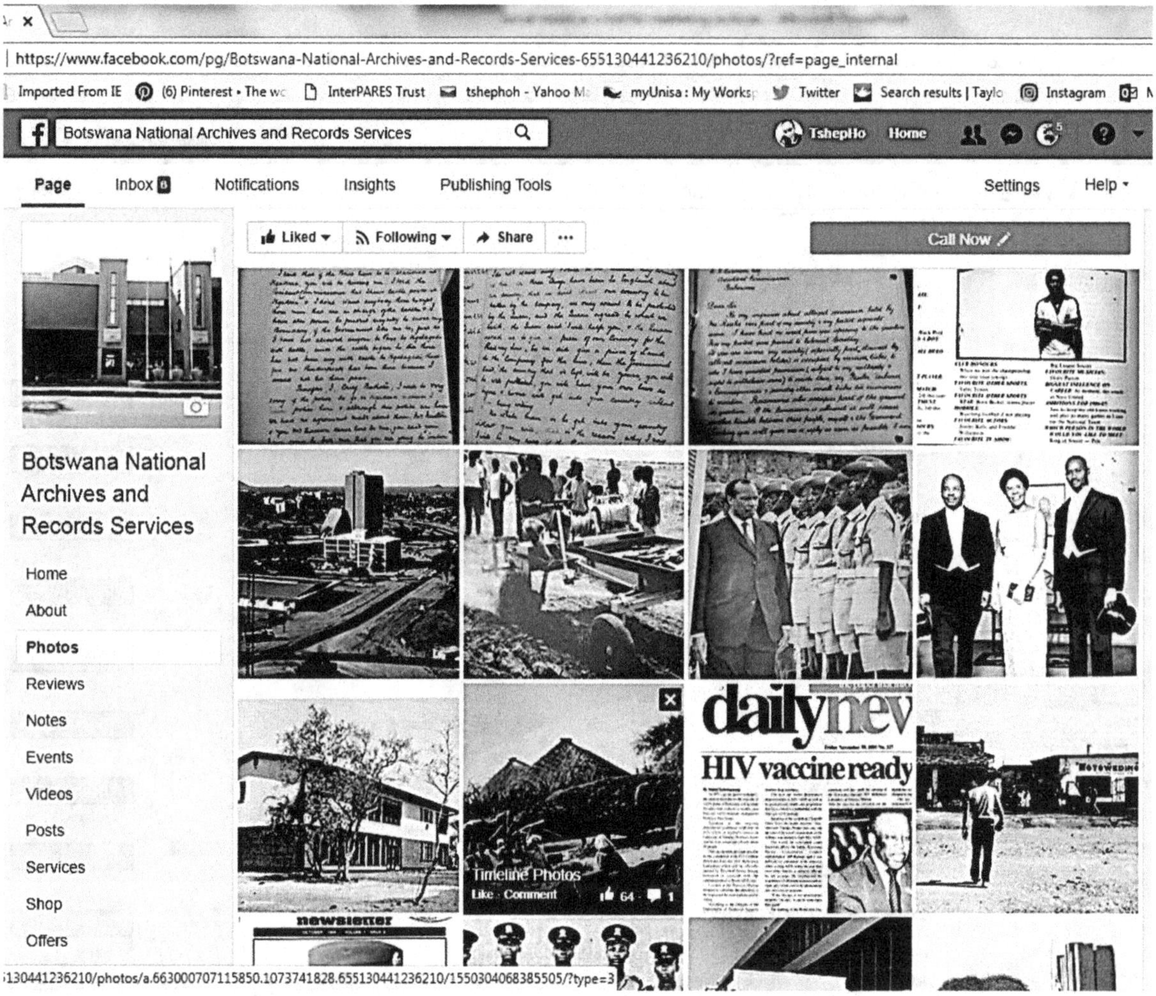

Staffing and Skills

The participants were asked whether they had staff dedicated to managing social media platforms, their number, and the requisite skills and whether they managed the pages on full time basis. They participants responded in Table 2.

BENEFITS OF USING SOCIAL MEDIA FOR MARKETING AND OUTREACH BY BNARS

The participants were asked to state the benefits gained from the use of social media. The following are the main reasons cited by the participants;

- Direct contact with the Archives' users.
- Increased archives usage.
- Improvement in the archives image by the public.
- Multiple access by our users and our potential users.
- Increased target groups that is both the old and the young.
- It's a good information sharing platform for archivists across the world.
- Services delivery is remotely performed.
- Effectiveness and efficiency in marketing our products and services.
- Immediate feedback.

Figure 3. Reactions on photographs far surpasses other status updates on BNARS Facebook page
(BNARS Facebook page, 2018)

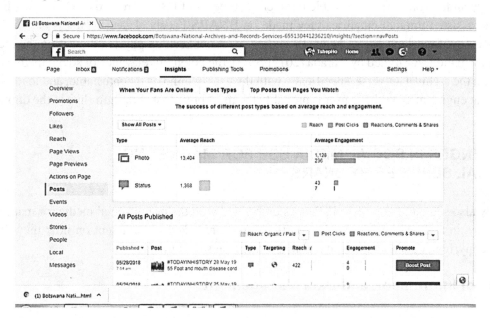

Table 2. Staffing and skills

Participant	Response
Participant A	We have five officers who are dedicated to managing social media pages. These officers do this job on part-time basis as they also serve as archivists in other divisions in the department. Yes we do have the requisite skills to maneuver social media platforms.
Participant B	Yes, 5 officers are dedicated to managing our social media platforms. We have limited skilled to run social media platforms as we have not received any training on social media.
Participant C	There are four archivists plus the Head of Archives Administration. They are full- time on the job. Full time I assume you mean they manage the platform on daily basis. We all have enough skills to post and interact with our clients.
Participant D	We have archivists who manage Facebook page and I think they have the skills required to manage the page. Roughly 5 archivists manage our pages. The knowledge we have is the one we have to operate our personal phones. We do not have the skills for example we failed to apply a watermark on our photographs so it's easy for people to use our photos for free.
Participant E	Five people manage our social media pages. They are not dedicated to social media full-time. Yes, the officers are all ICT literate.

Bountouria and Giannakopoulosa (2014, p. 516) have argued that archival services have realized the benefits of social networking and try to follow the trends of the society. This study showed that social media, especially Facebook enabled BNARS to achieve its mandate of promoting archives to a wider audience as it has been also observed by Crymble (2010, p. 129) that posting to a Facebook page or a Twitter account that has a reasonably large audience can be effective ways of drawing attention to upcoming events, a new blog post, interesting items in a collection, or a newspaper article promoting the institution itself. According to the United States Army Social media handbook (2013, p. 9), social media is more than just a platform to push command messages as social community Platforms such as Facebook and twitter help people bridge geographical gaps to connect, talk and interact and in the process be valuable as a communication strategy. Through their Facebook page, BNARS have received donations of private archives, for example which they might have not received with their traditional means of outreach activities. The Department was able to reach out to users and potential users outside the country and in rural areas. A sizable number of students of history, records and archives have been able to be assisted through enquiries they made on BNARS Facebook page. This is also in line with BNARS's aim of reaching out to the youth as they seem not keen on physically visiting the archives to access information. As argued by Garaba (2012, p. 26), the potential relevance of social media technologies within the archival universe, specifically with the user in mind, is incontestable, and lends weight to the fact that engagement with the user is probably the most prevalent paradigm shift in the digital world.

CHALLENGES IN SOCIAL MEDIA USE FOR MARKETING ARCHIVAL SERVICES BY BNARS

The study also sought to establish challenges embedded with the use of social media for marketing and outreach by an archival institution. The participants were asked to comment on how they dealt with privacy, copyright, data management and legal issues on social media.

Privacy of Information and Data Management

To explore privacy and data theft issues, the participants were asked to comment on how they ensured information privacy and measures in place to protect archives posted on social media platforms from data theft. They had the answers in Table 3.

Legal and Policy Framework

The researcher also asked the participants about the legal and policy framework that governs their use of social media. They responded as tabulated in Table 4.

Despite all the benefits BNARS enjoyed in using social media for outreach and marketing purposes, the Department is faced with issues of privacy of information, data theft and a weak legal and policy framework. As a result of weak or non-existence of the legal and policy backing, the Department was limited on what kind of information they could share with their users on social media whereby they resorted to only published information that was already public. The weak legal backing also exposed the Department to data theft and copyright infringement as Facebook allows downloading photographs shared on this platform without the knowledge of the owner. This exposed the department to data breaches. Even though the participants cited the National Archives and Records Services Act as well as the Copyright and Neighboring Act as laws that back their use of social media, a documentary analysis of these acts showed nothing that talks to managing digital information shared on cloud-based platforms such as Facebook and twitter. Even though BNARS has Facebook posting and Comments Guidelines, the guidelines are not adequate to cover pertinent issues such as privacy of data.

Table 3. Privacy of information and data management

Participant	Response
Participant A	There are no measures in place to ensure privacy or protect materials posted online.
Participant B	We make sure we do not post information that might breach privacy of individuals. There are no measures in place to protect the archives posted on social media as we have seen before other people posting the photographs we had previously shared on our pages.
Participant C	We ensure that all content that will be uploaded on the Facebook page shall be out of copyright, that is, copyright belonging to BNARS and of public knowledge. A process of engagement involving all parties concerned is followed where copyright issues maybe in dispute before any uploads are made to ensure that copyright laws are adhered to and those on intellectual property are not infringed. We also adhere to our Facebook posting and comments guideline. Watermarking was thought of as a means that could actually help stop people from abusing images posted but then, watermarking often tempers with the originality of the images. With developments in technology taking place rapidly there are no guarantees that security packages such as these will hold presently and in the future. BNARS will have to consider very carefully the materials that will be posted on the Facebook page by identifying those that will not present any challenges such as copyright infringement as opposed to those that are known to be common national images.
Participant D	I do not have an exact answer but I guess copyright and privacy issues in government are a concern for the Government Computer Bureau Department. To protect our data from theft we use water mark, besides most of the items posted are already in public domain.
Participant E	There is privacy policy in place. The archives we post on our social media platforms are not protected from theft.

Table 4. Legal and policy framework

Participant	Response
Participant A	There are no policies in place that govern our use of social media platforms.
Participant B	We rely on the National Archives and Records Services Act to make information available but the act is limited in terms of guiding information shared online like social media.
Participant C	We rely on the BNARS Facebook posting and comments guidelines, Copyright and Neighboring Act 2000 as well as the Cybercrime and Computer Related Act of Botswana.
Participant D	I do not know because BNARS Act does not cover social media.
Participant E	We do not have policies that govern the use of social media platforms.

The challenge is compounded by the fact that Botswana does not currently have Data protection legislation. This is despite the proclamation in the country's ICT Policy which states that the development of policy and possibly a combination of legislation and industry codes of conduct to deal with the protection of personal privacy, particularly in the context of cross-border data flow, health care and financial services and transactions (Government of Botswana 2007, p. 21). Franks and Smallwood (2014, p. 260) observed that if content-posting guidelines are not clear, then the informal nature of social media posts potentially can be damaging to an organization. In acknowledging the importance of security, privacy and skills impact on employees using social media, The North Carolina Office of the Governor (2012) have advised their agencies that in participating in social networking, they should;

- Provide security awareness and training to educate users about the risks of information disclosure when using social media, and make them aware of various attack mechanisms.
- Ensure employees are aware of Privacy Act requirements and restrictions. Educate users about social networking usage policies and privacy controls to help them better control their own privacy in any profile they use for work-related activities and more effectively protect against inadvertent disclosure of sensitive agency information, and
- Educate users about specific social media threats before they are granted access to social media websites.

IMPACT OF SOCIAL MEDIA PLATFORMS ON MARKETING AND OUTREACH SERVICES OF ARCHIVES

The study also assessed the impact of social media platforms for marketing and outreach of archives services by BNARS.

Public Engagement

The participants were asked on whether they measured their audience on social media platforms and if yes what they used the information for? All the participants confirmed that they kept track of the number of people reached out through statistics produced on Facebook. The information was used for reporting and planning purposes, to determine customers' preferences or get feedback from them and act on information that had a bearing on their collection development policy. The information also showed user needs and helped guide outreach strategies. One respondent indicated that high statistics demand that there was need to start a special unit to address issues of social media.

Participation and Engagements Trends

When asked on the trends in terms of participation and engagement observed on their social media platforms, the participants had the following responses in Table 5.

The researcher was able to get BNARS Facebook page metrics. The statistics show that people who liked BNARS page were from different countries, locations in the country and of different language background. Figure 4 shows insight on the kind of people interacting with the page.

Target Audience

When asked whether their social media efforts were targeted to any specific audience, Four (4) of the participants answered in the affirmative and said they target people who were conversant with the usage of social media and technology, the people who might not be able to physically visit BNARS such as the youth, users outside the country and users in rural areas as BNARS archives services are mostly in

Gaborone while only one participant denied that there is any target group. Figure 5 depicts that people in the bracket of 25-34 are the most users of BNARS Facebook page at 42%.

Table 5. Participation and engagements trends

Participant	Response
Participant A	Our users find the use of photographs more appealing.
Participant B	Our followers appreciate the kind of information we share of their past especially photographs.
Participant C	People have taken keen interest in the use of archives. Some share their stories with us on posts. This shows that indeed history is of great importance in their lives.
Participant D	Users respond to all our posts without fail every day.
Participant E	Persons who engage with us are mainly students of history and archives and records management as well as historians.

Figure 4. Showing the kind of people interacting with the BNARS Facebook page
(BNARS Facebook page, 2018)

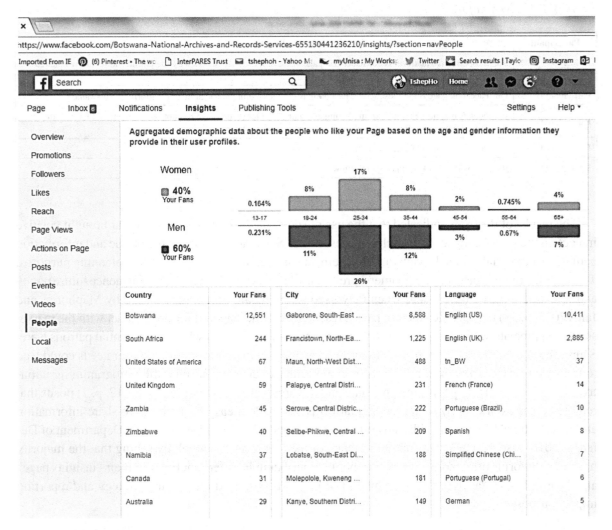

Figure 5. BNARS Facebook page users age rages and percentages
(BNARS Facebook page, 2018)

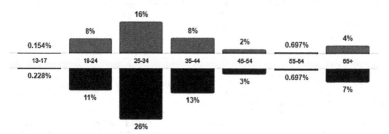

The Most Effective Social Media Platform in Promoting Archival Services

The participants were also asked to state which of their social media pages was most effective in marketing their services and the reason behind that. Table 6 shows the responses.

Table 6. Effective platform

Participant	Response
Participant A	The most effective platform is our Facebook page because it is easily accessed by the public and regularly updated unlike Twitter.
Participant B	Our Facebook page is the most active. Facebook is the most common social media platform in Botswana.
Participant C	Facebook is the most effective for marketing and outreach. Our twitter page has not been operational for a while that's why I have not indicated it as one of our social media platform.
Participant D	Facebook is the most effective platform we use.
Participant E	It has to be Facebook as it has more followers and we are more focused on it.

The results of the study indicated that the use of social media by BNARS has so far brought positive impact on their marketing and outreach services. BNARS was able to engage the public and information gathered from social media through that engagement has been used for reporting and planning purposes. This enabled them to determine customers' preferences and user needs which may influence future policy and direction which unlike before when they used social media as it was observed by Maphorisa and Jain (2013, p. 38) that BNARS did not have a research or marketing unit for pre-contact with the market so as to appreciate who are their customers/users/ readers/ clients and who their potential patrons were. Saurombe and Ngulube (2016, p. 43) are of the view that detailed information on user needs could lead to improved services and offer archivists an opportunity to develop fitting public programming initiatives that could get more people to appreciate and use archival resources. Garaba (2012, p. 7) posits that remote access as offered by social media platforms has made it easy for archives to share information about collections like finding aids and collection catalogs online. The United States Department of Defense (2016) also acknowledges the importance of metrics from Facebook by saying that the majority of social platforms offer more data, as Facebook, as an example, offers analytics in their "insights page" and Twitter has an "analytics" page which information is best used for guiding strategy and reporting impact purposes.

The study also revealed that although the Department had Facebook and Twitter accounts, Facebook was mostly used as the common social media platform in Botswana as is the case in most countries. According to Kallas (2018), Facebook jumped by 70 million monthly active users from 2.13 billion in December 2017 to 2.20 billion as of March 31, 2018. The rate of growth seems to continue at 20 million active users per month. Masilo and Seabo (2015, p. 118) observe that during the Botswana 2014 General election, the increased use of social media, particularly Facebook in Botswana as a mobilizing tool increased young people's interest in politics. A study by Mpoeleng, Totolo and Jibril (2015) on the perceptions of the usage of Web 2.0 technologies carried out among library staff of the University of Botswana showed that library staff had adopted some Web 2.0 tools such as Facebook, however some tools such as wikis, podcasts, Twitter, LinkedIn and blogs were not very popular. Instead of archives being viewed as a dark storage of archival documents, materials posted on social media by BNARS appealed to the public as shown by the number of likes and shares by their followers.

The study also revealed that BNARS was able to reach out to many users remotely through social media which works for BNARS as currently there is one central archival service in the country responsible for archives (Ngoepe & Keakopa, 2011). Users could send messages through Facebook messenger and be promptly assisted as revealed by this study. In agreement with this Theimer (2011, p. 61-62) has argued that the archivists of the social media era see their primary role as facilitating rather than controlling access whereby they use social media tools to invite user contributions and participation in describing, commenting, and re-using collections, creating so-called collaborative archives.

SOLUTIONS AND RECOMMENDATIONS

In the digital era it is imperative for archival institutions to utilize social media technologies to enhance their public programming activities (Garaba, 2012, p. 29). This chapter has established that outreach and public programing remains an important duty of archival institutions. Technological advances have brought in innovative and creative ways for archival institutions to reach a wider spectrum of users (Mnjama, 2010; Ngoepe & Ngulube, 2011). To be able to fully take advantage of the benefits brought about by social media platforms, archival institutions need to have a social media strategy or framework. Sinclair (2012) suggest a framework for social media outreach which comprises policies to direct general activities regarding social media use in government and a plan that discusses specific media to be employed by the archives which this chapter also proposes. Maphorisa and Jain (2013, p. 42) recommended that BNARS design its own website to reach out to the market throughout the world through World Wide Web platform. This study recommends the adoption and use of social media platforms by archival institutions for marketing and outreach purposes least they become irrelevant to the wider audience which prefers to access information online rather than physically visiting the archives.

It is recommended that archival institutions should have dedicated staff to manage social media pages as online users require prompt and quick service. In line with this, Maphorisa and Jain (2013, p. 41) also recommended an independent marketing and research division be established by BNARS and be allocated the necessary resources to enable it to perform effectively. The demand of online interactions requires that archivists be trained on these digital platforms in order to be able to deal with challenges that come with managing information online. Franks and Smallwood (2014, p. 258) have also argued that consistent training is crucial as social media is a moving target. The adoption and use of social media by archival institutions for marketing and outreach purposes calls for the relevant legal and policy framework to avoid issues of copyright, privacy and data breaches. The situation in Botswana is exacerbated by the fact that currently there is no access to information and data protection legislation though the right to privacy and access information are guaranteed under the Constitution of Botswana (Government of Botswana 1966). The Data Protection Bill was recently presented by Minister for Presidential Affairs, Governance and Public Administration which seeks to regulate the protection of personal data and ensure that the privacy of individuals in relation to their personal data is maintained (Mokwena, 2018). This study recommends the adoption of social media policies for archival institutions seeking to use social media for marketing and outreach purposes. Clear guidelines and monitoring mechanisms must be in place to control and manage archival materials before they are published on social media platforms (Franks & Smallwood, 2014, p. 267). The study also recommends that social media metrics should be used by those who engage on it to inform their social media strategies.

FUTURE RESEARCH DIRECTIONS

With its fluid nature, the digital world may change overnight bringing new challenges to archival institutions adopting the use of social media platforms for outreach and public programming. Social media strategies that may be adopted today may not necessarily work in the future. Future research opportunities may include exploring the perceptions of archivists towards the use of social media platforms in the archival profession and archives user needs assessment studies.

CONCLUSION

The chapter discussed efforts by the Botswana National Archives and Records Services (BNARS) in the use of social media platforms for marketing archival services. It closely analyzed the benefits and challenges embedded in the use of social media for marketing and outreach by an archival institution. By examining how BNARS have applied social networking platforms for outreach purposes, other archival institutions can determine how they may also use social media platforms to suit their outreach needs. The chapter concludes that though the use of social media platforms by archival institutions brings challenges to the traditional notions of archival practice, it is imperative for the archives to move with the times in order to stay relevant to their users.

REFERENCES

Batane, T. (2013). Internet access and use among young people in Botswana. *International Journal of Information and Education Technology (IJIET)*, *3*(1), 117–119. doi:10.7763/IJIET.2013.V3.246

Bertot, J. C., Jaeger, P. T., & Hansen, D. (2012). The impact of polices on government social media usage: Issues, challenges, and recommendations. *Government Information Quarterly*, *29*(1), 30–40. doi:10.1016/j.giq.2011.04.004

Bountouri, L., & Giannakopoulos, G. (2014). The use of social media in archives. *Procedia: Social and Behavioral Sciences*, *147*, 510–517. doi:10.1016/j.sbspro.2014.07.146

Clough, G. W. (2013). Museums, libraries, and archives in a digital age. *Smithsonian Institute*. Retrieved from https://www.si.edu/content/gwc/bestofbothworldssmithsonian.pdf

Creswell, J. W. (2009). *Research design: Qualitative, quantitative, and mixed methods approaches* (3rd ed.). Los Angeles, CA: Sage.

Creswell, J. W. (2012). *Educational research. Planning, conducting, and evaluating quantitative and qualitative research* (4th ed.). Los Angeles, CA: Sage.

Creswell, J. W. (2014). *Research design: Qualitative, quantitative, and mixed methods approaches* (4th ed.). Los Angeles: Sage.

Crymble, A. (2010). An analysis of twitter and facebook use by the archival community. *Archivaria, 70*, 125–151.

Curtis, R. (2011). Social media, libraries, and web 2.0: How American libraries are using new tools for public relations and to attract new users –fourth annual survey. *South Carolina State Library*. Retrieved from https://dc.statelibrary.sc.gov/bitstream/handle/10827/7271/SCSL_Social_Media_Libraries_2011.pdf?sequence=1

Franks, P., & Smallwood, R. F. (2014). Information governance for social media. In R. Smallwood (Ed.), *Information governance. concepts, strategies and best practices* (pp. 253–269). New Jersey: John Wiley & Sons.

Garaba, F. (2012). Availing the liberation struggle heritage to the public: Some reflections on the use of web 2.0 technologies in archives within the East and Southern Africa Regional Branch of the International Council on Archives (ESARBICA). *Information Development, 28*(1), 22–31. doi:10.1177/0266666911424074

Government of Botswana. (1966). *Constitution of Botswana*. Gaborone: Government Printer.

Government of Botswana. (1978). *National Archives and Records Services Act Cap 59:04*. Gaborone: Government Printer.

Government of Botswana. (2000). *Copyright and Neighboring Rights*. Gaborone: Government Printer.

Government of Botswana. (2007). *National Information and Communications Technology Policy (Maitlamo Policy)*. Gaborone: Government Printer.

Greener, S. (2008). *Business research methods*. London: Ventus Publishing.

InterPARES Trust. (2016) *Assessment of privacy-preserving and security techniques for records management in cloud computing*. Retrieved from https://interparestrust.org/assets/public/dissemination/NA18_AssessmentofPrivacy-PreservingandSecurityTechniquesforRecordsManagementinCloudComputing_FinalReport.pdf

Kallas, P. (2018). *Top 15 most popular social networking sites and apps*. Retrieved from https://www.dreamgrow.com/top-15-most-popular-social-networking-sites/

Kamatula, G. A., Mnkeni-Saurombe, N., & Mosweu, O. (2013). The role of archives in the promotion of documentary national heritage in Tanzania, South Africa and Botswana. *ESARBICA Journal, 32*, 109–127.

Maphorisa, O. M., & Jain, P. (2013). Marketing of archival reference services at Botswana National Archives and Records Services (BNARS). *International Journal of Academic Research and Reflection*, *1*(3), 34–42.

Masilo, B., & Seabo, B. (2015). Facebook: Revolutionizing electoral campaign in Botswana? *Journal of African Elections*, *14*(2), 110–219. doi:10.20940/JAE/2015/v14i2a5

Mnjama, N. (2008). Access to Records and Archives in Kenya. *African Research & Documentation*, *106*, 59–76.

Mnjama, N. (2010). Preservation and management of audio- visual archives in Botswana. *African Journal of Library Archives and Information Science*, *30*, 129–148.

Mokwena, N. (2018). MPs okay Data Protection Bill with reservations. *Botswana Guardian*. Retrieved from http://www.botswanaguardian.co.bw/news/item/3247-mps-okay-data-protection-bill-with-reser-vations.html

Mosweu, T. L. 2012. *An assessment of the court records management system in the delivery of justice at the Gaborone Magisterial District*. Unpublished master's thesis, University of Botswana, Gaborone.

Mpoeleng, D., Totolo, A., & Jibril, L. (2015). Perceptions of University of Botswana librarians on the potential of web 2.0 tools. Retrieved from https://www.ifla.org/files/assets/reference-and-information-services/publications/210-mpoeleng-en.doc1.pdf

Ngoepe, M., & Keakopa, S. (2011). An assessment of the state of national archival and records systems in the ESARBICA region. A South Africa-Botswana comparison. *Records Management Journal*, *21*(2), 145–160. doi:10.1108/09565691111152071

Ngoepe, M., & Ngulube, P. (2011). Assessing the extent to which the National Archives and Records Services of South Africa has fulfilled its mandate of taking archives to the people. *Innovation*, *42*, 1–22.

Ngulube, P., Sibanda, P., & Makoni, N. L. S. (2013). Mapping access and use of archival materials held at the Bulawayo Archives in Zimbabwe. *ESARBICA Journal*, *32*, 123–137.

North Carolina Office of the Governor. (2012). *Best practices for state agency social media usage in North Carolina*. Retrieved from https://files.nc.gov/dncr-archives/documents/files/best_practices_so-cialmedia_stateagency.pdf

Phologolo, A. (2015). Botswana National Archives and Records Services Facebook page. *Tshedimoso Newsletter*, (29).

Pule, T. (2015). BNARS embraces social media platforms. *Tshedimoso Newsletter, (28)*.

Samoulean, M. (2009). Embracing web 2.0: Archives and the newest generation of web applications. *American Archivist*. Retrieved from http://americanarchivist.org/doi/pdf/10.17723/aarc.72.1.k73112x7n0773111

Saurombe, N., & Ngulube, P. (2016). Perceptions of user studies as a foundation for public programming activities by Archivists from East and Southern Africa. *ESARBICA Journal*, *35*, 30–45.

Saurombe, N., & Ngulube, P. (2018). To collaborate or not to collaborate, that is the question: Raising the profile of public archives in East and Southern Africa. *Information Development, 34*(2), 162–181. doi:10.1177/0266666916684181

Simon, I. (2016). BNARS received private archives from the International Community. *Tshedimoso Newsletter*, (30).

Sinclair, J. M. (2012). *The interactive archives: Social media and outreach.* Unpublished Masters Dissertation, University of Manitoba, Manitoba, Canada.

Statistics Botswana. (2014). *Botswana household access and individual use of Information & Communication Technologies.* Retrieved from http://www.statsbots.org.bw/sites/default/files/publications/Botswana%20Access%20%20and%20Use%20of%20ICTs%202014%20Statistics.pdf

Tasmania Archive and Heritage Office. (2015). *Managing social media records.* Retrieved from https://www.informationstrategy.tas.gov.au/Records-Management-Principles/Document%20Library%20%20Tools/Guideline%2018%20Managing%20Social%20Media%20records.pdf

Theimer, K. (2011). What is the meaning of archives 2.0? *The American Archivist, 74*(1), 58–68. doi:10.17723/aarc.74.1.h7tn4m4027407666

United States Army. (2013). *Social media handbook.* Retrieved from http://www.jber.jb.mil/Portals/144/socialmedia/PDF/socialmedia-army-social-media-guide.pdf

United States Department of Defense. (2016). *Memorandum for military service public affairs chiefs.* Retrieved from https://www.defense.gov/Portals/1/Documents/pubs/Forging-Two-New-Links-Force-of-the-Future-1-Nov-16.pdf

United States Government Accountability Office. (2011). *Federal agencies need policies and procedures for managing and protecting information they access and disseminate, GAO-11-605 "What GAO found.* Retrieved from http://www.gao.gov/new.items/d11605.pdf

Washburn, B., Eckert, E., & Proffitt, M. (2013). *Social media and archives: A survey of archive users.* Dublin, Ohio: OCLC Research. Retrieved from https://www.oclc.org/content/dam/research/publications/library/2013/2013-06.pdf

KEY TERMS AND DEFINITIONS

Archival Institution: An organization that collects the records of individuals, families, or other organizations for preservation and future access.

Archives: Records which have been preserved for their enduring value.

Facebook: Social networking site that allows users to interact with other users.

Public Programming: Consented activities designed to enable interaction between an archival institution and its users.

Social Media: Online communications channels dedicated to community-based input, interaction, content-sharing and collaboration.

Social Media Platforms: Web-based technologies that enables the development, deployment and management of social media solutions and services.

Social Networking: The use of dedicated applications and websites to interact with other users of the same interests.

This research was previously published in the Handbook of Research on Advocacy, Promotion, and Public Programming for Memory Institutions; pages 182-204, copyright year 2019 by Information Science Reference (an imprint of IGI Global).

APPENDIX: INTERVIEW GUIDE

I kindly ask you to respond to the few questions below on a study that investigates the use of social media platforms for increased access and visibility by the Botswana National Archives and Records Services (BNARS) by illuminating efforts to use social media for marketing archival services, analysing the benefits and pitfalls/challenges embedded in the use of social media for marketing and outreach as well as the resultant impact. The data is to be used for academic purposes only. If you need clarity, please contact me at lydhoss@gmail.com

Efforts to Use Social Media for Marketing Archival Services by BNARS

1.   When did the Botswana National Archives and Records Services start using social media platforms?
     a.   What reasons led BNARS to use social media?
     b.   Which social media platforms are used for marketing archival services?
     c.   How often do you update your social media platforms?
     d.   What kind of information do you share on your social media platforms?
     e.   Do you have staff dedicated to manage these social media platforms? How many employees are responsible for these accounts, are they only dedicated to social media full time?
     f.   Do you have the requisite skills to manoeuvre social media platforms? Please explain.

Benefits of Using of Social Media for Marketing and Outreach by BNARS

2.   What are the benefits gained from the use of social media for marketing archives services?
3.   (Tick appropriate answer. You may tick more than one option):
     a.   Direct contact with archives' users
     b.   Increased archives usage
     c.   Improvement in the archives image by the public
     d.   Increased attendance at various events, and
     e.   Other (please specify)

Challenges That Come With the Use of Social Media for Marketing and Outreach by BNARS

4.   How do you ensure that the privacy of people involved in whatever information is shared on social media is protected?
5.   How do you protect archives you have posted on your social media platforms from data theft?
6.   What legal and policy framework back your use of social media?

Assess the Impact of Social Media Platforms for Marketing and Outreach of Archives Services

7. Do you measure your audience on social media platforms and if yes what do you use the information for?
8. What trends in terms of participation and engagement have you observed on your social media platforms?
9. Are your social media efforts targeted to any specific audience? Please explain
10. Which of your social media pages is most effective in marketing your services? Explain the reason behind this.

Thank you for taking time to complete this questionnaire!

Index

F

G

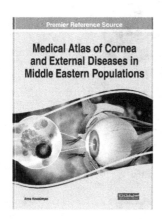

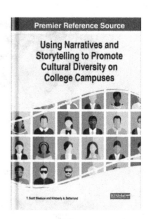

Printed in the United States
by Baker & Taylor Publisher Services